For more information on Allan Mallinson and his books,
see www.penguin.co.uk

Fight to the Finish

*The First World War –
Month by Month*

Allan Mallinson

BANTAM BOOKS

TRANSWORLD PUBLISHERS
61–63 Uxbridge Road, London W5 5SA
www.penguin.co.uk

Transworld is part of the Penguin Random House group of companies
whose addresses can be found at global.penguinrandomhouse.com

Penguin
Random House
UK

First published in Great Britain in 2018 by Bantam Press
an imprint of Transworld Publishers
Bantam edition published 2019

Maps by Lovell Johns

A CIP catalogue record for this book
is available from the British Library.

ISBN
9780857503800

Typeset in 8.7/12.63pt ITC Stone Serif by Jouve (UK), Milton Keynes.
Printed and bound in Great Britain by Clays Ltd, Elcograf S.p.A.

Penguin Random House is committed to a sustainable
future for our business, our readers and our planet. This book
is made from Forest Stewardship Council® certified paper.

MIX
Paper from
responsible sources
FSC® C018179

1 3 5 7 9 10 8 6 4 2

'Germany elected to make it a finish fight with England.
Now we intend to see that Germany has her way.
The fight must be to the finish.'

David Lloyd George, secretary of state for war
(later prime minister), September 1916

'The only wonder to the compiler of these records is that any sure
fact whatever should be retrieved out of the whirlpools of war.'

Rudyard Kipling, *The Irish Guards in the Great War*

CONTENTS

CONTENTS

CONTENTS

MAPS

Preface

The genesis of this book goes back many years, but to four years ago in particular, when, just before the centenary of the outbreak of the First World War, Simon Pearson of *The Times* asked me to write a monthly commentary of a thousand words or so on the course of the conflict. I am most grateful for Simon's advice and encouragement during that project, which in many ways has shaped this book. I have of course expanded on those monthly pieces, and – although each retains a certain unity – they have been edited with a view to reading as a continuous narrative rather than as discrete articles. This latter task has been the assured work of my copy-editor, Gillian Somerscales, who as ever (she has edited all my non-fiction save the first) has been the most diligent assayer of the text. I am, of course, indebted to Simon Taylor, my editor at Penguin Random House, who over very many years has steered my writing with the deftest of touches. I am most grateful once again to Auriol Griffith-Jones for her indexing, Liane Payne for the picture research, Lovell Johns Ltd for the clarity of the maps, Phil Lord for his design, Steve Mulcahey for another most striking cover, and Katrina Whone, managing editor, for pulling it all together as if it were no effort at all.

The text is not referenced or footnoted – very deliberately. This is not a polemical work or an academic treatise, whose propositions must be backed by scrupulous citations. It is a narrative designed to flow. Although some books are mentioned in the text itself, if every statement, quotation and allusion were to be catalogued, the multitude of primary and secondary sources would change not just the book's weight but its complexion.

At the end of the book, however, I offer – principally for the British reader – a short list of further reading.

Introduction

In the Time of the Breaking of Empires

From the opening shots to the signing of the Armistice, the First World War lasted some fifty-two months. It was fought on, or in the waters of, six of the seven continents, and in all of the seven seas. For the first time, the fighting was on land, at sea and in the air. It became industrial, and unrestricted: poison gas, aerial bombing of cities, and the sinking without warning of merchantmen and passenger ships by submarines. Military and civilian casualties probably exceeded forty million. During its course, four empires collapsed – the German, Austro-Hungarian, Russian and Ottoman. In all its military, political, geographical, economic, scientific, technological and above all human complexity, the First World War is almost impossible to comprehend.

Day-by-day narratives – excellent reference books – can be dizzying for the reader trying to make sense of the whole. Freer-flowing accounts help to convey the broader trends and factors, but offer less of a sense of the human dimension of time. The month is a digestible gauge. We remember months, because months have names, because they are linked to the seasons, and because they have their own characters. Looking at the First World War month by month reveals its complexity while preserving the sense of time.

Fight to the Finish is not intended to be a comprehensive account

1

of the fighting, nor of all the other factors in the war. It does not examine the conflict's causes or its consequences. It aims simply to give a picture of each of those fifty-two months: what was the predominant action, how and why it came about, and how it looked. The narrative, while not Anglocentric, is told in the main from a British perspective.

It is called *Fight to the Finish* because that is what David Lloyd George, the British prime minister for twenty-four of those fifty-two months, and minister for munitions and then secretary of state for war for the preceding eighteen, said that it must be. Such a demand – in effect, the Germans' unconditional surrender – required a national effort of unprecedented proportions. It was this that gave the war its unique and terrible face, which *Fight to the Finish* seeks to portray.

Prologue

The Alliances

1839: Britain, France, Prussia, Austria and Russia sign the Treaty of London, which requires Belgium to remain perpetually neutral, and by implication commits the signatory powers to guard that neutrality in the event of invasion.

1879: Germany and Austria-Hungary enter into a treaty: the Dual Alliance.

1882: Italy joins Germany and Austria-Hungary in the Triple Alliance. (In 1914 she would remain neutral, stating that the Triple Alliance was defensive and that both Austria and Germany had acted aggressively.)

1892: France and Russia enter into a treaty: the Dual Entente.

1902: Britain signs a treaty of mutual naval assistance with Japan to safeguard British interests in the Far East.

1907: After *rapprochement* with France (the Entente Cordiale), which settles years of colonial disputes, Britain joins Russia and France to form the Triple Entente. While France and Russia conclude treaties of mutual assistance, however, Britain has no formal treaty commitments.

PROLOGUE

1908: Austria-Hungary annexes Bosnia – formally still a province of the Ottoman Empire – which contains many Serbs. Serbia and her ally Russia protest strongly. An enlarged Bulgaria declares independence from the Ottomans.

1912: Britain signs a treaty of mutual naval assistance with France. In the event of war with a third party or parties, France will take responsibility for the security of the Mediterranean, while Britain will take care of the North Sea.

1912–13: A series of wars in the Balkans. Serbia emerges as the main beneficiary and a perceived threat to Austria-Hungary.

PART ONE

1914

'Over by Christmas'

28 June: Archduke Franz Ferdinand, heir to the Austrian throne, and his wife, visit Sarajevo in Bosnia, a province of the Austro-Hungarian Empire. A lone assassin, Gavrilo Princip, shoots and kills them both. Austria believes the killer is linked to the Serbian nationalist movement.

23 July: Austria-Hungary, with the backing of Germany, delivers an ultimatum to Serbia. The Serbs offer to submit to arbitration, but also begin to mobilize their army.

25 July: Austria-Hungary cuts diplomatic ties with Serbia and begins to mobilize.

26 July: Britain tries to convene a conference of the major European powers to resolve the situation. France, Italy and Russia agree to take part. Germany refuses.

28 July: Austria-Hungary declares war on Serbia.

29 July: Britain calls for international mediation. Russia urges German restraint, but then begins partial troop mobilization as a precaution. The Germans warn Russia, and then begin to mobilize.

1914 – 'OVER BY CHRISTMAS'

30 July: Austria shells Belgrade, the Serbian capital.

31 July: Russia begins full mobilization.

1 August: Germany declares war on Russia. France and Belgium begin full mobilization.

3 August: Germany declares war on France and invades neutral Belgium. Britain delivers an ultimatum to Berlin demanding withdrawal from Belgium. Germany ignores it.

4 August: Britain declares war on Germany. The declaration is binding on the British Empire, including Canada, Australia, New Zealand, India and South Africa.

6 August: Austria-Hungary declares war on Russia.

19 August: President Woodrow Wilson announces that United States will remain neutral.

23 August: Battle of Mons.

26 August: Battle of Tannenberg (East Prussia) begins.

5 September: Battle of the Marne begins.

19 October: Battle of Ypres ('First Ypres') begins.

29 October: Turkish fleet bombards Russian Black Sea coast.

1 November: Russia declares war on the Ottoman Empire.

5 November: France and Britain declare war on the Ottoman Empire.

1

AUGUST

To Arms!

Churchill makes a decisive move seven days before the war

Soon after 11 p.m. on 4 August the Admiralty flashed the signal to His Majesty's ships: 'Commence hostilities against Germany.' Earlier the War Office had sent telegrams to army headquarters bearing the single word 'Mobilize'.

The Foreign Office issued a statement explaining why:

Owing to the summary rejection by the German Government of the request made by his Majesty's Government for assurances that the neutrality of Belgium will be respected, his Majesty's Ambassador to Berlin has received his passports, and his Majesty's Government declared to the German Government that a state of war exists between Great Britain and Germany as from 11 p.m. on August 4, 1914.

Invading Belgium was merely a means to an end. General Alfred von Schlieffen (1833–1913), the former chief of the *Grosser Generalstab*, the great general staff, had devised a strategy for war on two fronts, which the Franco-Russian alliance made inevitable if Berlin

LONDON

ENGLAND

Dover
Nieuport
Ostend
Brug
Dunkerque
Calais
Ypres
Straits of Dover
Boulogne
Lille

Arras
Cambrai
Abbeville
Le Cat
Dieppe
Amiens
St Quentin

Le Havre
Rouen

PARIS

FRANCE

Chartres

THE SCHLIEFFEN CONCEPT

Five armies wheeling through neutral Belgium
and Luxembourg (and even perhaps the
Netherlands), with two more holding between
Metz and Mulhouse against an expected French
offensive (Plan XVII).

→ German troop movements

→ Anticipated French offensive

Orléans

were to declare war on either country. The Schlieffen Plan entailed a huge wheeling movement through neutral Belgium to bypass the strong defences in Alsace-Lorraine on the Franco-German border. Only in this way, he had told the Kaiser, could Germany defeat France quickly enough to be able then to send her victorious troops east to defeat the slower-mobilizing Russians.

By midnight on 4 August every branch of the British government was putting into action its chapter of the 'Red Book', a document without precedent that set out the instructions for transition to war drawn up over the preceding four years by the Committee of Imperial Defence. The first offensive action was taken by the Postmaster-General's department, whose cable ship *Alert* dredged up and cut, or else patched into the British network, the German communication cables in the Dover Straits, severing Berlin's telephone and telegraph connections with much of the world beyond the Central Powers, crucially the Americas. However, one of the most decisive acts of the war had been taken seven days earlier when the first lord of the Admiralty, the 39-year-old Winston Churchill, ordered the Grand Fleet, with all its reservists aboard after a practice mobilization, to steam 'at high speed and without lights' through the Channel to its war stations at the lonely Orkney anchorage of Scapa Flow. At a stroke the Royal Navy had gained mastery of the North Sea and the English Channel, without which no British army could be sent to France. While cruiser patrols from the east coast ports kept the Channel clear of nuisance raids, Admiral Sir John Jellicoe's Grand Fleet would ensure the *Hochseeflotte*, the German High Seas Fleet, stayed in port at Wilhelmshaven.

On the afternoon of 5 August a council of war met in the Cabinet Room. After much discussion the decision was taken to send an expeditionary force to France. Following the meeting the prime minister, H. H. Asquith, appointed Field Marshal Lord Kitchener secretary of state for war. Kitchener, doubting the prevailing military wisdom that the war would be over quickly, at once set out to raise a huge citizen army. Britain, unlike the other major European powers, did not operate conscription; it had a relatively small – though extremely well trained – long-service army, and consequently fewer reservists (former regulars who still retained a reserve liability) it could call up. Nevertheless, of the 100,000 men of the British Expeditionary Force (BEF) – four infantry divisions and a cavalry division – who would go to France as soon as mobilization was complete, some 60 per cent would be reservists. The Territorial Force comprised fourteen divisions, but these were primarily for home defence and could not be compelled to serve overseas. Some units volunteered almost to a man, but it would not be until November that territorials would go to France in significant numbers, and not until 1915 in formed divisions.

Mobilization and the subsequent move of the BEF to the principal embarkation ports of Southampton, Queenstown (Ireland) and Glasgow went like clockwork, thanks to the War Office's well-laid plans – which had come as a surprise to many of the cabinet, who had not been informed of the Anglo-French staff talks authorized by Sir Edward Grey, the foreign secretary, in 1906, by which they had been hatched.

The first British casualties of the war occurred early in the morning of 6 August when HMS *Amphion*, leader of the 3rd Destroyer Flotilla at Harwich, lost 150 of her crew after striking a mine laid by the *Königen Luise*, which the flotilla had sunk the day before off the Thames estuary. Nevertheless, advance parties of the BEF sailed for France the next day without mishap, the main bodies following a week later. The only military force ever to have left Britain other than by sea – Nos 2, 3, 4 and 5 Squadrons (sixty aircraft) of the Royal Flying Corps (RFC) – took off from Dover and crossed the Straits to Boulogne, followed the coast to the mouth of the Somme, and then flew upstream to Amiens. Not every aircraft made it, however: on 12 August, as the squadrons were leaving their stations for the staging field at Dover, a Blériot flown by Lieutenant Robert Skene, with Air Mechanic Raymond Barlow aboard, crashed on take-off from Netheravon airfield in Wiltshire, killing both men.

Thanks to the detailed railway movement plans drawn up by the British and French staffs under the supervision of the War Office's director of military operations, Major-General Henry Wilson, the BEF was more or less complete in its concentration area at Maubeuge, near the Franco-Belgian border on the left flank of the French armies, by 20 August. That same day, however, 90 miles to the north-east, the great fortress of Liège, literally pulverized by the huge siege guns produced in the Krupp and Skoda factories, fell to the German 2nd Army, signalling the beginning of the end of the Belgians' heroic defence of the River Meuse. Next day the BEF began its march north across the border towards Mons to close up with General Charles Lanrezac's 5th French Army and attack the Germans' right flank as they turned south, for the French commander-in-chief, General Joseph Joffre, persisted in his belief that the German main effort was in Alsace-Lorraine, and that their advance through Belgium would therefore be confined to the south-east towards Sedan and Verdun. This belief suited the French military doctrine of *offensive à outrance* – attack to the utmost, to excess even: Joffre had already launched his counter-offensive in Alsace-Lorraine (the famous 'Plan XVII'), where he believed he could disrupt the entire German campaign plan. His 1st and 2nd Armies hurled themselves into the former French *départements* (incorporated in the *Kaiserreich* since 1871), where the German 5th and 6th Armies were in fact preparing not to advance but to repulse the expected French attack. The German right wing, in Belgium, was far stronger than appreciated by Joffre – though not, strangely, by *The Times*'s military correspondent Colonel Charles à Court Repington, who on 12 August published a map showing detailed German deployments, concluding that 'the bulk of the German Armies about to operate against France is to the northward of Lorraine'.

The commander-in-chief of the BEF, Sir John French, though not entirely convinced by Joffre's appreciation, relied nevertheless on the assessments from the *Grand Quartier Général*, the French general staff, and was tardy in getting the RFC into the air to obtain his own strategic intelligence. At Mons on 23 August the BEF ran straight into General Alexander von Kluck's 1st Army, which had – to Joffre's astonishment – crossed the Meuse and turned south.

Fortunately, French, having learned the night before of the great numbers of enemy actually before him, had ordered his troops to dig in along the line of the Condé Canal amid the slag heaps and mining villages of the Borinage. The British army was about to fight a major battle in a built-up area for the first time. 'I took one look at it and thought what a bloody place to live,' said Private Jim Cannon of the 2nd Suffolks: 'I took a second look and thought what a bloody place to fight.'

The desperate encounter at Mons would also be the first test of the revolution in the army's rifle-shooting, prompted by its drubbing at the hands of the Boers a dozen years before. Fifteen aimed rounds a minute with the new magazine-fed Lee–Enfield convinced the Germans that the BEF had many more machine guns than hitherto supposed, though in fact each battalion (of 1,000 men) had just two. Wave after wave of German infantry was brought to a bloody halt by the rapid fire of two divisions of Sir Horace Smith-Dorrien's II Corps (Sir Douglas Haig's I Corps, guarding the right flank in the gap between the BEF and Lanrezac's 5th Army, saw little action that day).

Four Victoria Crosses were won at Mons, two of them by Lieutenant Maurice Dease (posthumously) and Private Sidney Godley (wounded, presumed dead, though taken prisoner) of the machine-gun section of the 4th Battalion Royal Fusiliers, for defending the canal bridge at Nimy, and two by sappers (Royal Engineers), Captain Theodore Wright (killed three weeks later) and Lance-Corporal Charles Jarvis, for laying demolition charges on the bridges under fire. Jarvis had left the colours in 1907 and was within months of the expiry of his reserve liability when he received his recall telegram.

Outnumbered and pummelled by heavier artillery, II Corps was forced off the canal towards evening. On learning that Lanrezac's army had also suffered a major reverse, and from the RFC that the Germans were manoeuvring to outflank the BEF on the left, that night Sir John French ordered a general withdrawal.

So began the retreat from Mons, which would continue for ten gruelling days until the Germans could be checked at the Marne. Smith-Dorrien would make a controversial stand at Le Cateau three days later when, having lost contact with Haig's corps the other side of the Forest of Mormal and the River Sambre, he stood his ground for a morning with three divisions (the 4th Division having just arrived from England) and the cavalry division, in the British army's largest battle since Waterloo. Though with some loss, II Corps imposed such a check on Kluck's 1st Army that the BEF was able to continue the retreat in reasonable order.

Schlieffen's Plan seemed to be going well, and not only on the Western Front. In the east, the German army, which expected to have to hold off Russian spoiling attacks as the bulk of the Tsar's forces – the reservists – slowly mobilized, not only held the attacks but mounted a spectacularly successful counter-offensive.

As soon as Berlin had declared war, two Russian armies, only partially mobilized, had at once marched into East Prussia – as vividly described in Aleksandr Solzhenitsyn's novel *August 1914*. Things began well for the Russians, whose 1st Army under General Paul von Rennenkampf defeated eight divisions of the German General Friedrich von Prittwitz's 8th Army at Gumbinnen on 20 August. Simultaneously Aleksandr Samsonov's 2nd Army moved to threaten the German rear.

Prittwitz panicked and announced that he intended withdrawing to the Vistula river, which would have meant abandoning most of East Prussia including the capital-fortress, Königsberg. He was at once replaced by Field Marshal Paul von Hindenburg who, with his new chief of staff Erich Ludendorff – names that would later become famous on the Western Front – immediately launched a counter-offensive. By 27 August Samsonov's 2nd Army had been surrounded in a double envelopment at Tannenberg; by 30 August his entire command had disintegrated, the Germans taking 92,000 prisoners and Samsonov committing suicide. A week later, Rennenkampf's 1st Army would lose another 100,000 at the Battle of the Masurian Lakes.

2

SEPTEMBER

'Miracle on the Marne'

The Schlieffen Plan is thwarted within sight of Paris

On Sunday, 30 August, exactly a week after the BEF's first, bruising battle at Mons, followed by six days of fighting retreat, the commander-in-chief, Sir John French, wrote in his diary: 'I have decided to retire behind the Seine to the west of Paris, if possible in the neighbourhood of St. Germain. The march will occupy at least 10 days.'

The massive German hook through Belgium, in execution of the 'Schlieffen Plan', had taken the allies by surprise, and the three French armies on the Franco-Belgian and Luxembourg borders were in full retreat. On their left the BEF had taken over 10,000 casualties; withdrawing from the fight would leave the French left flank in a perilous position.

When French's telegram announcing his intentions reached the War Office the next day, an alarmed prime minister, Asquith, told the secretary of state for war, Lord Kitchener, to go at once to France to 'put the fear of God into them'. Just after midnight on 1 September, Kitchener set off in uniform by special train from Charing Cross and fast cruiser from Dover to see his fellow field marshal.

As he crossed the Channel in the grey dawn, one of the BEF's most heroic actions was being fought at Néry, a farming village in the valley of the Oise. The 1st Cavalry Brigade had bivouacked for the night and were waiting for the early-morning mist to clear before continuing the retreat, the six 13-pounder guns of L Battery Royal Horse Artillery drawn up as if on parade, ready to move. When the mist lifted, however, the brigade found themselves over-looked by high ground 600 yards to the east, which the German 4th Cavalry Division had occupied during the night. The Germans at once opened a furious fire, cutting down L Battery's men and horses and destroying three of the guns. Led by the battery captain, Edward Bradbury, the survivors scrambled to unhook the other three and bring them into action, then fought an unequal duel for an hour in which two of the guns were destroyed, the ammunition ran out and Bradbury was killed. He and the last two gunners in action, Battery Sergeant-Major George Dorrell, at thirty-four a vet-eran of the Boer War, and 28-year-old Sergeant David Nelson from County Monaghan, were awarded the VC. After recovering from wounds both returned to service and were commissioned, Dorrell rising to lieutenant-colonel, and Nelson – killed in action in 1918 – to major. The VCs and No. 6 Gun, the last to remain in action, are on permanent display at the Imperial War Museum.

Later that morning Kitchener met French at the British embassy in Paris. The meeting was frosty, not least because the commander-in-chief thought it improper for the secretary of state to be in uniform. As a minister, Kitchener could not give him orders; as a field mar-shal, he could. In the event, persuasion was enough. French agreed to stay in the line and conform to the movements of General Lanrezac's 5th Army, remaining, in effect, under the operational control of General Joffre, the French commander-in-chief. Joffre, belatedly realizing that the German main effort was being focused not on Alsace-Lorraine but on Belgium, had at last begun to move troops by rail west from the Franco-German border, but had advised the government to quit Paris for Bordeaux.

Fortune now favoured him. The RFC, shepherding the BEF from

the air, together with their French counterparts operating from Paris, reported that the movement of German troops was shifting south-eastwards, away from the capital. And then a blood-stained map was found on a dead German staff officer, marked with pencil lines indicating that the German axis of advance was indeed south-east.

Not only did this perfect gift of intelligence indicate that Paris would not be invested, as it had been in 1870; it suggested the opportunity for a decisive counter-attack. By marching south-east, the Germans were presenting their right flank to the Paris garrison, now reinforced by the newly created French 6th Army under General Michel-Joseph Manoury, and commanded overall by the incomparable veteran 'colonial' General Joseph Gallieni, Joffre's mentor.

On 3 September, nevertheless, the BEF crossed the River Marne, the last obstacle on what Sir John French still regarded as a march to haven west of Paris. Sergeant David Brunton of the 19th Hussars, French's old regiment, recorded in his diary that he and his troop 'had a swim . . . washed underclothes, and dryed them in sun'. In thirteen days the BEF had marched nearly 200 miles – the infantry on their feet, the cavalry half in the saddle and half afoot. Which was the better off is debatable: an infantryman got an average of four hours' sleep in twenty-four during the retreat, a mounted man – cavalry or gunner – an hour less, for he had his horse to attend to before he could lie down, and before he could march again. Brunton's troop had had an eventful and bloody time, including the action at Néry, but, like most of the BEF, they just wanted to turn and fight rather than keep retreating. Some battalions of Haig's I Corps had yet to fire a shot.

Two days later, however, Joffre would literally have to beg Sir John French to join in the counter-attack. Having driven to the BEF's new headquarters, at Melun on the banks of the Seine in the south-east suburbs of Paris, the massive, usually imperturbable 'Papa' Joffre, having explained his plans, clasped his hands together and beseeched his ally: 'Monsieur le maréchal, c'est la France qui vous supplie.' French, reduced to tears, tried to reply but language failed him. Turning to his interpreter, he said: 'Dammit, I can't explain. Tell him all that men can do, our fellows will do.'

At first light on 6 September, therefore, 100,000 British troops (reinforced since Mons by two divisions) joined close on a million French to begin the great counter-offensive against the 750,000-strong German right wing on a front of 150 miles between Paris and Verdun. Gallieni even requisitioned 700 Parisian taxicabs to rush forward two regiments, including Zouaves (colourfully clothed light infantry) just arrived from North Africa. 'Eh bien, voilà au moins qui n'est pas banal!' he remarked ('Well, here at least is something out of the ordinary!').

The main weight of the counter-attack was in the valley of the Marne, and the turning back of what had looked like an unstoppable advance on Paris would be dubbed 'the Miracle on the Marne'. By 13 September the Germans had fallen back 60 miles to the River Aisne, leaving evidence of the sort of atrocities which the newspapers were reporting from Belgium: 'One town we passed through today was a pitiful sight,' wrote Sergeant Brunton. 'The Huns had played hell with it and many young girls violated.'

The swelteringly hot weather now broke and torrential rain swelled the streams lying in the path of the allies, gaining the Germans time to dig in on the high ground north of the Aisne, finally checking any further advance. Nevertheless the BEF would suffer 12,000 casualties in the next fortnight attempting to dislodge them, bitter losses when in the advance from the Marne they had taken fewer than 2,000.

Those 12,000 were indeed a heavy toll, but a week later 1,459 men and cadets would be lost in the space of an hour when a German U-boat torpedoed three British cruisers, *Aboukir*, *Cressy* and *Hogue*, prompting Asquith, in a curious anachronism, to tell the first lord of the Admiralty, Churchill, to mine the North Sea 'on a Napoleonic scale'.

Meanwhile, on 13 September the German commander-in-chief, Colonel-General Helmuth Johann von Moltke (the 'Younger Moltke'), in a state of nervous collapse, had told the Kaiser: 'Your Majesty, we have lost the war.' Next day he was replaced by the Prussian war minister, General Erich von Falkenhayn.

The allied counter-offensive was running out of steam, however, and the nature of the battle beginning to change, as Sir John French noted in a letter to the King: 'From now on the spade will be as great a necessity as the rifle, and the heaviest types and calibres of artillery will be brought up on either side.'

But for the moment the flanks still hung tantalizingly in the air, with 200 miles of open country to the west, and each side now desperately tried to outflank the other. With each attempt the lines would be prolonged west and north, in what would become known as 'the Race for the Sea', though the object was not so much reaching the coast as re-establishing a war of manoeuvre.

*

The defeat of two Russian armies at Tannenberg and the Masurian Lakes at the end of August and early September had been a major setback for the Triple Entente of Russia, France and Britain, but the Russian invasion of East Prussia had drawn off two German army corps from France and Belgium, to the advantage of the counter-attack on the Marne.

In the south of Poland, too, at that time the territory of the Tsar, the Russians got the better of their other enemy when Austria-Hungary, hitherto preoccupied with Serbia, launched its belated offensive towards Warsaw. Waiting for this very move were four fully mobilized and well-supplied armies. On 30 August, under Generals Nikolai Ivanov and Aleksei Brusilov, these mounted a counter-offensive which by the end of September had inflicted 130,000 casualties and forced the Austrians out of Galicia.

For their part the Germans, having checked the threat to East Prussia, could now switch troops to south-western Poland, where the Austro-Hungarian offensive had failed. Little progress would be made, though, for Russian mobilization was at last complete, and sheer numbers began to tell.

To the south, Austria-Hungary had made no better progress against Serbia, its first invasion brought to a rapid end on the Cer Mountain (15–20 August) and at Šabac (21–4 August) by the experienced Serbian General Radomir Putnik. In early September, however, Putnik's counter-offensive on the Sava river, in the north, had to be broken off when the Austrians began a second attack, against the Serbs' western front on the Drina river. Weeks of deadlock followed, tying down many Austrian troops on whom the Germans had been counting for operations against Russia.

The Schlieffen Plan was beginning to come undone on both the Western and the Eastern Fronts.

3

OCTOBER

The Wars of the World

The fighting spreads beyond Europe as imperial troops rally to the cause

By the middle of September, after the great allied counter-attack at the River Marne, almost at the gates of Paris, some believed the war on the Western Front was as good as won – that it would indeed be over by Christmas. Major-General Henry Wilson, the most influential officer in Britain's pre-war planning and now the BEF's deputy chief of staff, told his French counterpart that 'unless we make some serious blunder we ought to be at Elsenborn [across the German border] in four weeks'. The French general thought three.

They would make a serious blunder, however: under-estimating the Germans' power of recovery. All further allied advance was checked on the River Aisne; and it was during the ensuing 'Race for the Sea' that the BEF would fight its most desperate action to date, at the place that would become synonymous with British arms on the Western Front: Ypres.

General Joseph Joffre had formed a new army, the 6th, north of Paris, and was bringing his 2nd Army from the Franco-German border, where the fighting was less intense, to prolong his line north-west. The BEF now found itself sandwiched between French armies, rather than on the western flank as planned. Sir John French therefore asked Joffre to allow him to resume his position on the left of the French line. He was expecting the arrival of significant reinforcements, including the newly formed 7th and 8th Divisions (both regular) and the leading elements of the Indian Corps and the Indian Cavalry Corps, telling Joffre: 'My present force of six Divisions and two Cavalry Divisions will, within three or four weeks from now, be increased by four Divisions and two Cavalry Divisions, making a total British force of ten Divisions (five Corps) and four Cavalry Divisions' – in all, some 250,000 men.

The BEF also needed to shorten its lines of communication, and to that end shift its supply base from Le Havre to Calais or one of the other more northerly Channel ports.

Joffre acceded to French's request, and on 3 October the BEF began the move, towards Ypres in Belgian Flanders. However, the Belgian government, now in Antwerp with the remnants of the field army, Brussels having fallen, asked the allies for troops to prolong the defence of the city (which would also allow the BEF to reach the coast). The 7th Division was therefore diverted to Ostend and Zeebrugge, and Winston Churchill, as first lord of the Admiralty, was sent to Antwerp to assess the situation. 'I don't know how fluent he [Churchill] is in French,' wrote Asquith to his confidante Venetia Stanley, 'but if he was able to do himself justice in a foreign tongue, the Belgians will be listening to a discourse the like of which they have never heard before. I cannot but think that he will stiffen them up to the sticking point.'

At Churchill's urging a Royal Marines brigade and two more of the Royal Naval Division – reservist sailors not required for ships' crews, half-retrained as infantry (among them, hastily commissioned, Rupert Brooke) – were sent at once to Antwerp. The French then withheld their reinforcements, and with the city's defences disintegrating, the 7th Division, transported in London buses, some still bearing their metropolitan destinations and advertisements for soap, was ordered to cover the withdrawal of the Antwerp garrison. The city surrendered on 10 October, with Albert, King of the

Belgians, reputedly firing the last shot. Many Royal Marines and sailors were taken prisoner, or interned when they crossed into neutral Holland, but the bulk of the Belgian army managed to slip south to take up positions along the River Yser between Ostend and Dunkirk. Albert ordered the sea-locks at Nieuport to be opened to flood the countryside and thereby stem the German advance.

The allies had won the 'Race for the Sea'.

At Ypres, however – 'Wipers' in Tommy parlance – the duke of Württemberg's 4th Army, brought by rail from south-east Belgium, reinforced by fresh troops from Germany and from the siege of Antwerp, was making a determined effort to break through. The BEF halted the attacks, and on 21 October Sir John French, urged on by General Ferdinand Foch, whom Joffre had placed in local command of his left flank, ordered a counter-offensive.

It soon ran into trouble, hampered by a shortage of artillery shells and over-optimistic estimates of German strength. A month's desperate fighting would follow as the Germans made their own counter-attacks on the 'Ypres salient', 8 miles at its widest. The first regiments of the Territorial Force (those who had volunteered for service overseas) would be blooded in this 'First Battle of Ypres', notably the London Scottish, who lost half their strength in the fighting. The Germans also had their first sight of the turbans, pugarees and Gurkha pillboxes of the Indian Corps. At Hollebeke on 31 October Sepoy (Private) Khudadad Khan of the Duke of Connaught's Own Baluchi Regiment won the first ever Indian VC in an action almost identical to that in which Lieutenant Dease and Private Godley of the Royal Fusiliers had won theirs at Mons: 'The British Officer in charge of the [machine-gun] detachment having been wounded,' ran the citation, 'and the other gun put out of action by a shell, Sepoy Khudadad, though himself wounded, remained working his gun until all the other five men of the gun detachment had been killed.'

The situation looked so bad that Sir John French told Foch: 'There is nothing left for me to do but go up and be killed with I Corps.' Foch replied simply: 'You must not talk of dying but of winning.'

*

While the BEF was fighting for its life in Flanders, the war was spreading world-wide. British and German troops clashed in both East and West Africa, and South African forces invaded German South-West Africa (Namibia). Louis Botha, the South African prime minister, and his defence minister Jan Smuts, who as Boer commanders had been fighting Britain only twelve years before, had been quick to declare the dominion's support, despite armed opposition by German-sympathizers.

In the Pacific, cruiser warfare and operations against German colonies had begun at once with Australian, New Zealand and Japanese help, Japan having declared war on Germany on 23 August in accordance with the Anglo-Japanese naval treaty of 1902. The German cruiser *Karlsruhe* sank merchant ships in the Caribbean, while the *Emden* raided shipping in the Indian Ocean and bombarded the oil storage tanks at Madras.

On 29 October, the war took a critical turn with the entry of the Ottoman Empire on the side of the Central Powers. A secret Turco-German treaty had been signed on 2 August, but Constantinople had at first been hesitant to act. Berlin therefore decided to force the issue. The German battle-cruiser *Goeben* and light cruiser *Breslau* of Admiral Wilhelm Souchon's Mediterranean squadron had managed to give the Royal Navy the slip and reach the Dardanelles, and Souchon now took both vessels – under Ottoman colours – plus a Turkish squadron into the Black Sea, from where they shelled Odessa and Sevastopol.

With the allies' subsequent declaration of war on the Ottoman Empire, fighting would now spread to the Middle East, at huge opportunity cost in manpower and resources, not least those of India, Australia and New Zealand. The Russians too now faced a new front, in the Caucasus, in addition to those in East Prussia, Poland and the Carpathians, while the closure of the Dardanelles to shipping meant that armaments could not be sent to them via the Mediterranean. The road to the Russian Revolution was beginning to open up.

No two warships have ever had more decisive strategic effect than the *Goeben* and the *Breslau*.

4

NOVEMBER

The Sea Dog

A defeat for the Royal Navy in the South Pacific,
and then an emphatic victory in the South Atlantic

At 6.18 p.m. on 1 November, off the coast of central Chile near the port of Coronel, Rear-Admiral Sir Christopher Cradock, a bachelor Yorkshireman with a passion for foxhunting, signalled to the distant HMS *Canopus*, a pre-dreadnought battleship sent by the Admiralty to reinforce his South Atlantic cruiser squadron: 'I am now going to attack enemy.'

So began, wrote Winston Churchill, first lord of the Admiralty, 'the saddest naval action in the war. Of the officers and men in both the squadrons that faced each other . . . nine out of ten were doomed to perish. The British were to die that night: the Germans a month later' (*The World Crisis*, vol. 1, 1923).

The Battle of Coronel, still the subject of controversy, was the result of faulty intelligence, misunderstanding and miscommunication. After commerce raiding in the Indian and Pacific Oceans, Vice-Admiral Maximilian Graf (Count) von Spee's East Asia squadron had turned its attention to southerly waters. The squadron

CORONEL AND THE FALKLANDS

1914

→ Vice-Admiral von Spee's course

▶▶▶▶ Vice-Admiral Sturdee's course

```
0          miles          500
0          kilometres          1,000
```

Coronel

Battle of Coronel
1 Nov. 1914

ARGENTINA

CHILE

South
Atlantic
Ocean

Falkland
Islands

Battle of the Falklands
8 Dec. 1914

South
Pacific
Ocean

N

comprised mainly light cruisers, some of which were detached for independent action – notably the *Emden*, which in September had bombarded Madras – but had two modern armoured cruisers, the *Scharnhorst* and *Gneisenau*, crewed by the best men of the German fleet. In mid-September Cradock was told to prepare to meet Spee if he came into South American waters. However, his own squadron consisted of elderly cruisers manned largely by reservists, and whereas *Scharnhorst* and *Gneisenau* could each dispose eight 8-inch guns, six of which could fire on either beam, Cradock's flagship, HMS *Good Hope*, had but two 9.2-inch guns that could match their range, while his second cruiser, *Monmouth*, carried only nine 6-inch guns that could fire on the beam. The Admiralty, judging that not a single dreadnought-class battle-cruiser could be spared from the Grand Fleet, which was keeping the German High Seas Fleet penned up in Wilhelmshaven, sent south instead the elderly battleship *Canopus*. Her four 12-inch guns could easily deal with *Scharnhorst* and *Gneisenau*, but she lacked speed – 15 knots compared with *Good Hope*'s 23.

In late October, having intercepted signals from the cruiser *Leipzig*, Cradock concluded that she was the only one of Spee's ships to have reached Chilean waters, and so took the armoured cruisers *Good Hope* and *Monmouth*, the light cruiser *Glasgow* and the armed merchant ship *Otranto* round Cape Horn to intercept her, leaving the slower *Canopus* to escort his colliers. *Glasgow* scouted ahead to Coronel, where on 1 November, instead of just *Leipzig*, she found Spee's entire squadron.

In the coming darkness Cradock could have withdrawn to the cover of *Canopus*'s 12-inch guns 300 miles to the south, but he decided to stand and fight. Not the least of his reasons was that a fellow rear-admiral, Ernest Troubridge, was facing court martial for letting slip the cruisers *Goeben* and *Breslau* in the eastern Mediterranean the month before.

According to *Glasgow*'s log, 'the British Squadron turned to port four points together towards the enemy with a view to closing them and forcing them to action before sunset, which if successful would have put them at a great disadvantage owing to the British Squadron being between the enemy and the sun'. However, Spee used his superior speed to overcome the dazzle, putting his ships on a parallel course south. Within an hour Cradock's ships were silhouetted against the afterglow of the sun, which had now dipped below the horizon, while his own were scarcely visible against the dark background of the coast. At seven o'clock he opened fire.

The sea was high, adding to the difficulties the *Good Hope*'s and the *Monmouth*'s gunners faced, for their 6-inch guns were on the main deck, while the Germans' were on the upper. *Scharnhorst*'s third salvo put one of *Good Hope*'s 9.2-inch guns out of action, and shortly afterwards she exploded with the loss of all hands, including Cradock and his beloved terrier Jack. *Monmouth*, though holed and listing badly, refused to surrender and was shelled at close quarters by the cruiser *Nürnberg* until she too sank without survivors. *Otranto*, unarmoured and having only 4.7-inch guns, was incapable of taking part in the action, and managed to use her 18 knots to get away. *Glasgow* remained pluckily in action until darkness overcame her, when she too managed to escape. In all, the British had lost 1,654 sailors in less than an hour, the Germans none.

Coronel threw the Admiralty into a rage, for not only was it the Royal Navy's first defeat at sea in more than a century, it left Spee in command of South American waters and with a wide choice of alternatives. But Spee himself had doubts. When the German community in Valparaiso, where he had put in after the battle, pressed congratulatory bouquets on him, he replied: 'They will do for my funeral.'

This time the Admiralty spared no measures. While Churchill arranged for the Japanese navy to cover the South Pacific, the 73-year-old first sea lord, Admiral of the Fleet Lord (Jacky) Fisher, who had been brought out of retirement days earlier following the enforced resignation of the German-born Prince Louis of Battenberg, detached the dreadnought battle-cruisers *Inflexible* and *Invincible* from the Grand Fleet. After hasty refit at Devonport, these raced south under command of the square-jawed Vice-Admiral Sir Doveton Sturdee and, having rendezvoused with Rear-Admiral Archibald Stoddart's mid-Atlantic cruiser squadron at the Abrolhos Archipelago off Brazil, reached Port Stanley in the Falkland Islands on 7 December. Here they found *Canopus* undergoing repair to her boilers, but her guns ready for action, and began at once to coal.

It was not a moment too soon, for the day before Spee had sailed through the Straits of Magellan intending to destroy the signal station at Stanley. At about eight o'clock on 8 December his leading armoured cruiser, *Gneisenau*, with his younger son Heinrich on board, came in sight of Sturdee's guardship. 'A few minutes later a terrible apparition broke upon German eyes,' wrote Churchill. 'Rising from behind the promontory, sharply visible in the clear air, were a pair of tripod masts. One glance was enough. They meant certain death.' For only dreadnoughts had tripods – and eight 12-inch guns apiece.

But Sturdee's battle-cruisers, still coaling, could not immediately raise steam, and it was *Canopus*, beached on the mudbanks, that opened fire first as *Gneisenau* turned away to rejoin the main body of the squadron. Soon all five of Spee's ships were making full steam east then south, pursued by the cruisers *Glasgow*, *Kent* and *Carnarvon*, but it was not until nearly ten o'clock that *Invincible* and *Inflexible* could give chase. However, both ships, fresh out of dry dock, had a 5-knot advantage over Spee's, and in three hours closed to within 17,500 yards of *Leipzig* and opened fire. Spee now ordered his light cruisers to turn south-west, while *Scharnhorst* and *Gneisenau* turned north-east to cover their retreat. They opened fire half an hour later and scored a hit on *Invincible*, though the shell burst harmlessly on the belt armour.

British gunnery was poor at first, scoring only four hits out of more than 200 rounds fired, largely owing to the copious quantities of smoke generated. Sturdee therefore decided to put distance between the opposing squadrons and, as in Nelson's day, to seek the weather gauge, though not for steerage but to get upwind of the smoke. But Spee closed again to 12,500 yards to enable him to use his 5.9-inch guns, and firing continued for some hours, both sides now troubled by poor visibility. Damage to both *Scharnhorst* and *Gneisenau* mounted, however, while that to *Inflexible* and *Invincible* was negligible. *Scharnhorst* ceased firing at four o'clock and capsized a quarter of an hour later with not a single survivor, Spee going down with his flagship. *Gneisenau* was pounded for another hour and a half by both battle-cruisers, which had closed to just 4,000 yards, until her captain opened the sea-cocks and she too capsized, the British ships picking up 176 men from the freezing sea. Lieutenant Heinrich von Spee was not among them.

Sturdee's cruisers, which had given chase to the lighter ships, overtook and sank the *Leipzig* later that evening, pulling just eighteen sailors from the water. HMS *Kent* had earlier caught and sunk the *Nürnberg*, having exceeded even her design speed. *Nürnberg* had refused to surrender, and as she foundered by the head, a huddle of her remaining crew on the rising stern could be seen waving the German flag. All but seven of her complement of over 300 perished, including Lieutenant Otto von Spee, the admiral's elder son.

Only the *Dresden* escaped, but she was cornered three months later in Chilean waters, where she too was scuttled and her crew interned; they included Lieutenant Wilhelm Canaris, the future chief of Hitler's military intelligence service, the *Abwehr*. In December 1939 the German pocket battleship *Admiral Graf Spee*, named in honour of the victor of Coronel, would herself be scuttled in South American waters after a brilliant affair of gunnery and deception by Commodore Henry Harwood's cruiser squadron at the Battle of the River Plate, off Montevideo, when once again Churchill was first lord of the Admiralty.

With the fortuitous wreck of the *Karlsruhe* off the West Indies in November, the cornering of the *Königsberg* in German East Africa and the destruction of the *Emden* by HMAS *Sydney* in the Indian Ocean, by the middle of March 1915, as Churchill wrote, 'no German ships of war remained on any of the oceans of the world'. The consequences of their exclusion, he noted, 'were far-reaching, and affected simultaneously our position in every part of the globe'.

From now on the Germans' war against merchant shipping would have to be waged by submarine – activity which would do so much to bring the United States into the conflict – or else the High Seas Fleet would have to break out of Wilhelmshaven. This they would not try until the middle of 1916, when at the Battle of Jutland the Royal Navy forced them back into their North Sea haven for the rest of the war.

While the Royal Navy's distant drama of tragedy and revenge was being played out, the fighting at Ypres on the Western Front had become very bloody indeed as the Germans made desperate attempts to break through to capture the Channel ports. Reservists of every type, as well as dismounted cavalrymen and Indian troops, many still in their tropical uniforms, were thrown in to hold the line. On 6 November, Captain Arthur O'Neill of the 2nd Life Guards became the first MP (for Mid Antrim) to be killed – the first of nineteen. His youngest son would be prime minister of Northern Ireland in the 1960s. Casualties at 'First Ypres' to 22 November, the close of the qualifying period for the medal known colloquially as the Mons Star, were some 60,000.

Fighting on the Eastern Front, though, remained fluid. Having managed to defeat an Austro-Hungarian offensive in Galicia and a German attempt to take Warsaw, in early November Russian forces began a counter-offensive into Silesia. After heavy losses, however, both sides accepted they had gone as far as they could, and in early December the Russians withdrew to a new and stronger line closer to the Polish capital.

Meanwhile, in Mesopotamia, the British were striking the first blow against the Turkish army. On 7 November the 6th (Poona) Division of the Indian army landed at the mouth of the Shatt al-Arab waterway to secure the Persian oilfields, taking Basra a fortnight later. It would be another three and a half years, however, before the Turks were finally ejected from what is now Iraq.

5

DECEMBER

'Wipers'

Heroic resistance in Flanders as the home front comes under fire

December began exceptionally wet for the BEF on the Western Front. The incessant rain turned the stone-less soil of Flanders into 'a sort of liquid mud of the consistency of thick porridge', wrote the commander-in-chief, Sir John French, 'without the valuable sustaining quality of that excellent Scots mixture. To walk off the roads meant sinking in at once.'

The BEF of December 1914 was not, however, the same force that had crossed to France three and half months earlier. Reinforced by regulars from around the world, by troops of the Indian army and territorials, it was now nearly three times its original strength. But the casualties in the retreat from Mons, the counter-attack on the River Marne and the subsequent fighting on the Aisne, and above all in the Ypres salient, had borne heavily on the 'Old Contemptibles', as the pre-war regulars called themselves after the Kaiser had supposedly remarked that they were a 'contemptible little army' (he would later admit only that he might have said that Britain's army was 'contemptibly little' – which by continental standards it was).

The BEF had arrived in France with around 80,000 infantry, and by 22 November, the official end of the First Battle of Ypres, casualties of all kinds since the beginning of hostilities numbered 86,237. Most of these were in the infantry, and disproportionately high among the officers. The 1915 edition of *Debrett's Peerage* would be delayed for many months until the editors could revise the entries for almost every blue-blooded family in the kingdom.

Of First Ypres, that usually stern critic of British arms, and the most influential military theorist of the inter-war years, Captain Sir Basil Liddell Hart, wrote:

> No battle in Britain's annals has given clearer proof of fighting quality. It was a battle in the natural line of British tradition – a defensive attitude combined with timely ripostes. Thus it suited the nature of the troops who conducted it. If it did not directly fit their pre-war tactical training, predominantly offensive in imitation of the continental fashion, it appealed to their native instincts, which count for more than a fashionable dogma under the test of battle.

There were times when that fighting quality had faltered, but only momentarily, a reality the duke of Wellington himself would have recognized. Once, in the Peninsula, one of his staff pointed to some troops abandoning their position, to which he replied: 'Oh, they all do that at some time: the question is, will they rally?' Despite the mounting losses at Ypres, the regiments of the BEF always rallied. Their morale and superlative weapon skills – fifteen accurate rounds a minute with the Lee–Enfield magazine-fed rifle – were the decisive factors in the battle, said Liddell Hart: 'The little British Army had a corporate sense that was unique . . . "First Ypres", on the British side, was not just a soldiers' battle but a "family battle" – against outsiders . . . After the battle was over, little survived, save the memory of its spirit.'

But although First Ypres officially ended on 22 November, fighting did not, each side trying to gain local advantage. The Indian Corps won two VCs the very next day, and a third the day after.

Commanders, all too conscious of the loss of so many experienced officers and NCOs, as well as the worsening physical conditions, were determined to keep up the pressure.

Opportunity for offensive action now seemed to beckon when intelligence revealed that the Germans were transferring troops to the Eastern Front (the secretary of state for war, Lord Kitchener, told the cabinet there was 'nothing in front of them [the BEF] but men and boys'). The French commander-in-chief, Joseph Joffre, ordered his armies to renew the offensive, and asked the BEF to renew their partial attacks at Ypres without delay. Unfortunately, the Germans who had gone east had not taken their barbed wire with them. On 12 December Sir John French gave orders for a series of divisional actions, and to achieve surprise no artillery preparations were to be made, the infantry being issued instead with wire-cutters and mattresses with which to cross the obstacle belt.

The results were bloody and fruitless. Nor were they unpredictable, as Captain Billy Congreve of the Rifle Brigade (who would later win the VC, as his father had, before being killed on the Somme) with the staff of the 3rd Division, wrote in his diary: 'Yesterday we made an attack and, as we only put two battalions into it, the attack naturally failed. We had about 400 casualties. It is very depressing. I should have thought that we had learnt our lesson at Neuve Chapelle [in October] about unsupported attacks, but it seems not.'

Notwithstanding the weather and mounting casualties, attacks continued in this vein throughout December, and while the Germans were no less active at times, by the end of the month General Joffre could declare that there was now no possibility of their breaking through the allied line. However, while Berlin and London were coming to terms with fighting a long war, August's boast of 'over by Christmas' now a distant dream, Joffre remained convinced he could achieve an early and decisive victory in France. This disparity of views would lie at the root of the allies' problems in 1915.

From Churchill's perspective as first lord of the Admiralty the situation looked equally promising, if for a different reason. With German cruisers swept from the oceans after the battles of Coronel and the Falkland Islands, the *Hochseeflotte* for the moment skulking in its anchorage at Wilhelmshaven in fear of Jellicoe's Grand Fleet at Scapa Flow, and the submarine threat still relatively small, trade routes were now safe. But the commander of the *Hochseeflotte*, Friedrich von Ingenohl, now tried to lure Jellicoe into a skirmish, aiming to wear down his numbers and thereby even the odds for the great fleet action that he knew must come at some point. On 16 December he sent Franz von Hipper's scouting group, comprising five battle-cruisers (*Seydlitz, Moltke, von der Tann, Derrflinger* and *Blücher*) with a screen of light cruisers and destroyers, to bombard the North Sea ports of Scarborough, Whitby and the Hartlepools, in the hope that this would bring out a part of the Grand Fleet, which his own battleships, following up Hipper's group, would then ambush.

The Admiralty's signal intercept service, 'Room 40', had intercepted *Hochseeflotte* signals, however, and knew there was a sortie, if not its object. Jellicoe despatched Vice-Admiral Sir George Warrender's 2nd Battle Squadron, comprising six dreadnoughts, four battle-cruisers, four heavy cruisers, six light cruisers and eight submarines, to intercept Hipper's group. In the pre-dawn murk these ran into the *Hochseeflotte* itself, however, and Warrender's destroyers opened fire. Ingenohl, fearing torpedo attack and mindful of the Kaiser's injunction to avoid heavy losses, turned away and ran for port. Meanwhile Hipper's battle-cruisers had crossed the North Sea, and at 8.10 a.m. began bombarding the largely undefended ports, firing 1,150 shells in an hour and twenty minutes before escaping in the mist. They inflicted some 650 casualties, mainly civilian, including 137 killed of whom 78 were women and children. Scarborough in particular suffered much damage.

Public opinion and the press held the Royal Navy to blame for failing to prevent the raid, but the bombardment reinforced the image of German 'frightfulness' gained from the earlier atrocities in Belgium. 'Remember Scarborough' became a rallying cry for recruiting officers, as well as provoking outrage in the United States. The Kaiser's orders to the *Hochseeflotte* became even more restraining.

'As December passed,' wrote Churchill, 'a sense of indescribable relief stole over the Admiralty ... The mighty enemy, with all the advantages of preparation and design, had delivered his onslaught and had everywhere [on land and sea] been brought to a standstill. It was our turn now. The initiative had passed to Britain – the Great Amphibian ... It was for us to say where we would strike and when.'

*

The Pope called for it. The high command gave orders to prevent it. The Christmas truce of 1914 is perhaps the best known but least understood episode of the First World War.

What is incontrovertible is that on that Christmas Day British and German troops climbed out of their trenches along several stretches of the Western Front and met in no-man's-land on sociable terms. Why, and what this moment signified, are questions more complex than suggestions of incipient pacifism or war-weariness allow. Pope Benedict XV, elected in early September and appalled by what he called 'the suicide of civilized Europe', had from the outset urged a general ceasefire. 'The greatest and wealthiest nations,' he said, were 'well-provided with the most awful weapons modern military science has devised ... day by day the earth is drenched with newly shed blood and is covered with the bodies of the wounded and of the slain.' In early December he asked specifically that 'the guns may fall silent at least upon the night the angels sang' to allow negotiations for an honourable peace.

The belligerent powers dismissed the plea more or less peremptorily. For a decade the French government had been fervidly anti-clerical. Germany, despite Catholic Bavaria, was also unreceptive: the *Kulturkampf*, the aggressive secularization policy of the former chancellor, Bismarck, was of recent memory. Austria-Hungary, though 80 per cent Catholic, was deeply suspicious of Rome – which was not just the seat of the Pope but the capital of Italy, its erstwhile ally, now veering towards the Entente powers. Russia, being Orthodox, had always rejected claims to papal authority, and in any case, adhering to the old Julian calendar rather than the Gregorian, celebrated the Nativity on 7 January. Britain, for its part, retained the distrust embodied in the Book of Common Prayer: 'The Bishop of Rome hath no jurisdiction in this realm of England.' Indeed, despite the heroism of Irish troops (the first VC of the war was an Irish-born Catholic), the British army's leadership could be suspicious of the commitment of Catholic officers. As late as November 1917 the BEF's chief of intelligence, Brigadier-General John Charteris, would write to his wife: 'My chief opponents are the Roman Catholic people, who are really very half-hearted about the whole war.'

The western allies, France, Britain and Belgium, had fought the Germans to a standstill and were in no mood for peace negotiations. The French alone had lost 300,000 killed, and twice that number wounded, captured or missing. The front now consisted of continuous parallel lines of trenches from the North Sea to the Swiss border, and Joffre was determined to evict the invader from French soil before the German defences were strengthened. Senior officers of the BEF were therefore anxious to keep up the offensive spirit, and on 5 December, the General Officer Commanding (GOC) II Corps, Sir Horace Smith-Dorrien, issued instructions to his divisional commanders:

> It is during this period that the greatest danger to the morale of troops exists. Experience of this and of every other war proves undoubtedly that troops in trenches in close proximity to the enemy slide very easily, if permitted to do so, into a 'live and let live' theory of life . . . officers and men sink into a military lethargy from which it is difficult to arouse them when the moment for great sacrifices again arises . . . the attitude of our troops can be readily understood and to a certain extent commands sympathy . . . Such an attitude is however most dangerous for it discourages initiative in commanders and destroys the offensive spirit in all ranks . . . friendly intercourse with the enemy, unofficial armistices, however tempting and amusing they may be, are absolutely prohibited.

Joffre asked Sir John French to renew his attacks south of Ypres as quickly as possible to distract the Germans while he himself made preparations for the French army's counter-offensive. In mid-December, therefore, the British army made some of its most flawed and costly assaults of the war, notably at Messines and Ploegsteert (known inevitably to the troops as 'Plug Street'), and as a result by Christmas large numbers of dead of both sides lay unburied in no-man's-land.

Despite the orders against 'friendly intercourse', the static and routine nature of trench warfare and the proximity of the enemy – in some cases as close as 50 yards, which meant that they could be heard talking, and even their breakfast cooking smelled – made for curiosity. Because, too, the weather was particularly cold and wet, a degree of mutual respect developed among those enduring it on both sides. On 20 December there was a local truce on 22 Brigade's front when the Germans began taking in British wounded from no-man's-land, though there was no fraternization.

Meanwhile the festive spirit was being fuelled by the respective armies' postal services, with huge volumes of mail and gifts arriving for the troops from home. King George V sent a Christmas card to every soldier, sailor and nurse, and the Princess Mary Fund despatched a gift box to every soldier at the front, one for smokers and another for non-smokers. In her letter launching the scheme, the 17-year-old daughter of the King and Queen wrote: 'Could there be anything more likely to hearten them in their struggle than a present received straight from home on Christmas Day?'

The Kaiser likewise sent tobacco, and cigars for the officers and NCOs, and ordered 100,000 Christmas trees for the front, much to the dismay of his staff officers, who were appalled at the appropriation of transport for non-warlike supplies.

For both sides, therefore, Christmas approached with some degree of festal promise. For the British regulars in particular, 25 December had always been a holiday, with reduced duties and relaxed discipline whether in barracks or on active service. Traditionally the men were served tea in the morning by the sergeant-majors and dinner by the officers. Why should 1914 be any different?

At this stage of the war, too, the ground had not been churned-up into the moonscapes of the later years, and many parts of the line had a familiar pastoral look. On Christmas Eve the temperature plummeted, a peculiarly welcome event, for the liquid mud now froze solid. Getting out of the trenches was therefore easier and more inviting.

Many of the immediate accounts of what actually happened that night and on Christmas morning were rushed, confused or contradictory, while others, written long after the event, were overlaid with hindsight. To begin with there was no particular pattern beyond the shouted exchanges, or the signs – initially probably ironic – hoisted above the trenches wishing those opposite respectively a Merry Christmas or *Frohe Weihnachten*, and in places carol-singing and counter-singing. But on the whole it was the Germans who left the trenches first and advanced without their weapons to the wire in the middle of no-man's-land. The British seem to have responded out of inquisitiveness, and the sheer absurdity of milling around between the lines of trenches shows on the faces of those photographed (both sides prohibited cameras in the trenches, which accounts for the paucity of such photographs). Once footballs were produced, as happened here and there, the soldier's natural inclination to fun took over. In other sectors, however, the grim business of recovering the dead made for a more sombre encounter, with occasional exchanges of mementos, an attempt perhaps on the part of each side to proclaim its humanity.

Some British troops made full use of the opportunity to spy out the enemy's defences, as Brigadier-General Walter Congreve, commanding 18 Brigade near Neuve Chapelle, related in a letter home that day:

My informant, one of the men, said he had had a fine day of it & had 'smoked a cigar with the best shot in the German army, then not more than 18. They say he's killed more of our men than any other 12 together but I know now where he shoots from & I hope we down him tomorrow.' I hope devoutly they will.

There were instances of temporary, localized ceasefires between the French and Germans, and even the Russians and Germans (and

Austrians), but the Christmas truce of 1914 appears to have been a phenomenon principally of the British and German sector, probably for the simple reason that to the regulars of the BEF the war was not as 'personal' as it was for the French and Belgians, whose homelands had been violated and whose domestic life had been up-ended by mobilization. Indeed, when civilians in the rear areas heard of it the reaction could be hostile. Frank Richards, a former regular recalled to the colours, and author of *Old Soldiers Never Die*, recalls how his battalion, marching back to billets through Armentières on 27 December, were spat at by Frenchwomen shouting: 'You no bon, you English soldiers, you boko [*beaucoup*] kamerade Allemenge.'

Nor was there any consistency in the pattern of truces: General Congreve relates that while '1st [battalion] Rifle Brigade were playing football with the Germans opposite them, the next-door regiments fired all day.' The 2nd Grenadier Guards, for example, took many casualties in heavy fighting. The Commonwealth War Graves Commission's records show that two officers and sixty-eight other ranks were killed on 25 December (there is no record of those wounded or posted missing that day).

Disciplinary action against a number of officers was initiated, though it largely fizzled out with the renewal of attacks in the weeks following. There would be no repeat of the Christmas truce, in part because of the firm hand of authority on both sides, in part because of the growing bitterness of the fighting.

In reality, the Christmas truce was less romantic than it is frequently portrayed. In retrospect it was but a passing episode, a relic of pre-war soldiering which, while it appears to have left a profound impact on some of those who took part, in the majority of regiments of the BEF hardly registered a mention.

PART TWO

1915

Deadlock

19 February: Dardanelles campaign begins.

22 April: Second Battle of Ypres begins.

25 April: Gallipoli landings begin.

7 May: RMS *Lusitania* sunk by U-20.

23 May: Italy joins the war on the side of the Entente.

25 September: Battle of Loos begins.

14 October: Bulgaria declares war on Serbia.

6

JANUARY

Eastern Approaches

As the soldiers dig in on the Western Front,
the politicians look elsewhere to fight

The new year brought new thinking about how to prosecute the war. Winston Churchill, first lord of the Admiralty, wrote in a memorandum to the prime minister, H. H. Asquith:

> I think it is quite possible that neither side will have the strength to penetrate the other's line in the Western theatre ... My impression is that the position of both armies is not likely to undergo any decisive change – although no doubt several hundred thousand men will be spent to satisfy the military mind on the point ... On the assumption that these views are correct, the question arises, how ought we to apply our growing military power. Are there not other alternatives than sending our armies to chew barbed wire in Flanders?

'The military mind' of which Churchill was rightly suspicious was principally that of the French high command, which though understandably determined to evict the invader from French soil had no means of doing so except frontal assaults against the strengthening German defences. As the junior partner on the Western Front, the BEF would have little option but to support them. Indeed, this would be the story of the war until mid-1918, when British military strength at last reached rough parity with that of France, not least because the French high command had squandered so much of their own.

In the short term Britain's 'growing military power' consisted of those few regular troops still in overseas garrisons, together with territorials who volunteered for overseas service and 'colonial' troops, principally Indian, Canadian and Australian (the Canadian division, assembling in England, would cross to France in early February). In the longer term, the strength would be in the 'new armies' that Kitchener was raising through voluntary recruitment in Britain and Ireland. Formed in successive tranches of 100,000, known unofficially as K1, K2 etc., each was to mirror the original BEF. However, K1 would not be ready to take to the field for at least six months, K2 and K3 not for a year, there being neither the equipment nor the instructors to train them any more rapidly. But the question of where to send them was already exercising David Lloyd George, the chancellor of the exchequer. These new armies would be, he argued – correctly –

a force of a totally different character from any which has hitherto left these shores . . . drawn almost exclusively from the better class of artisan, the upper and the lower middle classes. In intelligence, education and character it is vastly superior to any army ever raised in this country, and it has been drawn not from the ranks of those who have generally cut themselves off from home . . . So that if this superb army is thrown away upon futile enterprises, such as those we have witnessed during the last few weeks, the country will be uncontrollably indignant at the lack of provision and intelligence shown in our plans.

Lieutenant-Colonel Maurice Hankey (a Royal Marines officer), secretary of the Committee of Imperial Defence and of the new 'war council', a slimmed-down cabinet attended by the first sea lord and the chief of the imperial general staff (CIGS), had recently circulated a paper along the lines of Churchill's memorandum of 14 December, 'The Apparent Deadlock on the Western Front', in which he argued that Britain should use the Royal Navy to project her power. On 1 January, therefore, Kitchener wrote to Sir John French:

> The feeling here is gaining ground that, although it is essential to defend the line we now hold, troops over and above what is necessary for that service could better be employed elsewhere. The question where anything effective could be accomplished opens a large field and requires a good deal of study. What are the views of your staff?

Sir John was alarmed. He and his French counterpart, General Joseph Joffre, estimated that although the Germans had suffered one and a half million casualties on both the Western and Eastern Fronts, they had a further 800,000 men in training. By March or April they would be able to 'wipe out their existing inferiority and even once again make themselves superior to us . . . It seems, therefore, of the utmost importance that we should take the offensive and strike at the earliest possible moment with all our available strength.'

Kitchener was not persuaded. December's losses, on both sides, demonstrated all too clearly the price and outcome of frontal attacks. He told the war council: 'An advance could only be made by means of developing a tremendous volume of artillery fire, and the ammunition for this is simply not available.'

The Russians, under pressure from the Ottoman Turks in the Caucasus, were calling for a diversionary effort to be made against Constantinople. Churchill, confident that Jellicoe's fleet could maintain its blockade of Germany and keep the *Hochseeflotte* penned up in its anchorage at Wilhelmshaven, having already eliminated the cruiser threat to the trade routes, believed that the Admiralty could spare some obsolescent warships to force the Dardanelles Straits and open up communications with the Russians in the Black Sea. This would also encourage Italy, Greece and Bulgaria, who were still sitting on the fence, to come in on the allied side.

Only a fortnight earlier the first naval VC of the war to be gazetted had been won by 26-year-old Lieutenant Norman Holbrook, who had taken his elderly submarine B11 under five rows of mines to sink the armoured frigate *Mesudiye*. The Dardanelles looked ripe for the taking; all it needed was equally bold action on the surface. Although the first sea lord, Admiral Jacky Fisher, was sceptical, on 13 January the war council instructed the Admiralty to make preparations for an expedition against the straits the following month. So began the ill-fated Gallipoli campaign.

Meanwhile the war was spreading with an apparent impetus of its own. Although it was not until 1918 that *The Times*'s war correspondent Colonel Charles Repington coined what would become the official expression 'First World War', as early as September 1914 the German biologist and philosopher Ernst Haeckel had written prophetically in the *Indianapolis Star*: 'There is no doubt that the course and character of the feared "European War" . . . will become the first world war in the full sense of the word.'

In January 1915, not only was the conflict drawing in troops from around the world – French colonials to the Western Front; imperial British forces to the Middle East for defence of the Suez Canal against the Turks, and to secure the oil fields of present-day Kuwait and Iraq – but the actual fighting was becoming global too. In his novel *All Our Yesterdays*, published in 1930, the former war correspondent H. M. Tomlinson describes in vivid prose the almost surreal extension of the conflict that had begun in a street in Sarajevo:

> Russians were hurling Kurds from the slopes of Mount Ararat. And at Basra, that port of the Persian Gulf for which Sinbad set sail, Sikhs had arrived from the Punjab, and Gurkhas from the Himalayas . . . to dislodge Ottomans who were entrenched in the Garden of Eden. The coconut groves of New Guinea were stormed by Australians . . . Far to the north of Singapore, by the Yellow sea, the Japanese landed in Shantung, and attacked Tsingtau, a Chinese city, though occupied by Germans, who were ordered by the Kaiser never to surrender that symbol of Germanic honour.

JANUARY: EASTERN APPROACHES

Yet while the allies were trying to contain the Germans, looking for a distant, strategic flank to turn, Berlin was only too keen to see the fighting spread in the hope that it would divert allied resources from the decisive European theatre. Although her cruisers in the South Atlantic, the Indian and Pacific Oceans had all met their end, there was still the dark continent in which to make war on land. From her colonies in West, East and South-West Africa, with native troops and a cadre of German professionals, Germany made war – notably in what are now Burundi, Rwanda and mainland Tanzania, under Colonel Paul von Lettow-Vorbeck – on British, French and Belgian colonies. In doing so she drew in, among others, South African troops under the leadership of two of Britain's former Boer adversaries, Louis Botha and Jan Smuts, whose readiness to rally to the British cause prompted armed rebellion by pro-German Afrikaner settlers.

'In the twilight aisles of the Congo,' wrote Tomlinson,

the pygmies knew of an ominous stirring among the leaves, by a terror unknown in their simple law. Negroes fought each other because of it on Lake Tanganyika. White men died on the red hot iron of burning ships sequestered in the mangrove swamps near Zanzibar; they pursued each other, with black levies, through East African jungles, and across the waterless sands of Namaqualand. African tribes, that had forgotten raw head and bloody bones through the gentle persuasion of the followers of Jesus of Nazareth, were dislodged from their mealie fields and hunting grounds because the Emperor of Germany had invaded Belgium.

7

FEBRUARY

Cruiser Rules

The U-boat campaign begins

No month of the war was to prove more fateful than February 1915. With stalemate on the Western Front, eyes were turning to other theatres – the Germans to the Eastern Front, the Ottomans and their German advisers towards the Suez Canal, and the British to the Dardanelles and beyond to the Black Sea.

A naval stalemate had also developed. The Grand Fleet at Scapa Flow in the Orkneys, and her standing cruiser patrols along the east coast, had neutralized the German High Seas Fleet, keeping the fruit of the Kaiser's great pre-war naval building programme, the 'Dreadnought Race', bottled up the other side of the North Sea at Wilhelmshaven. The attempt in December to even the odds by luring the Royal Navy into ambush with the bombardment of Scarborough and other ports on the north-east coast had ended in failure, and Admiral Jellicoe, conscious of being, in Churchill's memorable words, 'the only man who could lose the war in an afternoon', was consistently able to out-manoeuvre the Germans thanks to superior signals intelligence. On 24 January another cruiser raid was intercepted in what became known as the Battle of Dogger Bank, and although the Royal Navy was slow to follow up its success, the armoured cruiser *Blücher*, one of the villains of the Scarborough raid, was sunk with heavy loss of life. Her capsizing was filmed at close quarters by British destroyers, one of the earliest moving-picture records of the death of a warship. Ingenohl was promptly replaced as commander of the *Hochseeflotte* by Admiral Hugo von Pohl, a notably cautious officer.

While the Admiralty pondered how to tempt the *Hochseeflotte* into decisive battle, the Germans were determined to take the war underwater. U-boats had already sunk a number of allied merchantmen as well as warships, but had observed the so-called 'cruiser rules'. Under these rules, laid down by the Hague Conventions of 1899 and 1907, a submarine intending to attack an unarmed vessel was first meant to surface and allow the crew into lifeboats. Nevertheless, on 26 October U-24 had become the first submarine to attack an unarmed merchantman without warning when she torpedoed the French *Admiral Ganteaume* with 2,500 Belgian refugees aboard, her commander, Kapitänleutnant Rudolf Schneider, claiming that he had mistaken the Channel steamer for a troop transport. Then, on 30 January 1915, U-20, commanded by Kapitänleutnant Walther Schwieger, torpedoed and sank the *Ikaria*, *Tokomaru* and *Oriole* in the English Channel without warning, and on 2 February the German chancellor agreed to the request of the navy minister, Grand Admiral Alfred von Tirpitz, to launch unrestricted submarine warfare against all ships, including neutrals, bringing food or supplies to the Entente powers. That day an American diplomat at the embassy in Paris, John Coolidge, wrote in his diary: 'Another little merchant ship has just been sunk by the Germans, just at the mouth of the Mersey, which gives us all a horrid feeling. The Germans are so angry at not getting ahead that they leave nothing undone.'

American distaste at increasing German 'frightfulness' solidified into something stronger when on 4 February Berlin declared that the torpedoing of neutral ships 'cannot always be avoided', and that 'cruiser rules' would not always apply. This brought a sharp response from Washington, President Woodrow Wilson declaring that it was

49

an 'indefensible violation of neutral rights' and that the United States would take the 'necessary steps' to safeguard American lives and property.

There was some logic in Tirpitz's thinking, which was reinforced by Germany's own experience of the effects of the British naval blockade. For before the war there had been a widespread belief that Britain was wholly dependent on food imports from North America, the influential newspaper editor W. T. Stead declaring as early as 1901 that without them 'we should be face to face with famine'. But compared with the cruiser, the U-boat was not well adapted to commerce raiding or blockade. Its speed both on the surface and underwater was no greater than that of many a merchant ship, and its light gun was inadequate against larger vessels, some of which were now armed. For the new strategy of blockade to have any chance of success, therefore, now that all Germany's cruisers bar auxiliaries had been swept from the seas, the U-boat would have to exploit its trump card, the attack without warning using torpedoes, abandoning the stop-and-search rules that had hitherto safeguarded neutrals. On 19 February the Norwegian tanker *Belridge* was torpedoed by U-8 in the Dover Straits, the first neutral to be attacked without warning. Berlin again claimed that it had been fired on in error.

From 1 February, therefore, Berlin was almost inexorably set on a course of conflict with Washington. So too were Kapitänleutnant Schwieger and U-20: on 7 May they would sink the Cunard liner *Lusitania* off the south-east coast of Ireland with the loss of 1,200 passengers and crew, including 128 American citizens. And although President Wilson would be measured in his response, stating that 'there is such a thing as a nation being so right that it does not need to convince others by force that it is right,' his new secretary of state, Robert Lansing, would write in his memoirs that although it was another two years before the United States entered the war, after the sinking of the *Lusitania* he had had no doubt 'that we would ultimately become the ally of Britain'.

Meanwhile, at the urging of Churchill at the Admiralty, plans were under way to force the Dardanelles (the old Hellespont), the narrow (in places less than a mile) 40-mile waterway linking the Aegean with the Sea of Marmora and thence Constantinople, thereby opening up communications with Russia. Pre-war studies had concluded that this operation would be extremely hazardous, and both the Admiralty and the War Office had discounted it as an option, but stalemate in the west and increasingly urgent calls from the Tsar to take action to relieve the Turkish pressure on his southern flank had led to a reappraisal. The war cabinet, not least the war minister, Lord Kitchener, now had high hopes that seizing Constantinople would also have profound diplomatic advantages, encouraging Bulgaria and Romania to join the allies. However, the first sea lord, Admiral Fisher, remained sceptical, which did nothing to energize Vice-Admiral Sackville Carden, the commander charged with forcing the Dardanelles with a flotilla of elderly battleships. In fact, Carden himself had begun to doubt his original assessment that the straits might be taken by a methodical advance and systematic bombardment of the shore batteries, which Churchill had used to urge the war cabinet to approve the operation. On 16 February, therefore, the war cabinet decided to mount in addition a land operation to clear the shore batteries, and a substantial force under General Sir Ian Hamilton, one of the most highly regarded officers in the army, began assembling in Egypt for the task. It included both British regulars and reservists, two French brigades, Indian Army troops, and those of Australia and New Zealand on their way to France.

On 19 February Carden began the naval operation with the bombardment of the defences at Sedd-el-Bahr on the Gallipoli peninsula and Kum Kale on the Asiatic side of the straits. This was not successful, in part because of bad weather, and was quickly broken off before being resumed on 25 February at closer range. A party of Royal Marines landed the next day, along with a naval demolition party led by Lieutenant Eric Robinson. Turkish troops put up stiff opposition, but Robinson, alone and in his tropical whites, strolled up the Achilles Mound, the supposed tomb of the Greek hero of the

Trojan war, and under heavy fire proceeded calmly to blow up the two guns. For this and later acts of courage he was awarded the VC, the first of the Gallipoli campaign. Bad weather returned, however, and little progress was made subsequently, despite a more concerted effort in mid-March.

Worse still, surprise had now been lost, and the initiative no longer lay with the allies. A further month would elapse before Hamilton's Mediterranean Expeditionary Force landed at Gallipoli, with great loss of life and to no effect but to draw Turkish troops from the Caucasus, though by that time the Russians had been able to stabilize their southern front. The campaign would be one of the great lost opportunities of the war, and would have serious political and diplomatic repercussions.

Success was to come the allies' way in Egypt, however, doubly welcome after near-catastrophic losses by the Russians in Polish Masuria. The Suez Canal was the lifeline through which troops from the Empire passed to France, and in late January an Ottoman force of some 23,000, in large part Syrians but including a regular Turkish division, under the direction of Colonel Friedrich Kress von Kressenstein, mounted an offensive to block it. They crossed 130 miles of the Sinai desert with 5,000 camels as water carriers, using wells dug in advance by German engineers, but aircraft of the RFC and Royal Naval Air Service (RNAS) observed their advance throughout. On 3 February determined attempts to cross the canal at Kantara and Ismailia were decisively repulsed by Indian and Egyptian troops with the aid of naval gunfire.

Reassuringly, contrary to the hopes of the Ottoman high command and German efforts at incitement, the Muslim troops of the Egyptian and Indian armies showed no inclination to rise up against the British in support of a Turkish 'holy war'. Indeed, one officer of the 5th Battery Egyptian Artillery, Mulazzim Awaal Effendi Helmi, was killed in a particularly gallant stand at his gun during hand-to-hand fighting, and according to the despatch in the *London Gazette* would have been recommended for an award had he lived.

The repulse was not immediately followed up because the GOC of the Canal Defence Forces, Major-General Alexander Wilson, believed his troops were ill-trained for the task; but although it would be nearly three years before imperial forces cleared Gaza and entered Jerusalem, the defeat on the Suez Canal was the beginning of the end for Ottoman power in Palestine.

8

MARCH

Drum-fire

Neuve Chapelle: a taste of the battles to come

With the better weather and drier ground in early spring 1915 came renewed thoughts of an allied (Anglo-French) offensive on the Western Front. The moment appeared auspicious – 'particularly', in the words of Sir John French, in view of 'the marked success of the Russian Army in repelling the violent onslaughts of Marshal von Hindenburg, the apparent weakening of the enemy in my front, and the necessity for assisting our Russian Allies to the utmost by holding as many hostile troops as possible in the Western Theatre'.

This too was the opinion of his French counterpart General Joffre, who although having no official authority over the BEF carried the moral authority of the stronger ally. Joffre planned to reduce the great German bulge to the north-west made in the first months' fighting by attacking its extreme points in Artois and Champagne. If the lateral railways in the plain of Douai could be recaptured, he reasoned, the Germans, deprived of the means of supply and rapid reinforcement, would have to withdraw. And there was always the chance of breakthrough and the restoration of mobile warfare, the holy grail of the allied command.

There was for the British another reason too: in the words again of Sir John French's later despatch 'perhaps the most weighty consideration of all, the need of fostering the offensive spirit in the troops under my command after the trying and possibly enervating experiences which they had gone through of a severe winter in the trenches'. Certainly the Indian Corps, comprising the Lahore and Meerut Divisions, wanted to prove themselves. The courage displayed by the newly arrived sepoys in the fighting at Ypres in October and November was undoubted, but their commanders' tactical skill had been less convincing.

By March 1915, although it was still but a fraction of the size of the French forces holding the 400-mile line of trenches from the Belgian coast to the Swiss border, the BEF had grown to such a strength that it had been reorganized into two armies: 1st Army, commanded by the newly promoted General Sir Douglas Haig, and 2nd Army under General Sir Horace Smith-Dorrien. French delegated the planning of the British element of the Artois offensive – the attack at the village of Neuve Chapelle – to Haig and 1st Army, which consisted of IV Corps and the Indian Corps, while the exploitation was to be the business of Smith-Dorrien and 2nd Army. Logic would have suggested the roles be reversed – Smith-Dorrien, the infantryman, planning the set-piece attack, with Haig, the cavalryman, ready to exploit – but besides the actual positions of the armies in the line, Haig's stock stood particularly high after holding the line at Ypres in November, whereas Smith-Dorrien's decision to stand and fight at Le Cateau in August had become such a bone of contention with Sir John French that the peppery infantry general was to be increasingly marginalized.

Neuve Chapelle lay on the road between Bethune and Armentières, the ground flat and cut by drainage ditches. A mile beyond the British lines lay Aubers Ridge, which though barely 20 feet higher than the surrounding country gave a significant advantage in artillery observation, while some 15 miles to the south lay the far greater heights of Vimy Ridge. In consequence, perhaps, the German lines were relatively lightly held, the defenders being able to place greater reliance on their artillery to defeat any attack.

The French assault was to be at Vimy Ridge to threaten the road, rail and canal junctions at La Bassée from the south, while the British attack would menace them from the north. However, the attack on Vimy Ridge would be cancelled when Sir John French said he was not able to relieve the French IX Corps in the line north of Ypres to release them for the assault. Instead Joffre promised the BEF heavy artillery support.

Haig's preparation was thorough. Despite poor weather in late February the RFC had carried out much aerial photography. The Royal Engineers Survey Branch was therefore able to map the area over which the attack was to take place to a depth of nearly a mile, each corps receiving 1,500 copies of 1:5,000-scale (1 cm to 50 m) sheets. Neuve Chapelle was the first deliberately planned British offensive, and would provide something of a template for the BEF's future attacks on the Western Front: a scheduled artillery bombardment followed by infantry advancing at a fixed time, conforming as best they could to the fire plan.

Haig was able to concentrate 340 guns – as many as the BEF had taken to France the previous August – against the German salient at Neuve Chapelle, a ratio of one gun to every 6 yards of front attacked. But guns were one thing, ammunition another. The expenditure rate on the Western Front in 1914 had come as a surprise to everyone. At the end of September Sir John French had written to the War Office calling urgently for more shells, especially high explosive (HE), as the field batteries hitherto had fired only shrapnel. The master-general of the ordnance, Major-General Sir Stanley von Donop, a Royal Artillery officer who steadfastly refused to anglicize his name (his family had come to England when Bonaparte invaded Lippe-Detmold), replied: 'I am commanded by the Army Council to point out that they have provided in the first instance, and have also sent out, replenishments in almost every case fully up to the quantities of gun ammunition which were laid down before the war.' And a subsequent request elicited the reminder from the war minister, Kitchener: 'You will of course see that economy is practised.'

If this sounded bureaucratic, the War Office was in fact faced with a serious problem: even if it accepted the need for far higher scales of ammunition, where was it to find the shells? The ordnance factories did not have significant spare capacity, and building more or outsourcing to industry was not an overnight affair. Von Donop was worried about quality control, not least safety in both production and use. In September the French General St Claire Deville, co-designer of the famous *soixante-quinze*, the 75 mm field gun, had come to London with a new design for an HE shell that could be manufactured quickly from readily available components. Everyone was impressed except von Donop. After the conference Kitchener, asking why he had been so 'stuffy' about the design, received the reply: 'Because in my opinion it is unsafe.' In 1915, when perhaps as many as 800 French guns would suffer barrel explosions, deranging many of Joffre's plans, Kitchener told Asquith that had it not been for the restraining hand of von Donop they would have been 'hanged on the gallows of public opinion'. But what soon developed in the newspapers as 'the great shell scandal' would bring David Lloyd George to the fore at a newly created Ministry of Munitions, and would be one of the factors (the principal being the Dardanelles fiasco) that forced Asquith to form a coalition ministry in May.

Haig's artillery preparation at Neuve Chapelle was therefore limited to thirty minutes. Initially it proved effective enough. Though the night before the attack was wet and snowy, turning to damp mist on the morning of 10 March, the shock of the hurricane bombardment – what the Germans afterwards described as 'the first true drum-fire [*Trommelfeuer*] yet heard' – kept the defenders' heads down just long enough for the assaulting infantry to gain their first objectives. In Artois, too, the water table was so high that the German trenches were dug relatively shallow and built up with earthworks, making them more susceptible to HE. However, after the first set-piece attack the tempo faltered, command impaired by poor communications (there was no tactical radio) and the gunners unable to respond quickly to the infantry's needs owing to shellfire having cut the field-telephone cables. Haig sought to renew the advance by attacking where the original assault had failed, repeating the detailed preparation of the first day, which cost precious time. The casualties mounted. A German divisional counter-attack early on 12 March was beaten back but at heavy cost, and soon afterwards Haig cancelled further attacks and ordered the gains to be consolidated prior to a new attack further north. The shell shortage was now so acute, however, that this attack was soon abandoned but for a local effort by the 7th Division, which also failed, again with high casualties.

Indeed, the losses in many battalions were catastrophic. Of the 750 men of the 2nd Scottish Rifles (2nd Battalion the Cameronians) who went into battle on 10 March – many of the officers with swords drawn – three days later only 143 came out, led by the surviving officer, a second lieutenant, and the regimental sergeant-major. Their dead, wounded and missing included twenty-nine sergeants, a devastating loss of experienced NCOs. Their story is told in one of the finest studies of men in battle, *Morale* (1967) by the late Sir John Baynes, himself a former Cameronian.

In all, the fighting cost some 7,000 British and 4,200 Indian casualties out of the 40,000 who took part, and almost as many Germans. Heroism was common currency: one of the ten resulting VCs was awarded to Gabar Singh Negi of the Gharwal Rifles, a brigade whose tenacity in the attack had been particularly marked. His citation reads: 'During our attack on the German position he was one of a bayonet party with bombs who entered their main trench, and was the first man to go round each traverse, driving back the enemy until they were eventually forced to surrender. He was killed during this engagement.'

Yet if the battle showed no appreciable gain, the French at least were to become cautiously optimistic that the BEF might be reliable in offensive operations. Given the French obsession with the offensive, however, this would prove a distinctly mixed blessing.

9

APRIL
Gallipoli

The greatest stratagem of the war that ended in the greatest failure

As calls increased for conscription to be introduced, a popular song of 1915 mocked Charlie Chaplin, a British citizen, for refusing to enlist. It ended:

And his little baggy trousers
They want mending
Before they send him
To the Dardanelles.

Why the Dardanelles? Because no hardships on the Western Front could compare with those of the Gallipoli peninsula, which commanded the Dardanelles Straits and thereby maritime access to the Black Sea. The extremes of heat and cold, the lack of water, the rocky, inhospitable terrain with its deep gullies and ravines, the close fighting which left the dead unburied, and the flies and other vermin which spread epidemic sickness – Gallipoli was just the very worst place to do battle. John Masefield, later poet laureate, would

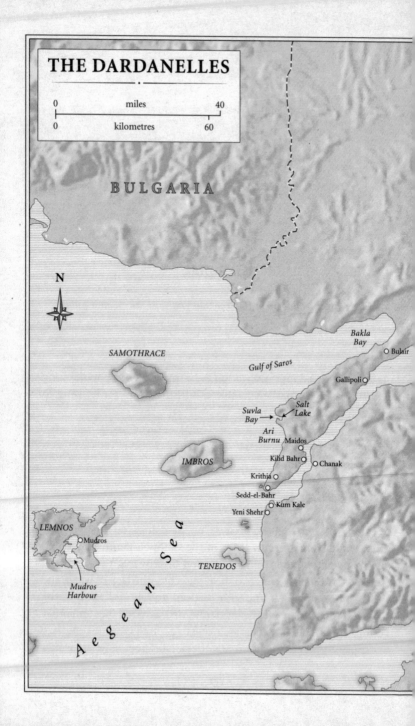

THE DARDANELLES

0　　　　miles　　　　40

0　　　　kilometres　　　　60

BULGARIA

N

SAMOTHRACE

Gulf of Saros

Bakla Bay

○ Bulair

Gallipoli ○

Suvla Bay →

Salt Lake

Ari Burnu

Maidos ○

Kilid Bahr ○

○ Chanak

IMBROS

Krithia ○

Sedd-el-Bahr

○ Kum Kale

Yeni Shehr ○

LEMNOS

○ Mudros

TENEDOS

Mudros Harbour

A e g e a n　S e a

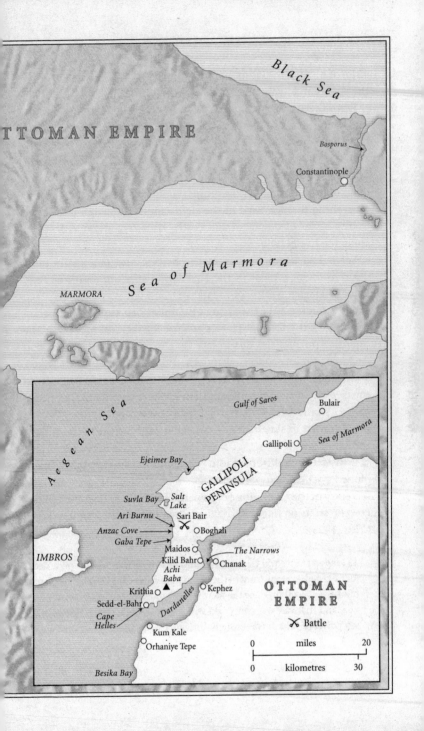

write of it: 'Men in Gallipoli in the summer of 1915 learned to curse the sun as an enemy more cruel than the Turk.'

From the start it had gone badly, although the margin of failure was much narrower than is sometimes supposed: success would have been possible with a few more resources, a little more skill, and a good deal more resolution at high level. The seaborne assault on 25 April by British, French, Australian and New Zealand troops quickly proved to be an over-improvised and bloody muddle, and everything that followed in the eight-month campaign little more than a series of desperate and costly, if heroic, attempts to overcome the initial failure.

Yet it had begun as one of the boldest and potentially most decisive strategic ploys of the First World War – indeed, the only allied stratagem worthy of the name.

On 2 August 1914 the Ottoman Empire had concluded a secret treaty with the Central Powers against Russia, and had taken the offensive in the Black Sea in late October. Britain and France had declared war the following month. With the situation in France and Flanders still fluid, however, little attention could be given to the new enemy except to strengthen the defences of the Suez Canal and to secure the oil fields of Mesopotamia. But as the Western Front turned to stalemate, the strategic gaze turned to the eastern theatre of war.

Winston Churchill, first lord of the Admiralty, vigorously championed a scheme proposed by Lieutenant-Colonel Maurice Hankey, secretary of the Committee of Imperial Defence, to turn the Central Powers' strategic flank. As he explained in volume 1 of *The World Crisis* (1923):

As long as France was treated as a self-contained theatre, a complete deadlock existed, and the front of the German invader could neither be pierced nor turned . . . [but] once the view was extended to the whole scene of the war, and that vast war conceived as if it were a single battle, and once the sea power of Britain was brought into play, turning movements of a most far-reaching character were open to the Allies ... the Teutonic Empires were in fact vulnerable in an extreme degree on either flank.

The Tsar had already appealed for an offensive against the Turks to take the pressure off his forces in the Caucasus, which would also, it was argued, encourage the neutrals, notably Bulgaria, to enter the war on the allies' side, as well as opening up an ice-free supply route to Russia, which was in desperate need of war materiel.

The war council accepted the Hankey proposal but, shy of providing resources at the expense of the Western Front, initially authorized only a naval operation to force the narrow straits. In mid-February, however, just before the naval operation began, they also authorized preparations for a landing lest bombardment of the shore batteries alone prove insufficient. This was the first grievous mistake: a joint operation, with surprise on the allies' side, might have succeeded, for at that stage the peninsula was not garrisoned very strongly; a naval and only then, in the event of failure, a sequential military operation with surprise gone risked disaster.

By mid-March the naval operation had indeed stalled, and the war council now sanctioned the landing.

General Sir Ian Hamilton, a clever, brave but diffident man, was appointed to command the Mediterranean Expeditionary Force (MEF). He had little time to prepare for what would be the first machine-gun-opposed amphibious assault in history. Nor had much preliminary planning been carried out at the War Office, for the General Staff had been sent to France with the BEF in August, and their replacements had not yet found their feet or gained the confidence of the secretary of state, Field Marshal Lord Kitchener. The first problem was that the MEF was scattered around the eastern Mediterranean and its equipment and supplies embarked haphazardly. Hamilton saw no alternative but to recall them to Egypt to reorganize and regroup before sailing for his advance base on the Greek island of Lemnos.

The Turks were by now thoroughly on the alert. By the end of

March they had reinforced Gallipoli to a strength of four divisions, with another two on the Asiatic shore, and the war minister, Enver Pasha, had appointed Lieutenant-General Otto Liman von Sanders, head of the German military mission, to command them. Sanders was supremely confident of his ability to repel invasion, 'if the English will only leave me alone for eight days'.

'The English' would in fact leave him alone for a whole month.

Against these six divisions Sir Ian Hamilton had only five. By far the best was the virtually all-regular 29th Division, Britain's strategic reserve. The Royal Naval Division, comprising Royal Marines and surplus naval ratings, had seen action at Antwerp but was ill-equipped and ill-trained. The magnificent Australian and New Zealand Army Corps ('Anzac'), consisting of one Australian and one mixed Australian and New Zealand division, under the outstanding Indian army Lieutenant-General William Birdwood, was as yet unblooded. The single, weak division of the French Corps Expéditionnaire d'Orient, formed of colonial troops, was also largely untried.

Hamilton had hoped for the 28th Division too, another regular formation, but Kitchener had promised it to Sir John French for one more offensive on the Western Front. He told Hamilton that in the coming months he could expect 'New Army' divisions – men who had flocked to the recruiting offices in August and September – and perhaps some territorials and Indian army, but these would be raw troops, fit initially only for defensive tasks and labouring.

Hamilton's choice of landing places was limited. The Gallipoli peninsula is only 10 miles across at the widest point and about 45 miles long. Cape Helles lies at the southernmost tip, overlooked by the heights of Achi Baba (709 feet), with Sari Bair ridge (971 feet) some 12 miles north overlooking both sides of the straits at the narrowest point (5 miles). There were a number of small sandy beaches at Cape Helles, as on the western side, but none on the eastern, which in any case was covered by fire from across the straits. There were no towns, just a few settlements, of which Krithia in the south and Bulair in the north were the most important. The roads were unmade tracks.

Given that his options were limited, not least by the inexperience of many of his troops, and given that the months of naval bombardment had forfeited strategic surprise, Hamilton tried to achieve tactical surprise by deceiving the Turks as to the actual main effort. While the 29th Division were to make the main landings at Cape Helles to capture the forts at Kilid Bahr, with the Anzacs landing some 15 miles up the west coast at Gaba Tepe to advance across the peninsula and cut off any Turkish retreat or prevent reinforcement, the French would make a diversionary landing on the Asiatic shore. The Royal Naval Division would also make a demonstration in the Gulf of Saros, which was, indeed, where Sanders expected the main effort to come.

The plan was sound, if pedestrian, but so much dispersal multiplied the chances of things going wrong.

The Anzacs did indeed gain tactical surprise by landing before dawn on 25 April without preliminary bombardment. But while they made some progress inland, casualties and the inexperience of commanders began to tell, and soon, in crude terms, their luck simply ran out, not least in finding themselves opposed by the Turkish 19th Division under command of the brilliant 34-year-old Mustafa Kemal Bey ('Atatürk' – first president of the post-war Turkish republic), one of the original 'Young Turks' who in 1908 restored the country's constitutional monarchy.

The experiences of 'Anzac Cove' would forge a strong national consciousness in the Australian and New Zealand troops, in turn carrying back to the home countries and, later, to the Western Front. The sense of 'mateship' was profound, as exemplified by the story of Private Jack Simpson, who had enlisted in Perth as a stretcher-bearer when war broke out. He had spent his boyhood holidays as a donkey-lad on the beach at South Shields, County Durham, and while bringing in casualties over his shoulder on the second day of the landings he saw an abandoned Turkish donkey and at once pressed it into service. In the next four weeks he would bring in over 300 casualties on its back. Colonel (later General Sir) John Monash wrote that 'Private Simpson and his little beast earned the admiration of everyone . . . They worked all day and night through-out the whole period since the landing, and the help rendered to the wounded was invaluable. Simpson knew no fear and moved unconcernedly amid shrapnel and rifle fire, steadily carrying out his self-imposed task day by day' – until on 19 May he was killed by a machine-gun bullet.

At Cape Helles the landings went badly from the outset. The 29th Division, under Major-General Aylmer Hunter-Weston, a Royal Engineers officer who though fearless had limited experience of handling infantry, impaled themselves on the cliffs and machine guns in broad daylight after a preliminary naval bombardment that left the defenders in no doubt as to what was happening. Only sui-cidal gallantry on the part of his regulars – the Lancashire Fusiliers would win six VCs 'before breakfast' – carried the day. One of the Fusiliers' VCs, Captain Harold Clayton, killed six weeks later, described the desperate scene at 'Lancashire Landing', as it was later dubbed:

> There was tremendously strong barbed wire where my boat was landed. Men were being hit in the boats as they splashed ashore. I got up to my waist in water, tripped over a rock and went under, got up and made for the shore and lay down by the barbed wire. There was a man there before me shouting for wirecutters. I got mine out, but could not make the slightest impression. The front of the wire was by now a thick mass of men, the majority of whom never moved again. The noise was ghastly and the sights horrible.

The battalion had started the day with 27 officers and 1,002 other ranks. Twenty-four hours later, just 16 officers and 304 men answered roll-call.

Yet despite the heroic efforts, 29th Division could gain only very limited beachheads. Indeed, at no stage of the campaign could Hamilton's forces drive further inland than a few miles. Planning had concentrated on the landings, with insufficient thought about what would happen subsequently, especially in the event of high casualties. By 5 May the division had lost half its initial strength, including two-thirds of its officers.

The Gallipoli peninsula would become a salient every bit as lethal as Ypres, with the added complications of supply across open beaches, water shortage, intense heat and insanitary conditions. As on the Western Front, barbed wire, machine guns and artillery put paid to tactical manoeuvre. The only alternatives would be head-on attacks or evacuation, the latter eventually conceded in January 1916. The bold move to break the stalemate of the Western Front had ended merely in its extension into the eastern Mediterranean. The campaign for mastery of the Dardanelles Straits cost the allies some 250,000 casualties, of which nearly half were from sickness, with over 40,000 dead. Turkish losses were roughly the same.

'That the effort failed is not against it,' wrote Masefield in his fine apologia *Gallipoli* shortly after the evacuation; 'many great things and noble men have failed.' But besides the strategic failure and the appalling losses, which in turn exacerbated the situation in France and Flanders, the Dardanelles campaign would have far-reaching political consequences. It spelled the end for Churchill as a voice in the direction of the war, and severely damaged the reputation and confidence of Kitchener. It forced Asquith to form a coalition government and set Lloyd George on course for the premiership. Above all, it reinforced the view that the Western Front was the only place in which the war could be decided. And with that would come the abysmal strategy of attrition, the wearing down of the enemy in bloody offensives that would prove equally costly to the allies themselves.

10

MAY

'Gas!'

The Germans tear up the rule book at the Second Battle of Ypres

Before the Somme became a byword for insensate slaughter, and the defining image of the First World War, it was Ypres that was the British army's centre of gravity on the Western Front.

Hard fighting there in October and November 1914 had cost the BEF some 58,000 casualties, most of them the irreplaceable regulars who could march all day, use cover artfully and fire fifteen aimed rounds a minute. By Christmas in many battalions there remained but a single officer and a few dozen soldiers who had heard the opening shots at Mons.

In the early months of 1915 the BEF had become a harlequin affair, reinforced by men of the Indian army, by territorials, by the few remaining regulars drawn from distant garrisons, and by Canadian regulars and militiamen, the first of the 600,000 of the Canadian Expeditionary Force who would serve on the Western Front. And aside from the futile blood-letting in March of the BEF's first independent offensive, at Neuve Chapelle, they had been able to rest, reorganize and train, so that in mid-April they could begin relieving the French in the Ypres salient.

The timing was unfortunate, however. General Erich von Falkenhayn, chief of the *Grosser Generalstab* – in effect, commander-in-chief – had authorized an attack on the Ypres salient as a strategic diversion from the German army's main offensive on the Eastern Front. With a limited objective, however – to 'pinch out' the salient rather than capture the important road junction of Ypres itself – and not wanting to commit too many troops, Falkenhayn decided, in flagrant breach of the Hague Conventions of 1907, to use chlorine gas. This had been developed and advocated for use as a weapon by the German Franz Haber, who would win the Nobel Prize in Chemistry in 1918 for his work on synthesizing ammonia for use in fertilizers and explosives – an innovation that helped prolong the war.

Though intelligence sources had suggested that gas might be used, the warnings were unspecific and therefore not paid much heed by the French general staff. In consequence, the strange mist that drifted across no-man's-land from the German line on the evening of 22 April towards the left (north-west) of the Ypres salient, where the trenches were still occupied by the French, took the defenders by surprise. Those who could, fled; those who could not, suffocated. Private Anthony Hossack of the Queen Victoria's Rifles, a territorial regiment, described the panic:

> Over the fields streamed mobs of infantry, the dusky warriors of French Africa; away went their rifles, equipment, even their tunics, that they might run the faster. One man came stumbling through our lines. An officer of ours held him up with levelled revolver. 'What's the matter, you bloody lot of cowards?' says he. The Zouave was frothing at the mouth, his eyes started from their sockets, and he fell writhing at the officer's feet.

A gap 4 miles wide had opened in the allied line, into which the Germans advanced, but hesitantly, for their high command seemingly had as little confidence in the new weapon as the French had belief in its existence, and had not conjured enough reserves to exploit the success. Fortunately, too, the Canadian division, on the French right – their first time in action – held their positions just long enough for British and Indian reinforcements to be brought up to check the advance.

Nothing could be done for the gas casualties, however, though Private Bert Newman of the Royal Army Medical Corps recalled his sergeant-major's desperate attempts to force Vaseline into the throats of men gasping for breath to ease the burning.

A German soldier who took part in the attack, Pioneer Willi Siebert, wrote:

> What we saw was total death. Nothing was alive. All of the animals had come out of their holes to die. Dead rabbits, moles, and rats and mice were everywhere. The smell of the gas was still in the air. It hung on the few bushes which were left. When we got to the French lines the trenches were empty but in a half mile the bodies of French soldiers were everywhere. It was unbelievable. Then we saw there were some English. You could see where men had clawed at their faces, and throats, trying to get breath. Some had shot themselves. The horses, still in the stables, cows, chickens, everything, all were dead. Everything, even the insects were dead.

Two days later the Germans released more gas, which struck the Canadian 8th Brigade near St Julien. With only the most primitive of anti-gas masks – towelling or handkerchiefs soaked in urine – the Canadian division paid dearly in the heavy fighting, with some 1,700 dead, 2,000 wounded and almost as many taken prisoner. One of the first of the Canadians' VCs was awarded posthumously to Company Sergeant-Major Frederick Hall of the Winnipeg Rifles, for repeatedly bringing in the wounded under fire. He and two other VC winners all came from homes on Pine Street in Winnipeg, subsequently renamed 'Valour Road'.

The gas attacks shocked public opinion on both sides of the Atlantic, as well as the authorities. Kitchener wrote to Sir John French:

> The use of asphyxiating gases is, as you are aware, contrary to the rules
> and usages of war. Before, therefore, we fall to the level of the degraded
> Germans [in retaliating] I must submit the matter to the Government . . .
> These methods show to what depth of infamy our enemies will go in
> order to supplement their want of courage in facing our troops.

This sentiment did not, however, prevent the British from developing their own – and better – chemical weapons.

Meanwhile the BEF were also facing the conventional logic of defence: if ground is worth holding in the first place, it is worth counter-attacking to regain if lost. And the greatest apostle of offensive action, General Ferdinand Foch, commanding French troops in the north-west and therefore with moral authority over the BEF, now ordered just this.

The counter-attacks began in earnest on 26 April. That day the Lahore Division suffered 1,700 casualties – over 10 per cent – without even reaching the German front line. The story was much the same everywhere, and General Sir Horace Smith-Dorrien, commanding the BEF's 1st Army, voiced his concern at the high cost of so little gain, suggesting instead that the line of defence be straightened and therefore shortened by withdrawing from the now even more constricted salient. Sir John French refused, though after another costly and futile attack by the Lahore Division, on 1 May, he authorized a limited withdrawal from its apex. Five days later, resenting this reversal, he took the opportunity to dismiss Smith-Dorrien and appoint in his place the less volcanic commander of V Corps, Lieutenant-General Sir Herbert Plumer.

The German attacks had dampened neither French's nor Joffre's ardour for the long-intended allied offensive. The two commanders-in-chief would stick to the plans made months before to attack in Artois, south of Ypres, notwithstanding the manifest shortage of artillery shells. 'Sir John, undeterred by the drain on his resources during his recent struggle,' wrote Kitchener's private secretary and biographer, 'was determined to adhere, on its broad lines, to his main plan. "The ammunition will be all right," he had told

Kitchener on May 2; he knew his men to be in as high fettle as ever.'

Kitchener was far from convinced but gave the go-ahead nevertheless, largely at Joffre's urging. Early on the morning of 9 May, therefore, the BEF attacked towards Aubers Ridge, while the French attacked towards Vimy Ridge – ground familiar from the Neuve Chapelle battle. Joffre said it was 'the beginning of the end'; the war would be over in three weeks, because Foch was employing a new tactic of prolonged and heavy bombardment instead of surprise. Six days' hard pounding by 1,250 guns along a 12-mile front held by four German divisions, and then eighteen French divisions would attack, with the BEF in support on the flank.

But the attack soon broke down, as all previous attacks had, except in the centre, where the corps commanded by General Philippe Pétain, later the hero of Verdun (and in the Second World War the 'arch-collaborator', president of Vichy France), broke through to a depth of 2 miles. However, the Germans managed to close the gap before reserves could be brought up to exploit the success, a pattern that would be repeated in every allied offensive for the next three years.

Progress in the British sector was just as disappointing. As Kitchener's private secretary noted: 'It was quickly and unhappily evident that Sir John [French] would be unable to make good the substantial support he had so manfully intended to lend. He could do little but to employ and destroy a considerable number of Germans, and capture – at sad cost to himself – some not very important trenches.'

Foch's troops suffered 102,000 casualties, but the BEF's were proportionately more: over 11,000 killed or wounded on 9 May alone, the great majority within yards of their own front-line trenches. Mile for mile, division for division, the Artois offensive saw some of the highest losses of the entire war.

But Sir John French knew where the blame lay – with the inadequate supply of shells, the result of the war council's giving priority to the Dardanelles campaign. And when he returned to his headquarters on the first day of the battle, in despondent mood having watched the stalling of the attack from atop a church tower, what should he find but a telegram from Kitchener asking him to 'hold in readiness for despatch to the Dardanelles via Marseilles by quickest route 20,000 rounds 18-pounder ammunition and 2,000 rounds 4.5-inch howitzer ammunition'.

In dismay he replied: 'This morning I commenced an important attack, and the battle is likely to last several days. I am warding off a heavy attack East of Ypres at the same time. In these circumstances I cannot possibly accept the responsibility of reducing the stock of ammunition unless it be immediately replaced from home.'

Kitchener was adamant: 'I will see that it is replaced [but] the state of affairs in the Dardanelles renders it absolutely essential that the ammunition which has been ordered should be sent off at once.'

The consignment was indeed replaced within twenty-four hours, but French was still dismayed, in part because he genuinely could not understand why industry could not supply more shells, or why the Dardanelles – a 'sideshow' – should have priority over his 'decisive theatre', but principally because he had a failed offensive to explain and consequently his neck to save. He therefore enlisted the support of the press, in the shape of Charles Repington, *The Times*'s influential military correspondent (dubbed 'the Playboy of the Western Front' because his promising career had been cut short a decade before as a result of a liaison with another officer's wife).

On 14 May Repington wrote an excoriating piece on the shell shortage under the headline 'Need for shells: British attacks checked: Limited supply the cause: A Lesson From France', and for good measure French also sent two of his personal staff to London to brief politicians, including Lloyd George and Arthur Balfour, leader of the Conservative opposition, in what Kitchener's private secretary called 'a minor coup d'état'.

Although it would redound to his discredit and, later, contribute to his dismissal, for the time being the 'shell scandal', on top of the Dardanelles setback, advanced French's cause: on 25 May Asquith reluctantly formed a coalition government, with Lloyd George leading a newly created Ministry of Munitions and the Tory cabinet ministers increasingly arguing for priority to be accorded to the Western Front.

Meanwhile the wearying attacks and counter-attacks at Ypres continued, with the largest discharge of gas on 24 May preceding a huge German push across a front of 4½ miles. Plumer's men, now with rudimentary but effective gas masks, were able to halt the enemy well short of the British line, and that evening Falkenhayn issued the order to cease all further attacks on the salient.

When Sir John French was relieved of command in December he would take the consolatory title 'Earl of Ypres'; but there was to be a Third Battle of Ypres, even bloodier and more futile, in 1917, known thereafter as 'Passchendaele'.

On 3 May 1915 Italy, having the previous August declared her neutrality on the grounds that the Triple Alliance was a defensive treaty and that Germany and Austria had waged offensive war, officially revoked the treaty. On 23 May she declared war on Austria-Hungary, though the declaration of war on Germany would not come until August 1916.

The acquisition of Italy as an ally, a considerable diplomatic coup, would add significantly to the Entente's naval strength in the Mediterranean, act as a beacon (for a time at least) to the wavering Balkan states, and divert Austro-Hungarian troops from the Galician and Serbian fronts. The Austro-Italian border was 400 miles long, stretching from the Stelvio Pass to the Adriatic Sea. Italian forces outnumbered the Austrian, which had to remain on the defensive while Russia resisted strongly, but the difficult terrain was in the defender's favour. The Italian commander-in-chief, Luigi Cadorna, a proponent of the frontal assault, planned to attack at once on the Isonzo river with the intention of sweeping across the Karst plateau into Slovenia, in turn threatening Vienna.

It was a grandiose concept, which, like similar plans hatched on the Western Front, took insufficient account of the defensive power of the machine gun and heavy artillery, and the variable quality of the available troops. The *Alpini* were tough mountain fighters, and the *Bersaglieri*, light infantry, experienced in recent wars against the Turks in Libya, but many of the conscripts from the south were ill-suited to the conditions.

Cadorna had some initial successes in his preliminary operations in late May and June, but as on the Western Front the fighting soon developed into trench warfare, though here the trenches had to be dug in Alpine rock and glaciers, and often at altitudes of 10,000 feet. It would become known as the 'White War'. In the first six months of his campaign Cadorna would launch four separate offensives on the Isonzo, each without appreciable success and costing in all some 60,000 dead and more than 150,000 wounded, a quarter of his mobilized forces.

11

JUNE

Those Magnificent Men

War in the air sees fiction turn into reality

No aspect of warfare saw greater advances between 1914 and 1918 than aviation, though progress before the war had been cautious. In H. G. Wells's futuristic novel *The War in the Air*, published in 1908, just five years after the Wright brothers' pioneering heavier-than-air flight, airships and flying machines did battle over New York, with the wholesale destruction of buildings, bridges and ultimately each other. In reality, the major powers were slower to exploit the Wrights' success than Wells prophesied. At the beginning of the war the British had fewer than 113 aircraft in naval and military service, the French 160 and the Germans 250 – and only Germany had a strategic airship capability.

By June 1915, however, Wells's original vision was beginning to take real form. In January the Kaiser had sanctioned an air campaign against military targets in Britain, including naval bases, fuel and ammunitions dumps but excluding royal palaces and residential areas. On 19 January, two 'Zeppelins', as they were invariably known, whatever their manufacture (Count Ferdinand von

Zeppelin's airships were aluminium-framed, while others, notably the Schütte-Lanz, were of wood), had attacked the Norfolk coastal towns of Great Yarmouth and King's Lynn, killing four civilians, and while the raids did little significant damage they caused much alarm. The Kaiser afterwards expressed the hope that 'the air war against England will be carried out with the greatest energy', and in May, therefore, the German high command took the decision to mount a sustained bombing offensive on the British mainland, especially the London docklands.

One of the reasons they were able to do so was the unexpected availability of most of the airships. The Zeppelins were not needed for scouting by the largely inactive German High Seas Fleet, and had already proved too vulnerable to anti-aircraft fire for use to support the army. Airships now began appearing regularly in the skies over the eastern counties, and on the night of 31 May the first attack on London was made, Zeppelin LZ38 dropping eighty-nine incendiary bombs and thirty grenades. Number 16 Alkham Road, Stoke New-ington, had the distinction of being the first house in the capital to be destroyed, though without casualties; LZ38 then turned south over Hackney and Stratford, where its bombs killed seven people and injured thirty-five. Nine RFC aircraft attempted to intercept it, but flying above 10,000 feet the airship was beyond their reach. Though this first attack was almost certainly a navigational error (the docks were the riper target), the bombing of civilian tar-gets now became routine, like the sinking of passenger ships by submarine.

On the Western Front, too, aerial warfare was developing apace. Before 1914 aircraft were regarded as an ancillary element at best, sometimes merely as an irrelevance. Tethered observation bal-loons and experimental dirigibles had been operated by the Royal Engineers since the Boer War, and their use in siege operations acknowledged, but the limited payloads of heavier-than-air machines and their dependence on good weather made them unreliable when it came to reconnaissance. On 27 September 1913 Charles Reping-ton of *The Times* quoted the opinion of Field Marshal Sir John

French, at that time CIGS, at the autumn manoeuvres, in which for the first time a relatively large number of aircraft took part: 'Aeroplane reconnaissance cannot always be depended upon . . . it may be mentioned that, owing to fog and mist on the morning of the 23rd [September], they were unable to leave their camp, although information as bearing upon the strategic problem was perhaps more urgently needed on that morning than on any other.' Cavalry would therefore remain the primary means of reconnaissance.

From 1912, however, both the War Office and the Admiralty had been trying to make up for lost time, with the active backing of their new ministers, Jack Seely and Winston Churchill respectively, who themselves took to the air at the controls of primitive aircraft (in Churchill's case with near-fatal results). In May that year the Royal Flying Corps was formed, comprising a naval as well as a military wing, and in August 1914, after conversion of the naval wing into the Royal Naval Air Service the previous month, four RFC squadrons with some sixty aircraft – BE2 (Blériot Experimental) biplanes, Blériot monoplanes, Farmans and Avro 504s – flew to France with the BEF. No 1 (balloon) Squadron joined them in 1915 when the war of movement had ended and the Western Front become entrenched.

The 'workhorse' BE2, a two-seater designed by Geoffrey de Havilland and built at the Royal Aircraft (formerly Balloon) Factory at Farnborough, had a maximum speed of 63 knots (116 km/h) at 6,500 feet, an operational ceiling of 10,000 feet and endurance of around three hours. Until the swivel-mounted Lewis gun was introduced in 1915 the observer was armed with a rifle, which was effective enough at the BE2's low speed, though equally at 63 knots the aircraft was vulnerable to ground fire. On 21 August, three days before the BEF's first battle at Mons, Sergeant-Major David Jillings, an observer with No. 2 Squadron RFC, brought down a German Albatros with a single shot near Lessines in Belgium. Next day he became the BEF's first casualty to enemy fire when small-arms fire from the cavalry division he was flying over wounded him in the leg. (He recovered, won the Military Cross (MC) the following year, and was later commissioned, rising after the war to the rank of group captain.)

Realizing almost immediately when fighting began that his cavalry could not penetrate the Germans' own cavalry screen to bring him information, Sir John French, now commanding the BEF, rapidly modified his earlier views, turning increasingly to Brigadier-General David Henderson's RFC squadrons to pinpoint the enemy. On 22 August, urged by Joffre to mount an attack to ease the pressure on the French army to his right at Charleroi, he replied that he could not commit to an attack before discovering what lay to his front – that is, 'until he got reports from his aeroplanes', as his deputy chief of staff recorded. French's trust in the RFC during the long retreat to the Marne over the next ten days saved the BEF from being outflanked or overwhelmed.

Bad weather had for the most part kept the German airships on the ground in the first days of the war, but on the night of 25 August Zeppelin Z9 dropped nine bombs on Antwerp, killing or wounding twenty-six people and damaging the palace in which the Belgian royal family had taken up residence. The RNAS detachment on fleet support in nearby Zeebrugge at once began sorties to try to destroy the airships at their moorings. On 8 October Z9 was wrecked in its hangar at Düsseldorf by two 20 lb bombs dropped from 600 feet by Lieutenant (later Air Vice-Marshal) Reginald Marix in a single-seater Sopwith Tabloid, one of the fastest aircraft of the time, having flown a zig-zag course from Antwerp, a straight-line distance of just over 100 miles – a magnificent early strategic use of air power.

When the war began, by and large only airships had radio. The aircraft of the *Deutsche Luftstreitkräfte* (German air force), as it became known, the French *Aéronautique Militaire*, and the RFC and RNAS communicated with the ground by signalling lamp. On 24 September, however, during the allied counter-offensive on the River Aisne, Lieutenants D. S. Lewis and B. T. James used airborne telegraphy (Morse Code) for the first time to direct artillery fire, their radio log beginning 'A very little short. Fire! Fire!', and ending forty minutes later with 'I am coming home now.'

The end soon afterwards of the war of movement at once increased the value of photographic reconnaissance. An experimental air photographic section was set up in January 1915, and this bore fruit in the BEF's first independent offensive, in March at Neuve Chapelle, when as a result of the RFC's extensive aerial photography the Royal Engineers Survey Branch was able to map the German trench system in considerable detail.

Aerial combat was also developing fast, and in June 1915 the so-called 'Fokker scourge' began. A monoplane (*Eindecker*) built by Fokker Flugzeugwerke GmbH in Schwerin, Prussia, designed by the Dutch-born Anton Fokker, incorporated an interrupter gear allowing a machine gun to fire forward through the propeller. This gave a pronounced advantage to the attacking aircraft, and losses to the Fokker *Eindecker* mounted alarmingly, the press referring to the lumbering BE2 in particular as 'Fokker fodder', until in April 1916 the allies produced comparable fighters, the British Airco DH2 and the French Nieuport II.

Meanwhile Zeppelin raids on London were increasing, almost with impunity. On the night of 13 October 1916 five airships would drop bombs killing seventy-one people. More and more RFC aircraft would be diverted from the Western Front and elsewhere to cover the capital and east coast ports.

But the Zeppelin was a large, slow target, and improved anti-aircraft artillery and searchlights, as well as aircraft able to fly higher, at night, to intercept them, began steadily to take a toll. As early as June 1915, Sub-Lieutenant Rex Warneford of the RNAS destroyed one with a bomb over the Belgian city of Ghent, for which he was awarded the VC. From the spring of 1917, therefore, the Germans would turn their attention to long-range bombers such as the twin-engined Gotha, which, flying at greater speed, could risk attacks in daylight. On 13 June that year a raid by twenty Gothas killed 162, and a similar raid less than a month later 57. By the standards of the Blitz in the 1940s these figures were small – in all, there were some 1,400 civilian deaths and 3,500 injuries during the war – but the effect on public morale was considerable, 300,000

Londoners routinely using the Underground for shelter overnight. Public opinion turned even more bitter towards Germany, demanding reprisal raids, and frustration with the RFC's inability to intercept or subsequently destroy the raiders grew. Both factors contributed to the decision the following year to form the Royal Air Force, thereby reintegrating the RFC and RNAS – which had begun the war as 'Cinderella' branches of the army and navy respectively – under unified command, but in an entirely independent service. When fighting ceased in November 1918 the RAF was operating 22,000 aircraft, most of them incomparably faster and longer-range than those that had left for France in 1914. In 1909 Louis Blériot had just managed to cross the English Channel in an aircraft little more powerful than a motorized kite. Only ten years later, in June 1919, two former RNAS and RFC pilots, Captain John Alcock and Lieutenant Arthur Whitten Brown, would fly a Vickers Vimy bomber across the Atlantic.

12

JULY

Askaris

War in Africa: a sideshow that inspired Hollywood

Africa had seen the first shots of the Great War between British and German troops, and in November 1918 it would see some of the last. Indeed, the small German force in East Africa would claim the unique distinction of not having been defeated in the field, returning to the Fatherland in 1919 like triumphal Roman legionaries from a distant campaign.

After the setbacks suffered by the allies in the spring offensives in France in 1915, July brought a welcome victory when the last German forces in German South-West Africa (Namibia), a territory six times the size of England and Germany's second-largest colony after German East Africa, surrendered to South African troops under the personal command of Louis Botha, the prime minister and former Boer commander.

Africa, though a military sideshow, had been dragged into the war because it was almost completely controlled by European powers. Berlin, expecting attacks on her colonies, also saw an opportunity to divert Anglo-French troops and resources from the Western

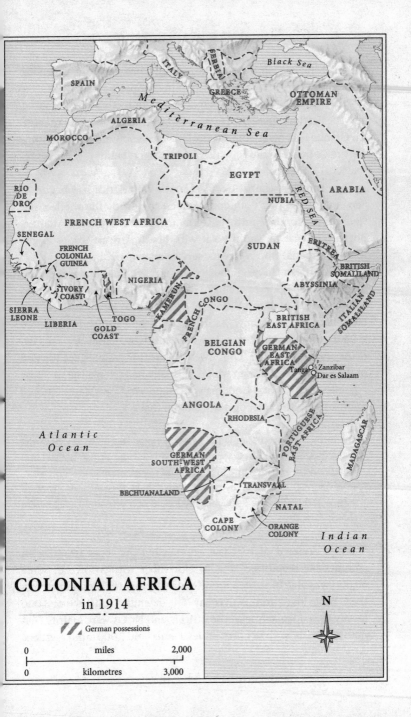

SPAIN

Black Sea

Mediterranean Sea

ITALY

SERBIA

GREECE

OTTOMAN
EMPIRE

ALGERIA

MOROCCO

TRIPOLI

EGYPT

ARABIA

NUBIA

RED SEA

RIO
DE
ORO

FRENCH WEST AFRICA

SUDAN

ERITREA

SENEGAL

FRENCH
COLONIAL
GUINEA

NIGERIA

KAMERUN

FRENCH
CONGO

ABYSSINIA

BRITISH
SOMALILAND

IVORY
COAST

SIERRA
LEONE

LIBERIA

TOGO

GOLD
COAST

BELGIAN
CONGO

BRITISH
EAST
AFRICA

GERMAN
EAST
AFRICA

ITALIAN
SOMALILAND

Tanga

Zanzibar
Dar es Salaam

*Atlantic
Ocean*

ANGOLA

RHODESIA

PORTUGUESE
EAST AFRICA

MADAGASCAR

GERMAN
SOUTH-WEST
AFRICA

BECHUANALAND

TRANSVAAL

*Indian
Ocean*

CAPE
COLONY

NATAL

ORANGE
COLONY

COLONIAL AFRICA
in 1914

/// German possessions

| 0 | miles | 2,000 |

| 0 | kilometres | 3,000 |

N

Front. Distances were vast, and a small force could tie down far greater numbers of troops here than in Europe.

However, the Royal Navy's rapid destruction of German cruisers, and the bottling-up of the *Hochseeflotte* in the North Sea by the British Grand Fleet, made communication and supply almost impossible for the German colonies, which increasingly had to rely on primitive local resources.

The campaign against German South-West Africa had begun in September 1914, with London's request to destroy the wireless stations crucial for the control of German vessels in the South Atlantic. Botha said that he could do it with South African troops alone, leaving imperial troops free for service elsewhere.

South African troops mobilized along the border under the command of Major-General Henry Lukin, a British officer seconded as inspector-general of the Union [of South Africa] Defence Force, and Lieutenant-Colonel Manie Maritz, leader of the commando (mounted irregular) forces. There was, however, much sympathy for the Germans among the Boers. Only twelve years had passed since the end of the Second Boer War, in which Germany had offered the two Boer republics both moral and material support. Now Maritz turned against the British, issuing a declaration that

> the former South African Republic and Orange Free State as well as the Cape Province and Natal are proclaimed free from British control and independent, and all white inhabitants of the mentioned areas, of whatever nationality, are hereby called upon to take their weapons in their hands and realise the long-cherished ideal of a Free and Independent South Africa.

Botha declared martial law, suppressing the 'Boer revolt' with considerable bloodshed, and in November with a force of some 50,000 was able to launch an offensive against the Germans across the Orange River from Walvis Bay. The defenders consisted of 3,000 locally raised *Schutztruppe* (the officers and NCOs were mainly German nationals, with a core of professionals) and 7,000 armed settlers, but Botha's methodical tactics quickly gained him the wireless stations, and in May the capital, Windhoek, surrendered without a fight. South African casualties were remarkably light, indeed fewer than in the revolt. It was to be the only campaign of the war planned and executed entirely by colonial forces. As a result, Deutsche-Südwestafrika would in 1919 become a South African possession.

Windhoek had in any case been isolated in August 1914 with the destruction of the powerful wireless station at Kamina in Togoland, Germany's smallest African colony, severing all radio communications with Berlin. Defended by fewer than 1,000 local police, the colony was invaded immediately after the outbreak of hostilities by British troops from the Gold Coast and French troops from Dahomey to the east. On 7 August an advance patrol of the Gold Coast Regiment ran into fire near the capital, Lomé, at which point Private Alhaji Grunshi became the first soldier in British service to fire a shot in the war. Resistance ended within a fortnight, though not without casualties on both sides. Grunshi was later mentioned in despatches, and in East Africa would win both the Distinguished Conduct Medal and the Military Medal.

He was among two million Africans who were to serve in the First World War, on three continents, either as soldiers or in labour corps. The French in particular used their colonial troops on the Western Front, but despite calls from Churchill and others, the War Office would not raise African battalions for service in Europe. In part this was because of the practical problems of language, training and command, but it also undoubtedly reflected a belief that African troops would not be able to bear the rigours of the Western Front in either the moral or the physical sense. Nevertheless, an estimated 300,000 Africans were to die, or be killed in action, over the course of the war.

Progress in the other German West African colony, Kamerun (Cameroon), was trickier. The British commander, Major-General Charles Dobell, had arrived off the coast in late September with a force of 13,000 largely local recruits, the majority French. Although the port of Duala fell without a shot, German troops withdrew inland to begin a sharp resistance in the forested interior. The local German commander urged Dobell to call a ceasefire to avoid the 'unsightly spectacle' of European troops killing each other in front of Africans. He refused.

More Entente troops entered the country from Nigeria and French Equatorial Africa, but by March 1915 Dobell's numbers had been so greatly reduced by sickness that for many months he was able to act only on the defensive. Operations dragged on until 1916, when the remaining German troops finally surrendered after last-ditch fighting in the Spanish-controlled province of Muni. Nevertheless, as commander of a successful independent campaign, Dobell would be one of those celebrated in John Singer Sargent's large group portrait *General Officers of World War I* (1920–2), now in the National Portrait Gallery.

The main – and least successful – allied campaign in Africa was in German East Africa (now Rwanda, Burundi and mainland Tanzania). Here, distances, climate, terrain and the resourcefulness of the German commander, Colonel Paul von Lettow-Vorbeck, combined to thwart the efforts of the Indian army, the King's African Rifles, and South African forces under Jan Smuts, one of the most famous commanders of the Boer War, and in 1914 also serving as his country's defence minister.

With scant artillery, a few hundred Europeans and 3,000 askaris – local black troops, commanded by German officers and NCOs – Lettow-Vorbeck conducted a masterly defence, defeating an Indian army expeditionary force in November 1914 at Tanga and, from 1916, waging a campaign of manoeuvre against a largely South African imperial force many times its size. Smuts's reputation might well have been tarnished by the setbacks had he not been recalled early and sent to London as South Africa's representative on the newly formed war council.

Lettow-Vorbeck was not, as is sometimes asserted, a convinced practitioner of guerrilla warfare. On the contrary, he was a Prussian officer in the orthodox mould who, having seen service with the international force suppressing the Boxer rebellion in China in

1900, and in putting down the tribal uprisings in South-West Africa in 1904, had developed a strong aversion to guerrilla tactics, which he saw as inimical to discipline. He favoured instead the classical German military doctrine of envelopment to try to bring about the decisive encounter, though he was always careful to avoid major pitched battles. In the end, the sheer disparity of numbers forced him to adopt hit-and-run tactics.

Karen Blixen, the Danish author of *Out of Africa*, with whom Lettow-Vorbeck formed a lifelong friendship after meeting her on a voyage to East Africa, later recalled: 'He belonged to the olden days, and I have never met another German who has given me so strong an impression of what Imperial Germany was and stood for.'

If the scale of fighting in Africa on land was small, that on water was smaller still, but not without drama. The Germans had controlled Lake Tanganyika since the outbreak of the war with three armed steamers and two unarmed motorboats. In June 1915 two British gunboats, HMS *Mimi* and HMS *Toutou*, each armed with a 3-pounder and a Maxim machine gun, were transported 3,000 miles overland to the British shore and, on 26 December, captured the 45-ton German steamboat *Kingani*, renaming it HMS *Fifi*. Soon afterwards, *Fifi*, with two Belgian boats, under Commander Geoffrey Spicer-Simson, sank the *Hedwig von Wissmann*, leaving only three German vessels on the lake, which in their turn were run aground or sunk by mid-1916. The war on the lake was the inspiration for C. S. Forester's 1935 novel *The African Queen*, memorably brought to the screen in 1951 by John Huston with Humphrey Bogart and Katharine Hepburn in the leading roles.

Lettow-Vorbeck also mounted spoiling attacks into the neighbouring British colonies of Northern Rhodesia (Zambia) and Nyasaland (Malawi), and Portuguese Mozambique. His only reinforcements during this time were men and guns from the cruiser *Königsberg*, which had taken refuge in the Rufigi river in October 1914. Indeed, for four years, with a force that never exceeded 14,000, and over an area of 750,000 square miles, he held in check some 300,000 imperial, Belgian and Portuguese troops, and was the only

German commander to invade British colonial soil with any claim to success. Never in the field of human conflict was so much tramped by so many after so few.

At the Armistice the *Schutztruppe* were still fighting, the only German troops to end the war undefeated, and in March 1919 Lettow-Vorbeck would be accorded the honour of leading 120 officers and NCOs in their tattered tropical uniforms on a victory parade through the Brandenburg Gate, which was decorated in their honour.

13

AUGUST
Suvla Bay

Another bold stratagem at Gallipoli fails through poor generalship

By the summer of 1915 not only was there stalemate on the Western Front and an unpromising situation on the Eastern, the campaign at Gallipoli was well and truly stalled. What had begun in the spring as a bold idea to use Britain's naval power to outflank the Western Front, forcing open the Dardanelles Straits to gain better communications with Russia, was becoming a byword across the Empire for incompetence and futility, an affair of trenches and barbed wire every bit as murderous as France and Flanders.

In part the blame could be laid with the commander-in-chief of the Mediterranean Expeditionary Force, Sir Ian Hamilton, a highly regarded if reticent man who had played poorly the bad hand dealt to him by the Admiralty and the War Office. But only in part: for when initial success eluded his force, London began starving him of the resources needed to recover the initiative. Despite the decisions of the war council in January and February, in part emanating from Lloyd George's particular demand that the 'New Armies' being raised should be used in a way that befitted the 'better class of man from which they are drawn' – in other words, elsewhere than the Western Front – by August no fewer than sixteen divisions had been sent to France, but only five to Gallipoli.

Nevertheless, Hamilton was determined to break the stalemate, using the same principle that had generated the Dardanelles campaign in the first place: turning the flank by amphibious means. He chose as his landing place Suvla Bay, 8 miles north of 'Anzac Cove', the bridgehead held by the Australian and New Zealand Army Corps commanded by the British Lieutenant-General William Birdwood. Suvla Bay was tricky to approach because of its shoals, but had plenty of room for boats to beach and, beyond that, a plateau mostly of salt marsh, so that the initial beachhead would not be as confined as at Anzac Cove, or at Cape Helles where the British landings had taken place.

Suvla was watched by just a regiment's worth of infantry – around a thousand men, lightly armed. Hamilton's plan was to reinforce Birdwood's corps for a renewed offensive to tie down the Turks around the heights of Sari Bair, and then land two fresh divisions – IX Corps – at Suvla: these, in conjunction with the Anzacs, would advance quickly across the peninsula and take the high ground dominating the Dardanelles 'Narrows'. The naval operation to force the straits could then begin anew.

Hamilton also wanted some younger generals fresh from the fight in France to command IX Corps and its two New Army divisions, the 10th (Irish) and 11th (Northern), and the 53rd (Welsh) Territorial, which would spearhead the landings. The first six months of the war had seen the rapid promotion of talent, and he asked specifically for Lieutenant-Generals Julian Byng and Henry Rawlinson. The War Office, however, was unresponsive. Because both Byng and Rawlinson were junior to the divisional commanders (who were already in place) on the peacetime gradation list, they appointed instead Lieutenant-General Sir Frederick Stopford, Lieutenant of the Tower of London. Aged sixty-one, Stopford had seen little actual fighting and had never commanded men in battle. It was a risky appointment at best, and at worse a reckless one.

Hamilton's intention was to open the operation with a diversionary attack by the British in the Cape Helles sector, then begin the offensive from Anzac Cove in early evening, with the landing at Suvla following in darkness, by which time the Australians and New Zealanders were to have broken out towards the Sari Bair heights. Because of the shoals in Suvla Bay, however, the plan for IX Corps had to be modified: 11th (Northern) Division would land in darkness south of Nibrunesi Point, the bay's southern headland, and 10th (Irish) Division within the bay the following morning, followed by the 53rd, with the immediate objective of seizing the ring of hills dominating the Suvla plain.

When Stopford was first shown Hamilton's plan in late July he thought it a good one: 'I am sure it will succeed and I congratulate whoever has been responsible for framing it.' However, there was now the most perverse, if well-meaning, of counsels. Stopford's chief of staff, the newly promoted Brigadier-General Hamilton Reed, a Gunner who had won the VC in South Africa, and come fresh from the Western Front, believed they lacked sufficient artillery: 'The whole teaching of the campaign in France proves that troops cannot be expected to attack an organized system of trenches without the assistance of a large number of howitzers,' he minuted.

For once, it seemed, lessons were being learned. But at Suvla, aerial reconnaissance had established that there were no entrenched positions. While this intelligence demanded wariness, especially if the Turks were to get wind of the landings in time to dig in, the wariness should not have dominated the planning. It did. Compton Mackenzie, author of the 1947 comic novel *Whisky Galore!*, was a counter-espionage officer with the Secret Service Bureau in the eastern Mediterranean, and recalled meeting Stopford and Reed on the island of Imbros during the planning:

Next to me was Sir Frederick Stopford, a man of great kindliness and personal charm, whose conversation at lunch left me at the end of the meal completely without hope of victory at Suvla. The reason for this apprehension was his inability to squash the new General opposite . . .

This Brigadier was holding forth almost truculently about the folly of the plan of operations drawn up by the General Staff, while Sir Frederick Stopford appeared to be trying to reassure him in a fatherly way. I looked along the table to where Aspinall and Dawnay [junior staff officers] were sitting near General Braithwaite [Hamilton's chief of staff]; but they were out of earshot, and the dogmatic Brigadier continued unchallenged to enumerate the various military axioms which were being ignored by the Suvla plan of operations. For one thing, he vowed, most certainly he was not going to advance a single yard until all the Divisional Artillery was ashore. I longed for Sir Frederick to rebuke his disagreeable and discouraging junior; but he was deprecating, courteous, fatherly, anything except the Commander of an Army Corps which had been entrusted with a major operation that might change the whole course of the war in twenty-four hours.

Slowly but surely Stopford began limiting the objectives of the landing. His final orders were imprecise, requiring only that the high ground be taken 'if possible', whereas in fact this was essential if the whole purpose of the Suvla offensive – cutting the Gallipoli peninsula and taking the heights above the Dardanelles Narrows – was to be achieved. Those who had to execute the orders now began to doubt how important the objective really was, and the necessary sense of urgency was lost.

Unsurprisingly the whole operation, launched on 6 August, miscarried. At Anzac Cove the attack had taken the Turks by surprise but then run out of steam, the commanders over-cautious, the troops over-burdened. At Suvla Bay the steam was never got up. Twenty thousand men were put ashore safely enough, if in places mixed up in the pitch dark, and for thirty-six hours there was nothing barring their way across the peninsula but at most 2,000 Turks with no machine guns, very little artillery and no reserves within 30 miles. The steep climbs beyond the plain were daunting but largely unopposed. Stopford, sleeping aboard the sloop HMS *Jonquil* during the landings, failed to recognize that his divisional commanders were more concerned to consolidate the beachhead than to push on, and when Hamilton himself at last realized what was happening he found that the naval arrangements had broken down and he could not leave his headquarters at Imbros.

In the confusion and hesitation casualties at Suvla began to mount – 1,700 in the first twenty-four hours, nearly as many as there were Turk defenders. On the second evening, the German adviser at Suvla reported to the head of the German military mission to the Turkish army, Liman von Sanders, in effect its commander-in-chief: 'No energetic attacks on the enemy's part have taken place. On the contrary, the enemy is advancing timidly.'

Sanders rushed reinforcements to Suvla, sacking the local Turkish divisional commander for failing to use his reserves and replacing him with Mustafa Kemal, the young general who would become Turkey's first president. When on 9 August, at Hamilton's urging, Stopford at last pressed forward his attack, the odds had almost evened.

Casualties began to mount, the fighting savage, the Turks giving no quarter with the bayonet. Three days later the 'Sandringham Company' of the 5th (Territorial) Battalion of the Norfolk Regiment, formed predominantly of estate workers from the royal residence and led by the King's land agent, the 54-year-old Frank Beck, were wiped out along with others of the battalion. It has long been believed that many of them were killed after capture. Their story was movingly told in the 1999 BBC dramatization *All the King's Men*, starring David Jason as Captain Beck.

There were moments of chivalry, though. Lieutenant John Still of the 6th East Yorkshires, a New Army battalion, recalled how, after he had been taken prisoner, a Turkish officer drew his pistol to shoot him and three others, when 'an Imam with a turban on . . . wrestled with him [the officer] and took his pistol away.'

It was soon apparent that all that had been achieved at Suvla was another beachhead that was going nowhere. Stopford and several of the divisional commanders were replaced, but the failure signalled the beginning of the end for the Dardanelles campaign. London now began to think of withdrawal altogether from Gallipoli, especially after Bulgaria entered the war in September on the side of the

Central Powers, ending any realistic chance of forcing a way into the Black Sea. Although Hamilton's staff came up with an estimate of 50,000 casualties to evacuate the peninsula, it was clear that the number would be higher if they stayed.

In October Hamilton himself was relieved of command. The Dardanelles Committee, as the war council had become (and from November simply 'war committee'), had wearied of the eastern adventure and now plumped for withdrawal at whatever cost. Yet on the night of 18 December, in a remarkable display of originality, field discipline and meticulous staffwork, the withdrawal from Suvla and Anzac would be carried out practically without loss, the final evacuation from Cape Helles following on 8 January, again without casualties. The penultimate officer to leave the beach at Suvla was the future Labour prime minister Clement Attlee, commanding a company of the 6th South Lancashires, another New Army battalion. The last was the divisional commander himself, Major-General Frederick Maude, who would command the expeditionary force in Mesopotamia with considerable success until succumbing to cholera in November 1917.

'Thus ended a sound and farsighted venture [the Dardanelles campaign] which had been wrecked by a chain of errors hardly to be rivalled even in British history,' wrote Captain Basil Liddell Hart, the pre-eminent military commentator of the post-war years. Erich von Falkenhayn, former chief of the *Grosser Generalstab*, testified in his memoirs to just what a strategic prize opening the Dardanelles would have delivered: 'If the Straits between the Mediterranean and the Black Sea were not permanently closed to Entente traffic, all hopes of a successful course of the war would be very considerably diminished. Russia would have been freed from her significant isolation.'

And in that case the events of 1917, culminating in the Russian Revolution, might have been quite different.

14

SEPTEMBER

Loos

An ill-starred offensive by Kitchener's 'New Army'

John Buchan's classic novel *Greenmantle* (1916), sequel to *The Thirty-Nine Steps*, opens with its hero Richard Hannay and his friend Sandy Arbuthnot convalescing from wounds received at the battle of Loos, two of the 50,000 casualties (twice those of the Germans) in one of the British army's bloodiest ever defeats.

Among the dead in the real battle was 2nd Lieutenant John ('Jack') Kipling of the Irish Guards, Rudyard Kipling's only son, who was just eighteen and had been in France for but a month.

The long-planned allied offensive of autumn 1915 was meant to snip out the great salient formed by the German line in northern France. It consisted of simultaneous attacks against both sides of the bulge, General Noël de Castelnau's group of armies making the main effort with thirty-four divisions in Champagne, while General Ferdinand Foch's were to strike near Arras, with the BEF carrying out a supporting attack on his left towards the mining town of Loos. At his final conference before the offensive, General Joseph Joffre, the French commander-in-chief, said they had 'a certain guarantee of success'. He was 'confident of a great and possibly complete victory'. The cavalry were to move up ready to pour through the breaches and 'make a relentless pursuit without waiting for the infantry, and with the frontier as their objective'. A four-day bombardment would suppress or destroy the defences.

The German commander-in-chief, Erich von Falkenhayn, did not believe an offensive was possible, and refused to reinforce either the Champagne or the Artois sector. Although for months there had been talk in the streets of Paris and London of a 'big push', and despite aerial reconnaissance and increased signal traffic indicating a build-up of troops, the *Grosser Generalstab* calculated that after their setbacks earlier in the year the French were in no condition to attack. This was not unreasonable, since it was the view of most French generals other than Joffre.

As the intensive shelling began on 21 September the local German commanders pulled back their forward troops to secondary positions, avoiding its worst effects. When the French attacked four days later, Castelnau's army group quickly over-ran the first line but then ran into serious opposition from the laid-back positions. For three days the French battered away at the German second line, giving Falkenhayn time to rush in reserves, until General Pétain, commanding the French 2nd Army, called off his attack in defiance of orders.

Not only did Castelnau's offensive in Champagne fail, its initial success had the perverse effect of hastening the failure of that in Artois, and therefore the BEF's. Seeing the spectacular progress on the first day, with its delusive promise of breakthrough and the victory he himself had been predicting, Joffre told Foch to halt his attacks temporarily but to 'take care to avoid giving the British the impression that we are leaving them to attack alone'.

The attack at Loos was the biggest the BEF had yet carried out: six infantry divisions and one of cavalry – more than had gone to France in August 1914 – with a further two divisions of the Indian Corps in support, under General Sir Douglas Haig commanding 1st Army, and three more divisions in reserve under control of the commander-in-chief, Sir John French.

Of the nine British infantry divisions, though, only five were regular. Three were 'New Army' divisions, two of which had not yet been in the trenches, and one was from the Territorial Force. This meant that although there was no want of courage and eagerness for the fight – the 'New Army' men had been the first to answer Lord Kitchener's call for volunteers in 1914 – too many of the troops were green. A year was hardly time in which to train an individual soldier, let alone battalions, brigades and divisions.

The Loos battlefield was uniformly flat and dominated by slagheaps. Joffre insisted it was 'particularly favourable'. Haig agreed, but in so far as it was particularly favourable for the defenders, not the attackers. His misgivings were to some extent allayed by the availability of a new and secret weapon: gas, the use of which had been approved by the cabinet in the wake of the German chlorine attacks at Ypres in April.

Haig's high hopes for his gas attack were to be cruelly dashed. Artillery gas shells had not yet been developed, so the chlorine had to be released from cylinders, and needed a breeze strong enough to carry it to the enemy's trenches but not so strong as to disperse it. The weather in the days before the attack, scheduled for 25 September, had been foul, with heavy rain. On the morning of the twenty-fifth, as Haig's intelligence officer Colonel John Charteris noted, 'There was not a breath of wind until 5 a.m.'; but the reports from the meteorological officer, Gold, 'had become pretty confident that the wind would be favourable'.

I went to D.H. [Douglas Haig] at 2 a.m., when we had just received a report from a distant station that made Gold reasonably hopeful. Our own report from the line was that it was dead still. At 3, when the decision had to be made, I took Gold ... to D.H. Gold was then more confident and D.H. ordered zero hour for 5.50 ... At 5 he came to our office with Fletcher [ADC]. There was quite a faint breath of wind then, and Fletcher's cigarette smoke moved quite perceptibly towards the Germans. But it died away again in a few minutes, and a little later D.H. sent down a message from the tower to 1st Corps to enquire if the attack could still be held up. Gough [corps commander] replied that it was too late to change. I was with D.H. when the reply was brought in. He was very upset.

Major-General Henry (later General Lord) Horne, commanding 2nd Division, ignored the advice of his gas officer not to release the cloud because of insufficient breeze: 'The programme must be carried out whatever the conditions,' he insisted. As a result his division, with their rudimentary gas hoods, suffered over 2,000 gas casualties, though mercifully only a handful were fatal.

In all, 140 tons of chlorine were released from 5,000 containers. Some of it did indeed serve its purpose. On the extreme right, where the 15th (Scottish) Division attacked, the gas carried well into the German lines, and the Scots nearly broke through, causing considerable consternation in the German command. The 47th (London) Division, territorials, despite heavy casualties also made good progress, in one case with unauthorized tactics. Disobeying orders, just before zero hour Rifleman Frank Edwards, one of the London Irish Rifles' football team, pulled a leather football from his knapsack and started to inflate it. 'Just imagine, as I did,' he later recalled, 'a party of London Irishmen, with our war cry of "Hurroo" charging across No Man's Land passing the ball forward to finish up the mad rush by leaping into their trench with the rifle and bayonet.' The ball got stuck in wire, but enough of the riflemen didn't, though Edwards himself was wounded.

Haig had no reserves to exploit these partial successes, however, having put all his forces into the attack, trusting to the early release of the extra three divisions by GHQ. These, however, had on Sir John French's insistence been kept 16 miles to the rear, which now meant an approach march throughout the night of 25–6 September. By dawn the men were already tired, with several miles still to go to the German front line. Congestion on the roads further slowed their progress. As the *Official History* put it, 'It was like trying to push the Lord Mayor's procession through the streets of London without clearing the route and holding up the traffic.' And two-thirds of the 'procession' (the New Army divisions) had never been in the 'streets of London' before – or, indeed, in a procession of any kind.

When the reserves eventually reached the front, again in heavy rain, they would make their attacks with inadequate artillery support against defences which the Germans had worked all night to strengthen. In the words of Sir Basil Liddell Hart, 'The attack broke down and the survivors broke back.'

Joffre, French and now Haig were determined to continue, for too many lives had been lost in what would otherwise be seen as a worthless sacrifice, and they were certain that the Germans had suffered at least as badly (in fact the total German casualties at Loos were around half the number of British lives lost). Over the coming days troops were brought to Loos from the Ypres sector, but unexpectedly strong German counter-attacks and more heavy rain checked all progress. Haig ordered the last attack on 13 October; fighting continued until 18 October when the offensive was formally closed down.

The *Official History* would conclude that the renewed attacks 'had not improved the general situation in any way and had brought nothing but useless slaughter of infantry'.

It was not only the number of dead that was significant, but also who they were. A large percentage were officers, many of them experienced regulars. Three divisional commanders (major-generals) were killed, three brigade commanders, and a staggering twenty-nine commanding officers – one in four of those taking part. Not surprisingly, the great majority of the latter were of New Army battalions: the less experienced the unit, the more visible its leadership had to be. While in the short term senior officers and battalion commanders could be replaced relatively easily, the junior leadership, the company officers, could not. The weakening of the battalions numerically was but a temporary setback, for battle-casualty replacements had been earmarked and in many cases were already in France at the base depots, but the loss of junior officers weakened the battalions far more in the long term. The typical 'bayonet' (attacking) strength of a battalion at this time was 650–750 men and 30–35 officers. In thirty-two battalions the loss of officers was over 50 per cent. The 8th Seaforth Highlanders and 12th Highland Light Infantry each lost twenty-three officers, and the 8th Royal West Kents and 8th Royal East Kents (The Buffs) – all New Army battalions – twenty-four. Six battalions lost over 600 men each, of which two lost almost 700. So grimly satisfied were the Germans with their machine guns that they called the battle *Der Leichenfeld von Loos*, 'The Field of Corpses of Loos'.

*

The subsequent failure to locate his son's remains would haunt Kipling for the rest of his life. His poem 'My Boy Jack', written in memory of his 'dear old boy', is one of his best-loved works. The eventual identification of his remains by the Commonwealth War Graves Commission in 1992 is still disputed.

Captain the Honourable Fergus Bowes-Lyon of the 8th Black Watch, the late Queen Mother's brother, also has no precisely known grave. Nor does Captain Charles Sorley of the Suffolks, who had left Marlborough College only two years before aged eighteen, already a published poet and in the opinion of John Masefield, later poet laureate, the greatest loss of all the poets killed during the war. His name is among the sixteen poets of the Great War commemorated on a slate stone in Westminster Abbey.

MY BOY JACK

Rudyard Kipling

'Have you news of my boy Jack?'
Not this tide.
'When d'you think that he'll come back?'
Not with this wind blowing, and this tide.

'Has any one else had word of him?'
Not this tide.
For what is sunk will hardly swim,
Not with this wind blowing, and this tide.

'Oh, dear, what comfort can I find?'
None this tide,
Nor any tide,
Except he did not shame his kind—
Not even with that wind blowing, and that tide.

Then hold your head up all the more,
This tide,
And every tide;
Because he was the son you bore,
And gave to that wind blowing and that tide!

15

OCTOBER

The Gardeners of Salonika

A new front opens in the southern Balkans

In a malaria-infested backwater, which at times both the allies and their enemies were wont to deride, two of the leading figures in British music and art found themselves among the ranks of a largely forgotten army.

Ralph Vaughan Williams, one of the greatest English composers of the twentieth century, and the celebrated painter Stanley (later Sir Stanley) Spencer were serving as medical orderlies on the Macedonian front, which would one day witness a spectacular allied counter-offensive precipitating a nervous breakdown in the German commander-in-chief, Erich Ludendorff.

In October 1915, however, such a feat could scarcely be imagined. For a year and more the doughty Serbs had held off a succession of Austrian attacks, but Berlin was keen for a knockout blow that would then allow the Austro-Hungarian army to put its full weight into defeating the more dangerous foe, the Russians, while fending off the Italians, who had entered the war on the Entente's side in May.

Italy's move, a considerable boost for the allies, was however

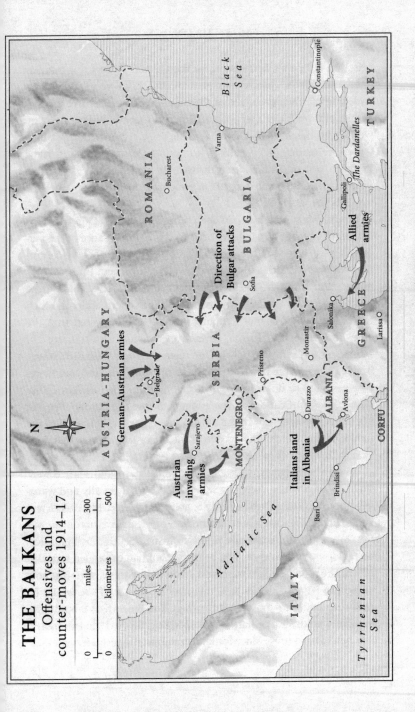

THE BALKANS
Offensives and counter-moves 1914–17

N

| miles | 0 | 300 |
| kilometres | 0 | 500 |

Tyrrhenian Sea

ITALY

Adriatic Sea

Bari ○

Brindisi ○

Italians land in Albania

Black Sea

ROMANIA

○ Bucharest

Varna ○

BULGARIA

Sofia ○

Direction of Bulgar attacks

AUSTRIA-HUNGARY

German-Austrian armies

○ Belgrade

Austrian invading armies

Sarajevo ○

MONTENEGRO

SERBIA

Priseno ○

Monastir ○

Durazzo ○

ALBANIA

Avlona ○

CORFU

Salonika ○

GREECE

Larissa ○

Allied armies

Constantinople ○

TURKEY

Gallipoli ○

The Dardanelles

offset by Bulgaria's declaration for the Central Powers five months later. The chief of the German general staff, Erich von Falkenhayn, had long planned a concerted German–Austrian offensive against Serbia, and on 2 October Sofia told Berlin that the Bulgarian army would join the offensive. Two days later the Germans and Austrians struck, Belgrade quickly falling, and on 14 October the Bulgarians launched a strong attack from the east. Against such a heavy, three-pronged offensive the Serbian army could do little but fall back towards the south and west.

The British and French had been promising direct aid to the Serbs for some time, but it had never been forthcoming because of the perceived greater need of the Western Front. Nor could they be certain that Athens, still officially neutral, would allow them lines of communication through Greek territory. Greece, in fact, seemed to be heading for civil war over the issue. The Serb commander-in-chief, the redoubtable Marshal Radomir Putnik, had suggested that the allies intervene via Albania, covered in the north by the army of Montenegro, a Serb ally, but this too seemed fraught with difficulties. Besides, the Entente had been trying to woo Bulgaria, and had therefore hesitated to do anything to drive her into the German camp. One of the justifications of the attempt to take the Dardanelles had been that it would draw in the Bulgarians on the side of the allies; the failure of that campaign was one of the major factors in Sofia's decision to throw in its lot with the Central Powers.

When the Bulgarians struck, however, Britain and France were quick to act, at once declaring war on Berlin's newest ally and warning troops at Gallipoli to be ready to go to Serbia's aid. But Greece was still divided. The king, Constantine, was pro-German (his queen was the Kaiser's sister), while the prime minister, Eleutherios Venizelos, was strongly pro-Entente. The country itself had expanded territorially in the recent Balkan wars, and stood to lose these gains if it now chose the wrong side. With Serbia now looking as if she would be over-run, and with no certainty where the Bulgarians would halt, Venizelos boldly but unilaterally invited the allies to send troops into southern Serbia (now Macedonia) through north-east Greece.

A force of two divisions, one British (the 10th Irish) and one French, under command of the French General Maurice Sarrail, was rushed across the Aegean from Gallipoli to the Greek port of Salonika. By the time they arrived, however, the mood in Athens had swung back against Venizelos, and the 10th Division found themselves under threat of internment, observed by German spies and hostile Greek officials.

In the event they were able to land unhindered, and found the port an altogether pleasant change from the beachheads of Gallipoli. Inland, however, the conditions soon proved just as bad. 'When you step out of Salonika you step into a virtual desert, roadless, treeless, uncultivated, populated only by scattered villages of the most primitive kind, inhabited by a low-grade peasantry,' wrote the divisional commander, Major-General Bryan Mahon.

> Two roads, in a condition quite inadequate to support heavy traffic, and three single lines of railway ran, at the most divergent angles possible, from Salonika towards the enemy's territory. Apart from these there was hardly even a track which in winter was possible for wheeled traffic. So that from the very beginning the Allied Forces have had to build up slowly, laboriously, the whole of the system of locomotion necessary for themselves and their supplies – piers, roads, bridges, railways – all have had to be created where nothing of the kind previously existed.

The 10th Division, soon followed by four more divisions from the BEF in France, much to the dismay of Sir John French, had arrived poorly equipped for the worsening weather. They had been sent to Gallipoli in August in cotton drill uniform to take part in what was expected to be the short and decisive operation at Suvla Bay, and had no greatcoats. As they struck into the mountainous interior, General Mahon found the weather 'most unpropitious for soldiering, cold and wet in winter, hot and feverish in summer . . . Winter, right up to the beginning of April, is a season of snow, rain, and, above all, mud.'

Indeed, during the next three years, casualties from disease and climate would be twenty times those from enemy action in this theatre. Salonika was one of the malarial black spots of Europe, and with the soldier's customary sardonic humour the Salonika veterans would name their newspaper *The Mosquito*.

The arrival of the Anglo-French force came too late to save the Serbs. Marshal Putnik ordered a general retreat through Montenegro into neutral Albania; of the 200,000 who began that arduous march, only some 125,000 would reach the Adriatic coast. Here, in a Dunkirk-like operation, they were embarked on allied ships, chiefly Italian, and taken via Corfu to join the Anglo-French force in Salonika. Over the next two years the 'Allied Armies of the Orient', as the polyglot force on the Macedonian front was known, would be joined by Russians, Italians, Czechs and troops from French Indo-China, and eventually by the Greeks themselves.

In December 1915, the Bulgarians having driven a wedge between the retreating Serbs and the allies, General Sarrail's force fell back from southern Serbia towards Salonika. There was a particularly sharp engagement with Bulgarian troops in the Kosturino Pass north of Lake Doiran, and for a while the situation looked dangerous, the chief of the Greek general staff warning Sarrail: 'You will be driven into the sea, and you will not have time even to cry for mercy.'

Despite the confusion and the worsening weather, however, the allies were able to establish a line of defence along the Greek border. Crucially, Berlin, anxious not to over-extend the effort and bring in the Greek army, told the Bulgarians that their troops must not violate Greek territory. The fighting subsided, and the Macedonian front settled into the uncomfortable tedium of watching and waiting, to the increasing frustration both of allied statesmen, who wanted to see more action there, and of the generals, who wanted to see the troops brought back to the Western Front. The soldiers themselves, like those in Italy in 1944 who were incensed at being called 'D-Day Dodgers', bridled at a jibe by Georges Clemenceau, the future prime minister of France, that they were 'the gardeners of Salonika' because instead of attacking all they did was dig. The Germans were just as contemptuous: with eventually half a million allied troops on the Macedonian front, Berlin would call Salonika the Entente's largest internment camp.

There were occasional bursts of small-scale fighting, however, some of it intense, as witnessed by the award of the VC in 1916 to twenty-year-old Private 'Stokey' Lewis of the Welsh Regiment, one of Kitchener's first volunteers, for his part in a savage trench raid. But with so little hard fighting until the autumn of 1918, Macedonia became the forgotten front. Certainly both Ralph Vaughan Williams and Stanley Spencer thought it so, and a none too congenial place either.

Although in his forties and a figure of national stature, Vaughan Williams had volunteered for the Royal Army Medical Corps almost as soon as the war began. After serving as a stretcher-bearer on the Western Front, he was transferred with his field ambulance to Salonika in November 1916. A fellow orderly, Private Harry Steggles, described sharing a two-man tent 'little less than the area of a double bed' with the editor of the *English Hymnal* and composer of *Fantasia on a Theme by Thomas Tallis* – known in the field ambulance simply as 'Bob':

> We had a groundsheet and blanket a piece and all our worldly goods included razor, comb, lather brush, also Isaiah and Jeremiah [which were] two empty pineapple tins in which we lit charcoal and after whirling them round and round like the old fashioned winter warmer we rushed them into the 'bivvy' and sealed up any air intakes we could find. I think we slept more from our rum ration plus carbon monoxide from Isaiah and Jeremiah than fatigue. One lost everything in these confined spaces, but Bob always gave up the chase with a grunt saying, 'Find it in the morning', and the great man slept.

One particularly filthy night however, Steggles recorded:

> We both sat with our knees drawn up in the 'bivvy' looking at a guttering candle, water creeping in, plus snakes, scorpions and centipedes. A few shells were sailing over which thrilled Bob, a typical Bairnsfather

'Better' 'ole' scene; when Bob suddenly said: 'Harry, when this war ends we will (a) dine at Simpson's on saddle of mutton, (b) see Carmen.'

They would indeed dine at Simpson's after the war, but *Carmen* eluded them.

Stanley Spencer, already an acclaimed painter of landscapes and allegorical subjects though still in his twenties, was serving with another field ambulance. Deeply if unconventionally religious, he was strongly affected by the experience of Salonika, which would have a profound and disturbing effect on his art. During his early months there, however, the landscape and colour thrilled him. 'I do wish I had my paints out here,' he wrote home. 'The pearly sky at sunrise (in winter), the deep blue sea, and the shadows of big ships along the surface, and the bronze hills beyond. The regular ridges of foam all gleaming in the sun like a Claude.'

His brush would find its real expression three years later in one of the most singular images of the conflict. In 1919 the War Memorials Committee commissioned him to paint a large work for their planned Hall of Remembrance. Though the hall was never built, the resulting work, *Travoys Arriving with Wounded at a Dressing Station at Smol, Macedonia, September 1916*, is now on permanent display at the Imperial War Museum. It recalls his time, he explained, in 'the middle of September 1916 [when] the 22nd Division made an attack on Machine Gun Hill on the Doiran Vardar Sector and held it for a few nights. During these nights the wounded passed through the dressing stations in a never-ending stream'.

Not until September 1918, however, would the Macedonian front show any return on the allies' huge investment of troops, when at last a spectacular counter-offensive would drive the Austro-Bulgarian forces out of Serbia, precipitating Ludendorff's breakdown and the weakening of the Western Front.

'It was upon this much-abused front that the final collapse of the Central Empires first began,' wrote Winston Churchill, an assessment confirmed by Ludendorff himself in his memoirs.

16

NOVEMBER

'Mespot'

The 500-mile British advance on Baghdad is turned back almost within sight of the city, leading to the most humiliating surrender of the war

'Winston is getting more and more absorbed in boilers,' the chancellor of the exchequer, David Lloyd George, had complained in 1913. The new first lord of the Admiralty's demands for an increase in the navy's budget to convert the fleet to oil propulsion thoroughly dismayed a Treasury struggling to fund the Liberal government's welfare programme. Besides, some argued, coal was to be had in abundance throughout Britain; oil propulsion would make the Royal Navy dependent on foreign supplies. Nevertheless Churchill got his way, and in July 1914, with just days to the declaration of war, he managed to secure for the Crown a 51 per cent controlling interest in the Anglo-Persian Oil Company, which itself had a 50 per cent interest in the Turkish Petroleum Company exploring resources in the Ottoman Empire, of which Mesopotamia was a part.

The British campaign in Mesopotamia – roughly, present-day Iraq – was first therefore about oil, lately discovered in large quantities around Basra and Mosul. However, the necessity of protecting the navy's oil supplies after Constantinople declared war on the Entente in early November was not the only factor: London and Delhi were concerned that Turkish agents would stir up trouble among India's Muslims, inciting them to *jihad*, 'holy war'. A campaign in Mesopotamia would demonstrate to Indian Muslims that the British were still in control, and also encourage an Arab revolt against Ottoman rule which would spread throughout the Middle East, easing the Turkish threat to the Suez Canal and hastening the defeat of the Ottoman Empire.

Mesopotamia derived its Greek name from its position between the two rivers Tigris and Euphrates, which meet at El Qurnah, 40 miles north of Basra, to form the Shatt al-Arab waterway which flows into the Persian Gulf at a complex delta. Baghdad, then the Ottoman administrative capital, lies on the Tigris some 550 miles upstream. For the most part the land is desert and very flat, the rivers flooding the immediate plains when the winter snows in the northern mountains thaw. In 1914 there were no roads to speak of, nor railways south of Baghdad, so strategic movement depended on the rivers.

The operation to secure the oil fields and pipelines around Basra and what would become present-day Kuwait was mounted by the army of India and directed from Delhi, rather than from London, the British army and its colonial reinforcements being already hard pressed in France and Egypt. 'Our Indian ewe-lamb,' the viceroy, Lord Crewe, called it. However, the mixed motives of the intervention had not made for clear strategic focus, and the operation began to over-reach itself. The best of the Indian troops and British regiments in India had anyway been sent to the Western Front, and many of the most experienced officers who remained, especially those on home leave when the war began, were redeployed to train Lord Kitchener's 'New Army' battalions. Nor was the Indian army equipped for intensive fighting, its divisions having for example only half the artillery of those in the BEF.

Early success had seemed promising. Basra, which the Turks evacuated, had been taken on 22 November by the 6th (Poona)

Division, and El Qurnah a fortnight later. Over the next few months the 'Indian Expeditionary Force D', as it was officially known, was therefore reinforced by a division and corps troops, and in March Delhi told its new commander-in-chief, the highly experienced Lieutenant-General Sir John Nixon, who in 1906 had succeeded Douglas Haig as Inspector-General of Cavalry in India, to 'retain complete control of the lower portion of Mesopotamia' and submit plans for an advance on Baghdad.

It made sense to expand what was little more than a toehold at the end of two strategic waterways along which the enemy would otherwise have been free to move, but 'the lower portion of Mesopotamia' was far from secured. In April the Turks had made a determined attempt to retake Basra, in which Major George Massy Wheeler of the 7th Hariana Lancers had won, posthumously, the first VC of the campaign. His medal, previously thought lost, was found in 2017 in the archives of the Brighton Museum, to which his widow had left it on her death in the 1950s.

In May 1915, despite the advice of the commander of the 6th Division, Major-General Charles Townshend, hero of the defence of Chitral on the North-West Frontier twenty years earlier, Nixon despatched two divisional columns upstream: while Townshend's moved along the Tigris towards Baghdad, Major-General George Gorringe's 12th Indian Division worked up the Euphrates, taking Nasiriyah on 25 July.

The ease of advance quickly proved deceptive, however, for it became increasingly difficult to supply the two divisions. And while Nixon's supply line grew longer, that of the Turks shortened accordingly, though he remained convinced that he could take Baghdad. Townshend continued to disagree. The 6th Division was tired, and its casualties to the enemy and the heat had not yet been made up.

The advance continued nevertheless, and at first Nixon looked vindicated. The Turks evacuated the bulk of their 10,000-strong garrison at Kut al-Amara, just 120 miles from Baghdad, leaving Townshend to take possession on 28 September, though not without some sharp fighting. As the division ploughed up the Tigris, the leading gunboat, *Comet*, commanded by Lieutenant-Commander Edgar Cookson, found the river blocked by dhows linked by wire hawsers and covered by heavy rifle and machine-gun fire from both banks. Having failed to sink the centre dhow by gunfire and then by ramming, Cookson, who only a fortnight before had won the Distinguished Service Order in an ambush, placed the *Comet* alongside and jumped aboard to set about the hawsers with an axe. Hit several times, for his courage and determination he would be awarded a posthumous VC.

The Admiralty and the War Office were now getting anxious. In a joint memorandum they warned against the diversion of troops to a campaign 'which cannot appreciably influence the decision as between the armies of the allies and those of the Central Powers'. The cabinet concluded nevertheless that success in Mesopotamia would offset the recent failure in Gallipoli, telling Nixon: 'Unless you consider that the possibility of eventual withdrawal is against the advance . . . we are prepared to order it.'

Although he had received intelligence that Baghdad was being reinforced by troops sent from Gallipoli, Nixon told Townshend to press on.

After waiting six weeks for resupply, Townshend resumed his advance and by 22 November had reached Ctesiphon, capital of the old Parthian empire, just 25 miles from Baghdad. But here his luck ran out. The Ottoman war minister, Enver Pasha, had appointed Baron Colmar von der Goltz to command the Turkish 5th Army in Mesopotamia. Goltz was a Prussian of the most determined kind, brought out of retirement in 1914 to serve as military governor of Belgium, where he had ordered reprisals against civilians to deter sabotage. When the 6th (Poona) Division attacked, they found a strong and well-sited defensive line awaiting them, and Townshend lost over 4,000 men, more than a quarter of his force. Without reserves, and with fresh Turkish troops arriving by the hour, all he could do now was begin a fighting withdrawal back to Kut.

This he did, and with some skill, reaching the town on 3 December;

but the remnants of his division were at once besieged by Goltz's now very superior forces, Townshend only just managing to get his cavalry and flying corps away before the old fortress-town was encircled.

Over the next four months three attempts to relieve Kut would be bloodily repulsed, including one in which the future Labour prime minister, and Churchill's deputy in the Second World War, Clement Attlee, who had earlier fought at Gallipoli, was badly wounded.

Attempts to buy off the Turks with upwards of £2 million came to nothing, but led to confused reports that their compatriots at Gallipoli had been paid to let the allied troops finally slip away in January. Indeed, General Nixon himself had earlier bribed his way past pro-Ottoman Arabs when his paddle steamer had become grounded.

Conditions at Kut in the winter of 1915–16 proved particularly severe. With casualties from disease and exposure mounting, and food about to run out despite resupply by aircraft for the first time in the history of war, on 29 April Townshend would be forced to surrender, at which point his last hope, General Nikolai Baratov's largely Cossack force of 20,000 advancing from Persia, turned back.

This defeat was a major blow to British prestige in both the Middle East and India. Kitchener tried to salvage some honour in a statement in the House of Lords by saying it had been only 'the imminent starvation itself [that] compelled the capitulation of this gallant garrison, which consisted of 2,970 British and some 6,000 Indian troops [and] followers,' commending them in their 'honourable captivity' and insisting that their surrender 'reflects no discredit on themselves or on the record of the British and Indian armies'.

The outcome would, however, reflect ill on British generalship. In the parliamentary inquiry that followed, Nixon was roundly blamed, as were the authorities in Delhi, and control of the campaign was taken over by London. Townshend was at first lauded for his skill in the withdrawal and for repelling all attacks on Kut, but when news began to emerge of the treatment of his troops in captivity – of the 11,800 men who left Kut with their captors on 6 May, 4,250 died either on their way to internment or in the camps that awaited them (many of them when released at the end of the war were as badly emaciated as those liberated from Japanese PoW camps in 1945) – compared to his own palatial captivity on the small island of Heybeliada near Constantinople, there was a storm of indignation. Kipling, in his poem *Mesopotamia* published in 1917, railed against the evasion of responsibility by many of the senior commanders and officials involved, and the subsequent closing of ranks:

Shall we only threaten and be angry for an hour?
When the storm is ended shall we find
How softly but how swiftly they have sidled back to power
By the favour and contrivance of their kind?

Though the army in Mesopotamia was eventually reinforced to nine divisions, with Kut recaptured in February 1917 and Baghdad falling the following month, the campaign would drag on until October 1918. Former US President Theodore Roosevelt's second son, Kermit, was awarded the Military Cross while serving with the (British) Machine Gun Corps, before transferring to the US army once America entered the war in April 1917. His father had repeatedly denounced President Woodrow Wilson's non-interventionism and the stance of Irish-Americans and German-Americans who put the interests of Ireland and Germany before those of America. A US citizen had to be 100 per cent American, he insisted, not a 'hyphenated American' juggling multiple loyalties. 'Teddy' Roosevelt would eventually be given permission to raise four divisions of 'Rough Riders', like those he had led in the Spanish–American war of 1898, though the scheme was dropped when Wilson decided instead to send an American Expeditionary Force to France.

17

DECEMBER

Casualties

After a year of dismal defeats, new men and old ideas are the future

As 1915 came to its melancholy close, the German auxiliary cruiser *Möwe* (Gull) slipped out of Wilhelmshaven on her first mission, to lay a minefield in the Pentland Firth near the Grand Fleet's anchorage at Scapa Flow. A few days later the battleship *King Edward VII* struck one of the mines and sank.

It was a dramatic lesson in the asymmetry of the new sea warfare: a capital ship of the Royal Navy, named after the late king, sunk by a converted banana boat lately named the *Pungo*, while the two great fleets in their havens eyed each other warily across the North Sea. 'We shall dig the rats out of their holes,' Churchill, first lord of the Admiralty, had said in September the year before; but it would be a full six months before the *Hochseeflotte* would accept battle with the Grand Fleet at Jutland. Meanwhile, with every other German surface warship sunk or incapacitated, Berlin's war at sea would be waged increasingly by auxiliary vessels like the *Möwe*, and more worryingly by the U-boats. It was a mine laid by a U-boat off Scapa Flow that in June 1916 would claim the highest-ranking casualty of the war, Field Marshal Lord Kitchener himself, when the cruiser *Hampshire* taking him on a mission to Russia sank with virtually all hands.

In December 1915 the curtain was also coming down on the Dardanelles campaign, the attempt to use sea power to turn the strategic flank, take Constantinople, open warm-water lines of communication with Russia, and encourage Bulgaria and Romania to join the allies. After a personal reconnaissance by Kitchener the previous month, the war cabinet had taken the decision to withdraw from Gallipoli completely.

In all, the attempt to force an entry to the Black Sea had cost the allies – British, Indian, Commonwealth and French – a quarter of a million casualties (over 40,000 dead), and the Turks the same.

The Dardanelles campaign had been deeply flawed, revealing defects in the direction of strategy and operations in Whitehall, as well as in the capabilities of Kitchener's newly raised battalions and some Commonwealth units and their commanders, who had been thrown into battle prematurely. Nor had it been the Royal Navy's finest hour, notwithstanding the individual skill and bravery of many ships' companies during the nearly twelve months of the campaign – and certainly not that of the first sea lord, Admiral Lord Fisher, who had first applauded the plans and then schemed against them, eventually just walking away from the Admiralty, prompting the prime minister to say that if he didn't return he would send a policeman to arrest him.

The navy's shining accomplishment, however, had been the achievement of its submarines. Having penetrated the Dardanelles Straits, with all the minefields, and the narrow, tricky waters of the Bosporus, even sinking Turkish warships in the harbour at Constantinople, for months British, French and Australian boats ranged widely in the Black Sea. By the time they were recalled in early January 1916, they had sunk some 50 per cent of Turkish merchant shipping.

The most spectacular casualty of the campaign was the navy minister himself, Churchill. When the original landings miscarried, and

Asquith was forced to bring the Tories into a coalition government, Churchill was deprived of the Admiralty and given instead a non-departmental position to keep him in the cabinet. Despite the initial setbacks at Gallipoli he continued to press for an offensive there, championing the landings at Suvla Bay in August to break the deadlock, and even after these failed he advocated holding on and reinforcing. When General Sir Charles Monro, who in October replaced Sir Ian Hamilton, recommended complete evacuation, Churchill remarked bitterly: 'He came, he saw, he capitulated.' And once the war cabinet had made its decision, Churchill, who held the rank of major in the Oxfordshire Hussars (Territorial Force), saw no further place for himself in government and instead put on uniform and reported for duty in France.

Yet Clement Attlee, whose younger brother Laurence also served at Gallipoli, remained convinced that Churchill had been right. In his memoirs he declared: 'I always held that the strategic concept was sound. The trouble was that it was not adequately supported. Unfortunately the military authorities were Western Front-minded.'

With the withdrawal from Gallipoli, attention would indeed turn back to the Western Front. Although the allies had taken the decision early in December to reinforce the Salonika front, Bulgaria having joined the Central Powers in a concerted effort against Serbia, and Italy had entered the war on the side of the Entente in May, opening up yet another theatre of operations, London and Paris regarded the Western Front as the only one on which the Germans could be decisively defeated. General Joseph Joffre, recently appointed commander-in-chief of all French armies in the field, intended keeping just enough troops in Salonika to prevent Greece from being over-run, and drawing troops of the Central Powers south and away from the Russian front, while mounting an early and decisive offensive in France. At the second inter-allied conference, held at Joffre's headquarters at Chantilly, north of Paris, from 6 to 9 December, the British and French agreed on a major combined offensive on the Somme, while Italy and Russia would mount their own offensives to coincide, and all agreed that whenever one ally came under clear threat, the others would immediately launch diversionary attacks.

Herein lay the seeds of some of the worst blood-letting of the war, for the most expeditious way of mounting a diversion was simply to bring forward the start date of the next planned offensive. As the Germans were bound to attack somewhere in 1916, there was a good chance that they would do so first, in which case the counter-offensives would to varying degrees be premature, therefore less well prepared and in turn less likely to succeed.

The British offensive on the Somme would, however, be under new leadership. For many months it had been plain to Kitchener and the war cabinet that Sir John French could not continue as commander-in-chief of the BEF. The Loos offensive in October had been badly conceived and executed, failures for which he had tried to shift the blame. His official despatch, published in *The Times* on 2 November, contained many errors, especially touching on the part played in the battle by General Sir Douglas Haig, commanding one of the BEF's three armies, and had seriously undermined his authority. French had also primed *The Times*'s military correspondent, Colonel Charles Repington, to write a supporting article suggesting that the battle might have gone better had French himself taken personal command rather than leaving things to Haig, whose 1st Army had taken the lead at Loos. Haig at once wrote to French asking for the despatch to be publicly corrected, which French refused to do. Thereafter Haig lost no opportunity to convey his view that French was not fit for command to anyone with influence – including the King through 'back channels', notably Lady Haig, a former lady-in-waiting to the Queen. '[French] is not only very ignorant of the principles of the higher leading of a large Army but is also lacking in the necessary temperament!' he wrote to Leopold de Rothschild on 9 December. 'He is so hot tempered and excitable – like a bottle of soda water in suddenness of explosion – that he is quite incapable of thinking over a serious situation and coming to a reasoned decision.'

The letter crossed with one from Asquith marked 'Secret', enclosed in three envelopes, which Haig received the following day at his headquarters at Hinges in the Pas de Calais: 'Sir J. French has placed in my hands his resignation of the Office of Commander in Chief of the Forces in France. Subject to the King's approval, I have the pleasure of proposing to you that you should be his successor.'

Kitchener had already told Haig what was afoot when he had been in London the week before, ostensibly taking a few days' leave. 'K' had also told him that he was recalling Lieutenant-General Sir William 'Wully' Robertson, the BEF's chief of staff, to be CIGS. This would provide Haig with a powerful ally in the War Office when the disastrous offensives of 1916 and 1917 began to give the cabinet second thoughts.

Kitchener also told Haig that Brigadier-General George Macdonogh, who until August 1914 had been head of the War Office intelligence division concerned with internal security (today's MI5), and thereafter the BEF's chief of intelligence, was to return to London as director of military intelligence. Macdonogh was brilliant. He and a fellow sapper – James Edmonds, who would become the official historian of the war – had gained such high marks in the staff college entrance exam in 1896 that the results, it was said, were adjusted to conceal the margin between them and their classmates (who included Robertson and Allenby). Macdonogh was a Catholic, however, Jesuit-educated, and deeply mistrusted by Haig and others. Although he would turn the intelligence directorate into a first-rate organization, his assessments would never be entirely accepted by GHQ in France. Haig preferred those of the man he appointed in Macdonogh's place as BEF chief of intelligence, Brigadier-General John Charteris – 'Haig's evil counsellor', as he became known – who increasingly fashioned his assessments to support his chief's decisions rather than challenge the assumptions on which they were made (perhaps the original 'dodgy dossiers').

To make matters worse, 'Wully' Robertson's replacement as the BEF's chief of staff, Major-General Launcelot Kiggell, was, it seems, wholly unable to make any impression on Haig and thereby gained the nickname 'the invisible man'.

The BEF was therefore to see in the new year with a most perilous team at its head, for while Haig himself lacked the imperfections he had complained of in Sir John French, he also lacked the qualities of humanity that had made French – at least until Loos – a well-regarded leader. After the war, Robertson would write of French, 'the little field marshal', that he doubted 'if any other general in the army could have sustained in [the BEF] to the same extent the courage and resolution which they displayed during the trying circumstances of the first six months of the war'.

On 18 December, French and Haig had a frosty handover meeting, 'in which Haig never for one moment unbent', said one who witnessed it. The outgoing C-in-C asked that Churchill be given a brigade to command.

That evening 'the little field marshal' dined at the Ritz in Paris with his military secretary, and next day at Boulogne was cheered all the way up the gang-plank by his old regiment, the 19th Hussars. Once back across the Channel he was created Viscount French of Ypres and of High Lake in the County of Roscommon, and made Commander-in-Chief, Home Forces.

There would be one more momentous act before the month, and the year, were out. On 28 December the cabinet agreed to lay before parliament the Military Service Bill. Every male British subject who on 15 August 1915 was ordinarily resident in Great Britain (the bill did not extend to Ireland), who had attained the age of 19 but was not yet 41, and who was unmarried or a widower without dependent children, unless he met certain exceptions was deemed to have enlisted for general service.

The bill would be passed with little opposition on 27 January: the first time in history that there was to be general conscription in Britain. The manpower thus assured, the stage was now set for the terrible battles of attrition that would characterize the rest of the war.

PART THREE

1916

'Pure Murder'

9 January: Final evacuation of Gallipoli.

21 February: Battle of Verdun begins.

31 May: Battle of Jutland.

4 June: Brusilov offensive begins (Eastern Front).

1 July: Battle of the Somme begins (with, on 15 September, the first use of tanks).

4 August: Sixth Battle of the Isonzo (Italian Front) begins.

27 August: Romania declares war on the Central Powers.

18

JANUARY
Enter Haig

After a year of failed offensives, the allies decided that the only way to victory was more offensives – but this time successful ones

On Christmas Day 1915 at his headquarters in St Omer in the Pas de Calais, General Sir Douglas Haig read a memorandum in the confidential papers left by Field Marshal Sir John French, from whom he had just taken over command of the BEF. It referred to armoured 'machine-gun destroyers' on 'caterpillars', which apparently had been the pet project of the then first lord of the Admiralty, Winston Churchill, who had recently left government and reported for duty with the army in France.

'Is anything known about the caterpillar referred to in Para 4, page 3?' he wrote in the margin.

A sapper on the staff of GHQ, Major Hugh Elles, was sent to England to find out.

For the time being, however, the new commander-in-chief had greater concerns than the Admiralty's experiments with 'land-ships', as they and the trench warfare branch of David Lloyd

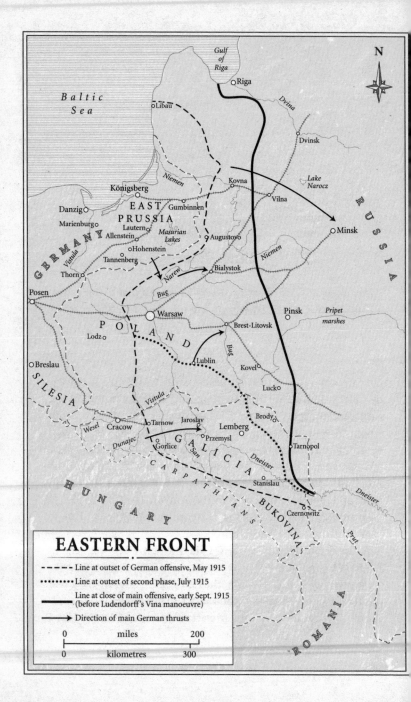

EASTERN FRONT

- – – – Line at outset of German offensive, May 1915
- ·········· Line at outset of second phase, July 1915
- ——— Line at close of main offensive, early Sept. 1915
  (before Ludendorff's Vina manoeuvre)
- ——→ Direction of main German thrusts

| 0 | miles | 200 |
| 0 | kilometres | 300 |

George's new Ministry of Munitions called them. At the Chantilly conference in December, the Entente allies had committed themselves to mounting major offensives in the coming year, and to hasten these offensives if one or other of them were attacked beforehand. Yet to 'wear down the Enemy and cause him to use up his reserves,' Haig noted in his diary on 18 January, 'all the Allies must start at once. But Russia may not be ready till later, say July. In that case Germany may turn on her and defeat her – she (Russia) may then make peace!'

The previous summer's offensives by the German and Austrian armies had pushed the Russians back to a line from Riga on the Baltic to Czernowitz on the Romanian border, which besides aught else had done nothing to encourage the Romanians, who were still sitting on the fence, to declare for the Entente. In this 'Great Retreat', which though well conducted was a severe blow to morale, the Russians had surrendered practically the whole of Poland (Warsaw had fallen on 5 August) and the Germans had taken three-quarters of a million prisoners. Indeed, by the close of the year, the Russian army since August 1914 had lost in all some four million men, with another million in that baleful category 'missing'. All thoughts in Paris and London of the 'Russian steamroller' slowly but surely destroying the German army on the Eastern Front were now gone. Worse still, although in September 1914 the Triple Entente powers had signed a pact 'not to conclude peace separately during the present war' in which they pledged that, 'when terms of peace come to be discussed, no one of the Allies will demand conditions of peace without the previous agreement of each of the other Allies', a separate Russian negotiated peace was now, as Haig noted, a distinct possibility.

After the failure of the Dardanelles campaign to open warmwater communications with Russia, the danger of a separate peace should certainly have been the predominant strategic concern. Yet the French commander-in-chief, Joseph Joffre, insisted there was no likelihood of Russian collapse, although he did see a need to draw off German troops from the east by mounting offensives in the west. In theory this was sound enough, except that the Germans understood the game and were not prepared to play it. Throughout 1915, because none of the offensives in the west had had the remotest chance of achieving break-through, given the Germans' agility in switching local reserves to seal any breaches in the line, the German chief of staff, Erich von Falkenhayn, had transferred only two divisions from the Eastern Front to the Western. Why should the allied offensives of 1916 be any more successful in diverting German divisions?

And yet there were voices in Vienna which argued that Russia, for all the setbacks she had suffered, was simply too powerful to overcome. At the beginning of January the Austrian chief of staff, Franz Conrad von Hötzendorf, confided to the Hungarian prime minister, Count István Tisza: 'There can be no question of destroying the Russian war machine; England cannot be defeated; peace must be made in not too long a space, or we shall be fatally weakened, if not destroyed.' For the German and Austro-Hungarian armies had suffered a million casualties on the Russian front in 1915, and despite the Austrians' recent success, finally, in over-running Serbia, the increasing alienation between the German and Austrian high commands was leading to cynicism on both sides, with some German officers complaining that 'We are shackled to a corpse.'

Conrad appreciated that the problem for the Russians was not, in fact, the absolute number of Austrian and German troops facing them – there were huge reserves, still, of Russian manpower – but the lack of arms and munitions with which to fight. This, as Conrad perceived, was not a problem beyond solution.

For a year it had seemed so, nevertheless. As early as December 1914 the chief of the *Stavka*, the Russian high command, Nikolai Yanushkevich, had written to the war minister, General

Vladimir Sukhomlinov, that the shortage of ammunition was 'a nightmare', as was that of war materiel in general. 'Why should we perish of hunger and cold, without boots,' his men were asking; 'the artillery is silent, and we are killed like partridges.'

On average the Russian army had one surgeon for every 10,000 men, and with medical staff stretched thinly across a 500-mile front, many soldiers were dying from wounds that on the Western Front would have been successfully treated. In June 1915 Yanushkevich wrote that because of the lack of shells 'the enemy can inflict loss unpunished' and that the fighting was 'pure murder'.

If the western allies couldn't or wouldn't help Russia directly, neither could she help herself. The closure of the Dardanelles in October 1914 had been calamitous – essential imports dried up, and her exports, largely grain from southern Russia and Ukraine, declined by over two-thirds – but it was not beyond the wit of a resourceful bureaucracy to cope with. The Russian bureaucracy was made for another age, however, and court intrigue was pernicious. In September the clique that dominated the Winter Palace persuaded the Tsar to dismiss the commander-in-chief, his cousin, the Grand Duke Nicholas, and to take command of the armies himself. This was unfortunate on three counts. First, although the grand duke was no strategist, his judgement of men was on the whole quite sound, which was not a quality that his cousin shared. Second, the Tsar's absence in the field left the Tsarina and her reactionary coterie to block all attempts at political reform. And third, as the cabinet, which had unanimously opposed the change, pointed out, any further reversals would inevitably be blamed on the Tsar himself.

Tsar Nicholas took no notice. (He never did.)

Social and industrial unrest then spread quickly, with food even in the capital becoming scarce. By the end of 1915 Russia was virtually ungovernable. The country desperately needed some military success to put heart into both the army and the civil population. Fortunately – in the short term at least, for in time it would highlight the hopelessness of the *ancien régime* and feed the appetite for revolution – the self-help system of *zemstva*, the semi-official councils which sorted out all manner of affairs in a local, pragmatic fashion, began to make the running. By the spring of 1916 they would bring about a significant improvement in the supply of armaments and munitions, and their welfare work began stiffening military morale.

There would also be some restorative military success, under the innovative cavalryman General Aleksei Brusilov, who in March was given command of the south-western front. His preparations for the offensive in the east promised at Chantilly would be far superior to those of previous commanders, envisaging the use of 'shock troops' to attack and infiltrate in small parties rather than, as before, en masse – tactics that the Germans themselves would later copy and perfect.

Meanwhile, Haig continued to work on a number of plans to fulfil the Chantilly pledge, notably to capture Ostend and Zeebrugge, which had become troublesome U-boat nests, as well as Joffre's favoured combined offensive on the Somme. All the plans were dogged by the same problem, however: how to overcome the deadly combination of barbed wire, machine guns and artillery which had created the stalemate of the Western Front. For the present, there seemed to be only one solution: more and heavier artillery. Indeed, a year later Haig would be no closer to finding a solution, prompting the commander of the Australian 3rd Division, the Gallipoli veteran Major-General John Monash (not a soldier by profession but a civil engineer), to state that 'the Western Front is first and foremost an engineering problem'.

There was, however, a glimmer of hope in Haig's Christmas-day marginal query about the 'caterpillar'. Major Elles would return from his research trip to England with encouraging news of a tracked device that could crush barbed wire, cross trenches and bring fire to bear on the enemy from behind steel protection. Churchill's 'Admiralty Landships Committee', set up in February 1915, had finally borne fruit, thanks to the engineering skill of William Foster and Co. Ltd of Lincoln, specialists in agricultural machinery. Fosters had tested a first design, little more than an armoured box on American tractor caterpillar tracks, in September, but it could not cross a gap of 5 feet – the average trench width – the tracks being prone to shed. Known as 'Little Willie', after either Fosters' chief engineer and managing director, William Tritton, or the British press's derisive nickname for the Kaiser's son, Crown Prince Wilhelm, the trial nevertheless suggested the solution to the tracking problem. A few weeks later Tritton sent a telegram in veiled speech to the Admiralty: 'New arrival by tritton out of pressed plate STOP. Light in weight but very strong STOP. All doing well Thank you STOP. Proud parents END.'

With Lieutenant Walter Wilson of the Royal Naval Armoured Car Division, Tritton had produced a completely new design with bigger tracks wrapped round a hull with forward-sloping 'prows' projecting beyond the crew compartment, a rhomboid giving the machine huge reach. Weighing 28 tons and variously known as 'Centipede', 'Mother' or 'Big Willie', the prototype was ready just three months later. On the night of 19 January, sheathed in tarpaulins and referred to as a 'tank', a deliberately vague term alluding to its boxy shape, it was taken to Burton Park outside Lincoln and the following day was put through its paces, crossing a trench 8 feet wide, climbing a 5-foot parapet and crushing barbed wire entanglements.

A week later the 'tank' was on its way by rail to Hatfield Park in Hertfordshire, seat of the Marquess of Salisbury – whose cousin, Arthur Balfour, had succeeded Churchill at the Admiralty – for demonstrations to the War Office out of public view. Yet although the tank would do all that was asked of it at Hatfield, Kitchener, as secretary of state for war, had his doubts, calling it 'a pretty mechanical toy but without serious military value'.

Fortunately, Major-General Richard Butler, an infantryman and Haig's trusted deputy chief of staff, whom Elles had primed beforehand, saw its potential straight away. Though the tank would be many more months in development, the Tank Corps itself had in effect been conceived that day on Lord Salisbury's golf course. Major (later Lieutenant-General Sir) Hugh Elles would become its first commander.

Left 'Churchill makes a decisive move seven days before the war.' Asquith had sent the 36-year-old Winston Churchill to the Admiralty as first lord in 1911 to overhaul its war plans. Churchill's unilateral decision on 28 July 1914 to send the Grand Fleet to its war stations at Scapa Flow gained crucial command of the North Sea. He is pictured here in a contemporary print discussing the options with Admiral Sir John Jellicoe, commander-in-chief of the Grand Fleet.

Bottom 'By 27 August Samsonov's 2nd Army had been surrounded in a double envelopment at Tannenberg; by 30 August his entire command had disintegrated, the Germans taking 92,000 prisoners.'

French cavalry on the move, with a dirigible of the *Aéronautique Militaire* keeping watch, during the 'battle of the frontiers', August 1914.

Above 129th (Duke of Connaught's Own) Baluchis near Hollebeke, Ypres, where on 31 October 1914 Sepoy (Private) Khudadad Khan of the regiment won the first ever Indian VC.

Above Churchill called the twin battles of Coronel (1 November) and the Falklands (8 December 1914) 'the saddest naval action in the war. Of the officers and men in both the squadrons that faced each other . . . nine out of ten were doomed to perish. The British were to die that night: the Germans a month later.' SMS *Scharnhorst* sinking (foreground) and her sister ship *Gneisenau* at the end of the Battle of the Falklands, as imagined in this sketch for a painting by marine artist Lionel Wyllie.

BOMBARDMENT OF SCARBOROUGH.
A wrecked shop in Prospect Road. The wife of the shopkeeper here was killed just inside door.

Left On 16 December 1914, in an attempt to draw out the Grand Fleet into ambush, German battle-cruisers bombarded the North Sea towns of Scarborough, Whitby and the Hartlepools, inflicting over 650 casualties, mainly civilian, including 137 killed of whom 78 were women and children. 'Remember Scarborough' became a rallying cry for recruiting officers, as well as provoking outrage in the United States.

Above Men of the BEF's hastily formed 7th Division, transported in London buses, some still bearing their metropolitan destinations and advertisements for soap, covering the withdrawal of the Antwerp garrison, 10 October 1914. The Belgian army, under the personal command of King Albert, would thereafter hold a tiny corner of sovereign territory north-west of Ypres, the last link in 'the race for the sea'.

Above 'Never in the field of human conflict was so much tramped by so many after so few': patrol of the 4th Battalion, King's African Rifles, British East Africa. For four years, with scant artillery, a few hundred Europeans and 3,000 askaris (local black troops, commanded by German officers and NCOs) plus bearers – a force that never exceeded 14,000 – Colonel Paul von Lettow-Vorbeck would hold in check some 300,000 imperial, Belgian and Portuguese troops.

Right 'Our Indian ewe-lamb', the viceroy, Lord Crewe, called it: the Indian Expeditionary Force D, sent in mid-November 1914 to secure the oil fields and pipelines of Mesopotamia. The campaign culminated in the capture of Baghdad in March 1917, though at much cost.

Left Artillery of the French *Corps Expéditionnaire d'Orient* in action at Kum Kale on the southern side of the Dardanelles Straits. The attempt to force the strait by naval action alone having failed, allied landings took place in April 1915 at the tip of the Gallipoli peninsula and on the Anatolian shore.

Below The 'White War': mountain gunners of the *Alpini*. Italy joined the Entente in May 1915 and immediately began offensive operations against the Austrians.

Below 'The use of asphyxiating gases is, as you are aware, contrary to the rules and usages of war,' wrote Kitchener in April 1915. 'Before, therefore, we fall to the level of the degraded Germans [in retaliating] I must submit the matter to the Government.' Men of (probably) the Cameronians wearing goggles and gauze masks, primitive defences against the chlorine gas released during the Second Battle of Ypres.

Left The Kaiser authorizes air raids on Britain (and unrestricted submarine warfare): King's Lynn, 19 January 1915. A Zeppelin dropped explosive and incendiary bombs on the Norfolk town, killing two – a boy of fourteen and a woman whose husband had recently been killed in France – and injuring fifteen.

Left Mass burials at the Old Church Cemetery, Queenstown (now Cobh). On 7 May 1915 a German submarine sank without warning the Cunard liner *Lusitania* off the south coast of Ireland with the loss of 1,200 passengers and crew, including 128 American citizens. The US secretary of state, Robert Lansing, would later write that although it was another two years before his country entered the war, after the sinking of the *Lusitania* he had had no doubt 'that we would ultimately become the ally of Britain'. As a consequence of the outcry, the Kaiser later rescinded his orders for unrestricted submarine warfare.

Right The forgotten ally. After a year of fighting the Austrians unaided, the remnants of the Serbian army would be evacuated from the Adriatic coast by allied ships and taken to the new front in Salonika (the Macedonian front). King Peter of Serbia – in bullock cart – on the march to the sea through the mountains of Albania before the combined Austro-German–Bulgarian offensive of October 1915.

German troops attacking at Verdun in February 1916 (**above**), and (**below**) French artillery, the famous *soixante-quinze* quick-firing 75 mm field gun, the mainstay of the heroic but tragic defence of the fortress-town. Falkenhayn's ploy to 'bleed the French army white' in defence of the emblematic national citadel would cost the German army dearly and lead to his own dismissal.

Left Tsar Nicholas II inspects his troops before the 'Brusilov offensive' in the summer of 1916. His decision to take personal command of the armies, contrary to advice, would contribute to his overthrow, and later murder (or, as the Bolshevists had it, execution) along with the rest of his family.

Left Jutland, 31 May 1916: the long-expected test of the Grand Fleet and Admiral Jellicoe – as Churchill said, 'the only man on either side who could lose the war in an afternoon'. The Grand Fleet outnumbered the enemy in dreadnoughts, so Admiral Scheer decided to take his six pre-dreadnought battleships too, less well armoured and three knots slower, reducing the *Hochseeflotte*'s overall speed, critical to both manoeuvre and fire-control. Here, the pre-dreadnought *Schleswig-Holstein* fires a salvo during the battle, showing the problem of observing the fall of shot.

Right 'Then I rode up-country to Feisal, and found in him the leader with the necessary fire, and yet with reason to give effect to our science.' So wrote T. E. Lawrence (of Arabia) of Feisal bin Hussein al-Hashimi, the future king of Iraq, here with his tribal bodyguard. The Arab Revolt in 1916 would play an important part in the Middle East campaign, particularly the continual harassing of the Hejaz railway.

Below The first day of the Somme, I July 1916: a rare photograph of men (probably the 34th Division) advancing with full equipment and rifles at the slope (on the shoulder) as per orders. They were not expected to have to fight to take the German trenches but merely 'walk-over' to occupy them, the greatest artillery bombardment to date having done the work. The reality was different: the artillery had failed to subdue the defences, or cut the barbed wire in no-man's-land. There would be some 60,000 casualties that first day, a third of them fatal.

Right The Somme. General (later Field Marshal) Sir Douglas Haig, commander-in-chief of the British armies in France and Flanders, tries to impress a point on the new war minister, Lloyd George, during the battle (probably September), with Joffre's support. The French munitions minister, Albert Thomas, looks on somewhat blankly. By this time 'LG' was changing his mind about the new C-in-C: 'Haig is brilliant,' he said later – 'to the top of his boots.'

A tale of two soup kitchens.

Left Hot food on the Somme: good logistics kept up the troops' morale even as losses mounted.

Below Hot food on the streets of Berlin: in 1916 the Royal Navy's blockade began to cause significant food shortages, which by 1918 were materially undermining the war effort.

19

FEBRUARY

The Blood Pump

The Germans gain the initiative with a strategic ambush at Verdun

In March 1916 the proprietor of *The Times*, Alfred Harmsworth, 1st Viscount Northcliffe, went to see the fighting at Verdun. 'This vast battle might have been arranged for the benefit of interested spectators,' he wrote,

> were it not that the whole zone for miles is as tightly closed to the outer world as a lodge of freemasons. Furnished with every possible kind of pass, accompanied by a member of the French headquarters staff in a military car, I was nevertheless held up by intractable gendarmes at a point 25 miles away from the great scene. Even at that distance the mournful reverberation of the guns was insistent. As the gentry examined our papers and waited for telephonic instructions, I counted more than 200 of the distant voices of *Kultur*.

Verdun was not the longest siege in history, but it was the longest battle: ten months of intensive fighting. 'Verdun was a whole war, inserted into the Great War, rather than a battle in the ordinary sense of the word,' said the distinguished academician Paul Valéry in a speech at the Académie Française in 1931 to honour Marshal Pétain, the man who had saved Verdun; 'It was also a kind of duel before the universe, a singular and almost symbolic tourney.'

Verdun was supposedly a trap laid by the Germans, but it turned out to be one in which they themselves were caught and maimed. Falkenhayn planned to use massed artillery as a mincing-machine rather than as a battering ram to break through the French defences. By attacking a place of national prestige, he hoped to draw the French reserves on to his guns like driven birds. In his memoirs he claimed that he sent the Kaiser a memorandum in December concluding:

> The string [of French defences] in France has reached breaking point. A mass breakthrough – which in any case is beyond our means – is unnecessary. Within our reach there are objectives for the retention of which the French General Staff would be compelled to throw in every man they have. If they do so the forces of France will bleed to death.

At first Falkenhayn had considered attacking Belfort, towards the Swiss border, but chose Verdun because it was a (French) salient and therefore cramped the defenders, and because it was close to one of the main German railway arteries, which meant he would be able to keep his troops well supplied. Verdun in 1916 was a town of some 20,000 astride the River Meuse on the old high road from Luxembourg and the Mosel to Paris, and one whose Roman name – Verodunum, 'strong fort' – suggested a long acquaintance with siege warfare. The place had been massively refortified after the débâcles of the Franco-Prussian war, and its prominence in the French national consciousness was such that Falkenhayn reasoned its loss would have so powerful a moral effect that it would have to be held 'at all costs'. A limited offensive would, he hoped, lead to the destruction of the French strategic reserve in fruitless counter-attacks, and the defeat of British reserves in an equally futile relief offensive, which, he told the Kaiser, would lead to the French accepting a separate peace.

Bad weather delayed the start of the offensive for a fortnight, but at 7.12 a.m. on 21 February, two 38 cm railway guns, known as 'Long Max' – naval pieces served by men of the *Kaiserliche Marine* – signalled the opening of *Unternehmen Gericht* (Operation Judgement): a bombardment by over 1,200 guns on a front of 12 miles astride the Meuse in the north of the salient. The intelligence branch at French GHQ had been warning of the buildup of troops – the Germans had concentrated more than 150 aeroplanes over the Verdun sector to prevent French aerial reconnaissance, itself an indicator that something was afoot – but Joffre, preoccupied with plans for his own offensive on the Somme, took no notice of the warnings. Besides, where was the prolonged preparatory artillery bombardment?

The German tactical plan was subtler than Joffre had imagined. It envisaged a continuous series of limited advances, each preceded by a brief (hours rather than days) but intense bombardment which would allow the infantry to take and consolidate their objectives before the French reserves could move up to counter-attack. When eventually they did counter-attack – as their doctrine required – the German infantry would be secure in the trenches and bunkers taken from the French, and their artillery could do its worst. But to minimize casualties in the attack, German patrols would first probe the defences to gauge the effectiveness of their artillery preparation before the main mass of infantry was launched, a tactic not seen before. On 21 February this revealed that the effect of the nine hours' bombardment varied, and so the main attack was launched on only a narrow sector, successfully but with limited gains. The following day the bombardment was repeated to greater effect and the French line buckled in several places.

Joffre was unperturbed. His operations branch assured him the offensive was a feint, perhaps to disrupt preparations for his own. In a sense they were right. The attacks *were* a feint: it would be the artillery strike on the French reserves that would be the real blow.

Joffre could not afford for this assault to be other than a feint, for he had earlier degraded the fortress by taking away many of its heavy guns. There had been representations in Paris that Verdun was no longer impregnable, which he had indignantly repudiated: 'I cannot be a party to soldiers under my command bringing before the Government by channels other than the hierarchical channel, complaints or protests about the execution of my orders.'

On the evening of the fourth day of fighting, General Noël de Castelnau, Joffre's chief of staff, became alarmed by the reports and asked permission to go and judge for himself. Joffre agreed and, as Castelnau set off to drive the 150 miles to Verdun, sent a telegram saying that any commander giving an order to retreat would be tried by court martial – exactly as Falkenhayn had calculated.

Soon after Castelnau arrived, Fort Douaumont, the largest and most elevated in the ring of nineteen forts that protected the town, now denuded of its heavy guns, fell with hardly a fight. Castelnau at once pulled the right flank back but ordered that the remaining line of forts be held, and transferred responsibility for the whole sector to General Pétain, commanding 2nd Army.

The story goes that Pétain, a sixty-year-old bachelor, had to be brought to the battle from the bed of a favourite Parisienne mistress by one of his staff. In any event, he was a good choice, if not Joffre's favourite; for, as an infantryman teaching at the staff college before the war, Pétain had rejected the mantra of *offensive à outrance* – mounting all-out offensives under any circumstances – urging instead the power of the defensive with the axiom *Le feu tue* (fire-power kills). As Pétain's deputy Castelnau appointed General Robert Nivelle, an artilleryman with a strong belief in the moral superiority of the infantry in the attack.

The tardiness of Pétain's promotion, owing to his unorthodoxy, now came to the army's aid. In August 1914 he had been a mere colonel commanding a brigade; he had therefore seen the new warfare from the ground up rather than from a headquarters where the temptation was to make the situation fit pre-conceived doctrine. After the failures of the autumn battles in Champagne, he had written a memorandum saying it was 'impossible to carry in one bound the successive positions of the enemy', and that offensives should be limited to the reach of artillery. He would now use this appreciation in reverse to defeat the German attacks.

His immediate problem, however, was supply, for the German guns had closed all but two routes into the salient – a light railway and the Chemin Bar-le-Duc. While ordering limited counter-attacks to slow the Germans on what was still a narrow front, Pétain set every available pick and shovel to work on widening and maintaining this one road. Motor lorries were soon bringing forward ammunition virtually nose-to-tail – by June, some 6,000 vehicles a day. Auguste-Maurice Barrès, politician and man of letters, dubbed it 'La Voie Sacrée', the sacred way, a name which defiantly stuck.

Falkenhayn in turn widened the frontage, on 6 March extending the attacks to the west bank of the Meuse. During the assault on Fort Vaux, Captain Charles de Gaulle, the future president of France, was wounded and taken prisoner. But the defence was now solidifying, not least through Pétain's own massing of artillery and relieving the infantry divisions before casualties and exhaustion had too great an effect. This called for ever greater numbers of replacements from elsewhere in the line, and as the weeks passed Joffre became increasingly anxious that it was disrupting his own plans. At the end of April he had to change his intended frontage of attack on the Somme from 25 to 15 miles, with thirty not thirty-nine divisions, and 300 rather than 1,700 heavy guns. In consequence the BEF would have to assume more of the burden on the Somme, because of the undertaking given at the Chantilly conference in December that whenever one ally came under clear threat, the others would launch counter-offensives.

On 26 May, Joffre went to Haig's headquarters to ask him to advance the date of the Somme offensive to 1 July to relieve pressure on Verdun. For three months the French had supported the whole weight of the German attacks there, he said, and 'if this went on, the French Army would be ruined'.

Haig had been planning on a start date of 15 August, by which time he would have 200 additional heavy guns and possibly some tanks, as well as more time to train his green 'New Army' divisions.

The Germans had not been having it all their own way, however. At the end of March, Crown Prince Wilhelm, commanding the 5th Army entrusted with the offensive, told Falkenhayn that the bulk of the French reserves had been exhausted and that it was now time to complete their destruction by the conventional methods of attack, using 'men, not merely . . . machines and munitions'. Falkenhayn agreed. But German casualties soon began to mount in the face of sacrificial resistance.

Joffre then came unwittingly to Wilhelm's aid by insisting that, for reasons of prestige, Fort Douaumont – though it had played no part in the initial defence, being stripped of armament – should be retaken. Against Pétain's better judgement, on 3 April Nivelle's corps tried to do so, with a predictably bloody lack of success.

The Germans renewed their attacks, capturing Fleury-devant-Douaumont on 23 June and threatening to break through. Nivelle, by this time commanding the whole Verdun sector, Pétain having been promoted to command the army group, issued an order of the day: 'Ils ne passeront pas!' ('They shall not pass!'). In the Second World War the motto would be worn on the uniforms of troops manning the 'Maginot Line', named after André Maginot, the defence minister, who had lost a leg at Verdun.

By now French casualties had reached 200,000, but German losses were almost as great. Still the 'blood-pump', as Falkenhayn called it, continued – attack after attack, counter-attack after counter-attack. The village of Fleury alone changed hands sixteen times between 23 June and 17 August. A *poilu* of the 65ème Division d'Infanterie wrote home:

> Anyone who has not seen these fields of carnage will never be able to imagine it. When one arrives here the shells are raining down everywhere with each step one takes but in spite of this it is necessary for everyone to go forward. One has to go out of one's way not to pass over a corpse lying at the bottom of the communication trench. Farther on, there are many wounded to tend, others who are carried back on stretchers to the rear. Some are screaming, others are pleading. One sees some

who don't have legs, others without any heads, who have been left for several weeks on the ground.

Despite Pétain's system of troop rotation, disobedience and desertion in the French army began to increase alarmingly.

The Germans, too, were becoming demoralized at their lack of progress; and not just in the west. Faced with a Russian resurgence – albeit an illusory one – in Galicia, under General Aleksei Brusilov, the fall of Gorizia to the Italians, and Romania's belated declaration of war on Austria-Hungary, the Kaiser replaced Falkenhayn at the end of August with the even more ruthless Paul von Hindenburg.

The fighting at Verdun would continue until 19 December, when a deceptively easy French counter-offensive devised by Nivelle regained much lost ground and forced the Germans to close down Operation Judgement. Unfortunately for both the French army and the BEF, Joffre having been elegantly relieved of command by the device of promotion to marshal of France, Nivelle would now emerge as the man purporting to hold the key to victory on the Western Front. His attempts to turn that key the following year would lead only to more huge losses, widespread mutinies in French units, and his own dismissal. It would then take all the humane skill of Pétain, recalled from the sidelines, to nurse the demoralized French army back to health.

In all, some 40 million shells would plough the ground at Verdun. Flying over the battlefield, the American pilot Edwin Parsons of the famous 'Lafayette Squadron' – volunteers flying for the French army before America's formal declaration of war – saw below him how

Nature had been ruthlessly murdered. Every sign of humanity had been swept away. Roads had vanished, and forests were fire-blackened stumps. Villages were gray smears where stone walls were tumbled together. Only the faintest outlines of the great forts of Douaumont and Vaux could be traced against the churned up background ... only broken, half obliterated links of the trenches were visible.

Some historians argue that Falkenhayn's 'trap' was a retrospective invention, his true intention always being breakthrough. In terms of attrition, however, he could claim some success: the French suffered well over half a million casualties in the two battles of 1916, and Haig was forced to attack on the Somme six weeks prematurely, with calamitous results. However, German casualties were so great that there would be no further major offensives on the Western Front until 1918. Indeed, it is probably only the collapse of the Russians the following year that enabled Hindenburg to hold on with any practical hope of victory.

20

MARCH
Q vs U

A 'Mystery VC' becomes the scourge of German submarines

At about seven in the morning of 22 March 1916, off Dingle in south-west Ireland, the German submarine U-68 fired a torpedo at what her captain probably took to be a British merchantman, the collier *Loderer*, 3,207 gross tons. The torpedo narrowly missed *Loderer's* bow, and she continued her same speed and course. Twenty minutes later U-68 surfaced 1,000 yards astern, moved to her port quarter and fired a shot across her bow. The 'collier' stopped, blew off steam, and launched a boat taking off some of the crew. The U-boat closed to 800 yards, whereupon *Loderer* – or rather HMS *Farnborough*, the 'Q-ship' into which she had recently been converted – raised the white ensign of the Royal Navy, uncovered her guns and opened fire with her 12-pounders, scoring several hits. U-68 began to dive. *Farnborough's* captain, Lieutenant-Commander Gordon Campbell, restarted her engines, steered straight for where the U-boat had submerged and dropped a depth charge, blowing the submarine's bow out of the water. *Farnborough's* gunners opened fire again, and U-68 sank by the stern with all thirty-eight of her

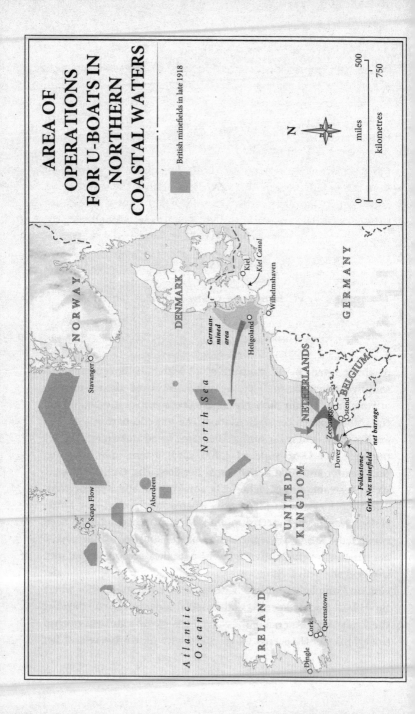

AREA OF OPERATIONS FOR U-BOATS IN NORTHERN COASTAL WATERS

British minefields in late 1918

N

miles
0   500

kilometres
0   750

NORWAY

Stavanger

Scapa Flow

Aberdeen

Atlantic Ocean

IRELAND

Dingle

Cork
Queenstown

UNITED KINGDOM

North Sea

Dover

Folkestone–
Gris Nez minefield

net barrage

Zeebrugge

Ostend

BELGIUM

NETHERLANDS

DENMARK

German-
mined
area

Heligoland

Wilhelmshaven

Kiel

Kiel Canal

GERMANY

crew. It was not the first loss of a U-boat to a decoy ship – *U-boot Falle* (U-boat trap), as the Germans called it – but it was the first to the newly developed depth charge, or 'dropping mine'.

No aspect of German 'frightfulness', whether reprisals against Belgian civilians, the shelling of seaside towns such as Scarborough, or the bombing of cities by Zeppelin – came as such a shock and posed so serious a threat as the U-boat campaign against merchant shipping. Before the war, Admiral Sir Jacky Fisher, the first sea lord, had warned that German submarines would flout the so-called 'cruiser', or 'prize', rules and sink merchantmen without warning, but the prime minister, Asquith, had refused to consider that a civilized nation would embark on such a 'barbarous practice in violation of international law'. The rules even prohibited leaving men adrift in open boats, though in practice, because submarines hadn't the room to take them aboard and couldn't spare men for prize crews (to take command of the ship and sail her to a friendly port), and because in the early months the U-boat's range was limited to coastal waters, where there was a reasonable chance of crews being picked up quickly, the convention was that the U-boat surfaced to warn the crew to take to the boats, before sinking the ship by torpedo or gunfire. In the early days some U-boat captains even displayed a degree of chivalry. On 20 October 1914, U-17, commanded by Oberleutnant zur See Johannes Feldkirchner, stopped the British steamship *Glitra* bound for Stavanger with a mixed cargo some 14 miles off the Norwegian coast. Feldkirchner ordered the crew to take to the boats and then, having scuttled the ship, towed them towards the coast, before a Norwegian patrol boat took over.

At the beginning of the war the *Kaiserliche Marine* had only twenty-four operational *Unterseeboote*, the Royal Navy about a hundred. Submarines relying on electric propulsion when submerged were still a recent development. Their first operational use had been with the Imperial Russian Navy in the Russo-Japanese war of 1904–5. Diesel engines gave them a surface speed of around 9 knots and charged the electric-motor batteries. Underwater they could make 15 knots for about two hours. In 1914 submarines on both sides were only around 150 feet in length and displaced about 400 tons. Armed initially with self-propelled torpedoes, once war began they were fitted with deck guns to force merchant ships to stop for searching, and to sink smaller ships that did not warrant a torpedo. The Germans also constructed specialized submarines with vertical mine tubes through their hulls to lay mines covertly.

Both sides saw submarines as adjuncts to the main battle fleet for patrolling, screening and offensive action against warships. On 22 September 1914 German U-boats sank three pre-dreadnought cruisers, *Cressy*, *Aboukir* and *Hogue*, in the North Sea with the loss of 1,400 men. A month later HMS *Audacious* was sunk off the north coast of Ireland by a surface-laid mine, at first thought to have been a torpedo, the only dreadnought to be lost to enemy action during the entire war. The Royal Navy's Grand Fleet at Scapa Flow in Orkney quickly became 'U-boat conscious', wary of torpedoes and mines, and its battle plans were increasingly characterized by caution.

The *Kaiserliche Marine* had never expected its U-boat service to make war on British commerce, even under the 'cruiser rules'. The prevailing view before 1914, at least among the Kaiser and his circle, was that if war came it would be over quickly. France would be rapidly defeated by the surprise offensive through Belgium, leaving the German army free then to deal with the slower-mobilizing Russians – the so-called Schlieffen Plan. Britain's 'contemptible little army' was too small to make any difference, and the Royal Navy could not affect the war on land. Besides, reckoned Berlin, the Grand Fleet would be held in check by the Imperial Navy's High Seas Fleet, the *Hochseeflotte*. War at sea, if it came to it, would therefore be a clash of titans – the dreadnought battleships – not a long-running affair of blockades and counter-blockades.

Germany's naval minister, Grand Admiral Alfred von Tirpitz, who saw a naval war with Britain as somehow inevitable and not necessarily connected with any continental clash, had always advocated submarine warfare against British merchantmen, in addition to trying to outbuild the Royal Navy in dreadnoughts. The Kaiser's qualms over sinking unarmed ships had nevertheless prevailed. In any case, the naval staff had estimated that some 220 U-boats would be needed to carry out such a campaign according to international law, far too many for the naval budget, whose first priority was the 'dreadnought race'. Soon after the war began, however, the commander of the submarine service, Korvettenkapitän Hermann Bauer, urged that his boats be allowed to attack British commerce without restriction on the grounds that Britain had already violated international law by its blockade. Not until 1915 would the Kaiser agree; and then, following the sinking of the Cunard liner *Lusitania* in May that year, with the death of many American passengers, he rescinded the order. Tirpitz continued to press for the restoration of unrestricted submarine warfare, until, frustrated by the Kaiser's vacillations, he resigned in March 1916.

The war on merchant shipping, including neutrals, therefore continued to be a perilous business for the German submarine service. A U-boat on the surface, even with its gun in action, was highly vulnerable to an armed merchantman, and even more so to the Q-ship, so called because they operated largely out of Queenstown (Cobh) in south-east Ireland. The idea of the Q-ship, like so many another in both world wars, can in part be credited to Winston Churchill. In November 1914, ignoring the niceties of the formal chain of command, the first lord of the Admiralty had telegrammed Admiral Sir Hedworth Meux, C-in-C Portsmouth, responsible for the English Channel:

> It is desired to trap the German submarine which sinks vessels by gunfire off Havre. A small or moderate sized steamer should be taken up and fitted very secretly with two twelve-pounder guns in such a way that they can be concealed with deck cargo or in some way in which they will not be suspected. She should be sent when ready to run from Havre to England and should have an intelligence officer and a few seamen and two picked gunlayers who should all be disguised. If the submarine stops her she should endeavour to sink her by gunfire. The greatest secrecy is necessary to prevent spies becoming acquainted with the arrangements.

The Le Havre submarine wasn't caught, but soon afterwards the Admiralty ordered its first dedicated decoy vessels, converted merchantmen. The possibilities of decoying were soon demonstrated by the Aberdeen fishing fleet, whose boats were being regularly harassed. On 5 June 1915 a dozen of them were fishing off Peterhead, among them the armed trawlers *Oceanic II* and *Hawk*, when U-14 surfaced in their midst. Days before she had sunk two Danish and Swedish freighters, both neutrals, and not noticing that any of the trawlers were armed she fired warning shots. Both *Oceanic* and *Hawk* returned fire, and U-14 began to sink; the trawlermen managed to pick up the crew of twenty-seven, though not the captain, Oberleutnant zur See Max Hammerle, who was killed when a shell hit the conning tower.

Despite the dangers, the U-boats had to wage war as best they could, for the *Hochseeflotte*'s surface warships were increasingly confined to tip-and-run raiding from their base at Wilhelmshaven, and Germany's armed cruisers elsewhere had long been sent to the bottom or else confined to the Black Sea. All that Tirpitz had otherwise were auxiliary cruisers – converted merchant ships – which were good at laying mines but not in a fight. U-boats would therefore be the mainstay of his *Kleinkrieg* ('small war') campaign to wear down the Royal Navy's numerical advantage or to divert warships from the Grand Fleet for trade protection. As the war went on, the *Kaiserliche Marine* poured resources into building more and more U-boats – 350 in all – increasingly sophisticated technically, ever larger and with greater range. Operating from their main base at Heligoland in the German Bight, from Ostend and Zeebrugge in Belgian Flanders, and in the Mediterranean, by 1916 U-boats were becoming not just an irritation but a menace.

Losses in merchant shipping mounted – a million and a quarter tons between October 1916 and January the following year. From February 1917, after the Kaiser had given in to the resumption of unrestricted submarine warfare, to April that year, U-boats sank more than 500 merchant ships, with latterly an average of thirteen each day. One ship out of every four that left the British Isles never returned.

Still the Admiralty would not adopt the convoy system. The first sea lord, by this point Admiral Jellicoe, would not divert the necessary escort vessels, judging that his destroyers had to remain with the Grand Fleet to screen the dreadnoughts if the *Hochseeflotte* tried to sortie in strength. Just as adamantly opposed were the merchant captains themselves, who did not want to be massed into an array of targets limited to the speed of the slowest ship. Only in May 1917, at the insistence of Lloyd George, now prime minister, were convoys formed, after which the losses began slowly to decline. Nevertheless, a month later, Jellicoe, in a mood of abject gloom, warned the cabinet that nothing could be done to defeat the U-boats at sea, and that unless the army could capture their bases on the Flanders coast he considered it 'improbable that we could go on with the war next year for lack of shipping'.

The Q-ships continued to operate even after the reintroduction of unrestricted submarine warfare, and by December 1917 the losses had significantly reduced; moreover, a new mine barrier in the Channel effectively closed this route for U-boats and inflicted heavy losses on the *U-Flotilla Flandern*. Over the course of the whole war, the German submarine service lost 178 U-boats in combat – 50 per cent – and 39 (11 per cent) to misadventure. How cost-effective the Q-ships were is uncertain. Twice as many were lost as submarines they sank, but this does not take account of their deterrent value. A U-boat commander was sparing of his torpedoes, and it is likely that many allowed smaller prizes to escape rather than risk surfacing to use the deck armament, only to find his submarine on the receiving end of concealed fire. Q-ship ruses grew ever more resourceful. One such was the trawler that towed a submerged submarine, connected by telephone. If a U-boat surfaced, the trawler engaged its attention while the submarine was released for attack. This ploy scored its first success in June 1915 when the Aberdeen trawler *Taranaki*, with Royal Navy submarine C24, sank U-40 off the east coast of Scotland.

Q-ships were also built with especially shallow draughts, so that torpedoes would pass underneath, or else their holds were filled with buoyancy aids and fire-suppressants to limit the damage if struck. After sinking U-68 by depth charge in March 1916, Commander Gordon Campbell became an ever more aggressive exponent of decoy tactics, believing that Q-ships must actually invite torpedo attacks in order to tempt U-boats to the surface to 'finish off' a stricken vessel. On 17 February 1917, off Cork, his audacity was rewarded when *Farnborough* was struck by a torpedo fired by U-83 at extreme range. Campbell had intentionally failed to evade the torpedo, and *Farnborough* took the blow in the hold, causing only minor injuries to some crewmen but serious damage to the ship. As U-83 surfaced, the well-rehearsed 'panic party' took to the boats with a great show of alarm and disorder while the gun crews manned the hidden weapons. When four lifeboats had been released and the ship was low in the water, the U-boat closed alongside. *Farnborough*'s remaining crew now sprang the ambush, opening fire at point-blank range with her 6-pounder and machine guns, killing the commanding officer, Kapitänleutnant Bruno Hoppe (who had sixteen sinkings to his credit). U-83 went down with just one survivor.

Only then did Campbell radio for help: 'Q5 slowly sinking respectfully wishes you goodbye.' In fact, with help she was able to beach at Mill Cove without loss. Campbell, who had joined the navy in 1900 from Dulwich College as a cadet of fourteen, was awarded the VC. The citation was deliberately vague: 'In recognition of his conspicuous gallantry, consummate coolness, and skill in command of one of HM ships in action.' The vagueness backfired, however, with the press referring to him as 'The Mystery VC', which led to reports that German agents had put a price on his head. He would survive the war nevertheless, with the DSO and two bars in addition to the VC, and afterwards rose to vice-admiral. His VC is held by his old school.

21

APRIL

A 'Stab in the Back'

The Easter Rising: the war comes to the streets of Dublin

In the early hours of 21 April 1916, Good Friday, the German submarine U-19 surfaced in Tralee Bay in the south-west of Ireland. Her captain, Raimund Weissbach, was familiar with Irish waters: the year before, in U-20, he had fired the torpedo that sank the *Lusitania*.

As daylight approached, U-19 lowered a boat, into which clambered Sir Roger Casement, a former member of the British consular service, and two men of the 'Irish Brigade' (a failed venture to recruit Irish PoWs to fight the British). Three months later, awaiting execution for high treason in Pentonville Prison, Casement, who had been knighted in 1911 for his humanitarian work in Africa and South America, but who had become disenchanted with colonialism and turned instead to Irish nationalism, would write to his sister:

The sand hills were full of skylarks rising in the dawn, the first I had heard in years – the first sound I heard through the surf was their song as I waded through the breakers and they kept rising all the time up to the old rath [enclosure] at Currshone where I stayed and sent the others

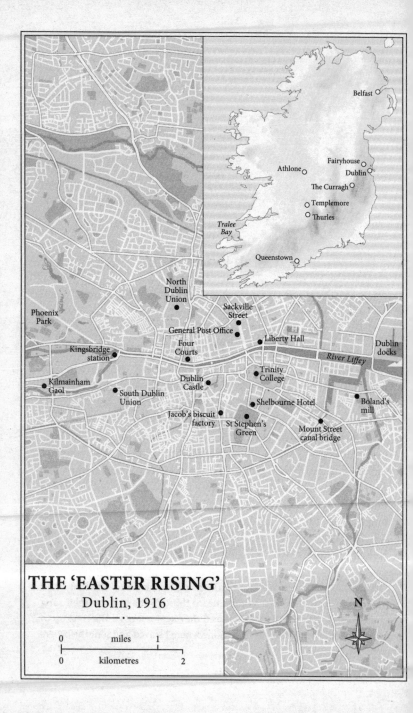

Belfast

Fairyhouse
Athlone
Dublin
The Curragh
Templemore
Thurles
Tralee Bay
Queenstown

North Dublin Union
Sackville Street
Phoenix Park
General Post Office
Liberty Hall
Kingsbridge station
Four Courts
River Liffey
Dublin docks
Kilmainham Gaol
Dublin Castle
Trinity College
South Dublin Union
Shelbourne Hotel
Boland's mill
Jacob's biscuit factory
St Stephen's Green
Mount Street canal bridge

THE 'EASTER RISING'
Dublin, 1916

N

| 0 | miles | 1 |
| 0 | kilometres | 2 |

on, and all round were primroses and wild violets and the singing of the skylarks in the air and I was back in Ireland again.

After encouraging discussions with the German embassy in Washington, Casement had been in Berlin to arrange support for the coming nationalist rebellion – 20,000 rifles and 10 million rounds of ammunition, ten machine guns, each with 100,000 belted rounds, plus explosives and hand grenades. It was less than he had hoped for, and, even more disappointing, would not be accompanied by any troops. With his encouragement, the German foreign ministry had issued an ominous statement, but it stopped short of action:

> Should the fortunes of this great war, that was not of Germany's seeking, ever bring in its course German troops to the shores of Ireland, they would land there, not as an army of invaders to pillage and destroy, but as the forces of a government that is inspired by good-will towards a country and a people for whom Germany desires only national prosperity and national freedom.

Were they having second thoughts about how ripe Ireland was for the 'stab in the back' to Britain? After all, there were 200,000 Irishmen fighting under the Union flag in France and Flanders, Salonika and the Middle East, many of them Catholics from the south. A Leinster man, Maurice Dease, had won the first VC of the war. Was England's difficulty really Ireland's opportunity, as the old nationalist saying went?

Casement had therefore tried to get word to Dublin to postpone the rebellion and disperse the weapons when they arrived. He had no idea if the message had reached the rebel leadership, however. Wracked by a bout of recurrent malaria, all he could do now was lie up in the ancient ring fort at Currshone, hope to evade capture – and dream of a united republic of Ireland.

In 1912 the Liberal government had introduced an Irish home rule bill. The Ulster Unionists, bitterly opposed to rule from Dublin, had raised a paramilitary body, the Ulster Volunteer Force. As a counter-force, the nationalists had raised their own, the Irish Volunteers. The Germans had supplied both sides with weapons. In August 1914, however, mainstream Unionists and Nationalists alike agreed to set aside the home rule question until after the war. Indeed, John Redmond, leader of the Irish Parliamentary Party, urged the Irish Volunteers to enlist in the British army 'in defence of right, of freedom and of religion', and to disprove the Unionist claim that, if given home rule, Ireland would inevitably stab England in the back in her hour of danger.

In April 1916, though, the war on the Western Front was not going well for the allies. Casualties were mounting, and the French were calling for a major British offensive to relieve pressure on Verdun. The effect of trouble at home on Irishmen serving in the army would have been incalculable, as would that of U-boats able to operate from bases in Ireland. Britain had had similar concerns about the 'stab in the back' during the Napoleonic wars, which had led to the 1800 Acts of Union.

Although 90 per cent of the Irish Volunteers – some 170,000 men – had heeded Redmond's call to enlist, others had allied themselves increasingly with hard-line groups such as the Irish Republican Brotherhood, Sinn Féin ('We ourselves') and the small but assertive Irish Citizen Army (ICA). By 1916, with conscription introduced in Britain and fears that it would soon follow in Ireland, these hardliners had decided the time had come for decisive armed action to gain not just home rule but independence. Their plan was to seize the centres of administrative power in Dublin and proclaim a republic and provisional government, hoping that popular support would help them defeat the authorities' inevitable reaction. Their leader and 'provisional president' would be the 36-year-old Patrick Pearse – barrister, teacher, and editor of the Gaelic League's newspaper *The Sword of Light*. Though a fervent Catholic, Pearse's interest in Celtic culture verged on the mystical, with a marked predilection for sacrifice. In 1915 he wrote of the war: 'The old heart of the earth needed to be warmed with the red wine of the battlefields. Such august homage was never before offered to God as this, the homage of millions of lives given gladly for love of country.'

But he had no military experience whatsoever. As one prominent Irish statesman wrote, 'Pearse saw the Rising as a Passion Play with real blood.'

Casement's 20,000 rifles left Lübeck on 9 April in the German freighter *Libau* masquerading as the Norwegian steamship *Aud*. Under command of Kapitänleutnant Karl Spindler with crew from the Imperial German Navy, *Libau* successfully evaded the Royal Navy's patrols in the North Sea and the western approaches to enter Tralee Bay on 20 April, Maundy Thursday. There was no one to meet them, however. Casement had left Wilhelmshaven in U-20 but the boat had developed steering trouble, and he had had to transfer to U-19, delaying his arrival. Worse, the Volunteers' high command, suddenly concerned about security, postponed the rendezvous by three days, to Easter Sunday, but had not been able to get the message to the *Libau*, which carried no radio. Spindler decided to leave, but the sloop HMS *Bluebell* intercepted *Libau* the next day, Good Friday, and took her to Queenstown near Cork. As they approached harbour, Spindler scuttled his ship.

Casement was arrested later that morning by the Royal Irish Constabulary (RIC). The Kerry Brigade of the Irish Volunteers set out to rescue him, but the leadership ordered them to 'do nothing': not a shot was to be fired before the rising was under way.

Meanwhile in Dublin confusion reigned. The rising had originally been planned for Easter Sunday, but last-minute disagreements between the groups led to order and counter-order, and it was postponed until Monday. The loss of the arms shipment greatly reduced the Volunteers' capability; the rising would now be confined almost exclusively to Dublin.

Just how much of a surprise the rising was to the authorities in London and Dublin is still uncertain. The Admiralty's signal intercept service, 'Room 40', was reading radio telegrams from the German embassy in Washington, where Berlin had opened an office to promote an Irish insurgency, and had warned the cabinet of the likelihood of the rising. Neither the civil nor the military authorities in Dublin received orders to increase security, however. The two police forces – the RIC and the Dublin Metropolitan Police – had their own intelligence divisions, but these were focused on crime rather than on insurgency. The military authorities had no intelligence network worthy of the name. The commander-in-chief, Major-General Sir Lovick Friend, even after learning of Casement's capture, saw no reason to cancel his Easter leave, and sailed for England the same day. Augustine Birrell, the chief secretary for Ireland, would tell the commission of inquiry afterwards: 'I always thought that I was very ignorant of what was going on in the minds, and in the cellars if you like, of the Dublin population.'

When, therefore, just before noon on Easter Monday, with the weather unseasonably warm and Dubliners in festive mood, the Volunteers and the ICA began assembling in the city, there were no troops on the streets. Some 900 rebels, in a mixture of grey-green uniform and 'mufti', moved openly towards their objectives, the key buildings dominating the routes into the centre – the Four Courts, Jacob's biscuit factory, the South Dublin Union, Boland's flour mills covering the approaches from the docks and railway station, and, most importantly, the General Post Office in Sackville Street, through which most telephone and telegraph communications in and out of the city passed. Pearse read out the proclamation of an Irish republic from its step.

'Captain' George Plunkett, who as a boy had been at the Catholic public school Stonyhurst with Maurice Dease, the first VC of the war, waved down a tram with his revolver, ordered on his Volunteers, took out his wallet and said 'Fifty-two tuppenny tickets to the city centre, please.' But the rebels were in deadly earnest. When a detachment of the ICA tried to march through the gates of Dublin Castle, seat of the country's administration, and Constable James O'Brien of the Dublin Metropolitan Police tried to bar their way, 'Captain' Sean Connolly shot him dead. Elsewhere a man trying to reclaim his lorry, commandeered by the rebels for a barricade, was shot and killed.

The police, unarmed, were in the main forced to quit the streets, but gave an accurate report of the situation to military headquarters in Phoenix Park. In the absence of the GOC, Colonel Henry Cowan began standing-to the Dublin garrison – with difficulty, for although the military guard had repulsed the attack on the castle, the rebels controlled most of the telephone lines, isolating the civil power. He then managed to get through to the Curragh, just outside Dublin, where there were two brigades, one of cavalry and one of infantry. Brigadier-General William Lowe, commanding the 3rd Reserve Cavalry Brigade, ordered three regiments less their horses (a fourth was already in Dublin for ceremonial and escort duty) to prepare to move. Cowan was also able to telephone the garrisons in Belfast and Templemore, and – crucially – the 5th Reserve Artillery Brigade at Athlone, 75 miles to the west, ordering reinforcements to the city.

The Great Southern and Western Railway rose to the occasion with impressive efficiency. Notwithstanding the diversion of trains for the races at Fairyhouse, the Dublin Society spring cattle show and a hurling match in Thurles, an official was able to report afterwards that

> at 12.25 pm on Easter Monday 24th April the military authorities telephoned the Superintendent of the Line to stop all traffic and to prepare military specials for the Curragh immediately. Empty specials left Kingsbridge [station] at 1.17pm, 1.45pm, 2.0pm and 2.6pm returning at once with troops, the last arriving at 5.30pm. Three thousand men were thus conveyed to the city.

None of these 3,000 were regulars in the true sense. The regular British army in Ireland had left for France in August 1914. What remained were the 'Special Reserve' battalions, whose primary role was to train battle casualty replacements for the eight Irish infantry regiments. These were based at regimental depots around the country, four of which were in Dublin and the Curragh. The cavalry brigade consisted of recruits undergoing training and men waiting to return to their regiments from courses of instruction or other postings, as did the artillery brigade, with its eight 18-pounder field guns. In Dublin there was a 'Kitchener battalion', the 10th Royal Dublin Fusiliers, in whose ranks were former Irish Volunteers who had heeded John Redmond's call to enlist. But in Ireland, unlike Britain, there was no Territorial Force. Cowan sent an officer in plain clothes to the naval base at Kingstown to get a wireless message to London calling for reinforcements. The War Office lost no time in ordering the 59th (2nd Midland) Division, territorials, to Dublin.

The Volunteers at the GPO drew first military blood when they ambushed a patrol of the 6th Reserve Cavalry Regiment sent to reconnoitre Sackville Street. Four troopers were killed and several wounded, but the rebels had opened fire prematurely and the patrol was able to withdraw. Lack of military experience would indeed be the rebels' undoing: besides poor tactics and field discipline, by occupying buildings and waiting for the army to assault, they surrendered the initiative. At St Stephen's Green the ICA's commander ordered his men to dig trenches, all of which were overlooked by buildings surrounding the square, ideal for the army's marksmen.

Brigadier-General Lowe arrived in the city centre in the early hours of Tuesday morning to assume overall command. He at once set about securing a line connecting the main station, the castle and Trinity College to divide the rebel positions north and south of the river. Many Dubliners were eager to help, pointing to where the 'shinners' (a blanket term for Sinn Féin and other republicans) were waiting. By midnight at the end of the first day, the dead numbered twenty-six soldiers, three policemen, eleven rebels – and fifteen civilians. Lord Wimborne, the lord lieutenant, declared martial law.

The noose began to tighten next day as men of the Royal Irish Regiment, the Dublin Fusiliers and the Leinster Regiment, with the dismounted troopers of the cavalry brigade, started to surround the various rebel positions. Overnight the cavalrymen had brought Vickers machine guns into the Shelbourne Hotel on St Stephen's Green, and quickly drove the ICA from their trenches. Midafternoon, the Royal Navy's gunboat *Helga*, which had sailed up the Liffey, opened fire on the flour mills with her two 12-pounders.

Four field guns from Athlone arrived soon afterwards and began engaging the barricades.

Lowe knew that it was only a matter of time before his artillery destroyed the strongpoints, but the 18-pounders had only shrapnel ammunition, not high explosive, and the process would therefore be slow and especially dangerous to civilians. By midnight of the second day, a further twenty-two of them, including several children, had been killed. Meanwhile, Lowe needed more troops to contain the rebels.

Public anger with the 'shinners' was growing, for many Dubliners had family fighting in France, and soldiers' wives found they were unable to draw their remittance money because the post offices remained closed. When the advance elements of the 59th Division, the 178th (Sherwood Foresters) Brigade, began arriving at the Dublin docks next morning, Wednesday, they were cheered by the crowds.

The Foresters had no practice in fighting in built-up areas, however, and quickly paid the price. Striking out for the castle, the leading troops ran into heavy and accurate fire on the approaches to Mount Street canal bridge from Volunteers under command of Eamon de Valera, the future president of Ireland. A firefight developed that lasted until early evening, when the Foresters were at last able to drive the rebels from their positions with grenades, which set several buildings alight. As night fell, thirty more soldiers were dead, and almost as many civilians.

A thick pall of smoke hung over the city centre next morning, the fires spreading. The *Helga* had been in action again, moving upriver to shell Liberty Hall. At about ten o'clock the 18-pounders began an indirect bombardment of Sackville Street, igniting the domestic gas supply and setting alight more buildings, forcing the rebels to abandon several barricades. Throughout the day more troops from the 59th Division arrived, and as darkness fell again much of Dublin's main thoroughfare was ablaze, with fires starting on the roof of the GPO.

Shortly after midnight, the absent GOC having been relieved, Lieutenant-General Sir John Maxwell, who a few months before had moved resolutely to counter the threat posed by the Senussi (an Arab Sufi sect) to Egypt from the eastern Sahara, arrived by warship to take command. He quickly confirmed Lowe's strategy, adding that he would accept nothing but the rebels' unconditional surrender.

Increasingly bitter fighting, with summary executions, continued all day and throughout Friday night. On Saturday morning, with the GPO now on fire, recognizing his men were surrounded and outnumbered, and 'to prevent the further slaughter of Dublin citizens', Patrick Pearse surrendered unconditionally. The city centre lay in ruins and 250 civilians were dead. As the rebels were marched off under escort some bystanders applauded them, but many more pelted them with stones and refuse, and shouts of 'Hang the bastards!'

Maxwell lost no time in exacting condign punishment. Over 3,000 men and women were arrested, although most were quickly released. Nearly 1,500 men would be interned in England and Wales. In courts martial a week later, ninety rebels were sentenced to death. Fifteen of them, including all seven signatories of the proclamation, had their sentences confirmed by Maxwell and were executed at Kilmainham Gaol by firing squad between 3 and 12 May, among them James Connolly, leader of the ICA, tied to a chair because of a shattered ankle. As Asquith told Parliament, 'A desperate plot was hatched for the disruption of the British Empire by means of an insurrection in Ireland. It was put into execution at a moment when England and Ireland were fighting for life against a foreign enemy. That enemy fomented and helped it with arms, money and promises.'

There was no doubting the offences – not least the killing of unarmed policemen – but the secret military courts (at least Casement was tried by due process, his case heard ultimately in the court of criminal appeal), the executions over a protracted period, and the heavy-handed, sometimes brutish, follow-up turned popular opinion increasingly in favour of the rebels. In January 1916 the war cabinet had concluded that thirteen divisions must be kept back from France and elsewhere for home defence and to keep the peace in Ireland. The Easter Rising only reinforced that costly diversionary decision.

22

MAY

The Victory that Looked Like Defeat

The long-anticipated clash of dreadnoughts in the
North Sea ends not as England expects

May 1916 would bring the long-expected clash of naval titans in a contest that the British public expected to be another Trafalgar – a decisive, strategic British victory. For the Royal Navy was incomparably the most powerful in the world; hundreds of millions of pounds had been spent in its pre-war modernization programme.

The issue was straightforward – control of the sea, a precept laid down three centuries earlier by the Elizabethan admiral and strategian Sir Walter Raleigh: 'Whosoever commands the sea, commands the trade of the world, commands the riches of the world, commands the world itself.' In 1916 control of the sea meant keeping Britain secure from invasion, allowing her warships freedom of action worldwide, and keeping open the trade routes to the British Isles for food and war materiel, while closing off those of the Germans. It underpinned the whole allied war strategy of building military strength on the Western Front and starving Germany. Loss of sea control – indeed, supremacy – would have meant national

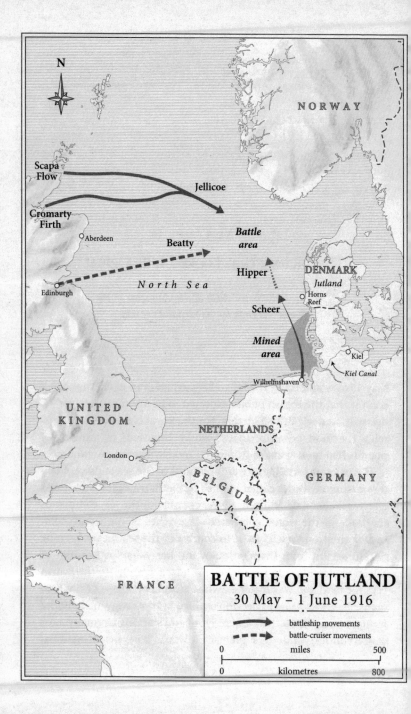

NORWAY

Scapa
Flow

Jellicoe

Cromarty
Firth

Aberdeen

Beatty

*Battle
area*

Hipper

DENMARK

Jutland

Edinburgh

North Sea

Scheer

Horns
Reef

*Mined
area*

Kiel

Kiel Canal

Wilhelmshaven

UNITED
KINGDOM

NETHERLANDS

London

GERMANY

BELGIUM

FRANCE

BATTLE OF JUTLAND
30 May – 1 June 1916

battleship movements

battle-cruiser movements

| 0 | miles | 500 |

| 0 | kilometres | 800 |

defeat. Winston Churchill, until mid-1915 first lord of the Admiralty, summed it up succinctly: Admiral Sir John Jellicoe, C-in-C of the Grand Fleet, was 'the only man on either side who could lose the war in an afternoon'.

Germany had tried to outbuild Britain in dreadnoughts, the revolutionary heavily armoured battleships, armed exclusively with big guns (initially 12-inch, increasing to 15-inch), named after the first of their class, HMS *Dreadnought*. Since her launch in 1906, however, Britain had managed to keep ahead in the 'dreadnought race' by almost two to one. Grand Admiral Tirpitz, Germany's long-time naval minister, knew that the *Hochseeflotte*, the High Seas Fleet, had no chance of victory in a straight fight with Jellicoe, and so his strategy was to wear down the Royal Navy's advantage by mines, torpedoes, opportunity skirmishes and ambushes, drawing in the dreadnoughts by deceit or provocation, of which the raid on Scarborough in December 1914 was the first and most infamous attempt. Two months earlier a mine laid by an auxiliary cruiser had sent HMS *Audacious* to the bottom. Since then, however, the *Hochseeflotte* had been unable to make much impression on the Grand Fleet's fighting strength, and both had settled into a routine of watching and waiting.

Like Nelson before Trafalgar, for nearly two years Jellicoe had confined the enemy's fleet to its home port – Wilhelmshaven and its connected bases. But unlike Nelson's blockade of Toulon, Jellicoe's had been a distant one. While his light cruisers, submarines, aircraft and dirigibles patrolled the North Sea, the main battle fleet kept largely to its base at Scapa Flow in the Orkneys, with a force of battle-cruisers (which had guns of similar calibre to the dreadnoughts but were not as heavily armoured, relying more on speed for protection) in the Firth of Forth under Vice-Admiral David Beatty.

Tirpitz had always wanted to use submarines as his prime strategic weapon. Pre-war calculations suggested that Britain would be brought to her knees in months, perhaps only weeks, if her food imports were intercepted. A good deal of these were carried by neutral shipping, however, and while surface ships of the Royal Navy could intercept neutrals bound for Germany, the *Kaiserliche Marine*, with the main fleet confined to Wilhelmshaven and all her other armed cruisers sunk in the opening months of the war, could not. Only U-boats could get into Britain's trade approaches – but their activities were restricted by the so-called 'cruiser rules', according to which a submarine intending to attack a merchant vessel was meant to surface, issue a warning and allow the crew to take to the lifeboats before sinking her. This was a dangerous procedure, for the U-boat was highly vulnerable on the surface, and Tirpitz was therefore a keen advocate of unrestricted submarine warfare – sinking without warning. In early 1915 the Kaiser had sanctioned this, but the international outcry, not least after the sinking of the *Lusitania* in May that year, had induced him to change his mind. In March 1916, frustrated by what he saw as the Kaiser's passivity, Tirpitz resigned.

The *Hochseeflotte*'s new commander-in-chief, Reinhard Scheer, while also an advocate of unrestricted submarine warfare, was now determined to take aggressive fleet action to whittle down the Royal Navy's superiority. By making a sortie in strength he knew he would bring Beatty's battle-cruisers, the Grand Fleet's reaction force, into the North Sea, and perhaps even some of Jellicoe's dreadnoughts as well. If Franz von Hipper, commanding the *Hochseeflotte*'s battle-cruisers, could tempt Beatty into a fight, he might be able to draw them and perhaps some of Jellicoe's main battle fleet, unsuspecting, on to the guns of his own dreadnoughts, reducing the odds for the next encounter. On 31 May, therefore, Scheer would personally lead the *Hochseeflotte* into the German Bight to bring on what would be the first (and, as it turned out, the last) dreadnought fleet action in history.

The relative strengths were certainly not propitious for Germany. Scheer had sixteen dreadnoughts to the twenty-eight that Jellicoe could bring out, together with Hipper's five battle-cruisers (against Beatty's nine), plus six light cruisers for scouting and thirty-one torpedo boats, as well as various supporting craft. He decided therefore to take his six pre-dreadnought battleships too, less well armoured and three knots slower, reducing the *Hochseeflotte*'s overall speed, critical to both manoeuvre and fire-control.

Scheer had a psychological advantage, however, for he had less to lose. The *Hochseeflotte*'s very existence fixed the Grand Fleet at Scapa Flow. But even if Jellicoe gained a Trafalgar-like victory, allowing the Admiralty to send ships elsewhere, it would not change the essential strategic situation: the economic blockade was already so effective that Germany was beginning to famish. On the other hand, Jellicoe could not risk losing superiority. While Scheer therefore could be bold, Jellicoe *had* to be cautious. And while Jellicoe could take calculated risks based on what he could see and reasonably anticipate were the actions of Scheer's surface ships, he could have no certain knowledge of where and in what strength lay his submarines. Gunnery did not trouble him, although Scheer's would prove unnervingly good; the mine (especially after the loss of *Audacious* in October 1914) and the torpedo did, factors that Nelson never had to consider.

One priceless advantage that Jellicoe possessed, however, was signals intelligence. When without warning the French fleet broke out of Toulon in March 1805, Nelson having withdrawn all but a few frigates to Sardinia for resupply, contact was lost for six weeks. In contrast, Jellicoe knew Scheer's precise sailing plans forty-eight hours before they were put into action, for the famed 'Room 40' at the Admiralty had intercepted and decrypted the *Hochseeflotte*'s radio traffic, revealing the operational plan and the sailing date. Jellicoe therefore left Scapa Flow, and Beatty the Firth of Forth, at last light the evening before, making for the German Bight to cut off and destroy as many of Scheer's ships as possible, but with the imperative of retaining overall superiority come what may. High winds made aerial reconnaissance all but impossible, so both fleets were relatively 'blind' once out of port.

At four in the afternoon of 31 May, Beatty's battle-cruisers, reinforced by the 5th Battle Squadron of dreadnoughts, ran into Hipper's battle-cruisers west of the northern tip of Jutland, beginning a running fight as Hipper turned south to draw them on to Scheer's battle fleet, with Jellicoe's squadrons closing fast but undetected from the north-west. The light cruiser *Chester*, scouting ahead of Rear-Admiral Horace Hood's 3rd Battle-cruiser Squadron, came under heavy fire from four of Hipper's light cruisers which killed or mortally wounded the crew of the forward 5.5-inch gun, leaving only the 16-year-old Boy 1st Class Jack Cornwell on his feet. Though gravely wounded, Cornwell remained standing by the gun throughout until the crippled *Chester* was ordered to break off the action and make for Immingham; he was taken to nearby Grimsby hospital, where he died. He was posthumously awarded the VC, the youngest recipient since 1860. His medal is on permanent display at the Imperial War Museum, as is the gun.

Beatty's battle-cruisers were also taking a beating. *Queen Mary* was soon hit by salvoes from the *Seydlitz* and *Derfflinger*. *Seydlitz*'s gunnery officer, Georg von Hase, noted:

> The enemy was shooting superbly. Twice the *Derfflinger* came under their infernal hail and each time she was hit. But the *Queen Mary* was having a bad time; engaged by the *Seydlitz* as well as the *Derfflinger*, she met her doom at 1626. A vivid red flame shot up from her fore-part; then came an explosion forward, followed by a much heavier explosion amidships. Immediately afterwards, she blew up with a terrific explosion, the masts collapsing inwards and the smoke hiding everything.

Both forward magazines had exploded, and she sank with all but nine of her 1,275 crew. Short cuts in ammunition handling owing to over-confidence were almost certainly the cause (too much cordite in the turret, and the anti-flash hatches kept open to speed resupply). HMS *Indefatigable* had blown up only minutes before, prompting Beatty to snap: 'There seems to be something wrong with our bloody ships today,' though what precisely he said and when, and what exactly he meant, are still disputed. However, as planned, Beatty now turned back north to try to lure Scheer towards Jellicoe's rapidly approaching dreadnoughts, a manoeuvre that Scheer could reasonably conclude was the result of the punishment that Hipper had inflicted.

During this 'run north', as it became known, Rear-Admiral Sir Robert Arbuthnot's 1st (Armoured) Cruiser Squadron plunged into the fight. Rear-Admiral Hood's 3rd Battle-cruiser Squadron had briefly engaged the light cruisers of the German 2nd Scouting Group, damaging several; now, with Nelsonian intrepidity, but unfortunately not the 'Nelson touch', Arbuthnot led his four pre-dreadnought cruisers straight at the damaged scouts. In doing so, he steamed into the middle of the fight between Hood's and Hipper's battle-cruisers, with Beatty's also closing fast and engaging. It was becoming what Nelson said he wanted before Trafalgar – a 'pell-mell battle' in which the Royal Navy's innately superior seamanship and gunnery would carry the day. However, armour-piercing explosive shells were infinitely more destructive than solid roundshot against oak. Arbuthnot's flagship, *Defence*, was caught in a deluge of shells from Hipper's battle-cruisers, detonating her magazines in a spectacular explosion. She sank with all hands – 903 officers and men. Of his three other cruisers, only one – *Duke of Edinburgh* – would survive the battle. *Warrior* managed to limp away, with most of her crew taken off before she sank, but *Black Prince* was lost with all hands too – 857 officers and men. Admiral of the Fleet Lord Fisher, the former first sea lord and architect of the dreadnought concept, called Arbuthnot's 'a glorious but not a justifiable death'.

Soon afterwards, Scheer's leading dreadnoughts began engaging Beatty's 'Barhams', as the Queen Elizabeth class ships were known after the fourth of the class – the fastest, most heavily armed of the dreadnoughts, also dubbed 'super-dreadnoughts'. Scheer believed he had caught an isolated portion of the Grand Fleet, and that he had his long-awaited opportunity for attrition. His hopes were shattered not long afterwards, however, when Jellicoe's ships, in one of which, HMS *Collingwood*, the twenty-year-old Prince Albert, the future King George VI, was serving, steamed into view. Sub-Lieutenant Prince Albert recorded:

We went to 'Action Stations' at 4.30 p.m. and saw the Battle Cruisers in action ahead of us on the starboard bow. Some of the other cruisers were firing on the port bow. As we came up the 'Lion' [Beatty's flagship] leading our Battle Cruisers, appeared to be on fire the port side of the forecastle, but it was not serious . . . The 'Colossus' leading the 6th division with the 'Collingwood' her next astern were nearest the enemy. The whole Fleet deployed at 5.0 and opened out. We opened fire at 5.37 p.m. on some German light cruisers. The 'Collingwood's' second salvo hit one of them which set her on fire, and sank after two more salvoes were fired into her . . . I was in 'A' turret and watched most of the action through one of the trainers telescopes, as we were firing by Director, when the turret is trained in the working chamber and not in the gun house. At the commencement I was sitting on the top of 'A' turret and had a very good view of the proceedings. I was up there during a lull, when a German ship started firing at us, and one salvo straddled us. We at once returned the fire. I was distinctly startled and jumped down the hole in the top of the turret like a shot rabbit!! I didn't try the experience again . . .

It seems that he was being characteristically modest: Sub-Lieutenant Prince Albert would be gazetted with a King's Commendation for his action during the battle.

But while the dreadnoughts on both sides were both taking and inflicting non-capital punishment, Jellicoe's battle-cruisers now suffered another catastrophic loss. Not long after the future King had jumped down the hatch, Rear-Admiral Hood's flagship, *Invincible*, famous for her part in the Falkland Islands victory of 1914, succumbed to *Derfflinger*'s gunnery, a shell penetrating her 'Q' turret (amidships) – the same mortal wound that had destroyed *Queen Mary* a few hours before. Of *Invincible*'s 1,021 crew, there were just six survivors, pulled from the water by attendant destroyers. Hood, great-great-grandson of Admiral Lord Hood, whom Nelson revered, was not among them.

Unlike life at sea, death at sea knew no privilege of rank.

Jellicoe's dreadnoughts were fast bearing down, however, and to extricate the *Hochseeflotte* from its perilous situation, Scheer now ordered a turn to the south-west, but twenty minutes later turned back towards Jellicoe's main force. Finding himself overmatched, he turned once more to break off contact, gallantly supported by Hipper's badly mauled battle-cruisers which charged the British line to cover the retreat. With darkness approaching, and Jellicoe's destroyers – he had seventy-eight in all – keeping up a ferocious if unequal harrying fight, Scheer's dreadnoughts eventually managed to break clean and make for Horns Reef, the shallows 10 miles off the westernmost point of Denmark. Jellicoe, sensing danger from a concerted torpedo attack by submarines if he pursued, broke off the battle – as he had agreed beforehand with the Admiralty he would do in such an event – and turned for home.

Scheer reached Wilhelmshaven in the early afternoon of 1 June. The *Hochseeflotte* had sunk more British ships than the Grand Fleet had sunk German (including six of the Grand Fleet's major ships to two of the *Hochseeflotte*'s, though neither side lost any dreadnoughts), and at once claimed victory, while Jellicoe was slower to return to Scapa and slower still to make capital of the fact that the Germans had been forced back to their anchorages. To the public it looked as if he lacked the 'Nelson touch', failing to win the complete victory that was in his grasp, and at a cost of 6,000 men. For although 'the fleet in being' – a naval force that extends a controlling influence without ever leaving port – had since Pepys's day been accepted strategy, the Royal Navy still maintained that in war its purpose was to seek out the enemy's ships and destroy them. And that was what England had expected.

The Kaiser declared that 'the spell of Trafalgar is broken.'

Yet Scheer's leading battleships had taken a terrible hammering, and over the weeks ahead the foreign section of the Secret Service Bureau (forerunner of the Secret Intelligence Service, MI6) was able to discover the extent to which the Grand Fleet's gunnery had disabled the *Hochseeflotte*. On 2 June the Grand Fleet had twenty-four capital ships in fighting condition, compared to only ten German.

Moreover, Berlin knew that Britain's shipbuilding capacity was much greater than its own, and that as the months passed the relative strengths would only increase in Britain's favour. After Jutland the *Hochseeflotte* would never again put to sea in real strength. Instead, the *Kaiserliche Marine* would increasingly place its faith and resources in the U-boat campaign, thereby hastening America's entry into the war.

23

JUNE

Pillars of Wisdom

The Army of Egypt stirs, and the seeds of the Arab Revolt are sown

'Is the army of Egypt guarding the Suez Canal, or is the Suez Canal guarding the army of Egypt?' asked the wags. For nearly two years British and imperial troops had been unable to do other than sit tight and repel desultory Turkish attacks across the Sinai, and by the Senussi Arabs, a Sufi political–religious order, in the eastern Sahara and Sudan.

The canal was a crucial artery of the Empire. Through this waterway passed men and equipment from Australia, New Zealand and India for the Western Front, and millions of tons of food and raw materials. There had been British troops in Egypt, nominally a province of the Ottoman Empire, since 1882 in what was known as the 'veiled protectorate', but after the Ottomans' defeats in Libya in the Italo-Turkish war of 1911–12, and in the Balkan wars of 1912–13, Constantinople had brought in German advisers to reform the Turkish army, as well as to modernize trade, commerce and communications, strengthening the Sultan's writ throughout the Levant, not least in Palestine.

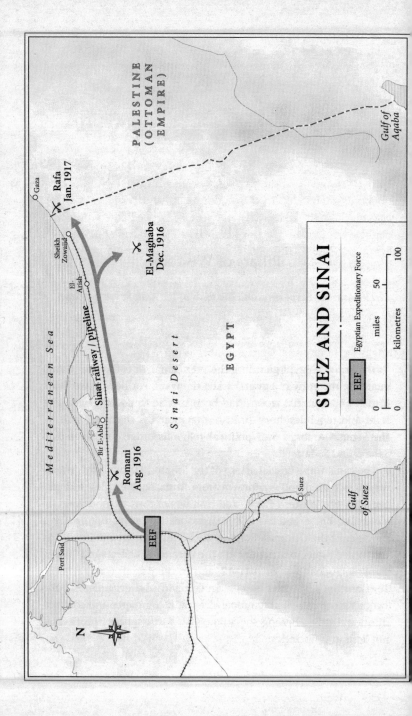

The elder Moltke had urged Bismarck to 'build railways, not forts', and this too was the Kaiser's strategy in his *Drang nach Osten* – his drive towards the east in search of new markets, oil and influence in Asia Minor, and for *Lebensraum*, 'room to live'. After Wilhelm's state visit to Constantinople in 1898, the Sultan had approved construction of the Berlin–Baghdad line, an extension of the German Anatolian Railway Company's system, with a further extension to Basra at the mouth of the Tigris, the head of the deep-water navigation of the Shatt al-Arab, and thence to the Persian Gulf. For commercial and strategic reasons Britain, France and Russia had objected – Britain, especially, seeing it as a threat to her position in Egypt and India. The Foreign Office succeeded in preventing the line's extension from Basra to the Gulf by persuading the Sheikh of Kuwait to repudiate Ottoman suzerainty and thereby the obligation to cede rights for building the line, in exchange for British protection; but in 1910, after a personal meeting between the Kaiser and the Tsar, Russia accepted the project on condition that no branch lines were built into Armenia and Kurdistan.

In August 1914, work on the railway had been well advanced, though large sections remained incomplete, especially between Aleppo and Baghdad, and the extension to Basra had not even been begun. A branch line to the port of Alexandretta on the Mediterranean had been built, however, which would prove useful to the German and Austrian submarines operating from there, as had connections with the metre-gauge line from Damascus to southern Palestine, which opened the way for an attack on Suez by routes that British warships could not dominate, and with the Hejaz railway, running 800 miles from Damascus through Arabia to Medina on the Red Sea, the canal route to and from India. Besides this challenge to British power, not only did the Berlin–Baghdad railway and its branches serve the *Drang nach Osten*, the project also bound Constantinople to the Central Powers, while the Sultan was only too pleased to strengthen the sinews of the increasingly rickety Ottoman Empire. Railways were therefore to play a part in the calculations and operations of the Entente which, if not on the scale of the Germans' great *Westaufmarsch* – the mobilization and deployment on the Western Front in 1914, the 'war by railway timetable' – was nevertheless just as crucial, and even more dramatic.

The Turks and Arabs of the Ottoman Empire were coreligionists but, like the constituents of the Austro-Hungarian Empire, were increasingly at odds with each other culturally. With an admixture of their advisers' Teutonic lack of subtlety, Ottoman rule became more and more repressive. Much-publicized executions of Arab nationalist leaders in Damascus played to London's advantage, and in January 1916, on the recommendation of Sir Mark Sykes, the amateur soldier and orientalist who with the French diplomat François Georges-Picot was to negotiate the eponymous agreement on post-war spheres of influence in the Middle East, the Arab Bureau was set up in Cairo to harmonize British political activity and keep Whitehall informed of 'the general tendency of Germano-Turkish Policy'. Among its political officers would be the remarkable desert traveller and archaeologist Gertrude Bell, and the eccentric orientalist and temporary soldier T. E. Lawrence – 'Lawrence of Arabia'.

The bureau's first success came in June when Grand Sharif Hussein ibn Ali al-Hashimi, guardian of the holy city of Mecca, entered into an alliance with Britain and France in return for military aid and a share in the dismemberment of the Ottoman Empire – which was no little diplomatic achievement for London, the Sultan having been trying for a year and more to inspire *jihad*, Islamic 'holy war', against the infidel, with its obvious threat to British India and her Muslim troops.

Sharif Hussein had about 50,000 men at his command, but only some 10,000 rifles. Supplying additional arms might therefore give the bureau considerable leverage, but the civil and military authorities in Egypt were slow to recognize the potential of such a move. The 'Great Arab Revolt' got off to a shaky start on 5 June when two of Sharif Hussein's sons, Ali and Feisal, attacked the Ottoman garrison at Medina, but then had to break off the attacks after three days for want of arms and ammunition. Nevertheless, on 10 June in Mecca, Sharif Hussein publicly proclaimed the revolt, seizing the city and driving the Ottoman garrison into the local fortress, while another of his sons, Abdullah, laid siege to the town of Ta'if 40 miles to the east.

Clans allied to Hussein now attacked Jeddah and other Red Sea ports. The Royal Navy sent a flotilla in support, including a sea-plane carrier, the former Isle of Man steamer *Ben-My-Chree*, and landed the first units of the Arab regular army – Ottoman army troops captured at Gallipoli, Mesopotamia or in the Sinai, who had subsequently volunteered to fight for the nationalist cause. T. E. Lawrence, still officially a staff captain in the intelligence section at army headquarters but now attached to the Arab Bureau, would join them in October, and the Hejaz railway, down which the Turks would send many thousands of reinforcements to try to recapture lost ground, became the focus of the Arab offensive, inspiring some memorable cinematography in David Lean's 1962 film *Lawrence of Arabia*.

Railways were also a preoccupation of Lieutenant-General Sir Archibald Murray, the new C-in-C Mediterranean Force (MF), responsible for defence of the Suez Canal. Towards the end of 1915 the Turks had begun extending the Palestine line into Sinai, while his own lines east of the canal were practically non-existent. In January 1915 Murray had been sacked as chief of staff of the BEF in France, and later appointed CIGS in London, only to be replaced in December by Sir William Robertson. Murray was a cerebral officer prone to breakdown under pressure, but evidently the secretary of state for war, Lord Kitchener, who until August 1914 had been the British agent (de facto viceroy) in Egypt, recognized his worth as a methodical planner and so reassigned him to Cairo with instructions to arrange the canal defences more economically and send as many as possible of the 300,000 men in Egypt, who included Gallipoli evacuees and newly arrived Anzacs, to France.

By June 1916 Murray had shipped out 240,000 of them, leaving largely territorial and Indian divisions and some mounted troops – in the main, Yeomanry and Anzac light horse. He had made a thorough appreciation of Ottoman railway capacity in Palestine and water supply in the Sinai, and concluded that he could adopt a more forward defence of the canal – at the choke points along the Palestine border – to shorten his line. In March he had set about preparations for an advance on El-Arish, including much track laying as well as greater use of camels. In January, to deal with the Senussi tribesmen in the Western Desert, camel-mounted troops had been raised, initially from Australian light horsemen recuperating after Gallipoli. Four battalions of what would be known as the Imperial Camel Corps were eventually formed, the 1st and 3rd entirely Australian, the 2nd British, the 4th a mix of Australians and New Zealanders, commanded throughout by the 38-year-old Brigadier-General Clement Smith of the Duke of Cornwall's Light Infantry, who had won the VC in Somaliland in 1904 and for several years afterwards served in the Egyptian army. In July, with the Senussi in retreat, Smith was able to turn east. Without the need of a cumbersome logistic tail, and much less reliant on wells and oases than horsed units, his cameliers were able to range deep in the Sinai desert.

Murray, however, like the other professionals in Egypt, was initially sceptical of the value of the Arab Revolt. In *Seven Pillars of Wisdom* Lawrence described him as of 'a very nervous mind, fanciful and essentially competitive', but after Sharif Hussein diverted a good deal of Ottoman attention towards Mecca, helping the MF to overcome the garrison at Bi'r ar Rummanah ('Romani') on the coast in August and thereby opening the way for the grand advance on El-Arish, Murray became more supportive.

The advance of his Egyptian Expeditionary Force through Sinai was a formidable effort of infrastructure – eventually some 400 miles of railway, 300 miles of metalled and wire-meshed roads and 300 miles of water-pipes, with drinking water pumped underneath the Suez Canal from the Sweetwater Canal in the Nile Delta, entailing the construction of filtration plants, reservoirs and pumping stations. Nevertheless, in December Murray took El-Arish, and Rafa, on the Palestine frontier, the following month.

These successes would do much to offset the failure of the

Dardanelles campaign, and the fall in April of the old fortress-town of Kut al-Amara in Mesopotamia, which came as a severe blow to the reputation of British arms, renewing fears of mutiny among Indian Muslim troops. (Lawrence himself was sent to see if there were any way of relieving Kut by 'indirect methods', including bribery.) Townshend's capitulation on 29 April after four months under siege might indeed have been fatal for British prestige had it not been for the exertions of the Arab Bureau, and then the renewed offensive from Basra by Major-General Frederick Maude, the last man to be taken off the beaches at Suvla Bay.

Back in Cairo, observing the initial setbacks to Sharif Hussein's campaign in the Hejaz, Lawrence got permission to go in person to see what could be done. 'I had believed these misfortunes of the revolt to be due mainly to faulty leadership, or rather to the lack of leadership, Arab and English,' he wrote in *Seven Pillars of Wisdom*.

So I went down to Arabia to see and consider its great men. The first, the Sherif of Mecca, we knew to be aged. I found [his sons] Abdulla too clever, Ali too clean, Zeid too cool. Then I rode up-country to Feisal, and found in him the leader with the necessary fire, and yet with reason to give effect to our science. His tribesmen seemed sufficient instrument, and his hills to provide natural advantage. So I returned pleased and confident to Egypt, and told my chiefs how Mecca was defended not by the obstacle of Rabegh [with its blocking force of Arab regulars], but by the flank-threat of Feisal in Jebel Subh.

Lawrence's chiefs in the bureau and HQ MF accepted his recommendations and sent him back as political and military liaison officer. Though (as he freely acknowledged) there were numerous other British officers serving under the flag of the Arab Revolt – a flag designed by Sir Mark Sykes as emblematic of Arab unity – Lawrence's was in large part the deciding presence.

By early 1917, with Murray having advanced to the Palestine border and Feisal's men gaining ground, the situation looked favourable for taking the fight to the enemy rather than merely standing on the defensive, despite London's determination to give priority to the Western Front. It would not be until June, however, with Murray's replacement by Sir Edmund Allenby, that the campaign was to gain real momentum. Feisal's irregulars would continue their diversionary attacks to the very end, October 1918 – although, knowing little or nothing about the Sykes–Picot agreement, he and Sharif Hussein did so in the belief that they had been promised an Arab caliphate stretching from Egypt to Persia.

24

JULY

Sixty Thousand Casualties before Breakfast

*The terrible first day of the offensive is followed by scarcely
less terrible weeks and months of fighting on the Somme*

'It was fine, cloudless, summer weather, not very clear, for there was
a good deal of heat haze and of mist in the nights and early mornings,' wrote John Masefield of late June 1916. He had served in
France as a hospital orderly before the Foreign Office engaged him
to produce war propaganda, sending him to the Somme to write an
account of the fighting for publication in America.

> At half past six in the morning of 1st July all the guns on our front
> quickened their fire to a pitch of intensity never before attained. Inter-
> mittent darkness and flashing so played on the enemy line from
> Gommecourt to Maricourt that it looked like a reef on a loppy day. For
> one instant it could be seen as a white rim above the wire, then some
> comber of a big shell struck it fair and spouted it black aloft . . .

The moment was arriving for 'the big push' which Sir Douglas
Haig had been planning since taking over as commander-in-chief

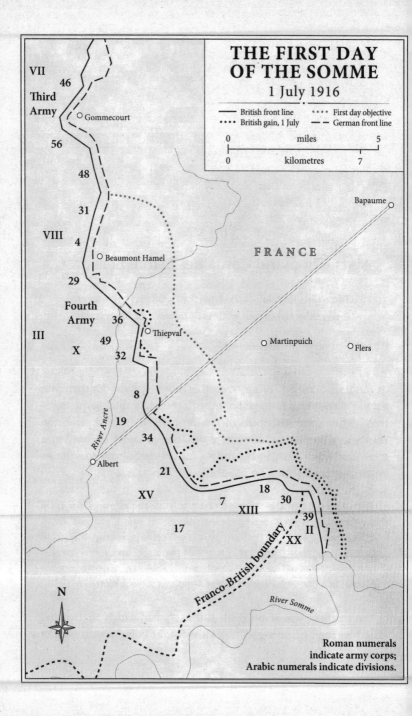

THE FIRST DAY OF THE SOMME
1 July 1916

—— British front line	•••• First day objective
•••• British gain, 1 July	– – – German front line

0 — miles — 5

0 — kilometres — 7

VII

Third Army

46

○ Gommecourt

56

48

31

VIII

4

○ Beaumont Hamel

29

Fourth Army

36

III

49

X

32

8

River Ancre

19

34

○ Albert

21

XV

7

17

XIII

18

30

39

II

XX

Franco-British boundary

FRANCE

Bapaume ○

Martinpuich ○

Flers ○

○ Thiepval

River Somme

N

Roman numerals
indicate army corps;
Arabic numerals indicate divisions.

of the BEF six months earlier. At the second inter-allied conference, in December at Joffre's headquarters in Chantilly, the British and French had agreed on a major combined offensive astride the River Somme, while Italy and Russia would mount their own offensives to coincide; but all had agreed that if in the meantime one ally came under clear threat, the others would launch diversionary attacks. The massive German offensive against the French at Verdun in February had therefore accelerated the various plans, and in the case of the Somme had significantly reduced the number of French troops taking part.

On 26 May, Joffre came to Haig's headquarters to urge him to begin his offensive without delay. For three months, said Joffre, the French had supported the whole weight of the German attacks at Verdun; 'If this went on, the French Army would be ruined.' They would not be able to hold out beyond 1 July.

Haig had been counting on 15 August, by which time he would have 200 additional heavy guns and possibly some tanks, a prototype having been demonstrated successfully in January. Going six weeks early would also carry a penalty in terms of training as well as materiel. Yet Haig felt obliged to accede to Joffre's plea. Besides, the Russians were doing a great deal to honour the undertaking they had given at Chantilly. In March they had attacked in Courland and Lithuania, an offensive which collapsed with heavy loss, and on 1 June, specifically at the request of Italy to relieve pressure on her armies in the Trentino, where the Austrians had launched an offensive, General Aleksei Brusilov had begun his long-planned attack in Polish Galicia.

There is still doubt as to exactly what the British high command thought it could achieve on the Somme. Haig had delegated planning and direction of the battle to Sir Henry Rawlinson, GOC 4th Army, a man he deeply mistrusted, setting him the task of capturing the high ground running from Montauban-en-Picardie through Pozières to Serre, and then securing positions linking Ginchy and Bapaume. The 3rd Army, to its north, would at the same time attack Gommecourt to draw away attention. An exploitation force consisting largely of three divisions of cavalry, some 30,000 horses, under Sir Hubert Gough, would thereafter pour through the gap created by the 4th Army to restore the war of movement which had been brought to an end in November 1914. To Haig the cavalryman, therefore, as C-in-C looking across the Western Front as a whole and seeking the all-important breakthrough, momentum was everything. Rawlinson the infantryman, as the tactical commander occupied by more short-term concerns, saw the attack as a more deliberate affair – rather a case of 'bite and hold'.

The problem for both men was the lack of experience in the troops who would carry out the attack, whether breaking through or 'biting and holding'. Put simply, the majority of Haig's men were green. The original BEF, largely regulars, had been destroyed as a cohesive force by the summer of 1915. Those who had survived the early battles were now filling staff appointments or commands in Kitchener's 'New Army' – the men who had answered his call to arms in 1914: 'Your Country Needs You!' These had been formed in successive tranches of 100,000, known unofficially as K1, K2 etc., each to mirror the original BEF, but this great expansion programme had never had enough instructors, materiel or time to undertake adequate training. The demand for reinforcements had brought them to France prematurely to fight alongside the remnants of the old BEF and the territorials who had volunteered to serve overseas. 'I have not got an Army in France really,' wrote Haig at the end of March, 'but a collection of divisions untrained for the field.'

How was this collection of untrained divisions supposed to deliver a crushing blow to the Germans only three months later?

The Somme does not belong to the poets, but they had a useful way with words, even in prose. In *Undertones of War* (1928), Edmund Blunden, an officer in a Kitchener battalion of the Royal Sussex, would write acerbically of the instruction issued by Haig's headquarters explaining how it was to be done: it 'assert[ed] the valuable creative principle that artillery and trench mortars cut the wire; infantry capture and consolidate the trenches. This promised to simplify the new warfare considerably.'

In fact the ambition for artillery went further. Not only would it cut the German wire in no-man's-land, it would also obliterate their fire and support trenches. Thus the infantry would not so much have to capture them, which might imply fire and manoeuvre, for which they had had scant training; they would merely have to occupy what was left of them. And because the trenches would have been destroyed, the infantry would not need to do anything but advance at walking pace across no-man's-land; so they could carry a greater weight of extra ammunition, water, rations and defence stores – up to 66 lb (30 kg) – in order to consolidate their gains.

The seven-day preparatory bombardment on the Somme certainly looked and sounded impressive: 1,500 guns firing 200,000 rounds a day (in the end, the shell count was nearer 1.7 million, since the French added their weight on the right); but because of the length of front to be attacked (18 miles in all) and the deficiencies in the number of guns for the task, their accuracy and the amount of high explosive as opposed to shrapnel, the inadequate fuses and the failure rate of ammunition (perhaps as many as one in three shells proved either duds or misfires), the German trenches would not be destroyed, nor the barbed wire in front of them cut sufficiently.

Lanes in the defensive wire laid by the British in front of their own trenches were to be cut by hand in the preceding days. In *Memoirs of an Infantry Officer* (1930), Siegfried Sassoon of the 1st Royal Welsh Fusiliers recounted how he spent a good deal of the day and night before the start of the battle crawling about trying to make wider gaps with his new wire-cutters, bought on leave at the Army and Navy Stores, so that the New Army battalion of the Manchester Regiment which was to attack from their trench might have a better chance: 'It seemed to me that our prestige as a regular battalion had been entrusted to my care on a front of several hundred yards.'

No proper testing of the theory that artillery could cut the wire and demolish the trenches had been carried out. Nor was there any plan – unlike the Germans' at Verdun – to assess the effectiveness of the bombardment before the infantry were sent over the top. Indeed, Haig specifically forbade reconnaissance on the grounds that it would 'lead to the loss of the boldest and best without result' – a strange tactical precept.

'In our trenches after seven o'clock on that morning,' wrote Masefield,

> our men waited under a heavy fire for the signal to attack. Just before half-past seven, the mines at half a dozen points went up with a roar that shook the earth and brought down the parapets in our lines. Before the blackness of their burst had thinned or fallen, the hand of Time rested on the half-hour mark, and along all that old front line of the English there came a whistling and a crying. The men of the first wave climbed up the parapets, in tumult, darkness, and the presence of death, and having done with all pleasant things, advanced across the No Man's land to begin the battle of the Somme.

The bombardment had of course told the Germans that an attack was imminent, and as soon as it switched to the support lines to allow the first wave to advance – in all, 100,000 men would go over the top that morning – German machine-gunners clambered up the ladders from their deep dug-outs in the chalk to open a devastating fire on them, supplemented by shrapnel from artillery batteries hitherto silent and undetected.

The result overall, if not without exception (the 36th Ulster Division, for example, managed to capture temporarily the formidable 'Schwaben Redoubt'), was calamitous. The north-country 'Pals' battalions – men from the same locality or trade who had been promised that if they joined up together they would stay together – fared particularly badly, and all the more tragically for the effect on the tight-knit communities at home when the telegrams began to arrive. The 1st and 2nd Barnsley 'Pals' (13th and 14th Battalions, York and Lancaster Regiment), attacking side by side in 94th Brigade, got nowhere but to a great many graves. The 1st Pals went over the top 720 strong; by the middle of the afternoon there were only

250 of them left. The 2nd Pals fared slightly better, losing 300 before the brigade commander called them off. Both battalions were lucky in one respect, however, for besides being in the support wave their brigadier was the 34-year-old Hubert Conway Rees, a regular infantryman robust enough to stop the attack. But it was too late for the battalion in front of them – the 11th East Lancashires, the 'Accrington Pals', 730 men from the close-knit cotton-mill towns of 'Blackburnshire'. After the first half an hour, 600 of them were dead, wounded or 'missing' (in other words, nothing remained of them after the shelling, for few had got far enough to be taken prisoner). Conway Rees wrote of his battalions:

> At the time this barrage really became intense, the last waves of the attack were crossing the trench I was in. I have never seen a finer display of individual and collective bravery than the advance of that brigade. I never saw a man waver from the exact line prescribed for him. Each line disappeared in the thick cloud of dust & smoke which rapidly blotted out the whole area. I saw a few groups of men through gaps in the smoke cloud, but I knew that no troops could hope to get through such a fire.

Elsewhere brigade and divisional commanders, whether from lack of information or want of Conway Rees's judgement, pressed the attacks regardless.

Some battalions famously kicked footballs into no-man's-land to lift the spirits. One Pals battalion, the 20th Northumberland Fusiliers (Tyneside Scottish), advanced as if on parade to the skirl of the pipes with all the innocence of the amateurs they still were. Pipe-Major John Wilson was 'marching erect, playing furiously, and quite regardless of the flying bullets and the men dropping all around him', wrote one man home. Wilson survived, but his uncle, in the same battalion, didn't: 'I did see poor "Aggy" Fyfe,' recalled a fellow Tynesider. 'He was riddled with bullets and screaming. Another lad was just kneeling, his head thrown right back. Bullets were just slapping into him knocking great bloody chunks off his body.'

As a man from one of the Pals battalions of the West Yorkshire Regiment wrote home: 'The battalion was two years in the making and ten minutes in the destroying.'

Sassoon, who a few weeks later would win the Military Cross, called that morning 'a sunlit picture of hell'.

The following day, Haig recorded in his diary that casualties were estimated at 'over 40,000 to date', adding that 'this cannot be considered severe in view of the numbers engaged [close on 200,000], and the length of front attacked'. The figures were unprecedented, however – almost as great as the total for the duke of Wellington's entire Peninsular campaign – and in any case were a serious underestimate. Some 40,000 had been wounded on the first day, but a further 20,000 had been killed. By comparison, those of the French and Germans had been light: the French some 1,600 killed and wounded, the Germans perhaps 12,000.

In the Battle of Loos the year before, there had been 40,000 British casualties for the gain of no significant ground, but in a fortnight's fighting, and the débâcle had led to the dismissal of the C-in-C, Sir John French. On 1 July 1916 very little ground was gained, nor was it held in the immediate German counter-attacks, but no one very senior was sacked, the blame devolving instead on regimental officers. And the Somme offensive would be pressed until the middle of November, the casualties mounting steadily, little ground being taken and no breakthrough coming. The new secretary for war, Lloyd George, would grow anxious, and then doubtful, but Haig would continue to assure him that progress was being made, that they were wearing down the Germans.

'We always felt that someone up above was ordering things, and that they probably knew more about it than we did,' wrote Captain Tom Adlam of the 7th Bedfordshire Regiment, another Kitchener battalion, who in September would win the VC: 'We just carried on.'

25

AUGUST

Exit Falkenhayn

Allied offensives on all fronts make the Kaiser begin to doubt

Of the several hundred thousand German casualties on all fronts in August 1916, the most significant was the chief of the *Oberste Heeresleitung* (supreme army command, consisting principally of the *Grosser Generalstab*, and also the Kaiser's military cabinet). But General der Infanterie Erich von Falkenhayn was not killed or wounded; he was sacked, and his dismissal would prove a turning point – perhaps *the* turning point – of the war.

Germany and her principal ally Austria-Hungary had come under increasing pressure throughout June and July. Falkenhayn's great offensive at Verdun, begun in February, had aimed at drawing in French reserves by capturing Verdun's prestigious forts, which, he calculated, were so prominent in the national consciousness that the French army would have no option but to counter-attack, and in so doing would be destroyed by massed artillery. The French had indeed obliged him, but their counter-attacks were in turn inflicting heavy casualties on the Germans. And, although the French commander-in-chief, Joseph Joffre, had desperately pleaded with

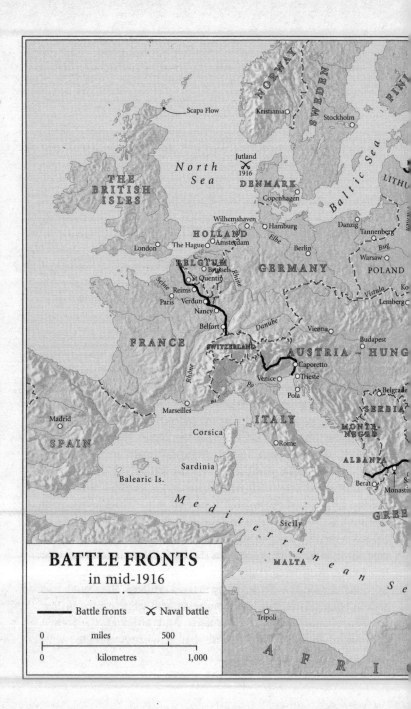

BATTLE FRONTS
in mid-1916

—— Battle fronts ✕ Naval battle

| 0 | miles | 500 |
| 0 | kilometres | 1,000 |

his British opposite number, Sir Douglas Haig, to bring forward the Somme offensive because he could not hang on much longer at Verdun, the French army had not broken. Falkenhayn had so far failed in his aim of 'bleeding France white'. Indeed, Verdun was proving as costly for the Germans as it was for the French.

On the Eastern Front the situation looked no more promising. On 4 June, General Aleksei Brusilov, commanding the Russian south-western army group – four armies consisting of some 600,000 men – had launched an offensive in Galicia, in what is now western Ukraine. In the first seventy-two hours his four armies advanced 50 miles, taking 200,000 Austro-Hungarian prisoners (entire Slav units surrendered) and several hundred heavy guns: infinitely more successful than the BEF's own offensive on the Somme a few weeks later, if ultimately no more fruitful.

At Joffre's urgent request, the Russians also attacked the Germans in the east, notably at Lake Naroch in present-day Lithuania, but here they were less successful, and the Germans were able to mount counter-offensives as well as reinforcing the Austrians. Nevertheless, Brusilov pressed his offensive throughout the summer, and though by the middle of August it was running out of steam, by then his four armies had taken some 375,000 German and Austro-Hungarian prisoners, a great deal of war materiel and 15,000 square miles of territory.

The cost in Russian casualties had been high – over half a million – and these would prove difficult to replace with troops of equal loyalty to the Tsar. Indeed, the offensive would prove to be the Russian high-water mark on the Eastern Front; but Brusilov's innovative tactics and operational art have earned high praise. Field Marshal Viscount Montgomery of Alamein, who in 1916 was an infantry major on the Western Front, would afterwards name Brusilov one of the seven outstanding fighting commanders of the war.

The Austrians had come under increasing pressure, too, on the Italian front. On 4 August, General Luigi Cadorna launched yet another offensive on the Isonzo river, where the future Fascist leader Benito Mussolini was serving as a corporal in the *Bersaglieri* (light infantry), and would be twice wounded, and where Ernest Hemingway would set his autobiographical novel *A Farewell to Arms*, in which an increasingly disillusioned American volunteer serves in an Italian ambulance unit. Unlike the previous five offensives here, however, all of which had ended in costly failure, this time there were marked gains, in major part owing to the masterly use of artillery – always the Italians' strongest arm (in the Crimean War *The Times*'s correspondent, William Howard Russell, had pronounced the artillery of the Piedmont–Sardinian detachment the best of the four allied armies). Before this Sixth Battle of the Isonzo, Cadorna had managed to bring forward in great secrecy 1,200 guns – 400 of them medium or heavy – and 800 bombards (heavy mortars), achieving surprise with a short (nine-hour) but intense bombardment before launching the main assault, unusually, in the afternoon. In five days the Italians forced the Austrians to abandon their bridgehead west of the Isonzo and captured Gorizia at the foot of the Julian Alps on the Slovene border.

And yet, although Austrian reserves had been sent east to counter the Brusilov offensive and further advance seemed possible, Cadorna could not exploit his victory. With no bridges left standing across the Isonzo, despite the brilliance of his engineers he could not get his artillery up quickly enough to break through the second defensive line, and on 16 August he closed down the offensive. Gorizia had cost him over 50,000 casualties – a third more than the defenders – and although these losses were fewer than the BEF had sustained on the first day of the Somme, 1 July, they came on top of the 220,000, a quarter of his then mobilized forces, suffered in the first five battles on the Isonzo. The Italian army was, however, learning. Indeed, it would now form the first 'shock troops' (preceding the famed German *Sturmtruppen*) to overcome forward defences by fire and daring – hence their nickname *arditi*, 'the daring ones', much lauded by the poet-aviator Gabriele d'Annunzio.

The British were learning, too, if not uniformly – and certainly not in the higher echelons. The attacks on the Somme had continued throughout July, the casualties mounting to 158,000, with a further 40,000 elsewhere on the Western Front, as the offensive degenerated into a series of seemingly uncoordinated localized battles that would go on throughout August. In one of these, George Butterworth, composer of *Banks of Green Willow*, was killed while in temporary command of a company of the 13th Durham Light Infantry, a 'Kitchener battalion', having won the Military Cross the day before.

The original front-line trenches were on relatively low-lying ground, overlooked – dominated, for the major part – by the German positions, especially at High Wood and Delville Wood, names immortalized in numerous regimental histories and Robert Graves's memoir *Goodbye to All That*. These gentle hills had been the objective of the first two days' fighting, Haig expecting to achieve a breakthrough so that he could launch Gough's *corps de chasse*, made up in large part of cavalry, into the open country beyond – what the less reverent officers (usually infantrymen) called 'galloping through the "G" in "Gap"'. In the event the cavalry remained penned in by barbed wire and machine guns just as surely as the 'PBI' (poor bloody infantry), only the 7th Dragoon Guards and a regiment of Indian cavalry, the 20th Deccan Horse, getting any sort of gallop – at High Wood on 14 July, and even then at a cost of 100 human casualties and 130 horses.

Fighting would continue through the whole of August and two weeks of September – gruelling fighting, some of it at night with imaginative tactics – before any of the BEF could start downhill on the far side of the ridges that had been the first day's objective, and the breakthrough would never come. A strange sort of routine set in during these weeks, at times almost surreal. In *The War the Infantry Knew*, Captain James Dunn, medical officer of the 2nd Royal Welsh Fusiliers, recorded how on 18 August

2.45pm was zero [hour] for a push through Wood Lance and High Wood by the 100th and 98th Brigades while demonstrations were made on the right and left. The gun-fire was over in little more than an hour. Through it all the Band of the 6th Welsh (Pioneers) practised: it's a good

Band, and plays good music of the 'popular' kind: a great din of guns made the strangest of obbligatos.

There were 'rumours of success everywhere', continued Dunn, but then 'At 7.30 we heard that "nothing had been gained," that "the situation is obscure".' Two days later it was the Fusiliers' turn to attack. Captain Robert Graves, not yet twenty-one, would be so badly wounded by a shell fragment through the lung that he was officially reported as having died of wounds. In fact, between 2 July and the end of August no more ground would be gained and held on the Somme than had been on the opening day of the offensive, and at the cost of a further 82,000 casualties.

The Somme was taking its mental toll, too. Dunn wrote of the increasing problem of 'shell shock', whether real, imagined or even feigned. Strange symptoms – paralysis, stuttering, inability to stand or walk, the 'shakes' – had begun appearing at the casualty clearing stations in 1915, starting a debate in both military and medical circles as to what it was, what had caused it and how it should be treated. The numbers were not then great, for the BEF in 1915 was still composed largely of regulars, or territorials who had volunteered to serve overseas – men who had been in uniform for some years, and were acclimatized to military life; Kitchener's 'New Army' battalions did not begin arriving in any numbers until the late summer. Although the battles of 1915 were bloody, they were not as relentless as those of the Somme, nor were the artillery bombardments on so industrial a scale. New drafts arriving at the front in August 1916, wrote Dunn, 'came in for enough shelling to light up the picture of "shell-shocked" and "gassed," for which two years of lurid journalese in the home papers had prepared the minds . . . so the Dressing Station near-by had many importunate applicants for admission'. He considered that 'the first duty of a battalion medical officer in War is to discourage the evasion of duty . . . not seldom against one's better feelings, sometimes to the temporary hurt of the individual, but justice to all other men as well as discipline demands it'.

The simultaneous and in part coordinated allied offensives – especially the continuing French counter-attacks at Verdun – were taking their toll on the Germans, and the Kaiser was getting anxious. Not the least of his concerns were the signs of unrest at home, in part the result of the Royal Navy's increasingly effective blockade: on 19 August, coal-miners in the Ruhr went on strike in protest at food shortages and rising prices. Then, on 27 August, the Entente gained a new ally – Romania. Bucharest, like Sofia the year before, had been wooed by both sides, but with over half the length of her border shared with Austria-Hungary, Bulgaria or occupied Serbia, and with the Black Sea closed for good to the western allies after the failure of the Dardanelles campaign, Romania had been understandably fearful of declaring her hand. In January the chief of the imperial general staff, Sir William Robertson, had minuted the foreign secretary, Sir Edward Grey, lamenting that diplomacy had not had much success of late (forgetting, rather, the Italian coup in May 1915), and Grey had replied not unreasonably that diplomacy in war depended on military success – and there had been precious little of that. But now it seemed that there *was* success – Brusilov's, Italy's, and on the Western Front. Even the nascent Macedonian front was beginning to look promising: the Bulgarians had invaded Greek territory, Athens appeared to be contemplating action (although it would be another ten months before the Greek government formally declared war), and allied reinforcements were beginning to arrive – including an advance party of a thousand Russians. On 27 August, therefore, Romania declared war on Austria-Hungary and at once sent troops into Transylvania, which had a large ethnic Romanian population. The following day, Italy, flushed with success at Gorizia and hitherto technically at war only with Austria, declared war on Germany.

It was all too much for the Kaiser. On 29 August he replaced Falkenhayn with Generalfeldmarschall Paul von Hindenburg (and his inseparable deputy Erich Ludendorff, who had parried the Russian blows with such skill), sending the former chief of the *Oberste Heeresleitung* to command the 9th Army on the Eastern Front. On the face of it Falkenhayn and his successor had much in common. Both were from the old Prussian nobility, both were infantrymen and both had seen service, though Hindenburg, some fourteen years Falkenhayn's senior (he had been recalled from retirement in 1914), had fought in Bismarck's audacious wars of unification. Whereas Falkenhayn was by nature cautious and calculating, however, Hindenburg was brusquely bold.

There would be a certain irony in Falkenhayn's rustication, for the following month he launched a dazzling counter-offensive against the Romanian army, entering Bucharest on 6 December. Field Marshal Montgomery ranked him alongside Brusilov as one of the 'seven outstanding fighting commanders of the war'. The other five were Mustafa Kemal ('Atatürk'), who had thwarted the Entente's Dardanelles campaign; Ludendorff, whose success on the Eastern Front the Kaiser now hoped to see replicated on the Western; the Australian John Monash, who in August 1916 was training his new division (3rd Australian) in England after the exertions of Gallipoli and Egypt, and whose star would begin to burn bright in 1917; and the British generals Herbert Plumer and Edmund Allenby, whose time was likewise still to come.

Hindenburg, who would slowly but surely become de facto Kaiser, lost no time in making his demands known. On the last day of August he sent a letter to the war minister demanding a doubling of ammunition output by May 1917 and a threefold increase in machine-gun and artillery production. The Western Front was to be put on hold through a massive system of defences in depth until the Russians had been beaten decisively by manoeuvre, whereupon he would turn the full resources of materiel and operational art on the western allies. Crucially, too, he pressed for the resumption of unrestricted submarine warfare, backing Admiral Scheer, commander-in-chief of the High Seas Fleet repulsed at Jutland three months earlier, who had already told the Kaiser that U-boats were the only way to bring Britain down. In so doing, Hindenburg would begin the chain of events that brought the United States into the war the following spring. And once America was under arms, a German victory in the west was but a pipe dream.

In the meantime, however, it would be a cruel irony that while Hindenburg and Ludendorff were discarding Falkenhayn's murderous *Ermattungsstrategie* (strategy of wearing down) for one of *Vernichtungsstrategie* (strategy of decisive victories), the French and British on the Western Front were doing the opposite – if not so much by design as by default. For although Haig and a succession of French generals would continue to talk about 'breakthrough' and restoring the war of manoeuvre, the reality – that for the time being, the power of defensive weapons rendered any such breakthrough impossible – turned the offensives on the Somme and in 1917 into the strategy of attrition: what Churchill called the 'dreary process of exchanging lives, and counting heads at the end'.

26

SEPTEMBER

The Rude Mechanical

The tank goes into action – with mixed results

No weapon was ever brought to the battlefield with more impressive speed and secrecy than the tank. After a year of trial and error with various caterpillar devices, on 20 January 1916 a prototype of the ultimate rhomboid-shaped design had been demonstrated to the Admiralty Landships Committee in Lincoln. A week later, the 28-ton machine, shrouded in tarpaulins and described on the bill of lading as 'water tank for Mesopotamia', was on its way by rail to Hertfordshire to be shown to the War Office and the cabinet – and Haig's deputy chief of staff, Major-General Richard Butler, who, having watched the demonstration, asked simply: 'How soon can we have them?'

The minister of munitions, David Lloyd George, at once loosened the purse-strings. By the middle of February, Fosters of Lincoln had been contracted to build fifty, and the Metropolitan Amalgamated Railway Carriage and Wagon Co. Ltd, Birmingham, fifty more, increased in April by a further fifty. On 15 September, barely eight months after its first outing in Lincoln, the tank – the name now officially adopted – would take part in what Haig hoped would be the decisive attack of his stalled Somme offensive: the battle of Flers-Courcelette, as it became known.

Finding 'crews' – a nod to the tank's naval origins – was a novel challenge. Each tank was to be commanded by an officer, with a further seven men as drivers, gearsmen and gunners. Including supports and replacements, 150 officers and 1,000 other ranks would be needed for the initial 100 tanks. Secrecy demanded they be recruited without knowing what exactly they were volunteering for – so how were they to be found? A cover name for the organization was needed, and found: the 'Heavy Section Machine Gun Corps'. Ernest Swinton, a Royal Engineers lieutenant-colonel who had been one of the first advocates of caterpillar traction, was given charge of raising and training the new force. He at once asked the War Office to 'select and warn personally, good fighting subalterns of resource and courage, conversant with motor cars or motor cycles', then set off round the officer-cadet schools and home-based battalions scouting for talent.

Similarly secretive arrangements were put in hand to find the other ranks. Advertisements appeared in *Motor Cycle Magazine* for men who could drive 'light cars'; recruits in training for other arms were suddenly told that former plumbers and gas-fitters should report to the orderly room. The best drivers came from the stalwart Army Service Corps, whose superior discipline would prove significant.

Recruits began assembling in some mystification at Bisley in Surrey, among them a number of transferees from the Navy's armoured car detachments; then, once a few training tanks were available, they moved to Elveden Hall in Suffolk, seat of the Guinness brewing magnate the Earl of Iveagh – 15 square miles of the best pheasant shooting in the country. When the Lands Branch of the War Office telephoned Lord Iveagh to tell him of its requisition, he had sighed resignedly and said that if anyone's shoot was to be spoilt it might as well be his. Tenant farmers and labourers were uprooted, old retainers were displaced from their almshouses, and Elveden School was closed. Three pioneer battalions, many of them Welsh miners, began work creating a mile-and-a-half-long replica of the Western Front, complete with shell craters, barbed-wire entanglements, dugouts and six lines of trenches. Security was tight. When Clough Williams-Ellis, the future architect of Portmeirion, and one of the Heavy Section's first subalterns, arrived at 'Elveden Explosives Area' (its cover name), he found cavalry, Indian troops and territorials patrolling three concentric perimeters, the area 'more ringed about than was the palace of the Sleeping Beauty'.

The first operational tanks appeared at the beginning of June. The 'Mark 1' came in two types: 'male', with two 6-pounder (57 mm) guns in side sponsons firing high explosive shells, plus three Hotchkiss machine guns; and 'female', with four heavier Vickers machine guns and a Hotchkiss. Each had 6–12 mm of armour – good protection against rifle fire and to some extent machine guns, but not much against HE. Motive power was from a 6-cylinder, 16-litre, 105 hp Daimler–Knight petrol engine driving the caterpillar tracks through three independent gearboxes. Steering required the tank to halt momentarily to disengage a track, and the first models had tail wheels to assist, though in action these proved ineffective and were soon abandoned. On level ground the Mark 1 could make 4 mph, with a range of about 25 miles before refuelling.

Crew conditions were appalling. The combination of engine heat, noise, exhaust fumes, and violent movement as the tank crossed broken ground made men violently sick even on short journeys. Injuries were common. It was difficult to communicate within the tank, and almost impossible without. The commander would have to dismount to reconnoitre a path through an obstacle, or to liaise with the infantry. The War Office specification for mechanical reliability was a mere 50 miles between failures, as the tank was meant to be a one-off weapon whose job would be done once the infantry broke through and the cavalry let loose. Unsurprisingly, therefore, given its weight, the inexperience of the crews, and the difficulty of keeping engine and gearbox lubricated when pitched at extreme angles, breakdowns were frequent.

Nevertheless, under Swinton's direction at Elveden things slowly began taking shape, with four companies, A to D, each consisting of four sections of three tanks – two male, one female – and another tank in company reserve, formed by late July. C and D companies would entrain for the Somme on 16 August. Few of the crewmen had ever heard a shot fired in anger.

Meanwhile, at his headquarters just south of Boulogne, Haig was having to adjust his plans again. Having launched the Somme offensive six weeks earlier than planned in response to pleas from the French, under severe pressure at Verdun, in late August he began planning a climactic offensive-within-an-offensive to break the deadlock. His intention was to establish a defensive flank on the high ground north of the Albert–Bapaume road, which bisected the Somme battlefield, while pressing the main assault south of it with the aim of breaching the German rear line between Morval and Le Sars. In essence it was the same idea as that of 1 July, but on a narrower frontage (8 miles as opposed to 18 miles), with a shorter but more concentrated preliminary artillery bombardment – and now with the game-changing tanks, for which lanes 100 yards wide would be left clear of artillery fire.

There were growing concerns about loss of operational surprise, however. Once the tank was used, the Germans would gain the measure of it, adjust their tactics, increase the distribution of armour-piercing rounds which snipers already used to penetrate sentry shields, and – worst of all – develop tanks of their own. Indeed, there were fears they were already doing so. After watching a demonstration near Amiens, the Prince of Wales, a titular subaltern in the Grenadier Guards, wrote to his father, King George V: 'I enclose a rough sketch of these land submarines or "Tanks" as they are called for secrecy. The Huns have no doubt got accurate drawings of them and have by now produced a superior article!!'

Edwin Montagu, the new minister of munitions (Lloyd George having become war minister after Kitchener's death at sea in June), told the cabinet on 12 September, just three days before the fresh offensive was due to begin, that 'there are rumours the Germans are making something of the same kind' and that his French opposite number had told him that his own army had placed an order for 800 tracked machines and urged that 'we should not put ours into the field until they were ready'.

The prime minister, Asquith, whose eldest son, Raymond, was serving on the Somme, had seen the tank for himself during a recent visit. Though unsettled by Montagu's intervention he decided to leave the decision to the man on the spot – Haig. The CIGS, Sir William Robertson, agreed, though he himself believed the tank should not be used until there were many more of them, and had told Haig so.

Haig, however, was desperate for some sort of success. He told Sir Henry Rawlinson, commander of 4th Army, who if not the actual architect of the Somme offensive was certainly its clerk of works, that 'when we use them [the tanks] they will be thrown in with determination into the fight regardless of cost'.

The problem was not only of numbers, though, but of ground. The Somme was not Suffolk, certainly not after two months' bombardment. The novelist John Buchan, serving as *Times* correspondent in France, likened it to 'a decaying suburb . . . pockmarked with shell holes'. Although the tank was designed to cross broken ground, the more slowly it advanced the more vulnerable it became. Nevertheless, by the end of August fifty machines had arrived in France, and Haig decided that they would support the attack on 15 September, distributed more or less evenly across the three assaulting corps, with six held for the reserve army.

Their arrival in the forward areas just before zero hour came as a surprise to most of the infantry. Indeed, some did not see them until the attack had begun. Private Arnold Ridley of the Somerset Light Infantry – and sixty years later, Private Godfrey of BBC TV's *Dad's Army* – was severely wounded in hand-to-hand fighting that day. He recalled: 'We in the ranks had never heard of tanks. We were told that there was some sort of secret weapon and then we saw this thing go up the right hand corner of Delville Wood. I saw this strange and cumbersome machine emerge from the shattered shrubbery and proceed slowly down the slope towards Flers.'

Some thought them comical, while others were impressed by the very thing that was perceived to be their weakness: 'It was her slowness that scared us as much as anything,' a territorial told a reporter afterwards. There was something unnerving about the tank's steady, relentless advance in the face of fire. Others saw nothing at all, for only twenty-two of the fifty tanks actually reached the start line, seven of which promptly broke down.

Most of those that did get into action paid dearly. Lieutenant Basil Henriques' tank came under intense machine-gun fire, forcing him to close the viewing slits:

> Then a smash against my flap at the front caused splinters to come in and the blood to pour down my face. Another minute and my driver got the same. Then our prism glass broke to pieces, then another smash. I think it must have been a bomb right in my face. The next one wounded my driver so badly we had to stop. By this time I could see nothing at all.

When the glass shards were removed from his face at a dressing station, Henriques kept a piece to have mounted in a gold ring to give to his wife.

Where two or more tanks managed to advance together there could be distinct success. The defenders of the half-ruined sugar-beet factory at Flers were forced out by concerted 6-pounder and machine-gun fire. But overall, little ground was gained that day. Rawlinson wrote in his diary: 'A great battle. We nearly did a big thing.'

The tank had at least demonstrated its potential, and production would now be stepped up. In November the companies were expanded into battalions, and in July the following year the Tank Corps was formed – some fifteen battalions. To some extent, the concern about the loss of surprise proved over-stated. Although the Germans would occasionally use captured British and French tanks, and eventually develop their own, they failed to recognize the worth of armoured fighting vehicles until after the war. They saw the tank as something to be defeated rather than emulated.

Flers-Courcelette cost the BEF another 25,000 casualties before Haig called off the offensive a week later. Perhaps the most significant casualty – in respect of its repercussions in public life – was not a tank man, however, but an infantryman. On 17 September, H. H. Asquith's second wife, Margot, received a telephone call. 'I went back into the sitting room. "Raymond's dead," I said to the servant. "Tell the prime minister to come and speak to me." '

27

OCTOBER
'Preparedness'

*As German U-boats reach American waters,
the tide begins to turn against isolationism*

Within hours of the declaration of war at 11 p.m. on 4 August 1914, British ships had dredged up and cut the German transatlantic cables. This was not for fear of direct US intervention but to disrupt the supply of war materiel for Germany and to thwart German propaganda, which might threaten supplies to the allies. In 1940, after the fall of France, Churchill in his great 'We shall fight on the beaches' speech looked to the moment when 'in God's good time, the New World, with all its power and might, steps forth to the rescue and the liberation of the old'. In 1914 neither London nor Paris had any thoughts that the United States would send troops to France; the US army was small, and few expected the war to be a long one.

President Woodrow Wilson had declared his policy of neutrality. In an address to Congress on 19 August he warned that 'the people of the United States are drawn from many nations, and chiefly from the nations now at war. It is natural and inevitable that there should be the utmost variety of sympathy and desire among them with regard to the issues and circumstances of the conflict.'

Wilson saw the conflict largely in terms of Europe's old dynastic wars, in which a New World democracy had no place save as an honest broker, for intervention would risk the still relatively young republic's cohesion (it was less than fifty years since the end of the Civil War):

> Divisions amongst us would be fatal to our peace of mind and might seriously stand in the way of the proper performance of our duty as the one great nation at peace, the one people holding itself ready to play a part of impartial mediation and speak the counsels of peace and accommodation, not as a partisan, but as a friend.

It would be some time before German 'frightfulness' – the ruthless occupation of neutral Belgium and the sinking of unarmed ships – and Berlin's clumsy meddling in Mexico led him reluctantly to the view that the conflict was more a struggle between rampant militarism and Enlightenment. Even after the sinking of the *Lusitania* in May 1915, with the death of 128 American citizens, Wilson's instinct was to persuade Germany to limit the war at sea, if only by unspecific ultimatums. At that point, Berlin had reluctantly complied, abandoning the policy of sinking without warning. In the campaign for re-election in 1916, the slogan in Wilson's camp was 'He kept us out of war!', though he never in fact promised unequivocally to stay out of it. In his acceptance speech for the Democratic nomination in September, he pointedly warned Berlin that submarine warfare resulting in American deaths would not be tolerated: 'The nation that violates these essential rights must expect to be checked and called to account by direct challenge and resistance. It at once makes the quarrel in part our own.'

There were other, more hawk-like voices. Many of these advocated not necessarily direct intervention – though some, like former President Theodore Roosevelt, one of whose sons was fighting as a volunteer with the British army in Mesopotamia, were strong advocates of joining the Entente – but 'military preparedness'. Organizations such as the American Defense League, the Army League and the National Security League were formed, championing universal military training. In 1915 military training camps for college students were set up in a number of states, and the idea of 'preparedness' began to gain traction in Congress. Wilson, however, continued to maintain that the National Guard was an adequate reserve force.

Nevertheless, in March 1916 Congress passed the National Defense Act. One of its major provisions was to grant the president power to place orders for war materiel and to force industry to comply. A Shipping Board was established to regulate sea transport and develop a naval auxiliary fleet. The Act also authorized an increase in the peacetime strength of the army to 175,000 men, and a contingency wartime strength of 300,000. Federal funds were also allocated for the National Guard, hitherto largely a responsibility of the states, and to bring it under professional supervision of the War Department. The future president Harry S Truman, who had served in the Missouri National Guard from 1905 to 1911, would rejoin when America declared war in 1917, seeing active service in France. At the same time, a Naval Act provided for construction of ten battleships, sixteen cruisers, fifty destroyers and seventy-two submarines. If the president was determined that the United States remain neutral, Congress wanted it at least to be a strongly armed neutrality.

In August 1916 Wilson conceded the establishment of the Council of National Defense, consisting of the secretaries of war, navy, labor, agriculture, interior and commerce, with the somewhat Delphic explanation that 'the Country is best prepared for war when thoroughly prepared for peace'. Then in October he appointed an advisory commission of business and industry leaders.

Yet he was increasingly frustrated by what he saw as British resistance to his calls for a negotiated end to the war, though his embryonic proposals were impossible for either side to accept (Pope Benedict XV made no progress either, and was reviled by both sides as favouring the other). There was also widespread distaste for the ruthless suppression of the 'Easter Rising' in Dublin, and its follow-up (the Irish-American vote was an important one for the Democrats), as well as anger at the blacklisting of eighty-seven US firms suspected of trading with the Central Powers.

The German decision in October to resume and intensify warfare on commerce was therefore something of an own goal. The problem was that the Battle of Jutland at the end of May had demonstrated that the German High Seas Fleet could not overcome the Royal Navy, and Admiral Scheer's hope of using U-boats to even the odds had been dashed in two subsequent attempts by the *Hochseeflotte* to draw the Grand Fleet on to a torpedo ambush. Scheer had therefore begun lobbying the Kaiser to reintroduce unrestricted submarine warfare and to expand the U-boat building programme. In October the Kaiser agreed to switch strategy from trying to wear down the Grand Fleet, instead diverting the existing U-boats to a blockade of Britain and building larger boats to take the war into the Atlantic.

The new chief of the German general staff, Paul von Hindenburg, was only too pleased to throw his weight behind Scheer's appeal to let his submarines sink merchantmen without warning, which he calculated would bring Britain to her knees in six months, for his troops and those of the other Central Powers were under real pressure. The Russian offensive led by Brusilov had made gains against the Austro-Hungarians; the German army was feeling the strain of the allied offensive on the Somme and French counter-attacks at Verdun; the campaign against the new Entente ally, Romania, was making heavy demands; and in the face of a counter-offensive by the allies on the previously inactive Macedonian front, the Bulgarians had fallen back towards Monastir in southern Serbia. However, at the insistence of the chancellor, Theobald von Bethmann Hollweg, who was anxious lest the Entente attract more neutrals – principally America – the Kaiser ruled that the U-boats must continue to issue warnings before sinking. On 24 March, a U-boat had torpedoed the *Sussex*, an unarmed Channel steamer, injuring several Americans (first reported as dead), and Wilson had threatened to sever diplomatic relations unless Germany abandoned attacks against passenger and merchant ships. Germany had complied, making the so-called '*Sussex* pledge' not to attack unresisting merchant vessels without warning, but with the proviso that Washington put pressure on London to observe international law while imposing its blockade. The 'pledge' had held through the summer, but largely because the main target of the U-boats had been the Grand Fleet.

Then, on 7 October, a U-boat made a dramatic entry into American waters. One of the *Kaiserliche Marine*'s newest and largest submarines, U-53, 715 tons, put in at Newport harbour, Rhode Island. Her captain, Hans Rose, paid courtesy visits to the admirals in port, who paid courtesy visits in return while Washington decided how to handle the affair. The harbour master pre-empted the formalities, however, by suggesting to Rose that there might be a problem with quarantine regulations, whereupon he promptly returned to sea to avoid being detained.

Next morning, 2 miles off the Nantucket lightship, U-53 stopped the American steamer *Kansan* by a shot across the bow; her papers revealing no contraband cargo, Rose let her go. An hour later U-53 stopped the *Strathdene*, a British steamer, sinking her by torpedo once the crew had abandoned ship. The Norwegian steamer *Christian Knutsen*, with a cargo of diesel oil for London, went the same way. The British steamer *West Point*, bound from London to Newport News, Virginia, was stopped at 11.30 and sunk by explosive charges after the crew had taken to the lifeboats.

Alerted by the Nantucket lightship, seventeen American destroyers raced to the scene, the first arriving late in the afternoon just as U-53 intercepted the British passenger steamer *Stephano* and the Dutch merchantman *Blommersdyk* – bound for Rotterdam but with orders to put in first at Falmouth, and therefore a legitimate prize. Their crews and passengers, including several American women and children, were taken off by the destroyers while Rose used his last torpedoes to sink both ships, having asked one of the destroyers to move aside to give him a clear line of fire.

Though the sinkings were carried out under the accepted 'cruiser rules', and no one was killed, the fact that they had occurred within sight of the lightship and in the presence of US warships made for unease in Washington and consternation in the press. Under the headline 'German sea code utter disregard for neutrals', the *Cornell Daily Sun* (New York state) declared:

> We are familiar with German denunciation of a British policy which aims to blockade the Central Powers, and, as we are eloquently informed, to 'starve German women and children into submission.' As an evident sign of a nobler faith, the German Government, through its irresponsible submarine commanders, sinks the flour which is destined for the women and children in Holland.

Roosevelt thundered that Wilson's 'ostrich policy' had earned the contempt of Europe. '[His] ignoble shirking of responsibility has been clothed in an utterly misleading phrase – the phrase of a coward – "he kept us out of the war." In actual reality war has been creeping nearer and nearer until it stares us in the face from just beyond the three-mile limit.'

With U-53 the Germans had also demonstrated a hitherto unsuspected reach, which alarmed both the British Admiralty and the US Navy. Washington's concern would only be exacerbated on learning that the German legation in Mexico was in discussions with the government to establish a submarine base in Mexican waters.

Mexico had been a troublesome neighbour for some time. Since 1910 the country had been in a state of revolution. Francisco 'Pancho' Villa, one of the most prominent of the revolutionary leaders, controlled much of the north-east, and in January 1916, angered by Washington's arms embargo against him, had killed several US mining executives in Chihuahua. Then in March Villa's forces had raided Columbus, New Mexico, killing sixteen Americans. Wilson ordered an expedition to capture him, but despite receiving assurances that it would be conducted 'with scrupulous regard for the sovereignty of Mexico', the Mexican president Venustiano Carranza regarded it as a violation of sovereignty and refused support.

Brigadier-General John J. 'Black Jack' Pershing, who in due course would command the American Expeditionary Force in France, led the raid but failed to capture Villa, skirmishing instead with 'Carrancista' forces. Another cross-border raid, into Texas, by Villa's forces in May brought more US troops into Mexico and another clash with the Carrancistas, this time in a major skirmish at Carrizal on 21 June which resulted in the capture of twenty-three US soldiers. Fearing that war was imminent, Carranza proposed direct negotiations and Wilson agreed, which for the time being eased tensions. Nevertheless, Hindenburg, who increasingly had the ear of the Kaiser, saw the potential of Mexico's diverting US troops and materiel if it came to war between America and Germany, and much to Bethmann Hollweg's dismay began manoeuvring accordingly.

Woodrow Wilson would be re-elected president in November with the narrowest of majorities. A fortnight after his inaugural address in March 1917 his cabinet would agree unanimously to declare war on Germany – just as the secretary of state, Robert Lansing, had predicted: that he 'had no doubt that after the sinking of the *Lusitania* we would ultimately become the ally of Britain'.

The challenge for Washington would be how to build an army capable of taking part in modern war, and where exactly to send it.

28

NOVEMBER

Attrition

*The 'butcher's bill' on the Somme begins to raise
differing doubts among politicians*

'Are we to continue until we have killed ALL our young men?'

In November 1916, as the Somme offensive spluttered on in rain
and snow, the Marquess of Lansdowne, who as foreign secretary in
1904 had negotiated the Anglo-French 'Entente Cordiale', put this
question in a bleak memorandum to Asquith's coalition cabinet. In
the four and a half months' fighting astride the River Somme,
420,000 British and imperial soldiers had been killed or wounded –
60,000 on the first day alone – along with nearly 200,000 French.
The furthest advance made was 7 miles.

They had, however, killed a lot of Germans. Indeed, because there
had been no breakthrough, the offensive had become one of attrition. Lacking sufficient artillery and opportunity for manoeuvre,
this *guerre d'usure* could be carried out only by frontal attacks against
an enemy in strong defensive positions. Trading life for life, even at
a favourable rate of exchange, was always going to rack up a heavy
butcher's bill, and although fighting techniques improved during

the course of the offensive, the obsession with capturing ground, in part driven by Haig's continuing hope of breakthrough, added further to the bill drawn on the 'poor bloody infantry'.

Although called 'the Battle of the Somme', the offensive was in fact a series of smaller battles across a frontage of some 25 miles. It had been conceived originally as a combined offensive, but with the French army under increasing pressure at Verdun, the greater burden had fallen on the British. After the failure of Rawlinson's 4th Army to break through on 1 July, Gough's Reserve (later renamed the 5th) Army took over the northern part of the battlefield, and from 2 to 13 July the two in concert tried to carry the assault into the German second main defensive position in what became known as the Battle of Albert.

Sharp fighting continued across the whole front for the rest of the month, Rawlinson managing to seize 6,000 yards of the German line between Longueval and Bazentin-le-Petit. From 23 July to 5 August, three Australian divisions of Gough's army fought a costly but eventually successful battle for the village of Pozières in order to open an alternative approach from the rear to the formidable Thiepval defences, while Rawlinson also tried to support the renewed French effort towards Péronne.

By mid-September, with the assistance of the new secret weapon – the tank – Rawlinson felt ready to assault the German third line of defences. However, though Flers and Courcelette fell, the advance was limited to about 2,500 yards on a 3-mile front, the Germans holding on to Morval and Lesboeufs for a further ten days, at which point the attack finally stalled.

Throughout, Haig remained confident of a German collapse. In part this was because his chief of intelligence, Brigadier-General John Charteris, in an effort to maintain Haig's morale, had begun to downplay reports of German strength and over-state reports of German weakness. Towards the end of September he told Haig that 'the Germans may collapse before the end of the year'. Captain (later Major Sir) Desmond Morton, from 1917 one of Haig's ADCs and after the war a member of the Secret Intelligence Service (and one of

Churchill's principal advisers in his so-called 'wilderness years'), wrote of the perverse relationship: 'Haig hated being told any new information, however irrefutable, which militated against his pre-conceived ideas or beliefs. Hence his support for the desperate John Charteris, who was incredibly bad as head of GHQ intelligence, who always concealed bad news, or put it in an agreeable light.'

On 26 September Haig launched Gough's 5th Army against Thiepval Ridge, which had hitherto defied all attempts at capture. Mouquet Farm and Thiepval fell, but fighting in the infamous Schwaben Redoubt went on until the middle of October, with the Canadian Corps continuing in their desperate battle for Regina Trench until 10 November. Further south, Rawlinson had made painful progress towards Le Transloy, capturing Le Sars on 7 Octo-ber, but in November the battlefield turned into a quagmire, and even Haig became doubtful that further attacks would bring about the enemy's collapse. However, he was about to attend an inter-allied conference, first with the other commanders-in-chief and chiefs of staff at Chantilly, Joffre's headquarters, and then with ministers in Paris, to discuss the strategy for 1917, and reasoned that if he could stage a late success, reducing the German salient between Serre and the Albert–Bapaume road in the Ancre sector, it would give him greater moral authority in the discussions – not least with Lloyd George, who as secretary of state for war was begin-ning to doubt both Haig's competence and the priority given to the Western Front as the decisive theatre of operations.

Gough, ever a 'thruster', readily agreed to one more push. On leaving his headquarters for Chantilly, Haig gave him instructions to limit his objectives in the event of serious setback, but without being specific. On 13 November, in appalling conditions, Gough attacked astride the River Ancre, north of Thiepval, and with great sacrifice the 51st (Highland) Division managed to take Beaumont-Hamel. The 63rd (Royal Naval) Division – Royal Marines, and naval reservists surplus to requirements at sea who had volunteered for land service – proved no less determined. They had seen action at Antwerp and Gallipoli, but were taking part in their first attack on the Western Front. Novices, perhaps, they were nevertheless exceptionally well led. The commanding officer of the Hood Battalion (their naval units were named after famous sailors – Drake, Nelson, Collingwood etc.) was the New Zealander Bernard Freyberg, much admired as a divisional and corps commander at El Alamein and Monte Cassino in the Second World War. During the Ancre attack he would win the VC – one of the fifty awarded during the Somme offensive – and gain the nickname 'Salamander' for his ability to live through fire. While the Naval Division captured Beaucourt, their losses were heavy. In the Hawke Battalion, only two officers survived unscathed. One of them, the future humorist, author and parliamentarian A. P. Herbert, drew on the experience for his first novel, *The Secret Battle* (1919), an unflattering picture of the way the war was fought.

In six days' fighting on the Ancre, 5th Army lost some 22,000 men, though the Germans' losses were considerably higher as they held on stubbornly to the northern part of the line. With mud claiming the few available tanks and making all communication difficult, by 18 November the battle had petered out. All it had achieved was the creation of a most unwelcome salient, and Haig now 'closed down' the Somme offensive.

For some, however, cut off by German counter-attacks, the fighting went on regardless. Perhaps the most tragically inspiring episode was the stand by ninety men of the 16th Battalion Highland Light Infantry, a 'Pals battalion' recruited originally from ex-members of the Glasgow Boys' Brigade (the first voluntary uniformed youth movement in the world), who were isolated in the Frankfurt Trench near Beaumont Hamel. On 21 November the Germans sent a party along the trench to take them prisoner, but were repulsed by small-arms fire. The following day – on which the Glaswegians' food ran out – the Germans attacked again, and again were seen off. The Glasgow men continued to fortify their positions, hoping for relief that evening, but attempts to reach them failed. On Thursday, 23 November, after a sharp artillery bombardment, the Germans attacked once more. They were driven back by the fire of the Lewis (light machine) guns, but the bombardment had killed several men, wounded many more and destroyed part of the trench, including the makeshift water reservoir of melted snow. Next day, the Germans attacked yet again, mortally wounding Company Sergeant-Major George Lee. As he was taken down from the parapet, Lee, who had been a foreman in the Glasgow roadways department, said three words: 'No surrender, boys.'

On the Saturday a small party of Germans approached with a white flag and a captured Inniskilling Fusilier who delivered a message from the German battalion commander: 'Surrender quietly and you will be well-treated. Otherwise you may take what is coming to you.' The few unwounded Highland Light Infantrymen took a vote and decided not to reply. After dark several of them crawled out to find water, while the rest waited for the attack, but the night passed quietly.

The following morning, Sunday, with one drum of Lewis-gun ammunition left, the remnants found themselves surrounded in force. The Germans rushed the position and quickly overcame the last few defenders. Of the original ninety Highland Light Infantry, there remained only some thirty wounded, many of them badly, and a handful of unscathed men to be made prisoner. Some were taken to the German brigade headquarters for questioning. On seeing the starving, filthy, frozen and exhausted 'Pals', the interrogating officer could not believe they had held out so long: 'Who are you and where have you come from?' Defiant to the end, they answered only with their number, rank and name.

They might well have said that they were the men, or in some cases replacements for the men (for the Glasgow Boys' Brigade Battalion had lost heavily on the first day of the Somme), deemed incapable on 1 July of doing more than advance in line to take the German trenches that would have been destroyed by artillery fire.

In his despatch to London the following month, Haig claimed the Somme offensive as a considerable success:

The enemy's power has not yet been broken ... [but] despite all the advantages of the defensive, supported by the strongest fortifications, [the German army] suffered defeat on the Somme this year. Neither victors nor the vanquished will forget this; and, though bad weather has given the enemy a respite, there will undoubtedly be many thousands in his ranks who will begin the new campaign with little confidence in their ability to resist our assaults or to overcome our defence. Our new Armies entered the battle with the determination to win and with confidence in their power to do so. They have proved to themselves, to the enemy, and to the world that this confidence was justified, and in the fierce struggle they have been through they have learned many valuable lessons which will help them in the future.

The Somme has its apologists still, for the offensive was not entirely futile. The Germans found it difficult to transfer divisions to reinforce their faltering offensive at Verdun. Their new commander-in-chief, Paul von Hindenburg, began to press the Kaiser to authorize unrestricted submarine warfare to bring Britain to her knees, a desperate measure which only brought the United States into the war. Early in 1917 German troops would withdraw some 25 miles to the *Siegfriedstellung* ('Fortress Siegfried'). The British army on the Western Front – predominantly 'green' troops, the men who had flocked to the recruiting offices in 1914 – had also learned a great deal about how to fight (those, that is, who survived).

Some 130,000 British troops had been killed, however, with irreplaceable losses among junior officers and experienced NCOs. German losses remain disputed, but they were significantly less, though they too lost much 'quality'. The withdrawal to the *Siegfriedstellung* would give them better ground to hold and a shorter front, allowing them to withdraw thirteen divisions into reserve. And while Hindenburg may have been prompted to urge unrestricted submarine warfare, the naval C-in-C, Reinhard Scheer, had been pressing for it since the Battle of Jutland at the end of May, and given the increasing success of the blockade in starving Germany of food and raw materials, the Kaiser could not have resisted the pressure indefinitely.

Nor was an offensive the only or even the best way to help the French at Verdun. Sending them heavy artillery and aircraft, and taking over more of the allied line to release French troops, would have been options better suited to Haig's situation and his green regiments. Above all, persuading the French to stop playing to the Germans' game plan by mounting costly counter-attacks to recover ground of no importance except to national (or, more correctly, to Joffre's) prestige would have preserved France's fighting strength.

In his memorandum to the cabinet, Lord Lansdowne wrote: 'No one for a moment believes we are going to lose this war, but what is our chance of winning it in such a manner, and within such limits of time, as will enable us to beat our enemy to the ground and impose upon him the kind of terms which we so freely discuss?' He concluded that a negotiated peace would be preferable – a proposal for which he would be reviled by politicians and soldiers alike. Lloyd George, soon to become prime minister, drew a different conclusion, however: fight the war with better strategy and different men at the head. Unfortunately, his efforts to do so would largely fail.

The losses on the Western Front in 1916 would haunt the British and French ever after. In November 1918 the allies would be too quick to accept the Germans' call for an armistice. In 1919 they would make a bad treaty at Versailles. In the 1930s the French would adopt the catastrophic strategy of the Maginot Line, and the British the policy of appeasement.

29

DECEMBER

The Welsh Wizard

Lloyd George becomes prime minister, and Haig becomes apprehensive

Making Lloyd George war minister was 'the greatest political blunder of Henry's lifetime', Margot Asquith had confided in her diary. After the death at sea of Lord Kitchener on 5 June, the prime minister had offered the War Office to Andrew Bonar Law, leader of the Tories and colonial secretary in the coalition government, but Bonar Law declined in Lloyd George's favour.

Margot saw this as an incipient coup. The failure of the Dardanelles campaign, the humiliating surrender at Kut al-Amara in Mesopotamia, and Jutland – the strategic victory that looked like defeat – had shaken public confidence. 'We are out,' she wrote: 'it can only be a question of time now when we shall have to leave Downing Street.'

The subsequent huge losses on the Somme for no appreciable gain only compounded the sense of drift in war policy. As Churchill wrote, 'the recovery of the Germanic powers in the East [with the defeat of the Brusilov offensive], the ruin of Roumania and the beginnings of renewed submarine warfare strengthened and stimulated all those forces which insisted upon still greater vigour in the conduct of affairs'. In September Asquith's son, Raymond, was killed, which made the prime minister even more withdrawn and difficult to approach. After the Somme offensive was finally abandoned in mid-November, criticism of his apparently half-hearted prosecution of the war became more vocal, echoed in a powerful editorial in *The Times* on 4 December. Two days later Asquith resigned and the King invited Lloyd George to form a government.

In France, the commander-in-chief of the British armies, Sir Douglas Haig, was in two minds about the change, writing to his wife that 'I am personally very sorry for poor old Squiff [Asquith was notoriously fond of drink]. He has had a hard time and even when "exhilarated" seems to have had more capacity and brain power than any of the others. However, I expect more action and less talk is needed now.' He was wary of Lloyd George, however, for the 'action' the new prime minister favoured might not accord with his own plans.

The government in Paris was under pressure too. French losses at Verdun and the Somme, 348,000 and 194,000 respectively, on top of the huge casualties in the opening weeks of the war and the futile counter-offensives of 1915, had brought the army close to exhaustion. On the first day of the Somme it had been 92,000 men short, but because the general staff had accelerated the call-up of 78,000 conscripts of the class of 1916, it was in reality 170,000 men below establishment. Replacements were increasingly difficult to find and to train, with even Catholic priests being called up for service as combatants. It was probably only his African troops that allowed Joffre to hang on until the fighting subsided with the onset of winter. On 12 December the prime minister, Aristide Briand, was forced to form a new administration, replacing General Gallieni as war minister with General Hubert Lyautey, the military governor of Morocco, and managed at last to manoeuvre Joffre out of his previously unassailable position by appointing him to a hollow command – 'general-in-chief of the French armies and technical adviser to the government', face-saving titles but little else – with the consolation of promotion to marshal of France.

In Russia the disintegration of the old order continued. In November the prime minister, Boris Vladimirovich Shtiurmer, was forced to resign, and on 9 December the State Council demanded the removal of the 'dark forces' and the formation instead of a government 'based on the confidence of the country'. Three weeks later, one of the most notorious of the dark forces, Grigori Rasputin, 'the mad monk', whose malign influence over the empress had become almost total, was murdered.

Yet these developments would not immediately curb the military ambitions for 1917. In mid-November, Joffre and Haig, together with the military representatives of the other allies, had agreed at the Chantilly conference to renew their offensives as soon as weather permitted. This was not what the political leaders, meeting at the same time in Paris, had wanted, believing that there could be no breakthrough on the Western Front and that the cost of the continuing strategy of attrition was too great; but they felt obliged to take the military advice nevertheless. They had favoured instead action on the Italian front, or else the Macedonian (Salonika), where a harlequin allied army – French, British, Italian, Russian and Serb – had recently begun a promising counter-offensive against the Bulgarian army. In late 1915, together with German and Austro-Hungarian troops, the Bulgarians had compelled the Serbian army, with their king, Peter, to retreat to the Adriatic through the mountains of Albania. The remnants of the Serbs had then joined the allied army on the northern Greek border, blocking the Bulgarians' advance into nominally neutral Greece. On 19 November 1916, the allies recaptured Monastir (present-day Bitola), the southernmost city of Serbia, and Lloyd George became convinced that there was now an alternative to battering against the brick wall of the Western Front.

One of those wounded during the Monastir offensive was Flora Sandes, the Yorkshire-born daughter of an Anglo-Irish clergyman. She had joined an ambulance unit in 1914 and had worked for eighteen months in a field hospital in Serbia, but during the retreat to Albania had enlisted in the ranks of an infantry regiment, rising to sergeant-major. Later commissioned and awarded Serbia's highest decoration, the *Orden Karađorđeve zvezde* (King George Star), her memoir of the retreat, with its Dunkirk-like evacuation in February 1916 and the move to Salonika via Corfu, was published in London later that year as *An English Woman-Sergeant in the Serbian Army*, with a foreword by the Serbian chief of staff, raising a good deal of money for Serb relief funds.

On 15 December, however, attention turned once again to the Western Front, where a spectacularly successful French attack at Verdun seemed to promise a change of fortune for the allies. Joffre's successor as commander-in-chief, Robert Nivelle, an artillery officer and a hero of the defence of the fortress-city (he had famously issued an order of the day which ended 'Ils ne passeront pas' – they shall not pass – a defiant slogan which in 1940 would be worn on the uniforms of the troops manning the Maginot Line), had planned in detail the attack by four divisions, with four in reserve, following a six-day bombardment by 800 guns firing over a million shells, directed in the latter stages with great precision by observation aircraft. The infantry's advance was preceded by a double 'creeping' barrage (one that progressed by successive bounds) – shrapnel from field artillery 70 yards in front of the leading troops, and HE 150 yards ahead, which then switched to shrapnel along the German second line to cut off retreat and interdict reinforcements. The German defence collapsed, with over half of the 21,000 troops in the forward divisions lost or taken prisoner in their dugouts. By the second night the French had consolidated a new line half a mile beyond Fort Vaux and 2 miles beyond Douaumont, the German line having in all been pushed back nearly 5 miles. When German officers complained about the conditions in the PoW cages, Lieutenant-General Charles Mangin, commanding the offensive, replied wryly: 'We do regret it, gentlemen, but then we did not expect so many of you.'

Briand believed that in Nivelle, a fluent Anglophone (his mother was English), he had at last found his Napoleon. He told Lloyd George that the general had sent telegrams from various places during the advance demonstrating that his objectives were being achieved exactly according to plan. Nivelle now proposed his grand design for 1917: an offensive on the Aisne, promising 'Laon in twenty-four hours and then the pursuit', with the British playing a major supporting role at Arras.

Meanwhile, in Berlin and Washington there was talk of peace. On 12 December Bethmann Hollweg, the German chancellor, called for negotiations without specific conditions or demands. On the surface, this appeared to reflect confidence in Germany's military position, the chancellor declaring that the Central Powers 'have given proof of their indestructible strength in winning considerable successes at war'. However, he knew that time was not on Germany's side. At home, the Social Democrats, the largest party, were increasingly demanding assurances that the country was fighting only in self-defence, not for conquest. Austria-Hungary, the principal ally, was becoming demoralized, notwithstanding the failure of the Brusilov offensive and the advances against Serbia and Romania.

Although Germany's armies now occupied substantial tracts of allied territory, the country faced a coalition with superior manpower resources and access to world markets, while the Royal Navy's blockade was slowly strangling her own economy and starving the home front. Desperate to break the military stalemate, Germany's military and naval leaders were pressing the Kaiser to authorize unrestricted submarine warfare, a course that Bethmann Hollweg feared (correctly) would bring the United States and possibly other neutrals into the war on the allied side. He reasoned that if the allies refused to open peace negotiations, it would be they, not Germany, who were seen as prolonging the war, thereby rallying the wavering Social Democrats to the war effort and screwing Austria-Hungary's courage to the sticking-place. Such a refusal might even mean that the United States would accept the unleashing of the U-boats – and, perhaps the greatest prize, it might spur the anti-war parties in France and Russia to press irresistibly for a separate peace.

Washington's peace initiative was more altruistically motivated.

President Woodrow Wilson, newly re-elected on a platform of keeping the country out of the war, had always seen himself as a mediator, repeatedly urging a discussion of peace terms, usually on some basis of the *status quo ante bellum* together with post-war disarmament. In 1915 and again in early 1916 he had sent his chief foreign policy adviser, 'Colonel' (an honorific peculiar to the Southern states; he had no military experience) Edward House, to Europe for talks with both sides. By way of encouragement, in May 1916 he pledged the United States to a post-war international security organization, a 'league of nations', and in December he called for the belligerents to state the exact objects for which they were fighting. In January 1917, sensing his own country's glide into war, he would make an impassioned plea for a 'peace without victory'.

Wilson was convinced that if either side won a decisive victory, this would simply re-ignite the arms races, alliances and secret diplomacy that in his view had caused the war in the first place. Sooner or later, he reasoned, another global conflict would occur: 'This is the last war of the kind, or of any kind that involves the world, that the United States can keep out of.' An end to the war that gave neither side full achievement of its aims, he believed, would enable a more enduring peace to be made through collective security. Events, however, would overtake his ideals, for once US troops were fighting in France, decisive victory could be the only object.

Notwithstanding the outcomes of the Chantilly and Paris conferences, Lloyd George was determined to take a firm grasp of strategy. The chief of the imperial general staff, Sir William Robertson, assured Haig that despite the talk of peace, prompted largely by the Marquess of Lansdowne's memorandum to the cabinet suggesting that victory was not possible without destroying the nation's vitality, the new prime minister was 'in real earnest to leave nothing undone to win the war ... [but] seemed to wish to pose as the prime instrument and mainspring of the actions of the Allies'. At their first meeting since taking office, on 15 December in the drawing room of No. 11 Downing Street, Asquith having been allowed a little grace to quit No. 10, Lloyd George told Haig that while he acknowledged the Western Front to be the primary theatre of operations, he 'could not believe it was possible to beat the German armies there – at any rate not next year'. This being the case, he wanted to transfer two divisions from France to Egypt for an attack on El-Arish and thence towards Jerusalem, and, temporarily, to send 200 heavy guns to Italy to help General Cadorna take Pola on the Adriatic.

Haig would have none of it, however: his armies were, he said, 'all engaged in preparing for next year's attacks'.

With 'Wully' Robertson strongly backing Haig, Lloyd George had little option but to concede. He would have to trust to General Nivelle's promise of 'victory without tears', and try to clip Haig's wings by placing him under command of Briand's new-found Napoleon.

Nivelle would prove to be no Napoleon, however, and 1917 would be even bloodier than 1916.

PART FOUR

1917

Defeat; and Deliverance

1 February: Germans declare unrestricted submarine warfare.

8 March: Russian revolution begins.

15 March: Russian Tsar Nicholas II abdicates.

6 April: United States declares war on Germany.

16 April: Nivelle offensive begins (preceded by Battle of Arras).

30 June: Greece officially declares war on Central Powers.

31 July: Third Ypres ('Passchendaele') begins.

24 October: Battle of Caporetto (Italian front) begins.

7 November: Bolsheviks overthrow Russian government.

11 December: Allenby enters Jerusalem.

15 December: Armistice agreed between the new Russian government and the Central Powers.

30

JANUARY

The Turnip Winter

*Economic warfare – the Royal Navy's blockade of
Germany – begins to bite*

By 1917, Germany had become, like Frederick the Great's Prussia
(according to Voltaire – or, as some have it, Mirabeau), 'an army
with a country attached to it'. A century earlier, in his seminal work
Vom Kriege (On War), the Prussian military theorist Carl von Clausewitz had concluded that 'war is an act of force . . . [which knows] no
logical limit'. In January 1917, Germany's military leaders, to whom
the Kaiser was now in total thrall, were about to prove Clausewitz
right – and with catastrophic results.

In his memoirs, General Erich Ludendorff, the power behind the
military throne of the chief of staff and effectual viceroy, Field Marshal Paul von Hindenburg, wrote that with the Entente's rejection of
President Wilson's peace initiative in December, 'the war had to continue and to be decided by force of arms. It was to be Victory or
Defeat.' Because the struggle was therefore now existential, 'the results
were further preparations on a large scale, the maintenance of our
determination to fight . . . and at the same time the employment of

223

every weapon in Germany's arsenal'. The German army, he believed, was 'completely exhausted on the Western Front, [nevertheless] our worn-out troops would have to take the offensive as early as possible, and on a greater scale than in the autumn of 1916, if they were to achieve ultimate victory'.

Ludendorff knew that the odds were increasingly against them. Although the Entente offensives of 1916 had all been checked, ultimately, 'the outlook for the coming year was exceedingly grave. It was certain that in 1917 the Entente would again make a supreme effort.' French losses at Verdun and on the Somme had been appalling, 'but she possessed in her colonies extraordinary resources of manpower'. Britain's army was yet to reach its full potential, and the Russians, in reorganizing their forces in the wake of the failed Brusilov offensive, had actually increased their strength. With the cooperation of the exiled Romanian army, re-equipped and retrained by the French, and Austro-Hungarian prisoners of war forming their own Slavic national contingents to fight for the Entente, the Russian bear looked as dangerous as ever. 'In every theatre of war the Entente was able to add to her numerical superiority enormous additional resources in every department of technical supply, and to destroy our troops on a still greater scale than had been achieved on the Somme and at Verdun.'

German strength, on the other hand, was diminishing. Verdun and the Somme had taken serious toll of the army, and the Royal Navy's blockade was sapping morale at home. Ludendorff railed against the civil authorities' lack of resolution to organize ruthlessly for war: 'The law left untouched labour that should have been devoted to the state.' Only men between the ages of seventeen and forty-five were liable for service. At Ludendorff's bidding, Hindenburg now demanded that the liability be extended to men between fifteen and sixty years, and, with certain exceptions, women. He largely got his way, and the so-called Hindenburg Programme introduced comprehensive control of labour, with a consequent doubling in output of war materiel.

Food production remained inadequate, however. Malnutrition,

even starvation, became widespread in the so-called *Kohlrübenwinter* – 'Turnip Winter' – of 1916–17, the blockade exacerbated by the strange inability of the civil authorities to regulate agricultural practice and prices. Farmers fed grain to their animals although its nutritional value as bread was four times that of grain eaten indirectly through meat (the 2 lb loaf had been enough for the pre-war working man's day). Prices incentivized farmers to slaughter stock rather than breed, so that there was a compounding shortage of animals and therefore of manure – resulting in smaller harvests and the need for more fertilizer to be produced by industry at the expense of explosives and other war materiel. Black-market prices rose, and *Reibekuchen mit Rübenkraut* (potato cakes with sugar beet syrup) – still today a curious favourite of German Christmas markets – became a staple in the towns (workers in rural areas tended to fare better). Ironically, it had been the Royal Navy's blockade of Napoleonic Europe a century earlier, cutting off the supply of cane sugar from the West Indies, that had stimulated the growth of beet sugar extraction. Soldiers returning to Germany for leave were shocked to find their families famished. Absenteeism and desertion increased, occasionally with offers of intelligence to the Entente.

Food was not only in short supply at home. Military rations were repeatedly cut, and the high command became increasingly concerned about the monotony of the diet. When the German army launched its last-ditch offensive on the Western Front in March 1918, many a unit's progress faltered on coming across bounteous allied ration dumps. There was also insufficient corn for the army's horses, which were quickly being worn out, so that industry had to produce more mechanical transport instead at the expense of armaments and aircraft production. In turn, the mechanical transport needed more fuel, placing even greater demands on logistics at the front. The cavalry were progressively demounted, their horses sent to artillery and transport units (the shortage of cavalry would play a part in the failure of the March 1918 offensive).

In January 1917, Ludendorff's assessment was bleak in the extreme: 'We could not contemplate an offensive ourselves, having to keep our reserves available for defence. There was no hope of a collapse of any of the Entente Powers. If the war lasted our defeat seemed inevitable.' Indeed, the army 'would not have been able to exist, much less carry on the war, without Roumania's corn and oil.'

The Russian revolution in March (February in the Russian, Julian, calendar) took Berlin by surprise, and would in large part be the German army's saving in 1917.

However, there was one weapon in Germany's arsenal that had yet to be fully employed. In October 1916 submarine warfare against merchant shipping, suspended after the sinking of the *Lusitania* the previous May, had been resumed, but under the so-called 'cruiser rules', with ships stopped, searched and then sunk only if carrying contraband and after the crews had been allowed to take to the lifeboats – a time-consuming and dangerous practice. After the Battle of Jutland on 31 May 1916, with the German surface fleet more or less confined to Wilhelmshaven and the Royal Navy's economic blockade therefore unchallenged, Admiral Henning von Holtzendorff, chief of the imperial naval staff, proposed a counter-blockade by U-boats, sinking without warning any merchant ship within designated 'exclusion zones'. Britain relied on imports of food and war materiel, and unlike Germany had no land borders across which a minimal supply could be maintained. In 1916 the *Kaiserliche Marine* had built over a hundred powerful new submarines able to range into the Atlantic, and a base for the lighter ones at Zeebrugge whence the cross-Channel transports could be attacked. Holtzendorff reckoned he could sink 600,000 tons of shipping per month. Two of Germany's leading economists, Gustav von Schmoller and his pupil Max Sering, a specialist in agrarian economics, stated that this would result in food riots, severe distress in trading areas and the collapse of the British economy, especially if Zeppelins bombed the grain depots in the Channel ports. Britain would therefore be forced to sue for peace, Holtzendorff argued, in which case France could not continue the fight.

The issue was decided on 9 January at a conference at GHQ in Pless Castle (present-day Poland), presided over by the Kaiser.

Theobald von Bethmann Hollweg, the increasingly marginalized chancellor, was sceptical of the naval and economic arguments and fearful of the reaction of neutrals – principally the United States, whose trade with the Entente was considerable, but also Denmark and the Netherlands. After the recent victories in Romania, however, Ludendorff was confident that Denmark and the Netherlands would have no appetite for war, and proposed merely that cavalry patrols on these borders be increased.

The chancellor seemed reassured, asking only that 'military measures which are to be taken with regard to the neutral boundaries, and particularly with regard to the Danish border, be such as not to carry the implication of excessive menace'. Indeed, he conceded: 'We should be perfectly certain that, so far as the military situation is concerned, great military strokes are insufficient as such to win the war. The U-boat war is the "last card." A very serious decision. But if the military authorities consider the U-boat war essential, I am not in a position to contradict them.' What, though, if America were to declare war?

Admiral Holtzendorff jumped up. 'I guarantee on my word as a naval officer that no American will set foot on the Continent!' It was an ill-judged echo of Admiral St Vincent's remark in the Napoleonic wars: 'I do not say the French cannot come [to Britain], I only say they cannot come by sea.' The same hubris, too, would prompt Reichsmarschall Goering to boast in 1939 that 'if one enemy bomber reaches the Ruhr, you may call me Meyer'.

Hindenburg, however, backed his naval counterpart emphatically: 'The war must be brought to an end rapidly, although we would be able to hold out still longer, but haste is needed on account of our allies [who were beginning to falter]' – to which Ludendorff added that the U-boats would bring 'some relief for the western front. We must spare the troops a second battle of the Somme.'

Besides, Hindenburg declared, 'We can take care of America. The opportunity for the U-boat war will never be as favourable again.'

The chancellor looked out of the window at the frozen pond in the park below, rubbed his hand over his clipped grey hair in a familiar gesture of uncertainty, then found his voice: 'Of course, if success beckons, we must follow.'

With his military advisers, and now also the chancellor, urging it, the Kaiser's decision was but a formality. Unrestricted submarine warfare was to begin on 1 February, he said, and 'with the utmost vigour' – at which point he signed the order and, followed by the high command, marched from the room to lunch.

Moments later Baron von Reischach, the *Oberhofmarschall* (Lord Chamberlain), entered the room and found Bethmann slumped in a chair. 'What's the matter?' he asked. 'Have we lost a battle?'

'No,' replied the chancellor, 'but *finis Germaniae*. That's the decision.'

In fact the *finis* was rather slower to begin than feared. The United States broke off diplomatic relations with Germany on 3 February, but President Wilson said he would take no further action unless Germany committed 'overt acts' by actually sinking American vessels. On the same day, the grain ship *Housatonic* was torpedoed off the Scillies. Ironically, she bore the same name as the first ship ever sunk by a submarine – the USS *Housatonic*, sunk by the Confederate submersible *Hunley* off Charleston, South Carolina, in 1864. But the grain ship *Housatonic* was sunk under cruiser rules, by Hans Rose of U-53, who had paid a 'courtesy visit' to Newport, Rhode Island the previous October before sinking several neutrals within sight of the Nantucket lightship a few days later. Rose stopped the *Housatonic* with warning shots, then sent his crew aboard to open the sea-cocks. They returned to the submarine with armfuls of soap, explaining that it was in short supply in Germany owing to the demands of the munitions industry for glycerine. Only when the *Housatonic*'s crew were in the lifeboats did Rose hasten her to the bottom with a torpedo.

Indeed, it would take another eight sinkings – and the discovery, through the so-called Zimmerman telegram (the 'suicide note written in farce'), that Germany was encouraging Mexico to invade – to provoke Congress into a declaration of war on 6 April.

Even so, it looked at first as if Admiral Holtzendorff's promises would be fulfilled. In January, under cruiser rules, his U-boats sank 368,000 tons of shipping; in February they sank 540,000; in March they almost reached the projected figure of 600,000 tons, and in April sank 881,000. Holtzendorff's mistake, however, was to assume that the Royal Navy – and soon the US Navy – would find no answer to the threat. Initially the Admiralty was reluctant to introduce convoys in the Atlantic, not least because the Grand Fleet needed the escort destroyers, but in May, Admiral Jellicoe, now the first sea lord, conceded to the demands of the prime minister, David Lloyd George. With the introduction of improved depth charges, a primitive hydrophone (developed by the New Zealand physicist Sir Ernest Rutherford) and more float planes, sinkings quickly fell back to pre-February levels.

Nor had Holtzendorff been alone among professional naval officers in believing that unrestricted submarine warfare would be decisive. In June 1917, a still sceptical Jellicoe told the war cabinet that nothing could be done to defeat the U-boats at sea, and that unless the army could capture their bases on the Belgian coast it was 'improbable that we could go on with the war next year for lack of shipping'.

However, by the end of the year the 'Dover Barrage', the mine and steel-netting barrier laid north of the Dover Straits, had been much strengthened, effectively closing the straits to submarines operating out of Zeebrugge and Ostend. Between May 1917 and November 1918, over two million American troops would be transported across the Atlantic in convoy, with fewer than 700 killed as a result of U-boat attacks.

Bethmann had been right: after 9 January 1917, it was *finis Germaniae*. The only questions were how, exactly, and when.

31

FEBRUARY

Biblical Terms

Lloyd George tries to turn attention to a land he knows

Raised in the strong evangelical tradition of Welsh Nonconformity, David Lloyd George had probably the best grasp of biblical geography of any British prime minister in history. At the Versailles peace conference after the war, he reduced the French premier, Georges Clemenceau, to silence by suggesting the British mandate in Palestine should run 'from Dan to Beersheba'. It was perhaps not surprising, then, that on becoming prime minister at the end of 1916, dismayed by the continuing slaughter on the Western Front, he should turn his eyes east to the Holy Land.

Initially he had to play his cards close to his chest, for the Germans on the Western Front could obviously not be beaten in Palestine, and the allied generals, not least the chief of the imperial general staff, Sir William Robertson, were intent on continuing their war of attrition in France. Lloyd George's motives were undoubtedly mixed. He had an instinctive dislike of the Turks and wanted Britain to play a greater role in the Middle East after the war. Diverting troops eastwards would also limit the generals' ability to mount offensives in France. Above all, perhaps, he wanted a victory somewhere – anywhere – to raise public morale in what was clearly going to be a long and bloody fight. 'Jerusalem by Christmas' (1917) became his objective.

However, the Ottoman Empire – its ethnic Turkish troops especially – had so far proved a far tougher adversary than expected. In January 1916 the Dardanelles campaign had ended in the humiliating (if brilliantly conducted) evacuation of the Gallipoli peninsula, and then in April the British army suffered one of its worst ever defeats when 10,000 British and Indian troops were forced to surrender at Kut al-Amara in Mesopotamia after a four-month siege. Yet Lloyd George had reason to be optimistic. General Sir Archibald Murray's meticulous logistic planning for the advance of the Egyptian Expeditionary Force from the Suez Canal across the Sinai desert into Southern Palestine was beginning to yield rewards. In December, Murray's British, Anzac and Indian troops, few of whom were regulars, had taken El-Arish, opening up the coastal road, and then, in January, Rafa on the Gaza frontier. It looked as if Lloyd George would indeed have a great victory for the public to celebrate, and long before Christmas.

The shame of Kut was also being expunged. The fortress-town, gateway to Baghdad, was about to be retaken. The campaign in Mesopotamia was primarily about oil, discovered just before the war in large quantities around Basra and Mosul; but there were also other considerations. Success here would discourage any Turkish attempts to foment discontent among India's Muslims, demonstrate that the British were still in control and encourage an Arab revolt against Ottoman rule which would ease the threat to the Suez Canal and hasten the defeat of the Ottoman Empire. Baghdad, therefore, Mesopotamia's administrative capital, some 300 miles upstream of Basra, was – and remained – a considerable prize.

After the surrender of Kut in April, London had taken over control of the campaign from Delhi, removing Lieutenant-General Sir John Nixon as head of the Mesopotamian Expeditionary Force and instructing his replacement, Lieutenant-General Sir Frederick

Maude, to consolidate around Basra. Maude, a systematic Cold-streamer and experienced general, ignored these instructions and began instead to plan the recapture of Kut. By December, having gathered reinforcements to form two corps (50,000 men), thoroughly reorganized his logistic support and at last put the medical services on a footing comparable with those on the Western Front, he persuaded the reluctant 'Wully' Robertson to authorize an advance.

Progress was slow initially because of heavy rain and Robertson's insistence – under the shadow of the Somme – on minimizing casualties. Nevertheless, on 24 February 1917 Maude drove the Turks from Kut, harrying their retreat with a flotilla of Royal Navy gunboats. Barely pausing to consolidate, two days later he renewed the advance and on 11 March took Baghdad.

With Mesopotamia apparently all but won and the Egyptian Expeditionary Force now through Sinai, it looked as if Britain was set to knock Turkey out of the fight, thereby changing the course of the war in the southern Balkans, drawing in precious Austrian and German reserves from both Western and Eastern Fronts and relieving pressure on Russia, about to erupt in revolution. Buoyed up with his success in taking Rafa, and believing Ottoman morale to be crumbling, on 26 March Murray launched a hasty offensive at Gaza, gateway to Palestine. However, the Turks, advised by the Bavarian Colonel Friedrich Kress von Kressenstein, and alerted by aerial reconnaissance to the attempts at encirclement, were not yet done. Murray, highly regarded as a staff officer but lacking the vital energy of a commander, tried to direct the battle from his headquarters railway carriage at El-Arish, 50 miles away. His divisional commanders, dismayed by mounting casualties and what appeared to be strong defences (though in fact they were thin), broke off battle after a single day's fighting.

The stakes were high, and Murray's report encouraged London to order another assault. The second Battle of Gaza, in mid-April, would be a more deliberate affair, in which tanks were used for the first time in the Middle East – but just eight of them, widely separated in a frontal assault 'to frighten the life out of them [the Turks]'.

Without adequate artillery support – though with another innovation, gas shells – against strengthened defences, the attack was no more successful than frontal assaults in France, and almost as bloody. In June, Murray would be relieved – as he had been from his two previous appointments – and replaced by Sir Edmund Allenby, whom Field Marshal Haig had just removed from 3rd Army in France.

Never did Haig do better service than in sacking Allenby from his European command. In November, adopting a plan devised by Lieutenant-General Sir Philip Chetwode, John Betjeman's future father-in-law, he would break through the Gaza defences by a surprise attack at Beersheba – where Abraham and Isaac had dug their seven wells, as Lloyd George would have known, and which now proved a vital watering place for the Desert Mounted Corps, foremost in the subsequent advance.

On 11 December Allenby would enter Jerusalem, dismounting to walk through the Jaffa Gate, a gesture received well by both Jews and Arabs. He had delivered Lloyd George what the prime minister called 'a Christmas present to the nation'. General Maude would not live to hear of it, however: he died in November, of cholera – by coincidence in the same house in Baghdad in which Colmar von der Goltz had succumbed to typhus eighteen months earlier.

32

MARCH
Alberich

Spirits soar as the Germans withdraw to the Hindenburg Line

'One night when we weren't being shelled we heard that the old Hun, as we called him, had pulled out his heavy howitzers and gone.' Henry Williamson, author of *Tarka the Otter* (1927), recalled the surprise and hopefulness in the trenches in March 1917 when Operation Alberich began. Not long afterwards, 'we saw the Bengal Lancers trot past us . . . a wonderful sight'.

As an 18-year-old territorial in the London Rifle Brigade, Williamson had volunteered to serve in France, spending the winter of 1914–15 in the trenches before being evacuated, sick. On recovering he was commissioned into the Bedfordshire Regiment, but specialist training and more sickness kept him in England during the Somme offensive. In March 1917, by then a lieutenant with the Machine Gun Corps, he was in the line just south of Arras when the Germans began pulling out. However, rumours that 'the Hun was packing up altogether' soon proved wide of the mark. Operation Alberich was a strategic withdrawal to more defensible ground.

The losses at Verdun and the Somme in 1916, and the Austrian setbacks on the Eastern and Italian fronts, had left the German army much weakened and short of artillery ammunition. Its 154 divisions on the Western Front were ranged against 190 French, British and Belgian (many of them much stronger than the Germans'), soon to be reinforced by the *Corpo Expedicionário Português* (Portuguese Expeditionary Force – some 55,000 infantry and supporting arms) and their independent heavy artillery corps. Against these forces, and certain that the allies would renew their attacks, in January 1917 Hindenburg decided to go onto the strategic defensive until he could find more troops. He told the Kaiser that they must 'let the U-boat commanders show what they can do'.

His chief of staff, Erich Ludendorff, advocated falling back to a new line of defence – the *Siegfriedstellung* ('Siegfried Fortress-Position') – to eliminate two salients between Arras and St-Quentin, and between St-Quentin and Noyon, which had been formed during the Somme offensive. The line – at its furthest point, some 30 miles back, and 90 miles long – had been reconnoitred as early as August 1916 in case of an allied breakthrough, and rudimentary trenches dug. Hindenburg now ordered that stronger defences be prepared. Not surprisingly, to the Entente these would become known as the 'Hindenburg Line'.

On ground of their own choosing, well away from the day-to-day fighting, industrial construction techniques could be used instead of digging under fire. Several hundred thousand men, including German and Belgian civilians and 50,000 Russian PoWs, laboured on the *Siegfriedstellung* throughout January and February. The defences consisted not merely of trenches (some of them 5 metres deep and 4 metres wide) but pillboxes – *Mannschafts-Eisen-Beton-Unterstände* ('iron-reinforced concrete shelters for troops'). These allowed machine guns to dominate the ground, obviating the need to rely on massed infantry rifles. Many were sited on reverse slopes, making them difficult to pinpoint, with a line of lightly defended outposts a mile or so in front to slow down any attack. It was a looser system of defence than the rigid lines of the Somme, making a 'battle zone' up to 4 miles deep, better able to absorb attacks, and in turn making the attacker more vulnerable to counter-attack. As the war went on, anti-tank ditches were also dug.

As well as providing the defenders with better ground to hold, by eliminating the two salients the move to the Hindenburg Line shortened the front by some 25 miles, releasing thirteen divisions into reserve.

The allies were not unaware of the activity. As far back as October the RFC had reported new trench lines far behind the Somme front, and the following month aerial photography revealed a complete new line of defences, 70 miles long, from Bourlon Wood north to Quéant, Bullecourt, the Sensée river and Héninel, joining the German third (reserve) line near Arras. This in itself was not indicative of the scale of Alberich; the British, too, were constructing precautionary fall-back positions. Even the forcible evacuation of thousands of French civilians (perhaps as many as 125,000, while the elderly, women and children were left behind with minimal rations) revealed nothing definite, for the Germans had never shown any qualms about uprooting potential spies and *francs tireurs* in the forward areas.

As winter drew on – the worst winter of the war, the frozen ground so hard that bursting shells were lethal at several times the usual distance – the construction was increasingly masked by bad flying weather. GHQ concluded that the work was tactical and routine. Indeed, until late January it is probable that Ludendorff – and thus Hindenburg – intended withdrawing to the new line only if there were an actual allied offensive. Besides, Field Marshal Haig and the new French commander-in-chief, Robert Nivelle, doubted that any soldier would willingly abandon ground, especially that on which he had spilled so much blood, however valueless or however much of a liability that ground had become. This assumption harked back to their historical understanding of battle – that he who was in possession of the ground at the end of the fighting was the winner. Ludendorff himself was only too aware of the moral effect of withdrawing, writing in his memoirs: 'It implied a confession of weakness bound to raise the *morale* of the enemy and lower our own.'

When at last, in March, Nivelle realized that the Germans were indeed retiring, and his staff warned that his own plans for an offensive would be seriously derailed as a result, he declared that 'if he had whispered orders to Hindenburg, the latter could not have better executed what he desired'. And as late as 17 April, Haig would tell the director of military operations at the War Office that it would be 'the height of folly for the French to stop [their offensive] now, just when the Germans had committed the serious fault of retiring, meaning to avoid a battle, but had been forced to fight against their will'.

However, the 'Alberich manoeuvre' was not merely a withdrawal; it also involved a scorched-earth operation. Nothing of use to the allies was to be left standing in the country abandoned. Houses were to be destroyed – whole towns and villages razed to the ground – railways dug up, bridges blown, road junctions mined, wells fouled or filled in (some may have been poisoned), even fruit trees cut down, and booby traps – ranging from simple pieces of duckboard in trenches which, when stepped on, would detonate grenades, to a huge delayed-action mine under Bapaume town hall – laid to make the allies wary of following up too quickly. Three- and six-inch steel 'crow's feet' – caltrops – were sown in the river bottom at every ford to puncture horses' hooves.

The operation was indeed well named. In German mythology, Alberich was the malevolent dwarf who guarded the treasure of the *Niebelungen*, and was eventually overcome by the hero Siegfried. Crown Prince Rupprecht of Bavaria, commanding the group of armies in the northern sector, learning of the scale and methods of the proposed operation, was appalled and contemplated resigning. He only stayed his hand because he thought his departure might suggest that a rift had developed between Bavaria and the rest of Germany. Churchill wrote that the Germans 'left their opponents in the crater fields of the Somme, and with a severity barbarous because far in excess of any military requirements, laid waste with axe and fire the regions which they had surrendered'.

Ludendorff saw the position rather differently:

We had to put up with the fact that the Entente turned our exceedingly thorough demolition of the territory and dispersal of the population to account, in order once more to call us Huns, and to play the organ of their propaganda with all the stops pulled out. One cannot blame them. Nevertheless, we had acted in accordance with the laws of warfare, and had not even gone as far as the belligerents in the American Civil War.

The actual withdrawal took place between 16 and 20 March and yielded more French territory than any action since the counter-attack on the Marne in September 1914. Indeed, it seemed at first to be an excellent opportunity for the British and French cavalry, including the Indian regiments that Henry Williamson saw, to have their long-awaited gallop at the enemy. But in following up the Germans – as far as their aggressive rearguards permitted (their artillery was perfectly ranged on every bridge and crossroads) – cavalry and infantry alike were shocked at the conditions wrought by the weather, their own guns and the scorched-earth policy. The divisional history of the 62nd (West Riding) Division, in which Williamson was serving, records that

> trenches as such did not exist, for they had been obliterated by the con-
> centrated fire of the guns . . . The front line was held by a series of posts
> and dugouts which somewhat resembled islands in a sea of mud. Shell
> holes pock-marked the ground, often overlapping one another and
> where pathways existed between them they were but a few inches
> wide. The holes were full of water and more than one man lost his life
> through slipping off the narrow pathway into the slimy mass which
> engulfed him.

The problem of getting up supplies was prodigious. After a while even the stocks of insulated telegraph cable, on which the entire system of communications relied, ran out. The Royal Engineers, ever resourceful, did their best to recover German wire, using wine bottles with the bottoms knocked out as insulators, fixed on pea-sticks. Pursuit was inordinately slow. Indeed, the cavalry frequently found themselves having to mark time while necessaries were got forward for the infantry and artillery, as well as having the greatest difficulty themselves finding feed and water for the horses. The Wiltshire Yeomanry reported that between 20 and 29 March, through shortage of forage, they lost twenty-two horses dead and thirty-five unfit for service.

Nor had the horses started the pursuit in the best of condition. Because of shortages of, and interruption to, shipping that winter, in part owing to the U-boats, the forage ration for the cavalry had been severely cut – from 12 lb of both oats and hay per day to 9 lb of oats and 6 lb of hay. It was not restored until late April, when in addition certain amounts of bran (not a great nutrient) and linseed were issued as a supplementary ration. The 9th Lancers had used thatch from their billets in lieu of hay.

Nevertheless, there were several brisk actions. On 27 March, the Canadian Cavalry Brigade, commanded by Brigadier-General J. E. B. (Jack) Seely, the former British war minister (who shared initials with the great Confederate cavalry leader J. E. B. Stuart), was ordered to take what remained of the village of Guyencourt. In the course of doing so, Lieutenant Frederick Harvey, of Lord Strathcona's Horse, won the VC – dismounted, displaying the skill that had made him an Irish rugby international. His citation recounts that

> a party of the enemy ran forward to a wired trench just in front of the village, and opened rapid fire and machine-gun fire at a very close range, causing heavy casualties in the leading troop. At this critical moment, when the enemy showed no intention whatever of retiring, and fire was still intense, Lt. Harvey, who was in command of the leading troops, ran forward well ahead of his men and dashed at the trench, skilfully manned, jumped the wire, shot the machine-gunner and captured the gun.

But in truth, in the two years of trench warfare the BEF as a whole had lost the habit of movement. Later that year, when again they were able to break out from the trenches – temporarily – General Edmund Allenby, commanding 3rd Army, would say they were like 'blind puppies', unable to make use of ground.

The British and French needed eight weeks to rebuild the roads, bridges and railways in the abandoned area before they could launch their own spring offensive – exactly as Ludendorff had intended.

As the year wore on, the Hindenburg Line would be progressively strengthened, extending eventually from the North Sea to the Vosges, in five distinct zones, or *Stellungen*, each bearing a name from German mythology: Wotan, Siegfried, Alberich, Brunhild and Kriemhild, with supporting lines Hunding and Freya. These were formidably strong positions in which to hold out against allied attacks, and to garner strength for their own great offensive in 1918.

Meanwhile, as the Germans settled into their new fortress-quarters, they were to receive an unexpected windfall. On 15 March (2 March in the old Julian calendar), as revolution swept through Petrograd, the Tsar abdicated. With the imperial Russian army and navy disintegrating, Ludendorff promptly withdrew ten divisions from the Eastern Front.

The following month, however, German fortunes would take a turn for the worse with the entry of the United States as 'co-belligerents' on the side of the allies. Berlin's window of opportunity to defeat what remained of the Entente would begin to close. Everything now depended on the U-boats' ability to starve the British, keep the Americans at arm's length and buy time for one last throw of the dice on the Western Front.

33

APRIL

The Cruellest Month

The great French 'Nivelle offensive' fails dismally, and with it the British, though the Canadians show their mettle

'Battles are won by slaughter and manoeuvre,' wrote Churchill. 'The greater the general, the more he contributes in manoeuvre, the less he demands in slaughter.'

After the Somme, the new prime minister, David Lloyd George, came to the same conclusion. His commander-in-chief on the Western Front, Sir Douglas Haig, offered only a repeat of the costly frontal attacks of 1916. Lloyd George thought him 'brilliant – to the top of his boots'.

But who might replace him?

In October 1914, as both sides dug in and stalemate developed, Lloyd George, then chancellor of the exchequer, called on General Noël Castelnau, commander of the French 2nd Army. How many troops did he have? asked the future prime minister. Nine army corps, was the answer. That was more than Napoleon had ever commanded in a single battle, replied 'LG'.

'Ah, Napoleon, Napoleon,' said Castelnau, with a sigh; 'if he were here now, he'd have thought of the "something else".'

In January 1917 the French prime minister, Aristide Briand, having finally managed to sideline the long-serving commander-in-chief Joseph Joffre, began singing the praises of a new Napoleon – Robert Nivelle. Like Napoleon, Nivelle was an artilleryman, and he appeared to have mastered the potential of the 'creeping barrage', which at last promised to allow the infantry to break through the German defences. At the inter-allied conference in Rome that month Briand told Lloyd George and Paolo Boselli, the Italian prime minister, that during the counter-offensive at Verdun in December, Nivelle had sent telegrams from various places during the advance demonstrating that his objectives were being achieved exactly according to his plan. Briand was sure that the grand offensive his new C-in-C was planning would be decisive. When the Italian C-in-C, Luigi Cadorna, suggested instead a combined offensive against the Austrians on the Italian front, 'LG', wary of promised breakthroughs in France, was at once enthusiastic. However, the chief of the imperial general staff, the gruff ranker General Sir William Robertson, argued that the priority must remain the Western Front. Unfortunately, Cadorna backed down, apparently impressed by Anglo-French military solidarity.

Lloyd George met Nivelle in Paris on his way back to England and, reassured by his confidence, invited him to London. Later that month Nivelle addressed the war cabinet in perfect English (his mother was British) and made a strong impression. When he left, Colonel Maurice Hankey, the cabinet secretary, wrote in his diary: 'Lloyd George would like to get rid of Haig, but cannot find an excuse.'

Instead, he proposed subordinating the BEF to the French high command for the coming offensive. Haig – since 1 January, by the express wish of the King, Field Marshal Haig – refused, arguing that Nivelle could rely on his best support but could not order him precisely how and when to give it. Lloyd George backed down, with some face-saving formula for all parties, but the episode left a bitter taste in Haig's mouth and did nothing to improve the prime minister's view of his new field marshal.

In March Nivelle began issuing peremptory instructions nevertheless, to which Haig objected both as a matter of military principle and because he did not 'believe our troops would fight under French leadership'. Resignations threatened, Haig writing in his diary that he 'would rather be tried by court martial', and although things quietened down, the row led to Briand's resignation.

It was while all this was going on that the Germans had decided to fall back to the *Siegfriedstellung* or 'Hindenburg Line'. As information about the move came through, many of Nivelle's own subordinates began urging him to abandon his plans. General Joseph Micheler, commanding the army group formed to exploit the anticipated victory, argued that the Germans were now in too strong a position. They had many more troops and artillery available for counter-attack, including those now being transferred from the Eastern Front after the Tsar's abdication and the near-collapse of the Russian army. He begged Nivelle to stand on the defensive instead and send troops to Italy to gain a victory there before the Germans did.

Nivelle was not deterred, however: 'Laon in twenty-four hours and then the pursuit. You won't find any Germans in front of you.'

Indeed, the more his generals voiced their concerns, the more vaunting became his predictions. They would break through 'with insignificant loss' and in three days at most would be in open country on their way to the Rhine: 'Nous les verrons Verdunés,' he claimed: 'We shall see them "Verdunned".'

On 24 March, Paul Painlevé, France's new war minister and a future prime minister, visited Haig and 'questioned [him] closely about Nivelle'. Haig was guardedly supportive, writing in his diary that 'I was careful to say that he struck me as a capable general, and that I was, of course, prepared to co-operate with whoever was chosen by the French government to be their C-in-C ... my relations with Nivelle are and always have been *excellent*.'

Haig's sense of soldierly solidarity when faced with a politician (especially 'an extreme socialist', as he described Painlevé) prevented his speaking his mind. Perhaps with the offensive only a fortnight away he believed the die was cast, and any doubts expressed only likely to do harm. It was a catastrophic mistake.

Still Painlevé was not convinced. Having heard the discordant voices (traditionally shriller in the French army than in the British), he tried to persuade Nivelle to heed his generals. This was an impossible proposition, and nonsensical too, for either a C-in-C was to be trusted to come to the best military judgement or he was not, in which case dismissal was the only option.

Nivelle threatened to resign. Painlevé, though a brilliant mathematician, could not find the formula or the confidence to – in effect – dismiss 'the victor of Verdun', and backed down. He would count it as the costliest mistake of his long political career.

At first things seemed to go well for the Nivelle offensive. The BEF, in its supporting role, was to make a preliminary attack along a 15-mile front at Arras and at Vimy Ridge to draw German reserves away from the coming French assault on the ridge of the Chemin des Dames above the River Aisne. This it began on 9 April, Easter Monday, in a snowstorm, spearheaded by 3rd Army under Sir Edmund Allenby. An early casualty was the poet and most lyrical of writers on the English countryside Edward Thomas, thirty-nine years old, not long commissioned and only recently arrived in France, who was killed in a forward observation post, spotting for the guns of his heavy battery.

Progress was encouraging nonetheless. The 9th Scottish Division advanced 4 miles, and the Canadian Corps under the British Lieutenant-General Julian Byng took Vimy Ridge, the dominating heights above the Artois plain, in one of the finest feats of arms in the entire war. This success did not come cheap, however. In the three days' fighting it took to consolidate their gain, some 10,500 Canadians – or 'Byng Boys' as they were soon known – were wounded, and 3,600 killed (the Germans, defending fiercely, suffered 20,000 casualties). What had given the assaulting infantry their chance was an unprecedentedly accurate three-week bombardment, during which many of them were able to shelter from the counter-fire unobserved in tunnels hewn in the chalk of Arras. Isaac Rosenberg, one of the few acknowledged greats of the war poets not to have been commissioned, was serving with the 11th Battalion, The King's Own, a 'Bantam battalion' (consisting of men under the 1914 minimum height of 5 feet 3 inches). In a letter home he wrote: 'We've been in no danger – that is, from shell-fire – for a good long while, though so very close to most terrible fighting. But as far as houses or sign of ordinary human living is concerned, we might as well be in the Sahara Desert.'

Once the attack began, a very precise creeping barrage screened the infantry's advance. It was devised and coordinated in large part by Major Alan Brooke – who in the Second World War would rise to become Field Marshal Lord Alanbrooke, Churchill's 'master of strategy'. British artillery techniques had by this stage become quite sophisticated, including gas shells that neutralized much of the German artillery. On the other hand, the few tanks available were dogged by mechanical failure.

Exploiting success was another matter, however, not least because of the congestion behind the British front, caused in part by the very troops who were to have been the instrument of exploitation – the mass of cavalry, which instead became a target for the enemy's guns. Fighting then descended to what it had been on the Somme – a slogging match, with mounting casualties on both sides (the Australians suffering particularly badly at Bullecourt due to the inveterate self-assurance of the 5th Army commander, Sir Hubert Gough). When the battle ended on 15 May, losses in the BEF had risen to 150,000. Indeed, the daily casualty rate was the BEF's heaviest of the entire war. The following month, Haig sacked Allenby. 'The Bull', as he was known, not entirely affectionately, had fallen foul of those both above and below him. His subordinate commanders felt he had pushed them too hard, while Haig blamed him for failing to break through. It would prove to be one of the most felicitous of Haig's decisions, however. Reassigned to command in Palestine, by Christmas Allenby would take Jerusalem from the Turks.

The French attack, when it came on 16 April – delayed several days by bad weather – faltered almost at once. The German defences were largely on the reverse slope of the Chemin des Dames and therefore hidden from observation, except by air, and although the French had mustered 1,000 aircraft, superior German fighter tactics and bad weather had negated the advantage (the BEF itself lost seventy-five aircraft in the five days preceding its attack). Nivelle's artillery bombardment, by an unprecedented number of batteries, was much less successful than he had predicted, leaving the German machine-gunners to dominate the crest. The French infantry failed to keep up with the creeping – in fact, more a 'running' – barrage, which advanced too quickly at 100 yards a minute, and the attack could get no further than the top of the ridge. By nightfall the infantry had advanced just 600 yards instead of the 6 miles promised in Nivelle's schedule. Of the 132 French tanks massed for the attack (mainly Schneiders), in action for the first time, 57 had been destroyed and 64 had become irretrievably bogged down in the mud.

As Micheler had warned, the Germans had been able to increase the number of divisions on the Aisne substantially – indeed, by a factor of four, so that the French were barely at parity, let alone with the usual superiority of three to one reckoned necessary in the attack. Operational security had also been poor, with divisional orders in some cases being copied down as far as battalion level, so that as soon as the Germans began taking prisoners they were able to piece together Nivelle's intentions. There were even suggestions that Nivelle's critics had leaked the plans – a suggestion that would have been unbelievably far-fetched but for the fevered state of the post-Verdun French army, which within a month would see widespread mutinies.

By 26 April, over 95,000 French wounded had passed through the casualty clearing stations. When the offensive was abandoned a fortnight later, the total number of casualties, dead and wounded, had risen to 187,000. Nivelle's days were numbered.

But who was to succeed him? Paris was badly shaken, and the right answer – the infantryman Philippe Pétain – seemed unthinkable, for he had long been the outsider, refusing to subscribe to the orthodoxy of *offensive à outrance* ('offensive to the utmost') and insisting on the power of the defensive. But some, at least, could see his qualities. At the end of April, the *Times* war correspondent, Charles à Court Repington, wrote anxiously to Lloyd George from Paris:

> I hear that influence is being brought to bear on your side of the water to oppose the appointment of Pétain to the chief command on the ground that he holds certain views which, in fact, he does not hold . . . [I] ask you not to credit the silly chatter which attributes to him a want of go and resolution.
>
> He sees the situation clearly . . . He will not promise the moon as others have done. In this last French offensive our friends have lost 120,000 men, equal to two thirds of the French class of a year, and are much depressed. Pétain foretold the failure to the War Council . . . He sees that we are practically on an equality with the enemy, and must wait until you in England, and the Americans, provide the superiority of force necessary for victory . . . He is against trying to do much with little, and prefers to do little with much . . . He will most certainly support Haig in every way, for the arrest of this mad Rheims offensive [Nivelle's] does not at all imply quietism and want of activity . . . Believe me that he is the best general in France.

Repington, dubbed by his detractors 'the Playboy of the Western Front', was wrong about many things during the course of the war, but not this. Although Pétain, who replaced Nivelle on 15 May, would not be able to contribute much in manoeuvre, he had the sense and courage to stop demanding slaughter.

Unfortunately, as the baton now passed to the British on the Western Front, Haig would not see things the same way.

34

MAY

All Goes Quiet on the Western Front

While the armies lick their wounds,
the allied high commands try to work out 'what next?'

In the wake of the failure of Nivelle's 'mad Rheims offensive', as Repington called it in his letter to Lloyd George, another inter-allied conference was held, in Paris on 4 May, at which 'LG' found himself having to put heart into the new French government, especially its head, Alexandre Ribot, prime minister for a fifth time since 1892. The BEF was now in some respects co-equal with the French army, if not in size then certainly in terms of fighting capability (and Britain's wider war effort – naval and economic – was also now vast); but it was still not strong enough to achieve any significant offensive success on its own. Ribot assured 'LG' that the French nation was still in the fight, but the French army had serious problems of morale to put right first. This job would fall to Pétain, and he would do it well, not least by heeding what every *poilu* was saying – that they would defend the trenches but they would not attack. He told Ribot that the only rational course was to stand on the defensive until conditions changed in favour of the offensive, which to his mind meant more British troops, but principally the arrival of the Americans – and tanks.

Haig, still offensively minded, saw all this as a green light to switch his own effort back to Flanders, and the scheme to take Ostend and Zeebrugge, the viperous nests of U-boats. The previous November, Asquith – then still prime minister – had told the CIGS, Robertson, that there was 'no operation of war to which the War Committee would attach greater importance than the successful occupation, or at least the deprivation to the enemy, of Ostend, and especially Zeebrugge' – and Lloyd George had, of course, been a member of that committee. Now, with 'LG' humbled – hamstrung, even – by having placed his faith in Nivelle, Haig turned the steering wheel to head north-west and put his foot confidently on the accelerator, telling General Sir Herbert Plumer, 2nd Army commander, to dust off the plans he had made a year ago (before, at Joffre's request, Haig had switched the effort to the Somme) for a preliminary attack to take the Messines–Wytschaete Ridge.

The lull in offensive operations was certainly a boon for the RFC, which had suffered so many losses in the previous month that it had become known as 'Bloody April'. Its numerical superiority over the *Deutsche Luftstreitkräfte* – 385 fighters to 114 – had been negated by the Germans' superiority in aircraft technology, organization and pilot training. The Albatros D.II and D.III outclassed most of the RFC's planes except the French SPAD VII and the Sopwith Pup and Triplane, which were few in number and spread along the front. The new generation of allied fighters was not yet fully ready for service, and attempts to rush new aircraft into action proved disastrous. On the first patrol undertaken by the Bristol F2a (a plane that in time was a match for the Albatros), four out of six were shot down in an encounter with five Albatros D.IIIs led by Manfred von Richthofen, the 'Red Baron', who commanded one of the innovative *Jagdstaffeln* (hunting squadrons). During that one month, the RFC lost a third of its fighter force (losses three times those of the Germans), the flying life-expectancy of its pilots falling to just seventeen and a half hours.

'Bloody April' would force the RFC to change its approach to aerial combat, just as the losses over the Somme had forced the Germans to do the year before. It was now accepted that well-trained pilots flying the best planes were more important than mere numerical superiority, and pilot-training schools were reorganized with experienced veterans as instructors.

The consequences of the 'mad Rheims offensive' were also felt further afield. As agreed at the Chantilly conference in November, the Italians had been due to make their own, concurrent, offensive on the Isonzo to keep the German–Austrian alliance at full stretch; but this had been delayed by organizational problems, and it was not until 10 May that the tenth Isonzo offensive was opened on a frontage of 25 miles: thirty-eight Italian divisions against fourteen Austro-Hungarian. By the end of the month the Italians had advanced to within 10 miles of Trieste, but a counter-offensive recovered virtually all lost ground. Cadorna finally closed down the offensive on 8 June, having suffered 157,000 casualties; the Austro-Hungarians lost only half that number. (A simultaneous offensive by French, British and Serbian troops on the Macedonian front was no more successful in its objectives, though much less bloody.) Morale in the Italian army had taken a serious blow, and Cadorna would attempt to restore it by massing his greatest number of divisions yet along the Isonzo for one further attempt to break through towards Trieste.

Meanwhile in Russia, although the provisional government announced that it would stay in the war, troops and peasants were declaring for the anti-war Bolshevik party in increasing numbers. On 16 April, Vladimir Lenin had returned from exile in Switzerland in a special train organized by the Germans. By November his leadership of the Bolsheviks would bring an armistice on the Eastern Front.

Only at sea – and across the Atlantic – did there appear to be good news for the allies. Finally, after much opposition from Sir John Jellicoe, the first sea lord, the Admiralty agreed to introduce the convoy system for merchant ships making the crossing from North

America. The decision would have an almost immediate impact: U-boat losses rose, while the rate of merchant ship sinkings fell equally dramatically. And although it would be several months before Admiral Holtzendorff's promise to the Kaiser that 'on my word as a naval officer . . . no American will set foot on the Continent' would be proved an idle boast, those American troops were already gathering. On 12 May, General John 'Black Jack' Pershing – who would prove one of the most thoughtful but resolute commanders in France – was appointed commander of the American Expeditionary Force. He had surmised something was afoot when on 3 May, at his headquarters on the Rio Grande, from where he was conducting operations on the Mexican border, he had received a cryptic telegram from the father of his late wife, Senator Francis E. Warren of Wyoming: 'Wire me today whether and how much you speak, read, and write French.'

On 18 May, Congress passed the Selective Service Act, enabling the registration and selective draft of men aged between twenty-one and thirty. By November 1918, Pershing would have at his call some two million troops.

35

JUNE

Messines

Victory in a well-planned, well-executed set-piece battle,
but a false promise of future success

At the beginning of 1917 the commanding officer of the Australian 3rd Division, Major-General John Monash – not a soldier by profession but a civil engineer – had astutely characterized the Western Front as above all an 'engineering problem'. Yet GHQ seemed to be tackling it as mobile operations at the halt. Haig continued to think in terms of a breakthrough that would restore the war of movement last experienced in the late summer of 1914, a war in which for some reason he believed the allied armies would have the advantage. Monash and a few others, their voices necessarily muted because there could be no open dissent, thought the situation more akin to siege warfare.

Indeed, the Western Front, with its continuous line of trenches from the North Sea to the Swiss border, had become the largest siege in history. The Germans laid siege to France, the allies to German-occupied Flanders and northern France. And like a gigantic ravelin of some medieval fortress, the German salient south of

Ypres, formed during the fighting in October 1914, threatened, and in some places overlooked, the movement of troops to its north.

For over a year the commander of 2nd Army, General Sir Herbert Plumer, had been working on plans to straighten out the line at Ypres, and much preparatory tunnelling work by the Royal Engineers (with Canadian, Australian and New Zealand engineers), assisted by former coal-miners in the infantry battalions, had been carried out. Undermining fortifications had long been one of the staples of siegecraft. In 1215 King John had famously laid siege to Rochester Castle, tunnelling under the great tower and hollowing out a large cavity, the roof supported with props. Into this his siege-workers packed brushwood and fattened pigs; they then set the chamber alight, and down came the tower. In the seventeenth century, gunpowder had added an explosive dimension to military mining, which soon developed into a specialist arm. Eventually, in 1856, the Corps of Royal Sappers and Miners were incorporated into the Royal Engineers.

With Haig now turning his attention to a major offensive at Ypres, eliminating the German salient became a priority, and he gave Plumer approval to mount a limited operation in early June to take the high ground east of Wytschaete and Messines.

Though Plumer, usually somewhat ponderous, could at times become emotional and even impulsive, he was a meticulous, experienced infantryman. His appearance – slightly portly, with bushy white moustache – entirely belied his capability. Haig almost sacked him shortly after becoming commander-in-chief, but had since developed a solid respect for his fellow officer. With the cloud of the Somme hanging over 4th Army commander, Sir Henry Rawlinson, 'Plum' was the only infantryman to whom he could turn at that level. Nevertheless, bruised by the experience of the Somme, and by Arras in April, Haig was anxious not to see another operation stalled through 'phasing', with deliberate operational pauses, and urged all speed in the attack. This suited Plumer, who although thoroughly realistic about what could be expected of infantry, wanted as short a battle as possible. Initially suggesting three days, as the furthest objective was just 3 miles he finally agreed to Haig's preference for a single day.

Such an ambitious aim would rely on the successful detonation of all the mines more or less simultaneously, followed immediately by the occupation of the shattered German defences. For no student of history, as Plumer and his fellow generals were, would have forgotten the disastrous delay before the Union infantry's attack at Petersburg in the American Civil War after the annihilating explosion of the long-tunnel mine under the Confederate defences.

In the wake of the detonation of the nineteen mines at Messines, therefore, Plumer planned for his infantry to advance in strength protected by a creeping barrage 700 yards deep which progressed at the rate of 50 yards a minute (half that of Nivelle's disastrous barrage at the Chemin des Dames in April), with tanks to help overcome any remaining strongpoints, and gas or flammable bombs from the new man-portable Livens projectors.

Three army corps would take part in the attack – two British (IX and X), and II Australian and New Zealand (Anzac) under command of Lieutenant-General Alexander Godley, an Anglo-Irish officer who had been commandant of the New Zealand Military Force (largely militia) before the war. Each corps comprised four infantry divisions, three of which would take part in the initial assault, with the fourth in reserve.

By early June, twenty-one mine shafts, a total of nearly 9,000 yards of tunnels, had been driven under the German lines across a front of nearly 12,000 yards, and packed with 400 tons of ammonal explosive at depths of between 50 and 100 feet.

Plumer had also studied the lessons of the Somme, not least the necessity of not taking it for granted that massed artillery achieved results. Precision was essential. With the help of the RFC, therefore, a very precise preliminary bombardment was opened on 8 May, followed by a heavier one beginning on 21 May. Some 2,300 guns and 300 heavy mortars fired in all around three million shells. The RFC and French air service had been able to provide the gunners with accurate maps of German artillery positions, and during the bombardment helped correct the fall of shot. By the time the infantry attacked on 7 June, 90 per cent of German guns in and around Messines had been destroyed.

It was by no means easy for the allied gunners, however. Captain Cyril Dennys, in a Royal Artillery heavy howitzer battery, spoke of the particular difficulties and danger of operating near Ypres. The guns could not be placed in a pit because the water level was too high, so a platform had to be made and sandbag walls built for protection. The ground was so devastated

> that the usual camouflage netting might give you away. So we would make the position look as untidy as the surroundings. We used to throw around bits of old sackcloth, sandbags, rum jars – and instead of putting the implements, the battery hand spikes and levers and things in neat order, we used to throw them about. We were told to do this by the RFC pilots. They said, 'For God's sake don't have any kind of order. Have your battery positions as untidy as you can and never allow your men to approach the guns along the same track, or they'll make a path that will be visible from the air.'

A long bombardment signalled to the enemy the intention to attack, of course, but Plumer turned this to his advantage. When a bombardment stopped suddenly, the Germans would at once scramble up the ladders of their deep dug-outs to man the machine guns in anticipation of attack. Plumer therefore timed zero hour, when the mines were to be detonated, at 3.10 a.m., when there was just enough light for a man to be seen from the west at 100 yards, but for the bombardment to cease at 2.50. The Germans, expecting attack, would rush to their defensive positions and then be caught by the explosions.

There was a thunderstorm in the evening of 6 June, but by midnight the sky had cleared, and at 2.00 a.m. the RFC began overflying the German lines to mask the sound of the tanks as they drove up to the start line. By 3.00 a.m. the infantry had reached their forward trenches largely unnoticed, thereby not attracting enemy shelling, and at 3.10 – zero hour – the nineteen mines were detonated over a period of twenty seconds, which magnified the shock and terror in the German lines, for the forward troops had known for months of the tunnelling and become increasingly apprehensive.

'The whole hillside rocked like a ship at sea,' recalled one Australian sapper. 'Then when we got to look at the craters, we saw there were lumps of blue clay as big as small buildings lying about . . . We thought the war was over.'

Major-General Charles Harington, Plumer's chief of staff, had shared that same sense of apocalypse when, at the final conference the day before, he said: 'I do not know whether or not we shall change history tomorrow, but we shall certainly alter geography.'

In London, Vera Brittain, auxiliary nurse and writer (of, among other works, her memoir *Testament of Youth*, covering the war years), felt 'a strange early morning shock like an earthquake.' Lloyd George heard it in 10 Downing Street. It was reportedly heard even in Dublin. The combined near-simultaneous explosions were the loudest man-made sound to that date.

Some 10,000 German troops were killed instantly. Those who survived unscathed were very badly shaken. Some positions were abandoned. Others were surrendered without a shot. But by this stage in the war, German defences had become 'elastic', designed to absorb punishment. The most forward line was relatively lightly defended, and troops were authorized to retire to more heavily defended lines half a mile behind if they came under heavy pressure – acting in effect as reconnaissance patrols, for communications (still predominantly line) were always precarious.

The combination of the artillery preparation, the mines, the creeping barrage and the tanks, and the improved organization and tactics of the infantry, quickly paid off. By 5 a.m. almost all Plumer's initial objectives had been taken. Only on the extreme left was there any appreciable delay as the territorials of the 47th (London) Division struggled to cross the Ypres–Comines Canal. The second phase of the attack began soon afterwards with the reserve divisions carrying on from where the initial attackers were consolidating, supported by tanks and field artillery that at last had their opportunity to gallop forward.

As was standard practice, the Germans counter-attacked the following day, but without success, and indeed with the loss of more ground. The counter-attacks continued, but with decreasing force, until 14 June, by which stage the entire Messines salient was in allied hands.

Messines was probably the finest set-piece action of the war, demonstrating what combined-arms planning and tactics could achieve. And although it begat over-optimism in Haig's plans for his big offensive at the end of July, it was a great boost to morale.

It was certainly not without cost, though: 2nd Army suffered some 24,000 casualties, including over 3,500 who were killed or died of wounds. But the Germans lost probably 35,000, including 7,000 prisoners. Compared with the 60,000 casualties on the first day of the Somme the year before (for the most limited territorial gains), the 'butcher's bill' seemed reasonable.

One of the most poignant losses was that of the Irish Nationalist MP Major Willie Redmond. His brother John, leader of the Irish Parliamentary Party, had urged fellow Nationalists to enlist to further the cause of home rule by proving their loyalty to the King. In November 1914, Willie Redmond had himself made a celebrated speech in Cork, standing at an open window of the Imperial Hotel. Speaking to the crowd below, he ended by shouting: 'I do not say to you, "Go" – but,' – taking off his hat – 'grey-haired and old as I am, I say "Come, come with me to the war!"'

By June 1917 he was a major in the Royal Irish Regiment, in the 16th (Irish) Division consisting in large part of former members of the Irish Volunteers, who had been formed before the war to counter the Ulster Volunteers raised to resist home rule. On 7 June, the 16th (Irish) advanced towards Wytschaete alongside the 36th (Ulster) Division consisting in large part of former Ulster Volunteers. The 57-year-old Redmond, a devout Catholic, was hit by shell splinters and fell in no-man's-land. He was found by an Antrim Protestant, Private John Meeke, a stretcher-bearer with the Ulster Division.

Though coming under machine-gun fire, Meeke managed to bandage Redmond's wounds before himself being wounded, whereupon Redmond ordered him to leave him and take cover. Meeke refused and managed to get him back to an aid post, but Redmond died that night of wounds.

At his burial next day, the Ulster Division formed a guard of honour.

36

JULY

'Passchendaele'

Ever more slaughter in Flanders fields

'Every brook is swollen and the ground is a quagmire. If it were not that all the records of previous years had given us fair warning, it would seem as if Providence had declared against us.'

So wrote Haig's chief of intelligence, Brigadier-General John Charteris, on 31 July 1917 at the beginning of the Third Battle of Ypres, commonly called 'Passchendaele' after the village and ridge that would become the culminating objective before the offensive was finally called off in November.

In the fortnight's preparatory bombardment, 3,000 guns fired four and a half million shells on the German defences. That barrage cost £22 million – in today's prices, £1.7 billion. The results overall were mixed. On the drainage system of west Flanders, however, they were tragically spectacular. As reclaimed marshland, the Ypres area was bound to revert to swamp if the system were destroyed. Worse still, according to Charteris, the records showed that in Flanders 'the weather broke early each August with the regularity of the Indian monsoon' – and in 1917 the weather proved true to its record.

Third Ypres followed a depressing pattern of strategic thinking on the Western Front – a pattern that had produced ever greater slaughter. In four and a quarter years' fighting on the Western Front, the allies 'spent' (casualties and losses) nearly eight million men, and the Germans (and to a limited extent Austrians) over five and a half million. Of all those years, 1917 was perhaps the bloodiest.

The strategy for 1917 had been determined at the inter-allied conference at Chantilly in December the previous year. At the urging of Joseph Joffre, the French commander-in-chief, he and his allied counterparts – British, Russian and Italian – agreed to apply again the same strategy that had failed in 1916. They would mount syncopated offensives on the three principal fronts to try to stretch the enemy to breaking point, and then exploit the situation that presented itself. All their training convinced them that, in the words of the British army's *Field Service Regulations*, 'decisive success in battle can be gained only by a vigorous offensive'. Haig in particular believed that the chief factor in success was, as *FSR* stated, 'a firmer determination in all ranks to conquer at any cost'.

The problem was that the situation on the Western Front had not materially changed since December 1914, when it seemed 'quite likely', as Churchill had written to Asquith, 'that neither side will have the strength to penetrate the other's line in the Western theatre'. The overwhelming advantage lay now, as it had then, with the defender.

Nevertheless, a weak French government acquiesced in Joffre's strategy, though the prime minister, Aristide Briand, despairing of the casualties at Verdun, managed to manoeuvre him out of command in the field, replacing him with Robert Nivelle, a man he called 'a new Napoleon'. Unfortunately, Lloyd George, who had just replaced Asquith in No. 10, fell for Briand's confidence – and, indeed, Nivelle's, not least for the latter's ability to explain himself in perfect English. Having lost confidence in Haig after the Somme offensive, 'LG' threw his weight behind Nivelle's proposed spring offensive on the Aisne and told Haig to put aside his misgivings and support the 'new Napoleon'. When that offensive failed, spectacularly, Haig emerged in a morally stronger position with London. He therefore began to develop his own ideas for a breakthrough near Ypres, ostensibly to clear the Belgian coast and thereby substantially reduce the menace from the U-boats – an enterprise that would resound strongly with the cabinet's conclusion in November that 'there is no operation of war to which the War Committee would attach greater importance than the successful occupation, or at least the deprivation to the enemy, of Ostend, and especially Zeebrugge'.

This war cabinet minute was not in itself a requirement for an offensive, rather an attempt to limit the ambitions for offensive action, and with the failure of the Nivelle offensive, the cabinet wanted to avoid another major blood-letting in 1917. However, by May that year, with Russia beginning to fall apart in revolution, the French army barely answering to discipline, the Italians increasingly hard pressed and no prospect of American relief for at least six months, they recognized that Britain would have to bear the burden not merely at sea and in the Middle East, but on the Western Front. There seemed to be no alternative to Haig's plans to reach the sea.

Nevertheless, a month before it was due to begin, Lloyd George warned Haig that 'a great attack which fails in its objective while entailing heavy casualties must necessarily discourage the British Army' as well as having a grave effect on public opinion in both Britain and France, and that the cabinet 'must regard themselves as trustees' for those serving and must see that they were 'not sacrificed on mere gambles'.

Haig assured the cabinet they need have no worries. And indeed, preparations seemed to go well. On 7 June, the British 2nd Army under General Sir Herbert Plumer launched a meticulously planned operation at Messines just south of Ypres with the object of straightening out the Ypres salient and taking the high ground that commanded the British defences and rear areas further north. From here Haig intended to launch his 'Northern Operation' – an advance to Passchendaele Ridge and thence, in conjunction with landings from the sea, including tanks, to the Belgian coast as far as the Dutch frontier south of the Scheldt.

Notwithstanding the success of the Messines operation, Lloyd George remained apprehensive. In his memoirs he wrote bitterly about Haig's over-optimism: 'The capture of the Messines Ridge, a perfect attack in its way, was just a useful little preliminary to the real campaign, an *apéritif* provided by General Plumer to stimulate the public appetite for the great carousal of victory which was being provided for us by GHQ.'

He was not alone in his concern. Ferdinand Foch, the new French chief of the general staff, told the senior British liaison officer, Henry Wilson, that 'the whole thing was futile, fantastic and dangerous'. Philippe Pétain, who had replaced Nivelle as commander-in-chief, believed that 'Haig's attack towards Ostend was certain to fail', and with heavy casualties.

However, the British CIGS, 'Wully' Robertson, who had risen from the ranks and had a reputation for bluff common sense, told the cabinet that Haig's plan 'should secure us against this mistake'. Haig himself assured the cabinet that he was 'fully in agreement . . . that we ought not to push attacks that had not a reasonable chance of success, but that we ought to proceed step by step'. He himself had 'no intention of entering into a tremendous offensive involving heavy losses' – although, as he told the cabinet, 'if the fighting was kept up . . . for six months Germany would be at the end of her available manpower'.

Still the war cabinet hesitated, but at this point Haig found an unlikely ally. Admiral Sir John Jellicoe, the first sea lord, said that nothing could be done to defeat the U-boats at sea, and that unless the army could clear the Belgian coast the losses of shipping were likely to be such as to render it impossible for Britain to prosecute the war for another year. Few but Jellicoe believed this, for most of the submarines were operating from bases in Germany, principally the island of Heligoland (which in 1890 Britain had exchanged for Zanzibar), but Haig was not a one to look a gift horse in the mouth.

Eventually the war cabinet gave him the go-ahead after he

promised he would halt the offensive if it became clear that his objectives could not be obtained. However, the criteria for judging whether those objectives were being obtained were not specified. The judgement would be Haig's, and Haig had a tendency to believe that failure to make progress was primarily a sign of lack of determined leadership.

As if to reinforce Haig in his conviction that his great 'Northern Offensive' was not only practicable but necessary, on its very eve he learned that three Russian armies – some sixty to seventy divisions – were in full retreat along a 150-mile front. Under the terms of the December agreement, a major offensive against one ally would bring about a prompt counter-offensive by all the others. He therefore felt justified in telling Pétain, who was nursing the French army back to fighting health after the terrible losses of 1916 and early 1917, that the policy the French C-in-C was advocating of standing on the strategic defensive until 1918, when the Americans would arrive in strength, would only serve the Germans, allowing them to concentrate all their reserves in the east and knock Russia out of the war before the winter. Now, Haig proclaimed, was 'the critical moment of the war'.

Clearly, therefore, he would press the offensive in Flanders with even greater determination than the cabinet envisaged, for as well as the questionable objective of relieving the U-boat threat, it now had a major strategic purpose.

In any case, he was confident of a breakthrough, telling his army commanders that 'opportunities for the employment of cavalry in masses are likely to offer'. And Hubert Gough, commanding 5th Army, a cavalryman and a 'thruster', was the man to create those opportunities. Gough rewrote the plan that Plumer had earlier devised, making provision to take rapid advantage of ground the Germans abandoned – one of the lessons of the Somme – and setting more ambitious objectives for the first day. Tanks in large numbers were to help the infantry forward. Tank supply had been stepped up after the Somme, and the Tank Corps, hitherto the Heavy Branch of the Machine Gun Corps, came formally into being on 27 July.

However, Tank Corps staff officers had been surveying the going for several weeks and were far from confident that the ground was suitable. The destruction of the drainage ditches had, wrote one, turned the Steenbeck, a stream that ran parallel to the front line, into 'a wide moat of liquid mud'.

The attack was scheduled to begin on 28 July, but was postponed for three days because Gough had not quite completed his preparations. On 28 July it began to rain heavily. Nevertheless, of the 136 tanks committed to the attack, all but two managed to reach the start line, which was itself a mechanical triumph.

Zero hour was 3.50 a.m., first light, to minimize the Germans' advantage in observation from the higher ground. A layer of unbroken low cloud meant that it was still dark when the infantry advanced – fourteen divisions, with the support of a French corps on the left, and one of Plumer's on the right, on a frontage of 11 miles.

Progress was mixed. Lieutenant Edmund Blunden MC, of the 11th Royal Sussex, advancing on the left, recalled:

> We rose, scrambled ahead, found No Man's Land a comparatively good surface, were amazed at the puny tags and rags of once multiplicative German wire, and blundered over the once feared trench behind them without seeing that it was a trench . . . German dead, so obvious at every yard of a 1916 battlefield, were hardly to be seen.

Towards the centre, north-east of Ypres itself, things were not so promising. Here the ground was more open, rising gently and dotted with fortified farms and concrete pillboxes that had scarcely suffered during the bombardment. The infantry had to overcome these one by one, with the help of those tanks that could get forward over the cratered and waterlogged ground. By the end of the day's fighting, half the tanks had been knocked out by fire or become 'bogged'.

German reserves poured forward throughout the day. Gough had planned that the RFC, which had had a gruelling two months' combat against the odds, would interdict their movement by bombing, and by machine-gunning – 'strafing' (from the German imprecation *Gott strafe England* – 'May God punish England') – but the low cloud largely prevented it.

Many of the initial gains in the centre and south were either lost to German counter-attacks or could not be exploited because of the exhaustion of the troops. The greatest success was achieved on the northern flank, by the French, and by XIV Corps under the diminutive but capable Lieutenant-General the Earl of Cavan, a Grenadier who had been recalled from retirement as a colonel in 1914 and who would go on to command an Anglo-Italian army with notable success in 1918 during the final offensive on the Italian front.

But nowhere was there any appreciable gain of more than 2 miles. Still Haig reported to the War Office that evening that the results were 'most satisfactory'.

The offensive would continue, though it would never get near the coast, in what Blunden would describe as a 'slow amputation'. Casualty figures are still disputed, but were probably around a quarter of a million on each side.

Blunden would survive the three and a half months' fighting at Third Ypres, and the war. Two of his fellow poets (though their names are not inscribed on the memorial in Westminster Abbey) did not survive the first day. Lance-Corporal Francis Ledwidge of the Royal Inniskilling Fusiliers, a fervent Irish Nationalist who had nevertheless answered the call to arms, was killed by artillery fire. Private Ellis Humphrey Evans of the Royal Welsh Fusiliers, better known by his Bardic name 'Hedd Wyn', a reluctant conscript, was fatally wounded by shrapnel. In September, he would be posthumously 'chaired' (made chief bard) at the national Eisteddfod, at which Lloyd George, a Welsh speaker, was present.

37

AUGUST

'O for a beaker full of the warm South'

*British reinforcements on the Italian Front find the food
strange and the fighting every bit as murderous*

As Field Marshal Sir Douglas Haig's armies battled throughout
August with the Germans and the weather at Third Ypres (Passchendaele), for others, attention was being called to the warm
south. In April, ten batteries of field guns and howitzers had been
sent from France to strengthen the Italian army's artillery on the
Isonzo, and several more of heavier calibre joined in August, some
direct from England.

For most gunners, the change was welcome. Hugh Dalton, who
would become Clement Attlee's chancellor of the exchequer in
1945, but who in August 1917 was a lieutenant with a siege battery
on the Italian front, expressed his delight at his new theatre of war:
'What worlds away is this country with its wonderful cloudless sunshine from the dismal flat lands of the Western Front!'

While the other ranks shared Dalton's sentiments as to climate
and scenery, however, they were not best pleased with the rations.
On the Western Front the Army Service Corps fed them good

British fare, but in Italy they were victualled by the *Regio Esercito Italiano* (Royal Italian Army): less beef, bacon, cheese and tea than they were used to in France, supplemented instead by macaroni, rice, coffee and red wine. The wine – 'Key-Auntie', as they were told to pronounce it – was appreciated, but many a letter home complained of the monotony of pasta and stew.

Haig had not wanted to send them anyway. He protested vehemently to the chief of the imperial general staff, Sir William Robertson, when given the order, arguing that it would jeopardize his coming offensive at Ypres; but Lloyd George was chary of the continued promises of breakthrough on the Western Front and wanted to shift the effort south, to either Italy or Salonika – or both. The Italian commander-in-chief, Luigi Cadorna, had also begun to warn that with the disintegration of the Eastern Front since the overthrow of the Tsar in February, there was a heavy buildup of not only Austro-Hungarian but also German troops on the Italian front. He was keen to mount another major summer offensive on the Isonzo, as promised at the inter-allied conference at Chantilly in November. It would be his eleventh offensive south-east towards Trieste (in Slovenia, then a province of the Austro-Hungarian empire) since Italy entered the war in May 1915: bloody, attritional fighting, sometimes with promising, but all too often temporary, gains.

In the Tenth Battle of the Isonzo, from 10 May to 8 June, Cadorna's *grigioverdi* ('grey-greens', the colour of their uniform) had almost broken through to Trieste, but were then pushed back almost to their starting lines by Austrian counter-attacks. Though Tenth Isonzo had inflicted heavy losses on the enemy, Cadorna now doubted he could mount an eleventh offensive unless reinforced. However, while the French and British had made contingency plans to send reinforcements if the Italians were attacked in overwhelming strength, as also agreed at Chantilly, both Robertson and his French counterpart, Ferdinand Foch, dug their heels in and refused anything more than artillery for an offensive.

Cadorna went ahead nevertheless, having managed to assemble fifty-one divisions and 5,200 guns. His object once more was the

Carso, the limestone plateau beyond the Italian bridgehead at Gorizia which had been captured exactly a year before. The preliminary bombardment – a single day, but intense – opened at 6 a.m. on 18 August. Unlike the struggle with the mud of Passchendaele, however, Dalton recalled that

> one had to guard against a dust cloud being raised by the blast of the guns, thus giving away our position to the enemy. To prevent this, we formed a chain of men every half hour to pass water-buckets from hand to hand, from the river just behind us down the sunken road, to lay the dust in and around the gun pits. But under an Italian August sun the ground soon grew parched and dusty again.

The Italian 3rd Army, under the duke of Aosta, son of King Amadeus of Spain (of the House of Savoy) and cousin of the Italian king, Emmanuele III, made good progress initially along the coastal plain, and 2nd Army under Luigi Capello, an outspoken general with a reputation as both a self-publicist and a 'butcher', advanced 7 miles in short order, taking five mountain peaks, over 20,000 Austro-Hungarian (and some German) prisoners, and most of the Bainsizza plateau south-east of Tolmino. However, 2nd Army's progress was so rapid that they outran their artillery and supplies, and Capello halted the advance to regain balance.

It was an unfortunate decision, for the Austro-Hungarians were probably at breaking point. By the time he resumed the offensive, resistance had stiffened, and his attacks, particularly in the mountains, were beaten back with heavy loss. Aosta's 3rd Army likewise was fought to a standstill. Cadorna again asked for heavy artillery to be sent from France, but the answer once more was 'no'. On 12 September he called off the offensive.

The 'butcher's bill' was a heavy one. The Italians admitted to 166,000 casualties: 40,000 dead, 108,000 wounded and 18,000 missing (prisoners of war or men subsequently accounted killed), losses some 25 per cent greater than in Nivelle's disastrous spring offensive on the Aisne. Morale in the Italian infantry fell noticeably. But the

Austro-Hungarians had taken serious casualties too, some 110,000: 15,000 dead, 65,000 wounded, 30,000 missing. Moreover, an additional 30,000 had been taken prisoner – a sure sign of collapsing morale – and a third of their artillery had been destroyed or captured.

Cadorna was now determined to mount a twelfth – and decisive – offensive as soon as he could make good his losses and gain reinforcements from the British and French. These both Robertson and Foch continued to refuse, having little faith in the remaining fighting spirit of the Italian army. Indeed, Haig demanded the return of 'his' artillery now that Cadorna's forces had gone back on to the defensive.

Unfortunately, however, the Austro-Hungarian high command would not wait for Cadorna to mount his Twelfth Battle of the Isonzo. Reinforced by more troops and up to 1,000 guns drawn from the disintegrating Eastern Front, as well as by five high-grade German divisions, including the *Alpenkorps*, in October they would strike a blow centred on Caporetto that would send the Italians in full retreat almost as far as Venice. Many more troops would then be sent from France to help them consolidate on the Piave than Cadorna had asked for in the summer (and with them, to the relief of 'Tommy', would come the Army Service Corps – and 'better' rations).

Meanwhile, during Cadorna's eleventh blood-letting on the Isonzo, London and Paris found themselves troubled by another Italian – the Pope, Benedict XV. Cardinal Giacomo della Chiesa had been elected to the papacy on 3 September 1914 at the comparatively young age of fifty-nine, probably for the very reason that the conclave of cardinals wanted a vigorous pope to deal with what Benedict himself would call 'the suicide of civilized Europe'. In his first encyclical letter, in November 1914, he had asked, albeit with a degree of circumlocution, but clearly referring to the invasion of neutral Belgium: 'Surely there are other ways and means whereby violated rights can be rectified. Let them be tried honestly and with good will, and let arms meanwhile be laid aside.'

But he had been more direct in his summary of the human

condition of Christian Europe: 'Race hatred has reached its climax; peoples are more divided by jealousies than by frontiers; within one and the same nation, within the same city there rages the burning envy of class against class; and amongst individuals it is self-love which is the supreme law over-ruling everything.'

Since he had made no concrete proposals, his appeal had brought no material response. He had then turned his efforts to limiting the war's spread, conducting behind-the-scenes diplomacy to prevent war between Italy and Austria. And because British diplomatic efforts were being made at the same time to persuade Italy to declare war on the side of the Entente, Benedict's initiative made him no friends in London.

In late 1915, after the Italians had entered the war, he had tried to broker a peace directly between Belgium, France and Germany. This foundered on the pact made in September 1914 by the Triple Entente powers (Britain, France and Russia) 'not to conclude peace separately during the present war'. Having failed in this, he had issued another general appeal for a negotiated peace, which was no better received than the first.

Benedict continued his efforts throughout 1916 and into the following spring, when he tried also to keep the Americans out of the war; and then, in August 1917, when it seemed as if all sides must be growing exhausted, he issued his most significant 'peace note'. In a preamble, he said that he wished

> no longer to dwell upon the general, as the circumstances suggested to us in the past: we want now to descend to more concrete and practical proposals, and to invite the governments of the belligerent peoples to agree upon the following points, which appear to be the bases of a just and lasting peace, leaving to the same governments to apply them at a specific level and to complete them.

These 'following [seven] points' ranged widely, and probably influenced President Woodrow Wilson's own 'Fourteen Points' speech of January 1918 proposing a basis for lasting peace (which, just as unrealistically as the Pope, if every bit as worthily, he called 'peace without victory').

Benedict's August peace note fell on no more fertile ground than his earlier initiatives. He had no influence in Russia, an Orthodox country, which was anyway imploding. Germany, though it had a sizeable Catholic population, especially in the south, was essentially Protestant, the land of Luther. France was as much anti-clerical as it was staunchly Catholic. Besides, Catholicism did not equate with ultramontanism: 'Holy Father, we do not want your peace,' was the message of one preacher in the church of La Madeleine in Paris. Austria-Hungary, the great Catholic empire, had long lost its soul to Berlin. Britain in many ways was still too close to the Spanish Armada and the Gunpowder Plot to regard Rome with anything but suspicion. And, indeed, Haig's diaries are disparaging of 'the Catholic people [certain officers]' whose hearts, he believed, were not in the fight. As for the Italians, their goal – the reason they had entered the war in the first place – was their ultimate unification, the repossession of *Italia Irredenta*, the parts of the territory still in Austrian hands; and it was, moreover, only forty-seven years earlier that Rome had been liberated from papal rule – by troops commanded by Cadorna's father. The Italian government mistrusted Benedict's motives, too (not entirely without reason), believing that in a negotiated settlement he would try to recover some of the former papal states. Italian newspapers suggested his name should not be 'Benedetto' ('blessed') but 'Maledetto' ('accursed').

Benedict's peace initiative would even be cited as one of the reasons for the Italian collapse at Caporetto. This, however, was another convenient excuse to distract from the failure of the Anglo-French high commands to regard the war on the Italian front as a continuation of that on the Western Front. Only with the 'crisis of the war', as Haig called it – the great last-ditch German offensive in spring 1918 – would the interrelationship of the two fronts be acknowledged by the creation of a *generalissimo*, Marshal Foch, to take supreme command of both.

38

SEPTEMBER

'Boom'

As Zeppelins and Gothas bomb London with impunity,
a new air service is conceived to counter them

While fatherhood of the Royal Air Force is usually attributed to Major-General Sir Hugh (later Marshal of the RAF Lord) 'Boom' Trenchard, who led the Royal Flying Corps on the Western Front, a paternity case could equally be brought against the South African Lieutenant-General (later Field Marshal Sir) Jan Smuts. In September 1917, daylight raids on London propelled his paper on the reorganization of aviation to the top of the war cabinet's agenda.

Jan Smuts had been a successful Boer commando leader in the South African War a decade and half earlier, but with the creation of the Union of South Africa in 1910 as a self-governing dominion, he had done much towards reconciliation. Indeed, in many ways he was as much an imperialist as his former adversaries. In 1914, when defence minister, he had put on uniform and taken command in the field against a Boer insurrection, then led operations against German South-West Africa (now Namibia), and later in German East Africa. In the spring of 1917 he came to London to take part in the first imperial conference of the war.

In late 1916, during the Somme offensive, Sir Douglas Haig, commander-in-chief of British armies on the Western Front, began pressing urgently for twenty more squadrons of aircraft. These could not be found, however, without borrowing from the Royal Naval Air Service (RNAS), and it became clear that something was wrong with the supply of equipment and trained personnel for the two separate air services. While the RFC was preoccupied with the war in France, the RNAS was growing anxious about the air defence of its dockyards and arsenals in Britain. Raids by 'Zeppelins', the generic name for German airships irrespective of manufacture, and by Gotha bombers, were increasing, including attacks on civilian targets. The RNAS had taken offensive action against the Zeppelins from the start, bombing the airship sheds at Cologne and Düsseldorf in October 1914. The success of these prompted the director of the Admiralty's air department, Captain (later Rear-Admiral Sir) Murray Sueter, to commission the aircraft manufacturer Frederick Handley Page to produce a longer-range machine capable of dropping a heavier bomb – as Sueter put it, 'a bloody paralyser of an aircraft'. The result was the Handley Page Type O, the first British strategic bomber, which came into service towards the end of 1916. Twin-engined, with a crew of four or five, it had a range of 700 miles, eight hours' endurance and a top speed of just under 100 mph, and could carry 2,000 lb (907 kg) of bombs.

The RNAS was, however, divided between those advocating long-range bombing and those who saw the priority as cooperation with the fleet. Meanwhile, air defence of Britain remained the responsibility of the RFC, though the army believed that operations in France and Flanders had priority. Zeppelins had bombed London in 1915 and 1916, killing 500 people, and the RFC had been forced to allocate – divert – twenty-seven squadrons, with over 400 aircraft and some 17,000 officers and men, to air defence. The Royal Artillery, too, increasingly had to divert anti-aircraft guns and searchlights to cover London.

The airships countered by attacking at dusk and in darkness, using factory and street lighting as guides before enforcement of the blackout (first ordered in London in October 1914 and extended across the whole of England in February 1916). The defending aircraft found them difficult to attack because they flew high and their top speed was about equal to their own. At the start of the war, aircraft could not climb fast enough to intercept a Zeppelin before bombs were dropped, and, defended by five machine guns, it was a dangerous enemy to close with. Nevertheless, it was an early model, a BE2c biplane, flown by Lieutenant William Leefe-Robinson, that brought down the first airship over England, at Cuffley in Hertfordshire on the night of 2 September 1916. Leefe-Robinson repeatedly circled the Zeppelin, which was illuminated by several searchlight beams, firing at close range into its belly until it caught fire. For this action, he was awarded the VC.

The Germans' periodic ascendancy in aerial combat on the Western Front – notably the so-called 'Fokker scourge' from June 1915 until the allies produced comparable fighters ten months later, and then 'Bloody April' (1917), when the German 'flying circuses' gained temporary mastery again – was a growing concern of both GHQ in France and the War Ministry in London.

The press began to agitate, too. On 31 October 1916, *The Times* thundered at Lord Curzon's Air Board, which had been formed in May to improve coordination:

It is a week since we called attention to the deplorable deadlock which has paralysed the Air Board, and everything which has come to our notice since has continued that warning. In our opinion the Board was always doomed to failure. We described it when it was appointed as 'one more stopgap, which can only succeed by a miracle'; and the miracle has not happened. The fact is that the Air Board has never possessed the willing confidence and cooperation of both the Services concerned, and it was never invested with the formal authority required to override them. That it has existed for months without open and notorious scandal we attribute, first, to the energy with which it has faced an impossible

Above U-boat warfare: U-86 wrecked after the war. Initially German U-boats operated under the Hague Convention's 'cruiser rules', by which the passengers and crew of an unarmed ship were warned before attack so that they could take to the lifeboats. After the Kaiser finally re-authorized unrestricted submarine warfare in January 1917, some U-boat commanders were pitiless in their attacks. On 27 June 1918, U-86 torpedoed the Canadian hospital ship *Landovery Castle*, then surfaced and machine-gunned the survivors in the lifeboats. In all, 234 medical officers, nurses, orderlies, wounded troops and seamen died. There were just 24 survivors.

Right The pilot and observer of an RE8 biplane of 59 Squadron RFC are briefed before a mission, St-Omer, 1917. In 1914 the RFC and RNAS could muster around a hundred aircraft for operational service. By the end of the war, the RAF, formed by amalgamating the separate services on 1 April 1918, had some 22,000 aircraft.

Left 'Lafayette we are here!' General John J. 'Black Jack' Pershing, C-in-C American Expeditionary Force, arrives at Boulogne in June 1917. The entry of the US into the war was the certain guarantee of ultimate victory, but exactly how this was to be achieved would cause much allied disagreement – as would President Wilson's ideas about the peace terms to be offered the Germans.

Above The collapse of the Eastern Front: Russian troops captured in the final 'Kerensky' offensive of July 1917, named after the chairman of the Russian provisional government. It was singularly ill-timed, after the February revolution: calls for peace were increasing, especially in the army, whose material capability and morale had been rapidly deteriorating since autumn 1916. The Germans were now able to transfer troops to the Western Front, and to reinforce the Austrians on the Italian front.

Left An army in defeat: the Italian front, October 1917. Reinforced by 'crack' German divisions, and using poison gas to devastating effect, the Austro-Hungarian army mounted a huge surprise offensive in the Julian Alps, with its *Schwerpunkt* (point of greatest effort) at Caporetto, now Kobarid in Slovenia. British and French heavy artillery, aircraft and then troops were rushed from the Western Front to help stem the tide, but the Italians were eventually able to halt the offensive on the Piave. The loss of sovereign territory was humiliating; however, a year to the day, the Italians would launch a counter-offensive that knocked Austria out of the war.

Right Ottoman machine guns in Palestine. General Sir Edmund Allenby's arrival as C-in-C in July 1917 reinvigorated the British and imperial troops of the Egyptian Expeditionary Force, which in the autumn swept north through Gaza and by Christmas had taken Jerusalem.

Above left 'Good God, did we really send men to fight in that?' Haig's chief of staff is meant to have said when he saw the ground over which Third Ypres ('Passchendaele') was fought. Men of the 4th Australian Division on a duckboard track passing through the remains of Chateau Wood, near Hooge in the Ypres salient, October 1917 – a landscape which Paul Nash's modernist *The Menin Road* (painted 1919) could hardly make more nightmarish.

Above right His 'Christmas present to the nation' (and to Lloyd George): Allenby entering Jerusalem on foot by the Jaffa Gate on 11 December 1917, the gesture of a shrewd, confident and arguably great commander. 'Only one man rides into Jerusalem,' he said simply (Jesus of Nazareth had, of course, entered the city on a donkey on Palm Sunday via the Golden Gate, on the east side).

Left Who was giving orders to whom? The Kaiser (*centre*) remained the commander-in-chief of the German army, but from late 1916 Hindenburg (*pointing*), chief of the *Grosser Generalstab*, began increasingly to direct the entire war effort, including industrial policy. Meanwhile, Ludendorff (*right*) acted increasingly as commander-in-chief of the armies in the field, directing military strategy. Ludendorff suffered a nervous collapse in October 1918, and shortly afterwards resigned. The Kaiser abdicated on 9 November. Hindenburg remained in post until July 1919. In 1925 he would become the second elected president of the German Reich.

Above A war of movement at last: Canadian troops on the Arras–Cambrai road, September 1918, with an abandoned Renault FT light tank, during the three-month allied counter-offensive – the 'Hundred Days' – which brought the Germans on the Western Front to their knees.

Left British Mark V tanks, carrying fascines to assist in trench and ditch crossing, advancing during the 'Hundred Days'.

Left British and Italian troops passing abandoned Austrian artillery in the Val d'Assa, 2 November 1918, after the victory at Vittorio Veneto. The following day, Vienna accepted the Italians' terms for an armistice

ove left To the victors . . . The Generalissimo, Foch *(third from left)* with his Western Front ¬-Cs: to his left Pershing, his right Haig, and on Haig's right, Pétain.

ove right To the victors . . . The fourth C-in-C, Diaz, who nursed the Italian army back to health er Caporetto, then on the battle's anniversary launched a counter-offensive that expelled Austrians from Italian soil and brought about their complete collapse. (The C-in-C of the cedonian front, Franchet d'Espèrey, answered in effect directly to the French government, to Foch.)

Left To the victors . . . the 'Big Four' at the Paris peace conference, 1919: Lloyd George talking to Orlando; Clemenceau ('Le Tigre') facing the camera squarely; and Wilson in elegant profile. Making peace as allies would prove every bit as tricky as making war, not least because Wilson sought a new approach to international relations in the post-war world – his famous 'Fourteen Points' – whereas the European allies were more concerned with weakening Germany.

THE ART OF WAR

No war before or since has been painted so much and in so many different styles. Official war artists were appointed early in the fighting to record the supreme human endeavour.

Above *Canadian Artillery in Action*: a 6-inch howitzer on the Somme, July 1916, depicted by the Toronto-born Kenneth Forbes. A combatant officer in the (British) Machine Gun Corps, he had been wounded and gassed, and thereafter appointed an official war artist. The painting shows the exhausting 'industrial' nature of the gunners' work – as well as the danger.

Below *The Zeebrugge Raid*, 23 April 1918, by Charles de Lacy. HMS *Vindictive* landing men on the mole by night, with others going ashore from the *Iris*, a Mersey ferry, behind; star shells illuminate the action, in which many a VC was won.

Above *Made on the Wing*: RAF scouts leaving their aerodrome on patrol over the Asiago Plateau, Italy, 1918, by Sydney Carline. Himself a pilot, Carline sketched the scene in watercolours from the observer's seat in the fourth aircraft.

Above *Charge of the [Australian] 3rd Light Horse Brigade at the Nek*, Gallipoli, 7 August 1915, by George Lambert. As a diversion in support of an attack by New Zealand troops, the 3rd Light Horse were ordered to take the Turkish trenches at 'the Nek', a narrow, sheer-sided ridge, at first light. The artillery bombardment was ineffective and the Turks stood-to their machine guns. Despite the losses in the first wave, the Australians pressed the attack, suffering nearly 400 casualties in a very restricted area. The attack, if not a model of tactical judgement, became a symbol of defiant Australian courage.

Above 'Good God, did we really send men to fight in that?' *The Menin Road*, by Paul Nash.

Below The man on whom it all depended, whether British, French, Italian or American – the NCO. *Grenadier Guardsman* (1918) by Sir William Orpen. The model was Sergeant Stanley Burton, of Hulme, Manchester – at the time of the painting, 35 years old. He had joined the Grenadiers in 1902; recalled to the colours in 1914, he was promoted sergeant in 1917 and won the Military Medal in July that year at Third Ypres.

task; and, second, to the supremacy which our airmen have lately achieved at the front. The public, and perhaps the Government, have been obsessed with this temporary triumph. There has been no long view of the reaction which will follow unless the organization of the Air Services – and especially the design, construction, and purchase of machines for both – is placed on a satisfactory footing.

Reaction of a sort came soon enough, as Zeppelin raids on London increased, almost with impunity. More RFC aircraft were diverted from the Western Front and elsewhere to cover the capital and east coast ports, and there was talk of forming a separate air ministry, and a separate air service, better to focus on air defence and strategic bombing. For the prime minister was acutely aware of his growing political predicament. The Passchendaele offensive was going nowhere but to even more graves, while the Germans were ranging almost at will over England; and the effects of the Royal Navy's blockade of Germany – which were steadily but surely undermining the enemy's ability to fight – were not discernible to the man in the street (or, indeed, to many senior military officers). A display of determination to deal with the aerial raiders by forming a separate force, and giving the Germans a taste of their own medicine by bombing, which would also supplement the work of the blockade, made both political and military sense.

Lloyd George was not without opposition at home when it came to strategic bombing, especially when it involved civilian deaths, which looked like reprisals. Bishops in the House of Lords spoke against it (as they would in the Second World War, notably after the bombing of Dresden). In April 1917, in retaliation for the sinking of two hospital ships, the RNAS bombed Freiburg. The Bishop of Ely declared bluntly that 'a policy of reprisals is essentially wrong.' On 13 June, 162 civilians were killed and 400 injured, including many children, in a daylight raid on London by fifteen Gothas. Seventy-two tons of bombs fell within a one-mile radius of Liverpool Street Station, while others fell at Fenchurch Street and in the East End. At a service for children killed in their schoolroom, the Bishop of

London, Arthur Winnington-Ingram, a strong supporter of the war effort from the outset (he had been a chaplain to the London Rifle Brigade – territorials – since 1901), echoed the protests, saying that he did not believe 'the mourners would wish that 16 German babies should lie dead to avenge their dead'.

RFC and RNAS aircraft had been barely able to get within striking distance of the bombers. When the Gothas returned on 7 July, the defenders made better contact, but only one was destroyed and the casualty list was still high at 57 killed and 193 injured. The *Daily Mail* reported that Britain had not been 'so humiliated since the Dutch Fleet sailed up the Thames in 1667' and called for the heads of those responsible.

The clamour for reprisals against German cities was as loud in Parliament as it was in the popular press and at Speakers' Corner in Hyde Park. William Joynson-Hicks, MP for Manchester North, and later a notably authoritarian home secretary, told Lloyd George: 'Every time the Germans raid London, British airmen must blot out a German town.'

Lloyd George decided he had to act. In June he had co-opted Smuts to the war cabinet, and now he asked him to carry out a study into the air defence of Britain, the air organization generally, and the arrangements for the higher direction of aerial operations. Smuts agreed at once. Indeed, he had already been consulting widely. The new chairman of the Air Board, Lord Cowdray, told him that aircraft production had so improved in late months that by 1918 there would be 3,000 machines surplus to known requirements, which would amply sustain an independent strategic bombing force. Within a month (on 17 August), Smuts had submitted his principal report to the war cabinet, recommending:

> We must create the new directing organization – the new Ministry and Air Staff which could properly handle this new instrument of offence, and equip it with the best brains at our disposal for the purpose. The task of planning the new Air Service organization [amalgamating

the RFC and RNAS] and thinking out and preparing for schemes of aerial operations next summer must tax our Air experts to the utmost.

The report met with a mixed response. The RFC and RNAS did not want to lose the connection with their respective services. Nor did Field Marshal Haig, and Admiral Sir David Beatty commanding the Home Fleet, want to lose command of their supporting aircraft, though the CIGS, Sir 'Wully' Robertson, and the first sea lord, Sir John Jellicoe, had no strong objection. Lloyd George began to have second thoughts, and, his spirits low with the news from France of the faltering Passchendaele campaign, in early September took a holiday. The press, not knowing of the actual Smuts report but hearing rumours of dissension in government and among senior officers, again began pressing for action, not least when the Germans mounted heavy attacks on London and the east coast over four successive nights at the end of September.

On 1 October the War Cabinet authorized retaliatory raids on Germany, though these proved slow in materializing. The following week, the cabinet received a paper showing that German aircraft production was increasing alarmingly, and on 15 October, during continued questions in Parliament, Andrew Bonar Law, Leader of the House of Commons, sensing serious disquiet, hinted at the formation of a separate service. It was confirmed in an official announcement the following day.

Much to Lloyd George's relief, but to the dismay of many, including 'Boom' Trenchard, who at this time opposed the concept of an independent strategic bombing force, in November the Air Force Bill would pass through Parliament with little opposition.

The Royal Air Force would formally come into being on 1 April 1918. The initials 'RAF', said those who opposed its creation still, stood for 'Royal April Foolers'.

39

OCTOBER
Caporetto

*A humiliating collapse of the Italian Front presages
victorious recovery a year later*

In October 1917, Freya Stark, who would later find fame as an
explorer and travel writer, was a 24-year-old nurse with the British
Red Cross on the Italian front. Her field ambulance just outside
Gorizia lay close to the junction of the 2nd and 3rd Italian Armies,
which for two years had been launching a succession of bloody
offensives astride the Isonzo River. Some of these had made gains,
some had been repulsed, and the eleventh, in August, had almost
broken through on the coast towards Trieste, then a city of the
Austro-Hungarian empire.

The Austrians had to date been standing on the defensive on
this, their south-western, front in order to concentrate their efforts
against the Russians and Serbs. With Russia in the grip of Bolshevik
revolution and her army disintegrating, with Serbia over-run, and
with Berlin willing to help, it was possible now to go on to the
offensive. Indeed, it was not just possible; it was necessary. Another
offensive by the Italians might just succeed.

OCTOBER: CAPORETTO

When the Austrian offensive was launched, on 24 October, across the entire front from Lake Garda to the Gulf of Trieste, but with especial force at Caporetto (today Kobarid, Slovenia) in the Julian Alps, 20 miles north of Gorizia, it would precipitate a general retreat that was only halted a few miles from Venice. 'Caporetto', as the whole battle (strictly, Twelfth Isonzo) is popularly known, became a byword for national calamity and humiliation.

Freya Stark would be lucky not to be taken prisoner. Separated from the main body of her unit, five days after the Austrians struck, in darkness and with only what she could carry, she managed to cross one of the last bridges over the Tagliamento just hours before Italian engineers blew it up. Though already exhausted by long hours of nursing the mounting casualties, she would have another 60 miles to cover until reunited with the rest of her field ambulance beyond the Piave River.

In mid-October, aerial reconnaissance and other intelligence had alerted the Italian commander-in-chief, Luigi Cadorna, to the buildup of enemy troops, and he had therefore instructed his army commanders to adopt a defensive posture rather than continue with plans for a further offensive. The newly appointed commander of 2nd Army, Luigi Capello, who had distinguished himself in the Italo-Turkish War in Cyrenaica in 1912 and in successive battles of the Isonzo, disagreed with Cadorna's strategy. His defensive measures were half-hearted to say the least, and not helped by his succumbing to a kidney infection in the days before the Austrians struck.

Nor was the northern part of 2nd Army's front, in which Caporetto stood, expected to be the Austrian *Schwerpunkt* (main effort). Indeed, it was viewed as something of a quiet sector and used almost as a rest area. Some of the units there were considered unreliable: many conscripts were disaffected factory workers from Turin, where there had been a general strike in August (in which the Italian Marxist Antonio Gramsci was active), with much violence. Officers in several units of 2nd Army were reportedly in fear of their lives, and many conscripts had agreed among themselves that if the Austrians attacked they would at once surrender.

In August, the German commander-in-chief, Paul von Hindenburg, by now in effect viceroy, had become increasingly anxious about Austria-Hungary's staying power. The empire – war-weary and fissile, composed as it was of disparate nationalities whose grievances seemed to be increasing – looked on the brink of collapse. Consequently, the new, young emperor, Charles I (Franz Joseph had died the previous November), and his new chief of staff, Arthur Freiherr Arz von Straußenburg, had little difficulty in persuading Berlin to come to their aid. There is no evidence that Hindenburg believed an offensive could knock the Italians out of the war completely, but a heavy blow might unnerve them to the point of abandoning future offensive plans. Sixteen divisions – nine Austrian and seven German, including the Austrian Edelweiss Division and the German *Alpenkorps*, specialist mountain troops – were therefore secretly assembled to form a new army, the 14th, under the German General Otto von Below.

The following month, experts from the *Grosser Generalstab* in Berlin, led by the chemist Otto Hahn, who would win the Nobel Prize for his discovery of nuclear fission in 1938, went to the Italian front to reconnoitre suitable areas for an attack by chlorine–arsenic and phosgene gas. They recommended Caporetto, where the junction of valleys on the upper reaches of the Isonzo, and the likely weather, would most favour the discharge. A good road running west to the Venetian plain also favoured the sector.

In the event, bad weather delayed the attack for two days, but on 24 October the wind dropped, and fog settled across much of 2nd Army's front. At 2 a.m., 900 *Gasminenwerfer* – mortars firing gas shells – were triggered electrically, at once shrouding the defences at Piezzo in the valley north of Caporetto in deadly vapour. Knowing that their gas masks were effective for at best two hours, many troops simply fled, though 600 were killed. Austrian troops were able to cross the Isonzo unopposed and begin the outflanking movement. All then remained quiet until 6 a.m., just before dawn, when a mortar bombardment was directed at the trenches over much of the 12-mile front, with particular intensity at Caporetto and downstream at

Tolmino. Forty minutes later, 2,000 artillery pieces opened fire, targeting especially the road along which reserves were already moving up to reoccupy the abandoned defences.

At 8 a.m. two large mines were detonated under strongpoints on the heights either side of the valley, and the Austrian–German infantry attacked using specialist 'storm-troop' tactics and the new model Maxim light machine gun. Mountain troops infiltrated the strongpoints and batteries along the crests of the ridges to protect the flanks of the main attack, laying reinforced telephone cable as they did so to maintain contact with the artillery. Among the German troops taking part was Leutnant (later Field Marshal) Erwin Rommel, whose Württemberg Mountain Battalion took three peaks south of Caporetto and 9,000 prisoners in just over two days. Rommel himself won the coveted *Pour le Mérite* honour for his aggressive spirit, and used the experience of the assault to develop his own ideas about offensive tactics, of which he wrote in his 1937 book *Infanterie Greift An* ('Infantry Attacks'), which was said to have helped persuade Hitler to give him command of an armoured division in 1940.

For the Italians, it was almost impossible to hold out against this well-planned and well-executed attack. Although they beat back the enemy on either side of Below's main thrust, the penetration – up to 15 miles by nightfall – began to throw 2nd Army into disarray. Many troops, believing the situation lost, threw away their weapons, declaring hopelessly: 'Andiamo a casa!' (We're going home!)

As the offensive gained momentum in the following days, and 2nd Army troops on the flanks of the main thrust fell back so as not to be cut off in the parallel valleys, Below's divisions reached the open plain, the high road to the great valley of the Po, and for a while it looked as if there would be a complete collapse. Cadorna ordered a general retreat, hoping to stabilize the front on the Tagliamento, but 2nd Army had in effect disintegrated.

No army in full retreat is a pretty sight, and the stories of Italian indiscipline (and worse) are unedifying, but in truth there would be similar scenes in Sir Hubert Gough's 5th Army in March 1918, when the Germans launched their great *Kaiserschlacht* offensive on the Western Front. The Italian army did rally, and largely of its own will and capability. Fortunately, to the right of 2nd Army was the duke of Aosta's 3rd Army, with its right flank on the Gulf of Venice. Aosta's men had withstood the attacks on their front, and now as they withdrew to avoid envelopment they were able progressively to take over enough of the front to make a junction with 4th Army, commanded by Mario di Robilant. Di Robilant, withdrawing from the Carnic Alps west of 2nd Army, had been able to take up a strong defensive position on Monte Grappa and extend east to the Piave, which was fortuitously swollen by the autumn rains. Here, in the second week of November, his and Aosta's 3rd Army were at last able to bring Below's 14th Army and that of the Austrian General Svetozar Boroević to a complete halt.

Meanwhile, putting into action the contingency plans drawn up earlier in the year, eleven French and British infantry divisions, plus heavy artillery and aircraft, were rushed to Cadorna's aid from the Western Front. Although – with the exception of some of the artillery – they would not arrive in time to take a direct part in the fighting along the Piave, they helped strengthen the front subsequently and, with further reinforcements, would take part in the counter-offensives the following year which led to the Austrians suing for peace.

For the time being, however, the price of sending allied divisions from France was to be Cadorna's sword. On 8 November he was replaced by his former chief of operations Armando Diaz, a humane and highly respected Neapolitan, who would now have to play the part of Pétain after Verdun, nursing Italian morale back to health.

Diaz's task was prodigious. When the fighting died down in late November, the army had retreated over 100 miles. The 670,000 men of 2nd Army were widely scattered: over 280,000 of them were prisoners of war and a further 350,000 were simply absent, while 40,000 were dead or wounded. Over 3,000 artillery pieces and a similar number of machine guns had been lost, along with huge quantities of munitions, food, animal fodder, petrol and medical supplies. By contrast, Austrian–German casualties, killed and wounded, were around 70,000.

While Diaz's task was as urgent as Pétain's before him, therefore, it was also more complex, not least in respect of the army's reputation. Commanding Freya Stark's field ambulance was George Macaulay Trevelyan, described later as 'probably the most widely read historian in the world'. Writing of Caporetto, he concluded:

In order to understand the nature of the phenomenon, before inquiring into its causes, it is necessary to realize that there were three distinct categories of conduct among the Italian troops. To confuse any one of these three categories with either of the other two is to misunderstand the whole affair.

First, there were a few regiments who, in accordance with a previously-formed intention, abandoned their duty, and surrendered on purpose. This was 'Caporetto' in the narrower and more strictly accurate sense, for it was only in that geographical zone that such betrayal occurred; but unfortunately Caporetto was the key to the whole strategic position.

When, consequently, a general retreat had been ordered, the second category of conduct was observable in a much larger number of men . . .

[Second Army] carried out irreproachably the difficult retirement across the Isonzo gorge and out of the hills; but as they proceeded over the plain, hustled by the victorious enemy pouring down on their flank from Cividale, they were gradually infected by the sense that all was lost . . .

The last scenes of the Second Army were a sad falling from what the same men had shown themselves two months before.

The third and largest category of all consisted of the troops who did their duty throughout. Most of, though not quite all, the Third Army from the Carso, and the Fifth, First, and Fourth Armies on the Cadore and Trentino fronts, saved Italy by holding fast where required, and retreating in order where necessary, so that the shorter line was success-fully established in the early days of November.

Many heroic feats of individual companies, regiments, and divisions illumined the worst hours of the Retreat. And some of the finest of these were performed by units of the Second Army itself, both in the mountain region of Matajur above Caporetto, and in the plain of Udine.

When Freya Stark herself crossed the Piave and stumbled into Padua to be reunited with her field ambulance, she had not bathed for a month, nor rested in sixty-four hours. She was amazed to find the place full of shops selling 'ordinary things', and people going about their business despite the growing number of military refugees. After taking a bath and some sleep, she ventured out and in one of the shops bought a chiffon blouse. 'It was the most frivolous and unwarlike thing to catch my eye,' she wrote in her diary. She had already written, 'I weep so easily now.'

40

NOVEMBER

Cambrai

The first mass tank attack gains spectacular results, but they are overturned in an impressive German counter-offensive

'Just a line. A big battle has begun & we are taking the leading part. In fact it could not have taken place without us . . .' wrote Lieutenant-Colonel J. F. C. 'Boney' Fuller, on the staff of the Tank Corps, to his mother on 20 November 1917. 'I believe the attack was one of the most magnificent sights of the war, great numbers of Ts forging ahead in line of battle followed by infantry . . . Elles our General led the battle in a T, flying our colours. I am glad to say he has returned safely, though the flag has been shot to tatters.'

The Battle of Cambrai was born of the disappointments of Third Ypres (Passchendaele). In July, just before the opening of his great offensive to break through at Ypres and capture the Channel ports, Field Marshal Sir Douglas Haig, a cavalryman, told his army commanders that 'opportunities for the employment of cavalry in masses are likely to offer'. Meanwhile, on the other side of no-man's-land, the German chief of staff, General Erich Ludendorff, an infantry-man, was convinced that 'trench warfare offered no scope for cavalry'. Indeed, he wanted to dismount them and give their horses to the artillery and transport: 'The wastage in horses was extraordinarily high, and the import from neutral countries hardly worth the consideration.'

But while Ludendorff saw the Western Front as siege warfare on an industrial scale, Haig, as a fellow general put it, regarded it as 'mobile operations at the halt'. Ever since succeeding Sir John French (also a cavalryman) as commander-in-chief in December 1915, he had constantly sought a return to the war of movement of 1914. In his view – and that of the army's 'bible', *Field Service Regulations* – decisive success in the field was to be achieved only by robust attack. In Haig's view, this meant an offensive leading to breakthrough followed by rapid exploitation, in which cavalry would be of the first importance.

Both sides had tried to break through in 1915, but without success, leaving their cavalry champing at the bit in frustration. It was the same again in 1916, first for the Germans at Verdun, and then for the British and French on the Somme. Fortunately, away from the front, minds had been at work on the problem of how to penetrate the German lines. In February 1915, Winston Churchill, then first lord of the admiralty, impatient with the War Office's lack of interest in mechanical trench-crossing devices, had himself set up the 'Admiralty Landships Committee' to investigate their potential. Seven months later, in September 1915, the first design was tested; by December a completely new and improved version was produced; and in January 1916 this first 'tank' was demonstrated to the War Office – which was sufficiently impressed to place an order for 100 of them, equipped with either 6-pounder cannon or Hotchkiss and Vickers machine guns. Thirty tanks went into action in the middle of September during the Somme battles; although most of them broke down prematurely, or were engulfed in the mud, nevertheless Haig recognized their worth and ordered several hundred more.

Opinions as to how the new weapon was to be used were divided. Some officers in the Heavy Section, Machine Gun Corps, the unit responsible for fielding the tank, believed from the outset that they should be used en masse and with a degree of independence. Inter-communication was only by hand or flag signals, however, and reliability remained a problem. Fosters, the Lincoln firm respon-sible for the development work, had been contracted for engineering tolerances of just 50 miles between breakdowns, which – allowing for movement to the start line from the railheads – did not envisage any great part in advancing. The War Office, and moreover Haig's GHQ, saw tanks essentially as battering rams to crush the initial defences – the multiple trench lines and fortified positions – in order to allow the cavalry to break out.

Haig certainly had high hopes of them at Third Ypres. He had some 140 available for the offensive, all but two of which made it to the start line without mishap. But the mud of Passchendaele would prove even worse than that of the Somme; soon the tanks were stuck fast, and once again the cavalry stood waiting in vain for the breakthrough.

Morale in the new Tank Corps, formed from the Machine Gun Corps on 27 July, fell, as did the confidence of the rest of the army in the tank. The corps needed to be given a fighting chance, on ground specially chosen – better drained and not pock-marked with shell craters. HQ Tank Corps therefore proposed an offensive towards Cambrai. However, planning for Cambrai – originally con-ceived as a raid, a limited action to show what the tank could do in the right conditions – soon fell prey to the continuing ambition for breakthrough and restoration of the war of movement. Not the least in ambition was another cavalryman, General Sir Julian Byng, recently appointed to command of 3rd Army after Haig had sacked Edmund Allenby, and now given responsibility for the battle as a whole. In 1757, one of his ancestors, Admiral John Byng, had faced a firing squad – *pour encourager les autres* – for failing to press his attack on a French fleet off Minorca. General Byng was not going to make the same sort of mistake.

He decided to throw all his divisions into the attack, and all his allotted fighting tanks – 380 of them (the Tank Corps now had 476 machines in all, including spares and various specialist tanks) – leaving himself without reserves. Haig placed virtually the entire Cavalry Corps, some 27,500 cavalrymen and their support troops, under Byng's command, with the intention that they should 'pass through and operate in open country'.

The preparations were prodigious. Some of the regiments had to march long distances to the assembly areas – the Queen's Bays, for example, 106 miles in five night marches. Oats and hay for the horses – 270 tons – had to be pre-positioned. 'Cavalry track battalions' were formed, largely of Indian NCOs and sowars (troopers) recently arrived in France as reinforcements, to make gaps in the barbed wire and fill in or bridge the trenches and shell holes to help get the cavalry forward in the wake of the advancing tanks and infantry. With pick and shovel, assisted by tanks fitted with grapnels to tear up the wire, they were expected to clear paths 60 yards wide to a depth of 5 miles, bridging twenty-six successive lines of trenches.

The battle began well. On 20 November, in an obliging morning mist and before a single artillery round had been fired, the massed tanks answered to the command 'Driver, advance!' Favoured by the absence of the usual artillery notification, and their own quite remarkable success in concealment during the build-up (aided by the RFC's local air superiority), the tanks took the Germans wholly by surprise. When the following infantry reached the forward trenches they found flasks of hot coffee at the firing step – breakfast hastily abandoned. On a 6-mile front, checked only at Flesquières, by midday Byng's divisions were able to penetrate 5 miles into the defences of the Hindenburg Line – further to date than anywhere on the Somme or in Flanders. By early afternoon, only a half-finished fourth line stood between 3rd Army and open country, and here there was a wide-open gap for several hours.

An advance of 5 miles, even a relatively easy one, was tiring, however. By now the tanks were crewed by men exhausted by noise, fumes and concussive vibrations, or were out of action owing to breakdown or enemy fire. The infantry could make no further progress without them, and if the infantry could make no progress, the cavalry certainly couldn't. Besides, for whatever reason – poor communications, lack of 'dash' in regiments that had been inactive for three years (recriminations would follow) – the cavalry were slow getting forward.

And they certainly *were* expected by the Germans. Leutnant Miles Reinke of *2 Garde-Dragoner Regiment* wrote home: 'We waited for several regiments of cavalry to sweep up and drive us towards Berlin. But this didn't happen, much to our surprise.' Indeed, expecting to be over-run at any minute, they had even abandoned Cambrai itself.

With no reserve of tanks and infantry to renew the attacks, Byng told his spent troops to dig in, and the cavalry, when they did come up in the afternoon, to hold along the St-Quentin Canal. German reserves began pouring into the breaches, and the following morning, after a night of icy rain, the British faced the predictable counter-attacks.

Haig sent more divisions to Cambrai, but it was too late. Byng's renewed attacks on 22 and 23 November quickly petered out, while with impressive speed, and largely undetected, the Germans massed twenty divisions for a counter-offensive. These came out of the morning mist on 30 November after a short, intense bombardment consisting of high explosive, gas and smoke – but with almost no tanks, for the Germans did not rate them. Using new infiltration techniques they thrust at both flanks of the salient created by 3rd Army's advance, breaking through in the south. Byng's infantry put up a resolute defence, and disaster was averted, but only with considerable loss, including Brigadier-General Roland Boys Bradford VC, MC – at twenty-five the youngest brigade commander of modern times, who had been in command for just three weeks.

Byng was now forced to abandon the greater part of his original gains. German casualties at Cambrai were around 50,000; the BEF's were 45,000 (of which 10,000 were dead), yet with nothing to show for it, just the sense of a 'near miss', a demonstration of what the tank could do in the attack if well handled. The church bells, which had rung in England on the first day to announce a resounding victory, had sounded prematurely.

A board of inquiry was held in London to examine how the spectacular initial success had turned into another costly reverse. Byng survived, as did Haig, though the perceived intelligence failures led to the dismissal of his chief of intelligence, Brigadier-General John Charteris.

However, the tank had at last proved itself. Production was now stepped up, and faster types were developed. From Cambrai on, it was seen as an essential element in the all-arms battle, which was itself the key to any sustained success on the Western Front.

As 'Boney' Fuller wrote to his mother, Brigadier-General Hugh Elles had led the Tank Corps into the battle 'flying our colours', which were 'shot to tatters'. The flag was in fact almost as famously improvised as the 'Star-Spangled Banner' at the defence of Fort McHenry. Nothing had been done about distinguishing colours for the Corps, and so just before the battle Elles went into a French shop to find material for a flag. Although stocks were small, he managed to buy some lengths of brown, red and green silk, which were then sewn together and flown from his tank, *Hilda*. Fuller suggested that the colours typified the struggle of the Corps – 'From mud, through blood to the green fields beyond.'

Ever after, the flag has been flown with the green uppermost.

41

DECEMBER

'How the devil can we finish this war?'

*Another year of failed allied offensives closes
with dismal prospects for the next*

New Year's Eve on the Western Front in 1917 was an occasion for 'fireworks'. In *Undertones of War*, Edmund Blunden, who had joined the army in 1915 almost straight from school and was now a captain in the Royal Sussex, with a Military Cross from the Somme, and still not fully recovered from being gassed in November, wrote of the 'successions of coloured lights ... but the sole answer to the unspoken but importunate questions was the line of lights in the same relation to Flanders as at midnight a year before. All agreed that 1917 had been a sad offender. All observed that 1918 did not look promising at its birth.'

It was certainly true of the Western Front – and indeed the Eastern and Southern: each new offensive in 1917 had failed. What was left of the Eastern Front was falling apart as Russia descended into civil war. On 15 December an armistice was signed between the new Bolshevik government and the Central Powers, and from the Baltic to the Black Sea the guns fell silent. On the Southern Front(s)

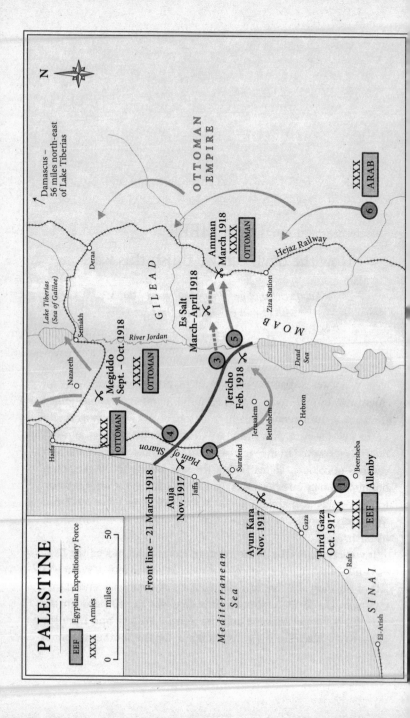

PALESTINE

EEF Egyptian Expeditionary Force

XXXX Armies

miles
0 — 50

N

Damascus –
56 miles north-east
of Lake Tiberias

OTTOMAN EMPIRE

XXXX ARAB ⑥

Deraa

Lake Tiberias
(Sea of Galilee)

GILEAD

Es Salt
March–April 1918

Amman
March 1918
XXXX OTTOMAN ✕

Hejaz Railway

Seriakh

River Jordan

⑤

③✕

Ziza Station

MOAB

Nazareth

Megiddo
Sept. – Oct. 1918
XXXX OTTOMAN ✕

Jericho
Feb. 1918

Dead
Sea

Haifa

XXXX OTTOMAN ✕

Sharon

④

Plain of

Jerusalem
Bethlehem

Hebron

②

Auja
Nov. 1917

Jaffa

Surafend

Front line – 21 March 1918

Beersheba

Ayun Kara
Nov. 1917

Mediterranean
Sea

①

XXXX EEF ✕ Allenby

Gaza

Third Gaza
Oct. 1917

Rafa

SINAI

El-Arish

a sizeable chunk of the north Italian plain lay in enemy hands after the Austro-German counter-offensive in October, and in December Romania, isolated after the Russian collapse, gave up the fight, releasing yet more Germans and Bulgarians for the Macedonian front. On the Western Front, the French were still licking their wounds after the ruinous Nivelle offensive, and the British, now the stronger ally, had been stopped in their tracks at Third Ypres (Passchendaele) – which was why the line of lights in Flanders had not advanced in a year. The Americans were arriving, but not yet in large numbers, and their troops were very green.

There had been good news further afield, however: Jerusalem, whence the Ottomans exercised their rule in Palestine, had fallen to British and Dominion troops of General Sir Edmund Allenby's Egyptian Expeditionary Force. Allenby himself entered the city on 11 December by the Jaffa Gate on the western side, but on foot rather than mounted in the traditional fashion of the victorious general. 'Only one man rides into Jerusalem,' he said simply, though Jesus of Nazareth had entered the city on 'Palm Sunday' via the Golden Gate, on the east side.

Jerusalem had fallen without a shot, too. Allenby had simply out-manoeuvred the Turks, and within a mere six months of arriving in theatre. Having been relieved of command of 3rd Army in France in June, in the wake of the failure to make progress at Arras, he had been chosen by Lloyd George to replace the hapless Sir Archibald Murray after the second failure to break through the Turkish defences at Gaza, which held the key to Palestine. Murray had been a serial failure – first as chief of staff of the BEF in 1914 under Sir John French, then as CIGS in London, and now as a commander-in-chief. He was, however, a methodical planner; it had been his eye for detail that had mastered the immense logistical challenge of crossing the Sinai desert and got the EEF to the other side. On the other hand, Allenby, 'the Bull', brought dynamism to the campaign. Although he was now facing Field Marshal Erich von Falkenhayn, who had worsted the Romanians in September before being made commander-in-chief of the Ottoman army group in Palestine,

Allenby was well served by his three corps commanders: the infantryman Lieutenant-General Edward Bulfin, the cavalryman Philip Chetwode, and the Australian Henry Chauvel – 'Light Horse Harry' – who, unusually even in the higher ranks of the Australian forces, was a regular.

In early November, Allenby broke the Gaza defences by a surprise attack at Beersheba, whose famed wells would prove invaluable to Chauvel's Desert Mounted Corps of 'Anzac' light horsemen and British Yeomanry. Now the pace could quicken, for hitherto, especially during the transit of Sinai, water had been a constant problem, and much reliance had had to be placed on the slower-moving camel for both reconnaissance and logistics.

Having opened the door to Palestine at Gaza, Allenby now pressed his advance on two axes, one towards Jaffa, the other towards Jerusalem. On 12 November four divisions of the Ottoman 8th Army counter-attacked in front of Wadi Sara Junction on the Jaffa–Jerusalem railway, but were held by the Australian Mounted Division fighting dismounted. In turn, the following day, Bulfin's XXI Corps, augmented by elements of Chauvel's, attacked and dislodged 8th Army who were deployed in hastily constructed but naturally strong defences. This and the failure of the Turk rearguards to check XXI Corps' follow-up in the coming days forced 8th Army out of Jaffa, while 7th Army withdrew into the Judean Hills to defend Jerusalem.

Despite a series of counter-attacks in the coming days checking the first attempt to surround Jerusalem, on 8 December Chetwode's corps, which had relieved Bulfin's in the advance, took the heights to the west of the city, and the Turks, now threatened with envelopment, gave up the ground that evening.

Exactly what happened the following morning is the subject of much anecdote. The mayor of Jerusalem, Hussein Salim al-Husseini, wanting to spare the city from bombardment, rode out to deliver the Ottoman governor's letter surrendering the city to Allenby's forces, but had difficulty finding anyone to accept it. In his memoir *The Romance of the Last Crusade: With Allenby to Jerusalem*, Major Vivian

Gilbert of the Machine Gun Corps recounts how the mayor's first attempt to hand over the letter – to a foraging cook, a certain Private Murch of 'one of the London regiments', met with failure. Murch's commanding officer had sent him into the village of Lifta to find eggs for breakfast. The cook, 'a miserable specimen', his clothes 'covered with grease and filth', wearing a misshapen helmet 'at least one size too small', and in boots so worn that his 'very big red toe' stuck out of one of them, got lost and stumbled into the mayor's party.

In broken English al-Husseini addressed him: 'Where is General Allah Nebi? I want to surrender the city please. Here are the keys; it is yours!'

'Murch' (Gilbert appears to have disguised his true identity) is supposed to have replied, in rich Cockney: 'I don't want yer city. I want some eggs for my hofficers!'

The mayor rode on and some time later came across two scouting sergeants, James Sedgewick and Frederick Hurcomb, of the 19th Battalion, London Regiment (Territorials). They too refused to take the letter, but sent word of it back. Eventually Brigadier-General Charles Watson, commanding the 180th (London) Brigade, came forward, found the mayor and rode with him to the city where a small but jubilant crowd met them outside the Jaffa gate. Watson formally accepted the surrender and returned to his headquarters, only to learn that the divisional commander, Major-General John Shea, a Bengal Lancer, was on his way to take the surrender instead. Watson therefore rode back to Jerusalem with the keys and asked the mayor to wait for General Shea.

Shea arrived by car not long afterwards and was warmly greeted by a now larger crowd. The mayor once again surrendered the city and both he and the general gave short speeches, to loud cheers.

On returning to his headquarters, Shea telegraphed to Allenby: 'I have the honour to report that I have this day accepted the surrender of Jerusalem.'

Allenby, however, appreciating that the moral significance of taking Jerusalem was far greater than its military importance, immediately telegraphed back that he would 'himself accept the surrender of Jerusalem on the 11th inst'. Shea again returned the keys to the mayor, and two days later Allenby made his pointedly humble entry. It was a gesture not lost on the Arabs, who had seen the Kaiser enter the city on a white horse during his visit to the Holy Land twenty years before.

Although it would be another ten months before the whole of Palestine was occupied, the fall of Jerusalem was indeed a fillip to British morale. In one respect, however, Britain's troubles here were only just beginning, for there were conflicting promises to be reconciled. Grand Sharif Hussein ibn Ali al-Hashimi, guardian of the holy city of Mecca, had been given to understand that by siding with Britain and the western allies against Constantinople, he would win unity and independence for the Arabs at the end of the war; in particular, that London would recognize the independence of a united Arab state comprising the Arab provinces of the Ottoman Empire, including all of Palestine. In May 1916, however, Britain, France and Russia had reached a secret agreement in which the major part of Palestine was to be 'internationalized', and in subsequent developments a letter sent secretly by Arthur Balfour, secretary of state for foreign affairs, to the British Zionist Baron de Rothschild promised support for the establishment in Palestine of a 'national home' for the Jewish people. The 'Balfour Declaration' would become one of the future League of Nations' first and thorniest problems.

To the high command on the Western Front, however, Palestine was a sideshow, for it occupied few Germans: only in France and Flanders could Germany be beaten, for that was where Germany's strength lay (though not, of course, its weakness). Yet how was the German army to be beaten after three years of failed offensives? General Émile Fayolle, who had been appointed to command the French central army group when Philippe Pétain was made commander-in-chief, before being sent to Italy in the wake of Caporetto, confided bleakly to his diary: 'How the devil can we finish this war?'

There were indeed some voices suggesting that the allies – in particular Britain – could not do so without self-defeating losses, and therefore should not try to end the war by force of arms. The most compelling of the advocates for a negotiated peace was the Marquess of Lansdowne, who in November 1916, as the Somme offensive dragged on with increasing losses, had put a memorandum before the cabinet forcing them to confront the scale of slaughter of the country's young men, arguing that continuing the war would destroy the nation's vital strength, and proposing that peace be negotiated on the basis of the *status quo ante bellum* – in other words, without annexations or reparations.

The memorandum was not well received, and when Lloyd George became prime minister the following month, Lansdowne was quietly dropped from the cabinet. For many months, however, he continued to try to persuade his former colleagues of his argument, before deciding to mount a public campaign. He invited the editor of *The Times*, Geoffrey Dawson, to publish a letter outlining his proposals for a negotiated peace, but Dawson decided that publication was not in the national interest. Lansdowne then offered the letter to the *Daily Telegraph*, which published it on 29 November 1917:

> We are not going to lose this war, but its prolongation will spell ruin for the civilised world, and an infinite addition to the load of human suffering which already weighs upon it . . . We do not desire the annihilation of Germany as a great power . . . We do not seek to impose upon her people any form of government other than that of their own choice . . . We have no desire to deny Germany her place among the great commercial communities of the world.

The letter was almost universally condemned as 'a deed of shame'. It was also probably unrealistic, for later research suggested that the German government's minimum peace terms would have been incompatible with Lansdowne's proposals, which would have been summarily rejected by Berlin. Field Marshal Haig, for one, countered by saying that the prospects for 1918 were 'excellent'.

If Haig's prediction was necessarily confident – he had the

morale of an army to maintain – it was nevertheless disingenuous. On 28 December, writing in his diary of his first proper meeting with General John J. ('Black Jack') Pershing, commander-in-chief of the American Expeditionary Force (AEF), Haig recorded that he had told the US general that he was expecting a huge German offensive to be mounted in the spring, that the 'crisis of the war would be reached in April', and that he had one question for Pershing: how might the AEF help?

What Haig could not yet have appreciated, however, was that there was soon to be a sea change in the allied direction of the war. On 16 November Georges Clemenceau, at seventy-six still the most dynamic of all French politicians – he was not known as 'the Tiger' for nothing – became prime minister. From an office in the war ministry, rather than the Matignon, the premier's traditional residence, 'Le Tigre' declared his policy in the simplest of terms: 'Je fais la guerre' – 'I [intend to] make war.'

He had once said that war was too important to be left to the generals; and he was now determined that he (and Lloyd George) would direct the strategy in the year ahead.

PART FIVE

1918

Finis Germaniae

3 March: Russia signs (peace) Treaty of Brest-Litovsk.

21 March: Germany launches spring offensive.

15 July: Second Battle of the Marne begins.

8 August: Battle of Amiens ('the black day of the German army').

21 August: Beginning of the 'Hundred Days' (allied counter-offensive).

24 October: Battle of Vittorio Veneto (Italian front) begins.

30 October: Turks sign Armistice (throughout Middle East); Bulgarians sign Armistice (fighting on Macedonian front effectively ceases).

3 November: Austria-Hungary signs Armistice (Italian front).

9 November: German Kaiser Wilhelm II abdicates and flees Germany.

11 November: Germany signs Armistice at Compiègne.

42

JANUARY

Peace without Victory?

'And I said to the man who stood at the gate of the year:
"Give me a light that I may tread safely into the unknown." '

King George VI made these lines famous by including them in his 1939 Christmas broadcast to the Empire. They begin the poem 'God Knows', written by the English missionary Minnie Haskins, later a tutor at the London School of Economics, and published privately in 1912. Had they been spoken by George VI's father, George V, at Christmas 1917, they would have been scarcely less apt. But unlike January 1940, at the gate of the year in 1918 there was indeed a man with a light wishing to share it: President Woodrow Wilson.

Yet Wilson was not so much answering the despairing question that the French General Émile Fayolle had confided to his diary as the new year came – 'How the devil can we finish this war?' – as proposing how the enemy might be persuaded to end it. The United States had entered the war in April 1917, Wilson insisting on the (largely symbolic) term 'co-belligerent' rather than 'ally' to define his country's status in the conflict, but up to now the US had been not so much a 'co-belligerent' as a non-belligerent. Except at sea, and in the air, US forces had seen little fighting. The American Expeditionary Force, under General John 'Black Jack' Pershing, was still in formation and training. The US army was having to expand even more rapidly than the British army had had to do in the first year of the war, the intention being to put a million men into the field by the end of 1918, starting from a regular army strength of at most 150,000.

Wilson's light by which to tread safely into the unknown came in the form of the 'Fourteen Points', which he put to Congress on 8 January 1918. The United States, he said, had entered the conflict as 'a war for freedom and justice and self-government'. While this was designed in part to appeal to domestic idealism, his intention was also to exploit the fragility of the enemy's 'multinationality'. The Central Powers principally comprised three multinational empires: the German Hohenzollern (the most homogeneous, but not without internal tensions), the Austro-Hungarian Hapsburg (the most polyglot, culturally and religiously diverse), and the Ottoman Turkish, which even before the war resembled the Roman Empire in its over-extended, terminal stages.

Wilson deliberately played to the growing ethnic unrest in the Austro-Hungarian Empire by promising independence and self-determination for all the nationalities involved, extending this to include those of the former Russian Empire, which since the Bolshevik Revolution in November 1917 was in a state of incipient civil war and had withdrawn from the allied war effort to negotiate a separate peace.

Eight of the Fourteen Points addressed specific territorial issues, the most important of which was that Alsace and Lorraine should be returned to France. The other six addressed the future conduct of international relations, prescribing an end to secret treaties; reciprocal and free trade; limits on national armaments; impartial adjudication of competing colonial claims; and 'freedom of the seas', an objective that would have the distinction of being opposed by Britain, France and Germany alike. Most significant, however, was Wilson's fourteenth point, that 'a general association of nations

302

must be formed under specific covenants for the purpose of affording mutual guarantees of political independence and territorial integrity to great and small states alike' – the League of Nations.

'The day of conquest and aggrandizement is gone by,' he declared, and it was 'this happy fact, now clear to the view of every public man whose thoughts do not still linger in an age that is dead and gone, which makes it possible for every nation whose purposes are consistent with justice and the peace of the world to avow now or at any other time the objects it has in view.'

In Wilson's call for a just and stable peace there were echoes of Pope Benedict XV's 'peace note' of August 1917, in which he called for 'peace without victory' – a note given short shrift by both the allies and the Central Powers. In truth, though, while Wilson's Fourteen Points offered a measure of succour to nationalists in the Austro-Hungarian Empire, who increasingly equated peace with their coming independence, they would do little to hasten the end of the war. They would, however, form the agenda for the peace conference in Paris that followed.

For the time being, largely at the urging of the British prime minister, David Lloyd George, the allied leaders strove to arrive at a more unified strategic approach to the war. At their emergency meeting at Rapallo in November 1917, after the débâcle at Caporetto, when the Italian army was thrown back almost to the Venetian lagoon, the French, British and Italian prime ministers approved the creation of a 'supreme war council' at Versailles to coordinate military policy, initially with respect to Italy, but also with a view to the strategy for the Western Front in the coming year. Lloyd George would rule out any idea of a renewed offensive in Flanders, advocating a policy of strategic defence until such time as the AEF could take to the field in strength and preferring any offensive to be against the Turks in Palestine and Mesopotamia instead. With intelligence of the transfer of increasing numbers of German troops from the Eastern to the Western Front, and knowing that the Germans could not afford to let the relative strengths (by some measures, 192 allied divisions to 169 German) turn decisively against them, especially with the continued erosion of civilian morale in Germany itself, all the allied leaders expected that the German chief of staff – effectively commander-in-chief – Erich Ludendorff, would mount a major offensive in early spring, and that, in Field Marshal Haig's words, the 'crisis of the war would be reached in April'.

For those in the trenches and the rest areas, however, January 1918 was just another month to be endured, the chief vexation now being not so much the Germans as the weather. Leonard Ounsworth, a gunner in a heavy battery of the Royal Garrison Artillery, recalled:

> The thaw started on January the 15th, with rain as well – so complete that the ground just collapsed. The end of the dugout just fell in and buried one of the cooks – he'd have suffocated if we hadn't got him out in time. Four of the guns were moved to Sorel [Somme] that day. They couldn't have picked a worse one for it, because by the time we got there the ground was an absolute quagmire.

Keeping up morale became an even greater priority: one way was foraging for ordnance, which was increasingly lucrative, with the shortage of metal in Britain putting a premium on salvage. In the Cambrai sector, Major Andrew Bain of the 7th Argyll and Sutherland Highlanders, a territorial battalion, recorded:

> I made a sort of salvage-price list, and distributed this to the four battalions in my brigade. It said 'For every rifle you'll be credited with two pounds; for a shell case, six pence; for ammunition about two pence a dozen for spent cartridge cases.' And that mounted up enormously. One month, the 6th Gordons, by just combing over the ground and picking up everything that was there, collected about six thousand pounds [£450,000 in today's prices].

With little prospect of serious action for a month or so, more leave could also be granted, sometimes for apparently exigent reasons. Captain Cyril Dennys of the Royal Garrison Artillery described how although he himself was 'very young', he believed that the sexual aspect worried some of the older men quite a lot. I mean, it made them jumpy. I remember there was one case where a captain who was getting on in age applied for special leave. You could get a week's special leave to go to Paris or somewhere. On his leave chit he was asked for his reason. He put quite boldly sexual starvation. And to everyone's surprise and delight he got his leave.

For the American Expeditionary Force, however, it was a time to familiarize themselves with trench routine and patrolling before the expected German offensive, although Pershing feared that 'the long period of trench warfare had so impressed itself upon the French and British that they had almost entirely dispensed with training for open warfare', and was determined therefore that the latter should be the focus of the AEF's training as soon as they were able to look after themselves when in the line.

There were practical problems, however. With the direct approach that had characterized American military thinking for at least half a century, Pershing saw his route on to German soil – key to winning the war – as the shortest distance between two points. That was through Lorraine (or, since 1871, 'Lothringen' to the occupying Germans), which meant that his starting place, and therefore the AEF's concentration area, had to be behind Verdun and the St-Mihiel salient: 'If the American Army was to have an independent and flexible system it could not use the lines behind the British–Belgium front nor those in rear of the French front covering Paris.'

When Pershing had visited GHQ on 28 December, however, Haig had asked him how the AEF might help in the event of a German offensive, 'the crisis of the war', for there were now almost 200,000 American troops in France, although as yet only one division had appeared at the front. Pershing was single-minded in his determination to keep the AEF as a discrete army under his own command, ready for the great offensive when the time came – and indeed, President Wilson had told him to keep his distance from the BEF – but Pershing was also a realist. Haig recorded in his diary, with evident relief, the AEF commander-in-chief's agreement that, if the situation became critical, he was ready to 'break up American divisions and employ battalions and regiments as draft to fill up our divisions'.

Who was to decide that the situation was critical was, of course, another matter.

There is no record of a comparable undertaking to the French, but while this does not signify any unwillingness, it does perhaps suggest a nascent, and not altogether surprising, Anglo-American 'special relationship' of the kind that was already developing between the respective intelligence branches. President Wilson's concern to keep the AEF at a distance from the BEF (exacerbated by the view of the CIGS, Sir William Robertson, who had urged that American troops be incorporated in units of the BEF as if they were simply British) and to look instead to the French, as the 'old ally', was all very well, but the *Grand Quartier General*, the French general staff, had proved reluctant to share intelligence. The head of the AEF's G2 (intelligence) branch, Brigadier-General Dennis Nolan, had therefore been turning increasingly to Brigadier-General John Charteris at GHQ, whom he found a much readier collaborator (though in January Charteris would be sacked because of the findings of the committee of inquiry into the failure of intelligence at Cambrai). Besides, the language and organizational differences with the French were already proving a hindrance to training, and so later that month Pershing decided to accept Haig's offer to take 150 battalions into the BEF to train. Initially one American battalion would be allotted to each British brigade, after which they would be progressively grouped into American regiments, the AEF's equivalent of brigades, and divisions.

By the end of January 1918, although inter-allied bickering and the mistrust between the British military leadership and Lloyd George continued, and while there was no consensus on precisely how and when the war would end, there was at least the confidence that unless 'the crisis of the war' was mishandled, there would come a peace with victory for the allies. The secretary for war, Lord Derby, went so far as to bet Lloyd George a hundred cigars to a hundred cigarettes that the war would be over by the next new year.

43

FEBRUARY

Doughboys

As the Russian front disintegrates further,
on the Western Front the Americans fire their first shots

In August 1917 the Pope had made his appeal for peace, declaring his neutrality to be 'appropriate to him who is the common father and who loves all his children with equal affection'. It brought him little filial warmth in response. In February 1918 it would be the turn of the Kaiser to speak of sacred matters: 'War is a disciplinary action by God to educate mankind,' he told the citizens of Bad Homburg, gathered in the courtyard of the castle, his summer residence for thirty years and now the place of his February *Kur*.

He had good news for them: the new People's Republic of Ukraine, detached from the Russian Empire in the wake of the Bolshevik takeover, had on the previous day signed a peace treaty. It signalled ultimate victory, he said, and in the meantime would bring them more bread, for Ukraine always had a surplus of grain. (In many parts of Germany, the flour was by now being supplemented with potato peelings and sawdust.) It was, indeed, the *Brotfrieden* – the bread peace. But he warned them too that Ukraine was 'shaken by a civil war . . . [and] could be overrun by the Bolsheviks and large parts of the grain could be carried away by the Red Army'.

Indeed, at the council of war that followed, the recent armistice with the Russians would be temporarily overturned in order to force the hand of the new government. Since the middle of December, the guns had been formally silent from the Baltic to the Black Sea (and less formally since the November ceasefire), but the peace negotiations at Brest-Litovsk were being deliberately drawn out, said Richard von Kühlmann, secretary of state for foreign affairs. General Max Hoffmann, chief of staff in the east and the guiding brain of the *Grosser Generalstab* throughout the campaigns against Russia, was convinced that both German and Austro-Hungarian forces must immediately take to the offensive again, 'otherwise these brutes [Bolsheviks] will wipe up the Ukrainians, the Finns, and the Balts, and then quickly get together a new revolutionary army and turn the whole of Europe into a pig-sty'.

The Kaiser agreed. There was, he told the war council, a world-wide conspiracy against Germany by Bolsheviks supported by President Woodrow Wilson, Freemasons and 'international Jewry'.

Not only was his proto-fascism a faulty assessment, however, it was inconsistent with recent German policy. It was Berlin that had brought Lenin by train from Swiss exile to Petrograd, and Berlin that had given financial backing to the Bolsheviks, including secret subventions to their newspaper *Pravda*. As for the Jewish conspiracy, what of the (by general estimate) 100,000 Jews serving in the German army, 12,000 of whom were killed in action and 18,000 of whom were awarded the Iron Cross?

Hoffmann was given the green light nevertheless, and on 18 February some fifty-two German and Austro-Hungarian divisions crossed the ceasefire line in *Unternehmen Faustschlag* (Operation Fist Punch). They quickly occupied Dvinsk in Latvia and Lutsk in north-western Ukraine, and soon found themselves advancing along the Russian railway lines against virtually no opposition. 'It is the most comical war I have ever known,' Hoffman wrote in his diary. 'We put a handful of infantrymen with machineguns and one field gun onto a train and push them off to the next station. They take it, make prisoners of the Bolsheviks, pick up a few more troops and go on. This proceeding has, at any rate, the charm of novelty.'

Lenin and his commissar for foreign affairs, Leon Trotsky, a Ukrainian Jew, gave in at once, telegramming Hoffmann to accept all the peace conditions demanded at Brest-Litovsk. With an open road before him, however, Hoffmann was not inclined to accept the capitulation, and prevaricated over the paperwork. On 20 February, German troops entered Minsk, the first city of Belarus and an important railway junction on the Warsaw–Moscow line, taking nearly 10,000 prisoners. 'There is no fight left in them,' wrote Hoffmann. 'Yesterday one lieutenant with six men took prisoner six hundred Cossacks.'

Indeed, during the next two weeks German troops would take the Ukrainian capital, Kiev, and Narva, the easternmost city of Estonia, less than 90 miles from Petrograd. When a German plane bombed the Fontanka embankment close to the Summer Palace, the Bolsheviks' governing council began quitting the city for Moscow, which was declared the new capital on 12 March. With the support, however, of the 39-year-old former editor of *Pravda*, Joseph Stalin, Lenin just managed to persuade his council to accept whatever terms the Germans offered, and on 3 March the Russian delegates at Brest-Litovsk were instructed to sign the punitive treaty that brought the war on the Eastern Front to an end, giving up Finland, Estonia, Latvia, Lithuania, Poland, Belarus and the whole of Ukraine.

Erich Ludendorff, in effect the C-in-C of the entire German army, could now switch even more divisions to the Western Front for what he intended to be the decisive offensive. And they would take with them an extra 2,500 artillery pieces and 5,000 machine guns captured in the recent fighting.

Meanwhile, in London, matters were coming to a head over the terms of reference of the British representative at the new supreme war council at Versailles – in effect a *generalissimo's* headquarters, controlling among other things the planned inter-allied reserve of thirty divisions. Although Lloyd George had been one of its chief proponents, the prime minister now found himself lumbered with three points of advice and decision – Versailles (where the permanent British representative was Sir Henry Wilson), GHQ in France (Haig), and the CIGS (Robertson). Maurice Hankey, secretary of the war cabinet, was at the council's meeting at the end of January and recorded that 'all gave different advice [creating] a worse state of chaos than I have ever known in all my wide experience'.

In the end, 'Wully' Robertson, who had never been a supporter of the idea of a supreme war council (he called it 'the Versailles Soviet'), resigned, whereupon Lloyd George made General Sir Henry Wilson CIGS, and appointed in his place at Versailles – double-hatted as deputy CIGS for supposedly greater control – Sir Henry Rawlinson, lately commander of 4th Army. This would do little to ameliorate the problem of differing advice, but it did at least remove one thorn from Lloyd George's side, for he had found Robertson increasingly difficult to work with of late.

For the rest, February on the Western Front continued as quietly as January, with just raiding and local attacks. For the Americans, however, it was the opportunity to see a little instructive action at last. In mid-January, the 1st US Division had entered the line in the St-Mihiel salient (French sector), the first complete division to do so. On discovering this, the Germans had launched several raids, killing, wounding or capturing a number of US troops. 'This thing of letting the Boche do it all is getting on the nerves,' noted one officer in his diary: it was certainly not 'the American way'.

On 13 February the AEF got its first opportunity to strike back, albeit in a limited way, when several artillery batteries took part in a six-hour bombardment prior to a French attack at Butte de Mesnil in Champagne. Then, ten days later, just south of Laon, two officers and twenty-four enlisted men took part in a raid alongside French troops, capturing several dozen Germans. In its report of the action, *The Times* commented that although 'the actual occasion was not of much importance, February 23 is one of the dates that will always be remembered in the history of the war'.

Another memorable date would be the fifth, but for a more melancholy reason – the loss of the former luxury liner *Tuscania*, pressed into service as a troopship, to a German torpedo off the north coast of Ireland, and with her of 166 US servicemen, the first to be killed on their way to Europe, together with 44 of her British crew. The German submarine UB-77 had sighted *Tuscania*'s convoy during the day and shadowed them until early evening, then under cover of darkness had fired two torpedoes, the second of which struck home, sending her to the bottom in four hours.

Elsewhere on the Western Front, one of the most famous – and certainly most controversial – American soldiers of the twentieth century was about to become the first to be decorated by the French. On 26 February, Colonel Douglas MacArthur, chief of staff of the US 42nd Division – 'the Rainbow Division' – had sought permission of the general commanding the line at Réchicourt to accompany a trench raid that night. His dress surprised both the raiders and one of the 42nd Division's ADCs who had slipped away to join in 'the picnic' as he called it. Instead of a steel helmet MacArthur wore his service cap, and rather than pistol, knife or club – the preferred weapons of a trench raid – he carried his riding whip. 'It's the orders you disobey that make you famous,' he told the ADC.

He was right. The raiders had a hard fight, but they returned at dawn with a large bag of prisoners, including a colonel whom MacArthur had taken in his personal charge and prodded back to the trenches with his riding whip. Though the seat of MacArthur's immaculate riding breeches was left behind on the wire, General de Bazelaire greeted the 38-year-old trench-raider with a kiss on both cheeks and pinned on him a Croix de Guerre. The story made the *New York Times* the following week, together with the opinion of the Rainbow Division's commanding general that 'Colonel MacArthur is one of the ablest officers in the United States Army and one of the most popular'. A fortnight later MacArthur would win the US Distinguished Service Cross in one of the 42nd Division's own raids, and by the end of the war was commanding the division whose name he himself had suggested – 'Rainbow' because it was made up of militia units from across America, rather than, as most of the others, recruited from a single state.

The AEF, for all their greenness, not least among the officers, were certainly creating an impression; and at the time of lowest ebb in allied morale – after the fruitless losses of 1917, and facing a massive and desperate German offensive – the impression alone was reassuring. When General Pershing visited GHQ at the end of December, Haig had been particularly impressed by his ADC, 'a fire-eater, [who] longs for the fray'. He was Captain (later General) George S. Patton.

As for the 'doughboys' themselves, they had, wrote Vera Brittain in *Testament of Youth*, 'an unusual quality of bold vigour in their swift stride'. While serving as a nurse at the British base at Étaples she saw for the first time a contingent of them marching down the road:

> They looked larger than ordinary men; their tall, straight figures were in vivid contrast to the under-sized armies of pale recruits to which we had grown accustomed. At first I thought their spruce, clean uniforms were those of officers, yet obviously they could not be officers, for there were too many of them; they seemed, as it were, Tommies in heaven. Had yet another regiment been conjured from our depleted Dominions? I wondered, watching them move with such rhythm, such dignity, such serene consciousness of self-respect. But I knew the colonial troops so well, and these were different; they were assured where the Australians were aggressive, self-possessed where the New Zealanders were turbulent.
>
> Then I heard an excited exclamation from a group of Sisters behind me. 'Look! Look! Here are the Americans!'
>
> I pressed forward with the others to watch the United States physically entering the war, so God-like, so magnificent, so splendidly unimpaired in comparison with the tired, nerve-racked men of the British Army.

Yet Pershing was still determined to take his time, and to keep the AEF as a discrete force rather than – except for training – integrating its divisions in allied corps. Notwithstanding his accommodating response to Haig's question when they had met on 28 December, he continued to stand aloof from allied planning, and would certainly not commit troops to the inter-allied reserve.

In mid-December, the French high command had noted a 'crisis of pessimism' among its *poilus*, and by mid-February the postal censors were reporting growing doubts about the Americans, and the *poilus*' 'anxiety' as to whether US cooperation would 'shorten the war or prolong it'. The late-February morale report observed bleakly: 'The depth of weariness is obvious.'

44

MARCH

Kaiserschlacht

The Germans' last hope of victory: a million-man offensive in the West

In his memoirs, General Erich Ludendorff, the man who by early 1918 was effectively running the German war effort and wielding increasing power over German politics and industry, wrote that at this point 'the condition of our allies and of our Army all called for an offensive that would bring about an early decision. This was only possible on the Western Front.'

The Royal Navy's blockade was beginning to cripple German civilian morale, as well as constricting supplies for the front. One deserter, Heinrich Fleischer, volunteered to work for the British Secret Service Bureau after going on leave to Berlin and finding his family 'white and emaciated, with nothing to eat but turnips and watery potatoes'.

If Ludendorff could not force a decision on the Western Front by the end of the year, a million and more newly arrived Americans would be poised to decide matters in 1919.

With the signing of the peace treaty with the Bolshevik government at Brest-Litovsk on 3 March, Ludendorff could now turn his

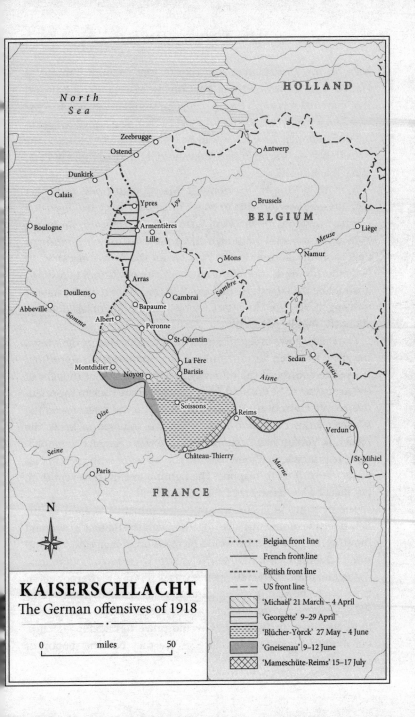

North
Sea

HOLLAND

Zeebrugge
Ostend
Dunkirk
Calais
Boulogne
Ypres
Armentières
Lille
Arras
Doullens
Abbeville
Bapaume
Albert
Peronne
St-Quentin
Montdidier
Noyon
Barisis
La Fère
Soissons
Château-Thierry
Paris

Antwerp
Brussels
BELGIUM
Liège
Mons
Namur
Cambrai
Sedan
Reims
Verdun
St-Mihiel

Lys
Meuse
Sambre
Somme
Oise
Aisne
Seine
Marne
Meuse

FRANCE

N

Belgian front line
French front line
British front line
US front line
'Michael' 21 March – 4 April
'Georgette' 9–29 April
'Blücher-Yorck' 27 May – 4 June
'Gneisenau' 9–12 June
'Mameschüte-Reims' 15–17 July

KAISERSCHLACHT
The German offensives of 1918

0   miles   50

back on the Russian front and transfer the remaining troops to France. 'I set aside all idea of attacking in Macedonia or Italy. All that mattered was to get together enough troops for an attack in the west,' he wrote. When he told the Kaiser that he planned to assemble 900,000 men for what would be called *Die Kaiserschlacht* – the Kaiser's battle – the reply was: 'Add another hundred thousand and make it a million.'

By withdrawing troops from the Macedonian front, and other measures, he was just able to do so. In January there had been 169 German divisions in the west against 192 allied ones. By March 1918 there were 191 (although the Americans were beginning to field more divisions too). Not only would *Die Kaiserschlacht* be, in Ludendorff's words, 'one of the most difficult operations in history', it would be the largest. He had also told the Kaiser that 'the state of training of the Army for attack enabled us to contemplate doing so about the middle of March'.

The training was as significant as the numbers. During the winter, the army had been forming units of elite *Sturmtruppen*, 'storm[ing] troops', to spearhead the offensive. 'The whole line of thought of the Army had to be diverted from trench warfare back to the offensive,' wrote Ludendorff, for they had stood on the defensive on the Western Front since mid-1916, when the attempt to break the French at Verdun had begun to falter. 'It was necessary to emphasize the principle that men must do the work not with their bodies alone but with their weapons. The fighting line must be kept thin, but must be constantly fed from behind.'

The light machine gun was to be the principal weapon in this new doctrine of the offensive, together with the flame-thrower and the rifle. The *Sturm* teams would be made up of men under thirty-five, including picked riflemen, who were withdrawn from routine duties and given better rations. Their task was not to overpower but to infiltrate, bypassing strongpoints to penetrate deep into the enemy's defences, leaving pockets of resistance to the second wave of more legionary infantry. They would prove formidably effective, but might have been even more so had they had the support of tanks. The one consolation to the allies was that the Germans had simply not thought these worthwhile enough to put into serious production, even after the experience of Cambrai, and fielded only a few dozen 'A7s' (named after the war ministry department responsible, the *Allgemeines Kriegsdepartement, Abteilung 7*), together with the same number of captured British Mark IVs. 'They were merely an offensive weapon, and our attacks succeeded without them,' reckoned Ludendorff.

Sturm tactics without sound operational strategy could not be enough, however. In December, Ludendorff's strategic adviser, Lieutenant-Colonel Georg von Wetzell, head of the operations section of the *Oberste Heeresleitung* (supreme army command), had written an appreciation of the situation on the Western Front. He was not greatly impressed with the expertise of the British army (including its imperial troops): the artillery, he said, 'like the British tactics as a whole, is rigid and stiff'. He thought the French much nimbler, 'just as skilful in the tactical use of their artillery as of their infantry', and their 'use of ground in the attack ... just as good as in the defence'. Their losses at Verdun in 1916 and the setbacks of the Nivelle offensive in 1917 had clearly taken their toll, though, and Wetzell thought the French 'not such good stayers as the British'. With the British, he concluded, 'we have a strategically [at GHQ level] clumsy, tactically rigid, but tough enemy in front of us'. The Third Battle of Ypres – Passchendaele – despite (perhaps even because of) all its terrible slaughter, showed that although French strength was on the wane, with growing British material strength and resolve, the Germans would now face an even harder fight.

Wetzell also pointed to the problem of maintaining the momentum in an advance through what he called the 'shot-to-pieces battle area' that had been left by the German withdrawal to the Hindenburg Line a year earlier, and the subsequent fighting. Moving forward the artillery would be especially slow. The logistical problems, already grave, would increase as the advancing troops got further from the railheads and depots, exacerbated by the shortage of both draught horses and mechanical transport (the Germans had 23,000 motor lorries, most with iron-rimmed wheels, compared with the allies' 100,000 with rubber tyres). Wetzell accordingly concluded that there would have to be 'operational pauses' in the offensive so that the supporting arms and services could catch up with the leading troops. These, however, would give the enemy time to reorganize their defences, aided by 'the excellent railway communications behind the front'. He warned, therefore, against hoping for a rapid breakthrough, urging instead a series of coordinated simultaneous attacks, in the hope that somehow the allied line could be prised apart.

For once, however, the allies would not be taken by strategic surprise. Any appreciation of the Germans' military situation could not fail to conclude that they now saw the war as a race with the American Expeditionary Force, whose drafts were arriving in the many thousands each month. Nor could aerial reconnaissance fail to pick up the signs of the German buildup, any more than the signals intercept service could miss the increased radio and telegraph traffic. Besides, by this stage in the war the allies had extensive human intelligence sources in Belgium and the occupied areas of France. The Secret Service Bureau operated a number of collection systems, one of the most successful of which was *La Dame Blanche* (named after the spectral harbinger of downfall in European myth), a network of train-watchers able to supply information on the movement of individual divisions, from which the bureau, together with the War Office's military intelligence directorate and the intelligence branch in GHQ, was able to put together a detailed German order of battle in north-west France and Flanders. The French had similar arrangements, including agents whom they inserted by air behind enemy lines.

On 19 February, *The Times* published a despatch from Harry Perry Robinson, its new war correspondent (its previous correspondent, the celebrated Colonel Charles à Court Repington, having resigned in a dispute with the proprietor, Lord Northcliffe, who wanted to distance the paper from Haig after the setback at Cambrai). Robinson explained:

The German offensive is now undoubtedly very near. Evidence accumulates daily, especially convincing being the statements of prisoners taken recently . . .

An immense amount of training for the attack has been going on. Of that we have been assured by our airmen. To escape observation, much of the training is being done in remoter areas . . .

The training is largely in the nature of open fighting, for the Germans seem to count on breaking our lines and getting the warfare into the open country behind, in which they are going to be aided by the use of gas, tanks and trench mortars. There will probably be no obliterating bombardment such as has preceded most of our great attacks, but in the days before the assault counter-battery shooting, both with gas and high-explosive shells, and long spells of destructive fire on trenches, communications, billets, and so forth. Immediately before the attack there will be only a short burst of fire, behind which men are to come over in one grand rush, while immense numbers of mobile guns and trench mortars will push up behind the supporting troops.

R. C. Sherriff, who served as a captain in the East Surreys, put the words of many a front-line soldier into the mouth of Lieutenant Osborne in his 1928 drama *Journey's End*, set in the run-up to *Die Kaiserschlacht*: 'We are, generally, just waiting for something.'

But GHQ did not know where, exactly, the Germans would attack. Ludendorff considered three options: in Flanders, to capture the remaining Channel ports; in the east, abreast Verdun, where the weakened French might this time be overwhelmed; or at the junction of the allied line between Arras and St-Quentin. The advantage of striking at the junction was that the enemy might retreat in diverging directions – the French to cover Paris, and the British along their lines of communication to the Channel ports, giving the latter very little manoeuvre room.

Forecasting the enemy's moves – as opposed to identifying his options and the relative merits of each – is more an art than a science, and therefore subject to the full range of human frailties. The forecast made by the 'E' (Enemy) Group of the British military staff at the allied supreme war council at Versailles would prove to be reasonably accurate, but was largely dismissed by GHQ as a result of the friction between the two headquarters.

To meet the expected attack, Haig, in order to cover the Channel ports, concentrated his strength in the north, while the French, to cover Paris, strengthened their positions to the south of the British. Three British armies – from right to left, 3rd (Byng), 1st (Horne) and 2nd (Plumer) – covered the two-thirds of Haig's front from Cambrai to the sea, some forty-six divisions in all. General Sir Hubert Gough's 5th Army, with just fourteen divisions, held the remaining third, from Cambrai to the Oise (4th Army, having had so many divisions withdrawn in late 1917, existed on paper only). Haig had thereby insured against the worst case, and had also strengthened Arras, a natural bastion and key communications centre, but in doing so he had left the junction with the French relatively weak. To compensate for this, GHQ sought to deceive the Germans with contrary intelligence, not least through the press. The *Times* article of 19 February accordingly also stated: 'So far as our front is concerned, especial attention is being given to sectors between Arras and St Quentin.'

Gough was not the subtlest of generals, and after Passchendaele morale in 5th Army was not the highest. In consequence, and also because 5th Army was relatively weak in numbers, Gough did not arrange his defences in the sort of depth that the Germans had at Third Ypres, and which Haig himself had stipulated. Gough appears to have believed rather more in the inherent superiority of a strongly held front line, and also that his infantry lacked the capacity for counter-moves under fire if held back in depth. Besides, GHQ's intelligence assessment was that the Germans had stood on the defensive for so long, and taken such a beating at Passchendaele, that they had lost the edge in offensive spirit. Consequently, nine out of ten of Gough's battalions were disposed within 3,000 yards of the front line – well within range of field artillery, and liable to be over-run or bypassed before they could adjust.

It was at this point of junction between 5th Army and the French that Ludendorff chose to strike – with the army group of the Crown

Prince. As late as 16 March, however, GHQ was sure that 'no significant attack is expected south of the Bapaume–Cambrai road'. A
week's shelling across the whole allied front had given nothing
away, and nor would its sequel in the five days following.

Then, at 4.40 a.m. on 21 March, a massive bombardment – the
new German technique of the *Feuerwaltz* (fire-waltz), a mixed bombardment of high explosives, smoke, tear gas and poison gas – was
opened on the foremost trenches and artillery positions along
40 miles and more of 3rd and 5th Armies' front. Operation Michael
(after the archangel depicted in Christian iconography in armour
with fiery sword in hand, trampling a dragon), the first phase of *die
Kaiserschlacht* had begun. At nine o'clock, Hartwig Pohlmann, an
officer in the 36th (Prussian) Division, left his dug-out after what he
described as 'a little breakfast' ready for the advance, but could see
nothing. 'It was thick fog. I thought, how can we attack in this?'

At 9.35, the creeping barrage began and Pohlmann told his
soldiers

> to hang on with one hand to the belt of the man in front, but they
> couldn't do that for long because the ground was very rough and we had
> to creep through barbed wire. So soon there was a pell-mell, but every-
> one knew that they had to go straight on ... As we advanced through
> the fog we suddenly heard guns firing behind us. We realised we had
> come out behind a British battery ... One of my men laid a hand on the
> shoulder of the British officers and said, 'Cease fire.' They were stunned.

If Pohlmann's recollections were coloured by the years, they certainly illustrate the confusion into which 5th Army was thrown that
morning. In just five hours, the Germans had fired a million shells
at 5th Army's sector – over 3,000 a minute. The British line began to
collapse, though there were many stubborn – heroic – pockets of
resistance. Near St-Quentin, the 16th Manchesters, a 'New Army'
battalion, were holding the line at what became known as Manchester Hill. Their commanding officer was Lieutenant-Colonel Wilfrith
Elstob, who was not yet thirty. A parson's son from Sussex, Elstob

had been commissioned in the first wave of volunteers in 1914 and promoted successively within the same battalion. He had told his men: 'Here we fight, and here we die.' The citation for his posthumous VC, won that day, ran:

> For most conspicuous bravery, devotion to duty and self-sacrifice ... During the preliminary bombardment he encouraged his men in the posts in the Redoubt by frequent visits, and when repeated attacks developed controlled the defence at the points threatened, giving personal support with revolver, rifle and bombs. Single-handed he repulsed one bombing assault driving back the enemy and inflicting severe casualties. Later, when ammunition was required, he made several journeys under severe fire in order to replenish the supply. Throughout the day Lieutenant-Colonel Elstob, although twice wounded, showed the most fearless disregard of his own safety, and by his encouragement and noble example inspired his command to the fullest degree. The Manchester Redoubt was surrounded in the first wave of the enemy attack, but by means of the buried cable Lieutenant-Colonel Elstob was able to assure his Brigade Commander that 'The Manchester Regiment will defend Manchester Hill to the last.' Sometime after this post was overcome by vastly superior forces, and this very gallant officer was killed in the final assault, having maintained to the end the duty which he had impressed on his men . . . He set throughout the highest example of valour, determination, endurance and fine soldierly bearing.

At two o'clock Gough gave the order to 'give ground' – to begin fighting a delaying action while the heavier guns were pulled back to escape capture. Soon, however, under the continued pressure of the *Sturm* troops and the sheer weight of artillery fire, 5th Army was in full retreat. By nightfall, after the Germans had fired some 3.2 million artillery and mortar rounds – at that time the greatest bombardment in history – the rearmost lines had been breached in several places, and the defenders south of St-Quentin driven right out. Within twenty-four hours the Germans would take nearly 150 square miles of the Western Front in some of the most spectacular advances of the war. It was not without cost, however: they had suffered some 40,000 casualties. British casualties were roughly the same, including 21,000 taken prisoner.

A young officer in the 2nd Yorkshire Regiment (Green Howards), Herbert Read – later Sir Herbert Read, the art critic and writer, and one of the thirteen war poets commemorated by name in Westminster Abbey – described in a letter to his future wife the frantic days that followed:

> We were rushed up to the line in the early hours of the morning, and from then and for six days and nights we were fighting as I never dreamt I would fight – without sleep – often without food and all the time besieged by hordes of the Boche. The Colonel was wounded during the second day and I had to take command of the battalion. We were surrounded in our original position and had to fight our way through. We took up position after position, always to be surrounded. On the whole the men were splendid and there were many fine cases of heroism. But our casualties were very heavy and we who have come through may thank our lucky stars eternally.

One of the thirteen poets who did not come through was Private Isaac Rosenberg. In 1915 he had enlisted in a 'Bantam battalion' consisting of men under the minimum (in 1914) height of 5 feet 3 inches. The Bantams were originally intended not for combat but for labour and support duties. Such had been the losses the previous year, however, that in March 1918 Rosenberg found himself with the 1st King's Own, a pre-war regular battalion, and on 1 April this diminutive Jewish infantryman from the East End was killed during night fighting near Arras. The American literary critic and Second World War infantry officer Paul Fussell would call Rosenberg's 'Break of Day in the Trenches' the greatest poem of the war.

Although there would be recriminations, 5th Army put up as much of a fight as could reasonably be expected in the circumstances. A German report stated: 'The [British] 7th Corps covered the retreat of the main body even to the extent of being destroyed itself.' Gough, however, would pay the price, not least because in part the circumstances were of his making. He was relieved of command on 28 March and replaced by Henry Rawlinson, brought back from Versailles.

At the end of December, Haig had told General Pershing that the crisis of the war would come in April. At the end of March, the crisis looked as if it were already come.

45

APRIL

'Backs to the Wall'

*The Germans almost break through in Flanders,
forcing Haig famously to reach for his pen*

The massive attack on General Sir Hubert Gough's 5th Army front
on 21 March was potentially as shattering for the cohesion of the
allied line as the Austro-German attack in October had been on the
Italian front at Caporetto. So ferocious was the initial artillery
assault and so innovative were the German infiltration tactics that
by 25 March three British divisions – the 16th (Irish), 36th (Ulster)
and 66 (East Lancashire) – each with losses of over 7,000, had
practically ceased to exist.

Unlike at Caporetto, however, the Germans on 5th Army's front,
while able to infiltrate and bypass locally, were unable to make the
big, bold, fast outflanking moves that had destroyed the unity of
the Italian line in the Alps and astride the Isonzo. Lacking both
cavalry (for a great many of Ludendorff's regiments had been de-
horsed to provide draught animals for the artillery and transport)
and tanks, when 5th Army began to withdraw – even at times
precipitately – the Germans could move no faster than their quarry.

One of the reasons was that a year earlier, in their own withdrawal to the Hindenburg Line, they had devastated the ground over which they now advanced.

It was the very problem that had prompted Ludendorff's strategic adviser, Lieutenant-Colonel Georg von Wetzell, to warn, during the planning of *die Kaiserschlacht*, against expectations of rapid break-through. Ludendorff had accordingly set no precise objectives, saying only that he intended to 'punch a hole into [their line]. For the rest, we shall see.'

After all, it had worked for him, and for Hindenburg, in Russia in 1914. And indeed, the men on the receiving end of Ludendorff's massive punch – both those of Gough's 5th Army and, increasingly, those to the north, on the right wing of Byng's 3rd Army – struggled to stem the German advance. Lieutenant Ulick Burke of the 2nd Devons, which though a regular battalion was by 1918 made up largely of conscripts, and whose officers in the main had joined since 1914 – men of Kitchener's 'New Army' – described the disori-entating experience of those days of constant retreat:

Then we halted, stayed where we were. We did as much defence work as possible and waited for them to come. Then they'd come on and we'd get the order – after we'd shot and killed quite a few – to retire. Well, we were retiring and retiring and we were never still. You never knew where you were going to pick up any food, where you were going to pick up ammunition, and some of the men got windy and really would have run. Now if an officer or a sergeant had behaved like that, the whole lot would have panicked. The only thing that kept them there was respect for your bravery and your attitude; you knew what you were doing and you were saving them all you could. And that kept them steady.

It was dispiriting, too, to be abandoning ground taken the year before. Sergeant-Major Richard Tobin, of the 7th (Hood) Battalion, 63rd (Royal Naval) Division, in Byng's 3rd Army, remembered how in late March they 'dropped into a trench . . . we knew of old. We had started to retreat on 21 March, and here we were back in the trench we had started to attack from on November the 13th, 1916.'

For this was the old Somme battlefield.

Here and there the speed of 5th Army's retreat actually became something of a problem for the Germans, for large parts of Gough's ordnance stores, with their abundant food and quantities of rum, brandy and whisky, had to be abandoned. For troops on increasingly short and unattractive rations, even the elite *Sturmtruppen*, it was sometimes simply too much to resist. As more than one historian has been unable to resist saying, the advance was slowed not so much by lack of German fighting spirit as by the abundance of Scottish drinking spirit.

Meanwhile in Paris something close to panic began taking hold, with Pétain, the French commander-in-chief, saying the war was as good as lost. The civilian population was already unnerved by bombing (on 8 March, Gothas had dropped 100 bombs on the city, precipitating the flight of 200,000 Parisians to the country), and the Germans were shelling the suburbs, now within the 70-mile range of their specially made Krupp railway guns.

The crisis, however, at last galvanized the allied leadership. On 26 March General Foch, the French representative at Versailles, had been instructed, in the words of the memorandum signed by Clemenceau and the allied plenipotentiaries, 'to coordinate the action of the allied armies on the Western Front'. Specifically, he was to form a common reserve and to use it to guard the junction of the French and British armies and to plug the potentially fatal gap that would have followed a German breakthrough. A fortnight later, with Paris looking as if it might fall, Foch was formally appointed *généralissime* (more usually, *generalissimo*): supreme commander. He now had strategic direction of all the allied armies on the Western Front, including the Americans, and in June his remit would be extended to cover the Italian front as well. This appointment meant that Ludendorff could not now divide the French and British armies, because Foch saw their cohesion as the greater priority than Haig's of covering the Channel ports. If it became necessary – and Foch told Haig and the supreme war council that he didn't believe it would – the armies would retire as one towards the Somme.

In this, Foch would be proved right. Ludendorff had indeed punched a hole into the allied line, but his offensive, 'Michael', had run out of steam. Despite attacks on the French line to fix their reserves in place, Pétain had, if somewhat belatedly, moved significant reinforcements to ease the pressure on Amiens, which was key to the continued cohesion of the allied line. Determined allied counter-attacks, including a magnificent mounted charge by a squadron of Lord Strathcona's Horse (Canadian Cavalry Brigade) at Moreuil Wood, together with the strengthening of a new line of defence, and handy reserves, halted the *Kaiserschlacht* just short of the city. After a fortnight's advances, in some places over 40 miles, on 5 April Ludendorff brought Operation Michael to a close.

Total British losses, including dominion troops, were 178,000, including over 75,000 taken prisoner, plus 1,300 guns and 200 tanks, while the French lost 77,000 and the Germans 240,000. But Amiens and Arras stood firm. Ludendorff would now turn his attention instead to the north, French Flanders, with the aim of pushing 1st Army (Horne) and 2nd Army (Plumer) back against the Channel ports.

The northern sector of the British line had been thinned out to reinforce the Somme, and the weakest link in this weakened sector was the Portuguese Corps, which held the front in the plain of the River Lys. Their morale was probably the poorest of any corps in the entire allied line, not least for the fact that home leave arrangements had largely broken down with the problem of shipping created by the need to bring US troops to Europe, and the submarine menace.

On 9 April, therefore – Ludendorff's fifty-third birthday, for which the Kaiser came to lunch at the *Oberste Heeresleitung* at Avesnes-sur-Helpe and presented him with a bronze figure of his imperial self – Operation Georgette began. After a short, sharp *Feuerwaltz* bombardment – high explosive, poison gas and smoke – fourteen divisions of Prince Rupprecht of Bavaria's army group (General Ferdinand von Quast's 6th Army) attacked along a 10-mile front towards the Lys at Armentières. Four divisions of well-rested *Sturmtruppen* assailed the Portuguese sector. So ferocious had been the bombardment, and so skilled was the assault troops' attack, that within an hour the Portuguese front line – apart from a few isolated positions – was taken, along with 6,000 prisoners.

The British troops on either side of the three-and-a-half-mile hole thereby opened up in the allied line were also soon on the retreat to avoid being outflanked – just as had happened at Caporetto. The Germans had released 2,000 tons of mustard and phosgene gas, incapacitating over 8,000 men, of whom many were blinded. The following day, Armentières fell (and despite a stout defence, Bailleul, across the Lys to the north-west, on the road to Dunkirk, would fall on the fifteenth). On the same day, Plumer's men were driven from Messines, whose capture he himself had masterminded nine months earlier, and would soon give up Passchendaele Ridge too, which had been won at such debilitating cost in November. The Germans now began to commit their reserves, and the situation became critical.

So alarmed was Haig that on 11 April he issued a 'Special Order of the Day':

Three weeks ago to-day the enemy began his terrific attacks against us on a fifty-mile front. His objects are to separate us from the French, to take the Channel Ports and destroy the British Army.

In spite of throwing already 106 Divisions into the battle and enduring the most reckless sacrifice of human life, he has as yet made little progress towards his goals.

We owe this to the determined fighting and self-sacrifice of our troops. Words fail me to express the admiration which I feel for the splendid resistance offered by all ranks of our Army under the most trying circumstances.

Many amongst us now are tired. To those I would say that Victory will belong to the side which holds out the longest. The French Army is moving rapidly and in great force to our support.

> There is no other course open to us but to fight it out. Every position must be held to the last man: there must be no retirement. With our backs to the wall and believing in the justice of our cause each one of us must fight on to the end. The safety of our homes and the Freedom of mankind alike depend upon the conduct of each one of us at this critical moment.

In fact, Foch remained firm in his conviction that the offensive was nothing more than a huge diversion in preparation for something more substantial elsewhere, and gave Haig only limited support. And although both 1st and 2nd Armies were forced to give ground, they were making the Germans pay dearly for it. Hauptmann Stefan Westmann, a medical officer with an assault battalion in Quast's 6th Army, described the sheer weight of machine-gun fire they faced, 'which was so terrific that the losses were staggering. We got orders to lie down and seek shelter. Nobody dared lift his head because they would machinegun us for any movement. The British artillery opened up and the corpses, the heads and the arms and legs flew about and we were cut to pieces.'

He also recalled his astonishment when his battalion over-ran a British field hospital near Merville: it was

> completely intact and there I saw for the first time since years the abundance of material, of equipment which we didn't know anymore about. Amongst other things I found cases full of surgical gloves. The German doctors had to operate with their bare fingers. They had to go into the purulent and contaminated wounds with their bare hands and the only thing to wash our hands with was a kind of sand soap. Two parts of sand, one part of soap. And here I found actually thousands of pairs of rubber gloves.

The war of materiel was beginning to show in every way.

Despite the initial success of Georgette, the Germans managed to advance only some 8 miles. Ludendorff closed down the offensive on 29 April, and began to think of a new line of attack – as Foch had predicted, against the French sector.

APRIL: 'BACKS TO THE WALL'

Casualties on both sides in April had been huge. In five weeks the BEF – technically now the 'British Armies in France' – had lost some 236,000 men (20,000 of them dead and 120,000 taken prisoner), the French around 90,000; but the Germans had lost an irreplaceable 348,000.

Although it was not yet apparent, the 'crisis of the war', which Haig had foretold in his discussion with General Pershing in December, and which he believed had come at the Lys, was past. The Germans had exhausted themselves, and were continuing to do so. They had also taken ground they could not possibly hold against a major counter-offensive by such abundantly equipped and well-supplied troops as the allies.

The appeal had already gone out to the Americans, however, to do all they could to hasten into the field. The chief of the army staff in Washington, General Peyton C. March, at once stepped up mobilization and declared: 'I am going to get the men to France if they have to swim.'

46

MAY

The Cruel Sea

A supreme effort is made to protect US convoys from U-boats

General March would baulk at nothing in his determination to strengthen the American Expeditionary Force. Troopships now sailed into the Atlantic filled to overflowing: tiers of bunks, each shared by three men, sleeping in shifts, reached the overhead (ceiling). Under March's leadership, from May until the Armistice in November, the US War Department despatched over a million and a half men to France.

Getting them there was one thing, however; getting General 'Black Jack' Pershing, the AEF's commander-in-chief, to commit them to battle was another. Even as the great German offensive looked set to continue, and with over half a million Americans already in France, he was adamant that he would not integrate trained battalions within British brigades, insisting instead on building them steadily into separate US brigades, divisions and corps. Haig gave vent to his frustration in his diary: 'I thought Pershing was very obstinate, and stupid. He did not seem to realise the urgency of the situation . . . [He] hankers after a "great self contained American

Army".' As the AEF had no commanders of divisions and corps, nor staffs, Haig believed it 'ridiculous to think such an Army could function alone in less than 2 years' time!'.

It had, after all, taken that long for the BEF to expand into something of the same; but the difference was that the BEF had made that transformation while also doing a great deal of fighting, in the course of which a very large number of men, and, crucially, of experienced officers, had been killed. At a meeting of the supreme war council at Abbeville on 1 May, attended by both Clemenceau and Lloyd George (as well as the Italian prime minister, Vittorio Emanuele Orlando, who had sent several divisions and aircraft to fight under French command), General Ferdinand Foch angrily demanded of Pershing: 'You are willing to risk our being driven back to the Loire?' Pershing, fearing that the French and British might be fought to exhaustion by the end of 1918, and that a great American army would then be needed to win the war in 1919, replied: 'Yes, I am willing to take the risk.' He was not, he said, willing 'to fritter away our resources in this manner'.

Though Foch was Generalissimo, this did not give him the power to direct how individual units and formations were to be used. His authority was to 'coordinate the action of the allied armies on the Western Front.' Lloyd George tried one final time, asking: 'Can't you see that the war will be lost unless we get this support?' Pershing was adamant, however. 'Gentlemen,' he replied forcefully, 'I have thought this programme over very deliberately and will not be coerced.'

But while the arguments went on as to how best the Americans could help win the war, the process of getting them to France looked increasingly vulnerable to demoralizing, even debilitating, losses at sea.

Operating out of Ostend and Zeebrugge, and from the specially constructed base on Heligoland in the German Bight, U-boats had initially had easy access to the English Channel. Almost as soon as war began, however, the Royal Navy had instigated counter-measures in the narrower waters, including the 'Dover Barrage', a belt of minefields and submarine nets between the Belgian coast and Dover, guarded by the 'Dover Patrol'. In late 1917 this had been shifted further south, and searchlights installed, to cover the 22 miles between Folkestone and Cap Gris Nez, so that by May 1918 the Channel was effectively closed to U-boats entering from the north.

The problem remained, however, the exit into the Atlantic via the Shetland–Norway gap. At the allied naval conference of September 1917 it was agreed to close this gap with mines, despite the technological and logistic challenge of mining water 900 feet deep. The component parts of 100,000 of the newly developed Mark 6 'antenna' mine, effective at the assumed maximum submarine depth of 200 feet, were to be manufactured in the United States and assembled in Scotland.

The Mark 6, a 34-inch diameter steel sphere with a buoyancy chamber and 300 lb of TNT, was a highly sophisticated device. The mine was connected to its 800 lb anchor box by a steel mooring cable coiled on a reel. Its depth below surface was controlled by allowing the cable to unwind as it was dropped from the minelayer until on reaching the bottom a sensor locked the reel so it would pull the buoyant mine below the surface, whereupon a float extended the antenna above the mine.

Ten rows of mines were laid at a depth of 80 feet to threaten U-boats on the surface, while submerged craft were targeted by four rows of mines at 160 feet and another four rows at 240 feet. Each mine had two safety devices to render it inert on detaching from its mooring cable. The first was an open switch in the detonation circuit that was closed by hydrostatic pressure 25 feet below the surface. The second was a spring that pushed the detonator away from the explosive charge into the buoyancy chamber unless compressed by hydrostatic pressure. Each mine contained a battery with a two-year life connected to a detonating circuit which could be initiated by any one of five parallel fuzes, four of which were conventional horns in the mine's upper hemisphere. Each horn contained a glass ampule of electrolyte to connect an open circuit if broken by bending the soft metal horn. The fifth and wholly innovative fuze was a long copper wire antenna with a float extending above the mine. A ship's steel hull that touched the antenna would form a battery, the seawater acting as an electrolyte to complete a circuit, with an insulated copper plate on the mine's surface actuating a detonating relay. The mines had five separate spring-loaded safety switches in the detonating circuit, held open by salt pellets that took twenty minutes to dissolve in sea water after the mine was laid overboard.

The US Navy, with Royal Navy support and cover, started laying mines in June 1918, and by November some 56,000 were in position. Within a month of beginning they had claimed the first U-boat. After the war the Admiralty calculated that twenty-three U-boats in all were lost to the 'Northern Barrage', and that it had also been a significant deterrent. The mines further demoralized the German surface fleet, too, whose mutiny in October would be a major factor in the call for an armistice. The cost of the mines was $80 million ($1.3 billion at today's prices) – harbinger of the American way of war.

Besides the minefields, the convoy system introduced in May 1917 was paying dividends. Not only did the escorts provide a strong deterrent to attack, with the improvement of depth charges and development of special equipment such as hydrophones, the convoys became an active means of destroying submerged craft. Aircraft were also an increasing deterrent to surface passage by U-boats, especially when in early 1918 the Germans shifted their attacks to coastal waters in an attempt to sink vessels after the convoys had dispersed to their intended ports of call.

Nevertheless, with the German High Seas Fleet effectively blockaded at Wilhelmshaven, the *Kaiserliche Marine* had no choice but to continue the submarine offensive. In May, Scheer sent six of the new long-range U-boats to operate in American coastal waters. By the end of the war these had sunk nearly a hundred ships, but they were mostly sailing vessels or small steamers, with no effect on General March's transportation plans.

The Admiralty, though, was not satisfied with largely passive measures. The justification for Haig's Third Ypres offensive – 'Passchendaele' – the previous year had been in part the prospect of taking Ostend and Zeebrugge and clearing out Holtzendorff's 'nest of vipers'. After the failure of the offensive to get anywhere near the ports, and the *Kaiserliche Marine's* concentration on attacking in coastal waters, in January the first sea lord, Sir John Jellicoe, was relieved – sacked – for what was perceived as growing defeatism. His successor, Admiral Sir Rosslyn Wemyss, instructed Vice-Admiral Roger Keyes, the new commander of the Dover Patrol, to undertake more vigorous operations in the Channel. Keyes, one of the few senior naval officers to come out of the Dardanelles campaign with any credit, needed no urging. The most spectacular demonstration of the new offensive spirit came in April with the 'Zeebrugge Raid', aimed at blocking the entrances to the Bruges (Brugge) ship canal in Zeebrugge harbour and to Ostend harbour some 15 miles down the coast, as well as inflicting as much damage as possible on both ports.

Devised and led by Keyes personally, the operation involved some seventy-five ships and began with superb symbolic timing at one minute past midnight on St George's Day, 23 April. A force of Royal Marines was to mount a diversionary attack on the mile-long Zeebrugge Mole, destroying the gun batteries, seaplane station and defences, in order to draw the Germans' attention from the main object, the blocking of the ship canal. The action was pure Nelson. The little force was carried to the mole by the old cruiser *Vindictive* and two River Mersey passenger ferries, the *Daffodil* and *Iris II*. *Daffodil's* task was to push *Vindictive* hard up against the mole, then to pull alongside the mole and disembark her marines.

The Germans, if not actually expecting the attack, were alert nonetheless. A smokescreen that had been laid by motor launches to cover the approach had been dispersed when the wind changed direction half an hour before the vessels arrived, and *Vindictive* came under fire as she approached, with many casualties among the storming party. *Daffodil* managed nevertheless to push *Vindictive* against the mole, but could not then disengage, and her marines had to disembark via the cruiser. *Iris II* was unable to land her marines directly on the mole either, and tried to get alongside *Vindictive* instead, but was only able to get a few men off before having to pull away.

At a quarter past midnight, the viaduct connecting the mole to the shore was severed by the submarine HMS C3 to prevent the Germans from counter-attacking. C3's commanding officer, Lieutenant Richard Sandford, son of the Archdeacon of Exeter, ran his boat, packed with high explosive, between the iron pillars of the bridge, had the crew taken off by motor boats, then set the fuzes. He was just able to get away before the explosion.

Meanwhile, three concrete-filled blockships were scuttled in the narrow access channel, though not in the intended positions. In the event, they would only obstruct the canal for a few days, for the Germans removed two piers on the western bank of the canal and dredged a channel through the silt near the sterns of the blockships, which allowed them to get two U-boats past at each high tide. The attempt to block the harbour at Ostend failed altogether when the blockships grounded too far out.

Keyes would make a second attempt in poor weather on 9 May, this time with *Vindictive* as the main blockship; but she too settled in the wrong position, and the entrance remained open.

Casualties at Zeebrugge were heavy for the numbers engaged: over 200 killed and missing, and 400 wounded. Not surprisingly, although in strict terms a failure, the operation was promoted as a victory, with the award of eight VCs, including one for Sandford of the C3, and numerous other decorations for gallantry. The 4th Battalion Royal Marines were deemed to have acted collectively with such valour that two of the VCs were awarded by ballot under rule 13 of the Victoria Cross Warrant, the last time that awards were made by this procedure.

Ludendorff was not to be distracted by pinpricks, however. Besides, he did not believe that the *Kaiserliche Marine* would now achieve anything worthwhile. This was, indeed, the ultimate reason for his great *Kaiserschlacht* offensive. On 27 May he renewed the attack, but this time in the direction of Paris – calling it Operation Blücher–Yorck after the duke of Wellington's great Prussian partner in scourging the French at Waterloo, and Field Marshal Ludwig Yorck, who with Blücher had led the Prussians in the storming of Paris the year before (and in whose honour Beethoven's *Yorckscher Marsch* is named). On a 24-mile front astride the old Aisne battlefield, in the early hours of the morning, 4,000 guns began yet another *Feuerwaltz* bombardment with HE, gas and smoke. In the French sector, along the Chemin des Dames, the Germans broke through to a depth of 12 miles, annihilating four divisions in the process. In just six hours, between Soissons and Rheims, the Germans reached the Aisne, destroying another four French and four British divisions. By the end of the following day a 40-mile-wide, 15-mile-deep salient had been driven into the allied line, and on the fourth day Ludendorff's men reached the Marne near Château-Thierry.

Elsewhere, however, the Germans were not having it all their own way. On 28 May the first entire American brigade would go into attack, at Cantigny on the Somme. The French army provided air cover and additional artillery support – a preliminary bombardment and then a creeping barrage – plus a dozen tanks and the new flame-thrower, which proved particularly effective. The Americans took the village and a hundred prisoners, though not without loss. It was, however, as great a symbolic success as a tactical one, and Pershing gave the order that no inch of Cantigny was to be surrendered. In the next three days the Germans made no fewer than seven counter-attacks, with poison gas, but the Americans held despite mounting casualties – over 1,000 by the time they were relieved, including 200 killed. The brigade commander, the 50-year-old Iowan Colonel Hanson E. Ely, recalled: 'They could only stagger back, hollow-eyed with sunken cheeks, and if one stopped for a moment he would fall asleep.'

Cantigny gave warning – to the Germans and allies alike – that the Americans, though recently arrived and still green in Western Front fighting, were not to be taken lightly. It also gave force to Pershing's argument for an independent US army command. At the meeting of the supreme war council at Versailles on 1 June, Pershing revealed that the planned strength of the AEF in 1919 was now 100 divisions. Although the point was not discussed, such a figure would place Pershing in the driving seat, perhaps even as *generalissimo*. It would also place President Wilson in an almost unassailable position from which to dictate terms of peace.

For the time being, though, Haig fumed in his diary, 'the ignorance of the Americans in all things connected with an Army [was] appalling'.

47

JUNE

The Bread Offensive

The war takes a turn in the allies' favour in Italy and the Balkans

While Ludendorff's attention was focused primarily on the *Kaiserschlacht*, his continuing offensive on the Western Front, he was only too well aware of the interconnection of the four discrete European fronts. In the east, fighting had effectively come to an end with the Treaty of Brest-Litovsk in March, and what troops remained there were a force of observation, except in Finland, where the Bolsheviks were reluctant to cede independence under the terms of the treaty. Ludendorff had sent the Baltic Division to assist the former Tsarist General Carl Gustav Mannerheim, later President of Finland, to eject the remaining Russian troops and put down the Finnish communists. By the end of May, German troops held both Vyborg (western Russia) and Narva (Estonia), respectively north and south of the Gulf of Finland. These Ludendorff intended to use as bases for an advance on Petrograd if it became necessary to overthrow the Bolshevik government, or to prevent the British troops sent to Murmansk in support of the 'White Russian' (anti-Bolshevik) forces from doing so themselves.

The Italian and Macedonian fronts had been quiet for many months, but Ludendorff was content: 'they formed the protection of our flanks, the Macedonian Front at the same time protecting the flank of Austria-Hungary', he wrote in his memoirs. This seemingly distant backwater was, however, rather less secure than he supposed, for morale in the poorly fed and ill-equipped Bulgarian army, which, with a stiffening of German generals, formed the major part of the Macedonian front, was beginning to ebb.

The capitulation the previous month of the Romanians, who after the Russian collapse were effectively surrounded and unable to continue the fight, had at first seemed propitious. The Romanian army, if not exactly agile, had been numerically strong. In July the previous year they had fielded eighty infantry and nineteen cavalry divisions and over 900 artillery batteries – some 800,000 men, with around a million in immediate reserve. The Treaty of Bucharest, signed on 7 May, allowed Ludendorff to withdraw several divisions from the Balkans, which added to his own reserves for the *Kaiserschlacht*. This, however, immediately weakened Bulgarian enthusiasm for the fight, for many army officers, seeing the Turks as the traditional enemy, had anyway tended to favour the Entente. Allied strength on the Macedonian front had received a boost in late 1917, too, with the entry of Greece into the war, and at the end of May the Royal Greek Army, though fielding only ten divisions, roundly defeated the Bulgarians in a two-day battle at Skra-di-Legen, north-west of Salonika.

The other factor on the Macedonian front was Serbia, which the Austrians and Bulgarians had over-run in 1916. The country remained turbulent, but extreme repressive measures had largely kept it in check. The Serbian army, though, having been evacuated via Albania and Montenegro by the Italian navy, had then been re-equipped by the allies and was also biding its time in Macedonia. Indeed, the manpower ratio on this southernmost front was now around three to two in the allies' favour (720,000 Serbian, French, British, Greek and Italian to 575,000 Bulgarian, German and Turk) – with even better ratios in artillery (two to one) and aircraft (ten to one).

Nevertheless, in March, the Austrians – who might have been

expected to reinforce their allies in the Balkans – had instead sent reinforcements to the Western Front to support the *Kaiserschlacht*: first artillery and then, in accordance with the new treaty of mutual assistance signed in May (the *Waffenbund* – literally, 'weapons federation'), several divisions. With ammunition in short supply, however, the artillery had soon returned to the Italian front; and the Austro-Hungarian army had received a boost after Brest-Litovsk with the repatriation of several hundred thousand prisoners of war, although some, notably the Czecho-Slovaks, heeding President Wilson's promise of national determination, had decided to join the allies – or, at least, the White Russians – instead. (Jaroslav Hasek, author of the semi-autobiographical comic novel *The Good Soldier Schweik*, was a member of this 'Czecho-slovak Legion' until, disillusioned, he defected to the Red Army.)

Yet while the boost in manpower was obviously welcome, it increased the logistic difficulties – notably food supply – with which the Austrians had been struggling for some time. Still, the Austrian chief of staff, General-Oberst Arthur Arz von Straußenburg, felt ready to go on to the offensive once more against the Italians, who were now strengthened by French and British divisions and holding firm positions on the Piave, to where they had withdrawn after the débâcle at Caporetto in October. Numerically, the two sides were evenly matched, but the Austrians' supply situation had become so acute that Straußenburg saw the offensive in part as the solution to his problems, for the north Italian plain beyond the Piave was a veritable storehouse. Indeed, the army began speaking of it as *das Brot Offensiv* – the bread offensive.

Meanwhile on the Western Front, Ludendorff, having closed down Operation Blücher–Yorck, the renewed offensive towards Paris, on 11 June, and then on 14 June its adjunct Operation Gneisenau, launched five days before astride the Oise, began hoping that 'relief on the Western Front might be secured in Italy itself'. The cost of the *Kaiserschlacht* was already enormous, with very little strategically to show for it. The Germans had lost 160,000 men in Operations Blücher–Yorck and Gneisenau alone, and although the allies had lost as many, they at least had had the satisfaction of success in halting the offensives.

Ludendorff's hopes of relief were soon to be dashed. On 15 June, the Austrians attacked, directing their main effort between Asiago, at the foothills of the Alps, and the sea. Straußenburg had some fifty-eight divisions available – almost 950,000 men, as many as Ludendorff had had at his disposal for the *Kaiserschlacht*. Facing him were fifty-seven divisions, but with a slight advantage in artillery – some 7,000 guns in all – and a considerable superiority in the air, with nearly 700 aircraft, including five squadrons of the newly formed RAF.

Two of the five British divisions hurriedly despatched to Italy in the aftermath of Caporetto had been recalled to the Western Front in March when the *Kaiserschlacht* began, but two were in the line. These held a front of about 5 miles south of Asiago, with the third remaining division in reserve, although influenza had rendered many troops sick. On 15 June the British divisions found themselves hard pressed opposing the Austrian main effort. In his despatch on the fighting, their corps commander, General the Earl of Cavan, one of the most capable senior British officers of the war – soon to be appointed to command a newly formed 10th (Anglo-Italian) Army – described how his front was attacked by four Austrian divisions:

[The line] was held by the 23rd Division on the right and the 48th Division on the left. On the front of the 23rd Division the attack was completely repulsed. On the front of the 48th Division the enemy succeeded in occupying our front trench for a length of some 3,000 yards, and subsequently penetrated to a depth of about 1,000 yards. Here he was contained by a series of switches [alternative positions], which had been constructed to meet this eventuality. On the morning of June 16th the 48th Division launched a counter-attack to clear the enemy from the pocket he had gained; this attack was completely successful, and the entire line was re-established by 9 a.m.

During the initial Austrian assault, Lieutenant Edward Brittain of the 11th Sherwood Foresters, brother of Vera Brittain, auxiliary nurse and author of *Testament of Youth*, was killed leading a local counter-attack. Brittain had won the Military Cross on the Somme and was highly regarded in the battalion, but it later emerged that his letters to England, intercepted by the censor, revealed that he had engaged in homosexual activity with one of his soldiers and that his commanding officer, Lieutenant-Colonel Charles Hudson, had been told in confidence that Brittain would face court martial when the battalion came out of the line. Hudson warned him obliquely, and it has been suggested that as a result Brittain put himself in the way of fire that first morning. Hudson himself, at twenty-six already with a DSO and bar as well as the MC, and barely four years older than Brittain, would win the VC that same morning, and be badly wounded in the course of doing so.

Opposite them was Lieutenant Ludwig Wittgenstein of the Austrian artillery, alumnus of Trinity College Cambridge and at twenty-nine already a philosopher of note. Almost killed directing the fire of his battery, he was decorated for bravery a third time.

Despite some local successes, however, the Austrians made no real progress that morning, or in the following days. Italian morale had recovered dramatically after Caporetto, in large part owing to the efforts, and personal qualities, of the new commander-in-chief, Armando Diaz. Under his leadership, commanders at all levels had taken to heart the lessons of Caporetto, adopting more 'elastic' tactics for the defence. Cavan himself noted that the

> High Command had ample reserves available and handled the situation with coolness and decision. Steps were at once taken to deprive the enemy of the gains which he had made. Torrential rains brought the Piave down in flood and added to the embarrassments of the enemy. Many of his bridges were washed away, and those which remained were constantly bombed by British and Italian aviators.

On a similar note, George Macaulay Trevelyan, who in 1918 was commanding the British Red Cross contingent in Italy, commented approvingly: 'Above all, the reserves were well handled, here locally as well as by Diaz on the grand scale. The Bersaglieri *ciclisti* were hurried up on their "push bikes" along the lanes to the threatened spot time after time, and never in vain.'

After a week, Straußenburg called off the offensive and withdrew his hard-won bridgeheads back north of the Piave. His casualties had been woefully heavy: nearly 12,000 dead, 80,000 wounded and 25,000 made prisoner. The allies had suffered too, with 8,000 dead, 30,000 wounded and nearly 50,000 made prisoner (many of whom were also wounded), but they remained masters of the field. As Cavan wrote:

> Not only was the original front line entirely re-established, but that portion of the right bank of the Piave, between the Piave and the Sile Rivers which had been in Austrian hands since November, 1917, was cleared of the enemy. Captured orders and documents proved beyond doubt that the enemy's plans were extremely ambitious, and aimed in fact at the final defeat of the Allied forces in Italy. The result was a complete and disastrous defeat for Austria.

Ferdinand Foch, the *generalissimo*, whose powers to coordinate and direct the allied armies now extended to the Italian front as well, pressed Diaz to mount a general counter-offensive to follow up his success. Diaz successfully argued against it, however. Like Pershing, he would not be hurried. When he mounted his grand offensive, he intended it to be decisive rather than merely exploitative. Besides, he argued, once the allies crossed the Piave they would face the same logistic problems that had confronted the Austrians. For the time being, therefore, content to bank the undoubted boost in morale his defensive victory had gained, Diaz ordered only limited actions to seize better start positions from which to launch his decisive offensive when the moment came. He could afford to take his time; the repulse was a catastrophic blow to the Austrian army's own morale and cohesion. From now on internal ethnic tensions would play an increasing part in the collapse of Austrian resistance.

Nor was it just on land that Italian morale received a boost that month. Just before the Austrian attack, the *Regia Marina* (Royal

Italian Navy) had sent the *Szent István* to the bottom of the Adriatic – the only dreadnought on either side to be sunk at sea by direct action. The allies had been strengthening the Otranto Barrage, making it almost impossible for even U-boats to get through the straits into the Mediterranean. The new commander of the *Kaiserliche und Königliche Kriegsmarine* (Austria-Hungary's 'Imperial and Royal' Navy), Rear-Admiral Miklós Horthy, who after the war would become Regent of Hungary, decided to force the barrage by bringing the blockade ships to battle. During the night of 8 June, Horthy left the naval base at Pola on the Istrian coast (in modern Croatia) with two of his four dreadnoughts, *Viribus Unitis* and *Prinz Eugen*, for the attack on the barrage, while his other two dreadnoughts, *Szent István* and *Tegetthoff*, were to sail the following evening to rendezvous with him further down the coast. At first light on 10 June, two Italian motor torpedo-boats (*Motoscafo armato silurante* – MAS) under Lieutenant-Commander Luigi Rizzo, returning from patrol off the Dalmatian coast, spotted smoke from the *Szent István* and *Tegetthoff* group making for the rendezvous. Rizzo at once turned his boats towards the smoke, closed rapidly to penetrate the escort screen and made a run for the dreadnoughts.

MAS 21's two torpedoes ran wide of *Tegetthoff*, but MAS 15's hit the *Szent István* abreast her boiler-rooms. Both boats then evaded pursuit by dropping depth charges in their wake.

Szent István's aft boiler-room quickly flooded, giving her a ten-degree list to starboard. Counter-flooding of the portside trim cells and magazines reduced the list somewhat, but the crew were unable to plug the holes, and the captain therefore steered for the coast at low speed. Water continued to penetrate the forward boiler room and eventually all but two of the ship's twelve boilers were doused, cutting off power for the pumps. In a further effort to counter the list her captain ordered the turrets to be trained to port and their ready ammunition thrown overboard. *Tegetthoff* then tried to take her in tow, but had to abandon the attempt when it became clear that *Szent István* was about to founder. She capsized just after six o'clock, some two and a half hours after being struck, with the loss of eighty-nine crew. The number would have been far higher had not the *Kriegsmarine* changed its policy just before the war to require all seamen to be able to swim.

Horthy called off the attack on the barrage and his fleet returned to Pola, where it remained for the rest of the war. Days before the Armistice, a second of his dreadnoughts, the *Viribus Unitis* ('United Forces', the personal motto of the former emperor, Franz Joseph), would be sent to the bottom – sunk at anchor by Italian frogmen in a daring raid. By then, however – although, with the Austro-Hungarian Empire disintegrating so rapidly, the *Regia Marina* was unaware of it – *Viribus Unitis* had been handed over to the provisional Yugoslav navy.

Soon after *Szent István's* sinking, a Russian dreadnought was also sent to the bottom by torpedo – but one fired from a Russian destroyer. The *Empress Catherine the Great*, launched in 1914 for the Imperial Russian Navy's Black Sea Fleet, had been renamed after the February 1917 Revolution *Svobodnaya Rossiya* ('Free Russia'). When the Treaty of Brest-Litovsk was signed, she had slipped out of Sevastopol for the greater security of Novorossiysk on the eastern shore of the Black Sea, but was scuttled on 18 June when the Germans demanded she be handed over under the terms of the treaty.

The writing was well and truly on the wall for the German *Kaiserliche Marine* too. After a fruitless foray into the North Sea in April to attack a convoy, in which the battle-cruiser *Moltke* was almost sunk by a torpedo fired by the Royal Navy's submarine E42, the High Seas Fleet was to remain inactive at Wilhelmshaven for the rest of the war. Throughout, the Imperial German Navy had lost none of its dreadnoughts, though they in turn had failed to sink any of the Grand Fleet's, with the exception of HMS *Audacious*, which had struck a mine off the north coast of Ireland. Only after the Armistice were any of the Germans' dreadnoughts sent to the bottom – by hand of their own crews interned at Scapa Flow.

48

JULY

Friedensturm

The Germans are finally halted on the Marne,
and Foch declares it time to go on the counter-offensive

By the middle of July 1918, the great and desperate German offensive on the Western Front – *die Kaiserschlacht* – had begun to stall. The military correspondent of the *Berliner Tageblatt*, Lieutenant-General Armand Baron von Ardenne, tried to put a favourable gloss on the situation:

> Our three great battles of assault from March 21st to July 15th caused the enemy losses amounting to 1,225,000 men. On July 15th our attempted surprise failed, and, despite his losses, the enemy's numerical superiority had increased. Then the German command, swift as lightning and without the least hesitation, knew how to find the transition to the now necessary, although momentary, defensive. That was a strategic masterpiece that merits admiration.

The 'strategic masterpiece' was no more than acknowledging reality, but credit was still due to the operations section of the *Oberste*

Heeresleitung, and in particular to its head, Lieutenant-Colonel Georg von Wetzell. During the planning for *die Kaiserschlacht* Wetzell had warned Ludendorff not to expect – and therefore not to attempt – any spectacular success, proposing instead that they take the line of least resistance rather than going for the seemingly most significant objectives. This offered the possibility of progressively prising apart the allied line. Ludendorff had accepted this in principle, but in the event had proved reluctant to break off attacks that appeared to be going well against what he considered to be important objectives. Having failed to make any significant progress in April against the northernmost sector of the British line (Operation Georgette), he had then devised a diversionary attack on the Aisne, hoping thereafter to be able to mount a second thrust towards the Channel ports. This part of the line was held by the French 6th Army under General Denis Duchêne and included the British IX Corps, which had been sent to what was supposed to be a quiet sector to recover from the March battles. It soon became apparent that an attack was imminent, however, and to counter the German infiltration tactics, but contrary to instructions, Duchêne massed his troops in the forward trenches. The three British divisional commanders, having suffered the penalties of forward defence against the new German tactics in Flanders, protested. Duchêne, an experienced infantryman, remained adamant.

The attack – Operation Blücher–Yorck – began at 1 a.m. on 27 May with another huge *Feuerwaltz* bombardment by some 3,700 German guns, saturating the gun emplacements, cutting field telephone lines and isolating the headquarters, and disorientating the defenders. Captain Sidney Rogerson of the Royal Sussex Regiment, attached to 23rd Brigade headquarters, described the scene:

> Crowded with jostling, sweating humanity the dugouts reeked, and to make matters worse headquarters had no sooner got below than the gas began to filter down. Gas masks were hurriedly donned and anti-gas precautions taken – the entrances closed with saturated blankets and braziers were lighted on the stairs. If gas could not enter, neither could the air.

349

The bombardment inflicted devastating casualties. The Germans were able to take the dominating ridge of the Chemin des Dames, while further east, near Rheims, they broke through and were across the Aisne in six hours. By 6 June they were within shelling distance of Paris, and Ludendorff, exhilarated by the prospect of reaching the capital (where the government was once again contemplating decamping to Bordeaux) tried to extend the offensive westward (Operation Gneisenau) to draw yet more allied reserves south, and to join up with his salient at Amiens. However, the French were ready for this, with defence in depth along the River Matz.

It was during Operations Blücher–Yorck and Gneisenau that the US Marine Corps fought its first large-scale action since its founding in 1775. For three weeks the 4th Marine Brigade, alongside the 3rd Infantry Brigade in Major-General Omar Bundy's 2nd US Division, checked the Germans at Belleau Wood, on the Marne. For the United States it was the largest battle since Appomattox (1865) in the Civil War. General 'Black Jack' Pershing, commanding the American Expeditionary Force, is supposed to have said afterwards: 'The deadliest weapon in the world is a United States Marine and his rifle.' It echoed a German intelligence report that described the marines as 'vigorous, self-confident, and remarkable marksmen'.

As before, in mid-June the combination of over-extended supply lines, exhaustion, stiffening allied resistance and counter-attacks brought the German advance to a halt, but at this point Ludendorff, either through desperation or, with Paris so close, genuine miscalculation, finally gave up on Wetzell's concept of seeking the most promising axis of advance. Seeing it was now or never, he gambled on sheer mass, and artillery bluster, though it would take him a month to garner the strength to do so. His grandiloquently named *Friedensturm* (peace offensive), he told the commanders of 1st, 3rd and 7th Armies, would draw the allied reserves south from Flanders, knock out the BEF, expand the salients and bring the Entente (and Americans) to the negotiating table.

By now, though, the allies were getting the measure of the new German tactics. Duchêne himself had been removed from 6th Army and replaced by the colonial artillerist Jean Degoutte, who after the Armistice would command the French Army of the Rhine, and the commander-in-chief, Philippe Pétain, insisted on what he called 'a recoiling buffer defence'. The idea was that, just as the hydraulic railway buffer absorbs impact, the lightly held forward defences would yield to the storm troops, who, outrunning the cover of their own guns and their impetus spent, would be stopped on a strong position in rear and pummelled by the defenders' artillery – the very system the Germans themselves had used to such effect at Third Ypres.

The *Friedensturm* opened on 15 July, but, warned by air reconnaissance and German prisoners, the French were ready. The warning did not come without cost, however, for aerial combat and 'strafing' of ground troops had been intense, and aircraft losses high. Earlier in the month, Major James McCudden VC, DSO and bar, MC and bar, MM – at 23, one of the most decorated British airmen or indeed British soldiers – had been killed in a crash following an engine failure; and before the month was out, one of the RAF's highest-scoring 'aces' and another of its most decorated officers, Major 'Mick' Mannock VC, DSO and two bars, MC and bar, was also dead, killed in a dogfight over the German lines. The day before the *Friedensturm* began, former President Theodore Roosevelt's fourth and youngest son Quentin, not yet twenty-one, was shot down and killed. (His other three sons were also in action, with the infantry and artillery.)

The loss of surprise had gone hard with the Germans. Herbert Sulzbach, adjutant of an artillery regiment in the 9th (Prussian) Division, recalled how the 'first French prisoners came in and told us they knew of our offensive. Our mood was not good after we heard this.' The French heavies shelled the *Sturmtruppen* even before they had left their primitive trenches. Machine guns cut them down savagely in the loose-knit forward defence zone, and then as they ran on to the main position – in the open, and beyond the covering range of their own guns – they were pulverized by every manner of artillery, not least the famous quick-firing *soixante-quinze*, tailor-made for the job.

East of Rheims the offensive stuttered bloodily to a halt, and although on 16 July, to the west of the city, under cover of darkness and smoke, the Germans did manage to get across the sacred Marne (the battle would be known officially as Second Marne) to threaten the Rheims–Epernay road – where the newly arrived 8th Italian Division suffered heavy casualties – by next day here too the attacks had petered out.

On 18 July, the French, with nine US divisions now fighting alongside them, and with British support on their left, counter-attacked. This time they used 'the Cambrai key' (so called after the British tank attack at Cambrai in November 1917): no preparatory bombardment to give away what was coming, enabling the tanks to gain the advantage of surprise, and then exceptional weight of artillery fire on the support trenches and battery positions. Crown Prince Wilhelm, the German army group commander, summed up the tactical shock: 'Without artillery preparation, simply following the sudden rolling barrage, supported by numerous deep-flying air-craft and with unprecedented masses of tanks, the enemy infantry – including a number of American divisions – unleashed the storm against the 9th and 7th Armies at 5:40 in the morning.'

Herbert Sulzbach recalled how his battery

> moved into the front line and were attacked by a barrage which was abso-lutely unbelievable. It was the worst barrage and the worst gunfire I ever heard, and I had been through the Somme and everything else since then . . . the gas attacks [were] fearsome. The gas stuck into the high grass so that even our horses had gas masks.

The French tanks were smaller, faster and more agile than the earlier models, too – the new Renault 'FT' (all Renault projects had a two-letter product code bearing no particular significance), armed with a 37 mm cannon or Hotchkiss machine gun in a revolving turret. (The British 'Whippet' tank, which mounted four machine guns and could make 8 mph, the speed of a trotting horse, had first gone into action in late March.) Aircraft in the ground attack role added to the Germans' discomfort. Sulzbach noted: 'Their aircraft were flying very low and seeing everything that we were doing and bombing us in daylight.'

Yet somehow the Germans managed to rally, and despite French advances of 5 miles on the first day, their counter-attack was eventually halted. For the Americans in particular, the Marne counter-attack was another sharp and salutary blooding. The Germans, especially when cornered, were still lethal – even to the bravest, corn-fed 'doughboy' if he was a novice in battlecraft, as many hastily trained recruits were. The French, by contrast, were now perhaps too wary; or, as the former infantry officer, historian of the war and military theorist Basil Liddell Hart put it, 'unlike the Americans they suffered too much from experience'.

Nevertheless, German casualties in the Marne battles were well over 100,000, with 25,000 more taken prisoner, and the critical loss of nearly 800 guns. Ludendorff was forced to abandon his Flanders stroke planned for 20 July, and his front was now over-stretched and under-fortified. It ran (in places meandered) over 300 miles – 70 more than when he had launched the *Kaiserschlacht*. Instead of the formidable defences of the Hindenburg Line and elsewhere, there were now vulnerable salients and primitive entrenchments. His losses since April had been staggering: perhaps as many as a million dead, wounded or missing. As early as 8 May, the chief of staff of Crown Prince Rupprecht's army group, Generalleutnant Hermann von Kuhl, had confided the grim state of affairs to his diary:

> Our supply of reinforcements and replacements is virtually exhausted . . . I doubt if further major offensives will be possible . . . The Americans are on their way. I am really doubtful if we shall be able to force a decision. We are not going to achieve a breakthrough – and then there is the issue of horses and the supply of oats.

The men on the ground knew it too, no matter how unprepared they were to admit it openly. Herbert Sulzbach said simply: 'We realised something had gone wrong, our losses were enormous . . . We realised it was the beginning of the end.'

Foch, however, the *generalissimo*, knew exactly what he had to do. On 24 July he told Haig, Pershing and his own senior officers: 'The moment has come to abandon the general defensive attitude forced upon us recently by numerical inferiority and to pass to the offensive.'

49

AUGUST

The Black Day of the German Army

The allies go on the counter-offensive

For nearly four years the guiding principle of the allied commanders – the thrusting Foch, the cautious Pétain, the dogged Haig – had been that only offensive operations could decide matters. *Field Service Regulations*, the British Army's 'bible', held that the chief factor in success was 'a firmer determination in all ranks to conquer at any cost'. But *Field Service Regulations* also made it clear that the situation had to be favourable for offensive action to be advisable: 'If the situation be unfavourable for such a course [a vigorous offensive], it is wiser, when possible, to manoeuvre for a more suitable opportunity.'

For nearly four years, however, the allies – Italy included, perhaps even Italy especially, if not for quite as long – had persevered with the doctrine of the offensive when the situation was not so much unfavourable as futile. Now, in the high summer of 1918, having lost countless hundreds of thousands of men in repeated attempts to make the situation fit the doctrine, rather than the other way round, the allies found themselves in a position where the situation really had – at last – changed to fit the doctrine. The high-water mark of *die Kaiserschlacht*, Ludendorff's own great and desperate offensive to knock out the Entente before the Americans arrived in overwhelming numbers – indeed, the high-water mark of the entire four-year German offensive in the west – was now visible; and soon would be heard its 'melancholy, long, withdrawing roar'.

The failure of Ludendorff's attack on the Marne in July – the *Friedensturm* or 'peace offensive' – would prove to be the *Kaiserschlacht*'s final battle. The subsequent German retreat to ground that they could hold was Foch's signal to begin the counter-push, if cautiously at first.

He had already been planning to reduce the salient at St-Mihiel, near the sector of the American buildup, and also to push the Germans back at Amiens to free the railway lines there from German artillery fire, for they were critical to the movement of reserves and supplies. Meanwhile Haig had been making his own plans (proposed by Henry Rawlinson) to attack at Amiens. When the BEF had at last managed to halt its own retreat after Ludendorff's offensive had broken 5th Army's front, Rawlinson's 4th Army had closed the gap astride the Somme, forming a junction with the French to the south. Throughout June, the British III Corps on the left, under Lieutenant-General Richard Butler, who had risen four ranks since commanding the 2nd Lancashire Fusiliers in 1914, and the Australian Corps under John Monash on the right, had made vigorous local counter-attacks. What these showed was that the tactics developed for offensive operations in the light of the experience of Third Ypres – re-organization of the platoon into assault parties and Lewis light machine-gun teams, well-rehearsed techniques of fire covering movement, and better all-arms coordination – were indeed battleworthy. The attacks also showed that the open, firm ground south of the Somme was especially suitable for a larger offensive.

Foch agreed to Haig's plan to attack at Amiens but insisted that the French 1st Army to the right also take part. Rawlinson objected at first as he wanted to use tanks instead of a preliminary bombardment – 'the Cambrai key' – so as not to sacrifice surprise, and the French 1st Army hadn't enough. The obvious compromise was reached: the French would not launch their attack until forty-five minutes after 4th Army went into action, so that their own bombardment would not begin before 4th Army's zero hour. North of the Somme III Corps would attack, with the Australian Corps under John Monash to their right astride the river, and the Canadian Corps under the 42-year-old Lieutenant-General Sir Arthur Currie to the right of the Australians and alongside the French. (In his memoirs, Lloyd George claimed that he seriously considered Currie, a militia officer – in civilian life an estate agent – as a replacement for Haig.) The Canadians, who were generally reckoned to be the best corps on the Western Front, were brought from Flanders especially for the operation. The move was conducted in great secrecy for, given the corps' reputation, had they been discovered the Germans would have assumed an attack was imminent. As deception, two Canadian battalions and a casualty clearing station were sent to Ypres with scant concealment, as well as a wireless unit to serve false signal intelligence to the German intercept stations.

By early August, aerial reconnaissance and artillery sound-ranging had located nine out of ten of the German batteries in the area. With the improved mathematical methods for 'predicted fire', these could be struck at zero hour without prior 'registration', the older technique of establishing the exact range and bearing by fire beforehand – visually observed, usually from the air, corrected, and the coordinates recorded. The disadvantage of registration was that it told the batteries they had been located, and prompted them to move. It also told the higher command that an offensive was probably imminent. Besides the mathematical improvements, predicted fire required very precise locating. Aerial photography was crucial, but sound-ranging had also become significant. The system developed had been one of the more impressive technical advances in gunnery during the war. Pairs of microphones were used to determine the bearings to the source of the sound. By calibrating the observed flash of the gun with the time of the sound's arrival at the microphone, the range could be calculated, and the intersection of the bearings gave the battery's location. The method had been perfected by the 28-year-old Australian Lawrence Bragg, who in 1915 had won the Nobel Prize in physics, and had subsequently been commissioned in the Royal Artillery.

Rawlinson's fire plan was devastating. At zero hour, as the tanks gained the initial surprise, 2,000 guns would open up counter-battery fire, bombard the German reserve trenches, and provide a creeping barrage for the infantry to shelter behind in the advance. A total of 450 tanks would take part, the Canadian and Australian corps each being allocated a brigade of 108 Mark Vs (the latest model), thirty-six Mark V 'Star' tanks adapted to carry a section of infantry with a light machine-gun team – and twenty-four unarmed tanks for ammunition resupply. A battalion of fifty Mark V tanks was allocated to III Corps, while a hundred 'Whippet' tanks each with four machine guns and a speed of up to 8 mph, plus several score armoured cars, were attached to Lieutenant-General Charles Kavanagh's Cavalry Corps, which, as at Cambrai, was to be held in close reserve for exploitation. Seventy more Whippets were sent to the French.

The security measures taken to mask the noise created by the deployment of all these machines were imaginative. In 1980, as the SAS prepared to storm the Iranian Embassy in London to release the hostages held by a group of armed militants, the noise of drilling as fibre-optic surveillance cables were introduced into the building was masked by getting air-traffic control to reroute passenger jets low overhead on their approach to Heathrow. It was a much-celebrated ruse, but not a new one. The night before the attack at Amiens in August 1918, the RAF's Handley Page bombers flew for hours over the front to drown the noise of the tanks coming forward.

On 8 August, just after first light, and in thick fog, the attack began. Private James Southey of the Australian Corps wondered

how we were going to get on. But, forward we pushed, and met comparatively slight opposition. Some Germans surrendered quickly. Others fought to the end. As we pushed on wondering where we were, the sun broke through and we began to see countryside that we hadn't seen for quite a time. It was unscarred, all sorts of cultivated land, and we began to feel, 'By Jove, the war's coming to an end. We're getting through.' And we had a feeling of great uplift about the whole job.

In the centre the Australians and Canadians advanced quickly – 3 miles by mid-morning – and by dusk, aided by the RAF's constant 'strafing' of the roads to harry the Germans as they withdrew and intercept reserves as they came forward, they had punched a 15-mile-wide hole in the forward defences south of the Somme. In all, that day, Rawlinson's 4th Army took 13,000 prisoners, and the French 3,000. A further 14,000 Germans had been killed or wounded. Losses in 4th Army – British, Australian and Canadian – were by no means light, however: nearly 9,000, including many tank crews. Corporal Harry Brice of the Canadian Engineers recalled coming across one tank that had been destroyed along with its crew by a German 5.9 howitzer that had depressed its barrel to fire at 15 yards' range. In doing so, it had also killed every one of the German gunners. As Private Southey said, some just fought to the end.

The cavalry had not been able to 'gallop through the "G" in "Gap"', however, for despite the success in punching a hole in the forward defences, no true gap had been made – or, at least, none that could be kept open. The Tank Corps staff had suggested letting the Whippets go ahead on their own, but both Haig and Rawlinson preferred to keep them in close support of Kavanagh's horsemen, for the lesson of Cambrai was that without machine-gun support the cavalry would be stopped in the rear of the battle area before being able to get a gallop in open country. Nevertheless some Whippets did break through into the German rear areas, playing havoc with the artillery. One of them, *Musical Box* (crews invariably named their machines, a nod, perhaps, to the tank's naval origins), commanded by Lieutenant Clement Arnold, roamed at will for nine hours, shooting up a battery, an observation balloon, an infantry battalion's camp and a divisional transport column, before being knocked out and set alight by an artillery round. The driver was killed as they tried to escape, but Arnold and his gunner were taken prisoner – and would have been despatched on the spot had it not been for the intervention of a German infantry officer, Ritter Ernst von Maravic. In gratitude as they were rescued from the homicidal *Feldgrauen*, Arnold gave Maravic his watch, a 21st-birthday present from his father. In 1931, Maravic made contact with Arnold, visited him and returned the watch.

In his memoirs, Ludendorff called Thursday, 8 August 'der schwarze Tag des deutschen Heeres' – the black day of the German army (literally, of the German armies). It was not so much the ground that the allies had taken, although that itself was impressive, as that the morale of his troops had so evidently buckled. Men had surrendered without a fight; and, as among the Russians in 1917, fleeing troops had shouted 'You're prolonging the war!' at officers who tried to rally them, and 'Blackleg!' (*Streikbrecher*) at reserves moving up.

When he received Ludendorff's report, the Kaiser said: 'I see that we must strike a balance. We are at the end of our reserves. The war must be ended.'

But while Wilhelm hoped to gain favourable terms, principally by appealing to President Wilson and his 'Fourteen Points', the proposals about which Britain and France had been so lukewarm, Ludendorff knew that the army would now face the hardest fight to prevent catastrophic defeat. His professional sense told him that the only feasible option was a strategic retreat like that of Operation Alberich (the withdrawal to the Hindenburg Line the previous year) to dislocate the allies' now inevitable counter-offensive. Indeed, some of Ludendorff's officers were already urging this very course. But how could he ask the army to retreat over the very ground that was still wet with their blood – and when he had just promised them victory (or at least peace) in the last big push?

To the allies, meanwhile, rapid and decisive victory did not yet seem a foregone conclusion. On 25 July, Henry Wilson, chief of the imperial general staff, had issued a memorandum entitled 'Military Policy 1918–19', in which he stated that '1st July 1919 should be taken as the date by which all preparations are to be completed for the opening of the main offensive campaign'. Indeed, even after such a promisingly large bag of prisoners on the first day, the Amiens attack had petered out in the days that followed, for the old problem of the Germans' being able to seal the breach faster than the attackers could exploit it had still not been overcome. Foch urged Haig to renew the attack, but Haig had at last learned the lesson of the Somme and Third Ypres – not to slog away at hardening resistance. Instead of returning to GHQ, however, the great and palatial 'War Office' at Montreuil-sur-Mer, Haig stayed near the front, forming a tactical headquarters, and showing a greater readiness to listen to his army and corps commanders when they advised against delivering unprepared attacks on new German positions. He now switched the main effort back north, to Julian Byng's 3rd Army, which had been preparing to attack at Bapaume, but told him to do '[no] more attacking than was absolutely necessary. Our object is to keep the battle going as long as possible, until the Americans can attack in force.'

On 21 August Byng launched his attack, and three days later 1st Army under Henry Horne joined in the general offensive north of Rawlinson's recuperating 4th Army. This rash-like spread of attacks now forced Ludendorff to do what his advisers had urged earlier – withdraw to the old Hindenburg Line as far south as Soissons.

But this time there would be no opportunity for the delaying tactics of Alberich – the demolitions, booby traps and general 'scorched-earth' policy that had made of it what Wetzell had called the 'shot-to-pieces battle area'. Nor would they be allowed to withdraw unharried: this time they would be pressed every mile of the way, not least from the air.

It was the beginning of what would come to be known as the 'Hundred Days' – a reference to Napoleon's bid for victory in 1815 (though he, of course, was unsuccessful) – which would culminate in the eleventh-hour ceasefire of 11 November.

50

SEPTEMBER

The Return Push

The Americans at last attack in strength

In September the Americans were at last ready to fight as a separate entity, rather than single divisions in support of the British or French. On 10 August, the American 1st Army had formally come into existence under command of General John J. – 'Black Jack' – Pershing himself, who also remained commander-in-chief of the growing American Expeditionary Force. 1st US Army comprised in all some 300,000 troops, and its first object would be to take the St-Mihiel salient, between Verdun and Nancy. In 1914 the Germans had driven this triangular wedge into the French lines towards the Meuse, effectively severing direct rail communications between Paris and the easternmost part of the Western Front. Reducing the salient would be the Americans' first independent task of the war.

Pershing decided to do this with two 'super corps' each consisting of four or five divisions, and a third of three divisions, with two smaller French corps in support. The main attack was to be made against the south face by the US I and IV Corps, with a secondary thrust against the west face along the heights of the Meuse by the smaller V Corps (including the French 15th Colonial Division). To fix the enemy in the salient, a holding attack against the apex would be made by the French II Colonial Corps, and in reserve Pershing would hold three strong American divisions.

To maintain air superiority and provide close air support, some 1,500 aircraft were placed under Pershing's operational control, 40 per cent of them flown by American crews, the remainder by British, French and Italian. Nine bomber squadrons of the RAF were also placed at Foch's call.

Pershing's Field Order No. 9, dated 7 September, was straightforward: 'The First Army will attack at H hour on D day with the object of forcing the evacuation of the St. Mihiel Salient.' It was the first time that the terms 'D Day' and 'H Hour' were used.

Ludendorff, however, increasingly short of men and bracing for the coming counter-offensive, had already decided to withdraw from the salient to shorten the line. By D Day, therefore – 12 September – much of the German heavy artillery had already been withdrawn, and the Americans' progress was deceptively swift. The assault was led by a body of over 400 tanks, largely French, but including an American brigade of 140 Renault FT light tanks commanded by Colonel George S. Patton, whose 3rd Army in the Second World War would famously skirt the same ground in short order. Patton wrote to his father afterwards that 'in war as now waged there is little of the element of fear, it is too well organized and too stupendous'.

Nevertheless, the infantry fighting was no less visceral than elsewhere, not least for its taking place in the foulest weather. Private di Lucca, of the 42nd US Division (the 'Rainbow' Division), described how, in the darkness, because of the deluge of rain that had filled the trenches the night before, 'we had to form a line by holding each other by our raincoats ... during a terrible barrage which had started fifteen minutes earlier. Everything was coming down – trees, stones, rocks, everything came over our heads in the trenches'. At dawn they went over the top. The Germans, di Lucca recalled:

came out of their trenches [and] we met one another like a bunch of animals. We lost our senses; we charged them with our bayonets. I saw a German, a six-footer, coming towards me – why he picked me I don't know. Anyway, I saw him coming. I don't know what gave me the idea, what gave me the strength, but as soon as he came near me, I turned my rifle by the butt, broke his thrust and I hit him on the chin. All of a sudden he was bleeding. He let go his arm, put his hand towards his chin to find out where the blood came from. That gave me a clear spot: I turned the rifle and I hit him in mid chest with the bayonet. I left the bayonet there till he fell down.

By 13 September, the leading units of the US 1st Army had met up with the French troops advancing from the west, and three days later, having nipped off the salient completely, Pershing halted the offensive. Its objective had been achieved with remarkably light casualties. Colonel George C. Marshall, Roosevelt's chief of army staff in the Second World War and afterwards Secretary of State in the Truman administration, was in September 1918 one of the operational planners in Pershing's headquarters, and had been anxious about US public opinion. He had reckoned that

fifty thousand (50,000) casualties was the percentage normally to be expected and hospitalization was prepared accordingly. Nevertheless, if we suffered that many casualties during the brief period involved, the American people, not accustomed, as were our Allies, to such huge payments in human life, would have seized upon the criticism of any Allied official as a basis for condemning our own Commander in Chief.

The actual figures proved to be a fraction of the worst estimate: some 4,000 Americans had been killed and 3,000 wounded – over twice as many casualties as the Germans; but the Germans had also had 15,000 men taken prisoner, and lost 450 guns.

In fact, Pershing had wanted to continue the offensive towards Metz, but this, along with Haig's own more northerly push, would have meant offensives on diverging axes, which, while posing a real danger to the Germans, would have failed to concentrate the allied effort. Pershing reluctantly agreed therefore to realign his axis of advance north and further west towards Sedan, which would mean attacking through the particularly difficult sector east of the Argonne forest. Unfortunately, not having time to switch all his experienced divisions to this new axis, he would have to use green ones. And these would pay the price.

When news of Haig's intention to attack the Hindenburg Line reached London, the cabinet feared another Passchendaele. The CIGS, Henry Wilson, sent Haig a telegram warning of the consequences of high casualties. In his diary, Haig sneered at his masters as 'a wretched lot of weaklings'. Fortunately for Haig, Foch now covered his back by issuing the simple directive: 'Everyone is to attack (Belgians, British, French and Americans) as soon as they can, as strong as they can, for as long as they can.'

London (and Paris) had appointed Foch to be *generalissimo*; they must now live with the consequences.

Foch's design was for a gigantic pincer attack on the great German salient between Verdun and Ypres – the ejection, no less, of the 'Boche' from France. The right pincer was to be the Americans in the Meuse–Argonne to draw away reserves from the Cambrai–St-Quentin sector and threaten the Germans' railway communications through Lorraine. The left (British) pincer would, if driven deep enough, likewise threaten the lines of communication through the Liège corridor. The French would support each pincer on the inner flanks, while a further attack by a combined Anglo-Belgian force at Ypres would tie down any loose German reserves.

On 28 September Pershing was able to mass nearly 3,000 guns for a three-hour bombardment of the lightly held German forward defence zone before advancing on a 20-mile front. In theory, the odds in his favour were overwhelming – almost ten to one – but his expectations of progress were to prove unrealistic. His green troops largely fell into the trap set up by the Germans' elastic defence, pushing on rather too rapidly without adequate artillery cover, and in the centre the advance began to falter. As Pershing's orders had been for the whole line to advance together, the rapid progress made by his troops on the flanks was soon to no avail, and the fighting developed into a slogging match. And in forest fighting, the defender always has the advantage. The situation report issued by 1st Army for 29 September read: 'It would seem that our troops are not well organized for an attack. The gaining of the objectives for the present, does not seem possible without undue losses unless time is taken to reorganize and prepare for a concentrated, simultaneous attack.'

Nevertheless, there were some notable examples of sheer fighting spirit. Perhaps the most famous was that of Sergeant Alvin York – memorably portrayed by Gary Cooper in Howard Hawks' 1941 film *Sergeant York* – a pacifist-leaning draftee from Tennessee who killed fifteen Germans and took no fewer than 132 prisoners all in the same frenzied firefight.

When eventually Pershing called a halt, in mid-October, 1st Army had suffered 100,000 casualties – almost the strength of the entire United States regular army before the war. No one who had seen green troops in action for the first time was surprised, but the scale of the losses, on a par with those incurred in the offensives of 1916 and 1917, and for equally little gain, was a shock none the less. Contrary to Marshall's fears, however, American public opinion did not immediately falter, or lose confidence in Pershing.

The BEF's pincer had been rather more effective, exploiting the lines of least resistance to pierce the German front and threaten strongpoints from the flanks. On 27 September, after a thunderous overnight bombardment in which, said a sergeant-major of the Irish Guards, 'Even the wurrums themselves are getting up and crying for mercy,' and again with the help of the early-morning mist, 3rd Army's left and 1st's right attacked on the Canal du Nord, penetrating on a narrow front and then spreading out fan-like to break down the sides of the breach. By nightfall the following day they had reached Cambrai, beyond the northern edge of the Hindenburg Line, thereby threatening to turn it. Stiffening German resistance brought things to a standstill, however.

The baton was now passed to Rawlinson's 4th Army, on the right of Byng's 3rd, which had been preparing to assault the line with 3rd

Army's support, but now found the roles reversed. A two-day bombardment had prepared the way: 1,600 guns, one for every 3 yards, the first eight hours with gas driving the defenders under cover, the next day and a half with high explosive keeping them below ground to avoid the need for further gas, which would have hindered the attackers when they went forward. On 29 September, one British and two American divisions of Monash's Australian Corps (the more recently arrived Americans having been attached for training) spearheaded Rawlinson's attack on a 9-mile front. Again, the Americans pressed bravely but without the battlefield 'savvy' that the British had acquired the hard way. They gained their objectives but at much cost, and had to be rescued by the Australians.

Meanwhile, in a move that would have been familiar to the duke of Wellington's men in the Peninsular War, the British 46th Division, under cover of the smoke-thickened morning mist and using collapsible boats (and life-belts taken from Channel ferries), managed to get across the St-Quentin Canal near Bellenglise and, with scaling ladders, climb the 50-foot scarp to capture the machine-gun posts which were supposed to command the obstacle. The Germans were taken entirely by surprise. Sappers following close behind patched up several bridges that had been only partially demolished. Then, thanks to the much improved staffwork at divisional and corps level, instead of the attacking troops continuing until exhausted, with the consequent loss of momentum, a fresh division was passed through to carry the advance beyond the rear line of the Hindenburg defences.

The 46th, originally a Midland territorial division, had had a poor reputation since the Somme, but had been reinvigorated by the arrival only weeks before of the forty-year-old Gerald Farrell Boyd, 'the ranker general', who had enlisted in the Devonshire Regiment after failing the entry exam for the Royal Military Academy Woolwich. Having won the Distinguished Conduct Medal in the Boer War as a sergeant, he had been commissioned into the East Yorkshire Regiment, and in 1914 had been serving as a captain on the staff – a promotion since the outbreak of war of five ranks.

With tactical opportunities now presenting themselves, regimental, brigade and divisional leadership was all-important. Lieutenant-Colonel Bernard Vann MC, an Anglican priest who had originally tried to join up as a chaplain but had been turned down because of prejudice against clergy from the Church of England's Anglo-Catholic wing, commanded one of Farrell Boyd's battalions, the 6th Sherwood Foresters. In September 1914, Vann, a Cambridge graduate who had played professional football for Derby County, had enlisted instead in the Artists' Rifles, and the following April had been commissioned in the Foresters. Almost four years to the day after enlisting, as he led his battalion in the attack at Bellenglise, he won the VC, in the words of the citation:

> For most conspicuous bravery, devotion to duty and fine leadership during the attack ... On reaching the high ground above Bellenglise the whole attack was held up by fire of all descriptions from the front and right flank. Realising that everything depended on the advance going forward with the barrage, Col. Vann rushed up to the firing line and with the greatest gallantry led the line forward. By his prompt action and absolute contempt for danger the whole situation was changed, the men were encouraged and the line swept forward. Later, he rushed a field-gun single-handed and knocked out three of the detachment. The success of the day was in no small degree due to the splendid gallantry and fine leadership displayed by this officer.

He would not learn of the decoration, however, for four days later he was killed leading yet another attack.

The 46th's breaching of the Hindenburg Line was one of the outstanding divisional actions of the war. It, and other successes at Ypres, now meant that the BEF were at last breaking into open country. Foch told Haig that the Germans could not resist the attacks for much longer, not least with the Americans going on the offensive continuously and 'learning all the time'. He was quite certain of it, indeed: 'Soon they will crack.'

51

OCTOBER

Tout le monde à la bataille!

*The Central Powers are assailed on all fronts,
and the Kaiser's regime crumbles*

At the culminating point of the battle of Waterloo, when his battered but defiant infantry had seen off Napoleon's last desperate attempt to break the allied line, the duke of Wellington took off his hat and waved it in the air to signal the whole line to advance. On 11 September 1918, Generalissimo Ferdinand Foch had done the same with his order: 'Everyone is to attack (Belgians, British, French and Americans) as soon as they can, as strong as they can, for as long as they can.'

Accordingly, across the entire Western Front, the allies had seized on the exhausted and much demoralized Germans and begun pressing them relentlessly. By the first week of October, the British (including all the dominion troops) were into open country. Two weeks later, in the Meuse–Argonne region, the Americans broke through the so-called Kriemhild Line and now threatened the great German railway base at Metz. The line's name proved to be prophetic, for Kriemhild, the wife of Siegfried in the Niebelung legends, was struck by a mighty sword-blow but said she felt no pain. It was only when she stooped to pick up a ring that her body fell into pieces. Everywhere, indeed, the increasingly desperate and erratic Ludendorff, de facto commander-in-chief of the German armies on all fronts, gave ground. His reserves were being pulled this way and that; a third of the entire German army spent September and October in or near slow-moving trains.

Even the dormant Macedonian front – tended by 'the gardeners of Salonika', as Clemenceau called them, for 'all they do is dig' – had come to life. Ludendorff had famously derided Macedonia as his greatest internment camp, but the allies had been steadily building up strength. They had lost the token Russian contingent there after the Treaty of Brest-Litovsk in March, but by that time had gained ample compensation in the nine divisions of the Greek army, Greece having in June 1917 finally been persuaded to join the Entente. By September 1918, the allies' advantage in manpower, artillery and aircraft on this southernmost front was overwhelming. The Bulgarians had begun to see the writing on their wall and were already preparing to quit Macedonia when the French General Franchet d'Espèrey, commanding the 'Allied Armies of the East', launched a two-pronged offensive in the middle of September, in which a Franco-Serbian army broke through at Dobro Pole. The fleeing Bulgarians were badly mauled by allied aircraft in the Kosturino and Kresna passes, and morale collapsed. The allies took Skopje, the capital of Macedonia, at the end of the month, by which time Bulgarian deserters had already reached Sofia and, with the Agrarian National Union, proclaimed a republic. The provisional government asked for an armistice, which Franchet d'Espèrey conceded on 29 September.

Austria's southern flank was now wide open, and Franchet d'Espèrey, who had made his name in the great counter-attack on the Marne in 1914, urged the supreme war council to let him press on north, believing that with an army of 200,000 he could cross Austria and Hungary, mass in Bohemia covered by the Czech Legion and take Dresden. Instead, Versailles told him to open up communications with Russia through Romania, while the Serbs retook their capital, Belgrade. The whole of the Central Powers' southern front was being systematically taken apart at the seams.

Ludendorff was literally prostrated by the news of the Bulgarian surrender. By some accounts he fell to the floor, foaming at the mouth. He told the Kaiser that the Bulgarian armistice had 'fundamentally changed the situation in view of the attacks being carried out on the Western Front', for to shore up his Balkan ally he had sent east his strategic reserve – several divisions – that could otherwise have been kept in France.

The situation in Germany itself was also becoming very ugly. The *Kaiserliche Marine* was increasingly restive, there were food riots in the major cities, and communist sentiment was rife and openly expressed. Indeed, to forestall revolution, the Kaiser sent for Prince Maximilian of Baden, a former major-general and prominent liberal, to be chancellor. On 3 October, the German government resigned.

Three days later, Haig visited Foch, who showed him one of the Paris newspapers, in which 'in large type was printed a note from Austria, Germany and Turkey, asking for an armistice at once, and stating their readiness to discuss conditions of peace on the basis of President Wilson's 14 points'.

It was somewhat premature, but in truth Ludendorff could find no succour from his remaining allies. With the climactic battle of Megiddo – ancient Armageddon, which according to the Book of Revelation was the place of the great battle at the end of time – Sir Edmund Allenby had chased the Turks out of Palestine, while in Mesopotamia, Lieutenant-General Sir William Marshall was about to make a final, successful push to secure the oil fields at Mosul. When the Bulgarians surrendered, the British Army of Salonika (Macedonia), under the shrewd Aberdonian Sir George Milne, turned east towards Constantinople. With nothing to stop Milne entering the Turkish capital, Enver Pasha and his cohort fled for Berlin, and on 15 October what remained of the Ottoman government asked for terms.

Next it would be the turn of the Austro-Hungarians to fall. Under Armando Diaz's judicious leadership, the Italians had roundly defeated their summer offensive on the Piave, Vienna having gambled what strength remained on a knockout blow. With French, British and American help, Diaz would now mount what would prove the decisive counter-offensive, launching it with exquisite theatrical timing, calculated to lift his own men and further depress the Austrians, on 24 October, the anniversary of Caporetto. The battle, known as Vittorio Veneto, after the small town at the furthest reach of the Italians' thrust, is sometimes dismissed as a walkover, the Austrians' morale having sustained a fatal blow at the Piave, but the Italians still suffered 30,000 casualties in the process.

Allied air power now began to assert itself conclusively. The ground-attack ('strafing') squadrons were never busier, even on the most distant fronts. Troops, guns and transport in the open were far easier targets than those in the years of entrenchments. In Palestine on 21 September the Turks had been caught in a defile north-east of Nablus and subjected to five hours' bombing and strafing, which, according to the official report, left them 'a dispersed horde of trembling individuals, hiding for their lives'. After the Italian victory at Vittorio Veneto at the end of October, the Conegliano–Pordonone road – the Austrians' principal escape route – was rendered impassable by aerial bombardment night and day. On the Western Front, although the terrain did not form many such defiles, the attacks were relentless nevertheless.

They were not pursued without cost, however; nor was the defensive fighting that preceded them. Between March and November 1918, for example, No. 80 Squadron RAF was in almost continuous action. Its average strength in pilot officers was twenty-two, and during this time a total of 168 officers were struck off strength (for all causes), a monthly attrition rate of 75 per cent. So high was the price the squadrons paid in those months that the losses would influence the RAF's post-war doctrine. Hugh Trenchard, the chief of the air staff, became convinced that the ground-attack role was not cost-effective, and would instead develop the concept of strategic bombing, the belief that the heavy bomber could win future wars without the aid of armies or navies.

With the steady collapse of all fronts, including the home, Prince Max of Baden had arrived in Berlin not a moment too soon. As the new chancellor, his first instinct was to ask for time to take stock, arguing that to seek an armistice was to make any peace initiative impossible. But on 3 October, with Ludendorff in despair, protesting 'I want to save my army' (a psychiatrist was called to Army headquarters after his foaming breakdown), Field Marshal Hindenburg, the titular chief of army staff and in effect pro-Kaiser, wrote: 'As a result of the collapse of the Macedonian Front . . . there is, so far as can be foreseen, no longer a prospect of forcing peace on the enemy.' Instead he insisted on an immediate appeal for an armistice.

A week later, however, Ludendorff had recovered his composure somewhat. The allies' advance on the Western Front was beginning to slow, and the resistance of his own troops seemed to be stiffening. Indeed, by 17 October there was such an improvement in the reports from the front that he felt able, without risk of precipitating rout, to order a general withdrawal to more secure positions to continue the fight.

Berlin's strategy now was to separate President Wilson from the other allied leaders, to try to negotiate with him on the basis of his apparently more conciliatory stance, rather than submit to what would be the far tougher terms of the Franco-British Entente. Wilson was not going to fall for that, however: he was determined that the German army be eviscerated to make sure there was no possibility of revanchism, although his reply to the German overtures confirmed his commitment to the 'Fourteen Points'. Ludendorff, whose mood swings must have been giving his psychiatrist and colleagues increasing cause for concern, but who realized the probable severity of the armistice conditions, now insisted that the war be carried on. When he learned that Berlin was not prepared to do this, he offered his resignation, which the Kaiser accepted on 26 October.

The long and, on the face of it, successful Hindenburg–Ludendorff partnership was finally broken – and acrimoniously – when the

Kaiser 'ordered' the field marshal to remain at his now largely ceremonial post. As the two men left the imperial presence, Hindenburg tried to console his old friend. Ludendorff, however, believing that Hindenburg should have insisted on resigning too, snapped back: 'You have treated me very shabbily.'

Adding to the ignominy of his 'betrayal', with revolution in the wind (workers' risings were spreading throughout Germany), Ludendorff had to lie low until, a week later, he was able to slip out of Germany for Sweden disguised in blue spectacles and a false beard.

Revolution was one thing, however; mutiny another. The *Hochseeflotte* – the German High Seas Fleet – had not made any sortie in strength since April. This prolonged inactivity while the army and submarine service were heavily engaged had done much to undermine both the morale of the ratings and the self-respect of the officers. Local mutinies had already resulted in executions, exacerbating the tensions, when the naval command conceived the truly Wagnerian solution of a *Tod Reit* ('Death Ride') – a desperate sortie by the entire fleet, some eighteen battleships, five battle-cruisers and supporting craft, with the aim of bringing every one of the Royal Navy's ships to battle.

The *Hochseeflotte* assembled in Schillig Roads, Wilhelmshaven, on 29 October to sortie the following day. That evening, however, the crews convinced they were to be sacrificed to sabotage the armistice negotiations, discipline dissolved. Next day, Admiral Franz von Hipper, who had succeeded Reinhard Scheer in command of the *Hochseeflotte* in August, cancelled the operation and ordered the squadrons to disperse in the hope of quietening things down. When *III Geschwader* (3rd Battle Squadron) returned to Kiel, however, their crews helped spark the more general mutiny of 3 November, which in turn spurred widespread military and civil upheaval, and a general strike in Berlin.

A Soviet Germany looked imminent.

52

NOVEMBER

The Eleventh Hour

The Central Powers collapse, and Germany signs the Armistice

At the end of October, with the German army in retreat on the Western Front, the Kaiser had left the *Berliner Stadtschloss* for the *Oberste Heeresleitung* at Spa in Belgium (quartered, ironically, in the Hôtel Britannique). Ostensibly to avoid the Spanish flu sweeping the capital, in truth it was because army headquarters was a safer place to be, not so much for Wilhelm II's health as for his life: the atmosphere in Berlin was as metaphorically febrile as it was literally.

On 2 November, the Austro-Hungarian army rapidly disintegrating, Emperor Karl I (as Karl IV, King of Hungary) abdicated. Next day, Vienna accepted the austere terms demanded by the Italians in return for an armistice. For two and a half years the Royal Italian Army had battled alone against the Austro-Hungarians – and then the Germans too – at altitudes never before seen, until the humiliating collapse of their Alpine front at Caporetto in October 1917. They had recovered by their own resourcefulness, with a little help from the French and British, and the following summer had defeated what was meant to be the Austrians' knockout blow. They had even

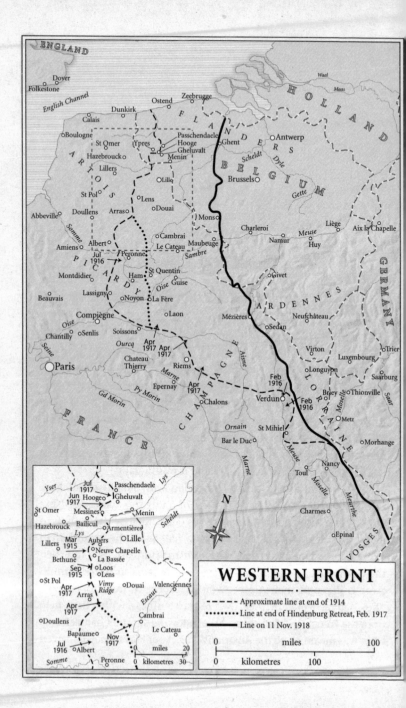

ENGLAND

Dover
Folkestone

English Channel

HOLLAND

Waal
Maas

Ostend   Zeebrugge

Dunkirk

Calais

Boulogne   St Omer   Ypres   Passchendaele   Ghent   Antwerp
            Hazebrouck   Hooge
            Lillers   Gheluvalt
                        Menin

ARTOIS   FLANDERS

                    oLille   BELGIUM   Brussels   *Scheldt*   *Dyle*

St Pol   Lens   *Gette*

Abbeville   Doullens   Arras   Douai

            Somme   oMons   Charleroi   Liège   Aix la Chapelle
Amiens   Albert   Namur   *Meuse*   Huy
                    oCambrai   GERMANY
            Jul   Peronne   Le Cateau   Maubeuge
            1916   *Sambre*
PICARDY   Ham   St Quentin   Givet   ARDENNES
Montdidier   *Oise*   Guise
        Lassigny   Mézières
    Beauvais   oNoyon   La Fère   oSedan
        Compiègne   oLaon   Neufchateau
            Oise   Virton   oTrier
Chantilly   oSenlis   Soissons   Longuyon   Luxembourg
        Ourcq   Apr   Apr   Saarburg
                1917   1917   Feb   Briey   oThionville
        Chateau   Riems   1916   oLonguyon   *Moselle*   *Saar*
        Thierry   *Marne*   Apr   Verdun   Feb   oMetz
Paris   Epernay   1917   1916
    Seine   *Py Morin*   Chalons   St Mihiel   LORRAINE   oMorhange
        Gd Morin   *Ornain*
FRANCE   CHAMPAGNE   Bar le Duc   Metz
                        Aisne   Nancy
                    Marne   *Meuse*   Toul   *Moselle*
                                                Charmes
                            N   *Meurthe*
                                            oEpinal   VOSGES

Yser   Jul   Passchendaele   *Lys*
        1917
    Jun   Hoogee   Gheluvalt
St Omer   Messines   Menin
                            Scheldt
Hazebrouck   Bailleul   Armentières
        Lys
Lillers   Mar   Aubers   oLille
    1915   Neuve Chapelle
Bethune   La Bassée
        Sep   oLoos
        1915   oLens
oSt Pol   Apr   *Vimy*   oDouai   Valenciennes
        1917   *Ridge*
    Arras   *Escaut*
        Apr
        1917   Cambrai
oDoullens
    Bapaume   Le Cateau
    Jul   Nov
    1916   1917   miles   20
    oAlbert
Somme   Peronne   0   kilometres   30

WESTERN FRONT

- - - - -   Approximate line at end of 1914
· · · · ·   Line at end of Hindenburg Retreat, Feb. 1917
─────   Line on 11 Nov. 1918

0   miles   100

0   kilometres   100

managed to send divisions to France to help stem the *Kaiserschlacht*, Ludendorff's own desperate final offensive, before launching their fight-back on the anniversary of Caporetto, recapturing all their lost ground and more in the battle known as Vittorio Veneto.

On the day that the last imperial Habsburg was leaving the Schönbrunn Palace for good, the German minister of the interior came to Spa to ask the Kaiser to abdicate too. Wilhelm rejected the idea out of hand. It would, he said, bring anarchy. Indeed, he declared his intention to lead his troops back to Germany in person to forestall revolution, and to go at once to the front to gauge for himself the troops' morale.

As ever, at the front the Kaiser saw what he wished to see. One of his personal staff, Count Detlef von Moltke, recounted: 'Near Ghent representatives from eleven divisions were greeted and decorated. The presence of the Kaiser had not been announced and the fresh and hardy and orderly appearance of the troops was all the more gratifying. The spontaneous enthusiasm of the soldiers on seeing their Commander-in-Chief was also most encouraging.'

Picked men about to receive decorations for bravery are not the best indicators of the general state of morale, but their commander-in-chief would return to Spa resolved to – as he saw it – do his duty to the army and the country.

That same day, 4 November, as fighting continued with barely remitting intensity – as if the frustrations of the trench years were being made up for with a vengeance – the most celebrated of the war poets, Lieutenant Wilfred Owen, was killed. He had recently returned to duty after convalescent leave in England, and died leading his platoon of the 2nd Manchesters during the crossing of the Sambre–Oise Canal. Only days earlier, Owen had been recommended for the Military Cross, which would be gazetted the following year.

On 5 November the Kaiser returned to Spa, where he learned of the *Hochseeflotte*'s mutinies at Kiel, the general strike in Berlin and the Social Democrats' vociferous demand for his abdication. He now began to have doubts, not helped by faltering communications with the capital. As Detlef von Moltke recorded:

Railroad connection with Germany began to be irregular and broken. Soon it ceased altogether. No train crossing the Rhine. Telegraphic and telephonic connection with Berlin became difficult. It appeared to be under some sort of censorial control and confidential messages could no longer be trusted. Finally we had to have recourse to air service. Two airships flew to Berlin, but none returned.

If communications with Berlin were difficult, Berlin had no difficulty communicating with Spa. On 9 November, the new chancellor, Prince Max von Baden, telegraphed that the Kaiser must abdicate, or else the cabinet would resign: 'revolution was extending on all sides, and the Social-Democrats could no longer hold the radicals under control,' Moltke recorded; 'the city and town officials in the large cities on the coast and in the western and southern portions of the Empire had assumed independent authority and . . . the Rhine and the great magazines of munitions and food along and east of this line had been seized by the revolutionists'.

The Kaiser, who had been joined by the Crown Prince, whose army group was covering the Ardennes approaches south of Liège, asked Hindenburg if he thought the unrest could be put down by force of arms. The Kaiser said that he himself was inclined to wait for the outcome of the peace feelers put out to the allies, and then lead the army back in person into Germany without announcing specifically that he would employ force against the revolt. However, Lieutenant-General Wilhelm Groener, who had replaced Ludendorff as *Erster Generalquartiermeister*, in effect commander-in-chief, told the Kaiser that the revolt had turned against him personally: 'The army will march home in peace and order under its leaders and commanding generals, but not under the command of Your Majesty, for it no longer stands behind Your Majesty.'

The Kaiser became angry. So did the Crown Prince's chief of staff, Major-General Friedrich von der Schulenburg, who was certain that 'no soldier of any rank would desert the Kaiser in the face of the enemy'.

Groener, a relatively low-born Württemberger, was neither impressed nor intimidated by the Junker's response: 'I have other information,' he replied stonily. Earlier and secretly, he had summoned fifty senior officers to Spa to discuss the feasibility of the Kaiser's plan.

At this darkest of moments, the telephone rang. Baron von dem Bussche, under-secretary at the foreign ministry, was calling from the chancellor's office to say that if the Kaiser did not abdicate at once the socialist Karl Liebknecht would be proclaimed 'President of the Republic'.

Wilhelm conceded. He would abdicate as emperor, he said, but remain King of Prussia. The news was telephoned to Berlin, but the message came back almost immediately: 'Too late. We can no more make use of that. By order of the Chancellor.'

The Wolff Telegraphic Bureau, the principal German news agency, then put out a communiqué which pre-empted further discussion: 'His Majesty, the Emperor and King, has abdicated, the Crown Prince has renounced the succession. Prince Max has been appointed Regent, and Representative Ebert [leader of the Social Democrats, and a moderate], Chancellor.'

That night the Kaiser left by train for exile in the Netherlands.

Meanwhile an armistice had to be negotiated. On 7 November Berlin had sent a telegram to the allied *generalissimo*, Ferdinand Foch, requesting a meeting. The following day the German delegation, headed by Matthias Erzberger, leader of the Catholic Centre Party, crossed the front line in five cars and were escorted for ten hours to Foch's private train in the forest of Compiègne, 35 miles north of Paris.

Erzberger was handed the list of allied demands. They amounted to complete surrender and demilitarization. He was given seventy-two hours to agree. There was to be no negotiation.

There were practical problems in communicating the military details to Spa, however. The 22-year-old Rittmeister (captain of cavalry) Count Wolff-Heinrich von Helldorf, one of the interpreters, volunteered to take them, but on reaching the crossing point at the front line, he found the fire too heavy and telephoned Compiègne to say he would have to wait till first light. Major-General Detlef von Winterfeldt, the German military representative, at once began making alternative arrangements: a French aircraft, trailing two white streamers in the hope of not being shot down, would fly them to Spa with the other interpreter. Eventually, though, Helldorf was able to slip through the lines in darkness, reaching Spa in mid-morning on the 9th, so the unique experiment of an airborne flag of truce was never attempted.

The following day, Sunday, Hindenburg sent the new chancellor, Ebert, a message urging that the armistice be signed even if the conditions he had just read could not be improved on. Meanwhile he set about composing new instructions for the delegation at Compiègne to try to negotiate better terms.

On receiving Hindenburg's message, Ebert telegrammed Erzberger instructing him to accept the terms as modified by Hindenburg's forthcoming proposals.

Ebert's telegram was followed soon afterwards by a much longer one from Spa specifying the improvements that Hindenburg sought to the military details. The delegation asked for time to decipher these before meeting the allied delegates to agree the final wording of the armistice document.

Tired, apprehensive men, laborious communications, and uncertainty as to what was really happening in Berlin made a classic recipe for misunderstanding. No sooner had the staff finished deciphering Hindenburg's instructions than a second telegram arrived from Berlin authorizing them to agree the original, unmodified, terms. To make matters worse, this was sent *en clair*, entirely compromising the improvements that Hindenburg sought. A note of farce then entered the proceedings when the allied delegation read the telegram and saw that it appeared to be signed not by Reichskanzler Ebert but by Reichskanzler Schluss. Foch did not know the name. He telephoned Paris. They didn't know the name either. Erzberger was summoned to explain. 'Schluss,' he told them, simply meant 'end of message'.

Nevertheless it was several hours before the German delegation were ready for the final meeting.

Shortly after two o'clock in the morning on Monday, 11 November, the parties assembled in the dining car of Foch's Wagon-Lits train. For the allies, there were Foch himself, the supreme commander, and the (British) first sea lord, Admiral Sir Rosslyn ('Rosie') Wemyss, and their principal staff officers. For the Germans, there were Erzberger, Count Alfred von Oberndorff from the foreign ministry, and their army and navy advisers Winterfeldt and Captain Ernst Vanselow.

Erzberger was in no position to make any conditional demands because the allies now knew that his instructions from Berlin were to accept the terms as given. He therefore tried reasoning, his concerns principally for the economic well-being of Germany. Starvation among the civil population would be exacerbated, he argued, if they were to surrender all the road transport and rolling stock as demanded. Foch was prepared to make a few concessions, as long as the central element of the Armistice – the surrender of territory – remained unaltered. If the Germans did not actually have 2,000 aeroplanes to surrender, he would settle for what they said they had – 1,700. If they couldn't without unwarranted hardship surrender 10,000 road vehicles in a fortnight, he would accept 5,000 over a longer period. He was certainly content to let them keep 5,000 of the 30,000 machine-guns demanded in order that they could fight the Bolshevists at home (and to grant some leeway in quitting Russia where 'Reds' threatened). And, as Lettow-Vorbeck's little army remained undefeated in East Africa, Foch was prepared to allow them time to withdraw rather than demanding immediate surrender.

'Rosie' Wemyss was rather less inclined to be accommodating when it came to the naval terms. Captain Vanselow, the naval representative, chosen probably for his legal acumen (before the war he had collaborated with the Swiss legal scholar Eduard von Waldkirch on the *Handbook of International Law*), pointed out that the *Kaiserliche Marine* did not possess 170 U-boats to surrender. Wemyss simply took back the document, crossed out the figure and wrote 'all submarines'.

Vanselow then said that the *Hochseeflotte* at Wilhelmshaven and Kiel should be accorded the same honours as Lettow-Vorbeck, as they too had never been defeated in battle.

'They have only to come out,' replied Wemyss tartly.

Erzberger and Oberndorff complained at the stipulation that the Royal Navy's blockade was to continue until a final treaty was agreed, claiming that this was unfair to Germany's women and children.

'Unfair?' snapped Wemyss. 'You sank our ships indiscriminately too.'

Indeed, some 11 million tons of allied and neutral shipping had been destroyed during the course of the war. Nevertheless, he said he would refer the matter to London.

The talking continued for almost three hours, until just after five o'clock the Germans said they were ready to sign. A fair copy of the signatory page was typed at once – with the rest to be typed up later – and signed by the delegates at twenty minutes past five, but officially recorded as five o'clock, to come into effect six hours later, at 11.00 a.m. Paris time – 'the eleventh hour of the eleventh day of the eleventh month'.

This demanded no mean effort of communications, on both sides. No official warning orders had been issued that hostilities might end soon, although the word was out that the Germans were seeking terms. On the contrary, offensive action continued across much of the front, if more cautiously than in the weeks before, as the allies could not afford to give the enemy occasion for second thoughts.

At 9.30 a.m. Private George Ellison of the 5th Royal Irish Lancers was killed in the outskirts of Mons, where the British army had fought its first battle of the war. Ellison, forty years old, from Leeds, in Yorkshire, had enlisted young but had left the army in 1912 on marrying, when he became a miner. Having a reserve liability, though, he was recalled to the colours in 1914, rejoining the Lancers, one of the first regiments to see action at Mons. Private George Ellison was the last soldier from Britain to die before the Armistice came into force.

The ceasefire order reached Captain Harry Truman of the US 129th Field Artillery just before ten-thirty. He sent at once for his battery sergeant, 'Squatty' Meisburger, who found the future president of the

United States of America 'stretched out on the ground eating a blueberry pie. Where he got the blueberry pie I don't know . . . His face was all smeared with blueberries. He handed me a piece of flimsy and said between bites, "Sergeant, you will take this back and read it to the members of the battery."'

Truman was following the old military maxim: bad news comes from the top; good news is passed down the chain of command.

But there were thirty minutes still to go, and they had a lot of ammunition prepared for use. In the next half-hour they fired as much of it as they could – 164 rounds.

At two minutes to eleven, the last soldier of the British Empire to die before the ceasefire was killed: Private George Price, twenty-five years old, of the 28th Saskatchewans (Canadian Expeditionary Force). His battalion had been ordered to secure the bridges on the Canal du Centre near Mons.

At 11 a.m. precisely the 15th Hussars, Field Marshal Sir John French's old command, a regiment that like many in the cavalry had hung on to its cherished traditions throughout the war, mustered its remaining trumpeters, fished out their obsolete instruments from the baggage, and sounded 'Cease Fire'. It was an extraordinary moment, for the ceremonial call (all calls were ceremonial, for the trumpet had long ceased to be carried in the field) had not been heard for over four years. Moreover, the regiment was mustered not a dozen miles from where they had heard the first shots fired on 22 August 1914.

In London, Lloyd George released the news at 10.20 a.m. A hundred and forty miles away in Shrewsbury near the Welsh border, as the church bells began ringing out the ceasefire at eleven o'clock, Wilfred Owen's mother received the telegram informing her of her eldest son's death.

Private George Ellison's widow, Hannah, would not learn for several more days that her husband had been killed that morning.

Some 700,000 servicemen from Britain and Ireland had been killed during the war, or had died while in the King's service, and 200,000 more from the dominions and India. In volume 4 of *The World Crisis*, published eleven years later, Winston Churchill reflected on the scenes of celebration he witnessed in London on Armistice Day:

> Who shall grudge or mock these overpowering entrancements? Every allied nation shared them. Every victorious capital or city in the five continents reproduced in its own fashion the scenes and sounds of London. These hours were brief, their memory fleeting; they passed as suddenly as they had begun.
>
> Too much blood had been spilt. Too much life-essence had been consumed. The gaps in every home were too wide and empty. The shock of an awakening and the sense of disillusion followed swiftly upon the poor rejoicings with which hundreds of millions saluted the achievement of their hearts' desire. There still remained the satisfactions of safety assured, of peace restored, of honour preserved, of the comforts of fruitful industry, of the home-coming of the soldiers; but these were in the background; and with them all there mingled the ache for those who would never come home.

Conclusion

The War to End All War?*

It is not possible to live in an English village – or indeed a Scots, Irish or Welsh one – without being aware of the Grim Reaper's harvest in the years 1914–18. The war memorials not only enumerate but also name the price of victory, sometimes in whole families of sons. The cost was indeed high – high enough in blood for Britain, but twice as high for France. How could it be otherwise with so many men under arms and for so long?

Need it have been *so* high, however? That is the question I address in *Too Important for the Generals* (2016). I maintain that it need not have been.

Was it a war of German aggression; were the Germans truly deserving of the *Kriegsschuld* (war guilt) verdict of the Paris peace conference of 1919, the basis of their agreement to pay reparations? Article 231 of the Treaty of Versailles specified:

The Allied and Associated Governments affirm and Germany accepts the responsibility of Germany and her allies for causing all the loss and

---

* In August 1914, the celebrated British author and social commentator H. G. Wells wrote a number of articles in the London papers, which subsequently appeared as a book entitled *The War That Will End War* – giving rise to the phrase 'The War to End All War.'

damage to which the Allied and Associated Governments and their nationals have been subjected as a consequence of the war imposed upon them by the aggression of Germany and her allies.

One historian, the Australian Christopher Clark, Regius Professor of History at Cambridge, has recently asserted otherwise. In *The Sleepwalkers: How Europe Went to War in 1914* (2012), he absolves Germany from peculiar guilt. The book sold well in Germany, because, said the German historian Hans-Ulrich Wehler, it served a 'deep-seated need [on the part of German readers], no longer so constrained by the taboos characteristic of the later twentieth century, to free themselves from the burdensome allegations of national war guilt' (*Frankfurter Allgemeine Zeitung*, 6 May 2014). Indeed, on the recommendation of the British ambassador in Berlin – who seems unilaterally to have repudiated Article 231 of the Treaty of Versailles – Clark received a knighthood for services to Anglo-German relations.

One wonders what the late Lady Thatcher would have made of this. She famously believed that too many ambassadors had 'gone native' in their eagerness to empathize. With a nod to Nietzsche, Professor Margaret MacMillan called her own meditation on the subject *The Uses and Abuses of History* (2009).* Perhaps there is scope for a further volume: *The Uses and Abuses of Historians*.

For a robust refutation of this revisionist idea of German innocence (which was, of course, an idea begun in Germany in the 1920s, and one that served the rise of the Nazis), it is well to consult the Anglo-German historian John Röhl's biography of the Kaiser.† I draw extensively on Professor Röhl's research in *1914: Fight the Good Fight* (2013), for it is compelling.

Indeed, there is a simple – but not simplistic – story that in a way sums up the whole question. In *The Origins of Totalitarianism* (1951), the German-born American political theorist Hannah Arendt relates

---

* Friedrich Nietzsche, *On the Use and Abuse of History for Life* (1874).
† Volume 3, *Into the Abyss of War and Exile, 1900–1941* (London, 2014).

an exchange between Clemenceau and the German representative at the Versailles conference: 'What, in your opinion, will future historians make of this troublesome and controversial issue?' asked the German. To which Clemenceau replied: 'This I don't know. But I know for certain that they will not say Belgium invaded Germany!'

It is not a case of there being two narratives, a British one and a German one, for that is to relativize the issue of truth versus falsehood in history. The facts of a case are not always apparent, but where they are, opinion must take note. The controversy is not so much between Britain and Germany as between truth-tellers and ideologues in both countries.

If for France and Britain, then, the First World War was not of their making, was the peace they made at Versailles as good as it might have been?

When the final treaty was signed, Marshal Foch despaired that it was 'not a peace but a twenty-year armistice'. He would die just ten years later – just ten years before his prophecy was proved true. In June 1944, writing in her syndicated daily newspaper column, 'My Day', First Lady Eleanor Roosevelt put it bluntly: 'We gave up unconditional surrender the last time ... and now [in the war with Germany and Japan] we have sacrificed thousands of lives because we did not do a thorough job.'

She was right – as indeed were her husband, President Franklin D. Roosevelt, and Winston Churchill in their declared policy 'this time' of unconditional surrender. As Cicero wrote: 'War should be so engaged in that nothing but peace should appear to be aimed at.'

For while it is still argued just how directly the Treaty of Versailles led to the Second World War, the Paris conference (its grander sessions held in the hall of mirrors at the Palace of Versailles) made a peace that was on the one hand too harsh and on the other too lenient. The allies' exhaustion after four years' fighting – the cost they had borne in blood and treasure – demanded territorial and financial reparations from the Kaiser and his Second Reich. Yet that same exhaustion conceded too much in the arrangements for the future self-government of Germany. And, being so exhausted, the allies would have no will in the years that followed to maintain armies great enough either to enforce the harshness or to safeguard the leniency. Foch saw it plainly. So did the young British Brigadier-General Archibald Wavell – later Field Marshal the Earl Wavell, of Second World War fame – who in 1919 wrote: 'After the "war to end war" they seem to have been pretty successful in Paris at making a "peace to end peace".' Others were saying the same, in several different languages.

If all do not agree that the war itself was *not* futile, despite its excessive cost, most seem to agree that the promise of peace was truly tragic. And so the debate as to the war's ultimate futility will go on.

PEACE AND FUTURE CANNON FODDER

The Tiger: "Curious! I seem to hear a child weeping!"

Annex A

THE ARMISTICE TERMS

Among its thirty-four clauses, the armistice contained the following stipulations:

Western Front:

- Termination of hostilities on the Western Front, on land and in the air, within six hours of signature.
- Immediate evacuation of France, Belgium, Luxembourg, and Alsace-Lorraine within 15 days. Sick and wounded may be left for Allies to care for.
- Immediate repatriation of all inhabitants of those four territories in German hands.
- Surrender of 5,000 artillery pieces, 25,000 machine guns, 3,000 mine-throwers, 1,700 aircraft (including all night bombers), 5,000 railway locomotives, 150,000 railway carriages and trucks, and 5,000 road vehicles.
- Evacuation of territory on the west side of the Rhine plus 30 km (19 miles) radius bridgeheads on the east side of the Rhine at the cities of Mainz, Koblenz and Cologne within 31 days.
- Vacated territory to be occupied by Allied and US troops, maintained at Germany's expense.
- No removal or destruction of civilian goods or inhabitants in evacuated territories and all military matériel and premises to be left intact.

- All minefields on land and sea to be identified.
- All means of communication (roads, railways, canals, bridges, telegraphs, telephones) to be left intact, as well as everything needed for agriculture and industry.

Eastern and African Fronts:

- Immediate withdrawal of all German troops in Romania, and in what were the Ottoman Empire, the Austro-Hungarian Empire and the Russian Empire back to German territory as it was on 1 August 1914. The Allies are to have access to these countries.
- Renunciation of the Treaty of Brest-Litovsk with Russia and of the Treaty of Bucharest with Romania.
- Evacuation of German forces in Africa.

At sea:

- Immediate cessation of all hostilities at sea and surrender intact of all German submarines within 14 days.
- Listed German surface vessels to be interned within 7 days and the rest disarmed.
- Free access to German waters for Allied ships and for those of the Netherlands, Norway, Denmark and Sweden.
- The naval blockade of Germany to continue.
- Immediate evacuation of all Black Sea ports and handover of all captured Russian vessels.

General:

- Immediate release of all Allied prisoners of war and interned civilians, without reciprocity.
- Pending a financial settlement, surrender of assets looted from Belgium, Romania and Russia.

Annex B

THE WAR FOR CIVILIZATION: THE RECKONING

Country	Total mobilized forces	Killed	Wounded	Prisoners and missing	Total casualties	Casualties as % of forces
ENTENTE AND ASSOCIATED POWERS						
Russia	12,000,000	1,700,000	4,950,000	2,500,000	9,150,000	76.3
British Empire	8,904,467	908,371	2,090,212	191,652	3,190,235	35.8
France	8,410,000	1,357,800	4,266,000	537,000	6,160,800	73.3
Italy	5,615,000	650,000	947,000	600,000	2,197,000	39.1
United States	4,355,000	116,516	204,002	4,500	323,018	7.4
Japan	800,000	300	907	3	1,210	0.2
Romania	750,000	335,706	120,000	80,000	535,706	71.4
Serbia	707,343	45,000	133,148	152,958	331,106	46.8
Belgium	267,000	13,716	44,686	34,659	93,061	34.9
Greece	230,000	5,000	21,000	1,000	27,000	11.7
Portugal	100,000	7,222	13,751	12,318	33,291	33.3
Montenegro	50,000	3,000	10,000	7,000	20,000	40.0
Total	**42,188,810**	**5,142,631**	**12,800,706**	**4,121,090**	**22,062,427**	**52.3**
CENTRAL AND ASSOCIATED POWERS						
Germany	11,000,000	1,773,700	4,216,058	1,152,800	7,142,558	64.9
Austria-Hungary	7,800,000	1,200,000	3,620,000	2,200,000	7,020,000	90.0
Turkey	2,850,000	325,000	400,000	250,000	975,000	34.2
Bulgaria	1,200,000	87,500	152,390	27,029	266,919	22.2
Total	**22,850,000**	**3,386,200**	**8,388,448**	**3,629,829**	**15,404,477**	**67.4**
GRAND TOTAL						

FURTHER READING

For an understanding of the war as a whole (even if contentious) – John Terraine's *The First World War: 1914–1918* (1984), though now rather dated, is a fine counter to the 'Lions led by Donkeys' school of Great War historiography. Sir Hew Strachan's (short) *The First World War* (2004) and Sir Michael Howard's shorter-still *The First World War* (2003, reissued as *The First World War: A Very Short Introduction* in 2007) are magisterial. So is Sir John Keegan's *The First World War* (1998). Niall Ferguson's *The Pity of War* (1998) poses interesting questions, but I prefer the answers in Strachan's, Howard's and Keegan's books. For straight chronology, with only the lightest touch of commentary (some of it poetical), Martin Gilbert's *First World War* (1994) is unbeatable. His *First World War Atlas* (1970) is indispensable.

The Western Front, which of course dominates British consciousness of the war, has generated books enough to sink a battleship. A number of British historians have made it almost their life's study. Gary Sheffield's work on Field Marshal Haig is crucial to any understanding of the conflict: his edition, with John Bourne, of *Douglas Haig: War Diaries and Letters 1914–1918* (2005) is as important as the probably better-known *Alanbrooke Diaries 1939–1945* in revealing the preoccupations of high command at any time. On the particular battles – First and Third Ypres ('Passchendaele') and the Somme – there has been much recent scholarship, but I still believe that General Sir Anthony Farrar-Hockley's two books – *The Somme* (1966) and *Ypres 1914: Death of an Army* (1967) are pacey, faithful and full of soldierly insight. *Passchendaele: A New History* by Nick

Lloyd (2017) is very fine. So is William Philpott's *Bloody Victory* (2009), on the Somme, as is his more general *Attrition: Fighting the First World War* (2014). On the final victories, Peter Hart's *The Last Battle: Endgame on the Western Front, 1918* (2018) is compelling, although he is considerably more approving of Haig's generalship than I am. For the French, of course, Verdun was the Somme and Third Ypres rolled into one; on these, Alistair Horne's *The Price of Glory* (2007) is essential.

The war in Africa is best read in two books: Hew Strachan's *The First World War in Africa* (2004) and Edward Paice's *Tip & Run: The Untold Tragedy of the Great War in Africa* (2007). The war in the Middle East has over the years produced many great books, not least of course that from the pen of T. E. Lawrence (of Arabia): *The Seven Pillars of Wisdom*. And *Allenby: A Study in Greatness* by General Sir Archibald Wavell, published in 1940 (to considerable criticism in some quarters, the feeling being that the C-in-C Middle East ought to be concentrating on beating the Italians rather than poring over page proofs), remains highly regarded. Of more recent scholarship, Rob Johnson's *The Great War and the Middle East* stands out.

Mark Thompson's *The White War: Life and Death on the Italian Front* is excellent.

Alan Palmer's *The Gardeners of Salonika* (2011) is a very fine account of the virtually unheard-of Macedonian Front.

And Gallipoli? Robin Prior's *The End of the Myth* (2009) and Peter Hart's *Gallipoli* (2011), each with its own focus and conclusions, are good places to start. L. A. Carlyon, an Australian author remarkably kind to the British, also offers a powerful account in *Gallipoli* (2002).

The Royal Navy has been less well served than the Army, for fairly obvious reasons: the work of blockade and counter-blockade is tedious and largely uneventful in comparison with the war on land, and, aside from the battles of Coronel, the Falklands and Jutland, there were no dramatic sea battles. So much of the story is about the preparations, and Robert Massie's *Dreadnought: Britain, Germany and the Coming of the Great War* (1991) is still the best analysis. Mike Farquharson-Roberts' *A History of the Royal Navy:*

World War I (2014) is concise, scholarly and readable, and has the added advantage of being written by a former Surgeon Rear-Admiral. As for Jutland, 'As well write the history of a ball,' as the duke of Wellington said of Waterloo. So many ships, so many salvoes – so many books. Nigel Steel and Peter Hart make sense of it – to me at least – in *Death in the Grey Wastes* (2012).

As for the service that saw the greatest acceleration and change – that of the air – E. R. Hooton's *War Over the Trenches: Air Power and the Western Front Campaigns 1916–1918* (2010) is definitive – and readable.

There were, of course, no British troops on the Eastern Front (though some found their way there in the wake of the Revolution). Norman Stone is a historian who, as they say, 'excites opinion'; I myself think his *The Eastern Front 1914–1917* (2008) is matchless in its Russian perspective – and entertaining.

PICTURE ACKNOWLEDGEMENTS

Any illustrations not specifically credited below are in the public domain or the copyright holder is unknown. Every effort has been made to trace copyright holders; any who have been overlooked are invited to get in touch with the publishers.

Section 1

Page 1: (*top*) The Print Collector/Getty Images; (*middle*) Library of Congress; (*bottom*) © Bundesarchiv, Koblenz Inv.-Nr.: Bild 183-R04335.

Page 2: (*middle*) National Maritime Museum, Greenwich, London; (*bottom*) The York Press.

Page 3: (*top*) © IWM (Q 57328); (*middle*) © The rightsholder (Q 67819); (*bottom*) © IWM (HU 95834).

Page 4: (*top*) GL Archive/Alamy Stock Photo; (*middle*) © TopFoto; (*bottom*) Forces War Records: https://www.forces-war-records.co.uk.

Page 5: (*top*) Bettmann/Getty Images; (*middle*) Popperfoto/Getty Images; (*bottom*) Archives/AFP/Getty Images.

Page 6: (*top*) https://www.learning-history.com; (*middle*) https://www.learning-history.com; (*bottom*) Karl Bulla/ullstein bild via Getty Images.

Page 7: (*top*) ullstein bild/ullstein bild via Getty Images; (*middle*) Military History Collection/Alamy Stock Photo; (*bottom*) https://rarehistorical photos.com.

Page 8: (*top*) Bain News Service/Ian Dagnall Computing/Alamy Stock Photo; (*middle*) New York Public Library/Science Source; (*bottom*) Science History Images/Alamy Stock Photo.

PICTURE ACKNOWLEDGEMENTS

Section 2

Page 9: (*top*) National Archives, USA; (*middle*) © IWM (Q 12167); (*bottom*) Keystone/Hulton Archive/Getty Images.

Page 10: (*top*) © IWM (Q 86646); (*middle*) Hulton Archive/Stringer/Getty Images; (*bottom*) Courtesy Library of Congress, Prints & Photographs Division, LC-DIG-ppmsca-13709-00127.

Page 11: (*top left*) Australian War Memorial; (*top right*) Universal History Archive/UIG via Getty Images; (*bottom*) Everett Collection Historical/Alamy Stock Photo.

Page 12: (*top*) Library and Archives, Canada; (*middle*) Henry Guttmann/Hulton Archive/Getty Images; (*bottom*) © IWM (Q 25968).

Page 13: (*top left*) SeM/Universal Image Group via Getty Images; (*top right*) Popperfoto/Getty Images; (*bottom*) Bettmann/Getty Images.

Page 14: (*top*) Canadian Artillery in Action, *c.*1915 (oil on canvas) by Kenneth Forbes (1892–1980)/Canadian War Museum, Ottawa, Canada/Bridgeman Images; (*bottom*) National Maritime Museum, Greenwich, London.

Page 15: (*top*) *British Scouts leaving their Aerodrome on Patrol, over the Asiago Plateau, Italy, 1918* (oil on canvas), Carline, Sydney (1888–1929)/Imperial War Museum, London, UK/Bridgeman Images; (*bottom*) *The Charge of the 3rd Light Horse Brigade at the Nek, 7 August 1915, 1924* (oil on canvas), Lambert, George (*fl.c.*1897)/Australian War Memorial, Canberra, Australia/Bridgeman Images.

Page 16: (*top*) *The Menin Road, 1919* (oil on canvas), Nash, Paul (1889–1946)/Imperial War Museum, London, UK/Bridgeman Images; (*bottom*) The History Collection/Alamy Stock Photo.

Illustration in text p. 388
'Peace and Future Cannon Fodder', cartoon by Will Dyson, *Daily Mail*, May 1919, © John Frost Newspapers/Alamy Stock Photo.

Index

*Page numbers in **bold type** refer to maps.*

INDEX

INDEX

INDEX

INDEX

TRANSWORLD PUBLISHERS
61–63 Uxbridge Road, London W5 5SA
www.penguin.co.uk

Transworld is part of the Penguin Random House group of companies
whose addresses can be found at global.penguinrandomhouse.com

Penguin
Random House
UK

First published in Great Britain in 2019 by Bantam Press
an imprint of Transworld Publishers
Corgi edition published 2020

A CIP catalogue record for this book
is available from the British Library.

ISBN
9780552176538

Typeset in 11.25/14.75pt Aldus by Jouve (UK), Milton Keynes.
Printed and bound in Great Britain by Clays Ltd, Elcograf S.p.A.

Penguin Random House is committed to a sustainable
future for our business, our readers and our planet. This book
is made from Forest Stewardship Council® certified paper.

1 3 5 7 9 10 8 6 4 2

For my boys, the true
Dark Knights of my world.

PROLOGUE

THE OUTDOOR CINEMA SCREEN in City Park cut out. The children's movie went black. Most of the thousand-strong crowd didn't notice, too busy playing in the fountains, a welcome respite from the sun's inhospitable rays.

Then a message started to flash on the screen, bold and threatening:

IMMINENT SECURITY THREAT. LEAVE CITY PARK IMMEDIATELY.

No 'please'.

No hint that this was optional.

Confusion rippled through the park. People stared at one another, wondering if this was some sort of joke. The screeching of car tyres and the overhead roar from two helicopters answered their doubts.

Police officers jumped from their cars with megaphones,

screaming for the crowd to disperse. They did not enter the park but kept to the perimeter.

At first, the shift was slow but the domino effect didn't take long to come into play and the few became the many. Bodies jumped from the pool and ran, some barefoot, others holding their shoes. Parents grabbed their children as the stampede began. Bradford was under siege.

ONE

Ten minutes earlier.

CITY PARK HAD NEVER been so full, the people of Bradford making the most of the July heatwave. Midday was approaching as the mercury soared past thirty, heading towards a forecasted record high of thirty-four. At its centre, the park's powerful fountains had created a magnificent pool of water, where adults relaxed at the edges and children waded in for water fights. Around the perimeter the restaurants were heaving. The Wetherspoon's pub had a queue two dozen deep.

Detective Chief Inspector Harry Virdee sat beside his mother, Joyti, and rested two cups of tea on the shallow wall surrounding the fountains. No matter the heat, it was always 'tea' with her.

'How much were they?' she asked, watching her four-year-old grandson, Aaron, splashing in the fountains.

'Does it matter?' replied Harry, shaking his head.

He watched his mother prise the lid from the container and frown at the colour. 'I knew it would be like this.'

'It's how people like it, Mum.'

'If I had a stall here and made my Indian tea, these English people would never drink this filth.'

'I'm English. I drink it.'

Harry's mother frowned. 'Your blood is Indian, your brain English.'

'I'm more English than you think. I stand in queues, prefer sandwiches to samosas and, most importantly, when you hit seventy, I'll be tempted to put you in an old people's home.'

His mother shook her head disapprovingly and sipped the tea, wincing at its taste. Harry slipped his arm around her and gave her a squeeze. God, he had missed this. With his brother, Ronnie, in India with his family, Harry was looking forward to a bit more time with his mother. He was determined today not to think of his father. Not if he could help it.

Harry's phone rang, interrupting his heat-hazed peace. He saw it was work and ignored it. These moments with his mother were precious; five years apart had been five years too many. Today was the first day of a fortnight's annual leave, and he would be creating memories he could call upon during those frequent

nights when his job dragged him to the city's darkest corners.

He kept his arm around his mother as she rested her head on his shoulder, both of them watching Aaron innocently splashing in the water.

Today, even more than usual, City Park was a vibrant display of Bradford's citizens. Women in burkas played with their children while beside them girls in Western swimwear were sunbathing. Boys, both Asian and white, had stripped off their tops and were flexing their muscles. Everyone was laughing and enjoying the weather.

'Do you like the watch?' his mother asked him.

Harry sighed, glancing at the Rolex on his wrist. 'It's a bit extravagant, Mum. You didn't need to.'

'Rubbish. You never had a proper wedding, so I never gave you a gift.'

Usually the watch stayed inside its box but when he met his mother he made a point of wearing it so she could see that he appreciated the extravagance. He'd looked up the value on the internet.

Five grand.

Harry wasn't a flash bastard and, while he did have a thing for watches, he'd never indulged it. A detective's salary didn't stretch that far.

Harry slipped off the wall and stepped into the water, soothing his sunburnt bare feet. He lifted Aaron and pointed towards the ice cream van.

'You want one?'

Aaron nodded.

'I think we'd better get dry first.'

'We come back here after, Daddy?'

'Maybe.'

Aaron kissed Harry's cheek. 'I love you, Daddy.'

Harry smiled and started towards his mother, who was ready with a towel. 'Love and affection when you want something, just like your mother.'

Harry's phone rang again.

Work.

Again, he dismissed it and flipped the phone to silent.

'Don't take the piss, I'm off,' he muttered to himself, annoyed.

As Harry's mother towelled Aaron, she took every opportunity to steal a kiss from him. Harry closed his eyes, taking a mental photograph. He hoped Saima would get here before his mother had to go.

She was due to meet Harry after Friday prayers.

Distracted from his son by an unfamiliar noise, Harry looked up to see a distant swirling of helicopter blades. More than one. As he saw them, the enormous cinema screen at the far end of City Park went black, before displaying a flashing red message, timed perfectly with the deafening roar of what appeared to be two military helicopters now almost directly overhead.

IMMINENT SECURITY THREAT. LEAVE CITY PARK IMMEDIATELY.

Only moments later, the same message boomed from the speakers.

Time froze in City Park. Everyone stared at the screen. Nobody moved.

The message sounded again.

Harry watched as, in agonizing slow motion, the panic started.

'Shit,' he said, feeling his phone vibrating in his pocket again. He pulled it out and put it to his ear, taking Aaron from Joyti and moving her out of the main flow of people as City Park started to fracture.

'What's happening?' said Harry. On the borders of City Park officers exited two armed-response vehicles, weapons raised, but came no further. More police vehicles were arriving every second and in the distance Harry could see uniformed officers pulling bright yellow tape taut to establish a cordon around the site.

The cinema screen now displayed another message, this one far more sinister: a skull and crossbones, a timer below them, counting down from twenty minutes. An obvious hack – there was no way that was protocol.

Harry listened to his boss, jaw tense, his eyes drifting down to his watch.

13.10.

Twenty minutes.

Before the call hit thirty seconds, he disconnected it, turned to his mother, tightened his grip around Aaron and said, 'Run.'

TWO

Pandemonium.

HARRY HAD NEVER WITNESSED anything like it.

People running in all directions. Screaming, shouting, adrenaline tangible in the hot, thick air.

Two helicopters continued to hover in the sky, not directly overhead, a little distance away. Harry knew there was only one reason for that – City Park was a blast zone. Police were ushering the public out of the area, loudspeakers bellowing for everyone to evacuate.

Terrorism.

Had to be.

Even Harry wasn't immune to the panic.

They'd only moved a short distance, people pushing past them, when his mother stopped, her face crippled in pain. Aaron started to cry in confusion.

'It's OK, little man, just a game we're playing,' he said.

'You go, Hardeep, get my boy to safety. I'm too slow,' Harry's mother said, panting, her hand gripping his.

'The hell with that,' replied Harry, lifting her arm and putting it around his shoulder. He threaded his hand round his mother's waist and tried to support her. It was her bad hip.

'Come on, Mum, I've got you.'

They moved slowly, too damn slowly.

Bodies glanced off Harry as people rushed forward and he saw several fall to the ground, skin grazing on concrete. Above them the sun continued its assault. Around them a mess of car horns, packed buses trying to move through stationary traffic. Everywhere was chaos.

Harry was struggling. Aaron grew heavier with each step, his mother pulling down his right arm. He felt as though he were back playing rugby, the second-row forward trying to support a collapsing scrum. He did what he did then, commanding her forward, pushing her with his arm.

They crossed the road, hit Hustlergate. She wouldn't last much longer – no chance she'd make it to the car.

In his peripheral vision, Harry saw people with mobile phones in their hands, social media no doubt awash with rumours. He could only imagine the speculation. His thoughts went to Saima but his hands were full and he had no chance to call her.

His mother finally stopped outside Waterstones, the

old wool exchange building, sweat pouring down her face, breathless.

She tried to push him away. 'You go, take my boy and leave!'

Aaron cried louder, his face red and not just from the heat.

Harry couldn't leave Joyti. He glanced for somewhere to hide.

From what? A bomb? A terrorist attack?

Joyti pushed him again. 'I said go!'

Harry looked around, utterly lost. He would not leave her. As he stared down the street opposite, Piece Hall Yard, a British flag caught his eye.

The Bradford Club.

He waited for a frightened crowd to tear past him, then made his move. His mother didn't resist.

They slowed as they turned off the main street, Harry afraid the cobbled path might hinder her further. The eerily abandoned street was a welcome interlude from the chaos behind. The chatter and pounding of footsteps on concrete faded. In the quiet, Aaron's cries reduced to a whimper.

'Hardeep, what is happening?' asked Joyti, panting.

'I don't know, Mum,' he replied, kissing Aaron and trying to soothe his little boy.

They reached the door of the Bradford Club and Harry tried to open it.

Locked.

He rang the bell and hammered on the door. His mum leaned against the wall, getting her breath.

Harry used the internet on his phone to find the club's telephone number and hit the Call button, praying reception in the area wasn't compromised. The phone started to ring. Harry kept pounding on the door.

'Hello?' said a frightened voice on the other end of the phone.

'This is Detective Chief Inspector Harry Virdee. I'm outside the club and I need you to open up. Now.'

'Why? What is happening out there?'

'Open the door or I'll be forced to arrest you for hindering an investigation.' It was a bluff but Harry didn't care at this point. He just needed to get inside. A Victorian building like this must have had a cellar, even an old air-raid shelter.

'I'm coming,' said the voice and hung up.

Harry immediately tried to call Saima but she didn't answer. He sent a frantic text, *Call me ASAP*, then glanced back to where they'd come from. He could see a chaotic stream of terrified people running away from City Park. As some fell, others jumped over them to escape.

Harry squeezed Aaron a little tighter, trying both to comfort his son and to keep the feeling in his left arm.

13.21.

Nine minutes until the countdown finished.

What was going to happen then?

The sound of robust Victorian locks being opened jarred his thoughts, then the grand wooden doors parted.

Harry grabbed his mother and pushed her inside, past

a grey-haired man. Harry quickly established he was Philip Jones, the fifty-three-year-old manager.

'Close the doors, Philip. Seal them,' said Harry. He let go of his mother, who almost fell into a nearby leather chair.

Harry switched Aaron to his right-hand side and shook out his left arm.

'Alone, Philip?' said Harry, hearing the locks being secured.

'Yeah. No one wants to be in here in the dark with the sun out like that.'

Harry placed Aaron into his mother's lap and turned to face Philip, now shaking both his arms to encourage blood flow. He looked around at the building, a spiralling staircase revealing three magnificent floors, 200-year-old architecture steeped in wealth and history.

'Is there a cellar here?'

'What the hell is happening?' said Philip.

'Do you have a cellar, Philip?' His tone was clipped as he massaged his shoulder, trying to recharge his muscles.

'Yes. Although, well, I haven't opened it in years.'

'Old air-raid shelter, right?' asked Harry, more in hope than knowledge. This place had survived two world wars and been a meeting point for wealthy wool merchants. Surely they would have had a shelter in it.

'I'm not sure,' said Philip.

'Where is it?'

'Down here,' said Philip, moving past Harry towards a shadowy oak-panelled corridor.

Harry picked Aaron up and helped his mother to her feet.

They entered a grand drawing room where Philip stopped in front of a massive wooden door. He struggled with four rusted bolts, pulling them free before opening the ancient door, grunting at the effort it took.

Darkness.

'Lights?' said Harry.

'Be surprised if they still work,' said Philip. He slid his hand along the left-hand side of the stone wall and flicked a switch.

A slight delay, then light breathed life into the void.

Harry pushed his mother inside but she hesitated. Harry checked his watch: 13.27. Three more minutes.

'You just leave me here, take Aaron with you,' she replied, clearly afraid.

'Not happening, Mum.'

Harry handed her Aaron, his face blotchy and streaked with tears. Harry stepped through the doorway on to a staircase that circled down into the cellar. It was easily wide enough for two people side by side.

Those Victorians knew how to design emergency cellars.

Harry flew down the steps, naked bulbs over his head illuminating the route. Satisfied they would be as safe as possible this close to the blast zone, he charged back up the staircase to his mother and told her to hold Aaron

tightly. Harry then picked her up, telling Philip to follow them and close the door.

The silence was disconcerting after the madness of City Park. They sat on the cold stone floor, their breath forming a white mist in the icy cellar.

'What now?' said Philip.

Harry put his arms around Aaron, checked the time and said, 'We wait.'

13.29.

One minute to go.

Harry hugged his family a little tighter, thinking of Saima. She wasn't far away, at the mosque observing Friday prayers, about a quarter-mile from City Park.

He watched the tiny hand on his Rolex ticking down the seconds until the time hit 13.30.

Harry felt the tremors first, then a deafening explosion that shook the ground. The light bulbs surged then popped simultaneously.

Joyti screamed.

THREE

SAIMA VIRDEE WAS ALMOST at the end of her Friday prayers, engaged in the final act of turning her head on to her right shoulder, back to the centre and then on to her left. Her eyes were drawn by the wide windows of the new Mehraj mosque, built on the site of an old wool mill that had been abandoned for decades. She could see much of the city from its elevated position.

More than just a place of worship, the enormous mosque had become a community hub. It had four levels. The basement, technically not part of the actual mosque, was an organized 6,000-square-metre space accommodating aid purchased from worshippers' charitable donations, which could be transported around the globe to areas often destroyed by war. On the ground floor was the grand hall, suitable for weddings and other religious gatherings. The first floor was for prayers, with separate male and female

areas, and the top floor housed an impressive white dome, modelled on the Taj Mahal.

Local and national press had described it as the most striking piece of religious architecture in the north, using marble from India, stone from Saudi Arabia and calligraphy artwork from Pakistan. Saima had fallen in love with the place.

She was whispering 'Assalamu alaykum wa rahma tullaah' when something happened. It felt like the foundations of the mosque shook and she heard the windows vibrate.

Saima hesitated, her head momentarily pausing and her eyes darting back towards the windows. Ahead the elderly lady leading Friday prayers also hesitated. Only a fraction of a pause.

'Assalamu alaykum wa rahma tullaah.'

The collective voice of the female worshippers had changed – a subtle change but Saima clearly heard it.

Fear.

What on earth *was* that?

Prayers completed, Saima left her mat on the floor and hurried out towards the doors, other women falling in behind.

They exited the hall into a wide, marble foyer to find the men already there.

The air filled with nervous chatter and loud cries for God to help them all as people started to turn away from the windows, rushing downstairs.

Saima was horrified to see an immense plume of black

smoke rising high above City Park, where a fire of herculean proportions was raging. A cloud of ash was beginning to block out the light. She chewed her lip, afraid, thinking of Harry and Aaron, her hand shaking, clawing at her pocket for her phone. For a few seconds, in her mind, the clamour around her faded to silence.

The ash cloud hit the mosque and everything went dark.

Screams came from the foyer. Shouts to close any open windows. People were running down the stairs. A fall, a scream, cries for help – other calls for calm.

Saima retreated into the prayer room.

Hellfire. It was a common enough word in Saima's childhood home and one her mother had used to frighten Saima into obeying God.

She tried to call Harry. No reception.

Her hands scrabbled to send a text.

Message failed.

She rushed to the rack where her shoes were and hurriedly put them on before charging back into the hallway. Saima pushed through the crowd, thinking only one thing.

Aaron.

She desperately needed to connect to Harry, her finger continually hitting Redial.

Just as she reached the ground floor the imam's voice came over the internal speakers.

'Please, everyone return to the grand hall. You must not leave the mosque, it is not safe. The doors are locked. Please make your way to the grand hall immediately.'

He repeated his request in Urdu. While some followed the order, others, including Saima, headed for the front door. She was dismayed to see people turning away from it, finding it locked.

With little option but to follow, Saima entered the grand hall but stayed at the back. When the time came to leave, she would be first out.

She never stopped hitting Redial, praying for mobile reception to return.

It took an age for everyone to convene inside the hall. Saima thought she heard men grappling with each other outside, several others appealing for calm.

She glanced out of the windows. The smoke was starting to lift. She couldn't prevent visions of the end of times flitting across her mind.

Imam Hashim, dressed in his usual Islamic robes, appeared on the raised stage at the front of the hall and the thousand-strong congregation fell quiet. A dozen or so men surrounded the doorway.

Saima heard her mother's voice again. *Hellfire.*

Imam Hashim stared into the crowd, face serious, arms resting by his side. 'We have been informed by the police that we cannot leave. The doors, my friends, are locked.'

FOUR

HARRY PLACED HIS SON in Joyti's arms. Aaron tried to resist, afraid, and Harry kissed his forehead. They were OK, but was Saima?

'I'll swap you a child for your phone, Mum,' Harry said into the darkness. He checked Philip was OK, relieved to hear he was. The force of the blast could have given the man a heart attack.

They had all survived. That was something.

What exactly had happened?

Harry unlocked Joyti's phone, his date-of-birth the PIN, and turned on the torch, breathing life into the gloomy cellar. He glanced at Aaron, wounded by the sight of his little boy's terrified face, tears streaming down his cheeks. He tried to call Saima.

No reception.

She was fine. Secure inside the mosque. He had to believe that.

Harry handed Joyti her phone and made to leave. 'Wait here for me to come back,' he said, reaching down to re-assure Aaron once more. 'Don't worry, little one. I'll be back very soon.' Aaron cried harder, alarmed Harry was leaving, but Harry had no choice.

Almost ten minutes after the explosion, he stepped outside the Bradford Club. He'd been expecting the July heat to hit him as he left but, even so, the force took him by surprise. The thick smoke made it worse.

Terrorism.

The smell made him recoil. Dust and ash coated his clothes immediately. Those famous images of 9/11 flooded his mind.

What had been hit to produce an ash cloud like this?

Harry dealt with fear every day but this was unfamil-iar territory. A bomb. Had to be.

He hurried down Piece Hall Yard, checking his sur-roundings constantly for threat. He felt vulnerable and didn't like it, particularly not with Aaron and Joyti so close by. He needed to get them to safety but he couldn't do that until he knew what he was up against.

Harry turned right on to Hustlergate and stopped dead in the street.

The clear blue skies were no more. An enormous mushroom cloud of black smoke had bloomed over City Park.

20

Visibility was poor. He could feel the heat from an angry fire but he couldn't see it.

Harry heard sirens in the distance, the sound of helicopter blades too.

He struggled with who to call first. His instinct was for Saima, not his colleagues at Trafalgar House, but it didn't matter.

No reception.

Harry imagined the cell masts were overloaded, the whole of Bradford calling their loved ones. Surely Saima would have been safe inside the mosque – it was far enough away.

Dismayed, he put the phone away and hurried into the smoke – towards the heat of a fire.

'Christ,' he whispered and inhaled a mouthful of smog that made him cough until he retched.

City Hall was on fire and the clock tower, which had survived the Second World War, had been destroyed.

City Park was no longer there. The fountains were no more. The entire landscape had sunk several feet below ground level. All the shops around the perimeter had been obliterated.

The park was a hole in the ground.

Locals had referred to the centre of town as a hole in the ground for more than a decade while they awaited an expensive regeneration project that had never material-ized. Now the phrase took on new meaning.

He hoped everyone had got out.

Dust, smoke and heat stung Harry's eyes and he raised his hands to shield them from an approaching gust of heavy air. The sound of sirens was growing ever louder. He doubled over and coughed a lungful of soot out of his system.

Forced to retreat, he saw people in doorways venturing to have a look, their faces filled with perplexed disbelief.

Harry was thinking so many things:

Was Saima OK?

How could he get his mother and Aaron to safety?

Was another blast coming? Again his thoughts went to images of the 9/11 disaster. Nobody had envisaged a second plane until it hit.

He turned back into Piece Hall Yard, now staggering from the cumulative hurt only smoke could inflict.

He couldn't bring Aaron out here yet.

In the club he locked the doors behind him and turned to see Philip standing unsure in the hallway.

'Detective? What's happened?'

Around an angry coughing fit, Harry told him what he had seen, then made for the cellar.

'Hardeep?' his mother said, voice sharp with concern before he reached the staircase.

'I told you to stay put.' He tried for stern but the sight of her face softened him. 'I'm OK, Mum.'

She threw her arms around him. Harry knew that embrace, a mother's desperation to keep him safe. It hadn't diminished with age.

'Seriously, Mum, I'm OK.'

'Daddy, I don't like it here,' piped up Aaron with his usual matter-of-fact delivery.

Harry stepped away from his mother and scooped Aaron into his arms, embracing him tightly.

Aaron recoiled a little. 'You smell funny, Daddy.'

'We're going to leave soon, baby. OK?'

'I want to go now,' said Aaron, burying his face into Harry's neck.

Harry turned to his mother and informed her in Punjabi, a language Aaron didn't understand, what he had seen. Philip looked confused and Harry simply nodded towards the front door, encouraging him to take a look.

Joyti's face mirrored the ones Harry had seen outside.

'I know,' said Harry.

'What . . . what are we going to do?' said Joyti, looking worriedly at Aaron.

'I don't know but I need to let Saima know we're OK. She'll be worried.'

He checked his phone.

Still no reception.

Harry was thinking of his next move. He lived a mile from here but needed to get Aaron further away than that. His mother lived in Thornton, a leafy suburb far enough away for Harry to feel they would be safe.

He could hear Saima's voice inside his head.

Get our boy to safety.

Harry kept tight hold of Aaron. Philip hadn't ventured

outside, looking afraid and unsure of himself. Harry told him of his fears about a secondary device and that he needed to make his own decision on whether to stay. To his mother he said, 'Come on, Mum, we're leaving.'

She stopped him as if reading his mind and said, 'Saima?'

Harry rubbed Aaron's back.

'She'll be safe at the mosque. Right now, I need to get Aaron and you to safety.'

FIVE

SAIMA STOOD AT THE back of the room, watching carefully.

Imam Hashim, at age forty one of the youngest imams in the city, stood centre stage in the grand hall of the mosque. Behind him was a large screen where a video clip had started to play – a clip also released on social media and, unknown to the worshippers, currently trending on Twitter.

It showed a dozen men, nothing more than silhouettes, sitting silently while a voiceover relayed their message.

Today we, the Patriots, unleashed the largest bomb to have been detonated on UK soil since the Second World War. We have planted a similar bomb inside one of the hundred and five mosques in Bradford. This bomb will be detonated should any worshippers in any of these mosques attempt to leave.

A wave of nervous whispers rippled through the crowd. Saima felt her heart racing, her mind a mess with worry for Harry and Aaron.

> *Our demands are simple. Bradford is home to a group who call themselves Almukhtaroon – the chosen ones. Their slogan is 'Death to the West' and they seek to impose their ways on the UK and its citizens. This group, led by a man called Abu-Nazir, incite religious hatred but they have so far managed to stay on the right side of the law. The UK government has tried and failed to secure prison sentences for leaders of the so-called Almukhtaroon, making a mockery of our justice system.*

Saima knew all about Abu-Nazir. He was a white convert to Islam, born and raised in Newcastle before moving to London where something had caused him to veer towards extremist ideology. He was considered a disgrace to the Islamic community. She watched the video, her mood souring.

> *No more. Today we issue this demand, that the leaders of Almukhtaroon are to be taken into custody and brought to us at the mosque where we have hidden the bomb.*
>
> *Once the bomb has been located, if the security services attempt to storm the mosque, we will detonate.*

If worshippers attempt to leave any mosque before we say so, we will detonate.

If any of our demands are not met, we will detonate.

The other hundred and four mosques in Bradford will be allowed to evacuate once the bomb's location has been verified by the police.

We are testing the Islamic community. Will they come together to ensure the safety of their worshippers? One hundred and five mosques will need to demonstrate that when a threat is brought to their doorstep, their resolve to protect one another is robust.

The wider community need to ask themselves a vital question: are the lives of four toxic individuals who seek to bring harm and division to the British way of life of equal value to the many lives of innocent Muslim worshippers?

Sacrifices must be made. Difficult decisions undertaken.

Our capabilities must not be underestimated.

This morning we provided a twenty-minute warning to evacuate City Park. We will not do so again.

We require the leaders of Almukhtaroon by 06.00 tomorrow.

Non-compliance will result in significant loss of life.

The transmission ended.

A stunned silence filled the room.

In spite of their predicament, Saima seized on the

positive news that City Park had been given a twenty-minute warning. Harry would have escaped with Aaron in that time, wouldn't he?

She had to believe it.

Saima had already lost most of her family by marrying Harry. She had a sister, Nadia, with whom she had become reconciled the year before, but they were not close. Truthfully, all she had was Harry and Aaron.

Saima saw life and death on a daily basis in the A&E department where she worked. She was able to keep her head in difficult situations, but this was on another level.

She was still clutching her mobile phone to her ear but the networks remained down. In the far window she saw smoke continuing to rise from City Park. Such appalling devastation.

Who could survive that?

The dread was twisting her insides, making it hard to breathe.

Nervous chatter was sweeping the room. A man at the front stood up and shouted, 'Why should we stay here like caged animals?' Others joined him.

Imam Hashim raised his hands and asked for calm. He was starting to lose the hall.

Saima didn't know what to think. There was simply no way they could keep thousands of people inside a hundred and five mosques. How on earth would the terrorists know if people left? The improbability of the Patriots keeping watch on all the mosques seemed clear to Saima.

Why couldn't the imam see that?

His voice boomed from the speakers, the microphone crackling. He ordered everyone to stay where they were and be calm. Saima had never heard him speak with such force. She didn't think anyone had.

The crowd fell into stunned silence.

'Let me speak. Listen to me. Then we can discuss our options,' he said.

He raised his hands for the dozen or so men who had stood up to sit back down. Hashim told the hall that the Patriots had given the security services advance warning of what was happening in Bradford before their broadcast had gone live on the internet – only a short window. The information had been cascaded to the mosques and an urgent decision taken to seal their doors. Nobody had known exactly what was going to happen and the consensus had been that the worshippers would be safest inside. Hashim was clear about what needed to be done now.

'We speak about solidarity. We hold charitable events for Palestine, Syria, Iraq and our Rohingya Muslim brothers and sisters. The persecution of our people is everywhere – a continual test. The intelligence is apparently extremely credible that one of our mosques contains an explosive device. Our responsibility is as a collective. If we walk out of our doors and somewhere in Bradford that bomb is detonated – because of *our* fear and *our* need to save *our* own lives – then we, as a community, will have failed. We have limited information on other potential threats. For

29

now, we are safest in our places of worship. The hour is dark, but if we panic it will become darker still. On our own doorstep, will we not save the lives of our neighbours?'

Hashim moved his head right to left, surveying the crowd, who had become subdued.

'I ask for your restraint. I ask you to trust this great city to defuse this unprecedented situation. Failure today will condemn us – across the world and inside our own minds. We must not act with haste.'

He paused. The room remained painfully silent, the atmosphere heavy.

'The doors have been sealed. You are not prisoners here. This mosque can never be viewed in such a way.' He pointed towards the window where ash from the blast was still clearly visible. 'Think about what might happen now. People may start hunting the leaders of the so-called Almukhtaroon. They may see every Muslim as a target. The Far Right may mobilize. These are uncertain times. Division is here, it has been building. Are we any safer out there than we are in here?'

He smiled, a warm, comfortable sight.

'You are thinking, what if this bomb is inside *this* mosque? I can see it in your faces. We will coordinate a thorough search, just like every other mosque is doing. What I ask from you is to remember that the other hundred and four mosques are with us. Now I ask those of you who insist you still want to leave, and put at risk thousands of lives, to raise your hand.'

He looked carefully into the crowd.

Hashim repeated the message in Urdu.

Nobody raised their hand.

'Thank you,' he said. 'Our time to show we can endure has arrived.'

He bowed his head and began whispering a prayer. In spite of her insides feeling like they were on fire, Saima focused on the prayer: the only thing she had now.

SIX

HARRY'S DECISION TO LEAVE the Bradford Club wasn't lightly taken. Again, his thoughts went to 9/11 and the second plane. If a secondary device detonated here, gas-main ruptures could lead to raging fires. Staying put and waiting to see what happened just didn't seem right.

The streets of Bradford felt alien to Harry as he hurried away from Piece Hall Yard, holding Aaron and supporting his mother. Philip had decided to stay put. Harry kept Aaron's face pressed into his body so he wouldn't inhale the thick, black dust swirling around them. His mother was struggling with her hip but forced herself on.

The smog enveloped them in a choke-hold. Aaron was starting to freak out, sensing all was not right.

And all the while, Harry knew he needed to get to Saima. She was at the mosque and would be safe. He couldn't rest, though, until she was with him.

Harry's car was at the Midland Hotel carpark. His mind was filled with questions about potential next targets. He couldn't see any danger here. It would be the shopping centre next, and they'd left that behind.

People's faces held disbelieving stares. Buttons on mobile phones were being pressed. Harry saw dismay that networks were still down.

He secured his family in the car then started it, maxing out the air-conditioning and ignoring Aaron's pleas for him to lower the windows. As they pulled out on to the road, the car still thick with summer heat in spite of the air-con, he saw an armed police car tear past, lights flashing, siren screaming.

Harry headed towards Upper Piccadilly, away from the city centre, reaching to turn the radio off. He needed a clear head.

More police cars tore past.

Above he could hear helicopter blades getting closer.

The roads were quiet, shock and fear keeping people away.

Harry ignored the traffic lights and the speed limits, cutting through the side streets, heading towards Thornton Road. He used one hand to unlock his mobile phone, scrolled to the Favourites and hit the top entry before handing it to his mother, the car veering as he did so.

'Keep trying Saima,' he said, ignoring another red light.

'It says Unavailable,' said Joyti.

From behind, Aaron started to whine about wanting his mum. Harry glanced at the clock: 14.05.

'Keep trying, Mum,' he said.

'Still nothing,' said Joyti, staring at the iPhone.

'Just keep pressing Redial,' said Harry, glancing at her to make sure she was doing it right. 'Anything?'

'No,' replied Joyti.

A speed camera flashed at Harry as the speedometer of his BMW tore past sixty on the forty-mile-an-hour road.

The flash made Harry wince.

Whoever had detonated that bomb was no ordinary terrorist.

Surely there was more to come.

SEVEN

THIS IS BCB RADIO'S Grace Chia reporting live from Brad-ford city centre, where a devastating explosion has reduced City Park from the well-loved mirror pool to nothing more than rubble and smoke. The heat of the fires raging through City Hall and the clock tower can be felt even from a good fifty or so metres away. Sources have told me that at around 13.10, a frantic twenty-minute warning was given to those in City Park, some two thousand people, to immediately evacuate. The cin-ema screen allegedly stopped playing a children's movie, instead flashing an urgent message for everyone to leave. Sources have confirmed that soon after, a further message featuring a skull and crossbones cast an entirely different light on this evacuation order. A video circulating on social media by a group calling themselves the Patriots, a seemingly new nationalistic group, has claimed there

is a bomb inside one of the hundred and five mosques within the city. This claim is as yet unsubstantiated and I understand this group is unknown to security services. They are demanding the arrest of the leaders of the well-known radical group Almukhtaroon, who were due to give a speech in Bradford tonight, but what is to happen after that is unclear. Almukhtaroon, of course, have long been a contentious topic, especially for the current Home Secretary, Tariq Islam, who failed to get the organization banned last year. Islam himself is in Bradford and, according to sources, was evacuated from Bradford City Football Club, where he was opening a new Asian football academy. At exactly 13.30, the bomb detonated. We do not yet know the extent of the damage caused. The emergency services are expecting a number of casualties, and we understand the Prime Minister has convened a COBRA meeting. As I stand here, smoke continues to bellow into the skies, and you can probably hear – raising her voice over the sudden noise – dozens of sirens behind me, police cars, ambulances and fire engines all desperate to save the lives of anyone trapped in the area.

Grace moved the microphone towards the centre of City Park. I don't know if you can hear that – almost shouting now – but there seem to be further explosions around the City Park area. The emergency services are ushering me away. I'm hearing something about a gas pipe.

EIGHT

HARRY PASSED THROUGH THE black iron gates of his brother Ronnie's grand Victorian house in Thornton. His brother was the model son, buying a big house and moving his elderly parents in with his own family. He'd even gone along with Asian hierarchy – this was his house, but while his parents lived there, they had the authority. It was not a house Harry was welcome in. His father had disowned Harry for marrying a Muslim and the rest of the family had been forced to follow. Harry had only recently been reconciled with his mother, but his father was a different animal entirely.

He hated being here. It was a place laden with the terrible memory of the night his job had brought him to this house to tell his brother and wife that their eldest daughter, Tara, had been murdered.

Harry did not want to leave Aaron here. He didn't trust his father not to react badly but he had no choice.

He turned to his mother and was about to speak when she raised her hand.

'He's my grandson,' she said fiercely in Punjabi, 'and, Hardeep, I love him more than I love you. He is *my* baby today and nothing your father says or does will change that. Put it out of your mind and go and get my daughter-in-law. Make sure your family is safe and I will do the same.'

Harry smiled. He needed to hear it. But he couldn't help glancing up at the house once more. He had been inside only once, when he had delivered the heart-breaking news about Tara. His father flashed before his eyes, his words from that night coming back to haunt Harry,

'This morning when I woke up, it was a good day. If I had known I would have to suffer seeing your face, in this house, on this day, I would have wished my own death.'

Harry grimaced. Punjabi could be such a coarse tongue, insults delivered with a force the English language could never muster.

Joyti put her hand on Harry's chin, forcing him to look at her. Harry realized she had seen the pain in his face.

'Today is not the day to think of the past,' she said firmly. 'Go and get Saima.'

He got out of the car, the humidity immediately sucking at his energy levels, and lifted Aaron from his car seat in the back.

'Listen, I'm going to leave you here with Grandma,' said Harry.

Aaron looked startled. 'No, Daddy, you stay here too.'

'I'll come back later with Mummy.'

'No, Daddy, I come with you.'

His pleading got to Harry, who felt a lump in his throat. He'd never left Aaron here before. The fact his father was inside and likely to treat Aaron with contempt troubled him deeply. At least they were surely safer here in Thornton than anywhere close to City Park.

Joyti arrived by his side and tried to take Aaron, who shied away from her, putting his arms tightly around Harry's neck.

'Daddy stay too!' he cried.

Joyti went to take him forcefully, which made it worse.

'Mum, leave it a minute,' said Harry, spotting a bright red ride-on mower parked on the grass. 'Aaron, look at that,' said Harry. Aaron did, and stopped crying immediately.

'Mum, I'm going to take Aaron with me so he can't play with the tractor,' said Harry solemnly, looking at Joyti.

She nodded, understanding the game. 'Yes, I put it here so Aaron could play with it, but if he is going with you, I'll have to lock it away.'

Harry saw the change in Aaron's face, eyes widening with excitement.

'Come on then,' said Harry, turning away from the tractor.

'No, Daddy,' said Aaron, struggling to get free.

Harry put him down.

Aaron looked at him matter-of-factly. 'I stay here . . . I play with tractor with Grandma and you get Mummy and come back?'

Harry shook his head. 'I don't know. You said you wanted to come with me?'

'No, Daddy, I sit on the tractor.' He paused, thought about it some more and added, 'I good boy.'

Harry crouched and ruffled Aaron's hair. 'OK. Because you're a good boy, I'll leave you here with Grandma.' He kissed him twice and stood up to leave, giving his mother one final look.

'Sunscreen's in his bag and make sure you give him lots of water.' Harry stared up at the house. 'And, Mum, make sure he's –' Harry struggled for this next word, an image of his angry father flashing across his mind – 'safe,' he said.

Joyti came across and took Harry's face in her hands, kissing him. 'Go and get Saima.' She let go of him, picked Aaron up and held him tightly. 'My life flows through his veins. Nothing and nobody is hurting this boy while I'm here.'

NINE

WEST YORKSHIRE ASSISTANT CHIEF Constable Steven Frost was no stranger to fast-moving operations in Bradford, but the sight he was looking at on his TV screen was unprecedented. The whole of City Park was no more. He had quickly established a Gold Command centre at the Dudley Hill police station to handle the emergency unfolding in his hometown. They'd evacuated Police HQ at Trafalgar House, less than a half-mile from City Park. Their switchboard had been forced to section off work to other centres around the country. It seemed like the whole of Bradford had hit 999 within the last hour.

They knew relatively little about what was happening but one thing was certain. Once this was all over, whatever *this* was, every decision he made would be scrutinized. This afternoon could come to define Frost's career, for good or for bad.

No pressure.

The regional counter-terrorism centre was located in Leeds and the assistant chief constable for that department, Peter Weetwood, was on his way.

Frost's current priority was avoiding any loss of life. All his officers who didn't need to be present at Gold Command were making their way to City Park. They would establish a hot zone where secondary terrorist activity might be imminent, a warm zone where casualties could be treated, and a cold, safe zone where operational teams could base themselves.

Frost also needed to try to prevent the media from getting ahead of him, no easy task in an age where social media could quickly manipulate the news. That meant making sure his officers weren't about to leak information to the press. It could jeopardize the whole operation.

The West Yorkshire Police had seen the video the Patriots put out on Twitter. They had also received a further video which had not been shared publicly. This second one showed a detailed, step-by-step demonstration of the make-up of a bomb, the bomb that was currently inside one of the hundred and five mosques of Bradford. A CTU bomb-disposal expert had briefed Frost on the video, giving an initial assessment that it looked credible. The assembly was flawless and had clearly been organized by someone proficient in bombmaking. Most importantly, the level of explosives it contained was enough to kill thousands.

'I've got no way of knowing if this is the bomb inside the mosque, sir,' he'd been told. 'I can tell you that if these are the Patriots on this video, then they know what they're doing. They're very much capable of carrying out their threats. Perhaps, even, of more.'

Frost picked up his phone, dialled the main switchboard and said, 'Get me the Prime Minister's office.'

TEN

THE MEHRAJ MOSQUE WAS opposite Forster Square retail park and the only way Harry could get to it was by driving past the blast site. Saima was the only thing on his mind as he stopped his car half a mile from City Park, where a yellow police cordon and two patrol cars were blocking the route. He showed his identification to uniformed officers and waited as they made a gap for him to pass.

Harry managed another quarter-mile before he was forced to stop. The roads surrounding the immediate perimeter of the park were blocked off by more police cars, these ones unmanned.

He started to jog towards City Park. He reached the site of the old Odeon cinema and immediately felt the heat, the air thick with smoke. The only way to reach the Mehraj mosque from here was on foot. Not far, if he cut through the side streets.

His phone rang.

Saima.

'Hey, I'm fine and Aaron is fine,' he said quickly, afraid reception would cut out.

'Oh, thank God!' She burst into tears.

Harry retreated into a dark side street, abandoned mills to both sides, afraid the sound of deafening sirens would alarm her.

'Saima, calm down, we might not have much time before reception cuts. Are you OK? Where are you now?'

She sobbed again and asked how Aaron was.

'He'll be playing with Ronnie's lawnmower for a good while this afternoon. Not a scratch on him.'

'Have you seen social media?'

'No. I've had no signal. What's going on?'

'You need to see the video on Twitter, Harry. I . . . I . . . can't explain.'

'I'm coming to get you first. Twitter can wait.'

'No, Harry. I can't leave the mosque.'

'What?'

'The terrorists have said nobody can leave any of the mosques or they will blow one up.'

Harry kept her on the line as he opened Twitter on his phone. He held his breath while it loaded, painfully slowly.

'Stay there, Saima, I can't afford to cut the connection with you. We might not get it back.'

It was the first thing in his newsfeed. He must have gone silent.

'Harry?'

He swallowed a lump in his throat, energy sapped from his body, and put the phone back to his ear.

'Yeah,' he said, completely flat.

'I don't know what to do.'

Neither did he.

'People are sweeping the mosque now to see if they can find anything.'

Harry put his head in his hands, closed his eyes.

'Harry? Are you there?'

'I'm here, Saima.'

'I can hear lots of sirens. Are you sure you're OK?'

'It's a mess down here. I was on my way to see you. Still am.'

Harry didn't know what else to do. He just wanted to be close to her.

'No,' she said firmly, almost angrily.

He knew what was coming.

'Aaron needs you. *That* is your priority. Not me. You cannot change what is happening or going to happen but you damn well can and bloody well will look after that boy of mine.'

'That boy of ours,' he said quietly. He'd seen the blast site, he'd been there for the warnings and now, with the Patriots' video, he knew there was nothing he could do to stop this.

'Promise me you will go back and look after Aaron.'

'Aaron's safe, I—'

'Harry Virdee, you swear to me now.'

He blew his cheeks out and stared up at the sky, angry smoke blocking out an even angrier sun. He couldn't find the words.

Saima's tone changed.

'You've always looked after me, Harry, but today it's about Aaron, not me.'

Harry said nothing.

Terrorism was not his expertise. As far as Bradford went, for now, he felt like a civilian, powerless.

'I'll look after Aaron,' he said.

'Promise me you will stay away from here. From every mosque in the city.'

'There's a mosque everywhere, Saima. What do you want me to do? Leave Bradford?'

'That's exactly what I want you to do. Take Aaron with you.'

She meant well but it irritated Harry.

'This isn't the time for your macho shit, Harry. You haven't promised me yet—'

'—and I'm not going to.'

'Harry—'

'—Saima, I don't want to fight with you. Not today.' His tone silenced her pleas. 'All I need to hear are three little words.'

'I trust you,' she said.

'Not those, you muppet.' He smiled.

'I love you.'

'I love you, too. Now hang up, conserve your battery and text rather than call – this is going to be a long day.'

'OK, OK,' Saima said, calmer than before. 'And for God's sake, stay safe. You know I can't raise our boy on my own.'

Harry sank to the ground, placing his phone on the warm concrete pavement. His phone beeped, notification of several voicemails. Harry saw they were all from his boss. He listened to the first one. A desperate plea for all hands on deck. Harry ignored it, unable to shake the fact that Saima was inside one of the mosques.

A Gold Command would be set up somewhere, probably Dudley Hill.

The Counter-Terrorism Unit would take control. Assistant Chief Constable Frost was no doubt shitting himself that this had landed on his watch, in his city.

Christ almighty – why Bradford?

He thought back to the Patriots' video.

One hundred and five mosques, one bomb.

Only Greater London and perhaps Birmingham had a higher number.

Harry picked up his phone to watch the video again when it started to ring.

Unknown number.

He answered, surprised to hear the Home Secretary, Tariq Islam, on the line.

'Harry, are you OK?' said Tariq, voice quiet, tone serious.

'Bloody wonderful. Was in City Park when the evacuation order came in and Saima is inside one of the mosques. So, yeah, I'm pretty fucking terrific. You?'

Tariq paused and when he spoke his voice was uncertain.

'I need you to come and meet me, Harry.'

He knew better than to ask for details on the phone. 'Where?' asked Harry, getting to his feet.

Islam told him.

He couldn't have heard it right.

'Your silence says everything, Harry, but you heard me just fine. Meet me there as soon as you can. We need to get a handle on this. I'll be waiting.'

The line went dead.

It hardly seemed possible, but Harry's day had just got worse.

49

ELEVEN

STANDING OUTSIDE HER HOME, Joyti had felt a deep unease as she watched Harry's car disappear out of the driveway.

Her husband would not be convinced to change his mind about Harry. To Ranjit, Harry was a disgrace. He would not forgive his Sikh son for marrying a Muslim woman.

Joyti understood her husband's position. Her acceptance of Saima had not been without its own challenges. The stereotypical depiction of Muslim women and their culture was not confined to white society.

Joyti held Aaron's hand a little tighter.

He was innocent, a beautiful product of Harry and Saima's relationship. And for her, all the more beautiful for looking just like her son. Being with Aaron brought back wonderful memories of Harry as a child.

Joyti started to cry and wiped her face immediately, not wanting Aaron to see.

Standing outside her home, she felt more afraid than ever.

'Grandma, you live here?' said Aaron, letting go of her hand, once again focusing on the tractor he was sitting on.

'Yes,' she said, and lifted the bag Harry had left her, unzipping it to find a bottle of children's sunscreen inside. She was grateful they were far enough away from City Park that the ash cloud from the blast was absent from the sky. She squirted some cream on to her hand and rubbed it into Aaron's face, then his arms. He didn't struggle but did close his eyes.

She stared at him, blinking hard, trying to regain her composure.

Ranjit could not hate Aaron, could he?

What kind of a man would that make him?

In truth, she was afraid of the answer to that question.

'Grandma, this your tractor?' asked Aaron, grabbing the steering wheel and making driving sounds.

Just like Harry, she thought. As a child, he would sit in Ranjit's car doing the same thing.

She nodded and stroked his sweaty head, the heat unforgiving. She needed to get Aaron inside. Sitting out here in thirty-plus temperatures wouldn't do.

'My daddy coming back? He going to drive it?' said Aaron.

Another nod of her head. Another stroke of his clammy hair.

Joyti gritted her teeth, the contempt she felt for her husband's stubborn position suddenly cold and venomous.

Aaron was *his* grandchild also. Surely he could not vent his rage on a child? If he did, Joyti would not tolerate it.

She looked up at her home.

Four walls and a roof.

Not a home.

Joyti hadn't felt like anywhere had been a true home since they had sold their corner shop and the flat they had lived in above it. They'd moved in here with Ronnie not long after. This place, whilst luxurious, felt cold without any memories of Harry.

A mother was incomplete without her children, that was how she felt. No matter what he had done. She was proud of him, always had been.

In some respects, even when Harry had chosen Saima over his family, deep down a spark of warmth had comforted her. He had chosen love over hatred. What mother could not be proud of a son making such a difficult choice? To simply judge a person on who they were.

Joyti looked at Aaron.

She leaned down and kissed him dozens of times until he recoiled, then picked him up, ignoring his cries to be left on the tractor.

'Ice cream inside,' she said, knowing exactly which buttons to push.

'Magnum?' he said, eyes wide, smile broad.

She nodded.

'I don't like white one.'

'I have chocolate,' she said, carrying him towards the front door.

'I have two, Grandma?'

'No.'

'At home, Mummy gives me two.'

'No she doesn't,' she said, squeezing his chubby cheeks.

Inside, Joyti took Aaron into the kitchen, sat him down and got a Magnum ice cream.

'No, I open it!'

She nodded and handed it over, unopened, sitting beside him.

Footsteps coming down the hallway startled her. Ranjit's shoes clicked on granite tiles. Joyti's heart began hammering, sweat prickled her temple. Her chest felt tight and a momentary light-headedness afflicted her mind.

She watched as Aaron bit into his ice cream, the sound of smooth chocolate breaking as Ranjit strode commandingly into the kitchen, chest stuck out, long hair loose down his back. He had learned of the blast and made his own assumptions, laying the blame firmly where it felt comfortable for him.

'Joyti! Have you been watching the news? Have you seen what these bastard Muslims have done now?'

TWELVE

QUEENSBURY TUNNEL.

This was Ronnie's domain. How in hell did the Home Secretary know about the place where Harry's brother buried the bodies?

Ronnie controlled the supply and distribution of heroin in a city second only to Greater London for its drug problem. Ronnie insisted he supplied only a clean product and claimed to be helping rid the city of dealers who cut the heroin with any old crap in the interests of making more money. Clean heroin, he said, was no more toxic than alcohol.

Harry hadn't given up the fight to bring his brother over to the right side of the law, but it was a long struggle.

He parked near the tunnel, BBC Five Live reporting from the 'Bradford terrorist attack' on the radio. He heard that Bradford City Football Club had been evacuated,

where Tariq had been, opening the new academy that encouraged young players from ethnic minorities to enter the game. The news report said the Home Secretary was currently en route back to Whitehall.

No he bloody wasn't.

Harry's brain couldn't handle any more stress right now.

How did Tariq know about this place?

Was he working with Ronnie, too? Harry pushed the thought from his mind. Tariq was the Home Secretary, of course he wasn't working with Ronnie. He was not, though, just a cabinet minister. Before entering politics, Tariq had been in the army, in an elite special forces group, no less. There were rumours that he had also been part of a covert group whose very existence was nothing more than speculation.

Eyes closed, hands gripping the steering wheel, Harry wondered if Tariq and his associates had ventured into the tunnel and found the bodies of the past.

The weapons hidden deep inside.

The secrets which could ruin them both.

Harry didn't like helping Ronnie out from time to time but blood ran thicker than water.

Harry exited his car, hurried to the boot and took off his expensive Rolex, shoving it in his laptop bag; the tunnel was no place for it.

As he looked down towards the entrance, it hit him. There was only one way Tariq Islam could know about

this place. He'd been wary of Harry and his methods since a high-profile case had thrown them together. Tariq must have had him watched.

Queensbury Tunnel was once a busy thoroughfare for passenger trains between the city and Halifax. The Highways Agency had been planning to fill it with concrete and consign it to the history books until a private investor had purchased it for a bargain price. Ronnie.

He used it to remind those bastards who dared cross him just what the entrance to hell felt like.

Dark.

Infested.

Forgotten.

Harry hurried down the steep, parched embankment, barren shrubs scratching at his naked arms. The city needed rainfall, especially today, he thought, remembering the fires raging in City Park. He jumped into the canyon, grateful for the shade.

Pulling a rusted, creaking doorway aside, Harry saw Tariq Islam with a torch on the ground pointing towards the concrete ceiling.

No suit and tie today. Still smart, though: white shirt, dark jeans. That shirt was too clean for this tunnel. Harry suspected Tariq never got his hands dirty. Not any more.

Harry left the door ajar, stepped inside and took up his place opposite Tariq, hands in pockets, waiting.

'Lots of questions, no doubt,' said Tariq.

Harry didn't reply. He didn't trust his voice not to betray how uneasy he felt.

'What needs to happen now, Harry, is a series of fast, extremely pressurized decisions which might shape the future of this city as well as the next decade's foreign policy and civil liberty programme.'

Harry raised his hand to silence Tariq. Then he pointed deep inside the tunnel where there was nothing but darkness.

'You know this isn't the place for politics. When you walk through that door' – Harry nodded towards the entrance – 'everything is off the record.'

Tariq nodded, arms folded across his chest now. 'You want to know how I came to find out about this place?'

Harry shook his head. 'It's obvious. You had me followed.'

Tariq raised an eyebrow.

'I helped you last year. I did you a massive fucking personal favour. Oh, and of course, while I was at it, I got you a career-high poll rating.'

Tariq chewed his lips, listening intently.

'We had an agreement' – Harry pointed to Tariq, his voice gaining an edge now – 'but you couldn't let it lie, could you? Put one of your team on me and realized one day this place existed. Have a snoop inside, did you? Find anything interesting?'

Harry's words were bitter, mostly because he didn't have a hand to play. Tariq knew everything about him.

'Some brother you have there,' said Tariq.

'In another life, you two would get along.'

Tariq nodded. 'Maybe. Something you said to me before really stuck out. Know what it was?'

Harry shook his head, waited.

'You said, Bradford isn't like anywhere else. You've got to stay in the shadows, become the city. Understand its energy, the good and the bad . . .'

Harry remained motionless, recalling those exact words.

Tariq continued, quoting him, '. . . and there are some dark times to come, maybe darker than we've ever known.' He paused. 'Remember that, Harry?'

'I do.'

'Almost like you were predicting the future.'

'This is Bradford. Its future is not without challenges. You know I had nothing to do with this. I was there with my little boy.'

Tariq unfolded his arms and stepped a little closer to Harry, blocking some of the light from the torch, silhouetting half his face. 'Dark times,' he repeated.

Harry stared at the one eye he could see, a sense of dread growing. 'Who the fuck am I speaking to here? The Home Secretary? The ex-special forces commander? Or someone else entirely?'

This time, when Islam spoke, it sounded altogether like military talk, pure facts, no padding – about as far removed from political speak as it got. 'One hundred and

five mosques, one bomb. Worshippers are afraid now but in a few hours they'll want to leave, some of them – maybe all. *Impossible* to contain so many people. The guy with a pregnant wife at home, the daughter with chronically ill parents, they're going to want to get back to their loved ones. We've got, I reckon, three hours before the Muslim community starts to crack. With the best intentions in the world, the imams, the police, the politicians, we can urge for calm but ten thousand people spread across a hundred and five sites? We can't control that.'

'Why am I here, Tariq?'

'We also have a blast site to contain,' Tariq continued, as if Harry hadn't spoken. 'A city to sweep for secondary devices and, amidst all that, four dickheads who refer to themselves as the chosen ones to locate and set up in a safe house, while troublemakers in Bradford, maybe even vigilante groups, try to compete with security services to track them down.' He paused, then said, 'Four dead or a thousand? That's what this might come down to if we cannot find that bomb and disarm it without the Patriots knowing.'

Another pause.

Harry had no idea where this might be going.

'We've got a deadline of six a.m. Sunrise.' Islam checked his watch. 'About fifteen hours from now. These . . . Patriots haven't destroyed this city and pulled off this plot without planning it for months. This might come down to choices we simply cannot make.'

'We?' said Harry, feeling the chill of the tunnel on his skin.

'Security services.' Tariq waved his phone at Harry. 'Twitter,' he said, shaking his head ruefully. 'Let me read you some tweets that sum this up.'

Tariq's finger scrolled through his feed.

'Let the bomb inside the mosque blow! New national holiday #takebackourcountry.'

It shouldn't have bothered Harry. Twitter heroes were cowardly people.

It did.

Tariq read another. *'Find the leaders of Almukhtaroon and make them Saints! #anothermuslimterrorist-attack.'* He scrolled for more.

'I get it,' said Harry.

'One more,' replied Tariq. *'Far Right brothers and sisters! Our day has arrived. #whiteandproud.'*

Harry put his hand out and lowered the phone in Tariq's hand.

Islam backed off, holding Harry's gaze. 'What happens if the security services find these four leaders of Almukhtaroon? They have no cards to play. The government does not negotiate with terrorists and that policy will not change simply because thousands of lives are at risk. There are always lives at risk. Either we will get them into safe custody and then pray we're able to disarm the bomb, or we somehow negotiate a truce with the Patriots. If the bomb blows, we will have the start of a new crisis in this country.

It could be a generation of nutters born from those who lost loved ones in this siege or a massive surge in popularity for the Far Right who will play on these fears. Either way, we lose.'

Harry knew Tariq was right.

Lose–lose.

With sudden clarity, Harry knew what was coming.

'There is one more option,' said Tariq.

Harry stepped back, leaning against the cold wall of the tunnel, a welcome distraction from the fear burning in his mind.

'If it does come down to the choice between four lives and thousands of lives, I want to be able to make that call, off the record. I need Almukhtaroon in my custody. To do that, I need someone to find them for me.'

THIRTEEN

SAIMA WAS STANDING BY the window in the foyer of the Mehraj mosque. From here she could see the ash as it continued to bloom into the sky from City Park, emergency services all around as fires burned in the distance. It looked like a war zone.

She continued to tap at her mobile. Joyti wasn't answering.

Why not?

Had something happened? She tried to phone Harry but his phone went straight to voicemail. Outraged, she kicked her foot against the base of the window.

Saima had managed to speak to her sister, who thankfully was not inside a mosque. They had shared an awkward conversation about whether Nadia should inform Saima's parents about her predicament. Their parents had moved to Pakistan soon after Saima had married Harry. That

had always been their plan but had been expedited by Saima's decision. The cultural shame, the damnation from the community. Saima had ordered Nadia not to inform their parents. She didn't need the added drama, today of all days.

She'd left the grand hall, preferring to watch what was happening outside. Inside, a search was under way, the men taking control because *clearly* women couldn't find a bomb.

Almost as worrying, dissent was rising. They all wanted to get out of this alive and unharmed. Yet all hundred and five mosques across Bradford would not stand together as one for long. In here, divisions were already forming. Saima heard people whispering about making a break for it.

Out the window she could see the one thing that might stop them. Dozens of officers creating a cordon around the mosque.

Somehow, amid all this chaos, she felt totally alone in the world.

She turned away from the window and glanced at the battery life on her phone: 33 per cent. She couldn't keep trying to call her mother-in-law. She couldn't just stand here, either.

Screw it, she was just as good as anybody else at searching.

Those men would accept her help whether they liked it or not.

FOURTEEN

HARRY HAD SPENT TOO many sombre nights in Queensbury Tunnel.

Usually as the voice of reason.

Now and again as something darker.

What Tariq was asking was impossible.

'Even if I wanted to, I couldn't. Almukhtaroon will be sought by every security service in the country. If they're smart, they'll already be in hiding.'

Harry pointed at Tariq's phone, still in his hands.

'Bet Twitter trolls are putting Almukhtaroon at the top of their most-wanted list. I might know this city better than anyone else but I also know when I'm out of my depth.'

Tariq turned his phone off, the screen fading to darkness, his face no longer illuminated by it.

'Out of your depth?' he said.

'Yes. The whole world is looking for four ghosts who could be anywhere in Bradford right now. How do we even know they are here?'

'They had an organized talk scheduled for this evening. It's on their Twitter page. They're around, all right.'

Harry glanced down the tunnel. 'Maybe so, but I'm beaten here.'

Tariq stayed silent.

'Anyway, murder's not my thing.'

'So, what then?'

Harry shook his head. 'Nothing.'

'I should be talking to your brother?'

'No. I mean, if I had these guys, I'd leave it to Bradford to choose their fate.'

'What do you think Bradford would decide?'

Harry thought about the city's intolerance for anyone who tried to bring it to its knees. If the four leaders of Almukhtaroon were left on the streets, they'd simply become part of its history.

'I think I'd be having dinner with my wife before the sun sets this evening.'

'Mob mentality?'

Harry started to reply, reconsidered and said, 'Street justice.'

'What if you had a head start?'

'I don't.'

'What if—'

Harry suddenly stepped towards Tariq. In the darkness,

he would have expected a lesser man to flinch. Tariq didn't move.

'My wife is in one of those mosques, my kid and my mother nearly got caught up in the blast, so, Tariq, why don't you just cut to the chase? What have you got on them?'

Islam looked at his watch.

Harry held his ground.

'I need to be briefed on the COBRA meeting within the hour,' said Tariq.

'Yet you'd rather be here, with me.'

'I'd rather not be at either. They'll assume I've been waylaid by the fallout up here. And all we need to stop Bradford from falling is four fuckers I can't do anything about because they're British citizens.'

He was starting to lose it and Harry didn't like it one bit.

'Abu-Nazir was born here, everyone knows that. The white Geordie ginger lad who moved to London, converted to Islam, went to Syria and returned with an English girl, Amelia Rose, also a Muslim convert. They set up Almukhtaroon.'

Harry knew the cases. They had caused a media sensation when the current Far Right leader, Tyler Sudworth, had a public altercation with Abu-Nazir, calling him by his English name, Kade Turner. Sudworth had handed out a beating to Nazir and all hell had broken loose as Almukhtaroon supporters and Far Right extremists had

locked horns. Arrests in their dozens had been made and Sudworth, the self-appointed 'saviour' of white people, had been jailed for six months, gaining an even larger following inside prison.

'Like we said, the security services lose either way on this one – with Almukhtaroon in safe custody or not,' said Tariq.

Harry felt his phone vibrate. A text from Saima.

You OK, and Aaron? What's happening out there? Everyone in here scared. So am I. Miss you. XXX

'I agree you can't win,' said Harry.

'But you can.'

Harry replied to Saima.

I'm fine. Aaron perfect. We'll get through this. We always do. XXX

He put his phone away and focused on Tariq. 'I don't follow.'

'Group-13.'

That got Harry's attention.

The covert para-military organization who officially didn't exist except in internet chat rooms, where arguments raged about who were deadlier, them or the USA's Navy Seal teams. He inched closer to Tariq, recalling speculation that the Home Secretary had once been a member of Group-13.

The men stared at each other.

In a tunnel rich with secrets, the silence they shared for

those few seconds told Harry everything he needed to know.

He inched closer still.

'Call them in,' whispered Harry.

'It is being considered. Most cannot be pulled from ongoing missions.'

Tariq stared past him into the darkness of the tunnel.

Harry felt the hairs on the back of his neck stand on end. 'What are you not telling me?' he said.

'It is more complicated. Group-13 don't engage with matters like this,' replied Tariq.

'Then what do they do?'

Tariq didn't answer that. 'If they get caught or pictured here – even a sniff of their existence – it opens up a box of explosives far more dangerous than what is currently ongoing in Bradford. I cannot say any more than that.'

Harry didn't understand. He turned around, looked into the darkness. Tariq arrived at his shoulder, both men now side by side.

'What's down there?' asked Harry.

'Nobody from Group-13,' said Tariq.

'So, who then?'

'Decision time, Harry. If you walk down there and find out, then you're involved until this siege ends, no matter the outcome. No going back.'

Aaron. Saima. He couldn't risk them.

'Why do I want any part of this?' asked Harry, focusing on the darkness.

'Because I think you want to be in control of what happens in Bradford today. To the city, to Saima, to your son.'

Tariq was right, of course he was.

Harry didn't want to leave this to chance. He held Tariq's stare for a moment, then stepped into the darkness.

FIFTEEN

THE LIVING ROOM OF the Virdee household was panelled with dark oak and had an ornate fireplace with brown Chesterfield couches either side. Joyti was standing by the living-room window, watching Aaron. He'd eaten his ice cream and was back on the tractor, pretending to drive. Ranjit was sitting behind her, the atmosphere strained, the silence deafening. Joyti had become accustomed to this over the years, always finding solace in standing by the window, watching the world go by. Joyti often used to find Harry standing as she was today, arms folded, deep in thought. Her boy.

She didn't know what to say to her husband. Ranjit had found her with Aaron and stormed out of the kitchen, muttering words and curses that made her relieved her grandson couldn't speak Punjabi.

For so long, her life had been about subservience, always

deferring to Ranjit. Even when it lost her a son. However, she had come to see that his was not the only way.

She couldn't – she *wouldn't* – allow Ranjit to take this from her. Her newly formed relationship with Aaron was more important than Ranjit's hatred of what Harry had done.

The stillness felt like a noose around her neck.

How to break it?

'Did you think when we first came to this country that we would ever live in a house with a little tractor to cut our grass?' she said, speaking in Punjabi.

Ranjit said nothing.

'You had two pounds in your pocket. We couldn't speak English. Do you remember how cold it was? How we yearned to go back to India?'

Still nothing.

Joyti smiled, focusing on Aaron, lost in his own little world. 'Do you think, in our fight to succeed, to make a life for ourselves and for our sons, we lost sight of the simple things that make life beautiful?'

She allowed the silence that followed to settle, wondering what was going through Ranjit's mind. He had only glanced at Aaron. Yet in that moment she was certain he had seen what had once taken her breath away – a carbon copy of their little boy. She might have been wrong, but she thought she saw in Ranjit a flicker of something that wasn't hate.

'He cannot stay here,' said Ranjit finally.

Joyti did not detect the usual force behind his words.

'There is nowhere else,' she replied, keeping her back towards Ranjit. If she saw contempt in his face, she didn't trust herself not to react.

'These people have very large families. There is always somebody there.'

'These people,' said Joyti, shaking her head.

'Muslims.'

'He is my grandchild – our grandchild. *We* are the family to look after him.'

'That man is not my son. Therefore, it is impossible for that boy to be my grandchild.'

'Well, a grandchild of mine must surely be one of yours also,' said Joyti, unable to keep a spiteful edge from her voice.

'You see what happened in Bradford two hours ago? Shall I put on the news for you, woman?'

She turned around to face him, irate. 'Did I see? *Did I see?* Take one look at me, Ranjit. I am covered in ash. We were there, in City Park, only moments before the bomb went off. Do you even care?'

'You see? They nearly take you from me! Nearly bring *more* suffering to our family, and still you entertain these people!'

Joyti steadied her voice. 'My son, his wife and my grandson are not simply "people". Harry saved my life this morning. You would have been proud.'

Ranjit swallowed hard, his eyes alight with rage. 'How many dead this morning? Do you know?'

'That has nothing to do with this.'

'They live in his house. Those who did this.'

Joyti was used to the tired, clichéd arguments. 'If you are referring to Saima—'

'Do not say her name in my house!'

'My house also,' she replied, turning back to face the window. It dawned on her that the bomb blast she had witnessed a couple of hours ago wasn't the most harrowing thing she would experience today.

Joyti could not have the same argument with Ranjit again. She had tired of trying to convince him Saima was not a terrorist simply because she was a Muslim. She focused on Aaron, who was now jumping up and down on the seat of the tractor. She envied him; such innocence, oblivious to the hate that existed in the world, in this room. She would do anything to keep it that way.

'He cannot stay here,' said Ranjit. 'If he does, I will leave and never return.'

She knew he meant it. His anger knew no compromise.

'My house is pure. We left Hardeep and his *filth* behind.'

The words sounded harsher in Punjabi. Again, she managed to remain calm. She paused a moment, thinking of her next move.

'OK,' she said, focusing on Aaron, feeling guilt at what she was about to do. She paused a beat then moved towards Ranjit, stopping in front of him. 'I will take him from this house but I want you to do something for me.'

'Which is?'

'I want your word – your kasam – that you will honour my request.' She knew he would not go back on his kasam, a sacred Asian promise made on penalty of death.

'Not until I hear what it is.'

Joyti mocked him, shaking her head. 'A man like you should be willing to do *anything* to protect his home.'

Ranjit got to his feet and nodded solemnly. 'You have my kasam.'

Joyti glanced back towards the window; another glimpse of Aaron, another pang of guilt. She had no choice but to try this.

'I will leave this house with Aaron, but before that, you must look that little angel in the face and tell him yourself that he is not welcome here.'

SIXTEEN

A FEW PACES INTO the tunnel, where the air grew colder still, Harry found an Asian boy, blindfolded and unconscious. He bent to check he was still alive, felt a strong pulse and backed away.

It wasn't the first time he'd seen someone like this in here. But he usually had Ronnie to thank for that.

He glanced at Tariq. 'Am I supposed to know who that is?'

Tariq set the torch on the ground. Water dripped from the roof of the tunnel, thudding to the ground by his feet. The air was chilly, enough to make Harry wish he had another layer on.

'No,' said Tariq, stuffing his hands in his pockets and staring down at the kid.

Harry waited for an explanation.

'One thing you learn in the army, especially special ops, is that in a crisis, fast decisions save lives. You

ponder, assess, hesitate too much and, more often than not, it's the difference between life and death. Sometimes it takes just a heartbeat.'

Harry crouched near the kid to get a better look.

Thin, almost painfully so. Long, delicate fingers wrapped around his knees. He looked bound, although it was difficult to see in the light of the tunnel. Patchy stubble.

Harry was certain he'd never seen him before.

'Who is it?' asked Harry.

'Your first impression of him?'

'Scared kid. Not much more to say.' Harry stood up. He wished Ronnie were here. Christ, he needed his counsel today. Ronnie might be the vicious one but he was also the smart one. IQ off the charts. When they were kids, he'd been headed for Oxbridge, until he'd gone to prison in place of Harry, protecting him from a murder charge – albeit one that had saved their mother's life after a bungled armed robbery at their corner shop.

Harry had never forgiven himself.

And now here they were, one brother upholding the law, the other breaking it. Complicated wasn't the word.

'Who's the kid?' asked Harry, pulling himself back to the present.

'It's Isaac Wolfe.' Tariq smiled, almost rueful, as if he'd hoped the name would trigger a response. When it didn't he unlocked his phone, accessed a video file and handed it to Harry, who only needed to watch the first few seconds before he hit Pause.

'What the fuck,' he whispered, looking from Tariq to the kid in disbelief.

The video was a typically vile broadcast by the leaders of Almukhtaroon.

Standing beside Abu-Nazir was Amelia Rose, the black widow mooted as his long-term partner and widely speculated to have been responsible for the recruitment of many vulnerable young Muslims to travel to Syria and join the 'resistance'. Then there was Fahad-Bin-Azeez, the muscle behind the pair's organization, and finally a young, naive-looking kid.

The same kid who was unconscious on the floor of the tunnel.

Tariq's voice was cold, his gaze steady, as he explained. While officials took advice on the legitimacy of the threat and pored over the Patriots' videos – both the one released on social media and the one sent directly to the police – Tariq had put his trust in a member of his close-protection team.

'How did he know where to look?' asked Harry.

'Intel on the police database.'

'How did he get access?'

'Trusted sources.'

'Auditable ones?'

'The security services got the video from the Patriots fifteen minutes before it was released to social media. The bastards gave us that window to get the message through to the imams in the mosques to seal their doors. I used it to

consider what would happen after the bomb exploded. Like I said, it's the decisions you make in the seconds after learning intel that can define what comes to pass. The police database showed Isaac had a record for assault and that he'd been in a youth detention centre until a year ago. His last known address was listed and we took a punt. Bingo.'

Harry rubbed a sweaty palm across his stubble.

This wasn't happening.

Tariq continued, calm, measured. 'I can't be anywhere near this for obvious reasons. Realistically, neither can Group-13. Manhunts are not what they do. Time is our main enemy here, Harry.'

Harry felt his blood boil. This was a major threat. He did not like Tariq's dismissive tone. He turned to voice his displeasure to find Tariq had his hand raised in anticipation.

'There are many things you don't know. Group-13 do not officially exist and even if I could speak to . . . certain people, they would arrive here far too late. The world's media is upon us, an entire city is in lockdown, and with every security service we have pulling together, Group-13 could not even be ghosts here.'

'And you think I can?' said Harry, perplexed.

Tariq looked around the tunnel. 'You seem to have a particular set of skills, which today might just give this city a fighting chance.'

With Ronnie in India, Harry had no leverage and no access to the muscle Ronnie employed. Harry's 'particular

set of skills' in this instance would just be his determination to keep his family safe.

'I'm alone here,' said Harry. 'You've got the wrong man.'

Irritation flashed across Tariq's face. 'If we walk away from this . . . mess and it all turns to shit, will you ever look back on this moment and forgive yourself?'

Harry thought of Saima.

Scared, alone.

He rubbed his hand across his face again, head hurting.

For the next fifteen hours, Almukhtaroon would be the most hunted people on the planet. Harry had seen the videos they put out on the internet. Abu-Nazir was a charismatic son-of-a-bitch and now, with everyone looking for him, he'd be rallying those closest to him, those he could convince to bring about carnage on the streets of Bradford.

Go out in a blaze of glory.

Harry folded his arms across his chest, a chill zipping down his spine. He sighed.

'What do I have from you?' he asked Tariq, without looking at him.

A hand on his shoulder, squeezing it firmly.

'Anything and everything I've got.'

Alone now, Harry had allowed Tariq to leave, having formed the loosest of alliances. Tariq had given him a cheap burner phone with his number programmed into the memory. It would be the only way they would communicate.

Tariq intended to set himself up at Gold Command. With Bradford on lockdown, he could not get out of the city back to Whitehall. Harry could only imagine what ACC Frost would make of that.

Harry had ventured deep into the belly of the tunnel and unearthed a bag Ronnie kept for times like these.

When someone needed to be broken.

Harry wouldn't do it here. Looking at Isaac and knowing his background, the tunnel might serve to deepen his resolve.

No. For this particular task Harry needed to change the game.

SEVENTEEN

TWO HOURS SINCE THE bomb had gone off and West York-shire Assistant Chief Constable Steven Frost had just finished his first full Gold Command meeting. Together he and his opposite number in the Counter-Terrorism Unit, Peter Weetwood, had established five critical areas to focus on.

1. Stabilize City Park and contain any ongoing terrorist activity.
2. Identify the previously unheard-of terrorist group calling themselves the Patriots.
3. Locate the four leaders of so-called Almukhtaroon and get them into safe custody.
4. Maintain police presence at as many of the 105 mosques in the city as possible.
5. Increase general police presence to ensure Bradford did not fall into civil unrest.

'I don't need to remind you all,' he'd said to the crowded briefing room just before he'd dismissed them, 'this is as serious as it gets. There is nothing too small to warrant our attention here. Everything is relevant. I want all eyes and ears open. And don't do anything stupid.'

The Prime Minister had offered him whatever resources he needed. Officers and patrols from Newcastle to Humberside were currently en route to Bradford. There'd soon be more police here than Frost knew what to do with.

The wild card was the hostage situation. Frost had thousands of people inside the mosques on lockdown. For now, the worshippers were afraid enough to stay there – uncertain of just what was happening in Bradford. He didn't think it would be long before that dynamic changed. If the mosques started to empty, the pressing question became whether to enforce the confinement, something that was only achievable once the added manpower from the north arrived.

Frost could not be sure of the risks involved. But he felt certain it wouldn't take much for things to go very wrong. He did not want that happening on his watch. For now, the safest place they could be was inside their mosques. The threat of the supposed second device had not yet been verified.

The blast in the park had been right next to Britannia House, where the city's CCTV surveillance was housed. It was currently offline, meaning most of Bradford was unmonitored. Work was frantically under way to restore

the network but that might take hours and, as the Patriots had made clear, the clock was ticking.

Frost knew all about Almukhtaroon. It was hard to forget their leader, the man known formerly as Kade Turner who, on converting to Islam, had taken the name Abu-Nazir. He now enjoyed a cult following – the white jihadi with bright ginger hair and a distinctly blond beard. He certainly made an impression.

The Home Secretary, Tariq Islam, had tried to prosecute both Nazir and his partner – and second-in-command – Amelia Rose eighteen months before, and suffered a humiliating defeat when the European Court of Justice ruled the UK had violated *their* human rights. The result had seen support for the Far Right surge.

The muscle behind the leaders was Fahad-Bin-Azeez, commonly referred to simply as Azeez. He was a former power-lifting champion who'd fled Somalia as a teenager and served time for petty thefts and grievous bodily harm. It was in prison that he had been radicalized by sympathizers of Almukhtaroon. Once released, he had joined the organization, quickly climbing the ranks until he sat alongside Abu-Nazir and Amelia Rose.

The fourth and newest senior member of the organization was just a kid: Isaac Wolfe. His role had seemingly been to attract a younger audience – angry teenagers, easy to manipulate. Isaac had recently been released from a youth detention centre and had spoken on social media about how his generation had been forgotten

by British society. He was the only one with a registered address in the city. It looked like it had been his mum's place, but she'd died not long before he'd been convicted. The other leaders of Almukhtaroon were listed as NFA – no fixed abode – which made them harder to track down, requiring intelligence. Officers were on their way to Isaac's home to take him into protective custody. Frost didn't have much hope they would find him there. His name was all over the news. While Frost was setting up the Gold Command room and delegating roles and priorities, Isaac Wolfe would have had time to escape.

For all Frost knew about Almukhtaroon, he knew next to nothing about the Patriots or what they were capable of.

Initial reports from City Park suggested no casualties, which Frost didn't believe. The blast site covered 4,000 square metres. City Park was nothing more than ash.

Without the twenty-minute warning to the public, the death toll might have been in the hundreds. Why give the warning? What sort of terrorist wanted to prevent major loss of life?

Frost played the YouTube video again. The national cyber agency hadn't yet sent through their analysis. The Patriots were targeting Almukhtaroon to show the rest of the UK that those with obvious animosity towards the country and its Western values would no longer be tolerated – this was extreme Far Right ideology.

Perhaps it was the inevitable outcome after so many years of terror attacks.

Frost didn't like the look of it. A damn slippery slope to total anarchy.

He saw it clearly. Gold Command had to secure Almukhtaroon before anyone else got to them.

EIGHTEEN

LOOKING OUT FROM THE front door at Aaron still driving the tractor, Ranjit could not quite believe his grandson was half Muslim.

His father would be turning in his grave. The man who had called Muslims a virus, who had declared them toxic, a danger to his family and to the world.

His father, though, had not seen this little boy, this tiny version of Hardeep.

He pushed the uncomfortable thoughts from his mind and focused on Aaron.

This had to be done.

Hardeep had no idea just how difficult he had made life for his father. People in his community had shunned him, even after he had disowned Hardeep. How could a senior member of the Sikh Temple have allowed this to happen?

Ranjit had stepped down from the committee. Some said he should have killed Hardeep.

He thought back to the night Hardeep had told him he was going to marry that wretched girl. There had been a moment of anger, Ranjit had drawn his sword, but Joyti had put herself between father and son.

Would he have done it?

He'd asked himself that question every day since.

And 'Aaron'. Who were they kidding? A white name for an already confused boy. He would grow older and embrace the Muslim faith. And then what? Aaron would go on to marry a Muslim and the Virdee bloodline would forever be ruined.

If the elders in India ever found out . . . it didn't bear thinking about.

He stepped from the house, the sunshine warming his face.

Ranjit approached Aaron, his hand reaching to scratch his forehead, his turban uncomfortable in the heat.

Joyti watched from the window, fists clenched, eyes watery. She was only now aware that she might have placed her boy in danger. Ranjit's demeanour was clear. He had opted to put his turban on, marching out to meet Aaron with his Sikh identity at the forefront.

She wanted to run outside and protect the boy as she watched Ranjit crouch in front of him so they were both

almost level with each other. Aaron stuck out his hand, smiling brightly.

He had never looked more like Hardeep.

A tear slid down Joyti's face, the tension unbearable as she watched her husband staring at Aaron, not saying a word.

She thought of Harry's words: *Look after my boy, Mum.*

Joyti felt her feet moving but stopped – she wanted to have faith in this moment, in this man.

She dug her nails into the palms of her hands, breaking the skin.

'Shake his hand, you shake it,' she hissed, trembling in anger, blinking away tears.

He didn't. He got to his feet and walked away, back towards the house, quicker than she had seen him move in a long time.

Joyti moved too, towards the front door.

She marched into the hallway, ready to unleash her anger at her husband, but was stopped dead as Ranjit barged past, their shoulders colliding. He wasn't quick enough that she didn't see his face. Or the tears sliding down it.

NINETEEN

HARRY PULLED UP AT an old farmhouse frequented by Ronnie when he needed a softer location to carry out some of his work. There was nothing for miles around, just field after field.

Perfect.

A quick sweep of the house confirmed it was empty.

Checking that the burner phone Tariq had given him was turned off, he went to get Isaac from the car.

The kid was still unconscious. For how much longer, Harry didn't know. Tariq said they had injected him with a sedative that usually lasted a couple of hours.

Harry carried him into the house and laid him down on an old leather couch in the living room.

He patted the boy down.

No mobile phone.

No wallet.

Nothing hidden under his Islamic robes.

Harry took in more details about the boy. He was extremely fair for an Asian kid, his skin was light and his dark hair had a red tint to it. Harry wondered if one of his parents might have been white. He checked Isaac's hands, feeling his pulse again. Harry frowned at the thumb on the kid's right hand, markedly thinner than his other. He'd seen this before.

What he really needed was robust intel on the boy and the only place to get that was Isaac's home, an address Tariq had given him.

Police would be there by now, tearing the house to pieces.

Removing his phone, Harry saw several missed calls, all from his boss, Detective Superintendent Clare Conway, but she didn't pick up when he called her back.

16.15.

Waiting around here for Isaac to wake up without a plan was futile.

Harry secured the boy's feet to the base of the couch using handcuffs, ensured his hands were still tightly bound and put a crude gag around his mouth.

The only thing that gave him a fighting chance was information. And the only place he was going to get that was at Isaac's.

TWENTY

PRAYERS FILTERED THROUGH THE Mehraj mosque's PA system as Saima made her way towards the basement. Full of aid boxes and constantly in a state of disorder, it was the obvious place to hide a bomb.

Saima had to take her mind off Aaron, left in the care of grandparents he barely knew.

She whispered for God to give her boy strength.

It wasn't just Aaron she was thinking of. Her mother's voice would not leave her mind.

Hellfire.

Marrying Harry had been bad. But the year before she had done something much worse.

Her life had been on the line.

She knew she'd had no choice. Saima had not forgiven herself for taking a man's life. And Harry . . . Ronnie . . . all the dark things they did, surely . . .

Was this the inevitable damnation for their sins?

She whispered another prayer and forced her mind to focus. She could do nothing with those thoughts now.

For the first time, all the mosques in Bradford were united. Sunni? Shia? Ahmadi? It didn't matter. It was only temporary, Saima knew that.

Once the bomb was located, what then?

Saima had a child who needed her – could she really put the solidarity of her faith before that? She knew she wouldn't be the only one having these thoughts.

The Muslim community spoke proudly of what it saw as its collective responsibility to care for one another. What better way to test that resolve?

She walked down a narrow corridor and checked her phone.

Nothing from Harry.

She wanted to try Joyti again but resisted. Hearing Aaron's voice would send her over the edge.

Saima arrived at a large set of automatic doors. They opened for her and she entered. Seeing the large wooden crates marked *Clothes, Dried fruits, Water* and *Canned goods*, she was reminded of an article in the local *Telegraph & Argus* about how the council was also using some of the space for its own aid programme, lauded as a cross-working collaboration between the Muslim community and the wider population of Bradford.

Hearing voices, she stopped. Men were checking the

boxes one by one. Many crates had been opened, with two teams of men taking responsibility for specific areas.

From the shadows, she watched as another was opened. A man was using a tool to remove what she assumed were metal clips, judging by the noise they made. It took a few minutes before several men carefully pulled the wooden cover free.

It was bottled water. They spent a few minutes inspecting it thoroughly, then moved on to the next.

Saima wanted to help but she knew these men would not take kindly to a woman interrupting their work. She was looking for something she could do when she heard a change in the other team's voices. She heard gasps and one of the men cursed.

Inside a mosque?

Their voices turned to whispers, then prayers.

She stepped out from the shadows, the men unaware she was there, creeping up behind them, peering into the container.

For a moment, she didn't know what had caused the commotion.

Wires.

Dozens of cylindrical structures.

Then it hit her.

'God help us,' she whispered.

TWENTY-ONE

HARRY ARRIVED OUTSIDE ISAAC Wolfe's home, a small terraced house on a side street not far from a large amusement park in Thornbury, and found it sealed off by a yellow police cordon, with two armed officers at the front door and uniformed constables on the street. He had taken his work laptop from the boot and checked to see if there was any pertinent information detailed for Isaac.

Harry imagined the CTU detectives inside. They wouldn't be searching the place thoroughly, more of a once-over. Technically, this was a 'locate and protect' exercise. Isaac hadn't broken any laws.

Unless, that is, CTU thought Almukhtaroon were complicit in an ongoing terrorist plot. It wasn't impossible. At any given moment, the Counter-Terrorism Unit was dealing with thousands of operations.

Harry called his boss. DS Clare Conway answered.

Judging from the noise in the background, she was at Gold Command. Phones rang, voices were raised, doors slammed.

'Harry? Where are you? Are you OK?'

He told her about his day, everything but his meeting with Tariq.

'Jesus, Harry, I was hoping to call you in but I can't have you working after that. You're sure you're not in shock?'

Her concern sounded genuine, but he heard the tinge of disappointment that she was a member of her team down.

'I'm outside Isaac Wolfe's house, Clare.'

'What? Harry, I don't expect you to be operational – not after what you've been through this morning. Not with Saima in one of the mosques. You're compromised.'

'Less sympathy, more focus, Clare. I'll let you know if it gets too much,' he replied flatly.

He heard her sigh in relief.

Harry thought she might have asked how he knew of the address – another reason he had used his laptop to log on. But she didn't.

'What has Frost tasked us with?' asked Harry.

'It's fluid, Harry. Right now it's finding the four leaders of Almukhtaroon and seeing if there's anything connecting them to the Patriots.'

Perfect.

'Who's in charge inside the house?' he said, opening the driver's door.

'DS Taylor, CTU.'

'Veronica Taylor?'

'Yes.'

'Got it. We were in the academy together. I'm going to assist, Clare. See if there's anything of interest.'

There were photos everywhere of Isaac and a woman Harry assumed to be his mother.

No sign of a father.

The place should have felt like a home but it was a mess. Dust swirling in the wake of the detectives, clothes and dishes everywhere and, in the kitchen, a bin overflowing with empty McDonald's milkshake cups. The sweet smell lingered.

Harry moved through the house with authority. Unlike the other officers, he was looking for something very specific – a weakness.

Upstairs, Isaac's bedroom was a typical teenager's room, full of clutter and disorder that had clearly been there even before the detective started rooting through everything. All over the walls were vibrant posters of superheroes – the Hulk, Superman and Judge Dredd.

DS Taylor handed Harry some paperwork. 'Get up to speed,' she said, not unkindly. The state of the house suddenly made sense. The batch of papers Harry was looking at included a death certificate. Isaac's mother had died from breast cancer two years ago.

Harry did the maths. Isaac had been taken into custody and placed in a youth detention centre two months after his mother's passing.

'Christ,' he called out as he leafed through the remaining papers. 'This kid got straight A* at GCSEs. He did four A levels, getting top marks. Puts him what? Highest one per cent of the country?'

DS Taylor grimaced at him.

'The house is clear, Harry. There's nothing here to help us find him. He could have gone anywhere.' She ran her hands through her hair. 'This is a nightmare.'

With resources at breaking point, she discharged the firearms officers, leaving two uniformed constables protecting the cordon.

'SOCOs are on their way from Wakefield but they'll be another hour. All of ours are out in City Park.' DS Taylor looked tired already. Harry could sympathize.

'I'm just going to look around, get a feel for all this. See you back at base.'

She nodded and took two steps towards the door before she turned back to him. 'Everything all right, Harry?'

Harry smiled at her. 'Fine. I was in City Park earlier – taking a while to shake it off.'

'I'm not surprised. Don't do anything stupid,' DS Taylor said as she left the house.

Alone now, inside Isaac's bedroom, Harry set to work, hoping for some information he might use to test Isaac's loyalties. This wasn't some stupid, impressionable kid. Something had gone badly wrong here. He just needed to find out what.

Lifting the mattress, a rage overcame him. Saima was

in one of those mosques, her life in danger because of these people. What he wanted to do was tear Isaac limb from limb, put him through the kind of pain guaranteed to get him talking and find out where the other three leaders of Almukhtaroon were.

It could take time. And he only had a little over twelve hours until the Patriots' deadline.

Harry systematically took the bedroom to pieces, starting with the bed and working his way around. He wasn't really sure what he expected to find.

The wardrobe was interesting. Traditional Islamic clothes for the most part, yet in the back, wrapped in protective plastic covers, he found designer clothing. No price tags. These were clothes that had been worn then carefully stored; they were clearly special to Isaac.

The desk was chaotic. Yet piled neatly to one side were several A4 drawing pads featuring incredibly detailed sketches of what appeared to be a comic superhero called Isiah. The character reminded Harry of Popeye, who would eat a can of spinach and transform himself from weed into hero. Isiah was identical, except he was Asian and ate lentils. His nemesis was a character called the Undertaker, a figure cloaked in black whose superpower was to be able to read other people's minds, control them and, if they did not comply, make them kill themselves. The detail was stunning. Harry put the drawing pads aside to take with him.

The bottom drawer had books on mindfulness and

spirituality alongside several blisters of medication. He pulled it out and emptied it on the bed.

The medication was recent, the labels only a week old. Propranolol hydrochloride 10mg and Amitriptyline 10mg tablets. Harry had no clue what they were for. Maybe the kid needed them. Harry wasn't about to be the one to kill him.

He made for the door. He couldn't risk being here when the SOCOs arrived.

He stopped in the doorway and turned around.

Something was missing.

He cast his eyes over the room once more.

Nothing religious.

No textbooks.

No teaching materials.

Absolutely nothing.

He looked at the posters, the all-action heroes. Judge Dredd was apparently the boy's favourite.

Something wasn't right here.

Outside, Harry put two large carrier bags in the boot of his car along with a change of Western clothing for the boy. He wasn't concerned the uniformed officers had seen him; they were too junior to think of it as anything other than a detective doing his job.

Harry Googled what Isaac's medication was for. He relaxed a little. For the first time, he felt like he was in the game.

He started his car and pulled away from the house.

He knew exactly how he was going to break the kid.

TWENTY-TWO

THE MEN WHO FOUND the bomb immediately locked the entrance to the basement. They had been shocked to find Saima there and surprised to see her hardly react.

This was Saima's worst nightmare.

Not being locked in a basement with a group of unfamiliar men.

Not being close to a bomb.

No. It was losing control of her destiny. Whether she left this mosque alive or not was in someone else's hands. Saima hated to feel powerless.

Someone had gone upstairs to discreetly alert the imam. They were awaiting his arrival – his counsel.

'What now?' one of the men said.

Nobody answered.

Saima took out her phone and saw that she had one bar of reception.

'We phone the police,' she said.

They turned to look at her.

Saima saw an opportunity to seize back some of the power the Patriots had taken from her.

'My husband is a police officer. I'll call him. We can't call 999 and report this. We need to know whoever we report it to won't leak it and encourage the other mosques to break out – it's this bomb that goes off if they do. How we control this information is critical.'

There were nods of agreement.

'And we should keep this to ourselves until such time as Imam Hashim is ready to inform the rest of the mosque. There's no knowing how people will react. If we have a stampede because people want to run, we might all die.'

She delivered her words with authority and clarity of mind.

Saima stared hard at the men in the room.

Some looked resilient. Others like they would run at the first chance they got.

It wasn't that Saima was not afraid. She absolutely was. But the fact the bomb was here was something she could not change.

Her heart was aching thinking about Aaron. Yet Saima had to focus on the one positive. Harry was out there. And Harry always came through for her.

Saima scrolled to Harry's number and hit Call. Three rings. Seven.

'Saima?' he said.

It sounded like Harry was driving. She told him to pull over, waiting until he had.

'What is it, Saima? Are you OK?' he said, clear concern in his voice.

She took a breath.

'It's here, Harry. The bomb. I'm looking at it.'

TWENTY-THREE

ACC FROST HAD ENOUGH on his plate without having to babysit the damn Home Secretary. Leeds Bradford airport had closed down as a result of the bombing, as had rail services. With no quick way to return to Whitehall, Islam had posted himself at Gold Command, promising to send COBRA real-time updates.

Frost had heard the exchange between Islam and the Prime Minister. As operational leader of this incident, he wanted to know everything, including what politics were at play. He'd been silently patched on to the call.

The PM did not want Tariq anywhere near this. Politicians needed to shift blame, he had said, especially if things did not go according to plan. This was no place for a Home Secretary, even if he was ultimately responsible for security arrangements within the UK.

Tariq wouldn't hear of it.

'I'm the first Muslim politician to have ever climbed this high. Bradford needs me to be visible, so to hell with the politics.' Frost would not have entertained his subordinate talking to him in this way. 'If I went running back to London, I would forever be remembered as the cowardly Muslim Home Secretary who fled for the sanctuary of Whitehall in one of the country's darkest hours.'

It would ruin him.

Tariq had cut the line before the PM could counter his argument.

Frost had put the phone down, pissed off on the PM's behalf.

Now Tariq was waiting in the conference room for Frost. He could wait a little longer.

Three hours post bombing and Bradford had been secured. Motorways into the city had road blocks. The official line was 'security protocols'. In reality they were doing two things: trying to stop the leaders of Almukhtaroon fleeing, and also stop an influx of potential protesters, Far Right or otherwise. Social media was rife with speculation of a demonstration later that evening.

Frost received updates from his team every fifteen minutes. The latest briefing was coming to an end.

'Nothing at Isaac Wolfe's house, sir,' said DS Taylor.

'Nothing?' he asked, incredulous.

She shook her head. 'The good news is that we've received confirmation that we have five hundred officers

from Humberside and the North East en route to Bradford as we speak.'

Frost nodded to dismiss her. He made his way to the conference room, where Tariq Islam was speaking with Peter Weetwood.

'This is really not what we need,' said Frost, closing the door. He could feel eyes on him – the whole floor stealing glances through the glass partition wall. Frost didn't close the blinds. They needed to see who was in charge here and it certainly was not the Home Secretary.

Tariq raised his hands passively and stepped away from Weetwood. 'Before you launch into some prepared speech—'

'Prepared speech?' Frost closed the gap between the two men and pointed angrily. 'We're three hours into this shit-storm. It's moving faster than anything we've dealt with before. The only prepared speech I have is the resignation I've wanted to submit since you fucked up policing in this country.'

Fucking politicians.

'Not the time or the place for politics,' replied Tariq, looking a little flustered.

Weetwood put a hand on Frost's shoulder, his attempt to calm the hostility.

Frost shrugged it away. 'Then why are you here?' he snapped at Tariq.

'If I was playing politics, I'd be on my way back to Whitehall. I'm here to be accountable.'

That stopped Frost. Accountable – he didn't think politicians knew the meaning of the word.

'Whichever mosque the bomb is inside will potentially have hundreds of Muslims inside, right?' said Tariq.

Frost nodded and beckoned for them all to sit down. He remained close to Weetwood, both men firm in their resolve not to fall victim to whatever game Tariq Islam was playing.

'If this goes badly, we need everyone to know that not only did we do everything in our power but that every rung of the ladder played its part. We're at a crossroads where both Far Right and religious extremists are vying for power. We cannot give it to either. The Patriots say that I failed to jail the founders of Almukhtaroon last year – that is my responsibility. Let me speak to them – let them know I am here and willing to negotiate.'

'Negotiate?' Frost and Weetwood spoke at the same time.

'Standard protocols went out the window the moment that bomb went off. I'm not saying I can give them anything but maybe talking about it buys us time.'

'And maybe the Patriots realize you are playing a game and all rules go out the window,' Weetwood said, almost to himself.

Tariq leaned closer, his face turned away from the glass wall of the conference room. He didn't want anyone outside to lip-read what he was about to say.

'Four leaders of Almukhtaroon dead or many, many innocent civilians. What if it comes down to that equation? We all know it might.'

Frost didn't say anything. He glanced at Weetwood, who avoided eye contact.

'How many officers do you have looking for them?' said Tariq.

'Over thirty.'

'How confident are you?'

A pause.

'Gentlemen, we are currently *off* the record.'

Frost shook his head. 'They go underground and it's a lottery. We might get one or two, but all four?'

'Is that our absolute priority at the moment, getting the four leaders of Almukhtaroon into custody?'

'*Safe* custody,' replied Frost.

'Damn it, Steven, we are off the record here.'

'What are you saying, Mr Islam?'

'I am saying that I do not believe that four lives are of more value than hundreds of lives.' Tariq gathered himself up. 'Gentlemen, I'm here to facilitate things which perhaps you can't sanction. All I need is for you both to stand up and walk out of that door if you are content for me to stay and explore every option. If not, remain where you are and we can debate some more.'

Tariq folded his arms across his chest and waited.

The men were interrupted by a harsh knocking on the door and a flustered-looking detective entered without

being asked. He told Frost that DCI Harry Virdee was on line two, apparently with crucial information.

Frost nodded and waited for the detective to leave before hurrying to a phone in the corner of the room. He put it on speaker.

'Virdee, sir. Saima found the bomb.'

TWENTY-FOUR

HARRY FELT NUMB. HE let the car idle in the driveway of the Queensbury farmhouse. The Mehraj mosque, Bradford's newest, was the largest in the city. If he were honest with himself, Harry hadn't been all that shocked when Saima had told him she'd found the bomb. There was no higher-profile location it could have been.

He had just finished his call to Frost.

'Do you think we can trust Saima to be our eyes inside there, Harry?'

'Absolutely,' Harry said. He wanted Saima distracted so she didn't go crazy worrying about him or Aaron. Frost needed someone with a cool head to relay information about the bomb to CTU and, as far as Harry was concerned, Saima was the perfect candidate. She dealt with pressure every day in her job at A&E.

'And do you think we could task her with taking

pictures and some video of the device?' Frost's voice was rich with concern but also sounded desperate.

Harry gave him Saima's number and told him he backed his wife to do it. He hung up, tried to call her and, unable to connect, sent her a text.

Frost is going to call. Head of this investigation. He needs help from inside the mosque and I trust you to do it. Stay in control, Saima. We will get through this. I love you x

Harry knew Saima was more than capable of the job.

How long could Frost contain this information?

Harry's heart was racing.

Inside the mosque, if the imam lost control of his worshippers, this might all unravel quickly. Frost was all over it, he knew. But he had more reason than ever to find the Almukhtaroon himself.

Frost had understood Harry's request, with his wife's life at risk, to stand down from this operation and return to his son. Harry had told him he'd return once he was certain Aaron was OK.

Time was against them. Saima had told him there were a dozen men with her. In Harry's experience, that was too many to contain a secret. Somebody would leak it. Then what?

Harry threw his phone on to the passenger seat, angry, an imaginary clock pounding inside his head. He looked down at the two McDonald's milkshakes in the passenger footwell. He'd bought them for Isaac on his way back, before Saima had called.

Was he putting his neck on the line for nothing?

Was he risking Saima's life by not handing over Isaac to Frost?

No, his boss would do this by the book. And Tariq was right – the book might not serve Harry in this instance.

He had little choice but to at least try, though he didn't like his chances of apprehending the other three leaders of Almukhtaroon before sunrise. Bradford had over three hundred thousand inhabitants; this was a fucking needle in a haystack.

Harry closed his eyes; his head felt like it was about to explode.

Christ, he missed Ronnie. Today of all days his brother's counsel would have been welcome. Last Harry had heard, Ronnie and his family were headed for the remoteness of Shimla – north India, a cooler climate than the rest of the blistering country. It was 11 p.m. in India. He'd tried to call him while waiting for the shakes at McDonald's – no reception.

He didn't like to ask himself what Ronnie would do in this situation. Harry wasn't keen to beat Isaac Wolfe to a pulp, not unless it was strictly necessary. He thought about the kid's stellar school grades, the untimely death of his mother and the stretch inside the youth detention centre. That was the key – who had he mixed with there and what impact had it left on the vulnerable boy? Harry thought of the sketches he had seen. Each one dated, and

all of them before his time in the secure unit – that was who Isaac Wolfe really was.

That was who he needed to find.

Harry entered the living room and saw Isaac awake, still secure, still gagged.

The boy glared at him, more in anger than fear.

Not a good sign.

A strong smell of urine hit Harry as he untied Isaac's hands but kept the cuffs around his feet secure.

A pool of piss around Isaac's feet.

Harry removed the gag, expecting rage, and got none. Isaac remained silent.

Harry placed the milkshakes on the table.

'Banana or strawberry?' he asked, waving them at Isaac. No reply.

He looked as though he'd been crying, eyes red raw.

He stuck the strawberry shake in his lap, retreated and sat on a chair opposite.

Isaac bowed his head.

It was the urine. The smell. The evidence of it around his ankles. The embarrassment alone made what Harry hoped to achieve that bit harder.

Harry replaced his shake on the table, took Isaac's from his lap and stooped to free Isaac's feet.

'This is very simple,' said Harry, backing away. 'If you try anything, anything at all, you'll force my hand and I won't be nice.'

Harry paused, then added, 'And trust me, this is me being nice.'

Isaac's head remained bowed.

Harry was struck again at just how immature the kid looked – a twenty-one-year-old who looked no more than sixteen.

'I know what you think this is, what you think is going to happen. If that were true, I wouldn't be telling you to go upstairs, take a shower, then change into some clothes I lifted from your place.'

Isaac met Harry's gaze, anger fractionally diminished.

Harry was impatient. He didn't have time for any of this. He knew though that force would make Isaac more resistant. It would make him shut down, revelling in the knowledge that all the Western hostility shit he had no doubt been brainwashed with was valid.

He forced a smile. 'None of this is going to be like you thought it was, Isaac. As soon as you've had a shower, drunk your milkshake and given me a chance to show you why, you'll see that the only person in control here is you.'

TWENTY-FIVE

ACC STEVEN FROST WAS in a peculiar situation. The fact Harry's wife was inside the Mehraj mosque with the bomb was both of great concern and, at the same time, offered an interesting opportunity.

Two further experts had given their views on the video of the bomb the Patriots had disclosed to them. They needed more information – a closer look, picture and video clips, maybe even a live stream. And for that, they now had a candidate. If Harry thought Saima was capable, Frost was more than happy to go along with that.

Council planning documents listed the new mosque as having a maximum capacity of 1,500 people. That number had made Frost's legs wobble.

It couldn't happen.

While they were waiting for estimates of how many people were inside, Gold Command had spent the past

hour discussing their strategy for the other hundred and four mosques, all of which were still under lockdown. According to the Patriots' demands, now they had located the bomb, they needed to let this be known, then they could begin to free those trapped in the other mosques.

Hashim would need to inform his followers and then, ideally, Frost would get high volumes of uniformed officers at each mosque in turn to ensure they evacuated in an orderly fashion and were subject to no hate-related attacks. The command room had now received solid information that the Far Right were making a beeline for Bradford.

Moving that volume of men around a stalled city would take time. And the longer Frost waited to evacuate the other mosques, the greater the risk they would break out of their own accord, triggering the bomb. He would not have that on his watch.

Frost did the only thing he could. He increased the manpower of the team he had tasked to liaise with the imams of the other mosques, ordering them to organize an orderly evacuation of their sites, but only once Imam Hashim had informed his worshippers the bomb had been located.

Frost may have been the Assistant Chief Constable and 'in charge', but this had all the makings of an impossible situation. He couldn't help but feel out of his depth. They were four hours into this mess and, so far, none of the Almukhtaroon leaders had been found. If they were smart, they'd have gone underground and wouldn't surface until after sunrise tomorrow.

His job was to protect their lives. Social media was already rife with death threats made against them from a whole host of angry groups – Muslims looking to defend their places of worship, Far Right activists jumping on the opportunity to incite hate, and smaller, local groups just wanting to cause bedlam. The four leaders of Almukhtaroon were currently the most hunted in the country. While Frost would have traded the bastards in a heartbeat for the people inside the Mehraj mosque, it was simply wishful thinking on his part. If he got them into protective custody, he wouldn't be able to hand them over to the Patriots. All he could do would be to send the military into the mosque. If he didn't capture them, he would not risk the population inside the Mehraj mosque and would still be sending the military in, before the deadline expired.

Damned if he did and damned if he didn't.

Lost in his thoughts, he didn't notice a junior member of staff knock lightly on his office door until he coughed politely.

'Yes?' he asked abruptly.

'Sir, we've had word from Imam Hashim.' He paused, as though unsure whether he should continue.

Frost waved him on.

'There are one thousand and nine people in the Mehraj mosque.'

Frost felt sick.

Senior military commanders were currently analysing their options with regards to the mosque and he had a

conference call with COBRA scheduled in fifteen minutes. He would have to let them know what they were dealing with.

First, though, Frost dialled Saima's number. DS Conway had offered to do it, having met Saima several times, but Frost needed to hear Saima's voice himself – feel her confidence, or lack of it. He hoped she was as resilient as Harry had suggested.

Her number failed to connect the first time. Second time, he heard it ring. In his peripheral vision, Frost could see the military commanders huddled together, working on their strategy – a hostile entry into the mosque. Unless they could disarm the bomb from the inside, it was inevitable. Frost desperately wanted to avoid that, for one main reason.

It was nothing more than a fifty–fifty chance.

His call connected.

'Is that Saima Virdee?' he asked.

'Hi, yes, it is,' she said. Saima's voice crackled noisily, her reception poor.

'This is Assistant Chief Constable Steven Frost. I—'

'I know who you are. Harry told me you would call.'

'I'm pleased. Are you able to speak in private?'

'Yes. I'm at the far end of the basement.'

'Good, because, Saima, we need you to help us.'

TWENTY-SIX

SAIMA WAS BACK INSIDE the grand hall, watching as Imam Hashim took to the stage to tell the rest of the mosque that the bomb had been found in their place of worship. She had many things running through her mind. She needed to send Frost pictures and footage of the bomb. The quicker they got this, the quicker it might all end. First the worshippers needed to know it had been found. A dozen or so already knew. They couldn't wait any longer in case it was leaked. Saima thought this was going to be the most important speech Imam Hashim ever gave. If he didn't secure the trust of his worshippers – if they panicked and went for the exits – this would all fall apart. It was why Saima had told Frost he would have to wait before she attempted what he had asked of her. He sounded dismayed but understood.

Saima noticed the mosque's committee members were

by the exits. She had also taken the time to glance out of the foyer windows and seen a considerable increase in police officers a short distance from the mosque.

She was also worried about Aaron. Had he eaten his tea? Was he OK? Saima wanted to call Joyti but this wasn't the time. She could not deal with Aaron sounding upset. The mother inside her felt dirty for thinking it but, for now, her focus was solely on Imam Hashim. Everything depended on how he broke the news.

Two men were standing either side of Hashim, mobile phones raised. He had told the hall what he was about to say would be live-streamed on social media.

Was that wise?

Saima feared the hall would descend into chaos once the news broke.

Hashim raised his voice, commanding everyone to be silent, and waited. He stared at the congregation and smiled. Speaking softly in English, he asked those who could translate into Urdu for non-bilingual worshippers to do so. He waited a few moments, then started.

'Our life is a test. We have read this many times, heard it spoken even more so. Today, our time to be tested has arrived. As Muslims, we speak of a collective responsibility to account for one another. This city works tirelessly to support our brothers and sisters caught up in war zones across the globe. Today a terrorist organization calling themselves the Patriots want to test this resolve. They think our collective responsibility is a show – nothing more. They do not

realize that, as Muslims, looking after one another is in the very DNA of our belief system. They mock us and want to show the world that we are nothing but liars!'

His voice changed, not quite combative but certainly more powerful. He paused, stared into the crowd and continued.

'Do you know what I see? A room full of a thousand united Muslims. A benchmark for solidarity and compassion – the very thing that makes us, as a community, unstoppable.'

The passion in his voice was mesmerizing. Saima felt the hairs on the back of her neck stand up. There were nods from around the room and murmurs that he was right.

'Have the other mosques emptied and abandoned our community? No! Have we panicked and turned on one another? No! Will we do so?'

His question was answered with a muted 'No'.

'Is that all you have to offer me?' He smiled and asked the question again, this time getting a more forceful answer. 'No!'

'We have built our lives around not only our faith but one another. So it is not with fear that I tell you all that the threat of a bomb located inside a mosque in Bradford has been verified.'

He quickened his speech, not giving the crowd time to react.

'And I ask you all to look at the life of our beloved

Prophet, peace-be-upon-him, and to analyse the many times he was tested. Every time, he overcame. Every time, he endured and came out stronger. Often it was by his peaceful actions and the wisdom of his words. Now, on perhaps the biggest stage our community might ever be given, we have the chance to show the world how we deal with adversity. How we come together to ensure our faith withstands this test. And withstand it we will.'

His words were working. The energy in the room was palpable. Saima observed hands being held, arms wrapped around one another as if they all knew what was coming.

Hashim continued, his tone softer now.

'Our mosque has been chosen to withstand this test. No greater test are we likely to face in our lifetime than this. It is time to ask ourselves how much we care for the safety of one another. These so-called Patriots want to see if a single person inside this room will put at risk the thousand-strong group that we are. If just one of us tries to leave, the bomb will detonate and the people who doubt the strength of our faith will be proven correct. The wider ramifications for the Islamic world will be crippling. Since we claim to feel the pain of our persecuted brothers and sisters around the world, is it nothing more than a show if we cannot, here and now, endure and stand together? We will be seen as traitors to the very message we work tirelessly to promote – service over self – and I ask you all here and now, are you all traitors?'

The deafening answer echoed through Saima's body.

Hashim asked them all again – this time louder, and the response in the room was equally loud.

The two men standing either side of Hashim turned their phones towards the crowd, getting the images of solidarity before focusing back on him.

'And to the Patriots I say – you have asked your question. And now you have heard our answer.'

He stepped closer to one of the phones, taking the microphone with him.

'A final message for Bradford. There is a resolve among Bradfordians not to allow division, hate and racism to prosper, irrespective of faith. Our time to unite as a city has arrived and, as ever, we will not go down without a fight. Let us show the world, once and for all, that this is truly God's own county.'

The mobile phones either side of him were lowered, the sermon over.

Hashim went back to his stand and stared into the crowd, looking for signs that his speech had pierced the heart of everyone in the grand hall.

Saima could see that it had.

Hashim asked them, with God as his witness, how many of them would go against his request for unity? How many would try to escape, knowing everyone else would almost certainly die?

The answer was unanimous.

Not a single hand was raised.

TWENTY-SEVEN

THE NEWS WAS OUT. Harry's newsfeed was alive with speculation about the bomb inside the Mehraj mosque.

He texted Saima.

How's things in there?

She replied immediately.

Calm for now. I'm in the basement about to send info to Frost. Everyone else upstairs. How's Aaron?

Fine. Call you later. Keep battery conserved. BE CAREFUL. Stop if you feel you cannot do it.

20% left. I got this. Promise me u will chk on Aaron.

Promise. Love you.

Love u 2. XXX

Harry only had 38 per cent of his battery life left, with twelve hours of this siege yet to play out. Not enough.

Isaac was in the shower, door open, window locked. Harry wasn't concerned with the kid trying to do a

runner but he sat in the hallway just outside the bathroom to make sure he didn't get any ideas. He had his police laptop open, accessing the Police National Database and seeing what information was listed on the other three leaders of Almukhtaroon. Abu-Nazir had an impressive record, mostly of 'disturbing the peace' by organizing demonstrations around the country. Amelia Rose had a decade-old record for drug use, but the real star of this shit-show was Fahad-Bin-Azeez. He had multiple entries for assault, grievous bodily harm and theft. Exactly the type of character Abu-Nazir targeted. None had listed addresses.

Harry put the laptop aside and examined the drawing pads he had taken from Isaac's house. Each sketch seemed to start with Isiah, a small, weak boy, getting bullied, then a kid from the local town would go missing – kidnapped by his nemesis, the Undertaker – requiring Isiah to eat lentils and explode into a hero to save the day. They were good, really good.

This kid had so much going for him.

What had gone wrong? What had made him join Almukhtaroon?

Pulling a gun he had lifted from Queensbury Tunnel from his pocket, Harry sighed. He thought of Saima inside the mosque, Aaron alone at his mother's house and the shit-storm out in the streets of Bradford. He couldn't afford to get this wrong.

* * *

At the kitchen table, Isaac greedily drank his milkshake. Harry hoped the sugar-rush would perk the kid up. Now refreshed and wearing jeans and a T-shirt, Isaac's previous bitterness seemed to have softened.

'I'm not helping you,' said Isaac, slurping the dregs of his shake.

Harry pointed to the drawing pads he had been reading. 'These sketches are good.'

He thought he saw a flash of pride but it disappeared as quickly as it surfaced.

'Reminds me of Popeye. He was one of my favourites as a kid – probably before your time. You know it?'

Isaac nodded.

'An Asian superhero. Don't get many of those. You should have tried to get these published.'

'Nobody wants to read about an Asian superhero. All we're good for is being terrorists.'

Harry shrugged.

'That what you think I am? A terrorist?'

'I've watched Almukhtaroon videos online. Death to the West. A new caliphate.'

Isaac held his gaze.

'Not exactly patriotic, is it?'

'The way the West lives is corrupt,' said Isaac forcefully. His expression didn't match his tone of voice. This was something he had been taught, not something he believed.

Harry's heart quickened. This could work.

'You know what's going on in Bradford right now?'

Isaac nodded. 'A little. Before I was taken from my house – before they injected me with that . . . stuff, they told me some people calling themselves the Patriots were terrorizing everyone. Bomb in a mosque? And they want us in return.'

'That's about right.'

Harry wondered what Isaac knew about the men who had lifted him. 'Any idea who took you from your house?'

'You guys? Police? Least that's what I thought until they hit me with that needle. So what's the deal? Are you here to deliver me to the Patriots?'

'No. I'm here on something different. You and the rest of your crew – Abu-Nazir, Fahad-Bin-Azeez and Amelia Rose – some friends you got there.'

'I'm not sharing anything with you. Torture me all you want.'

'Fine. Let's talk about you, then,' said Harry, flicking through the sketches. 'You believe all that stuff? A new caliphate? Death to the West?'

Isaac nodded weakly.

'Strange, because none of these drawings show that.'

'I believe it.'

'That's what I was hoping for.'

Isaac tensed in his seat. 'Why? So you can do me in?'

'On the contrary,' said Harry, standing up.

He turned his back and closed his eyes, thinking of the earlier bomb blast, the fear on his son's face, the YouTube

video of the Patriots' demands, and Saima sitting in the basement of the mosque sending pictures of the bomb to Frost.

He turned towards Isaac again and pulled his revolver from his pocket.

'I knew it,' Isaac spat, slamming his fists on the table, rage flooding his face. 'See a Muslim, take him off the streets and torture him – fucking typical of you pigs!'

This time, Isaac's rage felt real.

'Death to the West,' said Harry quietly, inching closer to Isaac. He stopped a foot short, got on his knees and turned the gun in his hand so he was holding the barrel.

'Thing is, Isaac, I don't think you're an extremist any more than I am.'

One of Isaac's drawing pads lay in his lap. Harry rested the gun on it, watching as Isaac's mouth fell open.

The kid was taking one medication to stop him wetting the bed and another to ease anxiety. The thumb on his right hand was a lot smaller than the one on his left. Harry guessed it was because Isaac still sucked it, just like Aaron did. Harry was betting Isaac wasn't about to blow his brains out.

He didn't have it in him.

'There are one hundred and five mosques under lockdown, and my wife is in one of them.'

Isaac's brow furrowed.

Harry nodded. 'That's right. My wife is Muslim. Saima. I know all about feeling marginalized and persecuted. Do

you know what I had to do to marry her? I left my family. I was disowned by my community – the Sikh who married a Paki and it ruined him. You're not the only one in this world on the wrong side of hate. You can choose to leave this place with me and do something good, be a hero. Thousands of innocent Muslims are trapped in those mosques: women, children, the elderly. They are all at risk. You don't need to be in Syria or Palestine to help the Islamic world right now. Today the fight is on your doorstep.'

Harry took Isaac's hand firmly and placed it on the gun, noting the tremble in it.

'You want to bring down the West? Now's the time. The gun is loaded. All you have to do is point and pull the trigger. You'll kill a serving police officer. Got to be worth some brownie points with Abu-Nazir. Or you can look me in the eye, see how much I want to save this city, my wife and all the people inside those mosques. Let's change the narrative and leave this house together. I told you: the only person in control here is you.'

TWENTY-EIGHT

SAIMA WAS STANDING IN front of the large shipping container that contained the bomb. Imam Hashim was by her side, holding a powerful torch, both of them alone in the basement. She needed him to help with this. Sweat was dripping down her forehead into her eyes in spite of it being considerably cooler down here.

Upstairs Hashim had left the worshippers in several large prayer circles and a trusted team keeping watch over them all. It was a smart move, and Saima had wished she could join them. She was silently praying, having doubts about whether she was the right person to do this.

Her phone began to ring, a Facetime request from Frost. She answered, hand shaking. Frost asked her if she was still OK to attempt this and when she confirmed she was, he handed the phone over to a man who identified himself as one of the CTU bomb experts, 'Paul'. He

spoke calmly and slowly, asking Saima first to switch off the torch on her phone and rely on the one Imam Hashim was holding.

She put the phone on speaker and listened carefully to instructions, then stepped slowly inside the towering wooden box. Her heart was pounding; it felt louder than Paul's voice coming from her phone.

Mouth parched.

Hands shaking.

She closed her eyes, whispered another prayer, then inched her way in. Hashim's torch was powerful, revealing six towering cylindrical shapes, filled with some kind of white substance. In the centre was a large, square contraption full of wires and lights with a keypad. A timer was counting down to the deadline of 6 a.m. It was that which was most disconcerting.

Saima knew nothing about bombs, yet something told her this was a sophisticated device.

Using her phone, she very slowly mapped out every inch of it, creeping ever closer. Her bladder suddenly felt heavy even though it was empty.

She focused now on the white material inside the glass cylinders.

'What am I looking at?' she asked, trying not to panic.

'Don't you worry about that, Saima,' said Paul. No matter how experienced Paul claimed to be, she heard the change in his voice.

'Paul, this only works if you tell me exactly what is

going on.' She didn't really need him to confirm what she was looking at: the cylinder directly in front of her was full of glass and nails. It was nerves that made her ask. Something to fill the silence in the claustrophobic environment of the box.

Paul asked her to focus on the computer-like device, which she did.

Saima angled her phone towards it and confirmed that she could see three red wires, three blue and two yellow. They streamed from the device towards the cylindrical containers.

Saima kept glancing at the one holding the glass and nails.

Designed to injure as many people as possible.

Since there was nobody down here, only she and Hashim would feel that pain.

Her mind was wandering and she asked Paul to repeat what he had just said. He did so. Saima crouched by the central device and tried to find a serial number or any markings of note. She found a ten-digit number and said it slowly and clearly, confirming it a second time. Paul asked her to wait. Her eyes once again found the glass and nails, though she tried not to.

What kind of sick bastards did that?

Paul returned and asked her to lift a small metal box next to the wiring and confirm whether she could see a way to take the lid off it. Saima didn't move. She didn't want to touch it.

She closed her eyes and wiped sweat from her brow. The need to urinate was becoming critical.

She could hear Paul's voice but not the words. Head spinning. Vision blurry. She recognized the symptoms of an impending faint. Without realizing it, she had been holding her breath.

Open your mouth.

Breathe.

She wiped a sweaty palm on her clothes, focused solely on the box and tried to lift it.

When she spoke, her voice was shaky. 'The top feels like it might come away. Do you want me to try?'

'Please. Take your time. Softly. If it resists, leave it be, Saima.'

'I need to put my phone down. Use both hands. Can I?'

'Can Hashim hold your phone so we can watch you?'

Saima saw the torchlight flicker as Hashim came carefully towards her. She saw his hand by the side of her face and handed him the phone, waiting until he had positioned it so Paul could see.

Carefully, Saima applied the gentlest of pressure and lifted off the top of the small rectangular box. It came away easily, revealing a maze of messily arranged wires and several lights, blue, red and opaque.

'Excellent,' she heard Paul say.

Feeling like they were making progress, Saima was about to replace the box when it started to beep, lights flickering.

'Shit,' she whispered, unclear what was happening. She nearly dropped the damn thing.

The torch light wavered, Hashim's hand suddenly unsteady.

The noise and urgent flashing of lights from the device continued before stopping abruptly.

Saima heard Paul's voice, firm, alarmed.

'Saima, stand absolutely still and do not move.'

TWENTY-NINE

ABU-NAZIR WATCHED THE NEWS with indifference. The imam's speech inside the Mehraj mosque had caused quite a reaction, *#Hashim* even knocking *#prayforBradford* off the top trending Twitter spot. For the moment, Abu-Nazir was not the most talked about Muslim person in the city. It wouldn't last long. He had just uploaded a video on to YouTube, an old one but one that always got a reaction before being deleted. A video demanding a new caliphate in the West. This time he reckoned it would be viewed millions of times before it got removed.

Timing was everything.

A documentary filmed in 2012, featuring the current leader of the Far Right, Tyler Sudworth, and Abu-Nazir, had been viewed over a million times since the blast in City Park. The two men had come together after a high-profile altercation to try to find common ground. They

had found none. Tyler Sudworth had been fierce in his criticism of Abu-Nazir, unable to comprehend why a white British national had crossed over to Islamic extremism. That was, however, Abu-Nazir's USP.

The documentary had been great exposure for Abu-Nazir, a primetime TV slot. Criticism of it had been widespread but by then the damage had been done.

The news went live to a woman from the BBC, reporting that armed police were now positioned throughout the city, forces from across Yorkshire pooling their resources. Skirmishes had been reported and footage was shown of clashes between Far Right activists and Asian youths.

Abu-Nazir smiled and turned the television off. He moved into the bedroom, checking on Amelia. She was still asleep, snoring lightly. He'd have to wake her soon.

It was over four hours since the bomb had gone off and he'd heard nothing from the boy, Isaac. He'd known where to come in an emergency. They had discussed it many times.

He doubted the boy would make it here now.

Every war involved sacrifice.

Even Isaac Wolfe.

THIRTY

ISAAC WASN'T SITTING ON the chair in front of Harry any more. He was standing over him, gun down by his side.

When he had moved to stand, just for the briefest of moments Harry had thought he might have seriously underestimated the boy.

The kid's eyes gave him away.

He couldn't pull the trigger.

Isaac's voice was shaky when he spoke. Bitter. Angry.

'You're mocking me, aren't you?' he spat.

Shit. If he lost the kid now, he'd never gain his trust.

'Just like the kids at school. Every girl I ever asked out on a date.' His voice was rising, eyes wet with tears he was trying hard to blink away.

This was bad. Very, very bad.

'I'm not mocking you,' said Harry gently. He kept his

body relaxed, tone calm, even though his knees were smarting on the floor.

'Yes you are!' said Isaac, raising the gun and waving it carelessly at Harry.

Great move, Harry. Give the kid a fucking loaded gun, then piss him off.

Harry shook his head slowly. 'You know that's not what this is, Isaac.'

'Then why give me the gun? To prove I'm too chicken to use it?'

Harry shook his head and smiled. 'On the contrary. To show you that if you wanted to, you could. Right now. Right here.'

Isaac's eyes softened a little but the tremble in his hand remained.

'That shit Abu-Nazir preaches – words are easy,' Harry went on. 'He's like any other hate-preacher out there, a second-rate asshole who preys on people he thinks are sheep.'

Isaac opened his mouth to object. Harry raised his hand, slowly.

'You're not a sheep. If you were, you would have pulled the trigger by now because that's what sheep do. They follow. What I'm offering you, Isaac, is a chance to put that gun down, knowing you had all the power and yet decided to share it with me. We can leave this house together and find the people we need to end this. We could save hundreds, thousands of innocent people inside those mosques.'

Harry calmly, steadily got to his feet. 'Twelve hours from now, that is the stuff people will be talking about. The boy who rose against the hate to save Bradford.'

Isaac smiled. It didn't reach his eyes.

'Sounds like a speech from one of those crappy nineties movies.'

'It is,' said Harry smiling. 'Thing is, just because it isn't delivered by a Hollywood golden boy, doesn't mean you can't believe it. Listen to the sound of those helicopters in the distance. Does it get any bigger than this? What greater stage could you ask for to play the hero?'

Harry tapped his forehead. 'Think about it. Everyone is expecting you to be one thing. Surprise them.'

Isaac's hand was starting to lower.

'Heavy, isn't it?' said Harry.

Isaac nodded.

'Lower it then. I'm not taking it from you.'

Isaac let his hand fall to his side. 'What's a police officer like you doing with a gun like this?'

'I'm not your usual type of detective.'

'You're a criminal, you mean?' said Isaac, raising an eyebrow.

It was a question Harry had asked himself a thousand times.

'No. I mean I get shit done.'

'And you want me to turn on my friends and help you find them?'

'What makes you call them friends?'

Isaac grunted and shook his head. 'They look after me. Look out for me.'

'How so?'

Isaac thought about it. 'We . . . they . . . you know . . . teach me things. Help me be a better Muslim.'

'Can I give you my honest opinion?'

Isaac nodded.

'The videos I've seen of you guys? You look lost. They're not making you a better Muslim. They're preying on your vulnerability.'

Isaac made to protest but stopped himself.

Harry moved slowly and picked up a sketch pad from the table.

'I read somewhere that writers and artists always need to show you what's going on, never tell you. I thought that was pretty good advice. *Show, don't tell*. I made it my thing in life – showed my boss I work like a dog, never just telling her. I show my Muslim wife that I love her by buying her a new prayer mat every year when it's Ramadan and waiting to eat with her when she's fasting. And today, I showed you by giving you that gun that I'm not full of shit. Looking at the sketches in this book,' said Harry, waving it at him, 'you're showing me that, deep inside, you want to be a hero.'

Isaac smiled dismissively.

'No? Play it out with me then,' said Harry. 'The bomb goes off and a thousand innocent Muslim people die. What do you think the fallout from that will be? It will

shape the future landscape of our country and God knows what the retaliation will look like. We live in an unstable world. This will turn everything to shit. It's the 9/11 of our times and we all know what happened there.'

'There's no way—'

'Turn on the TV. Have a look.' Harry was losing patience, painfully conscious of the time ticking by. He pulled his phone from his pocket, unlocked it and handed it to Isaac. 'Have a look at Twitter and tell me I'm wrong.'

Harry watched him, watched his eyes widen and his mouth drop.

'What do we have to do?' said Isaac.

THIRTY-ONE

FROST WAS ALONE IN the command room.

Of all the things Saima's exploration of the bomb could have revealed, he had not considered this.

A sleeper cell, clearly aligned to the Patriots, had run a diagnostic test on the bomb to ensure it had not been tampered with. A simple radio transmitter on the device was found to have a range of around a hundred metres. With the immediate area surrounding the mosque clear, only one option remained. The sleeper had to have been *inside* – a human sacrifice in case a special ops team entered the building intent on ending the siege. This was a failsafe that Frost could not counter remotely.

If a diagnostics test failed, the sleeper would know the bomb had been compromised and could then detonate the device. Bomb-disposal experts had suggested it could be triggered with a simple, battery-operated remote,

something they could not use technology to nullify. The Patriots had thought of everything. This blocked almost every move Frost could make.

They had no way of knowing when the sleeper might run a test or what might cause the sleeper to activate the bomb. The Patriots had a wild card.

His mind was a mess. He ran a sweaty hand across his face, glad to be alone, even if it was only for a few minutes. The military commanders had been informed of the development and were assessing their own protocols.

Saima had removed herself from the basement and together with Hashim returned to the grand hall. He admired her courage. She hadn't panicked when many would have.

Strong woman. Determined.

She needed to be. One thing was clear – the sleeper could have been anybody.

Except her.

That much he was certain of.

Which meant his only ally in trying to figure out who the hostile party inside the mosque might be was Saima Virdee.

He'd asked a lot of her already but there was no other choice.

Frost dialled her number.

THIRTY-TWO

AARON SAT AT THE kitchen table eating his tea.

He hadn't stopped asking for Mummy and Daddy since he'd come inside. Joyti had been forced to tell him they were still at work. She had tried to call Harry but his phone had gone to voicemail and she didn't trust herself to leave a message.

He would call soon.

Joyti watched Aaron neatly breaking off pieces of the chapatti she had made him and dipping them into a chickpea curry. Joyti had been surprised. She knew Saima cooked Asian food at home, yet seeing Aaron happily eating her curry had buoyed her dwindling spirits.

Her thoughts constantly flitted from the little boy in front of her to his parents, out there amid the chaos.

Why did Saima have to be inside the Mehraj mosque?

What would happen to Harry if Saima didn't make it through this?

Her heart ached for her son. She would do anything to stop his pain.

Ranjit didn't know Saima was in danger. He had lain on the sofa, door pulled to, with his eyes closed, ever since he had come in from the garden. Even on an ordinary day her husband was usually slave to the news channels. The fact this was happening on their doorstep and he wasn't interested told her one thing.

Her risk had paid off.

She left Aaron at the table and hovered by the living-room door.

'Would you like some food?' she asked Ranjit, stepping inside.

When he didn't reply, she touched his bare feet, squeezing them gently.

'Close the door,' he replied without moving. 'Leave me alone.'

She hesitated.

She had known what she was doing when she sent Ranjit outside to face Aaron.

Joyti clearly remembered the first time she had seen the little boy. The sight of Aaron had unlocked all the memories she had fought to bury.

Hardeep as a child, running around their shop chasing customers.

Hardeep as a child, sitting on her knee crying after a fall.

Hardeep as a child, falling asleep in her arms when he had been suffering a raging fever.

Memories she could not hold on to in the wake of Ranjit's decision to disown their son.

Joyti suspected the same thing had happened to her husband this afternoon.

'Let me help you,' she whispered.

'You cannot,' he replied. 'Nobody can. Now please shut the door and leave me be.'

Back in the kitchen, Joyti found Aaron licking his plate.

'Do you do that at home?' she asked, shaking her head.

'Mummy shouts at me,' he said with a smile.

'It's not nice.'

'I like it.'

'What else do you like?'

'Ice cream. Grandma always gives me ice cream?'

It wasn't really a question. He knew he would get one. Joyti saw him once a week and in those few hours she spoiled him rotten.

'I got to have bath soon,' he said matter-of-factly.

Joyti reached for another ice cream from the freezer.

She knew it wasn't right to let him have another but there were far graver things to worry about today.

'Would you like Grandma to bathe you?'

He nodded, biting greedily into the ice cream.

'What about sleeping here? Do you want to sleep with Grandma?'

Aaron thought about his answer, smiled and coyly shook his head.

'I sleep in my bed. I got my Batman blanket and my Pooh bear. He . . . he . . . sleeps next to me.'

Joyti nodded.

'Come on, Hardeep,' she whispered. 'I need you.'

THIRTY-THREE

HARRY CHECKED HIS PHONE.

Eight missed calls, six from his mother, two from Saima. No voicemails.

'Why don't you think about where Abu-Nazir might be hiding? I'll be a moment.'

Harry closed the living-room door and stepped out into the hallway, the most distance he could put between himself and Isaac. Saima answered immediately.

'Are you OK?'

'I am.'

'Where are you?'

'Imam Hashim's office.'

Her voice sounded shaky. Something wasn't right.

'What's happened, Saima?'

She told him what had happened with the bomb and of her follow-up call with Frost.

'A sleeper cell?' he said, amazed. 'Are you ... shit, I don't know ... "OK" seems like such a stupid word to use.'

'I'm OK. I mean, my life flashed before me but, to be honest, it's not the first time.'

She forced a laugh and Harry smiled. She was some woman.

'Frost asked me to ... help.'

'You good with that?'

'You know I am. How's Aaron?'

Harry smiled again. *Typical Saima, all about her boy.*

'I told you, he's with my mother.'

'Why aren't you there with him? How can you leave him alone for so long?'

'I'm working, Saima. Everyone needs to play their part today.'

'You need to get to your parents and put him to bed, Harry. He won't sleep otherwise.'

'Saima – my mother has looked after—'

'—did you leave his Batman blanket there? His pyjamas? His Winnie-the-Pooh?'

Christ, this wasn't going to be easy.

'He'll be upset and confused, Harry. Today must have been awful for him.' Her voice cracked. Harry hated to hear her this way.

'I can deal with everything that's going on. The mosque, City Park, the bomb, the sleeper – all of it. What I absolutely cannot deal with is my four-year-old in a strange house, afraid. You will go to that damn house,

Harry Virdee, and you will put my boy to bed – do you hear me?'

She was almost shouting now.

Harry took the breath he needed. 'Saima, he is my boy too. Do you think I would let him suffer? You have to trust my mother. I can't go and sit at home while this city burns around us and you're stuck in the mosque. What if something happens to you? What do I tell Aaron then?'

'You know I am not the priority here, Harry. Our son is the priority.'

'You are both my priority. Please, Saima—'

'Your father is there. God knows what he's said to Aaron. You know what he's capable of.'

It was the thing Harry had been trying not to think of. And now she'd said it aloud. Harry trusted his mother, but he also knew his father.

Was Aaron really safe there?

'If Mum needs me, I'll go back.'

It was a promise he knew he would be unable to fulfil.

'Saima, stop crying. I need you to hold it together.'

Harry glanced at the broken mirror, hanging clumsily next to the front door. He caught his reflection. The crack in the mirror distorted his image, cutting him in half right down the centre.

It was exactly how he felt right now.

'What did Frost say when he called? Did he give you any clues what to look for?'

Her voice steadied a little. 'He said to trust nobody.'

Harry wanted to give her some reassurance but didn't know what to say.

'I want to find who it is, Harry. It might . . . give us all a better chance.' She was right but the odds were against her: they were one in a thousand. 'How do I start?'

Harry told her the only thing he could think of. 'Try and find the calmest person in the room, Saima.' He paused then added, 'Or the one making the most noise.'

THIRTY-FOUR

ISAAC WOLFE COULD HEAR Harry on the phone in the hallway. The detective had taken the gun with him but that was OK.

Isaac put his hands across his chest and started to perform the Islamic nafl prayer, a quick form of worship that he used to charge his courage. Once finished, he remained on the floor, facing Mecca, eyes closed.

He had gained Harry Virdee's trust. It was a fragile allegiance but it was something.

The next few hours were about one thing.

Isaac Wolfe was going to reunite with his leader, Abu-Nazir, because he knew there was a much bigger nightmare to come.

One Harry Virdee would never see coming.

THIRTY-FIVE

HIS CALL TO SAIMA had barely disconnected when Harry phoned his mother.

She answered immediately and Harry heard in the background the one thing he absolutely didn't want to hear.

Aaron crying.

I should be there.

He closed his eyes, trying not to let his emotions over-rule his head.

'Hardeep, are you coming?' she said, clearly leaving the room judging by the sound of Aaron's cries fading.

'I can't, Mum. I just . . . can't.'

She paused for only a moment. 'It's OK,' she replied, her voice resolute. 'It's OK.'

'Has he eaten?'

'Yes.'

'Properly?'

'He had chapatti and curry and a Magnum.'

'He'll fall asleep when he's tired from crying, Mum. There's a dummy and a Batman blanket in the blue bag. Give them to him and lie next to him in bed.'

'He doesn't have any pyjamas, Hardeep.'

'It's warm, Mum, just let him sleep in his underwear.' Harry sighed. 'Mum, I need you to help with this. I need to know you can cope with him overnight. How's everything . . . else?' He couldn't bring himself to ask the question directly.

Her voice was fierce. 'Nothing is happening to Aaron whilst I am alive. You don't worry.'

'I need to go, Mum,' he said, fear pooling in his stomach. He wanted to throw his phone against the wall and smash the house to pieces. How could he not be there for his boy?

He hung his head. 'My phone might be off for a while, Mum. If it's urgent, leave me a voicemail, but only if it is urgent.'

'And Saima? Is she OK, Hardeep?'

'She's fine, Mum.'

'Almukhtaroon – tell me how you got involved with them? It's new, right? You were locked up until fairly recently. How did it happen? Tell me everything,' said Harry, checking his phone for the time: 18.25. They needed to move.

He was back in the kitchen with Isaac, his head still

cloudy for having spoken to his family. He knew this was the only thing he could do to protect them.

Isaac spoke hurriedly. His mother, Noori, was a second-generation Pakistani immigrant, born and raised in London. She'd been a shop assistant when she had become pregnant with Isaac. She and her boyfriend had moved to Bradford to escape their local community and the backlash for having a child out of wedlock.

The shame.

Isaac's father had died before he was born. He knew almost nothing about him.

Noori had changed her surname from Hussain to Wolfe, afraid her family would try to track her down. Afraid of what they might do if they found her.

'Why Wolfe?' asked Harry.

'She liked to read. Came across the name in a book. Plus, she thought it was safer to use a name nobody would think of.'

Isaac had worshipped his mother. She had worked two jobs to make sure he never wanted for anything. She had wanted him to become a doctor.

Harry thought about Isaac's stellar grades; the kid had been on his way.

Then, quite suddenly, his mother had been diagnosed with stage-four breast cancer. By the time she'd seen her GP it was already too late.

'Four months later, she was dead,' said Isaac.

Harry sighed; he still had Aaron's cries in his head.

'Just like that, she was gone,' said Isaac, his face blank. 'I was alone.'

They sat in silence for a moment.

'And the youth detention centre?' Harry ventured.

'Someone at school said something about her. I lost it.'

Isaac stopped. He didn't need to say any more. Harry imagined the rest.

The boy would have fallen on the wrong side of the government's Prevent programme, meant to tackle radicalization. Harry slouched in his seat, dismayed. Instead of helping Isaac, Prevent had put him on a darker path.

'Is that how you found Almukhtaroon?' asked Harry.

'Ironic, right?' Isaac allowed himself a smile. 'Abu-Nazir was visiting another kid inside. I asked some questions, he came to see me and, well . . . when I got out . . . he was there.'

Harry leaned back, scrubbing his palm across his stubble.

'He's a white guy,' he said, shaking his head. 'Didn't that strike you as weird?'

'It was because he was white that I listened. It felt like so much more of a statement coming from him.' Isaac glanced up at Harry but didn't stop talking. 'It felt like I had family again. The more Abu-Nazir taught me, the more I saw how unfair the world had become to the Muslim community.'

Harry struggled not to interrupt. This was textbook: lost Muslim kid falls victim to charismatic hate-preacher.

'How do we find the others?' Harry asked, voice firm. He wanted to find those fuckers now more than ever.

'First, I want to know what happens after that,' said Isaac.

'We negotiate with the Patriots.'

'They want us dead. That doesn't sound like a negotiation to me.'

Harry had been expecting the question. 'The Patriots will know that nobody is handing you over to be executed. If I were a betting man, I'd put my money on them asking you all to go on TV and stand down.'

Isaac slouched in his seat. 'Abu-Nazir would die first.'

Harry smiled. 'In my experience, when death actually stares you down, most men do what they can to stay alive.'

'I hope you're right.'

'What about Amelia? What is her role?'

'You've heard the stories, right?'

Harry had. She was known as the black widow, using her position as Abu-Nazir's partner to entice young, impressionable men to join the cause.

'Is she submissive to Abu-Nazir or are they equals?'

Isaac paused and just the fact that he did so gave Harry the answer. Abu-Nazir was not in charge.

'I got it. Let's move on to the muscle. Fahad-Bin-Azeez.'

Isaac's tone changed, now more serious.

'Nobody calls him that, just Azeez. And he is altogether different.'

Harry's leg started to twitch. He needed to get going but he couldn't rush this. Isaac had to be on his side, had to believe Harry was on his.

'He's the tough guy. I . . . I . . . don't really spend much time with him but Abu-Nazir says everyone's frustrations at how the Islamic world is perceived manifest differently, and that people like Azeez are necessary. Words get you so far, swords the rest of the way.'

'Those his words, are they? Abu-Nazir's?'

Isaac nodded. 'Azeez is huge. You're no match for him.'

'You just tell me everything you know about Azeez and let me worry how to take him down.'

THIRTY-SIX

JOYTI PUT HER PHONE away, wiped tears from her face and went back into the kitchen. Aaron was exactly as she'd left him. She hurried to him, ignoring his flailing arms trying to bat her away. Distressed, he called for his mummy. She held him close. His head was growing heavy with exhaustion and he nestled into her.

Her heart missed a beat.

She struggled to her feet, lifting Aaron with her. As she passed the living-room door, she saw Ranjit was not there. She went to the window by the front door. His car was gone.

Rage exploded inside her.

How could he hate Aaron for the sins of his father?

She gritted her teeth, pulled the chain across the lock and secured the top internal bolt. Her husband was not welcome any more.

Aaron continued to cry, tears from his warm face dampening her skin.

She took him upstairs, struggling with her hip, wincing in pain. She sat Aaron on her bed.

'We're going to sleep in here tonight, my boy. Just you and me.' She stroked his head to soothe him.

'No, I want my mummy,' he said, still crying.

'I know. But tonight you are going to stay here, with Grandma. Mummy and Daddy said so.'

Joyti handed Aaron his Batman comfort blanket and his dummy. His cries stopped for a moment.

'My blue 'jamas?' he asked hopefully.

Joyti grabbed a remote from the bedside cabinet and passed it to Aaron. She pressed a button and the bed moved underneath them, lowering them towards the floor. It was a specialist unit, for her hip.

Aaron took the remote, eyes lighting up.

'Do you want to sleep on this bed, tonight?'

He nodded. 'I keep this?' he said, shying away from her, afraid she might take the remote away.

'If you sleep in this bed, you can keep it.'

He nodded, sucking on his dummy, making it squeak. He really was the spitting image of Harry.

She jumped at the noise of the doorbell.

Ranjit.

'Grandma, somebody here?' said Aaron, still playing with the remote.

'It will go away soon.'

159

She could hear Ranjit's key in the door. The doorbell went again.

And again.

'Grandma, I don't like that noise.'

'You stay here,' she said and started towards the stairs.

At the bottom, she unlocked the door, ready to tell Ranjit he was not welcome.

She didn't have to.

Her husband stood on the doorstep, face grave, a large carrier bag in each hand. He raised them to show her. It was children's clothing.

And on top of the first bag was a pair of blue pyjamas.

THIRTY-SEVEN

HARRY GRIPPED THE STEERING.

If you fail tonight, everything will fall apart.

He'd sailed through the nearly empty streets. Now, close to the city centre, there were helicopters hovering above, police cars, ambulances and fire engines everywhere.

This was the biggest test the city had ever faced. The biggest test Harry had ever faced.

He headed for the side streets.

'How certain are you Azeez lives here?' asked Harry.

'It's the last place I know he was staying.'

'Staying?' said Harry.

'He moves around a lot. He's paranoid he's being watched. Works hard to stay under the radar.'

Harry thought of the Police National Database he had searched. *NFA*. No fixed abode.

Intelligence reports linked him with addresses around

Manningham, Leeds Road and Tong but this address on Back Lane hadn't been mentioned anywhere.

That needled Harry. He glanced at Isaac, the kid staring out the window. Could he really trust him?

'There,' said Isaac, pointing at the first house on the street: semi-detached, show-stopping front garden – red and yellow roses bordering a pristine lawn.

Harry drove past and parked further up.

Quarter past seven on the car's clock, and it was still daylight. This shit would have been so much easier in the dark.

'Are you sure this is the place?' asked Harry, not convinced. It was far from the shit-hole he had been expecting.

'Shared a taxi with him once. That's it.'

The garden was bothering Harry. Whoever lived there had poured a heck of a lot of time, effort and love into it. It wasn't the work of someone who drifted from place to place.

'Who else lives there?' he asked Isaac.

'I don't know. Family friend, he said.'

Harry stared at Isaac but saw nothing in his expression to make him think this was a set-up. His mind went to the gun Isaac had handed back to him.

'He wants to go back to Syria,' Isaac offered.

Harry thought of the recent headlines. Over a thousand young Muslim men had returned from Syria. Apparently, they were all on watch lists but, with resources badly stretched, those identified as 'low risk' had longer leashes.

With his connection to Almukhtaroon, it seemed unlikely Azeez would have been downgraded to low risk. Unless he had never been to Syria.

A dreamer, thought Harry. Azeez wanted the glory and camaraderie of combat but had been too chicken-shit to actually go there. He liked that theory. Maybe Azeez was nothing more than a playground bully.

Harry pulled a pair of handcuffs from the glove compartment and waved them at Isaac.

'You can't be serious?'

'I can't be scoping that place out worrying you might get a rush of blood to the head and do something stupid.'

'I'll come with you.'

'No.'

'I'm not wearing those.'

Harry sighed.

'You put a loaded gun in my hand and now you want to handcuff me in the car?'

Harry slapped the cuffs on Isaac, one across his right wrist, the other around the steering wheel. 'Finished with your speech?' he said.

Isaac looked despondent.

Harry got out of the car.

THIRTY-EIGHT

FROST HAD HIS EYE on the clock on the far wall: 19.30.

Two hours before darkness hit them. It would bring another complication. In this city, fading light usually brought fading hope. He was pleased Saima had sounded resilient when he'd asked her to help find the possible sleeper cell but Frost didn't have much hope. It was a one-in-a-thousand shot, a lottery.

One piece of positive news was that he had just received word there had been no fatalities from the blast in City Park. The twenty-minute evacuation order had been time enough for everyone to leave. Many people had been taken to hospital with minor injuries, most from the stampede to evacuate, some from flying debris. Bradford Royal Infirmary was in a state of emergency; other hospitals around Yorkshire were also receiving patients. A Gold Command had been set up for the NHS

trusts. The medical service, like the police force, was bracing itself.

One thousand and nine people were at risk inside the mosque.

A line of communication had been set up between Frost's team and the Patriots. It was an international phone number, which had been traced to an area of no-man's-land in Russia. What was clear, however, was that this was not a Russian operation. From them, this would have been an act of war, and the Soviets were far too cute for that.

No, this was the Patriots situating themselves in a place where the West had no allies to call on. It was smart.

Tariq had wanted to speak with them but Frost had not allowed it. He didn't trust the politician.

His team had found nothing on the Patriots. There were several low-level criminal groups around the country who used the nickname, none of whom had the capabilities to pull this off. Cyber experts had not been able to take anything from the video clips. The Patriots had left nothing but smoke.

Frost pinched the bridge of his nose. They were six hours into this crisis with no concrete leads. They hadn't tracked a single leader of Almukhtaroon and nightfall would make that all the more difficult. Worse, it would bring the vampires on to the streets. Frost had been updated that social media was rife with groups of anarchy-seekers on the streets of Bradford supposedly hunting Abu-Nazir. The enormous police presence in and around

the city centre and specifically now around the Mehraj mosque had detained dozens of locals, all seeking to stir up trouble. Maintaining civil order was becoming more challenging.

Even the brilliant Detective Superintendent Clare Conway, in charge of locating Almukhtaroon, could not bring Frost the good news he hoped for. She had many intelligence leads but, as yet, not a single member in safe custody.

The five hundred extra officers from Yorkshire and the North East had arrived and were now strategically positioned around Bradford, a bold, visible statement that the police were in charge. This thing was on a knife edge and if Bradford kicked off, they would have little hope of containing it.

He was waiting to hear from the detective superintendent responsible for evacuating the other hundred and four mosques but he had not yet checked in. Perhaps, Frost thought absentmindedly, there would be good news there. He couldn't sit about in his office waiting for the update.

Up on the second floor, Frost was searched by an armed military soldier.

Protocol.

Tariq Islam and special ops commander David Allen were standing in front of a large desk. Tariq's mobile phone was on the table, the line open to the government's COBRA committee.

Frost nodded for the men to start. The revelation of the

sleeper cell had made what he was about to hear a more pressing matter.

'We plan to enter the mosque through a sewage tunnel that gives access to the basement,' Allen opened with confidence. The Patriots had destroyed nearby access points with their bomb in City Park – intentionally or unintentionally, they could not be sure – which was slowing the operation considerably. A special ops team had gained access to the sewer system further out of town and were now one mile from the main line that would take them to the basement of the mosque.

Commander Allen spoke with the ease of a man who thought this was nothing more than a routine day in the office. 'We've dispatched a small robot armed with several cameras to trawl the route, make sure there's no unwelcome surprise waiting for our men down there.'

It would take a couple of hours, Allen went on. If it showed nothing of concern, the special forces team would look to enter the mile-long stretch at 22.30 with a proposed entry to the basement of the mosque at 23.00, giving them seven hours before the Patriots' deadline expired to try to defuse the bomb.

'What about the sleeper cell inside the mosque?' asked Frost, stepping towards the phone on speaker. 'If our contact inside cannot give us a name, can the bomb-disposal team disable it without the sleeper knowing?'

Allen didn't mince his words. 'No. But if we gain access, we have a good chance of disabling the device.'

The Prime Minister's voice on the phone interrupted them.

'Commander Allen, please define "a good chance".'

'All I can say, Prime Minister, is that looking at the pictures and video footage made available to us, we feel confident of a favourable outcome.'

Frost wanted to smile; Allen was just as good as the PM at evading direct questions.

The PM asked the Home Secretary for an update. He should have asked Frost, but this didn't trouble Frost. He listened closely to ensure the information was accurate. Five minutes later, the PM gave Commander Allen authorization to proceed and the phone call ended as a knock sounded on the office door.

'You wanted an update as soon as I could get it to you.' The young DS looked at Frost. She stopped talking, her face troubled.

'What now?' he said, realizing another body blow was imminent.

'I'm afraid the other mosques within the city have not been evacuated.'

'Why?' asked Frost, unable to keep the surprise from his voice.

Why the fuck not? he wanted to shout.

'Because, sir, they have refused to open their doors.'

THIRTY-NINE

SAIMA WAS SITTING ALONE in Imam Hashim's office.

Crying.

She couldn't help it. Much as she wanted to believe Aaron was OK, she needed it confirmed. She had tried to call Joyti, who hadn't answered. Saima didn't have the house telephone number, having never needed to call it.

How could she focus on what Frost had tasked her with – trying to locate the potential sleeper – when her mind would not focus on anything except images of her little boy crying, afraid, confused over why he was sleeping in a strange house without either of his parents?

The past six hours felt like a blur. The pace and adrenaline of first undertaking the search and then locating the bomb had made time fly. Now, sitting here, she finally had a moment to think of nothing but Aaron.

She called Joyti again. And again. But she did not

answer. Saima wanted to throw her phone against the wall and scream. This was her little boy. Surely Joyti would have realized that Saima needed to speak to him before he went to bed? For her, leaving the mosque was far from certain and she'd be damned if she didn't hear Aaron's voice one more time. Perhaps she was being overly dramatic. She didn't care.

If she got her head clear, she could do as Frost had asked. She had been calm on the phone with him – resilient even. They were all in this together and everyone needed to play their part. Before she could take up that challenge she needed a clear head.

Saima tried to Facetime Joyti. They had done so before; her mother-in-law knew how it worked. The call connected on the fifth ring and Saima's heart felt like it might burst from her chest.

Joyti's face appeared on screen, smiling but also with a degree of concern she could not hide.

Saima started to cry, more out of relief than anything else. She asked desperately about Aaron.

Joyti spoke to her in Punjabi, a language Saima was fluent in. 'He is fine. I put him to bed and he is asleep.'

'Let me see him, Mum.'

Joyti asked how she was but Saima shook her head and again pleaded to see Aaron.

'If he hears you, he'll wake up, Saima,' said Joyti.

'I won't say a word, I promise. I just need to see him.'

Joyti moved from wherever she was, taking the phone

with her. Saima had never been inside the house so she didn't have any bearings. Then the screen showed a bed, some distance away, as if Joyti were in the doorway. Saima could see Aaron's body, his head on a pillow.

She put her hand across her mouth, stifled her cries, then asked Joyti to go a little closer.

Now, with the phone right above Aaron, Saima saw him clearly. He had on some blue pyjamas she had never seen before, his dummy in his mouth, and looked to be sound asleep.

Saima cried hard, using her hand to absorb the noise, her whole body shaking. She just needed to get this out – be done with it.

Joyti slowly withdrew from the bedroom and made her way downstairs, arriving in the kitchen.

'Beti, are you OK? Tell me.'

Beti – daughter.

'I'm OK, Mum,' said Saima, not showing herself on the screen, simply speaking into the phone.

'I . . . I . . . am praying for you, Beti. Everything will be fine.'

Saima couldn't speak any more and remained silent. Joyti seemed to sense this and tried her hardest to put Saima at ease. 'He had all of his tea, Saima, no problems. Ranjit even went to the shops and bought him new clothes and a toy – you have nothing to worry about. Like I told Hardeep, your boy is now my boy and with my life I will protect and look after him.'

After the call Saima put the phone by her side, put her hands over her face and let it all out. Aaron had looked so peaceful asleep, not a care in the world. Just as it should be.

Hearing Joyti's calm voice, speaking as perhaps only another mother could, had made Saima want to speak to her own mother, something simply not possible. Instead, she reached for her phone and dialled her sister, Nadia. She answered immediately and was alarmed to hear Saima sounding so upset.

'I'm OK, I just, you know, being away from Aaron and trapped inside this place is getting to me.'

Nadia asked what was happening and Saima told her she didn't know, that as far as she was concerned, it was just a waiting game. Then she got down to the real reason for the call.

'Listen, Nads, if . . . you know, things should not go so well in here, if the worst happens, Harry is going to need your support. You're the only family I've got.'

Nadia tried to be positive and told Saima she was being silly – that everything would be OK. It was the only thing she could say.

'I know all that, Nads, but still, should it not happen that way, promise me you'll be there for Harry. That you'll do what you can.'

Nadia gave Saima her word, swore on her life.

Finally, Saima asked her for one more thing. Something she had never done before. She asked Nadia to call their mother in Pakistan and to tell her that Saima still loved her

and that she was sorry for all the heartache she had caused everyone by marrying Harry. And that, if this situation resolved itself, she wanted to try and reconnect.

Nadia fell silent and Saima knew it was because what she was asking would perhaps not be met with the response she wanted.

'I don't care if it is not received well, Nadia. Just promise me you will do it.'

Nadia said she would.

Having disconnected the call, Saima wiped her face and took a few minutes to compose herself, mind now cleared.

Saima Virdee had work to do.

FORTY

THIS IS TREVOR HOLMES reporting for ITV news from For-ster Square in Bradford, where just behind me you can see the iconic Mehraj mosque, confirmed to be the location of a second explosive device inside a city already devastated by a major blast earlier in the day. As you can see, there is a dramatic police presence around the mosque with the cordon having been extended in the past hour. We have been forced almost a quarter-mile away.

The breaking news we have just received is that the other hundred and four mosques within the city have not evacuated, in spite of being allowed to do so by the ter-rorist organization calling themselves the Patriots. We understand that the very young and elderly have left these sites but the majority of the worshippers have remained in situ.

With thousands of police officers throughout the city

and indeed around those mosques, this breaking development seems to go against the advice of the security services who, we understand, are in urgent talks with the imams of those mosques to find out what exactly is going on. One thing remains certain: with darkness approaching, Bradford has a very long night ahead of it.

FORTY-ONE

HARRY APPROACHED THE REAR of the property.

There were clothes on the clothesline but he couldn't see anyone in the house itself. Harry opened the rear gate and hurried down the path to the house.

The back garden was as perfectly tended as the front, not a blade of grass out of place.

Must take hours.

He was about to peer through the window next to the back door when he saw the handle move and the door flung open in front of him. A short, thin, black guy appeared in the doorway, a rucksack over one shoulder, heavy carrier bags weighing down both hands.

Couldn't have been Azeez; this guy hadn't seen a gym in his life.

He stopped, face aghast at seeing Harry in his doorway. Before Harry could react, the man charged at him,

catching him off guard. Harry stumbled as the man flew past him, still carrying all three bags.

All Harry could think as he leapt after the stranger was how ridiculous he looked running for freedom carrying two cheap carrier bags, both ready to split any second.

Harry reached him in four powerful strides. He grabbed him, one arm around his neck, the other snaking around his torso.

'Police.'

The man whimpered and dropped the bags, then, to Harry's astonishment, burst out crying.

The skinny black guy had identified himself as Roderick Manuel Alfonso. His driving licence said he was forty-two and it was registered to this address.

He continued to cry as Harry secured him to a kitchen cabinet door with a second pair of handcuffs.

The rest of the house was empty. Azeez wasn't here.

'What's your deal?' said Harry, opening Roderick's rucksack.

Clothes. Toiletries. A few hundred quid in cash.

The carrier bags each contained a laptop, which confused Harry. Surely the laptops would have been better in the rucksack and the clothes in the cheap plastic bags? This guy wasn't thinking straight. He was frightened.

'Azeez? You know him?' asked Harry.

Roderick continued to cry. It was starting to piss Harry off.

'You sick? Crazy? Or you in mourning?'

Everything about this bloke was off. His T-shirt was on back to front, his belt undone, one of his socks blue, the other red. Harry prodded him with his finger.

'You want to dial that shit down?'

Roderick didn't.

Exasperated, Harry grabbed the key from the back door and told Roderick he'd be back.

'Never seen him before,' said Isaac, looking as perplexed as Harry.

'Didn't think this was our guy,' replied Harry. 'I'm gonna take a proper look around. You see if you can calm him down.'

Harry locked the back door, taking the key with him. As he passed the staircase, he also checked the front door was secure. He didn't think Isaac was going to bolt but wasn't willing to take the risk.

The house was pristine. Rows of tiny porcelain ornaments were perfectly aligned on the mantelpiece in the living room. Plumped cushions on the sofa made a diamond formation. More of a show home than one where people lived. Upstairs was just as bad. Harry hurriedly searched both bedrooms.

The second had a wardrobe full of clothes for a man much bigger than Roderick.

Thirty-six-inch jeans.

Seventeen-inch collars.

Everything else either XL or XXL.

Seemed Azeez might have been here after all.

He was halfway down the stairs when he stopped. He could still hear Roderick crying.

Something wasn't right.

Surely not?

He went back upstairs. Back in Azeez's bedroom, he went for the bed. Duvet tucked tightly under the mattress, pillows snug underneath the duvet – more like a hotel than a home.

Harry pulled the duvet free. Dust swirled around his face. He backed off, coughing, blinking it out of his eyes.

Harry went to the other bedroom and did the same thing. No dust this time. He examined the pillows. Both well worn.

Harry frowned. He gave the room a little more focus. Blackout blinds on the windows, wires hanging loose behind the TV – a USB-to-HDMI cable. He found a mini-tripod down the back of the TV cabinet. Whichever camera it had once held had been connected to the TV screen. Amateur video at its best.

He opened the first bedside cabinet.

Empty.

Harry moved around the bed to the second and pulled it open.

There it was.

FORTY-TWO

RODERICK ALFONSO CONTINUED TO cry like a baby in his kitchen.

Harry grabbed a chair and sat down opposite him.

'Stop that,' said Harry, showing him his police ID. 'I'm Detective Virdee from the Homicide and Major Enquiry Team.'

'Oh shit, oh Jesus! Honestly, I didn't know he was going to do it. I tried to stop him!'

Harry held up a hand. He couldn't show his alarm at the man's response.

'Do what?' said Harry. 'Who are we talking about here? Let's start at the beginning.'

Harry saw the shift in the man's demeanour, the narrowing of his eyes and the realization that Harry might not know what he was talking about.

He wiped his eyes with his free hand and shook his head. 'Nothing.'

Harry wasn't about to let him get away with that.

'What do you do?'

'Huh?'

'Job?'

Roderick shook his head. 'I'm on disability.'

'You ran away from me pretty quickly.'

'I . . . er . . . took my painkillers just before you arrived. They . . . help.'

'Who do you live here with?'

'I live alone.'

'I don't think so.'

'I do.'

Harry slapped him. He didn't have time for this shit.

Roderick didn't cry this time. He sat there, stunned.

'I really hope I don't have to do that again,' said Harry, leaning a little closer and dropping his voice.

'You . . . you . . . can't do that as a police officer!' said Roderick.

Harry slapped him again. Harder.

'If I have to do that a third time, Roderick, something in your face is going to break.'

Roderick's eyes seemed to darken.

Isaac hung back behind Harry.

'He was right,' said Roderick quietly. 'This country *is* diseased. Infected.'

Harry said nothing.

When the silence hit a minute, he reached into his pocket and removed the items he had found in Roderick's bedside cabinet.

A handful of Viagra tablets, a gimp mask and a nipple clamp.

He dropped them one by one on the floor in front of Roderick.

'They're going to have a right old time with you in prison, aren't they? So is it you or Azeez who gets to wear the mask?'

Roderick didn't need to reply. Harry saw the answer in his face.

Harry pointed to the laptops stuffed inside the carrier bags, the ones Roderick had been running with. 'Bet there's a lot of saucy shit on those. Saw the leads hanging from the TV. No video camera, mind.'

Roderick glanced at his rucksack, realized his involuntary mistake then looked away. Harry opened it and dumped the contents on the floor. A silver Sony camcorder clattered on to the tiles.

'I don't really give a shit about your sex life, Roderick. I want to know where Azeez is. You tell me that and you can get back to running wherever it was you were going.'

Harry waved the camera at him, placed it on the table.

Roderick looked at the dustbin.

'Something in there you don't want me to find? Something worse than what's on that camera?'

Suddenly Roderick stood, pulling open a drawer beneath the cabinet he was cuffed to and brandishing a knife.

Isaac stepped back, just out of reach, eyes searching for Harry's, who ignored him and folded his arms across his chest.

'Really?' he said, frowning.

Roderick was waving the knife wildly at Harry, eyes glazed over, face twisted into a frightening snarl. Gone was the cry-baby.

Harry picked up the chair he had been sitting on. 'This only ends one way,' he said, raising it to throw at him.

Roderick shook his head. He was frightened and angry. Maybe the guy was mad.

Harry tightened his grip on the chair. Once he threw it, Roderick would have to drop the knife to use his hand to defend himself. Harry would put him down with a swift kick to the balls and then, well, he'd be forced to play a little dirtier.

Harry never got the chance.

Before he could do anything, Roderick started laughing, shouting something incoherent in what sounded like Arabic before closing his eyes and putting the knife to his neck. Then, without hesitation, he cut his own throat, eyes wide and crazy.

Isaac stood frozen in disbelief.

Harry stood there, chair still raised, stunned, blood haemorrhaging everywhere as Roderick collapsed to his knees, wavering slightly before slumping to the floor.

FORTY-THREE

JOYTI VIRDEE ALWAYS FOUND the act of making Indian tea soothing. Allowing water to boil, adding loose tea, cardamom and fennel seeds, then a generous amount of milk, and allowing it to simmer. The longer it simmered, the richer the tea. Her mind was on Saima. Trapped inside the mosque.

Alone.

At least she had seen that Aaron was asleep. Not that it had been easy. Aaron had cried incessantly, exhaustion finally taking over. Joyti doubted he would wake until morning.

Today she allowed the tea to simmer for a quarter-hour longer than usual, her mind now going to Ranjit.

He had been to the supermarket, bought Aaron clothes and a toy. Nothing from the usual range, everything from the premium line. A small detail but an important one, she felt.

Joyti turned off the stove, poured two cups through a

tea strainer and carried them into the living room along with a packet of Ranjit's favourite, custard creams.

Her husband was sitting quietly at the table by the window, staring outside, the brightness of the day starting to fade. She left the door wide open; if Aaron started to cry she needed to hear him. Joyti doubted he would. She had rarely seen a little boy as tired as he had been.

She placed the cups on the table and sat down opposite Ranjit. He didn't look up.

'Tea,' she said softly, jolting him from his thoughts. He looked in her direction, momentarily confused. She nodded towards the table. He hadn't eaten anything all day.

The silence lingered.

Joyti blew gently into her cup, the heat rising from the tea.

'You know, when our son bought us this house, I was so pleased,' said Ranjit finally, taking his tea, leaving the biscuits.

'It's a lovely house,' she replied.

'I liked the view. The hills in the distance. It reminded me of the place I grew up in Punjab after my family had been forced to leave Lahore.' Ranjit looked down into his teacup. 'When I was a child, I wished I could run over the hills because I had heard stories there was gold on the other side.'

Joyti listened quietly, unsure why Ranjit was telling her this. She knew how the partition of India had affected her husband's family. One day they had woken up to find themselves living in the newly formed Pakistan. It had taken only three days before the looting had started. The

British had fled, leaving Sikhs and Muslims to engage in a bloody conflict on both sides of the border.

'We left our home on a Friday. I always remember it because I could hear the mosques sounding their call-to-prayer.'

He laughed uncomfortably and took a sip of his tea.

'My mother was carrying my younger brother' – Ranjit paused – 'Charanjit.'

Joyti had never heard the name, had never known her husband had a younger brother.

'You—'

'He was my mother's favourite.' Ranjit spoke over her. 'Youngest always is.'

She smiled. Even Ronnie knew that Harry had always been her favourite.

'Charanjit was my favourite too. He used to sleep in my bed at night and when it got too hot I would fan him until he slept.' Ranjit wiped his eyes. 'We left Lahore on this Friday. We had heard from our neighbours, a Muslim family called Baig, that we were not safe any more. They were good people. We used to go to their house for Eid dinner and they would come to ours when it was Vaisakhi. This Friday, though, they told us to leave because we were in danger. And we did, in the baking heat. My father, two older brothers and my mother. My mother carried Charanjit until she became too tired. Then I carried him.'

He wasn't drinking his tea any longer, but he gripped the cup as if the room had grown cold.

'He was so heavy,' said Ranjit, his voice now just a whisper.

The expression on her husband's face was one Joyti had never seen before.

'There were thousands walking with us. We heard whispers that vandals were coming – to rape the women, kill the children – and the heat . . .' Ranjit shook his head. 'It felt like we were walking through fire.'

He got up from his chair and moved towards the dark corner of the room, as if the pale light from the window was burning his eyes. His voice had changed. Was it pain? Or fear?

'Charanjit stopped moving in my arms on the eighth day.' He placed his hands on the wall as if the wind had been knocked from him and he could no longer stand.

Joyti went to him but she didn't embrace him. She didn't know how. Why had she never heard this story before? In all their years of marriage?

'We . . . wanted to cremate him but there was no wood. Nothing to make a fire. So . . . so . . .' Ranjit broke down. 'We laid him down by the road – next to other children – and covered his body with leaves . . .' His voice trailed off.

Joyti wrapped her arms around her husband.

'We left him there! He was such a pure, innocent child. He should have been cremated so his spirit could have returned in the next life as something worthy! We could not do this for him. We . . . had to keep walking!'

He smashed his fists against the wall. 'What kind of God could allow that to happen?'

Another crack of his fists on the wall.

'My father kept pushing us to walk – he never cried. He just kept us moving. My mother, a part of her died that day. She was never the same again.'

Joyti hugged him as tightly as she could, feeling his body starting to shake, her tears soaking into his shirt.

'Those bastard Muslims took Charanjit's life. They took my mother from me! They ruined us. Homeless, penniless and now incomplete.'

Joyti heard a wheeze inside his chest, a sound she knew only too well. She moved to the shelf above the mantelpiece and snatched his inhaler, pushing it into his hands.

Ranjit put it to his lips and inhaled deeply, repeating it several times, keeping his body in the corner as if afraid to step out from the shadow.

'Charanjit had a birthmark behind his right shoulder. A perfectly formed circle.'

Joyti felt her head swim.

'That . . . that . . . child upstairs,' he said, continuing to cry.

She looked at him, pained.

Ranjit pointed upstairs. 'That boy, I swear to you, Joyti . . .' He balled his hands into fists. Not bitterness but pain. He stared at his wife, disbelief on his face.

'That boy upstairs has the same birthmark as Charanjit. I want more than anything to take him in my arms, kiss him, inhale the sweetness from his skin and never let him go! But I cannot.'

FORTY-FOUR

SAIMA WALKED UP AND down the grand hall, pushing a cart filled with food – the one thing the Mehraj mosque was not short of. As people ate, the edginess that had existed inside the room seemed to settle.

Saima had not offered to help cook in the kitchen, instead volunteering to distribute food. It gave her the chance to walk among the worshippers.

A sleeper cell? What did that even mean? Everyone she had so far seen appeared to be perfectly normal. A few faces she recognized; most, however, she did not.

The room had fragmented into four clear groups. The elderly, men, women and youngsters. The differences between them were stark. Saima was concerned about the last group – the young boys looked anything but passive. Tensions were rising – boredom, too much social media

and, the most worrying aspect, anger. The older men seemed to be on it – watchful.

Saima had been drawn towards the women in full burkas first, but then questioned it. Trying to be objective, was it not too obvious for the sleeper to be wearing a burka? There were half-a-dozen women dressed in the outfits. Saima had approached them, spoken with them and left, unfazed.

Imam Hashim entered the room, pushing a cart full of drinks. He caught her attention: smiling, embracing those who needed it. He was the epitome of a man in control.

Christ, she was being cynical, but Harry's words filtered into her mind:

Look for the calmest person in the room . . .

Hashim was certainly that.

She thought back to her attempts at analysing the bomb, Hashim by her side. He had been the perfect example of calm.

Finished with the food cart, Saima made her way back to Hashim's office, located at the right-hand side of the stage. She had left her phone on charge inside.

Having double-checked he was still at the other end of the grand hall, Saima sat down at his desk. She opened the drawers and found nothing more than religious texts. The computer was on and she moved the mouse, bringing the screen to life. Saima clicked on the email icon and scanned a few of the most recent emails.

She frowned. They were in Arabic, which Saima couldn't

understand. She glanced at the keyboard – also Arabic. She took a few moments to figure out which the Send button was, then forwarded the last five emails to herself. Saima unplugged her phone, checked the emails had landed then deleted them from Hashim's Sent folder.

Nothing to it.

She moved to the couch and used Google Translate on her phone to decipher the emails. It took a short while to figure them all out. Once she had, she could hardly believe her own eyes.

Imam Hashim.

Saima stood up, alarmed, the phone shaky in her hand. She tried to call Harry but it went to voicemail. Saima needed to tell someone what she had found.

Frost.

She scrolled to his number and was about to hit Call when the office door opened and Hashim strode in.

He closed the door then turned to look at her, clearly annoyed.

'Put your phone down, Saima.'

She stared at him, uncertain.

He pointed to the corner of the room.

Saima turned to see a small, dome-shaped CCTV camera, fixed in the ceiling. She hadn't realized it was there.

Hashim showed her his phone: real-time footage of them both.

Saima's thumb was poised to call Frost. Hashim closed the gap.

'Give me your phone, Saima.'

'I won't.'

'Let me explain.'

She pointed at him, outraged. 'You cannot do this, Hashim. I will not let you.'

FORTY-FIVE

NEITHER HARRY NOR ISAAC moved.

Blood pooled around Roderick's body, the knife by his side. Harry couldn't stop replaying how quickly and unhesitatingly it had happened. What the hell had made Roderick so afraid that he had slit his own throat?

Harry looked away. In his experience, only a very specific type of fear or mental illness could make a man do such a thing.

'You OK?' said Harry, looking to Isaac.

'I'm not the one who just slit my own throat,' replied Isaac, voice surprisingly calm. Harry didn't like what he saw in Isaac's eyes. Something dark surfaced then disappeared.

'Most people react after they've witnessed something like that.'

Harry wanted to add, *Especially ones who take medication for anxiety.*

Isaac met Harry's gaze. 'I don't know what you want me to say. I'm not sure what just happened.'

'Makes two of us.'

'Aren't you going to check his pulse?'

Roderick's arm was dangling awkwardly, still cuffed to a cabinet door. Harry unfastened the cuffs and put them in his pocket. 'He's as dead as anyone I've ever seen.'

'So, what now?'

'Why are you so calm about this?' Harry grabbed Isaac by the arm.

'I don't know what you expect. I'm supposed to cry? Faint?'

'All that and more.'

'Sorry to disappoint.' Isaac shook him off.

'He did that because he was afraid,' said Harry. He stepped around the blood, still pooling on the floor.

'Are you going to call an ambulance?' said Isaac.

'No.'

'Are you really a police officer?'

'Yes.'

'You don't act like one.'

Roderick had been staring at the bin just before he killed himself. Harry removed the lid. He couldn't see anything except the black bin bag. He carried it into the living room, away from the blood, Isaac following behind.

Harry emptied the contents on the floor.

Four pieces of cardboard, four plastic sheaths.

'Shit,' whispered Isaac.

'We need to move quickly,' said Harry, alarmed.

This time, he was comforted by Isaac's tone. If the kid hadn't reacted to what they were looking at, Harry wasn't sure he could have continued to work alongside him.

'You start down here. I'll do upstairs. Tear the place apart,' said Harry.

Isaac was still mesmerized by the contents of the bin: four empty packages that had each clearly contained a large kitchen knife. 'What am I looking for?'

'Azeez has a location in mind. He's dreamt of this, obsessed about it, and most importantly coveted the location. We only covet areas we know well. In this house is a clue to where the sick fuck is headed. We need to find it, Isaac. *Fast.*'

Isaac could hear Harry tearing the house apart upstairs. He was doing the same down here. They needed to find Azeez. Without him, Isaac couldn't get to Nazir, to safety.

He was angry at himself for letting the detective notice his reaction to Roderick's suicide.

Isaac knew Harry didn't trust him.

What he also knew, though, what he had experience of, was that desperation often left a man exposed. Vulnerable.

He wasn't about to underestimate Harry Virdee.

Isaac was banking on the fact that Harry would underestimate him.

* * *

Upstairs, Harry ransacked both bedrooms, not completely focused. It was distracting, having part of his brain concentrating on Isaac downstairs. Harry had always had a sixth sense when it came to people. The kid wasn't toxic, but there was something deeper going on that Harry didn't like.

For now the only question Harry needed an answer to was: could he trust Isaac not to have a pop at him?

For now.

Harry discovered a few photos of Azeez. Vanity snaps of him on a beach. Nothing that gave him any clues to where Azeez might be headed.

Wherever Azeez was going, he intended to kill.

He should call this in. What would he say? How the fuck had he got here, and what about Isaac?

The bastard had to be local. Probably close enough to go on foot. Someplace small yet with enough people to cause headline-grabbing casualties.

Isaac's voice startled Harry from his thoughts and he hurried downstairs.

'Found something?' said Harry, rushing into the living room.

'Payslips.'

Harry took them from him. The last three months. Each was for four hundred pounds, for part-time employment.

Harry checked the front, found the address.

'Oh, Jesus,' he said, stuffing them into his pocket. 'Come on.'

Harry grabbed Isaac and together they headed for the back door, stepping past Roderick's body.

Outside they ran for the car, Harry praying they were not too late.

Quebec Nursing Home, Dementia Specialists.

FORTY-SIX

QUIET.

What happened now?

'Why didn't you tell me?' Joyti asked finally. They were sitting back at the table.

'Poured dirt in the grave,' he replied. It was an old Indian saying. When bad things occurred, you simply buried the facts and never spoke of it again.

Joyti's heart broke for her husband.

'When I first saw the boy,' said Ranjit, pointing upstairs, 'I thought I was seeing things.'

Ranjit reached for his now cold tea.

'When I heard him crying, my chest started to ache.'

'We've shared so many burdens, Ranjit. Why not this one?'

'I didn't want to believe it had happened. I didn't want to remember.'

'How old were you?' she asked.

'Eight,' he replied. 'I was too young to know loss like that. And I saw it every day in my mother's eyes.' Ranjit looked at Joyti. 'You and her share the same look of sorrow. The day Hardeep left, your eyes became like hers.'

Joyti winced. She wanted to ask him why, then, had he not understood her pain? Why had he banished their son? It wasn't the right time.

'How could I do to you the very thing that was forced upon my mother?'

Joyti looked away. He had understood what she was thinking.

'I must be a real tyrant,' he said, 'not to have afforded you the opportunity my mother never had – just to be a mother to your child, to protect him and love him, no matter what.'

Joyti wiped a tear from her face.

'I saw what the Muslims could bring – the pain, the loss' – he paused – 'the suffering.'

Joyti opened her mouth but Ranjit raised his hand.

'On the day terrorists descend on Bradford to ruin this city we call home, a boy arrives in my house to torment what little life I have left.'

'Torment?'

Ranjit nodded. 'Until I stared at his little face, I thought I had suffered all I had to suffer.'

Joyti leaned forward and put her hand on his.

'So, nothing changes?' she said softly.

'I want to go upstairs and crawl into bed with him, Joyti,' said Ranjit, starting to cry again. 'I want to wake him up, take him into the garden and fly a kite with him, like I used to do with Charanjit.'

'Then do it!' said Joyti, putting her hands together as if in prayer.

Ranjit slammed his hand on the table, making tea spill from both their cups. 'I cannot, woman!' he cried.

Joyti allowed her tears to soak her face.

'What kind of sick man must I be that I cannot go upstairs and embrace that boy? My heart and mind are working against each other. I wish I were dead, Joyti—'

She got up to go to him but he stormed past her, hesitating by the living-room door, hammering his fist into his chest, the sound sickening.

'My bones are too old, my mind too stubborn and my heart too weak to do what you ask. I am,' he said coldly, 'dead inside.'

FORTY-SEVEN

HARRY SCREECHED HIS CAR to a stop outside Quebec Nursing Home, yelling for Isaac to follow as he got out.

It wasn't a small place. At least thirty rooms, he thought. Thirty vulnerable targets.

It appeared peaceful but Harry knew better than to feel relieved yet.

'Shouldn't we call for backup?' said Isaac.

'Not until we actually have a problem.'

If Azeez was here and had not yet carried out his attack, Harry needed to detain him himself. But if he found a knife-wielding lunatic in there, he'd be forced to call this in.

Tariq Islam's voice boomed loud in his ear.

The government does not negotiate with terrorists and that policy will not change simply because thousands of lives are at risk.

They looped around the side of the nursing home, Isaac

201

on Harry's heels. He wasn't sure what use, if any, Isaac would be. Or if Azeez was even here. He could never really be sure in his job, but two decades of policing told Harry Azeez would be inside. He had to try.

Thirty vulnerable elderly patients. It'd be a tragedy of the worst kind.

The back entrance, like the front, had automatic double doors and a window either side: four panels of glass. Curtains were drawn across the first two. Peering through the third panel, Harry saw a brutish figure, tall, broad, skin dark against his white vest. He was tying up a member of staff, the last of five. Harry spied a knife in his hand, another down the back of his jeans, handle sticking out. The room was full of elderly residents, most looking bemused. A few appeared to be shouting at Azeez.

He grabbed Isaac, put his fingers to his lips and nodded for him to have a look.

'Azeez?' said Harry, giving Isaac a few seconds even though he knew the answer.

'Yes,' replied Isaac, mouth dropping open.

Harry tried the door but it was locked for the night.

'We need to hurry,' said Isaac, panic clear in his voice.

In the rush to get here, Harry had left everything in his car.

He was unarmed.

Harry returned to the window. Azeez was still with the staff. A car pulling up behind drew his attention and he turned to see a blue Ford Focus parking in the rear

carpark. A young woman in a yellow healthcare uniform got out.

Nursing home staff.

Isaac moved with Harry, both of them rushing towards her. She saw them coming, tensed and turned to run.

'Wait!' called Isaac, but she was on the move, sprinting. And now screaming in panic.

Harry flew past Isaac, reached the girl and threw one arm around her, putting his other hand across her mouth.

She bit down, her teeth puncturing his skin.

Harry cried out in pain as she bit harder, shaking her head from side to side like a pit-bull. Then the girl moved her head backwards, butting Harry in the nose.

He let go, stumbling, as she ran for her car. Isaac came towards Harry, who waved him away.

'Go after her!' he snapped at the boy.

Harry blinked away tears and touched his nose.

No blood.

Back in her car, the young nurse reversed wildly.

Harry hurried in front of the car, struggling to get his police ID from his jacket with his injured hand.

He heard the gear change, no doubt from reverse into first.

Isaac moved out of the way but Harry stood firm, waving a pair of handcuffs and his identification in desperation, hoping Azeez had not seen any of this out of the window. Hoping they had not triggered his attack.

Harry saw something in the young woman's eyes shift.

She wasn't bluffing.

As the car came at him, Harry dived out of the way. He felt a gust of air brush by him, the car closer than he wanted it to be.

She was gone.

Harry, on the floor, groaned. He'd fucked it up.

He heard Isaac approach, offer his hand, which Harry ignored.

In his other hand, he waved a set of keys at Harry. 'She dropped these. Want to bet one of them opens that back door?'

FORTY-EIGHT

THEY ENTERED A KITCHEN, a lingering smell of cooked onions. He saw what appeared to be three empty trays of shepherd's pie on a worktop, waiting to be washed up.

Harry could hear Azeez's voice from the room next door, loud and angry.

'Weapon,' whispered Harry to Isaac, pointing for the kid to have a look and gesturing for him to be discreet.

Isaac pulled the kitchen drawers open on one side, Harry on the other. The bite the nurse had inflicted on his hand was bleeding. It hurt like a bitch. Harry grabbed a cloth and pressed it firmly against the wound, wiping blood clear. He'd been bitten before, by a drug addict several years ago. A fleeting memory of seeing Saima in A&E, of antibiotics and a dressing, flickered across his mind. He focused on the task. Surely there must be a knife around here.

Had Azeez been in here and secured them all?

'Come on, come on,' he whispered, hearing Azeez in the other room. He was becoming increasingly irate. He crept to the door and nudged it with his foot, thankful it didn't creak.

Azeez was about twenty feet away, muscles taut, sweating heavily in the heat. He was now standing proud in front of the residents, a knife in each hand. The cook, judging by her apron, was on her knees at his feet, eyes fixed on the floor.

The sight angered Harry, white hot fury rose in his chest.

These innocent people.

Azeez gesticulated wildly as he shouted. Harry couldn't hear his words, he was too focused on the knives in his hands. Every few seconds, one of them would find its way to the blonde curls of the cook cowering on her knees.

Azeez was enjoying this – his moment of glory, his time to exert control and feel all-powerful. Harry clenched his teeth; he was going to tear this bastard apart.

'Harry, we should call for backup,' Isaac said, fear in his voice.

The residents' faces were a mixture of bemusement, fear and blankness. Some looked unfazed and Harry was momentarily grateful that they might be too unwell to realize what was happening.

Azeez grabbed the cook's hair suddenly and yanked her head back, raising a knife.

'Shit,' whispered Harry. He turned to Isaac. 'This goes bad, don't be a hero. Call 999.'

'Let me help you.'

'No. He can't know you're here.'

'Why?'

'No time,' said Harry impatiently, 'just do it. You hear me?'

Isaac nodded.

Harry was ready to enter when something on the counter caught his attention. He flipped the lid of a small pot and stared at the contents.

That could be useful.

Harry put the container in his pocket.

He stepped into the corridor.

Azeez's head snapped up at the noise. He glared at Harry, pointed a knife at him, eyes cold with rage.

Harry walked towards Azeez, lifting an empty chair on the way.

'I am Detective Chief Inspector Harry Virdee. Hello, Azeez.' He stopped about ten feet away, poised to throw the chair, nothing more than a distraction technique.

Azeez waved a knife at Harry. 'Drop it.'

Harry glanced at the cook; she was unharmed. He replaced the chair on the floor.

Harry and Azeez held each other's gaze, their eyes burning, both motionless.

Then Harry smiled and started to laugh.

FORTY-NINE

'DO YOU WANT TO tell me what this is about?' Hashim asked Saima.

She didn't know what to say. Her face was flushing and she couldn't meet his gaze. He didn't know there was a sleeper cell. Frost had told her to keep that vital piece of intel to herself. All she had told Hashim was that the bomb had been too complex to disable. She thought she had delivered the lie well enough.

Hashim sat at his desk, calm as you like. 'These are extraordinary times we find ourselves in,' he said, clicking a few buttons on his keyboard, then turning his computer screen to face her. Sky News – live footage of the Mehraj mosque. Her eyes narrowed as she saw the enormous police presence.

Saima knew they might be planning a break-in to try to save the worshippers, to try to defuse the bomb. Frost

had hinted to her it might be coming but knew he couldn't confirm it.

'With all this going on, I find you acting like some sort of spy? Did what happened in the basement not build some trust between us?' He sounded genuinely wounded, looking at her with a critical eye. 'Are you something far removed from what you appear to be, Saima Virdee? A spy for these Patriots; someone I should detain?'

He was really turning this on her? Saima was outraged. 'You are so full of shit.'

She regretted the profanity and glanced at the canvas of Mecca on the wall behind Hashim. Saima grabbed her ears and whispered, 'Toba astaghfar.'

I seek forgiveness from Allah.

'Assume it has been given, Saima. Now, I'd like an answer to my question,' said Hashim.

She sighed. 'I wanted to send an email. My mobile has no reception, but I couldn't use your keyboard, it's in Arabic.'

Hashim gave her a menacing smile.

Saima knew she'd been rumbled.

'How long should we play this game?'

She nodded at the computer, still streaming the live feed from outside the mosque. 'You're very calm, considering what's happening out there.'

He didn't respond.

Saima couldn't stop thinking about the emails she had

read. It was time to confront him. 'I know what is going to happen in a few hours. You cannot! Think about what you and the other mosques are doing!'

'You do not know anything, Saima.' His words were delivered with real anger.

Saima came across to him, determined. Frost had told her the sleeper cell would have a simple device no larger than a car-key-sized remote.

'I wonder, would you turn out your pockets if I asked you to?' she said.

'Are you asking?'

'I am, unless you have something to hide, Imam.'

Hashim shook his head in dismay.

'Fine,' he said, standing up and emptying his pockets.

A mobile phone. A wad of twenty-pound notes. Rosary beads.

Saima stared at him, waiting.

Hashim smiled and turned his pockets inside out, showing her they were indeed empty.

'Do you intend to frisk me? Inside a mosque?' he said, bemused.

She didn't reply. Her eyes never left his.

'Really, Saima, this is very improper,' he said, raising his arms. 'Do what you must. We are not leaving until we both understand each other.'

She couldn't frisk him. It was a step too far. He'd called her bluff.

Saima backed away, retaking her seat.

Hashim reclaimed the contents of his pockets and sat down, waiting.

'Who else knows why the other mosques have not evacuated?' she asked him.

He stared at her hard enough that she was forced to drop her gaze.

'You're looking for a sleeper cell,' he said. It wasn't a question.

Saima didn't reply.

'You are not the only one with influential contacts outside this mosque. I know just as much as you. But it is right that they trusted you.'

'How did you know?' she said, looking at him.

'Like you, I have people on the outside whom I trust. And they trust me to find such a person.'

Saima saw what he was contemplating. 'You think it might be me?' she said incredulously.

'You're snooping around my office.'

'With good reason. I saw your emails – care to explain them?'

'No.'

'And you say you have nothing to hide.'

Hashim's face hardened. 'Do not meddle in things you have no knowledge of.'

'Or you'll what?'

'First, tell me what you have learned about the sleeper cell.'

'Nothing. I'm looking for a needle in a haystack.'

'As am I. And since we seem to be the only two aware of this, it would be far wiser to tackle it together.'

Saima pointed at his computer, her anger palpable. 'I don't trust you.'

Hashim shook his head. 'Fine. I will tell you something you do not know but only if, right here and now, you swear to keep it secret.' He pointed to the canvas of Mecca behind him. 'With God as your witness, swear that what we speak of in this room will go no further.'

'If it does not put anyone's life at risk.'

'Nobody inside *this* mosque.'

Hashim didn't say any more.

Saima glanced at the painting of Mecca. She swore an oath of secrecy.

Hashim stood up and made his way to her, perching on the desk.

'You're a brave woman, Saima. Lots of heart. Guts. Determination. I saw that in the basement. Clearly, important people outside trust you, and I will too.'

Hashim told her about the emails.

She was about to protest when he raised his hand then pointed to the canvas behind him. 'Have faith,' he said, simply.

Saima struggled, went to say something but stopped. *This was too much.*

'How do we find this sleeper, so that the things I have told you do not come to pass?' Hashim retook his seat. 'I know everyone inside this mosque.'

'Everyone?'

He nodded. 'Some for many years. Some more recent.'

'Nobody new?'

'No.'

'Are you sure?'

'Why do you think I have been moving through the crowd so often? Why I am handing out food and drinks and engaging in prayer circles?'

'Could someone be hiding in the building?'

'They could. We have swept it twice. Another search is under way.'

'Have you told anyone about the sleeper?'

'There is nobody to trust.' Hashim pointed towards the grand hall. 'Somewhere down there is our shaitan, Saima. In plain view.'

Shaitan – devil.

'It's time we worked this through together because soon what I have confided in you will come to pass.'

FIFTY

AZEEZ TIGHTENED HIS GRIP on the cook, shaking her head a little as he lowered the other hand to her throat, blade only inches from her skin.

'Don't come any closer,' said Azeez.

'You're quite something, aren't you?' said Harry, calming his laughter so he could speak. He reduced the distance between them.

'You cannot stop me,' said Azeez.

'Sure I can.'

Harry focused on the cook. From near the front of the hall, a few elderly residents, those still with their marbles, shouted for Azeez to put down the knives.

'What's your name?' he asked.

'Ellie,' she said.

'Everything's going to be fine, Ellie.'

'Hey!' snapped Azeez. 'Are you fucking stupid?'

Harry nodded. 'Clearly,' he said, before facing the elderly audience. 'This will all be over in just a few minutes, folks,' he said calmly. He turned back to Azeez and started laughing again.

Azeez looked angry and confused.

Harry searched for the words, something to injure Azeez, the more offensive the better. He needed Azeez to come for him.

'Ellie, he's not going to kill you. I doubt this gay boy can do anything except bend over.'

A shift in Azeez's eyes. Slight, but Harry saw it.

'Oh yeah, I know all about you. Got your boyfriend in custody. He likes to talk. In fact,' said Harry, stepping even closer, 'he showed us some footage on his laptop and that cute little camcorder.'

He stopped talking for a moment, allowing the silence to fill in the details in Azeez's mind.

'Radical Islamic warrior likes to take it up the arse. I'm guessing you're not banking on a one-way ticket to the promised land?'

He saw Azeez's grip on the cook's hair slacken.

'I'm going to upload the shit I've seen to the net. I reckon we could go viral. What do you think?' Harry put both his hands inside his pockets, making himself as unthreatening as possible.

Azeez lowered the knife a fraction.

'I've got my hands in my pockets and *still* you're afraid to come at me?' Harry got on his knees, taking the piss.

'All those muscles. All that rage and you're afraid? Try it. Let's see just how tough you are.' Harry paused, hesitated, then forced himself to add, 'Faggot.'

What happened next was quick but Harry felt like it occurred in slow motion.

Azeez let go of Ellie, who fell to the floor at his feet. He stepped past her, face contorted, spit spraying from his lips as he cried out.

Harry clenched his fist around the pot of chilli powder in his pocket and flipped open the lid with his thumb.

Azeez was on top of Harry, knife raised, ready to strike. Harry closed his eyes and threw the powder forcefully into Azeez's face before rolling quickly away.

Azeez screamed.

Harry had learned this technique at his corner shop, seeing his father defend himself against at least three armed robbers this way. Chilli powder in a corner shop couldn't be classed as an offensive weapon, but it worked.

Harry got to his feet and watched Azeez drop both knives, hands clawing at his face.

He waited until Azeez had done all the damage he could, powder rubbed firmly into his eyes, his nose, his mouth, then picked up the knives from the floor as Isaac emerged from the kitchen.

'You OK, kid?' said Harry to Ellie, helping her up and inspecting her neck.

No wounds.

She muttered something incoherent, moving away from Harry towards the crowd of elderly residents.

Harry turned to Isaac and held up a finger. He didn't want Azeez to know Isaac was here.

There was only one way he could do this.

He picked up a chair and swung it at Azeez's head. One swift crack and he was out cold.

'He'll be fine,' Harry said in response to Isaac's concerned expression.

Harry had two of the Almukhtaroon leaders in his custody.

And ten hours to find the others.

FIFTY-ONE

HARRY PULLED THE CAR round to the rear entrance of the nursing home and opened his boot. The wound on his hand was pulsing and he thought that by now the nurse who had bitten him would have reached a police officer. It wasn't a pressing concern. She wouldn't have known the altercation was related to Almukhtaroon. Officers would record it as an opportunistic assault and with everything else happening in Bradford right now, it would be low priority.

His altercation with Azeez had happened so quickly that Isaac had not had the chance to call 999. For now, they were still in the game.

Azeez would know the location of the other two leaders of Almukhtaroon but the bastard was unlikely to crack. Harry didn't believe the 'Saviour of God' would respond well to pain. It would simply harden his resolve to die as a martyr.

'Everything calm?' Harry asked Isaac as he went back inside.

Isaac nodded. 'I can't believe he was ready to kill all those people.'

The boy appeared shell-shocked, as if the capabilities of the Almukhtaroon were only now dawning on him.

Harry put his hand on Isaac's shoulder and squeezed it. 'Now you see why we need to keep going and find the others.' They locked eyes and Isaac nodded firmly.

Isaac handed Harry a green first-aid box, nodding at his hand. 'That nurse took a chunk out of you, didn't she?'

'Hell hath no fury like a woman scared,' replied Harry, smiling, taking the box from him.

'The cook is throwing up in the other room. Support staff are with her – care workers.'

Harry sighed and opened the box. 'Is there CCTV in this place?'

Isaac shrugged.

Harry nodded for him to go check. 'Ask the staff.'

Isaac hesitated. The sound of retching coming from down the hall.

'She's throwing up, not dying,' said Harry, waving him away.

The first-aid box proved useful, some antiseptic and a bandage. 'Bingo,' whispered Harry, opening the bottle of TCP and moving to the sink. He poured it over his injured hand, wincing.

Isaac re-entered the room. 'No CCTV,' he said.

219

'Good,' said Harry, grimacing.

'That hurt?'

'No shit, Sherlock.'

'There's some paracetamol in there, too.'

'Take it with you.'

Harry pointed to a small cardboard container. 'What are those? Plastic gloves?'

Isaac nodded.

Harry lifted out a pair and shoved them in his pocket. For later.

He held out his hand and instructed Isaac how to dress it, thinking of the numerous times he'd seen Saima do this.

Saima.

He had to get her out of there.

'Pull it tighter,' said Harry as Isaac reached the end of the bandage.

Azeez was where Harry had left him, cuffed to a radiator and unconscious. He'd been out for a while now. There was a chance Harry had misjudged the blow and seriously injured him. He should have used his elbow. Harry had searched him and found no more weapons but had found a small version of the Koran in English stuffed inside Azeez's back pocket. Harry had put it in his car. He had an idea for later on.

'Here,' said Harry, struggling. 'Help me.'

Together, they lifted Azeez into the boot of his car.

Back inside, Harry went to the room where the staff were holed up. They were all young girls and all of them foreign nationals. They hadn't registered who Azeez was.

They had tried to call 999 when Azeez had first become violent, shouting and screaming incoherently, but he had stopped them. Harry assured them he would call this in but explained that, with what was happening in the city, officers might not respond until tomorrow.

Harry drove fast past police vans with flashing lights, officers in full riot gear. He tried to call Saima but his phone was showing no reception. The networks must be down again.

He saw a phone box and pulled over, killing the lights but leaving the engine running.

'What is it?' asked Isaac, looking concerned.

Ordinarily, Harry would have headed to Queensbury Tunnel, but there would be road blocks in his way. He couldn't risk it, not with Azeez in the boot. He might wake up any moment. And Harry hadn't taped his mouth shut. He needed to confirm he wasn't injured from the blow before restricting his oxygen supply.

Harry needed a secure location.

He needed Tariq Islam to pull some strings.

Tariq . . . He'd been at Bradford City football stadium earlier. The place had been evacuated. Locked down.

Harry smiled.

'Wait here,' said Harry, turning the engine off and exiting his car, heading towards the phone box.

Isaac sat quietly, watching Harry. He closed his eyes, steadied his breathing.

221

Watching Harry take down Azeez had been quite something.

There was a determination inside of Harry Virdee. It meant Isaac could not, even for a second, risk underestimating him. He'd been worried that Virdee wouldn't be able to pull this off, but they would soon be on their way to Abu-Nazir and Amelia. Using Harry as a vehicle to get to Abu-Nazir was his only shot and, with Azeez now secure, Isaac knew that all that stood between him and his leader was his ability to pretend he wanted to help Harry.

He could do that.

Harry checked the time: 20.30.

Nine and a half hours to go.

He searched his contact list, pulling up a familiar name. Ben Mitchell, Bradford City FC.

He stuck 50p in the phone booth and dialled.

Dead tone.

'Shit,' whispered Harry and tried again.

He was about to try a third time when he stopped. 'Idiot,' he hissed. The mobile networks were down. If Harry's phone wasn't working, then neither was Ben's.

Harry went back to his mobile, this time looking for the landline number.

Six rings.

Eleven.

'Hello?' said a voice.

'Ben?'

'Who's asking?'

'Harry Virdee.'

'Jesus, Harry, what's going on?' Ben sounded more angry than scared.

'Arma-fucking-geddon.'

'Tell me about it. World's gone crazy.'

'How's it where you are? Armed police? Squad cars? Is the stadium on lockdown?'

'No, Harry, it's a wasteland out here. No one about. I mean, we had the evacuation alert a few hours back, like, got everyone out, but since then I've been told to pretty much lock everything up and piss off home.'

'So, why haven't you?'

'You think I'm leaving my stadium to hooligans who think they can take the piss while the police are busy elsewhere?'

That was Ben all right. Bradford City Football Club first, everything else second.

'Are you alone?' said Harry.

'Yeah. Why?'

'I need a favour.'

'Heard that before.' Ben sounded tired but also as though he was smiling.

'Can you open up the delivery entrance for me? I need to drive my car inside. I'll explain when I get there.'

Harry looked back to the car, mood darkening.

It was time to find out what was really happening inside Isaac Wolfe's head.

FIFTY-TWO

HARRY PULLED INTO THE delivery bay of Bradford City football stadium. He watched the massive metal gates closing in his rear-view mirror, plunging the car into an eerie darkness.

'You a football fan?'

Isaac shook his head.

'Welcome to the best football club in England,' said Harry.

'Isn't this dangerous?' Isaac asked. 'We're less than a mile from City Park.' He unfastened his seatbelt.

'This place has already been evacuated, swept and signed off. Nobody is coming back here any time soon,' said Harry, switching off the ignition and waiting.

Lights flickered overhead as a stocky old-timer appeared in the doorway through to the main building.

'Come on,' said Harry. 'This is us.'

Harry walked towards Ben. Ben was now in his sixties and he'd once owned the bakery next to Harry's dad's corner shop. It had been Harry's first paid summer job, cracking eggs, mixing cake batter and – the worst part – making the filling for the meat pies. Ben pulled him into a firm embrace.

'Weird to be here when it's dead,' Harry said.

'Not for me. Open up, lock up. This is how I like it.'

Ben stepped to the side of Harry and stared at the passenger seat of the car. 'Who's the kid?'

'Helping me with enquiries about what's going down in the city.'

Harry was banking on the fact Ben wouldn't recognize Isaac. He might have seen fleeting images on the news but at least his age group didn't obsess over social media like the younger generations. Besides, the images on the news were of Isaac wearing traditional Islamic robes. He looked vastly different in Western clothing.

'Usual cop shop not good enough?'

Harry dropped his voice. 'I could do with this staying between us.'

Ben nodded and held up his hand, all five fingers spread wide, and folded his little finger and his thumb across his palm. 'I owed you five favours. We're down to three.'

'Who's counting?' said Harry, slapping him on the shoulder.

'Me. How's my boy getting on?'

Harry had got Ben's son a job on the force. He wasn't exactly cut out for police work but he was trying.

'Gareth's doing fine, I hear,' said Harry. He'd heard the opposite but there was no point hurting the old man's feelings.

Harry watched Ben's expression as Isaac got out of the car. Ben nodded at the boy, no sign he registered who he was.

Harry told Isaac to stay put and moved to the boot with Ben.

'Got a parcel in here, Ben. Don't want to freak you out so, ahead of time, I'm going to let you know this' – he pointed at the boot – 'is one of the assholes these guys who call themselves the Patriots want.'

Ben raised his eyebrows, mouth dropping open a little. He said nothing.

'We good?' said Harry.

Ben nodded. 'I trust you,' he said. 'You do whatever you need to bring this home.'

He was about to open the boot when Ben said, 'Truth be told, can't say I much disagree with what the Patriots are doing.'

Harry paused. He didn't look at Ben, afraid his face would show that he hadn't liked what he'd just heard.

'I think there's a lot of innocent people at risk,' said Harry.

He waited for a response and got none.

Harry popped the trunk.

Azeez's feet came screaming towards him and hit Harry firmly in the chest, knocking him to the ground.

Harry fell backwards and hit the floor hard, seeing Azeez trying to flip his body out of the trunk. Isaac didn't move but Ben did. He grabbed the lid of the boot and slammed it shut, the sharp edging hammering into Azeez's thighs.

There was a piercing cry but Azeez didn't stop.

Rookie mistake, Harry – should have seen that coming.

Ben hammered the boot into Azeez again but he kept coming. Ben started to retreat.

Azeez couldn't see – eyes shut tight, presumably still burning from the chilli powder. Blind and cuffed, he was hardly a threat, apart from his flailing limbs.

Harry got up and brushed himself down. 'There's an easy way and a hard way,' he said calmly. Isaac remained by the passenger-side door. Harry raised his finger to his lips, glaring for Isaac to get back in the car. He didn't want Azeez to know he was there. Harry had plans for them both.

'Fuck you,' spat Azeez, his head moving side to side, eyes still closed.

'You can walk or be carried,' said Harry, stepping closer. He touched Azeez on the arm and moved swiftly to the side as Azeez tried to headbutt him. Harry dodged it and moved behind Azeez, grabbing him around the neck with one arm, his other snaking around his body to grab his balls. Harry squeezed.

'Like I said, walk or be carried.' The potency of the

chilli powder made Harry's eyes water. He could only imagine the pain Azeez was in.

He felt Azeez's body relax. He had given in.

Harry went back to his boot and got the Koran he had found on Azeez from his laptop bag. He saw his Rolex, thoughts momentarily going to his mother and Aaron.

Focus, Harry.

Harry secured Isaac in the car using handcuffs, ignoring the kid's protests. He didn't want to burden Ben with babysitting him and, moreover, Harry needed a clear head for what he was about to do.

Bradford City Football Club had a small prison cell inside the stadium, used in times gone by when fans became out of control and stewards needed somewhere to hold them, waiting either for the match to end or the police to arrive. It was now used to store pallets of plastic water bottles.

Ben opened it up for Harry and wandered off, clearly not wanting to know more than he already did.

Harry shoved Azeez to the floor, leaving the handcuffs in place, and pulled a bottle of water from one of the cases. He poured the contents across Azeez's face, using his other hand to clean the chilli powder from his eyes. He told Azeez to open one eye at a time. Harry gently poured water over them.

'Blink as fast as you can,' he said.

It took around five minutes and at least five bottles of

water before Azeez could keep his eyes open. The whites of his eyes were red raw – almost like they were bleeding. He looked like some kind of demon.

'Can you see?'

Azeez nodded. He was breathing heavily, Harry thought more from tiredness than anything else. The anger was still there but Azeez knew he wasn't about to escape.

'Painful, no?'

'Fuck you.'

Harry put his hand in his pocket and pulled out the pot of red powder. 'Heard a story once,' he said, crouching by Azeez and keeping the chilli powder in sight. 'My old man told it to me. When he lived in India, this thief broke into his home and tried to steal some money. My grandad – head of the village – was pretty well stocked. He had a rifle and a handgun. He collared this prick but he didn't shoot him.'

Azeez stared at the chilli powder.

'They didn't put it in his eyes. They stripped him bare and rubbed it into the crack of his arse and all around his cock.' Harry laughed. 'Sadistic, right? They sat him down and hauled a massive paving slab on his lap so he couldn't move. No squirming or jumping up and down on the spot.'

Harry moved to a broken slab of rock in the corner of the room and placed the pot of chilli on it so Azeez could see it. 'Something like that anyway.' He tugged the disposable gloves he had taken from the nursing home from his other pocket and put them on the ground.

He really hoped he wouldn't need them.

Harry whistled. 'Apparently, he screamed for over three hours before he passed out.'

'Who are you?' Azeez grunted.

'I told you. A cop.'

'Cops don't act like you.'

Harry leaned back and relaxed. 'Guess I'm a little different.'

'So, you approve of what is happening in Bradford then?'

'Do you want to leave this place?' Harry ignored his question. 'I'll make you a deal.'

Azeez spat on the floor. 'I'd rather die.'

'I know. Die a martyr, all for the cause. I'm not asking you to help me find your mates.' Harry held his gaze. 'Cards on the table? I've always wanted to have a one-to-one with someone like you.'

Azeez raised his eyebrows.

'An extremist nutter.'

'You are so ill-informed. I pity you.'

Harry reached for Azeez's Koran and placed it on his lap.

'This is very simple. You tell me which page, section, chapter states that you can kill innocent people, like you were going to do back at the nursing home, and on my life I'll release you.'

FIFTY-THREE

SAIMA HAD MOVED AWAY from the grand hall into the foyer, her head throbbing.

Finding the sleeper cell was not something she was going to manage. The more she looked, the more she convinced herself she was seeing things that were not there.

Darkness was starting to set in across the city now and Imam Hashim had told the congregation he had been advised to close the shutters outside the windows. The mechanical noise of steel slowly descending across the glass was startling. Once they were closed, they would no longer be able to see what was happening outside. Saima imagined an increase in police personnel, floodlights erected and, somewhere in the darkness, plans being finalized for a full-out tactical assault should the Patriots' demands not have been realized.

Saima watched the view she was looking at slowly

vanish. With a final clang of metal Bradford disappeared. A momentary feeling of claustrophobia hit her and she hoped the finality of seeing the windows black out did not push the congregation inside the grand hall into a panic.

She was spinning her phone in her hands, thinking of Imam Hashim's emails and his explanation for them. She believed him, no question there, but was struggling with keeping it from Frost. He needed to be warned.

Could he stop it from happening?

Saima doubted it. The police were surely already at breaking point.

Harry wasn't answering his phone, no doubt up to his neck in part of the investigation. She had hoped that with her life at risk, his priority would have been keeping himself out of harm's way, focusing on being there for Aaron if this all went to hell.

She knew it was unlikely. He didn't have it in him to stand down.

Downstairs four men continued to guard the front doors. She moved into the corner of the foyer, back against the wall so she could see if she had company, and called Frost.

He answered immediately, her calls no doubt being prioritized. She spoke softly and quickly, confirming there had been no progress on the sleeper cell.

Then Saima told him why the other hundred and four mosques had not emptied.

And why Frost had less than three hours to counter it.

FIFTY-FOUR

THE JAIL CELL WAS a claustrophobic, nightmarish space. The air was close and suffocating, sweat dripping down Harry's face. He waited.

When another minute trickled by and Azeez had still said nothing, Harry took the Koran back.

'Funny that. You can't tell me where it says you can kill a room full of innocent elderly people.'

Harry held the book high and spoke a couple of lines that Saima frequently quoted to him. *'And do not kill one another, for God is indeed merciful unto you.'*

'My wife is Muslim. She recites those lines to me, usually when people like you, terrorists, do something like the shit you tried tonight.'

Harry tried again. *'The first cases to be decided among the people on the day of judgement will be those of bloodshed.'*

233

Azeez raised his head.

'Oh, you've read that bit?' said Harry.

'The bloodshed has been that of our people for many years.'

'Your people? And who are those? Homosexuals? Refugees?'

Azeez smiled. 'I know the voice of the shaitan and it is yours.'

Harry sighed. 'Profound of you. So, this devil of yours, is it him that inspires you to kill the innocent?'

'Fuck you.'

'There I was, trying to be respectful and not use bad language in the presence of your holy book. My wife would have my tongue if I disrespected it that way at home.'

'She's not a Muslim if she is married to a kaffir like you. She's a fucking slut.'

Kaffir – disbeliever.

Harry calmly placed the Koran on a stack of water. Usually he'd have knocked Azeez's teeth out for the remark but he couldn't show this weakness. Azeez would never stop if he saw it. He grabbed a bottle of water, opened it and took a long gulp, wincing that it was warm, like the humid air they were trying to breathe, the two men cramped together in that tiny space.

'Homosexuality?' said Harry, replacing the Koran in Azeez's lap. 'That allowed?'

Azeez was looking at the Koran. He remained silent.

'Not like you can hide that sort of thing, is it? I mean,

the Almighty knows everything, right? So, when you're filming your best moves with your boyfriend, he knows about it.'

Harry pointed at Azeez. 'Shall I go and fetch the laptops we got from your place? Play you a few clips? Jog your memory?'

Azeez was starting to breathe heavily. He tensed as if he were about to charge but Harry pointed to the chilli powder in the corner of the room.

'Be a good little boy and settle down.'

'What do you want?'

'To know where Abu-Nazir and Amelia are.'

'I don't know.'

'Sure you do.'

'Even if I did, I would never tell you.'

'So, you do know and you're not telling me?'

'I know my rights. I don't have to talk to you.'

'Your rights?' said Harry, bemused, unable to hide the smirk on his face. 'Now you want to talk about rights.'

'I want my fucking lawyer.'

Harry removed the Koran from Azeez's lap and walked out of the cell, placing it in the hallway out of view. It was Saima's influence, not his own superstition.

Back in the cell, he pulled the plastic gloves over his hands and grabbed the chilli powder. He moved quickly over to Azeez and tried to yank his jeans down. Azeez started to thrash. He was strong, his torso thick with muscle.

Harry couldn't manhandle him and backed off.

'I warned you. Unless you want another blast of this in your eyes, you better calm down and let this happen. If you start talking, we stop.'

Azeez was grunting with rage. Harry came closer with the pot of chilli powder. Azeez turned his face away and stopped kicking out.

Harry pulled Azeez's jeans down, then his boxers. Quickly, he flipped him over, kneeling into his back, pinning the big man to the floor. This wasn't going to be easy.

He poured chilli powder into his gloved hands.

'Last chance. Either tell me where Abu-Nazir is or I'm going to light you up from the insides.'

Harry yanked Azeez's head off the floor and got a barrage of abuse. He let go.

'Have it your way. I'm not going to lie to you – this is going to *burn*.'

FIFTY-FIVE

JOYTI CHECKED ON AARON for the third time in an hour. She was sure he would sleep right through the night but couldn't help herself checking.

She entered the living room, where Ranjit was sitting on the floor, in a dressing gown, hair loose on his shoulders. He hadn't eaten much, spoken even less and spent over an hour in the shower. When he had emerged, he had asked Joyti to do something she had not done for years. Massage his head with coconut oil and comb his hair.

Joyti sat behind him, his head in her lap, and poured oil into her palms, rubbing them together, then started to massage Ranjit's scalp. He relaxed, eyes closed.

The house was eerily quiet.

After a moment he said, 'How much of your life have I taken from you?'

'Don't say such things,' she replied, tutting.

'I have though, haven't I?'

'No.'

'You've always served my needs. Always listened to what I said. You never fought me. Even when I banished Hardeep.'

She hesitated. Joyti couldn't remember the last time her husband had said her son's name without despair or hate.

'Why ask these questions of me now?' she said, pouring more oil into her hands.

'I'm just a man, Joyti,' he said, sighing.

'I don't know what you mean.'

'I'm not as strong as you. Women have always been stronger. Stronger will. Bigger hearts. You never stop giving and men never stop taking.'

'Stop this foolish talk,' she said. 'You gave a lot to this family.'

She couldn't find a better reply.

'I ask you again, how much of your life have I taken from you? Be honest.'

Joyti thought back to the years of not having seen Hardeep. Of missing her grandchild being born. Of feeling . . . incomplete.

Ranjit grasped her hand. 'Your silence tells me I am right. Do you know what I was thinking about in the shower?'

Joyti moved her husband's face to the side and continued to massage his scalp, stroking the skin on the side of his wrinkled face. 'What?' she said.

'I was thinking why I didn't die last year when I had my heart attack.'

She tutted again. 'What has gotten into you?'

'I should have. My heart stopped for more than a minute. Until she saved my life.'

She.

Saima. He still couldn't say her name.

'She did her job,' said Joyti.

'She did more than that. She' – he paused, eyes closed – 'showed me her spirit.'

Joyti's hands stopped.

'What you saw, was it' – now she had to think carefully about her words – 'a good thing?'

Ranjit took a moment replying. 'It was,' he said.

Joyti's lip quivered. Something had changed today.

'You have stopped,' said Ranjit.

'I . . . need some more oil,' she replied, lifting the bottle.

'What is she like?' asked Ranjit. Joyti blinked back tears. Her answer had to be the right one or she might end a conversation she had never thought she would have with her husband.

'She is like Harry.'

'Go on.'

'Big heart. Loving. Tough.'

'Tough?'

'Mmm.'

'I suppose they have loved together and lost together. They would be similar.'

Ranjit raised his hands, putting them on top of his wife's, holding them where they were on his head. 'Sum her up for me in one sentence.'

'Why?' she said, feeling him squeeze her hands.

'Humour me.'

'Why only one sentence?'

'My father always told me that if you cannot sum up another person in one sentence – often one word – then that person is not to be trusted.'

Joyti thought hard. 'I will if you will do the same for me first.'

Ranjit laughed, a tired, empty sound. 'That's a good answer.'

They kept their hands holding each other's.

'I can give you one word or one sentence,' he finally said.

'You choose.'

He nodded, squeezed her hand a little harder and said, 'Pure.'

She smiled, glad he couldn't see her crying behind him. 'Charmer,' she said.

'I haven't heard you say that in a long time.'

'Because you haven't been.'

'True.'

'My turn, is it?'

He nodded.

Joyti thought of Saima. She had only really known her for the past year, their relationship still felt so new. She

knew what she was made of, what Saima was capable of. She saw that in Harry's eyes when he talked of her.

'Sacrifice,' she said finally, letting go of Ranjit's hands and resting hers on his temple, stroking it. 'Is it a good word?'

Ranjit nodded.

FIFTY-SIX

HARRY TOOK ISAAC OUT to the centre of the football pitch, a lone floodlight highlighting the stand. His eyes were drawn upwards. He could hear helicopters continuing to circle in the distance. His thoughts turned to Saima. Daylight had faded, leaving vivid streaks of purple in the sky. On any other day it would have been something to savour. Now he only wondered if the darkness would bring further complications inside the mosque.

In the far corner of the field, a solitary light was on in Ben's office, visible through the vast windows. He was busy deleting the last sixty minutes of CCTV recordings and then disabling the system. Harry had made sure of it.

Isaac appeared sullen.

'Azeez didn't tell me anything,' said Harry.

'I told you he wouldn't. Beating him up won't help.'

'I hardly touched him.'

Isaac looked at Harry and raised an eyebrow.

'I've given him something to think about but I doubt he will talk,' said Harry, resigned.

'What now then?'

'Plan B. You.'

Isaac looked confused.

'He trusts you, right?' Harry asked.

Isaac nodded.

'I'm going to throw you in the cell, hands and feet taped, but I'll leave a little slack between your wrists. You can't ask him straight out where Abu-Nazir is because he'll get suspicious. Instead, ask him for a safe location for you guys to escape to. Get *him* to offer up the information. By that time, you'll have worked your hands free, you can loosen his restraints and make a break for it.'

'You said he's in a locked jail cell.'

'I'll leave the keys in the outside of the door. One twist and you're both out. Soon as I hear the lock, I'll head in and drag you outside to teach you a lesson. From there, we'll go wherever Azeez wanted you to go.'

Isaac was nodding, his demeanour a little softer.

Harry sighed and shook his head. 'I . . . can't have you going into that cell looking as you are.'

'Huh?'

'Unmarked.'

It took a few seconds for the penny to drop.

'You see that you cannot go in unharmed?' Harry pressed his point.

243

Isaac shrugged. Harry didn't take his eyes off him, making it uncomfortable. Finally, Isaac nodded, reluctantly.

'You see that door over there?' said Harry, pointing past the boy. As soon as he turned to look, Harry punched him in the face.

FIFTY-SEVEN

HARRY BUNDLED ISAAC INTO the cell and shoved him to the floor next to Azeez, who was still handcuffed and gagged. The boy's nose was bleeding, his T-shirt stained heavily. He'd been angry, outraged, when Harry hadn't even allowed him to tend to the wound.

'Got another of your mates, Azeez,' said Harry, kicking out at Isaac and just missing. 'You don't look so good. Feel like talking yet?'

Azeez's face was pouring with sweat, the chilli no doubt now fully absorbed into his body.

Harry held up a bag of ice he had lifted from one of the freezers in the food concourse. Azeez's eyes lit up and he mumbled something incoherent into the gag around his mouth.

Harry placed the ice on the floor, inches from Azeez,

and lowered the gag, pulling back just in time to avoid being bitten.

'You fucking pig!' Azeez spat.

'I bet your ass is hotter than the sun right about now. You remembered where Abu-Nazir might be yet?' asked Harry.

Azeez swore every profanity Harry had ever heard, eyes bulging with fury. Harry could not even imagine what damage the chilli was doing to his insides. He opened the packet of ice, pulled out an ice cube and popped it in his mouth, holding it between his teeth so Azeez could see it. Harry spat it on the floor.

'Such a waste,' he said.

Harry removed another, repeated what he had done.

Azeez was panting heavily, the lower half of his body wriggling on the floor.

'You see this, Isaac,' said Harry, standing up and gesturing at Azeez. 'This is what you've got to look forward to. I'm popping out, going to buy some extra-hot chilli powder.'

Harry exited the cell and secured the door.

'Twenty minutes.' He smiled.

Isaac waited for Harry's footsteps to recede.

Alone now with Azeez, he stared at the ceiling.

He was doing the right thing.

He was sure of it.

But Isaac was tired.

He started to struggle with the tape securing his hands. There was plenty of give. Blood continued to drip from his nose.

He'd been pissed off when Harry had struck him, even more irate when he'd tripped over his own feet and hit the ground.

Whatever it took to get back to Abu-Nazir.

Azeez continued groaning like a dying man. After witnessing what Azeez had been about to do at the nursing home, Isaac found it hard to feel sorry for him.

'I'm getting us out of here,' said Isaac, playing along with Harry's instructions. 'Do you know where we will be safe?'

Azeez wasn't listening. Sweat poured down his face. He looked delirious.

It took only a few minutes for Isaac to get his hands free. He wiped the blood from his face and pinched the bridge of his nose, squeezing hard, then turned to Azeez.

'How . . . how did you . . .?' said Azeez, momentarily sobering.

Isaac couldn't free Azeez's hands but he did, for the sake of keeping this charade alive, loosen the tape around his feet.

'Ice,' said Azeez desperately, nodding towards it.

Isaac grabbed the bag.

'You need to help me,' Azeez whispered, head bent low.

Isaac was unsure. 'How?'

'Take my jeans down, open the ice and let me sit on it.'

'Do you know where Abu-Nazir is? We need to get out of here and get somewhere safe.'

Azeez shook his head. 'Don't know.' He nodded at the bag of ice. 'Open it. Help me. Quickly.'

Isaac opened the bag of ice and pulled at Azeez's jeans, hesitating at his underwear.

'My boxers. Pull them down.'

He watched as Azeez lowered himself on to the ice, letting out a sigh of relief.

'Please,' he said, nodding towards his crotch.

Isaac scooped several cubes of ice which had fallen from the bag to the floor and threw them into Azeez's lap. Azeez sighed in satisfaction.

'Well, look at you two.' Harry's voice interrupted them.

Isaac flinched as Harry entered the cell, grabbed him by his hair and dragged him to his feet.

'Slippery little bastard, aren't you? Getting out of your binding.' He threw Isaac out of the cell. 'Stay put or you know what you've got coming.'

Harry turned back to Azeez, who had his eyes closed. He seemed hardly conscious of what was going on around him.

Harry kicked at the bag of ice. 'Shall I take that with me?' he said.

Azeez opened his eyes. He looked far worse than Harry would have expected. Desperate.

It was enough.

'Well?' he asked when they were out of earshot.

'Saville Tower, Dewsbury,' Isaac said confidently.

'What?'

'That's what Azeez said.' Isaac held his gaze.

'There's no way,' replied Harry.

'That's what he said. Come to think of it, I've heard that location mentioned before.'

'Everyone knows Saville Tower. I'm not buying it. The bastard is lying. Sending us to our deaths.'

Isaac shook his head. 'He gave me a number. Said we can call Abu-Nazir once we're free to check he's still there.'

Harry punched the number into his phone. 'You remembered it in one go?

'077 is standard. Next six are a mixture of mine and my mother's dates of birth and the last two are the year I left school. Easy.'

Harry was impressed.

'It's how smart people remember information; align it with something personal. There's books written on it.'

'All right, all right. Don't get too clever.'

He wanted to trust Isaac but something here didn't add up, he could feel it.

'Saville Tower makes no sense. Even the Yorkshire police officers don't go without armed backup. I don't get it. A notorious Far Right tower block – the one location Abu-Nazir would stick out like a whore in a nunnery.'

Isaac shrugged. 'I don't get it either.'

Harry went to his car and removed the burner phone Tariq had given him earlier. He handed it to Isaac.

'I need you to confirm he's there,' said Harry.

'You don't think me calling him is going to be suspicious?'

Harry shook his head. 'You're alone. Scared. You need a secure location until all of this dies down.'

The cheap handset didn't have a speaker function. Harry dialled the number Isaac had told him before handing it over, staying close and trying to listen, but he couldn't even hear the dial tone. He made Isaac hold the phone away from his ear so he could listen.

The call connected. The timer started to count down.

'It's Isaac. I need help.'

'Where are you?' came the muffled reply.

Harry had listened to Abu-Nazir's videos on YouTube but, truthfully, it could have been anyone on the other end of the line.

'Near the football stadium. I ... need to get out of Bradford. Everyone is looking for me.'

'Are you alone?'

'Yes.'

'Azeez?'

'I'm not sure.'

'Saville Tower. Call when you arrive.'

The line went dead.

Isaac handed the phone back to Harry.

Abu-Nazir hadn't given a location in the tower, but he

wasn't stupid. He'd have eyes watching. If Isaac did arrive, his identification would be confirmed before the number of a flat was given.

It's exactly what Harry would have done.

Saville Tower? Harry kicked the wall in frustration. Something wasn't right.

But it was all he had.

FIFTY-EIGHT

POTS AND PANS.

The worst job in the kitchen but one Saima was happy to do now.

For the past hour she and Imam Hashim had been working together to check the worshippers in the mosque, desperately trying to find the sleeper cell, neither with any real notion of what to look for.

Everyone had to contribute to the night's efforts and she was happy to play her part. It brought some welcome respite from the searching. But her mind wouldn't ease.

There were several women with Saima, all of them strangers. They cleaned in silence, everyone's minds clearly elsewhere. Saima wiped sweat from her brow. At home, Harry did the washing-up. Said it gave him time to think calmly about his day. She'd never argued – having

a dishwasher husband was more than most of her friends could say.

Friends.

Her mind wandered again.

Before marrying Harry, she'd had a lot of friends. They'd grown up together, taken Koranic lessons, dodged the vicious auntie at the mosque.

After she'd married Harry, the shame had been too much for her friends and family. It had seemed easier to let everyone go.

Now, apart from her sister, Saima had mostly white friends who had no clue about everything she and Harry had been through. She wondered if Nadia had called their mother and told her what Saima had said about being sorry. Guilt was something Saima had got used to carrying but her current predicament had made it feel heavier than ever. If this siege ended badly, she wanted her conscience clear. She wanted her parents to know she had tried.

Saima said goodbye to two women who had finished their cleaning, leaving just her and one other. She hurried up. The last thing she wanted was to be left alone here. She squeezed some more washing-up liquid on to her scourer, turned the hot water on and kept scrubbing.

God only knew what Harry was doing in Bradford. He'd sacrificed so much to be with her. She worried he'd be cracking skulls, trying to bring this standoff to an end, to get her out of here alive. There had been a time when she'd known nothing of Harry's willingness to bend the

rules, of his complex relationship with his brother Ronnie, of what Ronnie did.

Maybe ignorance really was bliss.

Her stomach was tied in knots. All she wanted was for Harry to be safe. With Aaron.

Distracted, her hand found its way directly underneath the hot tap. 'Shit!' she cursed, retracting it. Skin red raw. Heat spreading up her wrist.

The lone woman left with her called out, asking if she was all right.

Saima didn't reply, instead turning off the hot water, turning the cold on and pushing her hand under it: standard scalding protocol. At times like this she was glad to be a nurse.

Fifteen minutes was protocol but she wasn't standing down here that long. Five would have to do. She timed herself: 22.25.

The woman came over to see if she was all right.

Saima didn't recognize her.

'Are you OK?' said the woman. She was wearing a burka but with her face uncovered. Wisps of black hair escaped her headscarf. Her complexion was so fair it made Saima think she might be a convert.

Saima nodded. 'Took my eye off the hot water. Just a minor scald,' she said. 'I'm Saima.'

'Maria.'

'Are you all done?'

'Thankfully.'

Maria started on Saima's remaining two pans.

'You don't have to do that,' Saima said.

'Can't leave you. Imam said not to stay alone.'

Saima was pleased. The enormous kitchen was now a ghostly space, all shadows and secrets. 'Thanks.'

'Shit day, isn't it?'

'And the rest. Do you have family outside?'

'Yes. They're freaking out.' Maria's smile was kind as she scrubbed.

Saima adjusted her hand under the tap. 'Kids?'

'Not yet. You?'

Saima couldn't stand the iciness of the water any longer and withdrew her numb hand. 'A four-year-old boy, Aaron.'

'Precious,' said Maria, turning the tap off. She grabbed a towel from the side and started drying her hands, the sleeves of her burka inching up.

Saima frowned, noticing something unusual on Maria's wrist. She stared at her a little harder. Burka. Hair covered. No visible jewellery. Saima focused again at her wrist. Maria noticed where she was looking.

'Can you pass me that towel, please?' said Saima.

Maria didn't move, a momentary thing, nothing more.

'Sure,' she said, handing it to Saima.

Saima took the towel, drying her hands. She was thinking fast. 'Couldn't do me a favour, could you?'

'Sure,' said Maria, watching Saima intently.

'Could you grab one of those bigger dishcloths and

255

wrap it around my hand like a makeshift bandage? The heat from this burn is going to needle me all night.'

A pause.

'I work in A&E. I don't want the skin to break and scar.'

Saima had to know if she'd been mistaken.

'Sure,' Maria replied, grabbing the dishcloth.

Saima raised her hand and turned her palm up.

As Maria started to dress it, Saima manoeuvred her hand so that Maria's wrist turned with hers, her sleeve moving up just enough.

'What the hell are you doing?' snapped Maria, forcefully shrugging Saima's hand away.

A whole sleeve of tattoos.

Forbidden in Islam.

Sometimes girls got a small one somewhere discreet, on the hip or back, but Saima couldn't think of anyone she knew who had a full sleeve.

'Sorry! I love tattoos but I've never had the courage to get one,' said Saima.

Maria pulled her sleeve firmly back over her wrist.

'Don't worry about the bandage,' said Saima, turning to leave. She needed to get to Imam Hashim, needed to tell him she'd potentially found their sleeper cell. 'It won't stay on long anyway.'

She felt a firm grip on her arm.

'Very clever, Saima Virdee.'

How did she know her surname?

'But you should have left this well alone.'

FIFTY-NINE

THIS IS GEMMA WILES reporting live for BBC News from the Mehraj mosque in Bradford. Darkness has been banished by several large floodlights erected around the perimeter of the mosque. The police presence here is, as you would expect, considerable, and within the last ninety minutes it has greatly expanded. Our sources tell us this is in preparation for an influx of Islamic worshippers from the other hundred and four mosques within the city, who have not officially evacuated their places of worship but intend to amass here, in Forster Square retail park, to hold a midnight vigil in a show of solidarity with the people trapped inside the Mehraj mosque. We understand senior police officials are in urgent talks with the mosques, concerned that such a large gathering could stretch police resources beyond their limit as well as provide a clear target for Far Right supporters. Social

media appears rife with examples of clashes between the Far Right and Bradford's Asian population, which, as yet, have not ignited something larger. With no leaders of Almukhtaroon in custody and a growing feeling of despair inside the city, Bradford has a difficult night ahead . . .

SIXTY

HARRY KEPT AWAY FROM the city centre, taking the route through Clayton towards Wibsey. From there he'd go via Cleckheaton towards Dewsbury. He had left Azeez bound and secured in the stadium's prison cell. Ben would be there all night but he didn't want him involved.

Harry's injured left hand was throbbing, the bite the nurse had inflicted on him starting to sing. The wound hadn't clotted yet, blood still fresh. Damn thing was too deep and needed stitches. He'd retied the bandage, pulling it tighter.

This side of Bradford seemed calm, a world away from the chaos of City Park. No flashing lights. No helicopters, armed police or tactical units. Just . . . Bradford.

'Are you OK, Harry? You don't look good.' Isaac fidgeted nervously.

'We're going to attempt to lift Abu-Nazir and hopefully

Amelia from Saville Tower. If I felt OK about that, I'd be a fool.'

'Maybe we shouldn't go. Call in the real police?'

Harry snorted. 'Real police? What the hell do you think I am?'

'I don't know, but I do know you don't act like a policeman.'

'I get the job done. That's why they asked me to round you lot up.'

Harry regretted the slip of the tongue immediately.

'Us lot?' said Isaac, contempt in his voice.

'I didn't mean it like that.'

'Yes you did.'

'Really? That's what you're going to take issue with right now?'

'"You lot." That's everything that's wrong with how the world sees Muslims.'

'Fuck off. I married one.'

'Doesn't stop you lumping us all together, though, does it?'

Harry pulled the car over, tyres screeching, and grabbed hold of Isaac.

'What the fuck do you know about how I see the world? You think I enjoy putting my life on the line knowing that if it goes south, my son might wake up tomorrow without a mother or a father?'

Harry shoved him roughly into the passenger door.

'I'm doing this so a thousand innocent Muslims don't

get incinerated, one of them my wife. I'm doing this because if that bomb goes off we'd see a new generation of nutters, all inspired to seek revenge. Do me a fucking favour and park your sanctimonious, everyone's-against-the-Muslims crap.'

Harry pulled the car back on to the road, his blood pumping.

None of this was about Isaac. It was Saima. He had no idea what was happening inside the Mehraj mosque. Harry hadn't called her, afraid it would derail his focus.

And Aaron. Was his boy OK in that house? He couldn't let himself think about it. It was too much to contemplate.

Abu-Nazir and Amelia. They were his best shot at ending this. Christ, he hoped the bitch was there with him.

The atmosphere in the car was thick.

He pulled the car over again and switched off the engine. Both of them sat in silence.

'I shouldn't have done that,' said Harry.

'It's fine,' Isaac whispered.

'We're about to enter the most dangerous estate in the north of England. This isn't the time for us to fall out.'

Isaac nodded.

Harry restarted the car and continued on their route, the atmosphere still strained.

He needed a plan. They could not just rock up at the tower.

He wished he could call in Ronnie's men. What Harry could have done with that kind of backup! But they'd

never do anything without his brother's say-so. And he still couldn't get through to him.

They entered Dewsbury in silence, Saville Tower visible ahead. Harry drove past, circled around and stopped fifty yards from the entrance to the cul-de-sac.

One way in.

One way out.

'What now?' said Isaac.

Harry switched on the burner phone Tariq had given him and handed it to Isaac. 'Call Abu-Nazir. Ask him which flat he is in.'

The conversation was short. Isaac confirmed he was a mile away and Abu-Nazir simply said, 'Flat 420,' and hung up.

Only two words spoken – impossible to say whether it had been Abu-Nazir or not. Harry pulled out his own phone, the battery dying, and Googled Saville Tower and flat 420.

It was on the top floor, meaning it afforded a sweeping view of the area.

'Stay here,' said Harry, dismayed. He removed the keys from the ignition.

'Where are you going?' said Isaac.

'For a walk.'

Outside, the day's heat continued to radiate from the tarmac as Harry walked on the road past the entrance. Saville Tower loomed large.

Harry loitered on the far side of the pavement, casually looking over at the entrance, searching for ideas.

He had once been involved in an armed raid on Saville Tower after a body had been thrown from the top floor. The operation hadn't gone well – more lives had been lost and the IPCC investigation was still ongoing.

The raid had, however, thrown up something Harry had since forgotten.

S.S. Singh Convenience.

How did an Asian-owned corner shop exist in the most Far Right block in the north?

The lights were still on. The closing time on the fascia was listed as 00.00.

Bingo.

SIXTY-ONE

ONE HOUR TO GO before the other hundred and four mosques in Bradford emptied for a planned midnight vigil near the Mehraj mosque. The game of tactical chess was on a knife edge. Frost could not stop the approximately ten thousand worshippers from convening in Forster Square, and he didn't have the manpower or resources to control such a crowd. For now, it was in the hands of police and community-liaison teams, while here, on the second floor, Frost was in a secure room with a military escort outside. With him were Tariq Islam and Commander Allen, everyone focused on a laptop computer screen.

This was it: the special ops' attempt to use the sewer systems to gain access to the basement of the Mehraj mosque. The robot had not revealed anything suspicious about the access route. Neither had two police dogs. Frost wasn't overly reassured by the canines. Water in the tunnels was

what reduced the operation's probability of success. But they were ready to give it a go.

Two teams of six men were deployed. One team would enter the basement, the other would remain on standby in the tunnels.

Frost watched the computer monitor showing the dark, confusing footage of the special ops team navigating the murky sewage tunnels underneath the city. His eyes were focused on them but his mind was running wild. It was 23.10. In fifty minutes' time, Bradford would have the sort of march on its hands that could result in chaos. His officers were strategically placed to ensure a smooth passage and stop a growing Far Right element from intervening.

He hated what was happening, but conceded it was a smart move by the Islamic community. A worldwide audience would see them unified and peacefully supporting their fellow worshippers, trapped in the worst of all nightmares. However, if the Far Right got to them, the police would lose control.

Frost didn't have any of the four leaders of Almukhtaroon in safe custody.

Saima had not been in touch with any progress from the inside.

The monitor showed the special forces team making slow, measured progress. Frost was about to ask Allen how far out they were when a loud explosion on-screen almost made his heart stop.

The visual went blank.

Commander Allen, with a radio in his ear, stepped away, asking for an urgent update.

Frost held his breath as Allen listened carefully before removing the device and turning to face him.

'The Patriots just blew the tunnel.'

SIXTY-TWO

HARRY, HEART IN MOUTH, watched Isaac enter the estate. If the kid was playing him and wanted to escape, this was his chance.

He was relieved when the boy entered the corner shop. Harry waited a couple of minutes then exited his car, heading towards the store.

The entrance to the estate had graffiti sprayed on the wall. *Christ was a white man.* It summed up the estate perfectly – too stupid to realize Christ had been Middle Eastern with a skin colour more closely aligned to Harry's.

He went to check the time, realized his watch was in the car and momentarily paused.

You've got a five-grand Rolex in your boot in the worst area in Yorkshire.

Too late for that now. He checked his phone instead: 23.03. Nothing from Saima or his mother.

Harry entered the corner shop and saw Isaac on the far side, looking at the sweets.

Sweets at the back? This place was all wrong, not least the bizarre midnight closing hour. Shelves of booze, right next to the exit. On this estate? It was an invitation to steal it. Coffee, deodorant – all the things people bought regularly were near the door, at eye level.

Harry had been raised in a corner shop; this shit was second nature.

What kind of amateur was running this place?

Mr Singh looked no older than Harry, sitting behind the counter, bright orange turban, neatly trimmed beard. No protective glass between him and the customers. Nothing to stop anyone jumping over the counter to rob him.

All wrong.

'Hey,' said Harry, taking a closer look around the store.

No CCTV cameras.

What the fuck?

Singh didn't take his attention off his mobile phone. In Harry's experience, the half-hour prior to business end was critical – prime-time for robberies. Singh didn't give a shit.

'What do you need?' asked Singh.

His voice was pure Yorkshire, just like Harry's.

'A word,' said Harry.

Isaac loitered near Harry, in the periphery of his view.

'A word? The fuck I look like to you? Citizens' advice? You're either buying or not. If not, piss off. It's late.'

As Harry got closer to the counter, prepared to push

Singh a little harder, he saw why the shop didn't have CCTV and probably why he wasn't concerned with anyone attempting to shoplift.

Two powerful-looking Alsatian dogs were sitting on the floor beside him.

Harry smiled. Smart move. One dog to chase anyone who dared to steal, one always by Singh's side.

There were many threats Harry Virdee could negotiate. Big bastard dogs were not one of them.

'Either buy something or, like I said, piss off,' said Singh, focus still on his mobile phone.

'Can you close up?' said Harry.

That got Singh's attention. He glanced at Harry. Then at Isaac. Then at his dogs. The message was clear: Harry had no control here.

'I'm Detective Harry Virdee.'

'Then you definitely ain't welcome on this estate. What are you? Stupid?' Singh stood up. The dogs stood up with him. 'You ain't got backup because it's all in Bradford, sorting out that Paki shit-storm. Anyway, if you were a detective, you'd know cops don't come into this estate without armed backup.'

The dogs started to growl.

Harry put his hand in his pocket for his identification.

'Don't bother with ID,' said Singh. 'On this estate, you can get passports so realistic, you and I could piss off to Syria without anyone giving us a second look.'

Harry folded his arms across his chest.

The dogs growled a little more.

In his periphery, Harry saw Isaac back away.

'I'm going to count to three,' said Singh. The dogs stood tall, ears raised, mouths hanging open.

Alone with Singh, Harry would have bent him in half and dropkicked him out of the store.

'One,' said Singh.

But he couldn't find a way to argue with the dogs. He turned to see Isaac almost by the front door. Clearly the kid was afraid.

'Two.'

Harry let the pause linger. He didn't think Singh was bluffing. Not on this estate.

Just as Singh opened his mouth to say 'Three', Harry leaned a fraction closer, dropped his voice and said, 'Bet the Q5 moves on this estate. What are you shifting? A thousand £10-wraps a week?'

Singh stayed silent.

'I'd hate to put a call in to Enzo and tell him you've been unhelpful. That shit finds its way to the top of the food chain, and well' – Harry glanced towards Saville Tower – 'plenty of middle-men who could run this operation. Maybe even this store. Where would you be without a supplier?'

Enzo was Ronnie's number two and a name known to only very few people. He handled the streets while Ronnie handled the business: distribution, pricing and management of heroin.

Q5 was the latest code for the pure-heroin wraps Ronnie distributed.

Singh's eyes darted around the store, panicked now.

'You think I'm bluffing? You want me to call Enzo?' said Harry, removing his phone.

'You a cop?'

Harry nodded. 'You think this shit gets moved without someone on the inside knowing?'

Singh placed one hand on each of his dogs. Both of them stopped growling.

'What the fuck are you doing here?' said Singh, still not quite sure how to proceed.

'I need your help.'

'I don't help pigs, connected or otherwise.'

'I'll get you ten per cent off your next delivery.'

Singh sniggered. 'Like you have the power to make those decisions.'

'You want to try me? I can discount it or I can hike it. And if you really piss me off, I'll cut it completely. You've got sole distribution here and you want to chance all that for your fucking ego?'

Singh didn't reply.

'Close the fucking store, lock the dogs out back and let's do what needs to be done here.'

Singh nodded towards Isaac.

Harry beckoned him over and said, 'He's with me.'

SIXTY-THREE

THEY WERE ALONE IN the kitchens.

Just as Saima had been ready to strike, Maria had pulled a small, simple-looking electronic device from her pocket and waved it at her, ordering her to sit down.

The remote was just as Frost had said it would look. Hard to believe that little thing could detonate a bomb.

Saima had followed instructions.

Maria didn't amount to much: slight, and shorter than Saima. But if Harry had taught Saima anything, it was that underestimating people was one of the most foolish things you could do.

'How did you know my surname?' asked Saima, sitting on the floor, back against the wall. Maria was standing in front of her, out of reach.

'It doesn't matter, does it?'

Saima shrugged. It was obvious there was a leak some-where in Frost's unit. 'So, what now?'

Maria stood a little taller. 'I'll tell you when you need to know. If you choose to play games, this will all end sooner than anyone wants.' She waved the remote at Saima.

'I don't believe killing a thousand innocent Muslims is going to help you and the Patriots make your point.' Saima knew her best bet was to keep talking and to keep listening. Imam Hashim would notice soon enough that she hadn't returned from the kitchens.

'Sacrifice, especially on a scale like this, will mean what we stand for cannot be ignored. Things will change.' Maria's eyes were cold.

'And what things are those?'

'Taking back control of our country.'

Saima tapped the back of her head against the wall, beating a steady rhythm to keep her brain focused. 'If we're all going to die, doesn't hurt to tell me a little bit about yourself, does it?'

'I don't think so.'

'So, what then? We just stay down here in silence?'

Saima stopped tapping her head against the wall and focused on Maria.

'In a little while, once I'm sure you understand what's at stake, we are going to go back upstairs to rejoin the crowds, and you and I are going to be close. Like sisters,

arms linked, inseparable. If you go to the toilet, I'll be handing you paper to wipe. Got it?'

Of course she did. She nodded at the remote in Maria's hand. 'You're in control here.'

'I know. And if you force my hand, I will do what I was sent here for, without hesitation.' Maria pulled a mobile phone from her pocket and waved it at Saima. 'I text every thirty minutes, code words. If anything happens to me, they will know. So don't get any stupid ideas.'

'And if you do not get the leaders of Almukhtaroon?'

Maria raised her hand, pointing upstairs. 'Then a higher power will decide our fate.'

Saima forced a laugh. 'You are threatening to kill a thousand innocent people yet you believe in God?'

'The fight for the survival of every religion on the planet has involved far more bloodshed than this. Do not be so foolish as to kid yourself into thinking death does not play a part in creating a new world order.'

Saima got to her feet slowly. 'A new world order? Is that what you're about?'

'Yes.'

'And you achieve that by persecuting Islam?'

Maria shook her head and smiled. 'You are so naive. This has nothing to do with religion. Today is simply the biggest calling card we could have created.'

Saima shoved her hands in her pockets. 'Since you seem to know everything about me, you'll know that I need to call my husband and check in.'

'Nice try.' Maria stooped, removed Saima's phone from her pocket, dropped it on the floor and stamped on it, hard enough that it shattered.

Saima let out a wounded cry.

Aaron.

Harry.

'Since we are sisters now, Saima Virdee, the only person you need to talk to is me.'

SIXTY-FOUR

HARRY AND SINGH WENT out to the storeroom, full of newspapers and stock, leaving Isaac alone in the shop. Harry was painfully aware midnight wasn't far away, leaving just over six hours to bring this thing home. He felt the pressure starting to weigh on his mind.

'I deal with Enzo,' said Singh. 'Don't know shit about you. What do you want anyway?'

'Access to the tower.'

'What the fuck for?'

'Need to lift someone.'

'Who?'

'None of your business.'

Singh moved an outer of detergent off a wooden stool and sat down, one dog sitting obediently next to him. The other had stayed in the shop with Isaac.

'You know how hard it is to live on this estate as a

brown man? I've earned my place. Got the locals' trust, built a business—'

'—based on drugs.'

'Fine. But I still created this place the hard way.'

'Bullshit,' said Harry, more forcefully than he intended. The Alsatian growled. Harry softened his tone. 'No one here's buying newspapers from you. Your booze display is mostly cheap cider. Fag sales are way down. The drugs are your lifeline. And I can take it away.'

'Get Enzo on the phone,' said Singh, his tone sharp. The dog growled a little louder, stood up.

'He's busy.'

'Then you best return when he's not.'

Harry was getting annoyed. 'If I walk out of your shop without the help I need, I promise you – I give you my fucking kasam – your business is over.'

'What do you need to know?' said Singh reluctantly.

'Not everyone can know you're a dealer or some fucker would have snitched on you by now. So how do you exist here?'

'Done time. Ain't a Paki. The tower knows the difference between me and them.'

'You mean Muslims?'

Singh smiled.

Harry didn't bite.

'If I walk out there, to the tower, how long will I last before they come for me?' said Harry.

Singh shook his head slowly. 'Which flat?'

277

'Four twenty.'

'Top floor. That's a lot of eyes to pass.'

'Can it be done?' said Harry impatiently.

Singh nodded. He was studying Harry closely.

'When I do a drop-off, I wear my yellow turban. It's bright enough anyone can see it. And I take one of the dogs with me. They all give me space, no fucker messes about. If I go for a walk with a blue turban, people scatter, hide or flush their drugs – means we've got cops on the estate.'

'Genius,' said Harry, genuinely impressed.

'I'll give you the yellow turban. Take one of the dogs. That will give you your shot. Thing is, if it gets ugly, dog's not going to protect you. Just as likely to take you down. Their loyalty is to me.'

'Come with me then,' said Harry.

Singh shook his head. 'Two of us is unusual. They'd smell a rat.'

Harry sighed heavily and nodded towards Isaac. 'That mean I can't take the kid with me?'

'You can take him. Young white kid with me wouldn't be a red flag.' Harry was thankful Isaac was fair enough to pass for white.

Harry glanced at the dog. 'He going to come without ripping me to pieces?'

'If I hand him over to you. Make it clear you're friendly.'

'Can I take him inside the tower?'

Singh shook his head. 'He won't go inside with you but

278

he will get you there. When you've reached the tower, take his lead off and push him back in the direction of the store and say my name forcefully. He'll come home. You're on your own when you come out.'

'They'll think I'm you, though, right?'

'I never walk around here without my dogs. They might notice. They ain't academic these lot but they're street smart and razor sharp with it.'

Harry covered his face with both hands and rubbed it wildly, mind throbbing, feeling tired and irritable.

'If I can make your life easier, what's it worth?' said Singh.

Harry lowered his hands. 'Easier?'

'You can get to the top floor without even entering the tower.'

'How?'

'Fire escape.'

Harry stared at him, waiting for the catch.

'There's a security code for the bottom gate that gives you access.'

Singh stopped talking.

'How much?' said Harry.

'Five grand.'

Harry laughed. 'You best try again.'

Singh stood up suddenly and pushed Harry hard enough that he hit the shelving behind him with some force. Tins of food fell to the floor and the dog barked noisily, the other running through from the shop.

Harry saw Isaac peering around the counter, alarmed. He looked apt to do a runner.

Fear invaded Harry's body. The dogs were ready to tear him to pieces.

Singh yelled for them to stand down.

'You want to rock up in here, throw Enzo's name around to get an audience with me, then ask for my help – shit that puts everything I've built here at risk. And when I want payment, you try to tell me I'm taking the piss?' Singh jabbed a finger hard into Harry's chest. 'Don't take the fucking mick with me, Harry Virdee. Either cough up five grand cash in used notes or' – he pointed towards his front door – 'get the fuck out.'

Harry was annoyed at himself. He should have seen this coming.

He could get five grand from Ronnie once this was over. He held up his hands apologetically. 'You're right—'

'Price just went up to ten.'

Harry wanted to react, mood souring. Singh was taking the piss but Harry would give this man everything he had to get Saima home safely from the Mehraj mosque.

'Fine,' he said coolly.

'I don't do credit.'

'You think I carry ten grand around with me?'

'I don't give a fuck if you do or don't.'

The dogs growled again at Singh's raised voice.

'Look, I give you my word—'

'Your word isn't worth ten grand to me.'

If the dogs hadn't been there, Harry would have been making a very different type of deal with Singh.

'I can give you a five-grand deposit now,' said Harry. 'My watch. In the car. Rolex. Brand new.'

Singh looked unsure.

'It's legit. You can Google its value.'

Singh nodded. 'Thing is, Harry, I know something about watches, so it better not be some Kirkgate-market rip-off or our deal is off and you can forget about Saville Tower.'

SIXTY-FIVE

KESH – UNCUT HAIR.

   Kara – steel bracelet.

   Kanga – the comb.

   Kaccha – cotton underwear.

   Kirpan – steel sword.

Ranjit Virdee had observed the five Ks of Sikhism. He had lived as good a life as he thought possible.

He had drunk alcohol, smoked cigarettes and allowed his faith to lapse when he had first arrived in England, desperate to make a new home for his family. The memories of partition had never allowed him to forget his bitterness towards the Muslims who had hurt him. There wasn't a single day when he didn't think about his baby brother, Charanjit. That last kiss on his cheek, feeling his skin wet with Ranjit's own tears before walking away. Was it his mother screaming or had it been him?

He couldn't remember.

Ranjit stared at the items on the dining table, blinking away tears.

Upstairs in Ranjit's home slept a little boy with the same innocence as Charanjit. The same birthmark.

The same ability to warm the coldest souls.

He raised his hands and covered his face, letting the tears come, body shaking.

What kind of a man could not embrace a four-year-old child?

What kind of monster had he become?

He was tired, so very, very tired. Ranjit didn't want to live this way any more. Was he a good Sikh or simply a bitter, twisted old man who had given priority to his 'standing' within the community rather than his role as a father?

Hatred was wrong in Sikhism. The scriptures said it, explicitly. And yet . . .

He didn't deserve life.

He didn't want it any more.

For over seven decades he had hidden the memory of Charanjit lying still and beautiful by the side of the road so deep in his soul that at times he had hoped it was nothing more than a vivid dream. He could no longer pretend.

Ranjit ran his hands through his hair, the oil Joyti had massaged into his scalp soothing. He lifted his sword from the table, his sacred kirpan, turned the blade towards his chest, then used both hands to steady it.

He didn't want this life any more. Didn't deserve it.

Whatever he was, man or monster, he was already dead inside. This was simply progression of that.

Hardeep may have betrayed him but Ranjit had inflicted that hurt on Joyti. She was a good woman, undeserving of the type of man he had become. Without him, she could live freely.

She loved their grandson, their daughter-in-law. Ranjit thought back to when he had met Saima, when she had cared for him in hospital. She had asked him for forgiveness for marrying his son. She had stretched out her hands, wanting to touch his feet and say she was sorry.

He pushed the tip of the sword against the skin of his naked chest, the steel cold.

'If you touch my feet, with your hands, I will be forced to cut them off . . .'

How could he have said such a thing when she had saved his life?

He bowed his head, closed his eyes.

Monster.

She would never forgive him. He could not ask her to.

With hands shaking, Ranjit knew this was a sin but he had already committed so many.

Tomorrow, he would not awaken.

Finally, he would be at peace.

The sound of Joyti's voice stopped him. He felt her body brushing against his shoulder as she came to his side.

'Walk away, Joyti,' he said quietly. 'You do not need to see this.'

'Open your eyes,' she replied, the touch of her hand on his head.

'I have seen all I ever want to see in this lifetime.'

'Open them, Ranjit. Now.'

Her tone stopped him. He turned to look at her.

Ranjit dropped the blade.

SIXTY-SIX

CRUNCH TIME.

Harry still couldn't be sure that Isaac was trustworthy. He might have gone along with him because he genuinely wanted to help capture Abu-Nazir and Amelia, or he might have had something else in mind altogether. At this point, Harry didn't have much choice but to trust him. He was only one step away from having the leverage Tariq Islam needed.

What happened once he delivered all four leaders of the Almukhtaroon to Tariq?

Harry didn't know.

Handing over his Rolex to Singh had not been easy. He'd made it abundantly clear to Singh that he intended to come back for it.

Singh secured his yellow turban to Harry's head. It didn't feel natural. He may have been born into a traditional Sikh family but wearing the turban felt alien.

Harry glanced at his reflection in a small, dirty mirror in the storeroom. His breath caught in his throat.

He'd always thought he looked like his mother, yet now, with the turban, he was struck by how much he looked like his father.

'Here,' said Singh, handing Harry a yellow high-visibility jacket. 'Part of the programme.'

Harry slipped it on.

'This better be how it's done,' he said, aware how easy it would be for Singh to set him up. They'd be dead men.

'It is,' said Singh flatly.

'Spotters?'

'Few and far between at this time.'

Singh grabbed Harry's hand and placed it on the dog, telling the dog firmly that Harry was going to take him for a walk. He spoke to the dog as if he were a child on a naughty step.

He clipped a lead on Oscar and handed it to Harry.

'Oscar needs to know you are in charge. There is a hierarchy with dogs. You've heard of the expression "top dog"?'

Harry nodded.

'Dogs are subservient only if they know who is top dog. That needs to be you. No need to fuck around and yell at him. You speak firmly, if needed, but he shouldn't need obvious command. As long as he feels you are in control and not afraid, you'll have no issue. Got it?'

Harry nodded.

'Don't nod like a frightened schoolgirl.'

'I got it,' said Harry firmly. He pulled a little on the lead, feeling the weight and power of the dog.

'It's five hundred yards to the tower. They'll be watching. You might hear some whistling. Four short, sharp blasts. If that happens, raise your left hand high, then lower it. Keep your fucking head down. Got it?'

'Yes,' said Harry, trying his best not to show his nerves at having Oscar on a lead. He wasn't a dog-lover. Didn't mind them but didn't trust them not to take a chunk out of his body. He'd been there several times on the job.

'When you reach the tower, take the lead off Oscar, command him to go home and make your way to the fire escape. The code is 0666, sign of the devil.'

Singh smiled. It wasn't a warm expression.

Harry didn't find it funny.

They moved into the shop, the dog pulling, its weight considerable. Harry tightened his grip on the lead. Isaac jumped out of the way, clearly also not a dog-lover.

'One thing,' said Singh, putting a firm hand on Harry's shoulder.

'What?' said Harry, turning to look at him.

'Shit goes bad in there? Don't come back here for help. Doors are locked until morning. Got it?'

Harry walked away. 'Come on, Isaac. We're done here.'

Five hundred yards to Saville Tower.

The night was still warm, meaning the youngsters from the estate were likely to be out wandering the streets.

They walked with intent, the dog on Harry's right, Isaac on his left. Oscar seemed to know exactly where he was going, head high, pace brisk.

Harry had taken his crowbar from the car and stuffed it down the front of his trousers, the lip sticking out of his waistband but easily concealed by the high-vis jacket.

The houses they passed were in a sorry state. The rendered walls were decaying, slates missing from roofs, gardens unkempt and full of rubbish. As consistent was the area's fierce allegiance to the flag of St George. There were also National Front banners: a fascist group from the eighties.

Harry spotted a used syringe lying in the gutter.

Nice place.

'Kids up ahead,' whispered Isaac.

'Head down. We walk straight past them.'

'They'll see you're not the corner-shop keeper,' said Isaac urgently.

'You give them too much credit. Singh and I are two brown men with turbans and stubble. We all look the same.'

They approached the group of teenagers, cigarettes in mouths, bottles of cider in hands, the smell of marijuana in the air.

Harry and Isaac passed them without incident. He wasn't sure if it was the presence of the dog or if Singh strolling towards the tower was just a routine occurrence. Harry imagined it was a little of both.

He relaxed as they approached the building. It loomed in front of them.

As Singh had promised, Harry heard the whistle. Four sharp blasts. He raised his left hand high then lowered it.

'You OK?' he asked Isaac. The boy nodded, clearly uneasy. Harry stooped and unfastened Oscar's lead, commanding him firmly, 'Home.'

The dog immediately ran away, leaving Harry and Isaac to hurry towards the metal staircase.

Harry punched in the code. 0666.

This better work.

He hit the green button and the metal gate clicked open.

'Come on,' said Harry, pulling Isaac in behind him.

They closed the gate and climbed the stairs, the sound of their feet echoing on the steel treads.

When they reached the first floor, Harry stopped, turned to Isaac and raised his finger to his lips. He slowed his ascent, gentler footsteps, taking them two at a time.

They were more than halfway up before they hit their first obstacle.

A young lad, maybe eighteen, pissed up and smelling strongly of marijuana, was sitting in their way, cider in hand, spliff burning on the step by his side.

'Yo, Big Singhy. Late-night fix? Someone must need that shit baaaaaaad,' he said, smiling at Harry, completely unaware he wasn't Singh.

We all look the same.

'Something like that,' said Harry, pushing past the boy, who let them pass.

They arrived quickly and without incident at the top of the tower block. Harry could hardly believe his luck.

No incidents. No drama.

The gate at the top wasn't locked. Harry nodded for Isaac to follow him and together they crept along the walkway. Harry glanced down at the estate. No one had come after them.

The door to flat 420 was unlocked.

A lapse or a trap?

They knew Isaac was coming.

Abu-Nazir was the most hunted man on the planet right now. He wasn't leaving his door unlocked. Harry tried to calm the panic rising in his chest.

'You go in first,' he said to Isaac.

The boy looked afraid and didn't move.

'They're expecting you.' Harry pulled him close. 'I'm right behind you.'

He nudged Isaac towards the door, pulling his crowbar from his jeans.

Harry followed him in, keeping close.

Two doors either side of him, both open.

Bedrooms. Empty, unlived in. Harry didn't like this. Didn't feel right.

He heard a television playing in the living room. Sky News. They were reporting, live from Bradford. And voices.

Harry grabbed Isaac and stopped him entering.

He pointed back the way they had come but Isaac didn't listen. Before Harry could stop him, he opened the living-room door and disappeared inside.

'Shit,' cursed Harry and went after him.

Two men were sitting on a couple of shitty couches. Not a care in the world.

'Isaac.' A sickly-white man stood. Ginger hair, blond beard.

Abu-Nazir.

He was dressed in Western clothing, which made sense. No way he got inside Saville Tower dressed in traditional Islamic robes.

The other man got to his feet. In his hand was a stun gun.

The weapon was not the most alarming thing.

Tyler Sudworth. Founder of the Far Right group the Pure English Society. In a room with Abu-Nazir? What the fuck was going on? Where was Amelia Rose?

'Come.' Abu-Nazir held out his arms to Isaac.

Isaac stepped into the embrace.

Sudworth slapped Isaac on the back and raised the stun gun at Harry.

Harry's eyes went wide but his feet wouldn't move. He couldn't believe what he was seeing.

'No,' said Isaac firmly and lowered Sudworth's arm.

Harry breathed a sigh of relief.

Isaac took the weapon from Sudworth.

The boy turned to face him and simply said, 'Harry Virdee, I'd like you to meet my father, Abu-Nazir.'

If Harry's jaw could have hit the floor it would have.

How the hell had he not seen it?

And Tyler Sudworth?

'You lose, Harry,' said Isaac, shooting 50,000 volts into the detective's body.

SIXTY-SEVEN

JOYTI VIRDEE HAD AARON in her arms, asleep.

Ranjit couldn't help but stare at the birthmark on Aaron's shoulder. Everything about the boy reminded him of Charanjit.

Joyti moved quickly, not allowing him to speak, lowering the sleeping boy into Ranjit's lap, forcing him to cradle him, protectively.

Ranjit had started to recoil but as soon as Aaron's warm body touched his skin, everything changed. He held his breath, afraid Aaron would wake up and start crying. He did no such thing.

Ranjit kissed the boy's forehead, then his cheek, before turning his face to stop his tears from hitting the boy.

Joyti wrapped her arms around his body, her lips on his face, whispering in his ear, 'Let it go, Ranjit. Let it go.'

He gritted his teeth, confused.

Ranjit Singh Virdee felt – alive.

Aaron was the very reincarnation of Charanjit.

Ranjit kissed his forehead again. He didn't want to let Aaron go.

Joyti sat beside him, took his face in her hands. 'Let it go,' she said again, crying silently.

'How do I do that?'

Joyti pointed to the five items on the table, touched the sword and said, 'Embrace your faith.'

'My faith got me here.'

'Foolish man,' she said bitterly.

He shook his head in disagreement.

'Who laid the very first stone of our holiest site, the Golden Temple? Do you even remember?' said Joyti.

Ranjit thought about his answer. 'It was a Muslim saint, Sai Mian Mir.' The story came back to him and his eyes widened in realization.

'Our holy book, the Guru Granth Sahib, contains the work of two Muslim saints, Sheikh Fareedji and Bhagat Kabir Ji. Partition does not change these indisputable facts, yet for so long you have focused all your pain on what happened with your family, and the wider implications of partition. Was it any easier for the Muslims making their way into the newly formed Pakistan? How many of their women laid their children to rest by the side of the road?'

This was a conversation Joyti had wanted to have with her husband for many years. Once Harry had married Saima, she had gone back to the roots of their faith.

Historically, Sikhism and Islam were more closely linked than most people realized.

'Do you remember who our very first guru, Guru Nanak's best friend was? Who accompanied him on his travels across the world?'

Ranjit shook his head but Joyti saw in his face that he knew the answer.

'Bhai Mardana Ji – a Muslim.'

Ranjit's face started to crack and she saw him desperately trying not to break down. Her play was bold, the truth hurtful, the history unquestionable.

Truth was something Ranjit had been cowering from for years.

Everything Joyti said was true but the world had changed. It was true that Sikhism's and Islam's origins were not steeped in hatred but had been polluted by, first, the partition of India and, second, the current hysteria surrounding Islam. When Ranjit arrived in this country, he had Muslim friends. They had worked together, eaten together and gone out together. The war in Kashmir, a disputed territory between Pakistan and India, had strained their relationships but they had all allowed themselves to become that way.

'I'm lost, Joyti. I don't know who I am any more.'

'You are the man I married.'

'I don't know who he is.'

'I do. A strong man who sacrificed for his family. Worked hard. Loyal. Disciplined. And now . . . lost.'

'I want to go to sleep and never awaken.'

'Look at the boy in your arms.'

'I cannot take my eyes off him. I want to wake him up. I want him to hug me, call me Grandad and put his hands on my face.'

'You can have all of those things.'

He was crying again, wiping his eyes frequently.

'She will not forgive me.'

'Say her name, Ranjit.'

'I cannot.'

'Why?'

'I just cannot,' he said, starting to lose it.

Joyti took her grandson from him, allowing Ranjit to place his head in his hands. He cried hard and painfully.

'I gave her nothing but hate. And I did hate her, Joyti, I . . . do.'

'No. You hate yourself.'

He didn't reply.

'The community shame. Honour. What people would have said. All of that created the hate. Not Saima. Tell me I am wrong.'

Still crying, he relented. 'You are right.'

'Is it better to take your own life than finally show just how strong a man you can be? It will take everything you have to create a new chapter in our lives, with this little boy at its centre. That is what our faith will give you.'

He wiped his face, eyes red, spirit broken. 'I don't know how.'

Joyti pointed to the knife on the table. 'If having a

Muslim friend was good enough for the Guru, if a Muslim laid the first stone that made our holiest site, why can a Muslim not save your life, tonight?'

He stared at her.

'That's right,' she said, kissing the side of Aaron's face. 'Our grandchild is half Muslim, half Sikh, but he is all ours. You can look on him as a true message, one steeped in history and legend. A boy to close a gap so large nobody thought it could be done. Why does he have the same birthmark as your brother had? Why does his face reduce your hate to nothing more than a memory?'

She saw the realization in his face.

He shook his head. 'I don't know what to do.'

'Do you trust me?'

'Always.'

'Come with me.'

'Where?'

'Just come.'

She walked away and Ranjit followed her.

Upstairs, Joyti laid Aaron on her bed and lay down next to him, leaving a large enough gap for Ranjit.

'You have to choose. If you lie on this bed, you leave the hate and the past standing where it is. If you turn around and leave, then tomorrow morning, even if I do not find your body slumped at that table, you will forever be dead to me because right here, right now, a choice must be made.'

Joyti stroked Aaron's face, then looked at Ranjit.

'Choose,' she said.

SIXTY-EIGHT

THE EXPLOSION IN THE sewage tunnel had put a stop to special forces' plans to enter the mosque. No one had been injured. The tunnel had collapsed a few hundred yards in front of them. It had been a measured device, just enough force to block the route but not enough to have attracted attention or caused damage above ground. It had proved one thing. The Patriots were way ahead in this game. They'd clearly had a long time to plan this and knew every move the security services would be making.

Frost was back in the command room, getting updates on the ten-thousand-strong Muslim crowd heading for Forster Square retail park. As they'd promised, the mosques had begun to empty, everyone heading for one enormous stand of solidarity in Bradford with the world's media watching. Frost had no choice but to allow the peaceful demonstration to take place.

Limited CCTV had now been restored so he had real-time feeds coming in, showing a slow procession of Islamic worshippers holding candles, happy to take up position in the retail park the police had cleared for them.

Community leaders had tried to dissuade them from marching but to no avail.

Frost wondered how hard they'd really tried. He had spoken at length with several imams, advising them that this demonstration would use police resources desperately needed elsewhere, but they knew they had extra men in from all over Yorkshire. No, this was going to happen.

He'd left Counter-Terrorism ACC Peter Weetwood and Commander Allen speaking with COBRA downstairs. They had one final tactical option left to them.

A full-out assault on the mosque.

If the clock ran down too far and the powers-that-be made the call, they would storm the building. It was risky. There were many unknowns to factor in, not least the as yet unidentified sleeper cell inside the mosque. The easiest thing was to open the doors and allow the worshippers to run. That seldom went well. With only six hours remaining and none of the leaders of Almukhtaroon in custody, Frost and other senior members of this operation, Tariq Islam included, were forced to plan for an interception that might only have a 50/50 chance at success.

Frost was hoping for one thing.

That Saima Virdee came through for him.

SIXTY-NINE

HARRY CAME TO, HANDS cuffed behind him, feet tied and what felt like masking tape across his mouth. The skin on his chest burned where Isaac had Tasered him and his brain was foggy. The throb in his hand from where the nurse had bitten him was no longer the most painful injury he had.

The living room was empty, just a small lamp in the corner throwing shadows across the floor.

A clock on the wall said 01.00.

He'd been out cold for half an hour.

Isaac had double-crossed him. He must have been planning this all along.

And Abu-Nazir was his father?

Harry had been completely blind-sided. Or had his mind been so preoccupied by Saima, Aaron and the scale of everything unravelling in Bradford that he had simply missed all the signs?

Where the fuck were they all now? If they'd left, this was over. The thought spurred him to life and he tried to move, only to find his hands cuffed to the radiator.

What about Amelia Rose – where was she?

The fog lifted from Harry's head. And what the hell had Far Right activist Tyler Sudworth been doing here with Islamic extremists? He tried to focus.

The room was bland. Two shitty grey couches, a withered armchair and a small dining table with only two chairs. The TV was an old box unit, cased in a wooden frame. No pictures on the walls. Nothing personal.

This wasn't a home, this was a meeting point.

For what, an extremist reunion? In fucking Saville Tower?

Harry dropped his chin on to his chest, waiting for an idea.

At home, he often sat on the floor, as he was now, talking to his son at eye-level. Usually it was Aaron telling Harry off for not playing right.

Harry closed his eyes, but he couldn't think of his son. It was too hard.

Of course, his brain went straight to his wife. Saima was resilient, not the type to be cowering in the corner crying or praying for salvation. He smiled. It was one of the reasons he'd married her. She possessed a fierce type of determination – never the victim, always the fighter. God, he hoped she was all right.

The handcuffs seemed to have been threaded behind a

metal pipe creeping out of the floor, connecting the radiator. There was about a foot of space, giving him a little slack. Harry wrapped his hands around the pipe and pulled at it.

Solid.

He leaned forward, using his weight.

No give at all.

He opened his eyes and looked for what was in reach but there was nothing. Just a loose socket. Electricity. He wasn't fucking around with that.

He hated the sensation of helplessness, blood pressure rising, sweat breaking across his body. Panic wasn't his thing. Harry moved his hands away from the pipe, to the radiator itself, just enough slack to get his hands behind it.

He leaned forwards and pulled.

Movement.

Harry tasted the bitter, acidic glue from the masking tape, grimaced and pulled harder. He gritted his teeth, adjusted his body and pulled again, leaning into the radiator, groaning. The handcuffs dug painfully into his skin, metal cutting sharply. Harry applied as much force as he could for as long as he could, feeling the radiator give a little before he ran out of steam.

Panting, he leaned back against the wall, light-headed. Then he adjusted his position, scrambling on to his knees and moving his feet behind him so they were touching the wall.

He pulled at the side of the radiator with everything he had, feet pushing off the wall. The cuffs screamed at his

skin. His thoughts were of home: Aaron and Saima – their faces, their smiles, the feeling of Saima lying next to him.

A burst of energy, like an electrical current, charged through his muscles and Harry screamed into the masking tape. His body collapsed forwards. He turned and saw the radiator had come off its brackets. But there was a robust metal bolt pinning the radiator to the pipe. There was no way the cuffs were going to slide away past it. All he had done was create a mess.

His thoughts were disturbed by the sound of the front door closing.

Abu-Nazir entered the room. 'Having fun, I see.' He squatted in front of Harry and tore the tape from Harry's mouth.

Harry spat at him. Abu-Nazir simply wiped it from his face before slapping Harry, much like his father might have done. 'That was rude,' he said. Abu-Nazir retreated two paces.

'They'll be coming for me,' said Harry. 'The world and his dog.'

Abu-Nazir laughed. 'Such hollow threats. Isaac told me everything. You don't know if you're a cop or a renegade. I'll tell you what you are: you're a sacrifice to try and save Bradford.'

He brought a chair over to Harry, placed it in front of him and sat down, this time remaining out of spitting distance.

'You came here to take me in so that, if it came down

to it, you could take my life to save all the people in that mosque – including your wife, I hear.'

Harry stared at him, surprised.

'The British government does not negotiate with terrorists, but then they also cannot allow a thousand people to die while the four of us go free.' Nazir laughed. 'Got to love the laws in this country. If I walked into a police station right now, I'd be the safest person in the world. Make sure enough people see me, put it out there on social media and just . . . wait. What's your gut saying? I'd be safe or traded in?'

Harry didn't answer. The government wouldn't condemn four men to death, not even if it meant saving a thousand. Tariq Islam had been right – even Abu-Nazir knew it.

'I reckon an angry ethnic mob would tear the police station apart until they got us. That might be interesting.'

'What about Tyler Sudworth?' said Harry.

Nazir's face changed. Not angry, just different. 'It was unfortunate you had to see that.'

'Not like you were hiding him. You knew we were coming.'

'I knew Isaac was.'

'Isaac knows about Tyler?'

'Of course. He's my son – he knows everything.'

Harry was confused. It must have been clear on his face.

'You still don't get it, do you, Harry?'

'Why don't you explain it to me?' Harry felt anger rising inside his chest. He pulled on the handcuffs again but in vain. 'How does the most hated religious preacher in the north get a flat in Saville Tower?'

Abu-Nazir sniggered. 'People are such fools.'

Something sparked inside of Harry, a thought so ludicrous he dismissed it before it gained traction.

'Have you read the Bible?' said Abu-Nazir.

'What?'

'Let's see how clever you really are, Detective Virdee. Tenacious, no doubt, but smart? I'm not so sure. So, to my question: have you read it?'

'No.'

'Heard of the devil?'

'Of course.'

'Could he exist if God didn't?'

Of all the conversations Harry had envisaged, this had not been one of them.

'Simple enough question, Harry. Is the existence of the devil based on the assumption of a God?'

'What?'

Abu-Nazir sniggered. 'You really are just as thick as everyone else.'

Harry glared at Abu-Nazir, confused.

'Yin and Yang. Good and bad. Two sides of the same coin or opposing forces? I guess it depends on where you stand.'

Harry frowned.

'The Far Right have a clear mandate in this country, one which exists because of Islamic fundamentalism. Without them, we would have little purpose. Little way of ensuring our message held meaning.'

Couldn't be. 'Get the fuck out,' said Harry. 'You're bluffing.'

'People so easily believe that a man with a beard and a basic grasp of Arabic who rants and raves about infidels and martyrdom could be a fundamentalist. The fact I'm white makes people take notice and want to follow me, but more importantly it keeps the Far Right strong because one of their own has crossed over to the dark side. Quite above all that, it brings in more money than you could ever imagine.'

Harry swallowed hard. 'You're telling me, that you, Abu-Nazir, leader of the Almukhtaroon Islamic fundamentalist group, are in fact a member of the Far Right?'

'Is it so hard to believe?'

'You had a child with an Asian woman.'

'The bitch was hot and I was young and stupid. When I found out she was knocked up I tried to make it work. But her family? Shit, those people are from the dark ages. Opened my eyes. Put me on the right path.'

'You are some piece of work, aren't you? And the boy? Your son?'

Abu-Nazir smiled. 'Blood is thicker than water.'

SEVENTY

THE LIGHTS IN THE grand hall had been turned off, leaving only dim lamps around the perimeter. Most people were lying down but many were still awake, sitting in small huddles, talking.

Hardly any mobile phone screens lit the darkness. Saima assumed most people's batteries were dead.

Maria was close by her side. They'd been escorted from the kitchen by two committee members sweeping the building. They hadn't noticed anything unusual.

As they passed the worshippers looking for a small, private area to rest, Saima heard the whispers from a group of men crowded around a mobile phone. The remaining hundred and four mosques in Bradford had emptied at midnight, their congregations heading for Forster Square, a few hundred metres from the Mehraj mosque. It would be one of the largest peaceful protests ever organized by the Muslim

community in England, as many as ten thousand. As Hashim himself had told Saima in his office, this was an opportunity on a global scale to show how united the Muslim community within Bradford were, and furthermore the images of thousands of Muslims in candlelit silence would be a far more powerful image to relay across the world than a mosque surrounded by military. That needed to be the defining image of this siege – not fear and isolation but hope.

Saima followed Maria to a small empty space on the floor adjacent to the female washrooms.

'You should try and get some sleep,' said Maria.

'You're kidding, aren't you?'

'Hardly. You look exhausted.'

'Keeping secrets is exhausting.'

Maria ignored the jibe and sat down, her back against the wall.

Saima took a place next to her.

'Don't you have a soul? Don't you fear God?' Saima whispered, staring into the crowd.

'I'm not here to have a theological debate with you. Either go to sleep or sit in silence.'

'Or what? You'll detonate the device?'

Maria didn't reply.

Saima pointed to a nearby group of four elderly women. 'I see them in Bradford Royal every week – the cancer department. They are not suffering, they come to give comfort to those who are. Make them tea, talk to them while they undergo chemotherapy.'

Again, nothing from Maria.

'And those,' said Saima, pointing to another group. 'They teach young women in Bradford how to sew and mend garments.'

Maria remained quiet and perfectly still, as if she were in a trance, eyes open, breathing calm. Saima thought she looked like someone about to enter a state of deep meditation.

'There are so many good people in this room. They don't deserve what you are threatening to do to them.'

They sat in silence for a while until Imam Hashim made his way over to them. Maria grasped Saima's arm, squeezing it tightly.

'Saima, I wonder if you might do me a favour?' he said, kneeling by her side.

'Of course,' she said, trying to shift her position but unable to because of Maria's grip.

'A lady needs an insulin shot. She missed her dose earlier. Could you help? She's a little confused.'

Maria tightened her hold on her arm.

'Of course,' said Saima. She looked at Maria and smiled. 'It would be weird if a nurse didn't help someone in need.'

She delivered the statement with enough bite that Maria relaxed her grip. 'I'll come with you, Saima. I can't get comfortable here.'

Saima stood up, thinking fast.

How could she tell Hashim about Maria?

The two women followed him to his office. Maria had

hold of Saima's arm again. Leaning closer as they approached the door, she hissed, 'Be smart.'

Inside the office, an elderly woman was sitting on a couch, holding an insulin pen. Saima spoke to her in Urdu.

Was this her chance?

Surely Maria wouldn't understand the language?

She glanced at Maria. She had the greatest poker-face Saima had ever seen.

Saima took the insulin pen from the woman and asked what dose she took. The old dear said she didn't know, her son always took care of it for her.

The pen contained a long-acting insulin. Saima dialled it down to a low dose and administered it. She could always give her more if needed. She sat beside her and told Maria she had to wait a few minutes to ensure the woman was all right, something she'd made up to buy time.

'I hear the gathering of the other mosques is under way,' said Saima to Hashim.

He nodded. 'Roughly ten thousand worshippers holding candles in Forster Square. Faith will see us through this dark night.'

Saima nodded, racking her brains for an idea.

'Will you get some sleep?' she asked him, with emphasis on the word 'sleep'. It was clumsy but all she could think of.

Maria made her way towards Saima.

'This looks pretty comfortable,' she said, tapping the back of the couch. 'Why don't you sleep here for a while? You must be exhausted,' she said pleasantly to Hashim.

He shook his head. 'I'm responsible here. I fear when the clock enters the final two hours, things may well become unstable.'

The elderly woman beside Saima thanked her, kissed her cheek like her mother would have done and stood up to leave. Hashim escorted her to the door, keeping it open for the other women to follow. As they left, he turned to Saima and said, 'Do we need to talk about anything?'

Maria arrived by Saima's side, within earshot of a reply. Saima sighed and said, 'No. Nothing to discuss.'

She went to leave the room, paused and had a last shot at trying to relay that Maria was the sleeper by turning to Hashim and speaking in Urdu. 'Do you think the white people of this city will be with us tonight or against us?'

It was the most measured thing she could think of in the circumstances.

Maria, though, beat Hashim to a response, taking Saima gently by the arm and replying in perfect Urdu, 'This white woman is with you and that, my friend, is all that counts.'

SEVENTY-ONE

AFTER EVERYTHING THAT HAD happened, it all came down to money.

Harry thought of the documentary he had watched of Tyler Sudworth and Abu-Nazir. They'd seemed friendly, joking about their positions – one the saviour of the Islamic world, the other of the Western world.

Like yin and yang, they were opposites. One could not exist without the other. Abu-Nazir had jump-started Tyler Sudworth's political career. And without Tyler, Abu-Nazir would not have half the media focus.

The bastards had played the system perfectly and become wealthy in the process. Membership fees for Almukhtaroon, 'donations' from sympathizers around the world. As for Tyler, he was paid huge fees for public-speaking engagements highlighting the dangers of, among others, Almukhtaroon.

Saville Tower was a place Tyler was known to frequent, home to a lawless brotherhood who would never speak to the police or media. Tyler Sudworth's very own kingdom.

'This is Tyler's place, isn't it?' said Harry.

Abu-Nazir smiled.

'When things get hot, this is your safe haven. The last place anyone would look.'

'The thing about a brilliant illusion, Harry, is that you never see it coming or figure out how it happened.'

'I don't buy it.'

'We don't need you to. Your belief doesn't pay the bills.'

'Is that what this is about?'

'That's what everything is about.'

'Bullshit.'

Abu-Nazir snapped his gaze up at Harry. 'Are you really this naive?' His tone was disdainful. 'Money makes the world go around. Religion's a close second. Wars line the coffers of governments and, on the streets, identity politics pay our wages. Tyler fights for the white people of this country, and me' – he paused – 'I fight for the persecuted.'

'You don't talk for the majority. Neither of you do.'

'We don't need to. He gets money from foreign agencies. Don't you know? Nationalism is in. Big business. He clears seven figures propelling hate speech. Not a bad way to make a living, opening your mouth.'

'You twisted son-of-a-bitch.'

'Why? Because I make a living out of filling a void?'

'You're playing with people's lives.'

'No, governments play with people's lives. I've been there. Iraq. Afghanistan. Syria. Human lives have a value, I've seen it. And it's not as much as you think.'

Harry was beginning to see just what kind of monster Abu-Nazir truly was.

Far from stupid.

Far from textbook.

Harry found a flaw in the argument and told Abu-Nazir what he had stopped Azeez from doing at the care home. 'What about that? Azeez's hatred seemed pure. Didn't seem at all like he was playing a part to me.'

'Oh, he isn't,' said Abu-Nazir, getting off his chair and walking around the room. 'The man is angry, always has been. Combine that with his confusion about his sexuality—'

'—you knew about that?'

'—of course. It fuelled his anger. I knew he'd come in handy when the time arrived. Today was that moment. He was a pawn protecting the king. He had no idea what we truly stand for.'

'You're some piece of work. How does killing a care home full of pensioners serve any purpose?'

'It would have strengthened Tyler. In turn, that strengthens me, because the backlash against all Muslims would have been profound, not just the extremists. Those disillusioned turn to me. Between us we talk to millions of people—'

315

'Millions? You arrogant prick.'

Abu-Nazir waved away Harry's remark. 'Social media, the news and our hallowed freedom-of-speech laws take care of it. This, Detective Virdee, is how you play the game these days.'

'What about the innocent people inside the mosque in Bradford?'

'A thousand Muslims die every day in other parts of the world, usually fighting each other. If that happens in Bradford in a few hours' time, I'll view it as a good day for this city.'

'You twisted fuck!' Harry lunged forward, straining at the chains of his handcuffs.

Abu-Nazir retook his seat and removed the stun gun from his pocket. 'I wonder how many times I'll need to knock you out with this before it's all over.'

'This is over for you. Now that I know, soon everyone will.'

Abu-Nazir leaned a little closer and changed the tone of his voice to mimic a news headline. 'Abu-Nazir and Tyler in secret pact!' He chuckled. 'Your claims would disappear into the bottomless news canyon. Do you have proof of these wild allegations? Because one million YouTube subscribers say I'm right and you're wrong. Fake news is everywhere, don't you know? No proof. No credibility.'

Abu-Nazir had him.

'You need to let me bring you in,' said Harry. He saw no other way out of this. 'Like you said, you'll be safe there.'

'Don't be stupid.' Nazir pointed the stun gun at Harry. 'Time to go to sleep, there's work to be done.'

Harry could do nothing except brace himself.

'Wait,' said Isaac, entering the room and joining Abu-Nazir. 'Let me do it. I owe him a lot more than just one shot.'

Abu-Nazir handed him the gun, beaming. 'Boy's a chip off the old block.'

'Isaac, think about what you're doing,' said Harry, desperate.

Isaac smiled, crossing the room to bend low over Harry.

'You read my sketches but you didn't understand them, did you?' he whispered.

His brow was furrowed in anger. Harry recoiled.

'Isiah, my hero, you think he's me?'

Harry nodded, confused.

'His nemesis – what is he called?'

Harry thought back to the sketches. 'The Undertaker.'

Isaac dropped his voice a little more, leaned closer. 'And what was Abu-Nazir's name before he converted to Islam?'

Harry thought back to the police database, the news reports, anything.

Kade Turner.

An anagram for 'Undertaker'.

'And what's the Undertaker's weakness? His Kryptonite?'

Electricity.

Harry finally understood. He thought of Isaac's bedroom – the posters of superheroes, the detailed sketches of 'Isiah' saving the world. Of his wardrobe, with

Isaac's Western clothing safely tucked away – not discarded but something to come back to at some point. Harry saw who the kid really was.

Isaac smiled, winked at Harry and got to his feet. He turned around, raised the stun gun and, this time, sent 50,000 volts into Abu-Nazir.

SEVENTY-TWO

THIS IS DOMINIC BELL, reporting live for Sky News from Bradford, where thousands of Muslims have amassed in Forster Square retail park, holding candles and chanting prayers for their fellow worshippers inside the Mehraj mosque. We are in the twelfth hour of this hostage situation, with no obvious breakthrough to report. We cannot show you live footage of the mosque but I can tell you that the police presence here continues to grow and I've seen at least four military vehicles in the area. I can tell our viewers that while skirmishes have been reported and arrests made, the feared large-scale disturbances between the Far Right and the approximately ten-thousand-strong crowd of peaceful Muslim worshippers have not, as yet, materialized. As this siege looks to enter its final few hours, we can only hope that a peaceful resolution awaits us all.

SEVENTY-THREE

HARRY STARED AT THE body of Abu-Nazir, unconscious on the floor, Isaac standing over him.

He was no stranger to fraught relationships between a father and a son but there was nothing Harry could say here.

Isaac pulled a set of keys from his father's pocket, set the stun gun on the floor and came to Harry, unable to make eye contact. He simply unlocked the cuffs and stood.

Harry scrambled to his feet as Isaac hammered several brutal kicks into Abu-Nazir's side. After the third strike, Harry made to intervene but Isaac pushed him away.

Another kick.

This time, Harry wrapped his arms around the boy and pulled him back, hard enough to lift him clean off the floor.

Isaac was crying.

Harry sat him on the chair and went across to Nazir. Satisfied he was still alive, Harry handcuffed him to the radiator where he had been, then quickly searched the rest of the house.

The first bedroom told him everything.

Earlier it had been empty but now he found an unconscious blonde woman in jeans and T-shirt on the bed, hands and feet bound with tape. She must have entered the place after they did. Perhaps a lookout, outside the flat. Harry checked her pulse. She looked a lot like the images of Amelia Rose he'd seen online. He returned to the living room, where Isaac was once again kicking the hell out of Abu-Nazir.

'Hey, hey, hey,' said Harry, pulling the kid away. 'I get it, you want him dead, but that's not how this is going to go.'

Isaac didn't resist Harry's intervention and went thundering into a chair next to a table on the other side of the room.

'I got the headlines. You want to give me some of the fine print?' said Harry.

Isaac's eyes didn't leave Abu-Nazir. Whatever this was, it ran deep.

Harry thought back to Isaac's file and to what Abu-Nazir had told him.

'Let me have a stab at this. Your father fucked off as soon as your mother got pregnant. He had no contact with

you until recently. What I need are the details that connect what just happened here.'

Isaac's body suddenly relaxed. He leaned forward, put his hands on the table, head on top of them. 'I don't know what happens now. I never thought about that part.'

Harry went to the window, peered outside. Even though the hour was late, Saville Tower was still alive.

Isaac started talking behind him. 'He's an awful human being. My mother said he always was, that's why she lied and told me he was dead. I didn't know his identity until she got cancer. Then she told me everything: how she'd moved to Bradford to get away from her community and the sense of shame, but also to escape him. He was a shit.'

Harry turned to face the boy. Isaac lifted his head from the table.

'He told me he stayed in London. Joined the army but was dishonourably discharged after a few years. The rest, well – it is what it is.'

Harry sat beside the boy. He spoke softly. 'Do you know what he was discharged for?'

'Being a coward.'

'How so?'

'Didn't tell me. Gave me some bullshit about being wounded in battle. Not a chance – there's more to it than that. And that bitch in there, Amelia, she knows. She's just like him. The fucking Rose and Fred West of identity politics.' Isaac smiled ruefully. 'You know, he told me I'd got my artistic streak from him. Said he used to sketch.

322

I started the Kade Turner/Undertaker thing soon after realizing exactly what he was. Showed him my drawings. He was too stupid to figure it out.'

He hadn't been the only one. Admittedly, it had been well hidden, but now all the drawings Harry had seen made perfect sense.

'When did you realize he was working with Tyler Sudworth?'

'Six, maybe seven months ago. He told me to sell my mum's house and give him the money so we could grow Almukhtaroon, and I agreed. I put it on the market. All he wanted was the money. I fooled him. I devoted myself to his every word, gained his trust. I always knew there would come an opportunity. You gave me that tonight.'

There was so much Harry felt he needed to say to the boy, so much Isaac probably needed to work out. That was a problem for another time. Four and a half hours until the Patriots' deadline. *Time to see this out.*

'What now?' said Isaac, going to the window, parting the curtains slightly and staring out over the feral estate.

Harry joined him. Five hundred yards to freedom.

'Now, Isaac Wolfe, we get the fuck off this estate,' he said.

SEVENTY-FOUR

HARRY HAD PUT ABU-NAZIR and Amelia on the couch in the living room. They had both come around now, their mouths gagged to stop them from screaming, hands tied in front of them. Isaac was in the kitchen. Harry needed to keep father and son apart. The less conflicted Isaac was, the better.

What mattered now was getting the hell out of Saville Tower. Harry was conscious that Tyler Sudworth might return at any point. He also wanted to call Saima and give her some hope that things might be changing, but the best thing he could do for her was to get Abu-Nazir and Amelia Rose to Tariq Islam – from there, he didn't know what would happen.

Harry had to get Abu-Nazir and Amelia to walk out of the tower without drawing attention to themselves, and to do that he needed to put one of their lives on the line.

Which one?

Harry went to the kitchen, closed the door behind him.

'How long have Nazir and Amelia been together?' he asked.

'Why?' Isaac was clearly surprised at the question.

'Do they love each other? Or are they just fucking?'

'He told me they've been together for years.' Isaac shrugged.

'So, they're solid?'

'Pretty much. Why?'

'We need to get out of here but they obviously won't come willingly. This estate will tear us to pieces if we're seen. If we put our heads down, walk hard, we are five hundred yards from freedom. At this hour, we'll pass maybe a handful of kids, all probably pissed or high.'

'Let's go then.'

Harry shook his head and nodded back towards the living room. 'I need to . . . encourage them.' He grimaced.

'Tell me, Harry.'

He told him.

'Jesus,' Isaac said, shaking his head. 'That's . . . I don't even know the right word.'

Harry nodded. He simply didn't have any other choice. Had there been only one of them, he could have thrown them over his shoulder and made a run for it – five hundred agonizing yards. But with two people and time desperately short, this was crisis mode.

'Which one?' asked Isaac.

Harry grimaced again. 'Can't do that to a woman. Does she care enough about him to put his life first?'

'I think so.'

'Really?'

'She loves him. No question.' Isaac stopped talking but Harry could tell he had something else to say. 'What if . . . you go too far? We need them . . . in one piece for later.'

It was a possibility. 'I'll play it as safe as I can.'

'Do it.'

Harry paused. 'He's your father. You sure . . . about this?'

Isaac opened a kitchen drawer, rummaged through it and handed Harry a large kitchen knife. He said nothing. Didn't need to. His face said it all.

Back in the living room, Harry crouched in front of Abu-Nazir and Amelia. He focused, building his rage, and his courage.

Saima inside the mosque.

His son alone.

City Park reduced to ruins.

One thousand innocent lives.

The couple stared at him, clearly unsure what was happening. It wasn't just the knife Harry was twisting in his hand but the blood that rushed to his head and his short and heavy breathing, as if his chest were on fire. Harry Virdee was angry.

These two were afraid of him. Exactly what he needed.

'You guys love each other?' he asked, mood souring.

Amelia made to speak, the gag muting her. Nazir too. Harry wasn't interested in conversation. The longer he knew as little as possible about them, the better. Hard decisions were coming his way. He didn't want to see the human side of either of them if he could help it.

'We're going for a walk. Out of here, down the fire escape, then across the yard to my car. Quickly and orderly. I don't intend to fail, not when I'm so close, but logic dictates you'll both try and stop me. Create a commotion. Try to run.'

Harry focused on Amelia.

'Do you love him?' he said, pointing the knife at Nazir.

She nodded. Tears streaming down her face.

Harry believed her.

'Only way I guarantee neither of you try to fuck with me is to put a clock on one of your lives. I'll give you the choice, Nazir.'

Harry brought the blade to his own face, stroking his stubble with it, eyes burning with anger.

'You want to take this for team Almukhtaroon or should she?'

His muted response sounded like he was offering himself up.

'Just a nod or a shake of the head.'

Abu-Nazir nodded.

'I'm going to cut you, Nazir. Badly. It'll need attention and if we don't reach my car quickly, you'll die.'

327

Harry held up a cloth and waved it at him. 'I'll wrap a tourniquet around the wound; give you a borrowed lease of life. It's a few hours until the Patriots' deadline expires. You won't die in that timeframe. If you fuck me around and we don't get off this estate, the last thing I'll do is rip that tourniquet off you so you don't make it either.'

Harry turned to Amelia. 'You best follow my orders. Don't think I'm not capable of doing the same to you. My wife's inside the Mehraj mosque. I'll be damned if my kid's growing up without his mother.'

Harry grabbed Abu-Nazir, who started to struggle.

Harry flashed the blade towards Amelia. 'Should I pick her instead?' he snapped.

Abu-Nazir stopped fighting it.

Then, to the sound of Amelia's muted screams, Harry raised the knife, took aim and plunged it hard into Nazir's flesh.

SEVENTY-FIVE

SAIMA WAS FIGHTING OFF sleep.

Like so many of the congregation around her, she was determined to see this through.

Maria was still by her side. Saima had watched as she typed out a message and pressed Send.

'I check in every thirty minutes, Saima. Do. Not. Test. Me.'

Saima had no way of overpowering her without the people Maria was working with finding out. Who knew what might happen then?

She needed to get Maria's identity to Frost or, at least, inform Imam Hashim. She could not let the identity of the sleeper go unknown.

But she had no phone. And she couldn't get anything out of Maria. She was guarded, controlled and focused.

Her head hurt. Every idea she conjured turned out to be a dead end.

'I need the loo,' said Saima, unable to sit still any longer. Maria pocketed her phone and got to her feet.

The washrooms were generously proportioned to allow for worshippers to wash before prayer. There were four rows of toilets, each a dozen long. The doors were all closed. Maria nodded Saima towards the row nearest the sinks.

'Keep the door open,' she whispered.

'I can't pee with you watching me,' replied Saima.

'Door open,' repeated Maria and shoved Saima towards a cubicle.

Saima didn't really need to pee. She entered the cubicle and turned to face Maria, who had both hands in her pockets, no doubt one on her mobile, the other on the device which would remote-detonate the bomb. Saima couldn't read her face, it was blank.

The two women held each other's gaze for a moment. When Saima didn't back down, Maria said, 'Fine. Door closed. You don't open it in ninety seconds, I'm coming in.'

Saima moved to close it. Just as she did, there was the sound of breaking glass at the far end of the toilets.

Maria's eyes darted to her right as Saima ran from the cubicle.

There it was again. Quieter this time.

Saima's mind went into overdrive. Either this was a rescue attempt or it was someone trying to escape. Either

way, with Maria here, one hand on her remote, she didn't like it.

At the end of the last row of cubicles, Saima stopped and saw a teenage boy holding a small marble ornament, standing on the toilet to reach the small window. Unlike so many of the larger windows, it did not have a shutter.

'No! Stop!' said Saima.

At the sound of her voice, the boy panicked and began to squeeze himself through the tiny gap, catching his bag and his clothes on the remaining glass. Saima reached out for him, jumping on to the toilet seat and managing to grab his foot.

'You can't!' she shouted. 'What about the rest of us!'

He kicked out at Saima, catching her in the chest. She fell from the toilet seat, crashing into Maria, both women hitting the floor. They landed hard. Saima's head cracked on the marble and the world started to spin. Maria gathered herself immediately, phone to her ear.

She said one word, calmly and clearly: 'Breach.'

SEVENTY-SIX

FOR ACC FROST, THOSE eight seconds after the mosque window was smashed would forever be etched on his memory.

He was called to the CCTV banks immediately, in time to hear the voice of one of the snipers over the radio.

Frost watched as a young man ran from the mosque, full-pelt towards the police cordon, head down, arms pumping furiously by his side.

He heard the voices shouting, urgent, ordering him to stop.

Frost saw the bag in his hand.

The guy kept running. He didn't hesitate.

They had clear protocols for this.

Eighty metres.

Sixty metres.

Despite their shouts, the guy wasn't stopping.

'Target acquired.'

At the sound of the sniper's warning, Frost's blood ran cold. His eyes never left the screen. If he was a hostile, if he reached the police cordon, if that resulted in any loss of life . . .

Fifty metres.

That was a lot of 'ifs'.

Forty.

More voices ordering him to stop.

Thirty.

Frost could hardly breathe, then he heard the words no Gold Commander ever wanted to hear.

'Shots fired. Man down.'

333

SEVENTY-SEVEN

THE HUMIDITY HIT HARRY as soon as they stepped out on to the dark walkway on the top floor of Saville Tower. Abu-Nazir went first, Harry just behind him, then Amelia, escorted by Isaac.

Harry had tied a tourniquet around Abu-Nazir's arm to stem the bleeding. Neither were gagged – it would draw too much attention. The wound on Abu-Nazir's arm was enough to keep them both compliant. The sooner they got out of here, the sooner it got tended to. Harry had the knife in his pocket. He'd warned them both that if they tried anything cute, he'd end this for them right now. Looking at the fear in their faces, he knew they believed he would do it.

With the yellow turban back on his head, Harry was alert to everything around him as they headed towards the fire escape.

His heart was racing.

He didn't trust Abu-Nazir or Amelia not to try something. Harry paused. Should he have gagged them? He still had time. He glanced down at the estate. The night was dark but there were signs of life on the street below. The red tip of a cigarette on the street corner, the glow of a mobile phone, the interior light in a car. No, gagging them was an obvious red flag. Harry would have to hope the threat to their lives was enough.

They reached the end of the walkway and Harry glanced back to Isaac. He didn't know what Amelia was capable of, or whether Isaac would be able to handle it.

Harry pushed Abu-Nazir towards the metal staircase, but he resisted. Harry hissed in his ear. 'Either walk or I'll throw you down and watch as you break every bone in your body.' He nudged him hard and held back a little, observing him move reluctantly.

Their pace was slower than Harry would have liked. He couldn't hurry them without drawing attention.

Halfway down, the same kid they'd met on the way up was now lying comatose, a needle and syringe by his side. He was the only person they encountered.

They hit the bottom and moved through the metal gate. Harry had allowed himself a small breath of relief but he regretted it when he saw what was up ahead. A parked car, internal lights on, suspension bouncing. Someone was having a good time. At least the two people in the car would be more interested in what they were doing than in four people walking by.

As they passed, Nazir dodged over to the car and, before Harry could stop him, he raised his leg and hammered his boot through the driver's-side window. Glass exploded, the sound deafening.

'You fucking prick,' said Harry, as Nazir dropped to the ground. Harry turned to see Amelia had followed suit and she was also now on the tarmac. Isaac looked shell-shocked. The back door of the car flew open and a young, wiry skinhead got out, pulling his jeans back on.

Nazir started to yell, nodding at the wound on his shoulder.

On the other side of the car, a young woman got out, in just a bra and short skirt. She started screaming at Harry – every curse he'd ever heard.

The tower started to wake up. Lights came on in windows. Shouts from the hallways.

Harry had badly misjudged this. He'd lost control.

Momentarily stunned, he didn't notice the young lad step over to him until he'd been punched in the stomach. He crumpled to the ground, winded.

Shadows formed silhouettes in Harry's peripheral vision.

'Oi, why's Singhy on the floor?'

'What the fuck have you done to Singh?'

The guy who had hit him searched Harry's pockets, removed the knife. 'It ain't Singhy.'

'Course it's him.'

A crowd had gathered around them.

Harry got his breath back, rolled over and scrambled to his knees. The turban fell to the floor.

Abu-Nazir shouted, sounding panicked, 'That Paki's a groomer – taking my girl for his mates. Got to stop him!'

Amelia joined in, backing up the claim.

Harry was thinking desperately of his next move.

Don't ever go into Saville Tower alone. Mandatory armed backup.

Harry didn't want to say he was a cop.

Amelia did it for him. 'That pig is fucking setting us up! Protects groomers! He's a bent copper! He raped me!' She spat towards Harry and the pantomime was complete.

The crowd started to murmur disbelief – no way a copper would come here alone, especially at night.

'Groomer!'

'Do him!'

The lad who had struck Harry, early twenties maybe, raised his hands and the crowd fell silent.

Ring leader.

He had tattoos of tears dripping from his left eye down his cheek. Stony-faced, pronounced jawline. He cocked his head to one side.

'Joe,' said the boy.

'Harry,' he replied.

'You a cop?'

Harry nodded.

'Groomer?'

'No. She's just kicking off cos she's under arrest.'

337

'What's the charges?'

'Soliciting.'

'And him?'

Harry didn't want to reveal Abu-Nazir's identity and they hadn't clocked it yet. 'Every bitch needs a hound.'

Joe sniggered and pursed his lips. 'Nobody comes into the Tower without a pass.'

'Singhy said I—'

'Singhy doesn't run this tower,' said Joe, pointing up at the building.

'And you do?' said Harry, unable to hide the smirk from his face. *You're just a boy.*

Isaac stood back, looking lost.

Harry's eyes darted between Joe and the crowd gathered around. Girls chewing gum, boys in hoodies with hands in pockets. Everyone was calm and nobody had their phone out. He'd heard that when shit kicked off in the tower, they'd learned not to film it.

'I got four tears,' said Joe, touching his face. 'One for each pig I put down.'

Harry sighed. Last thing he wanted was a fist fight.

'You wanna leave the Tower, you've got to earn it.'

'If I was white, would the rules be the same?'

'If you were white, Apu, you wouldn't have been stupid enough to try this in the first place.'

The girl who had been in the car came across to Joe. She ran her hands across Joe's chest, dragging her nails.

'Show him, baby,' she said to him.

Joe smiled and said to Harry, 'You put me down, you walk. Saville Tower rules.'

The crowd started to whoop and cheer.

Joe smiled. Touched the tears on his face.

Harry wasn't stupid. Joe had struck him hard. The kid knew what he was doing. Harry glanced at his bandaged left hand. He stood little chance.

Joe cocked his head to the side. 'You want to try, Harry, or lie down now and let the crowd have some fun?'

More jeers.

Another car pulled up beside them, its lights illuminating the area, music pumping loud. The crowd bounced to the music. They were ready for some entertainment.

A sense of despair crept over Harry.

The car's music system got cranked up, bass booming now.

Girls were dancing to the tracks, boys grinning, and all the while Joe kept smiling.

Harry pulled Isaac to one side and dropped his voice. 'This shit goes sour, take your chance and run.'

'Are you kidding? What about . . . everything else?'

'Find my colleague, DS Conway. Tell her everything.'

Harry moved towards Joe. 'Let's get this over with.'

Louder jeers from the crowd – a carnival atmosphere now. Didn't matter that across town thousands of lives were at risk. Here in Saville Tower it was all about this moment.

Joe danced to his left. The kid was light on his feet.

Harry stood firm, flexing his injured hand.

The kid flashed his fists in front of Harry, left–right jab hitting air. He smiled and touched the tattoos on his face. Four tears, one for each pig he'd put down.

Soon to be five.

SEVENTY-EIGHT

HARRY FELT A LIGHTNING-QUICK left jab followed by a thunderous right hook into his stomach. Air disappeared from his lungs. His vision blurred as he felt a third blow to his jaw. He was weightless until he hit the ground heavily.

Pain.

He struggled on to his side, air rushing back into his lungs.

Harry had expected feet to kick him when he was down but Joe had backed off. He and his girlfriend were celebrating his win.

Harry looked around. Nazir, Amelia and Isaac were still in the crowd, secured by some of Joe's entourage. He half wanted Isaac to make a run for it and get help, fearful that Joe was not a man he could beat. The only way he was getting out of this was to play dirty.

He wasn't going to die here, that was for damn sure.

Harry stood up. The crowd cheered. He massaged his side and touched his nose. His hand came away red with blood.

Joe's girl moved away and Joe smiled again.

Arrogant shit. Harry just needed to get close enough.

Joe danced around Harry, stayed out of range.

Slowly, Harry moved his right foot, pressing his toes into the ground and releasing his heel from his shoe.

Joe smiled, pearly white teeth flashing.

Harry inched closer. He threw out a left jab, slow and clumsy. Joe saw the punch coming a mile away. The crowd laughed.

Joe turned and laughed with them.

Harry flashed out another jab, his fist landing inches from Joe's face.

Before the kid could laugh at him again, he kicked out towards Joe. His shoe flew from his foot. Joe ducked.

With his opponent low and distracted, Harry lurched forward and threw as hard a punch as he could towards Joe's liver.

The kid was too quick and moved out of range.

A flash of fists.

Agony.

Blood in his mouth, tarmac under his cheek. And Joe was on top of him, angry, possessed.

Hands around Harry's neck, squeezing.

Joe's eyes were full of an anger Harry didn't understand.

The world started to fade, his life being choked out of his body. Harry could do nothing.

The music suddenly stopped.

Joe pulled his hands away, allowing Harry an urgent breath, but kept a knee on his face. The crowd parted anxiously.

Harry heard dogs.

He saw Singh standing there, both of his Alsatians on a lead, straining to break free, barking aggressively.

Joe stood up, turned towards Singh and raised his arms as if to say, *What the fuck*?

Harry rolled over, trying to breathe, scanning the crowd for Abu-Nazir, Amelia and Isaac. They were at the back, surrounded by Joe's thuggish mates.

'Got to back off, Joe,' said Singh.

'The fuck has this got to do with you, Singhy? This is Tower business.'

'That prick owes me money.'

'So?'

'So, you do what you normally do and it makes collecting impossible.'

'You want me to back off so you can collect twenty quid from this pig?'

'If it was pocket change, I wouldn't have got off my couch to come out here. He owes me first. Your debt comes later. You know that's how it is around here.'

Joe looked around for support.

'Stand down, Joe.' Singh pointed at Harry. 'He doesn't

pay then I'm ten large out. And that means prices are going to have to go up around here because I'll need my debt clearing.' Singh paused then added, 'Business is business.'

Joe's shoulders slouched. Whatever dealings he had with Singh, they were important enough that he had to back off.

'You help him get in here?' said Joe.

Singh pointed towards Abu-Nazir and Amelia. 'Those two fuckers need clearing off this estate. We don't need that kind of heat around here. That's bad business for everyone.'

'Who are they?'

'Ghosts. They were never here.'

'And if I say no?'

Singh didn't need to reply. He loosened the leads a little and both dogs bared their teeth.

Harry struggled to his feet. Each breath rattled and his nose wouldn't stop bleeding.

'OK, Singhy,' said Joe through gritted teeth. 'Pig's yours.'

SEVENTY-NINE

ABU-NAZIR AND AMELIA WERE in the back seat of Harry's car, tape Harry had got from Singh's store over their mouths. Nazir seemed to have realized the wound in his shoulder was not as critical as Harry had made out earlier.

Harry stood a little distance from his car now, trying to call Saima, news reports of a shooting at the Mehraj mosque filling him with dread. Her phone, as before, was dead.

'If anything's happened to you . . .' His words trailed off. He switched phones, reaching for the burner Tariq Islam had given him, and made the call.

Tariq answered on the first ring.

'The shooting at the mosque. What happened? Is Saima OK?'

The background noise was chaotic, clearly the Gold Command room. Tariq was evasive.

'I get it, you can't talk. Is she OK?' Harry asked again.

'Yes,' he said. 'Ops took a shot at an escapee. Can't say any more.'

Harry drew his hand across his face, suddenly exhausted. 'I've got what we need. All four. Tell the Patriots. I'll call again shortly.' He turned off the phone. He needed to think – choose what his next best move would be.

Isaac approached him, looking concerned. 'Joe beat you up pretty bad. Your mouth is still bleeding.'

It wasn't Harry's mouth that was the problem but his chest. Felt like cracked ribs. Every time he took a breath it sent pain pulsing through his body.

'Just a scratch,' replied Harry, though even his rebuttal was delivered with a wince.

Singh struck a match and lit a cigarette, the end burning a furious orange.

'Appreciate the help back there,' said Harry.

'Fuck your thanks,' replied Singh, pinching the cigarette from his lips. 'Protecting my debt. Joe puts you in a coma, I kiss my ten grand goodbye.'

'Thanks anyway. Kid was untouchable.'

'No argument there. Only way a twenty-year-old can run that place. Ain't a man in that tower gets anywhere near him.'

'Seems you can.'

Singh sniggered. 'My dogs have their own reputation. Now you best piss off.'

Harry turned to Isaac and nodded at the car. 'Get in,' he said.

'One thing,' said Singh.

Harry turned to see him holding his phone up.

A flash as he took Harry's picture. Then two more of Abu-Nazir and Amelia in the back of Harry's car.

'Perfect,' he said, checking the images and smiling.

'The fuck's that for?' said Harry, irate.

Singh flicked his cigarette to the floor and stepped away. 'You've got the most hunted bastards on the planet. Reckon this shit you're doing is off the books.' He waved his phone at Harry then put it in his pocket. 'Insurance on your debt.'

'I gave you my word; my watch.'

Singh nodded. 'Still a pig, though. And you can take a pig out of its pen but, know what? It's still dirty.'

EIGHTY

THE PATRIOTS WERE ON the line.

'This is ACC Frost.'

Less than an hour since that sniper had pulled the trigger. News outlets were running wild, speculating that one of the terrorists had been shot dead.

Mustafa Khan, the escapee, had been taken straight to hospital. The sniper had missed the critical shot, hitting him in the shoulder, taking him down, not out. He was the only earner in his family, with a pregnant wife and elderly parents. The pressure had got to him.

This was going from bad to worse. The reality was, as the deadline diminished, there would be more incidents like this.

'You tried the tunnels, Frost.' The voice was disguised, just like before. 'How did you like our little surprise down there for your men?'

348

Frost said nothing. There were four other departments listening in, he couldn't put a foot wrong.

'And now this. Is the one who escaped dead?'

Frost had a decision to make. The Patriots wanted to hear Mustafa was dead but he couldn't guarantee his organization was without leaks.

'Serious injury. The prognosis as yet unknown,' he said.

'You made the right call. Otherwise we may have had to act on it ourselves.' The voice paused. 'Do you have the four leaders of Almukhtaroon?'

'It is an ongoing operation.'

'You have three hours.'

The line went dead.

EIGHTY-ONE

INSIDE THE MOSQUE, EVERYONE who had been sleeping was now awake. An hour since the boy had been shot and everything appeared to be fracturing.

The gunshot had caused a ripple of hysteria.

The army were about to storm the mosque and everyone would die.

Because someone had escaped, the bomb would detonate.

Saima watched in horror as a surge of people, maybe two dozen strong, tried to storm the foyer from the grand hall. It sounded like they were being rebuffed and the doors were slammed shut.

Maria removed her phone and hurriedly typed a text.

Saima tried to get the phone from her. Had the enormous room not been so chaotic, someone might have seen the women engage in a struggle.

Maria swept Saima to one side and, before she knew it, Saima crumpled to the ground, unable to breathe. She hadn't even seen the blow.

Unable to move, she could do nothing except watch Maria's fingers dance across her phone before answering a call. As more people headed out of the room, Saima couldn't hear Maria's words. The phone was replaced, then Maria sat down on the floor beside Saima and said calmly, 'If they leave, this ends.'

As if the death of over a thousand people was routine.

Imam Hashim's voice boomed across the speaker system now, pleading for quiet and saying he had urgent news he needed to share with everyone.

Saima, her breath recovered, heard raised voices outside. The doors of the grand hall opened. The people who had tried to make a run for it returned, clearly irate. There were more people keeping leavers in than trying to leave themselves. For how much longer, Saima didn't know. She focused on the stage.

Hashim didn't mince his words. 'This is very simple,' he said, hands raised, tone aggressive – a different approach from before. 'If we break up in here and fall apart, we will lose. Do you not think these people want us to escape? So they can kill us all? So far we have stood together. Now, as we enter the final three hours of this standoff, we cannot – we must not – fail!'

Hashim had a remote in his hand and used it to turn on the large screen behind him, a live feed from an Arabic

news channel covering the ten-thousand-strong crowd in Forster Square, candles held high – one enormous sea of light.

'Our friends did not return home when they were able. No. They are with us and the security services outside this building are doing everything they can to end this siege. We must play our part!'

A dissenting voice from the crowd interrupted. 'Doing everything they can – killing an innocent man!'

There were wide-reaching murmurs of agreement.

'Nobody has been killed. The boy who fled was not seriously injured. We are not the only ones under extreme pressure. We have a chance here – but if we give in and leave, then we each seal our own fate and that of everyone in this room. Quite simply, we all die. At least give yourselves the best chance you can.'

He pointed to the screen again. 'Have you ever seen such a coming together of our people? Are they trying to storm the mosque in outrage? Are they engaging in fights with those Far Right protesters behind them? No. They pray for us and with us.'

Saima didn't think his words were having the impact they needed. For the first time, he looked tired and uncertain. Moreover, the congregation was now clearly divided.

Saima felt that the closer they got to 6 a.m., the greater the chance of a mass exodus.

And for the first time she started to think of having her own shot at leaving.

EIGHTY-TWO

HARRY'S RIBS HURT. HE was forced to take slow, shallow breaths of air.

He'd checked his face in the car mirror. Cut eye, bust lip, blood-crusted nose. It was a long time since Harry had been in a fight like that. He flicked his eyes to the rear-view mirror and saw Abu-Nazir and Amelia staring at him.

What now?

Isaac had asked him twice. Truthfully, Harry didn't know. Every mile he put between himself and Saville Tower should have brought some peace but he knew he was heading towards the unknown. It could all be about to get a whole lot worse.

'Where are we going?' asked Isaac.

'Back to Azeez.'

'And then?'

Harry didn't reply. He swallowed, gagging at the taste of blood in his mouth.

'Are you OK?' Isaac's voice was uncertain.

'Marvellous.'

He didn't know how to talk to the kid just now. The Patriots wouldn't care that Isaac wasn't a true extremist. They wouldn't want to hear his story.

'You're worried about what happens to me now?' Isaac asked.

Harry's head was starting to pound.

As he entered Bradford, Harry pulled off the main road, once again using the side streets to reach the football stadium.

The Patriots' words were replaying in his mind.

Sacrifices must be made.

Difficult decisions undertaken.

Harry glanced at Isaac, conflicted.

Sacrifice.

EIGHTY-THREE

BACK INSIDE THE FOOTBALL stadium, Harry pushed Abu-Nazir and Amelia into the prison cell. They'd given up protesting through the tape over their mouths by now.

Azeez sat delirious in a pool of water, the ice bag just visible underneath him.

Harry took a photo of all four of them together, Isaac holding a copy of today's newspaper they'd found dumped by the food stands in the concourse. He could hardly believe he had them all. Isaac joined him outside the cell and Harry closed the door, locking it and handing the keys to Isaac. He trusted him fully now.

'Stay here and keep an eye on this lot for me.'

Harry made his way back to the concourse and found an exhausted-looking Ben standing by his car. Harry nodded towards the large metal gates.

'On the way in, saw a first-aid sign in the window next to that exit.'

Ben nodded. 'Player treatment room.'

Harry doubled over as a bolt of agony shook his insides.

'Christ, Harry, are you OK?'

He took a moment, the world going a little dizzy. He wondered just how many ribs Joe might have cracked.

'Any painkillers in that place?'

'I reckon so.'

Harry moved towards the room, keeping his breathing short and shallow. Ben unlocked the door. Harry scoured the room, seeing a small metal cabinet fixed to the wall. It had a sticker on it: *Controlled drugs*.

'You got the key to that?'

Ben shrugged, looking a little sheepish.

'Do you?' asked Harry, more insistently.

'Only supposed to open it when the team doctor's present. Laws and all that.'

'You can say I forced you.'

Ben seemed to understand the urgency. He flicked through his keys, found the right one and opened the cabinet, stepping aside. 'I'll have to say you made me do it, Harry.'

'You do that.'

Harry found several boxes of tablets and a bottle of liquid. He snatched at the bottle. Morphine solution 10mg/5ml. He had heard Saima speaking about the drug so many times, a common painkiller in A&E. There was also a small book in the cabinet: *Record of Administration*. He scanned

it, seeing multiple entries – players' names and the same dose repeated time and time again: 10mg/5ml, with only one entry saying 20mg/10ml.

Hell with it. He unscrewed the top. Out of the corner of his eye he saw Ben looking grave. 'I know what I'm doing,' said Harry.

He swigged a mouthful, reckoning a tad over 10ml. He was a big lad and the pain in his chest was killing him.

'What have you heard about what's happening out there?' said Harry, closing the cabinet and sticking the bottle of morphine in his pocket.

Ben looked unimpressed.

Harry waited for an answer.

'Whoever got shot outside the mosque isn't serious. Media reported on it a few minutes back.'

That was smart, thought Harry. If it were true. Quicker they dispelled the notion of a dead worshipper, or a dead terrorist, quicker the heat got taken out of this.

'Them Muslims are in Forster Square. Holding candles.'

Harry heard the disapproval.

'Far Right reckon they are making a stand too. Fucking city is going to hell.'

Sitting alone in the dugout, Harry stared into the emptiness of the stadium. The morphine was starting to kick in, the edge taken off his pain.

He had 4 per cent battery left on his phone and dialled Saima. Straight to voicemail. Again.

357

Harry put his phone away and removed the burner unit, needing to call Tariq. Only thing was, Harry didn't want to hand over control of Almukhtaroon. With the shooting outside the mosque and the enormous crowd of Muslim worshippers in Forster Square, everything was primed for anarchy. Would it change Tariq's resolve? Would he be compromised by all of this? Harry didn't trust politicians at the best of times and the Home Secretary had proved to be a slippery son-of-a-bitch. Harry wanted to speak to the Patriots himself. Christ, he'd done all the work thus far, he'd be damned if he just handed it all over. For him, this was about Saima. He dialled Tariq, who answered immediately.

'Secure?' Harry said.

'Yes. Where are you?' replied Tariq, voice shaky.

'Close. I need to speak to the Patriots. Right now.'

'Why?'

'Because I said so.'

The line went silent.

'Bradford's unravelling. If it kicks off, we all lose. Time to end this, no compromises. You've got three minutes to get me the number or I walk into a police station with all four of these bastards and end this right now. Make it a much larger headache – four dead or a thousand?' Harry hung up.

There was nothing more to say.

It was a bluff. No way had he come this far just to hand Almukhtaroon over to the police.

The phone in his hand started to ring. Harry rejected the call and typed a hurried text.

Two minutes now. Send the number.

How could he know if he was doing the right thing? How could he know Saima would come home safely? He couldn't. And he hated it.

Harry's phone beeped a text message. A phone number. Harry didn't hesitate. He called the Patriots.

An international dial-tone.

'I have what you need,' he said, wincing as a sharp bolt of pain stung his ribs.

A pause.

'Civilian or security?' The voice was disguised.

'Civilian,' said Harry, afraid if he said he was on the force it might complicate things.

'We require photographic proof.'

'I have it.'

Harry was given another number to text the picture to and did so quickly.

The call disconnected.

He closed his eyes, focusing on the pain – his face, his ribs, his hands – anything not to think about Saima and what was happening inside the mosque.

He jumped at the noise of his phone ringing.

'Are you willing to kill them?'

Harry considered his response. 'I—'

'Either they die or everyone inside the mosque dies. If you won't decide, we'll put it to the people. You have ninety minutes.'

The line went dead.

EIGHTY-FOUR

IT ALL CAME DOWN to this. Four lives against a thousand. Just as Tariq Islam had said it would.

Harry had wanted control. Now he had it.

Isaac was the problem here. A choice between the other three and a thousand inside the mosque was no choice at all.

He couldn't sit here and think about it, a decision had to be made. He walked reluctantly back towards Isaac.

Harry heard noises coming from the cell, two voices.

But they were bound and gagged. Everyone but Isaac.

Was he . . .

Harry rounded the corner, saw the cell door open, keys in the lock, Isaac crouched beside Amelia. He squeezed inside the room.

'I had to take the tape off Amelia,' Isaac said. 'She was throwing up, would have choked if I hadn't done it.'

Amelia was drained of all her colour, eyes closed.

'Shame you didn't leave it five minutes,' replied Harry. It would have made at least one decision easier for him.

'There's a complication.' Isaac dropped his gaze to the floor. Fidgeting with his hands.

Harry looked at Amelia again. Pale. Vomiting. The realization hit him.

'Go on,' he said, energy draining from his body.

'She's pregnant,' said Isaac.

EIGHTY-FIVE

NINETY MINUTES BEFORE THE deadline and ACC Frost had a nightmare on his hands – either a nightmare or a lifeline, depending on how he could swing it.

A picture had emerged on Twitter of the four leaders of Almukhtaroon, secure, alive. None of them looked to be in a good way but somebody had them.

It seemed the photo had been posted by the Patriots themselves. It was followed by something else. Frost had stared down at his phone.

We, the people of this great country, will decide the fate of Bradford. Take back control!

4 leaders of Almukhtaroon dead?	96%
1000 innocent people dead?	4%

3,650,863 votes

It was increasing every minute, the early morning hour no deterrent. The world continued to watch Bradford.

The photo had inspired another raft of calls to the Gold Command hotline. Sightings of the Almukhtaroon leaders right across the city. No way Frost's men could act on them before deadline.

Most would turn out to be dead ends.

Right now, in a small room on the second floor, no windows, no glass panels, locked away from eager ears and prying eyes, Frost, Tariq Islam and Commander David Allen were deep in conversation.

'Can we get this vote pulled?' Tariq Islam paced the floor.

'We're looking into it but it isn't a quick thing to do,' Frost responded. He hated that Tariq was in the room.

'What else?' Tariq asked.

'We try to find them,' Frost said. 'We've got people analysing the photo now. We find them and we bring them into custody. We can't sit by and let the masses vote on an execution like this.'

The social media vote could not be ignored. With each passing second thousands were voting, baying for blood.

If Frost apprehended Almukhtaroon, that would be the end of the matter. They would be put into safe custody. They had not broken any laws.

The three most powerful people in this operation had one simple decision to make.

To uphold the rule of law.

Or to break it.

EIGHTY-SIX

HARRY HAD HAULED AMELIA out into the main concourse by the food stands, freed her hands and given her some water. Isaac had followed behind.

'Easiest way for you to get out of this is to play the pregnancy card.'

She'd been crying, eyes blood-red, blonde curls stuck to her face.

'My phone,' she said meekly.

Harry removed it from his pocket.

'Turn it on. The pin is 300979. Access my diary. Thirty-first of July. Midwife appointment. In my photos, go back a week or so – you'll find a picture of me holding a positive pregnancy test. That's how I told him, Abu-Nazir. If you need more, my latest orders on Amazon will tell you the rest.'

It was all there.

'You're not even three months and you're buying baby things?'

'It's my first. I'm excited.' Her voice was flat.

'Fuck,' said Harry, slamming her phone on the counter. 'Fuck me!'

Isaac slumped in a chair.

'Take us to a police station. Let us walk inside. Wash your hands of this,' said Amelia.

'My wife's inside that mosque.'

'Is she pregnant?'

Harry didn't reply.

'Call her. Ask her what she would do.'

All he wanted was to hear Saima's voice. He swayed a little on his feet, exhausted.

'Hands,' said Harry, gesturing for Amelia to raise them.

'Who cuffs a pregnant woman?'

'Says the bitch who put us all here.'

She suddenly exploded from her seat and slapped him, hard.

It shouldn't have hurt. The blows Harry had taken from Joe had done real damage. Her slap sent a thunder-bolt through Harry's jaw into his brain. She went for it again but this time Isaac intervened before Harry could. They tussled and Harry grabbed for her, twisting one hand behind her back and slapping the cuffs on.

'This is your half-brother or sister,' she screamed at Isaac. 'Can you live with yourself knowing you condemned them to die?'

She tried to lash out again. Harry wasn't sure if she wanted to get to him or to Isaac but he stopped her.

'Sit down or I'll lie you down,' said Harry.

She slumped into the chair, eyes raging.

Harry told Isaac to back away.

God only knew what this was doing to the kid's mind. He was alone, no one left in the world, and now he had the promise of a sibling. However much he hated his father, this would surely be too much for him.

Harry reached for his phone to try Saima again when a commotion from behind drew his attention.

'Armed police!'

He turned, horrified to see half a dozen officers with MP5 machine guns rushing towards him.

Military. Not police.

This was serious.

'On your knees! Hands in the air!'

One went to Isaac, a second to Amelia. Two came for Harry.

'Down! Now!'

Christ, how had they found him?

He kept his eyes up as he lay on the floor.

Ben stood in the doorway, arms folded. Harry had believed he could trust him. So much for old friends.

This was over.

EIGHTY-SEVEN

HARRY WAS LOCKED INSIDE the prison cell with the four leaders of Almukhtaroon. They were practically on top of one another, all handcuffed and gagged, watching the military guards outside their cell.

One hour to the deadline. And no cards left to play. Harry hoped the Patriots were bluffing.

His body was tired, aching, ready to switch off, but his brain was on high alert. Voices at the end of the corridor grabbed his attention. One he recognized. Tariq Islam.

Military personnel, faces still covered, grabbed Harry by the shoulders and led him outside, locking the cell behind. He was marched down the corridor into a small, dank room where his hands were freed and the tape over his mouth removed.

'You look like hell,' said Tariq, alarmed.

'What the fuck is happening?' Harry winced with the

effort of speaking. He looked to Tariq's left, to a man in khaki he didn't recognize, and raised his eyebrows.

'This is Colonel David Allen, elite military commander.'

'So?' said Harry, massaging his ribs. The morphine seemed to be wearing off, his insides feeling like they were once again being squeezed.

'I'll leave you two to talk this through,' said Allen and left the room.

'You want to sit down? Look like you need it.'

'Get on with it,' said Harry, staying where he was.

'I understand from your mate Ben that the kid may have been helpful.'

'He isn't like them.'

Tariq nodded. 'Amelia told our guys she's pregnant. That true?'

'Seems so.'

'Fuck,' whispered Tariq.

Harry shuffled to a chair and perched on the edge. 'It's over.' *Saima.* 'Can you get the military to storm the mosque?'

Tariq shook his head. 'High probability it will blow.'

'So, we do nothing?'

Tariq sighed. 'Up until twenty minutes ago, we had a play here,' he said, nodding back the way Harry had come. 'Until Ben dialled 999 and blew this wide open.'

Harry hung his head, foolish to have thought with everything going on that Ben wouldn't have recognized

Almukhtaroon. If Harry had been in his shoes he would have done the same thing.

Harry turned towards Tariq, then back the other way, trying to find a position in which he felt slightly less pain.

'Before you came in, Allen and I shared a call with the Patriots.'

'Oh?'

Tariq closed the gap between them. 'We told them we have Almukhtaroon. That the woman is pregnant and we wouldn't bring her to the mosque.'

'The mosque?'

Tariq frowned. 'They said they'll release two hundred and fifty worshippers for each member of Almukhtaroon.'

'If you're not giving them Amelia, they'll only release seven hundred and fifty people?'

'They want the people responsible for making the UK less secure. I'm the Home Secretary, in charge of law and order, the one who tried and failed to prosecute Almukhtaroon.' He took a deep breath. 'The Patriots want four people. I'm going to take Abu-Nazir, Azeez and Isaac into the mosque and try to settle this myself.' Tariq waved his phone again at Harry. 'That's what has been agreed.'

'Who signed off on this?'

Tariq said nothing.

Harry understood. Tariq had made a deal with the military commander.

Frost didn't have a clue. He would think the Almukhta-roon had been lost to the night. Tariq, once again, was taking matters into his own hands.

'You've got a daughter,' said Harry.

'I'm betting my diplomacy works inside that mosque.'

'None of them will go willingly.'

'They won't know. Blindfolded, gagged, earplugged, handcuffed. They'll think we're doing our jobs and taking them into safe custody.'

Harry put his head in his hands. 'You can't do this.'

'If I fall with Almukhtaroon and it saves a thousand people, there's nothing better I can do with my life. Allowing a thousand Muslims to perish will ruin this country.'

Harry didn't push it any further. His thoughts, perhaps selfishly, were now on Saima.

'The mosque must have a cordon around it. How many officers on the ground? Few hundred? How the fuck are you going to get anywhere near it with your captives if Frost hasn't signed this off?'

'I don't know yet, Harry. I was hoping you might help me.'

EIGHTY-EIGHT

THIRTY MINUTES TO THE Patriots' deadline.

Harry was alone with Commander David Allen while his men, together with Tariq, got Almukhtaroon ready to leave.

What they were discussing was nothing short of mutiny.

'That's the plan,' said Harry, trying not to show Allen he was in agony.

Allen cracked his knuckles, his bulky frame seeming to fill the room. 'I've worked with my men for a decade. I know what they can deliver, and the degree of certainty. Now you want me to place all of my faith in you?'

Harry wanted to close the gap between them but didn't want to stand, afraid he'd collapse. His chest felt like it was fracturing. What he really needed was another morphine hit but the armed officers had taken the bottle from him when he'd been thrown in the cell.

'I secured Almukhtaroon. Hardly a walk in the fucking park.'

'That's what got you in this room.' Allen walked across to Harry. 'Stand up.'

Harry delayed it a second, gritting his teeth, trying to disguise it from Allen, and stood up. He stared the commander in the face.

Allen put his hands out, one on each side of Harry's ribs, and pressed lightly.

Harry collapsed on to his chair and only partially suppressed a scream. He slid off it, ending up on the floor.

He rested his head on the tiles, eyes closed, unable to look at Allen.

'You're a mess.'

Harry took a few short, shallow breaths. 'Your men took some morphine from me. Another hit and I'll be fine.'

Allen crouched by Harry's side. 'I don't doubt you're a special kind of police officer. Hell, I know a soldier when I see one. I also know when a man's beaten.'

'Help me to my feet,' said Harry.

Carefully, Allen did so.

Harry put his hands on Allen's shoulder, not just for stability but because he wanted him to know he still had something left in the tank.

'Fine, I'm hurt. Almost down, but know what keeps me going? The thought of my wife in that mosque. My kid at home and my city on its fucking knees. I'll be damned if

I let a little pain stop me now. You've heard my pitch – it's the best thing we have right now. Put me in the game. I won't let you down, sir.'

The men measured each other, Harry determined to show Allen he was able to see it through. *Bradford couldn't go down like this.*

Allen lowered Harry's hands from his shoulders. 'No commander wants to send his troops into a fifty–fifty. Know this, though, Harry. If you get to the doors and the hostages are not released, we will be forced to come in. Everything is set. I hope it doesn't come to that. I'll get you your morphine.'

Allen tried to step past Harry but he didn't move.

'The weapon I asked for? Do you have one? It's our only way in.'

A pause.

Allen nodded reluctantly and walked out of the room.

EIGHTY-NINE

HARRY SWIGGED AT THE liquid morphine.

'Easy with that stuff,' said Isaac.

Harry sealed the bottle and put it in his pocket, keeping his back towards Isaac so he couldn't see how badly he was struggling.

Broken ribs, for sure.

Outside Abu-Nazir and Azeez were being loaded into a Bradford City football van. Amelia had been left in the prison cell under armed guard.

'Did Tariq fill you in?' said Harry.

'Yes.'

'If we pull this shit off, you'll be able to sell your sketches for enough money to never work again.'

Isaac came to Harry's side. 'We need to go. Are you sure you can manage?'

Harry ignored the question. 'Did Allen show you . . .

the weapon? Are you sure you got it? This is all on you now.'

'I can do this.' He put his hand on Harry's shoulder.

Tariq entered the room, phone in hand, and waved it at Harry. 'Are you all good?'

Harry nodded. 'Make the damn call.'

NINETY

SAIMA WAS INSIDE IMAM Hashim's office with Maria.

His face said it all – how had he not noticed her?

He handed the phone back to Maria. The call had been short, the Patriots claiming Almukhtaroon were soon to be brought to the mosque and that this was over.

Maria spoke dispassionately. 'As you heard, with each member of Almukhtaroon to enter the mosque, we will release a quarter of the followers. Your job is to tell every-one this is happening, organize them and ensure they do as we say.'

Hashim sat still, stunned into silence.

Saima felt he was thinking the same thing she was: could they really make it out of here alive so easily? Just walk out?

'What about me?' she said to Maria.

'You're of no interest to me any more. You and Hashim

will be in the last group to leave. All we want is Almukhta-roon.'

'Why?' replied Saima.

Maria waved her phone at her. 'Six million votes have been cast. The people have decided.'

NINETY-ONE

THE BRADFORD CITY MINIBUS had blacked-out windows. Almukhtaroon were in the back, out of sight. Harry watched as Commander Allen raised his hand to the guard on the street. The military had control of the main route from Valley Parade stadium to the Mehraj mosque, a half-mile journey mostly straight down Midland Road. Each roadblock had stood down on Commander Allen's instruction.

They pulled up at the final blockade, the mosque directly ahead. To their left were hundreds of officers in full riot gear. It wasn't this that distracted Harry. It was the sight of thousands of people holding candles in Forster Square.

In the distance behind them, Harry could just see the Far Right protesters, placards raised.

The sound was deafening. Chants, shouts, a low hum of prayer.

Allen turned to Harry. 'Ready?'

Harry nodded.

'I need to hear it.'

'We're set,' replied Harry forcefully. The morphine hadn't properly kicked in yet but he did have a warm, calm sensation in the pit of his stomach.

Allen turned to the row of seating behind him. 'Isaac – this is it.'

The boy looked tense. 'I'm ready.'

Allen handed Isaac a white-phosphorus grenade. Same size and shape as a regular one but instead of an explosive, it would release a noxious cloud of gas, the phosphorus burning people's eyes, temporarily blinding them. It was the perfect decoy.

'You pull the pin out, hold it safe while you get past the cordon. You only replace the pin when the mosque doors open and worshippers start to emerge. If they do not come out, I will authorize a full-out assault. At that point, you'll need to run.'

Isaac nodded, trying to appear resolute.

Allen confirmed the plan with Harry then turned to Tariq. 'Anything to add?'

'No,' he said, unlocking his phone and holding it to his ear. It was time to call the Patriots.

'We are here. Bradford City football van. At the perimeter. When we get to the front of the mosque, we'll stand aside to let the worshippers out.' Tariq hung up. 'We're on. As agreed, they are going to release seven hundred

and fifty when we're at the door. The remaining two hundred and fifty worshippers will be held until we're inside the mosque. Harry, you'll wait outside and, once everyone is out, you retreat to the cordon with Allen. It's just the four of us going in.'

'Let's make this happen,' said Allen, as armed personnel approached the vehicle, weapons raised.

'God speed to you, boys,' he added, and opened his door. Isaac followed suit. The officers saw their commander and awaited instruction, weapons lowered.

That all changed the moment Isaac raised his hand, removed the pin from the grenade and shouted, 'Stand down! Or I'll drop the grenade and we all die!'

Harry was by his side, Azeez and Abu-Nazir between them, unaware of what was happening, the blindfold, gags and earplugs in place. Harry braced himself for gunshots.

Allen and Tariq raised their hands, Allen shouting at his men, 'Stand down! He has a live grenade!'

Radios crackled, officers backed away hurriedly, putting maximum distance between themselves and Isaac.

Harry heard the noise of the crowds fall away, replaced by something else . . . the murmur of uncertainty. They'd seen something change at the perimeter but the van was obscuring their view.

Allen stepped towards his men, arms raised. 'We don't have control here. Back away, allow these men through the cordon!'

Harry was holding his breath, eyes on Isaac. He leaned closer and hissed, 'Don't look at them. Focus on the front door of the mosque. Walk forward slowly.'

Isaac yelled again for everyone to back away, voice shaky, hand trembling.

They had no choice, unaware it was only a phosphorus grenade. Having pulled the pin, his hand was now effectively a dead-man's switch. If he was taken out, he'd drop the grenade and they would all die.

'Move,' hissed Tariq as a gap in the cordon opened ahead of them.

Harry knew Gold Command would be getting these images live over CCTV. Frost would be shitting himself. *How the hell had this happened?*

They would claim that Allen and his men had stormed the football club and been caught by Isaac holding a grenade. They'd been forced to stand down and obey Isaac's demands for him and his crew to enter the mosque and end the siege.

They would tell them how Isaac Wolfe had turned on Almukhtaroon.

If they saw this shit through, he would emerge a hero.

Harry had simply gone after the Almukhtaroon as instructed by his superiors. In the chaos of the night, they were banking on Frost forgetting that Harry had signed off.

And Tariq? He'd figure out his part.

Allen had joined his team now, relaying orders Harry couldn't hear, but he saw the guards lower their weapons.

He wondered how many snipers in strategic positions around the mosque currently had their weapons focused on Isaac's head.

They couldn't shoot. It would be certain death for all of them.

Isaac shouted for Allen to walk them through the cordon. They wouldn't do anything stupid with their commander at risk.

They moved quickly but in an orderly way, Allen at the front, then Harry escorting Azeez, Isaac behind him, grenade raised, and finally Tariq with Abu-Nazir. It had been Allen's decision to put Isaac in the middle so a sniper's shot was more unlikely.

Halfway, Azeez stumbled then slumped to the ground.

'No sudden movements!' yelled Allen, turning to see what had happened.

Harry couldn't drag the bastard to his feet – he didn't have the strength left to do it. Allen stepped up, lifted Azeez from the floor and dragged him along.

Harry turned to Isaac. 'You good?'

'Ready to throw up,' he replied, pale and shaky.

They arrived near the entrance of the mosque about four minutes after they had broken through the cordon. The noise behind them was incredible, as if the whole city were whispering as one.

'Here we go,' said Harry, turning to Tariq. 'Do it.'

They removed the blindfolds from Abu-Nazir and Azeez's faces and took out their earplugs. Azeez barely

knew what was going on, lost in a delirium. Nazir was a different animal. He started to struggle, realizing what was about to happen.

'Hey,' snapped Harry, stepping towards him. 'You mess this up and your wife and kid die. Back at the stadium, there's a gun at Amelia's head. Here, there's probably a dozen snipers itching to take you out, so stand the fuck down!'

Nazir's face screwed up in rage but he stopped fighting his restraints.

Tariq put his phone to his ear.

'What now?' said Harry.

'We wait,' replied Tariq.

Harry looked up. The sun had almost fully risen and he could see hundreds of armed guards, thousands of supporters and protesters in Forster Square, cameras trained on the entrance of the mosque, helicopters some distance away.

The entire world was looking at them, there on that step.

Harry checked the time on his phone: 06.00, the time the bomb should have gone off. For now, they had stopped that happening. He focused on the doors – they needed to open.

There were several clangs of metal and then the doors of the mosque were flung open and a steady stream of people started to walk hurriedly from the building, hands raised.

Harry held his breath, looking for Saima.

'It's working,' hissed Tariq, smiling.

Allen spoke hurriedly into a mic – Harry assumed it would be his team on the ground, ready to intercept the worshippers and take them into custody. They had to be certain nobody from the Patriots was among them.

It felt like an achingly long time for the seven hundred and fifty worshippers to exit.

Harry hadn't seen Saima. He'd seen many women emerge, and had assumed Imam Hashim would have prioritized getting the women out. Why hadn't Saima been among them?

Tariq's phone rang. He answered, listened to a short message then turned to Harry and Allen. 'They said that's seven fifty released. The rest when I take these three inside.'

Harry dropped his voice and leaned in to Isaac, who was shaking. 'Replace the pin in the grenade now.' Harry put a hand on his shoulder. 'I don't want you dropping that thing in there. Tariq reckons he can swing this.'

'He said he won't let them kill me.' Isaac was trying not to cry.

Harry nodded and lowered his voice to no more than a whisper so Tariq could not hear him. 'If you know it's going bad, pull the pin, throw it and run as fast as you can. You got that?'

Harry moved his body to block Isaac from the view of the crowds as he replaced the pin in the grenade. Last thing he needed was Isaac's head being taken off.

He raised his own hands above his head as he watched the four men disappear through the open door, Tariq

hesitating, turning around to face the crowd, the hundreds of camera lenses no doubt displaying this on the world's media.

It would be all over the internet in moments.

Alone now with Allen, Harry dropped his gaze to the floor as the doors reopened and another stream of people started to walk out, heads down, hands raised, pace urgent.

Whether it was the adrenaline or the morphine, it didn't matter, but Harry couldn't feel any pain as he stepped closer, watching for Saima.

'Come on, come on,' he whispered.

He glanced down the path towards the bottom, where worshippers were being searched by military personnel and ushered quickly away.

Something hit him.

The crowd.

The cameras.

The global media attention.

He glanced back to the front door, looking again for Saima.

Harry stepped a little closer to the entrance. The fact this thing might be drawing to a close gave him a sudden moment of clarity. He started to see things in a way he hadn't before. *Holy shit.*

The flow of people started to slow and, just as it ended, after a delay of no more than a few seconds, Saima Virdee stepped outside.

She saw Harry and started to run towards him.

'No!' he shouted, hands raised, alarming the few followers in front of her. 'Keep your hands up, Saima – walk slowly!'

She stopped, raised her hands and walked apprehensively towards him.

Harry patted her down quickly then threw his arms around her, kissing her.

'It's over,' he said.

She started to cry. 'God, I was so scared.'

'Harry, that's it, let's get out of here.' Allen's voice was calm and commanding.

In that moment, with his wife in his arms, and Commander Allen at his side, the noise of the past seventeen hours disappeared from his mind.

Harry Virdee understood. He had been played.

The bastard.

It was the way Tariq Islam had paused in front of the doors and turned back to the crowds, raising his hands like some sort of Messiah figure.

This had all started with Tariq Islam handing Isaac Wolfe to Harry. And now his sacrifice would be the enduring image of this siege.

Islam would be coming out of that mosque alive.

He pushed Saima towards Allen. 'Get her out of here.'

'Harry!' she said.

'Saima, I know what I'm doing. You have to trust me.'

'The hell you do,' said Allen, putting his hand on Harry.

He shrugged him away. 'Get my wife out of here.'

Harry walked to the entrance, hearing Allen dragging an outraged Saima away. Harry had been played and now, realizing his own life was not in any danger, he was going to put things right.

He opened the door and disappeared inside the Mehraj mosque.

NINETY-TWO

HARRY ENTERED THE MOSQUE calm and determined.

It was the twenty-minute warning the Patriots had given. Zero casualties in City Park. Tariq had placed himself centre stage for the whole operation, both on and off the books. Managing every angle. And just as the deadline had been reached, he had negotiated his way into the mosque after all the hostages had been released.

The question was – why?

Harry arrived in the main foyer, a spiral staircase to his left, two lifts to his right. The shutters were drawn across the floor-to-ceiling windows, blocking any snipers from seeing what was happening.

Which way?

Saima had told him the bomb was in the basement. Would Tariq have headed there? Harry needed to make a decision and fast.

He ran down the stairs. Inside the basement he found Isaac, Azeez and Abu-Nazir all out cold on the floor, hands and feet crudely secured with some sort of wire. He hurried towards them and checked for signs of life. They were all still breathing.

He found the white-phosphorus grenade in Isaac's pocket and shoved it in his own.

Suddenly he heard voices up ahead. Tariq Islam and one other.

He walked quickly towards them, rounding the corner to find an enormous wooden box, the bomb nestled inside.

'You should have stayed outside, Harry,' Tariq said.

Tariq stood with a young white woman.

She had to be one of the Patriots.

'You better start talking, and fast, Tariq,' said Harry.

Tariq shook his head, dismayed. 'Search him for a weapon and a phone.'

Harry removed the grenade from his pocket and pulled the pin, holding it high. 'Try it.'

Tariq frowned. 'Really?'

'You put me through hell, for what?'

'Put the pin back in and I'll tell you.'

Harry did no such thing. 'Tell me now.'

'It's a white-phosphorus grenade, Harry. It's not going to kill us.'

'Maybe. But it'll put you down while I cuff you both.'

Harry pointed at the bomb, the large screen displaying a timer that had stopped with only six seconds remaining.

'Start talking,' said Harry.

'This is Maria. She's a member of Group-13. One of my most trusted officers.'

'*Your* officers?'

'You never leave Group-13.'

Harry lowered his arm but kept his fist squeezed around the grenade, the pin still pulled.

'Power, Harry. That's what this is about. When I walk out of here, I'll be the hero of this saga, the most recognized face on the planet. It all but guarantees me the Prime Minister's job.'

Harry crept closer, eyes scanning the floor space for options and finding none.

'Power? Being Prime Minister doesn't buy you power. It isn't like being the President.'

'Not yet,' said Tariq, intercepting Maria, who had stepped towards Harry, Taser raised. 'You want to put the pin back in the grenade?'

'No.'

Tariq shrugged and spoke quickly and succinctly. He told Harry the world was changing. Powerful Far Right groups were emerging in the USA and all across Europe. And all the while, elitist career politicians with not an ounce of experience in the real world continued to dictate the country's policy in a twenty-first century unrecognizable from the one they'd imagined as children.

'We're headed for some major problems, Harry.'

The woman inched closer to Harry, Taser by her side.

Once she was in striking distance, she was going to go for him, grenade or not.

'Better tell your pooch to stand down,' said Harry, nodding towards her.

'She has nothing to lose, Harry.'

'Radiation exposure in Korea,' she said. 'I've got maybe a year.' Her eyes shone.

The sacrificial lamb.

The perfect sleeper cell.

They were so close now that if Harry dropped the grenade, the phosphorus-burn would also injure him. They were calling his bluff and, if it came down to it, he didn't know what the right call would be.

'What makes you so different from those politicians?' Harry pointed the grenade at Tariq. 'You seem more dangerous to me than anyone else.'

Tariq smiled. 'You just don't know when to quit, do you?'

There was a moment of silence as they all waited for one of them to make a move.

Tariq turned to Maria. 'Show him.'

'What?' she said.

'Show him why we did all this.'

She stared at him, incredulous.

'Either he's dead or one of us,' said Tariq.

'Are you sure?' she said.

Tariq nodded. 'I wouldn't have got him involved otherwise.'

Maria open a video on her phone.

'Drop the Taser and kick it away,' said Tariq. 'Give him the phone and let him watch it properly. Once he's seen it, he'll re-pin the grenade and we can get on with things. We can't be that far off a military raid.'

She did as he asked.

Harry retreated a little, hit Play and watched the clip. At first, he darted his attention between Tariq, Maria and the phone.

Two minutes in, he forgot they were there.

It showed the Prime Minister, Thomas Match, in conversation with two well-known billionaire businessmen and Tyler Sudworth. Their expressions said they were very pleased with themselves. The men congratulated each other on finding a scapegoat for the country's hardships, said how useful the immigrant population of the UK had been for them. They talked of targeting the Muslims, how satisfied they were with Abu-Nazir and his progress, and of growing hostility in the UK towards the immigrants. They spoke of social and ethnic cleansing, and returning the country to its indigenous roots.

The world had seen this before, in the 1930s and 40s.

All this hatred. It had come from these men.

These men in power, these men running the country.

The video didn't look or feel doctored. And Maria and Tariq had had no way of knowing in advance they might need this. They hadn't known Harry would be here.

He put the pin back in the grenade, placed it on the floor and said, 'How do we stop this?'

NINETY-THREE

'EXTREME SITUATIONS CALL FOR extreme measures. This is the only way we walk out of here.'

Harry didn't like Tariq's plan. Tariq wanted Maria to execute the three leaders of Almukhtaroon still unconscious on the floor.

'I get it, but I can't sign off on the boy's murder,' Harry said.

Tariq suddenly pushed Harry, both hands landing flush on his chest, pain ricocheting through his ribs.

'You don't get sign-off. And I don't have time to run you through every minor detail. For now, Harry, you're either with us or against us. No civilians have died today – don't be the first.'

Harry wasn't sure he wanted to know the rest.

'The boy leaves with us. You'll say he was an embedded operative who helped bring Almukhtaroon down. You'll

give him an award, a fucking medal if need be.' Harry glanced towards Abu-Nazir and Azeez. 'How'd you explain those two being killed, though?'

Maria pulled a gun from under her burka and put it to her own head. 'Do you know what radiation poisoning is like to die of?'

A true sacrificial lamb.

She handed the gun to Tariq. 'Better to die at the hands of my compatriots, civilized and honourable, than let my body burn from the inside. And it will cement Tariq's position as a true hero today.' She pointed towards the ceiling. 'He saved a thousand people.' She gestured to Isaac. 'Saved our insider.' Finally she put her finger to her temple. 'And took out the terrorist who killed Nazir and Azeez.'

Tariq stepped in front of her, looking at Harry. 'I need you to walk away.'

Harry rubbed his hand over his stubble, scratching it wildly. He opened his mouth to object but Tariq stopped him.

'Walk the fuck away and take the boy with you.'

There was nothing more to say or do.

Harry took one final glance at Maria, at the bomb behind her, the timer frozen on 00:06 seconds, and walked away.

He lifted Isaac from the ground, pain shrieking through his body. He had to put him back on the floor and drag him around the corner instead.

He waited. It felt like an age before Harry heard two gunshots: Abu-Nazir and Azeez.

Now for Maria.

Harry closed his eyes.

He wondered if Tariq would feel anything. He was far more complex than Harry had ever given him credit for.

Group-13, a brotherhood like no other.

A third gunshot.

There was a short delay before Tariq emerged, walking purposefully.

'You rescued the kid, didn't see what happened. The rest is on me. Got it?'

Tariq hit the button for the lift.

Isaac was coming around now and Harry managed to unbind his hands and feet.

Tariq crouched beside Isaac, tone soft and compassionate. The change in his demeanour was astonishing to witness.

This guy was something else.

'You're safe. It's over. Harry got you to safety. Abu-Nazir and Azeez were killed by the Patriots before I could neutralize that threat. We'll debrief you fully when we are out of here. You OK to walk?'

Isaac simply nodded and Harry wondered if he'd registered that his father had just been killed. Perhaps the kid was in shock.

The three of them entered the lift heading for the ground floor.

They walked to the main doors of the mosque.

Tariq put his hand on Harry, halting him before they stepped through the doors to freedom.

'They'll take you to hospital and you'll be reunited with your wife. At some point tomorrow they'll want a debrief from you but I'll see you before then and we'll get this thing straight.'

Harry turned to leave but Tariq kept his hand firmly on his shoulder.

'OK?' he said.

Harry stared at Tariq's hand until he removed it. 'I got it.'

NINETY-FOUR

JOYTI VIRDEE HAD NOT really slept at all. She'd been watching the television on mute in her bedroom. Behind her, Ranjit was sleeping next to Aaron, arms cradling the boy.

Joyti had almost woken him up when the news had shown some kind of military operation under way at the Mehraj mosque. The footage had been cut short and, less than an hour later, it was all over.

Saima had called Joyti, crying. She'd cried even harder when Joyti had told her that her little boy was sleeping soundly.

Joyti looked over to her husband and her grandson, asleep on the bed. If she had known how to take a photograph on her phone, she would have. This was an image she never thought she would see.

What happened now was anybody's guess but right

here, in this moment, Joyti felt a sense of peace she wanted to cling on to.

The clock by the bed started to beep loudly for its 07.45 alarm and disturbed both Ranjit and Aaron's sleep. She hurriedly turned it off and watched, heart in mouth, as Aaron sat up, rubbed his eyes and . . . smiled.

'Grandma, you still here!' he said, alert and happy.

Yesterday and all its worries were already gone from his mind.

Aaron turned to Ranjit and stared at him, perplexed. 'You sleep in my bed?'

Ranjit smiled. 'I did. I was scared of the dark. I needed you to look after me.'

Aaron thought about this and nodded. 'It's OK. I get scared sometimes. I look after you.'

Ranjit glanced at Joyti and she knew in that instant that something had changed.

'You need a shave,' said Aaron.

Ranjit nodded. 'I like my beard. Do you want to touch it?'

'No. I don't like beards. Too scratchy. My daddy has a small beard. He rubs it on my face.'

Joyti lifted Aaron into her arms, allowing Ranjit to get out of bed. 'Does my little hero want breakfast?'

'I want my mummy.'

'She is coming. She will have breakfast with us too.'

Joyti glanced at Ranjit, who didn't respond.

What now? How did they move on from this?

Ranjit nodded to the window. A police car pulled up in the drive, the back door flying open.

Saima Virdee ran towards the house.

Harry laboured behind her, moving slowly.

They were safe.

Ranjit sat down on the edge of the bed, rubbing his hands along his knees. He looked anxious. 'I think this morning I will have my tea upstairs.'

Upstairs.

He didn't want to come down to see Harry and Saima.

Ranjit came across to Joyti and took Aaron from her. He kissed him and simply said, 'Goodbye, my little prince. You have lifted an old man's heart.'

NINETY-FIVE

THIS IS AMANDA MAWSON reporting live from Bradford where, in spite of the terrorist incident being brought to an end, a large police presence remains throughout the city. Transport links have reopened with Leeds Bradford airport announcing the resumption of flights.

Behind me you can see the Mehraj mosque, scene of one of the most audacious hostage situations we have experienced in modern times, and certainly the most high profile this country has ever seen. I can report that the bombing of City Park resulted in no casualties and while we understand that sixteen people remain in hospital, their injuries are not thought to be serious.

There are questions over what exactly happened inside the basement of the Mehraj mosque. No official statement has been given, but our sources have told us that both Abu-Nazir and Fahad-Bin-Azeez were killed

in whatever took place when Home Secretary Tariq Islam and Detective Chief Inspector Harry Virdee entered the mosque. Indeed, social media is full of unverified images of three bodies being stretchered from the building. As yet, the identities of those victims, especially the third one, remain unconfirmed.

With a conference scheduled for 2 p.m. at the Midland Hotel, the world's press is firmly camped inside Bradford. Just who are the Patriots? What will happen to the followers of Almukhtaroon? Do the security services expect a backlash and potential counter-measures from the Far Right?

This siege may have concluded, but for Bradford the past twenty-four hours will surely be only the beginning of a lengthy, complex investigation . . .

NINETY-SIX

HARRY HAD BEEN ADMITTED to Bradford Royal Infirmary.

Broken ribs. He had undergone several scans and numerous vials of blood had been taken from him. Eventually he'd even been given an injection of morphine.

He was getting used to that shit.

He was in a large, comfortable side room. Outside he could see Saima ensuring everything to do with his treatment was in order. As yet, they hadn't spoken of what had happened in the basement of the mosque. Saima should have been at home but had refused to go. He could see Aaron sitting at the nurses' station, playing with a stethoscope, several nurses fussing over him.

Harry needed some sleep but his eyes were on the TV hanging above his bed. Sky News was broadcasting live from the conference hall of the Midland Hotel, journalists

and television crews from all major channels reporting simultaneously.

ACC Frost and Tariq Islam took to the stage. Frost looked the more serious man. Harry knew why. He needed the streets of Bradford to calm, to end viral rumours on social media. It was . . . necessary. Last thing Bradford needed were reactionary forces, Far Right or otherwise, hitting the streets. This city knew all about that.

Harry had spoken to Frost but hadn't debriefed him. He hadn't known what to say.

Isaac had been taken into custody and Harry had made it damn clear he was not to be treated as hostile, and ensured Tariq had relayed the same message. Harry had not disclosed that Abu-Nazir was Isaac's father. That revelation could come later.

Frost opened up by running through key events of the past twenty-four hours, nothing the audience didn't already know. Camera shutters clicked ferociously, fingers tapped on laptops and pages of notebooks were ruffled. He spoke for under five minutes, ending his segment by stating that Harry had been an active member of his team, tasked with securing the leaders of Almukhtaroon, and had been compromised in the line of duty, which resulted in him being forced into the Mehraj mosque with Tariq. What happened thereafter, he said, was part of an ongoing investigation. He stepped aside for Tariq.

Harry couldn't bear looking at him and turned away from the TV. This was a game Tariq had played at such a

high level that Harry could not allow it to go unanswered. He would not.

That, though, was for later.

Tariq covered some of what Frost had already said, then, as Harry had expected, he made his move for political power.

'. . . what I will say is that the past twenty-four hours have reaffirmed the current political climate in the West. What I can tell you all is that what has come out of this is the revelation that Abu-Nazir and his partner, Amelia Rose, were in fact members of a covert Far Right organization and created the smokescreen of Almukhta-roon to conceal that reality. They used our fears to propel their own narrative and, indeed, their bank balance.'

There was a surge of incredulous chatter within the room. Tariq raised his arms, asked everyone to be calm and continued.

'We live in a time where identity appears to be up for grabs. Where people are asked to pick a side depending on their ethnicity or religious values. This goes against the very ideology of a tolerant society. These divisions have been building for some time and we, not only as govern-ment but more widely, have allowed it to happen. Across Europe, Far Right gains have been building, no doubt aided by troubling messages coming from the United States.'

Tariq stared into the audience and paused. 'What hap-pened inside the basement of the Mehraj mosque is currently under investigation and I cannot tell you any

more than you have already heard. What I can say, however, is that it resulted in over a thousand innocent UK civilians being unharmed. I, for one, hold that above everything else.'

Another pause as he allowed the journalists to digest what he had said. Not quite condoning the death of Abu-Nazir but not far away.

'A thousand innocent UK civilians. Not a thousand Muslims or Asians or ethnics or any other word you want to use. But a thousand of us. We need to fix this country. Communities need to come together and embrace the common ground. Not by playing catch-up or continuing to do what has gone before, but by radically overhauling systems that encourage and tolerate division, whether financially or religiously. No more committee meetings and think-tanks and white papers. Simple, practical solutions. People first. People always. People together.'

Harry stared at Tariq, feeling like a grandstand finish was nearing.

'I have heard people saying that Bradford is broken. It is not. This country is broken. And I will finish by saying this. Starting tomorrow, I'm going to damn well fix it.'

He stepped aside as journalists fought for the right to ask the first question. Harry had heard enough and reached for the remote just as a journalist shouted out: 'Home Secretary, is your speech laying down the gauntlet for a prime-ministerial challenge?'

NINETY-SEVEN

TARIQ ISLAM WAS SITTING in Harry's room, his close-protection detail loitering outside on the ward.

Saima had taken Aaron home, closely followed by a security detail of her own. The media had swarmed around the house but she'd refused to stay in a hotel.

Tariq looked as tired as anyone Harry had ever seen.

'Two cracked ribs, I heard.'

'Three, actually.'

'I'm sorry, Harry. You need to know I mean that.'

'Park your bullshit elsewhere.'

Tariq leaned forward in his chair, hands clasped together, head bowed. 'You know what the real job of government is?'

'Its only job is to serve.'

'You're right. But not the people. Government serves itself.'

Harry raised his eyebrows.

'Westminster is the oldest old-boys' network in the world. Unlike other countries, we've never had foreign rulers – never been invaded or occupied. Westminster is still "Empire". You either embrace it or you're shown the door.'

'Get to the point, Tariq.'

'That video you saw was a snippet of a much bigger picture, Harry.'

Harry struggled to sit up.

'How did you get that video?'

'Group-13 has never officially existed. And yet, over the past eighteen months, my ex-colleagues have started to mysteriously disappear, presumed dead. I'm a threat to those men and they're trying to send me a message. That video was covertly filmed by Group-13. When you come after us, we don't take it lying down, but this is a complex war we are fighting.'

Harry was confused. 'What do you mean, you're a threat?'

'I'm going to be the first Muslim man to become PM. And I don't fit with their rhetoric.'

'So you did do all this for power?'

Tariq got up from his chair and walked to the window, keeping his back towards Harry.

'No. I did it because behind closed doors the people who really run this country – the billionaires and finance companies who control the economy – are talking about

overseas conflicts again. Yemen, Syria, another cold war with Russia. America continues to isolate itself in the most nationalistic of ways and here in Blighty we are, for the first time in generations, completely alone. I did what I did to make myself impossible to ignore and to force real, meaningful change. I'm going to go hell for leather after the hard-line right-wing societies and political entities to break them down but, at the same time, do the same with groups like Almukhtaroon. Abu-Nazir may have been playing a game to swell his bank account but there are others out there, true fundamentalists ready to take his place. I want a complete crackdown on all sections of hate speech and toxic nationalistic views. This country cannot afford to become like Italy, Spain, France, Holland, Germany, where the Far Right is growing in political power. We, Harry Virdee, are heading not only for another financial recession but this time also for a possible "cleansing" of UK passport holders. It's not for nothing that the current Prime Minister cut the policing and national security budgets by 20 per cent. How the fuck are you going to operate robust intelligence and security with cuts like those? It's not chance or an oversight. It's social cleansing.'

Tariq returned to Harry, stopping by his bedside. His face was flushed, eyes narrow, the tiredness replaced by something worse: a frightening resilience.

'You don't know this world of power like I do, Harry. There are plans in the most elite of circles, including government, to slowly move the centre ground to the right.

Look back through history. Every hundred or so years, times change. Populations do. People turn on one another. I did what I did because I aim to topple the PM, and that will start tomorrow with a press conference like no other. I'll berate the toffs and the career politicians as pen-pushers with no real allegiance to the British way of life. I walked into the mosque with you so that that image would be the one that gets me the power I need to create real, progressive change. The whole world is talking about Tariq Islam and it's not my fucking ego I'm polishing, it's my credentials to be the first man of colour, the first Muslim, to become PM in the UK. And my job will be to bring communities closer together and push the Far Right back to the fringes. Otherwise, we are all fucked.'

Harry's head was hurting. Some things made sense, others didn't. Why did they involve him? Why hadn't Group-13 just taken out Almukhtaroon themselves?

Tariq told him that had been the plan but, as he had already suggested, they were being systematically wiped out. Two days before, several key members of the organization had disappeared, ones critical to this operation.

'Everything was set. You were never part of this plan. No offence, but it's way above your pay grade,' said Tariq.

He told Harry that without their usual manpower, they had lost control of Almukhtaroon that morning. Only Isaac remained on their radar and he'd been the lowest rung. Tariq had targeted the only man he knew who stood a chance in Bradford.

Harry.

The remaining members of Group-13 were flat out ensuring the bigger plan with the mosques and security services went accordingly. Moreover, Harry was expendable; they were not.

'Thanks,' said Harry.

'You asked for the truth.'

'Why tell me all of this? Surely a bullet is what I should get. I could end you in a heartbeat.'

Tariq waved his phone at Harry. 'Globally I'm at ten million tweets. We live in a world of fake news. You wouldn't get far.'

Harry hated to admit it but Tariq was right.

'I'm telling you all this, Harry, so you don't stay up at night asking yourself questions you don't have answers to.'

Harry shook his head. 'No, it's more than that.'

Tariq smiled. 'It is more than that. Last year, in one monumental night for Bradford, with all the odds against you, Harry Virdee managed to pull off one of the greatest abductions and murders of our time. The best thing is, nobody knows it happened. You have a very specific set of skills, a very specific type of brother. There is one thing I am damn certain of . . .' Tariq helped himself to a glass of water, as if building up to what he had yet to say.

'In every major city in the UK I am making inroads. Putting "my people" in places they need to be, whether government officials or . . . otherwise. We need to cleanse this country in a far more radical way than politics

currently allows. The world has changed. We either change with it or get left behind. Courts, jails and reform were before the digital age. Before the top one per cent of the world's elite fucked the rest of us. The one place I don't have eyes is Leeds Bradford, the fourth-largest catchment in the UK and a place I have no one I can trust to come with me on this journey.'

Harry shook his head. 'After what you did today—'

'—zero civilian casualties! Two people who deserved to die got their comeuppance and I put to rest a woman who asked me to end her life the way she wanted. Fine, I upset and frightened thousands of people and we had a few minor injuries but – perspective! Better twenty-four hours of turmoil then twenty-four years.'

'What was inside that bomb? Actual explosives?'

'Examination of the device will show it was fake. An extraordinary bluff.'

Tariq went back to his chair and removed his jacket from it, putting it on. His eyes looked so sore they almost made Harry's water.

'You're pretty golden, Harry. The brass doesn't have shit on you and you were just as much the hero as I was. You broke some rules? It was an unprecedented scenario.' Tariq pointed to the window and smiled. 'I've plans for Bradford, Harry. Plans for you. Don't judge me before you have heard them.'

NINETY-EIGHT

HARRY WAS HOME, SITTING in his living room, once again watching the news. Bradford remained the headline story.

This wouldn't be forgotten. A terrorist event of this scale would be subject to many 'commissions' and 'inquiries' over the coming years.

There were questions the public would want answering.

Who were the Patriots?

Would Tariq Islam stand trial for murder?

And many they would never know to ask.

Would Maria's identity lead back to Tariq Islam?

Would his role in this ever come to light?

Harry had none of the answers.

Saima had put Aaron to bed and entered the room, bringing with her a pen and piece of paper. She kicked the footstool over towards Harry and sat opposite him.

'Divorce?' said Harry, trying to crack a joke. He'd told her all about Tariq Islam but Saima hadn't said much.

She didn't smile.

Harry muted the television.

Saima placed the pen and paper on her lap, then said, 'How come we always end up here?'

'Here?'

She nodded towards his ribs.

'Bones mend.'

'Don't use that macho crap with me.'

Harry shrugged. 'But they do.'

'This city is going to ruin us, Harry. Don't you feel it?'

He didn't reply.

'We need a fresh start. No drama.' Saima put her hands on him. 'All I care about is my boy and my husband. The past forty-eight hours, in all this madness, I saw what really matters. I had so much time to think of you and Aaron alone, without me. Then about what might happen if I got out and something happened to you. I don't want to think that way any more.'

'I doubt I'll have a job anyway, Saima. I broke every rule there is.'

Saima rolled her eyes. She lifted the pen and began to write. Harry peered past her at the TV, where a picture of him and Tariq Islam outside the mosque had a bold caption beneath it: *HEROES*.

He turned it off. You put everything on the line and got a few newspaper headlines, yet when all this died

down, he was certain that the only thing in his future was a misconduct charge.

Saima handed him the paper she had scrawled on.

He stared at it and didn't react.

Just two lines.

'You don't need to be the saviour of this city any more. Gotham can find another Dark Knight. You've done enough. We just need to be "us", and everything else we'll figure out. Will you sign it, please?'

Harry didn't move. He focused on the paper, on Saima, then back on the paper.

'Are you really asking this of me?'

Her expression said it all. In fact, it said more than Harry cared to see.

Saima was right.

He wasn't going to win here. Thoughts of Tariq Islam and his own brother, Ronnie, rolled across his mind.

Bradford's future was . . . uncertain.

Saima touched his hands and smiled. 'It's time. It is.'

Harry took the pen from her and scribbled his signature where she had left him space.

I, Hardeep Singh Virdee, formally tender my resignation with immediate effect from the West Yorkshire police force.

EPILOGUE

TARIQ ISLAM HAD BEEN true to his word and Isaac Wolfe was now something of a celebrity. The boy who pissed his pants and took anxiety medication was a distant memory.

Harry was standing by his side as Isaac laid a bunch of flowers on his mother's grave in Undercliffe Cemetery. The evening was warm and quiet, just the two of them by the headstone.

Harry had attended several meetings with Isaac and Tariq, where their story had been locked down before being shared with security services. Isaac had been given the chance to seal his file so that the fact Abu-Nazir was his father never came out.

He'd declined.

The other version was far stronger: the boy who had gone undercover to become a spy, putting his country first, his toxic father a distant second.

The spin-machine had been hard at work.

Isaac had sold his comic sketches to a publisher for seven figures and was now one of the most eligible bachelors in England.

'Not half bad for eighteen hours' work,' said Harry.

Isaac smiled. 'Every time someone asks me whether I'm still a spy I say, "No comment" and it increases my social media reach by a few thousand.'

Harry put his arm around the kid. 'The world could do with a few more brown heroes.'

Isaac turned to Harry and hugged him. 'Like you, you mean?'

'Hey, don't squeeze me too tight. Ribs, remember?'

'Sorry,' said Isaac, breaking the embrace.

'I mean what I said. The shit you did out there – you're the real hero in all of this.'

Isaac put his hand in his bag and pulled out a handful of photocopied sketches. 'Here, I wanted you to see these first, before I submitted them to my publisher for next week's edition.'

Harry took them and tried not to laugh. It made his ribs scream. 'Are you kidding?' he said.

'Time Harry Virdee, or should I say Harri Verde, got his own edition.'

Harry flicked through the pages. 'I don't know what to say. Is this libellous?'

'It's all good stuff. Now *you're* famous.'

'Do I get any of that seven-figure action your publisher gave you?'

'Name your number.'

Harry waved the pages at him. 'I'm content with this. Nice touch.' He stuck out his hand and Isaac shook it. 'Farewell, Isaac Wolfe. London won't know what hit them.'

'You'll come visit, right?'

'Some time. For now, Bradford will do just fine.'

They shook hands, a few gentle slaps on the back, a bond they wouldn't easily forget.

'Someone told me you handed in your resignation – is that right? Or fake news?'

Harry went to answer, paused, then glanced around the cemetery. 'We're a long time dead, no?'

Isaac didn't reply.

Harry smiled. 'Don't worry, Isaac Wolfe. Whatever happens, I'm pretty certain Bradford hasn't seen the last of me yet.'

ACKNOWLEDGEMENTS

This one was tough! A seismic plot, which did indeed push me to my limits as a writer.

Huge thanks to my incredible editor, Darcy Nicholson. I'm not sure how we continue to do this! You push me to my limits and I appreciate it more than you realize. We are breaking boundaries and creating the sort of fiction that I always dreamt of writing. You work so hard on these books with me and continue to be my secret weapon. The entire team at Transworld is amazing, especially the copy-editing team. Thank you all, so much.

To former DCI Steve Snow, for allowing me to hound you, probably more than I should! I know I break the rules with my plots, but the fact that you are always there, guiding, advising and constantly trying to help me create the high-end drama I love to write is invaluable. Long may it continue! I've got to be honest, sitting there

and watching your expressions as I twist and turn the plots is great fun! As you've told me before, 'If you were not a writer, Amit, I'd probably nick you . . .' Stay retired, Steve! We have much more work to do!

To Rob Glover, for running me through a detailed plot strand which ultimately didn't make the final cut – but rest assured, it's coming!

Michael Shackleton, at Bradford City Football Club, for the generous access. Come on, the Bantams!

Dr Jasjit Singh for assisting me with the finer points of Sikhism and Asian culture. I am so glad to have you on #teamVirdee!

My agent Simon Trewin for the continual support and for always being at the end of a phone.

To the 'Red Hot Chilli Writers' – Ayisha Malik, Vaseem Khan, Abir Mukherjee, Imran Mahmood and Alex Khan. Keep smashing the clichés, guys! A wonderfully supportive space to be part of. Also, for the humorous hours of 'bakwas'. Keep it coming!

My family – I know it's hard when I'm writing and I 'disappear' into the fictional world I've created.

To the city of Bradford. Thank you for continuing to support Harry – he will always keep you safe!

Finally, my wife. This one was bruising! I couldn't have done it without you constantly telling me; 'one more page, one more chapter, one more hour . . .'

You are the only person I write for and I couldn't do it without you. Four books done and I've fooled you with

the twists and turns each time! Seeing the look on your face when you finally read, 'the end' is the only reason I keep doing this.

I've said it before, I'll say it again:

Keep doing what you do – it makes me do what I do.

STREETS OF DARKNESS
A. A. Dhand

A body has been found.
And it's not just any body.

Detective Harry Virdee has been suspended from work just as the biggest case of the year lands on what would have been his desk. But he can't keep himself away.

Determined to restore his reputation, Harry is forced to take to the shadows in search of notorious ex-convict and prime suspect, Lucas Dwight. But as this murder threatens to tip an already unstable city into full-scale riot mode, Harry finds his preconceptions turned on their head as he finds out what it's like to be on the other side of the law . . .

'Outstanding – relentless, multi-layered suspense and real human drama make this a crime debut to relish.'
Lee Child

'A tense slice of neo-noir that has won Dhand comparisons to both BBC drama *Luther* and HBO's *The Wire*.'
Observer

'Dhand's *Streets of Darkness* are in Bradford and they sure are dark . . . The blood count is high but the novel deserves attention for its sheer inventiveness and unbridled energy.'
The Times

GIRL ZERO
A. A. Dhand

A routine call brings Detective Inspector Harry
Virdee face-to-face with something no one should
ever see – the cold body of his beloved niece.

He's immediately banned from working the case, but
there's no way Harry can walk away while the monster
who killed his flesh and blood is still walking the streets.
But before he can find the killer, he must tell his
brother, Ronnie, the terrible news.

Impulsive, dangerous and frighteningly well
connected, Ronnie will act first and think later. Harry
may have a murderer to find but if he isn't careful,
he may also have a murder to prevent.

'A story as fresh as today's newspaper
headlines – and all the more potent for being so.
Fierce, fast-paced and vivid.'
Mail on Sunday

CITY OF SINNERS
A. A. Dhand

It is a cold and miserable Yorkshire morning.
The streets are not yet busy. Police cars hurriedly
pull up in the centre of town. But the sirens
are eerily silent.

A body has been found, elaborately and
painstakingly positioned to send a message.
But why? And to who?

DCI Harry Virdee doesn't yet know that this
murder is the first of many. He doesn't yet know
that, as he approaches the crime scene, the
killer is watching him.

There's a lot he doesn't know yet.

Harry is on the hunt for a serial killer.

'Fearless'
Sunday Times

'Tense'
Observer

dead good

For everyone who finds a crime story irresistible.

Find out more about criminally good reads at Dead Good – the home of killer crime books, drama and film.

We'll introduce you to our favourite authors and the brightest new talent. Discover exclusive extracts, features by bestselling writers, discounted books, reviews of top crime dramas and exciting film news – and don't forget to enter our competitions for the chance to win some cracking prizes too.

Sign up:
www.deadgoodbooks.co.uk/signup

Join the conversation on:

ALLAN MALLINSON

1914: FIGHT THE GOOD FIGHT

It took just a month from the assassination in Sarajevo on 28 June 1914 for the huge armies of Continental Europe to be on the march. In his vivid, compelling and rigorously researched history, Allan Mallinson examines the century-long path that led to war, the vital first month of fighting, and speculates, tantalizingly, on what might have been had wiser political and military counsels prevailed . . .

TOO IMPORTANT FOR THE GENERALS

'War is too important to be left to the generals' snapped future French prime minister Georges Clemenceau on learning of yet another bloody and futile offensive on the Western Front. Why did the First World War take so long to win – and why did it exact so appalling a human cost? In his superbly researched, brilliantly argued and captivating history, Allan Mallinson provides controversial and disturbing answers to these questions that have divided military historians for nearly a century.

'Mallinson . . . combines the authority of a soldier-turned-military historian with the imaginative touch of the historical novelist'
Lawrence James, *THE TIMES*

'A wonderful series' Professor John Röhl,
biographer of the Kaiser

'I could not believe that [there was] anything new to say . . . but how wrong I was!' Professor Sir Michael Howard, formerly
Professor of the History of War, Oxford

ONE WAY OUT

A. A. Dhand

CORGI BOOKS

To the memory of my mother and my step-father.
Those we love travel with us always.

L

ONE

To be serious only about sex
Is perhaps one way, but the sands are hissing
As they approach the beginning of the big slide
Into what happened.

John Ashbery

1

Early spring, the new millennium, a young woman walks backwards along the deck of a boat. She goes slowly, is bent almost double, holds in her left hand a ladle and in her right a pot of hot pitch. From the spout of the ladle she pours a thin ribbon of pitch into the seams where all yesterday she tapped in lengths of oakum with a mallet and bosun's chisel.

So it begins, simply, with work.

The boat is raised on wooden stilts, the deck twenty feet above the ground, that hard standing of rubbled concrete and brick where the warmth of the new season has brought out unlikely patches of pale flowers, their roots in shallow veins of earth. Around the boat is the yard, a place where ships were once built – ferries, coal-lighters, trawlers, a wooden minesweeper during the war – but now given over to the servicing and maintenance of pleasure craft, some on their stilts, others tied up at the pontoons. There is a sound of power tools, radios, the now-and-then rapping of a hammer.

She is alone on the deck. For the work, for ease of movement and access, the mast has been unstepped, and all the rigging, together with stanchions and guard rails, has been removed and stowed away. When she finishes one seam she immediately begins the next. In the pot, the pitch is cooling. As it cools it thickens. She will have to stop at some point soon to light the gas-burner in the galley and heat it again, but not yet.

Below her, standing in the shadow of the boat's steel hull, a young man is dipping bolts into white lead and softly singing to himself. He is tall, blue-eyed, patrician. His fair hair, luxurious at a distance, is already starting to thin. His name is Henley but he is known and prefers to be known as Tim. There is some question, still unresolved, as to whether he and the girl on deck will sleep together.

He pauses, a bolt in his gloved fingers, calls up, 'Maud! Maud! Where art thou?' and getting no answer, grins and goes back to his work. He does not know her well but knows she does not do banter, does not in fact seem to understand what it is. This he finds funny and endearing, a trick of character, a benign absence, to be numbered among those things he most likes about her, such as the bluntness of her blunt brown stare, the curls of her hair that are flicks and half-curls because she cuts her hair short as a boy's; the inked lettering on her arm (the underside of her left forearm), a surprise the first time you see it that makes you wonder what other surprises there might be. The hint of Wiltshire in her voice, the way she sucks on a cut but does not mention it, the way her breasts are not much larger than peaches and hard, he thinks, as peaches. Yesterday, when she pulled off her jumper, he saw for the first time two inches of bare belly above the waistband of her jeans and felt an entirely unexpected seriousness.

They are both members of the university sailing club. The two others who came down with them have driven back to Bristol, perhaps, thinks Tim, to give them a bit of space, a bit of privacy. Is that what Maud thinks too? That the scene is set?

He can smell the pitch she's using. Also the faint sweet rotten smell of the river, the old piles, the mud, the amphibious vegetation. This is a drowned valley, a place broken to the sea, salt water heaving in and out twice a day under banks of dense woodland, at high tide lapping the roots of the trees, at low tide leaving little creeks of thigh-deep mud bare and glittering. In places, further up river, old boats have been scuttled and left to find their way back to nothing – blackened staves, blackened freeboard, some so old and rotten they might have carried Vikings, Argonauts, the first men and women of the world. There are herring gulls, egrets, cormorants, a resident seal that rises without warning at the side of boats, eyes like a Labrador. The sea itself is not in view but it's not distant. Two curves of the river bank, then the harbour, the town, the castles on the headlands. Open water.

Outside the boat shed a figure in red overalls and welder's goggles is standing like a boxer under a fountain of blue sparks. By the offices, a man in a suit is leaning against an iron pillar, smoking. Tim stretches – a luxurious feeling – but as he turns back to his work, to the boat, there is a movement through the air, a blink of feathered shadow, that is also a movement across the surface of his eye like a thorn scratch. There must have been a noise too – no such thing as silent impact – but whatever it was, it was lost in the hissing of his own blood and left no trace of itself.

He is staring at the ladle, which has come to rest by one of the patches of white flowers, pitch drizzling from the scoop. Maud herself is further off, face up, her arms flung above her head, her head tilted to the side, her eyes shut. It takes an immense effort to keep looking at her, this girl newly dead on the rubbled brick, one shoe on, one shoe off. He is very afraid of her. He holds his head between his gloved hands. He is going to be sick. He whispers her name. He whispers other things like fuck, fuck, fuck, fuck . . .

Then she opens her eyes and sits up. She's looking, if she's looking anywhere, straight ahead to the old boat shed. She gets to her feet. It does not appear difficult or painful though somehow she gives the impression she is reassembling herself out of the bricks and flowers around her, rising out of her own dust. She starts walking – bare foot, dressed foot, bare foot, dressed foot – twelve or fifteen steps until, without warning, she crumples to the ground, face down this time.

The welder has been watching it all through the tint of his goggles. He shuts the valves on the tank, pushes up his goggles and starts to run. The other man, the one smoking outside the office, is also running, though more awkwardly, as if running was not really his thing or as if he did not want to be the first to arrive. The welder kneels beside Maud's head. He puts his lips close to the ground. He whispers to her, rests two fingers on her neck. The man in the suit crouches, Arab style, on the other side of her, the cloth of his trousers tight over his thighs. From somewhere a bell has started to sound, high-pitched and continuous. Others are coming now, more yardsmen in red overalls, the woman from the marina office, somebody in salopettes who must have just come off one of the boats on the pontoon. 'Don't crowd her!' says the welder. Someone, breathless, passes forward a green box. Three or four times the woman from the office says she has called the emergency services. She says emergency services rather than ambulance.

At some point they all notice Tim, the way he is standing there fifteen feet away as if nailed to the air. They notice him, frown, then look back at Maud.

2

No stanchions, no guard rail. And she was, perhaps, affected by the fumes from the pitch. The ambulance could be heard coming from a long way off. It had, among other things, to cross the river. When they arrived, the paramedics put a neck brace on Maud then turned her like some precious archaeological find, a bog girl old as Christ, fragile as ashes. Once she was stabilized, one of the paramedics sat Tim on the back step of the ambulance and explained to him that he was suffering from shock but that he wasn't to worry because his girlfriend was doing pretty well, all things considered. They were going to drive up to the top of the valley to meet the helicopter. The helicopter would fly her to the hospital in Plymouth. She would be there in about half an hour.

When Tim wakes to himself, when the shivering stops and his head begins to work again in a way he can recognize, he is sitting in the marina office with a tartan blanket round his shoulders. Pot plants, filing cabinets, maps of the river. A poster, sun-faded, of a sailing boat, one of the old kind of racing yacht, low, over-can-vassed, a dozen crew sitting along the windward side, legs dangling. The woman who called the ambulance is talking in a low voice to the man in the suit. She brings Tim a mug of tea. It's scalding hot and undrinkably sweet. He sips at it then stands and folds the blanket. It takes him a moment to shrug off the idea that he too has been injured, that there is an injury he should find and look at. He thanks the man and the woman (he is nothing if not polite – those schools!) then goes out to where his old Lancia is parked and drives to Plymouth.

It's nearly dark when he arrives. The hospital seems among the most terrible places he has ever been. He cannot find A&E. He stands for a time in the lit doorway of the genito-urinary unit until a porter asks him if he is all right and points out his way – a path between bushes that leads to a forecourt where ambulances are clustered around wide, rubber-fringed doors.

At reception the woman behind the glass wants to know what he is to Maud and after a pause he says he's a friend. She won't tell him Maud's condition, her status. He thinks she probably doesn't know. He sits in the waiting room on a worn red bench. An elderly couple is sitting near him. They have the look of people who have recently escaped from a bombed city – or what he ima-gines such people would look like. A half-hour passes. He goes back to the desk. The woman has been replaced by another woman. This one is friendlier.

'Hold on,' she says. She calls the nurses' station, somewhere on the far side of the swing doors. 'Stamp,' she says. 'Came in on the helicopter this afternoon?' She listens, she nods. 'Yes,' she says, 'OK . . . Yes . . . Yes . . . A friend . . . yes . . . right . . . Thanks.' She puts the phone down. She looks at Tim and smiles.

Maud is in the hospital for three nights. Her first night is on ICU, then they move her to an assessment ward in an older part of the hospital. From the windows of the ward you cannot see the sea but you can see the light from the sea. Ten women either side of the room, one behind screens with a voice like a child's, so obese she cannot bear to be looked at.

Maud's parents, alerted by the hospital, visit from Swindon. They're both schoolteachers, busy people. They have brought a bag of Maltesers with them and some magazines from which certain pictures have been carefully cut out and already, perhaps, laminated on the machine in the kitchen, images of the physical world or pictures illustrative of the human condition, those aspects most readily taught to schoolchildren. Her mother calls her Maudy, her father polishes his glasses. In the middle of speaking to them Maud falls asleep. Her parents look at her, the wax-white face on the pillow, the bandages on her head like a skull cap. They look round to see if there is anyone calm and medical who might take charge of things.

When she leaves she has a cast on her leg and a pair of crutches. Tim drives her back to Bristol. He has spent the last three nights in a hotel near the docks where Chinese seamen wandered the overheated corridors in their underwear, a wide-hipped strolling from room to room, every room with its door open, parties of men strewn on the beds, smoking and watching television.

He stows her crutches in the back of the car. She is very quiet. He asks if she wants the radio on and she says she doesn't mind. He wants to know if she is in pain. He asks if she remembers anything. He says he is sorry, and when she asks why he says he doesn't know. He's sorry anyway. Sorry she's hurt.

Her flat is on Woodland Road, not far from the university biology department where she is doing her master's degree. She has lived there for at least six months but to Tim, when he has followed her up the stairs, the place has an oddly uninhabited air. He has sisters – the twins – and certain ideas about the spaces girls live in, the scented candles on the mantlepiece, dresses on hangers hanging from the backs of doors, throws, wraps, photographs in heart-shaped frames. He can see nothing of this at Maud's. There are two pairs of trainers and a pair of walking boots lined up in the little hallway. In the living room the furniture is three types of brown. There are no pictures on the walls. Light from the street drains inwards through a big window and falls onto a carpet of the kind intended to endure all insult. Everything is tidy. If there's a smell it's just the smell of the building itself.

She sits in one of the armchairs, her crutches on the floor beside her. He makes tea for her though there is no milk in the fridge. She is pale. She looks exhausted. He says he thinks he should stay the night on the sofa, unless of course there was someone else she could call. 'You're not supposed to be alone,' he says. 'Not for the first twenty-four hours. It's in the notes from the hospital.'

'I'm OK,' she says, and he says, 'Yes, well, you're probably not. Not yet.' Her cupboards are bare. He hurries out to do some shopping. In the supermarket he wonders if he is taking advantage of her, that far from being just a helpful friend he is in fact a manipulative scheming shit. This thought does not go deep. He fills the basket, pays and strides back to the flat, city wind in his face.

He cooks a cheese soufflé. He's a good cook and the soufflé is light and appetizing. She thanks him, eats three forkfuls. She sleeps upright in the chair. It's slightly boring, slightly worrying. When she comes to, they watch television for an hour then she goes through the door to her bedroom. He cleans up, lies awake on the sofa under his coat. He would like to find a secret diary and read her secret thoughts. Her sex fantasies, her fear of loneliness, her plans. Does she have a diary? His sisters have diaries, volumes of them, mostly with little locks on them, but he's pretty certain Maud does not and that if she did she would not be recording her sex fantasies, her fear of loneliness. Through the netting over the window he sees a smudge of moon and when he shuts his eyes he sees Chinamen drifting like cigarette smoke.

He is woken by the noise of Maud throwing up. She has made it to the bathroom; the door is open, the light on, a hard light. He has a back view of her in her nightshirt, bent over the pink sink. She doesn't have much to bring up. He hovers by the door waiting to catch her but she has wrapped her fingers round the taps, has braced herself.

The Infirmary is a five-minute drive, certainly at this time of night. They admit her straight away, wheel her off in a wheel-chair. He doesn't get to say goodbye or good luck.

When he returns the next morning he is told she is on Elizabeth Fry, a ward on the fifth floor at the front. He goes up flights of stairs, broad green steps, a window at every turn, the city opening out as he ascends, revealing itself as several cities, dozens perhaps, each wrapped around the bones of what it grew from. He cannot find Maud at first. The patients in their beds, in their gowns, are all strangely similar. He walks slowly past the ends of beds until he finds her in an annex with five others, her name and date of admission written on the whiteboard above her head.

She already has a visitor, a woman with long grey hair worn free, a pair of leopard-print kitten heels on her big feet. She is gently holding one of Maud's hands and keeps her hold as she turns to look up at Tim.

'She's asleep,' says the woman. 'She's been asleep since I got here.'

'But she's OK?'

'As far as I know.'

'It's probably what she needs.'

'Sleep?'

'Yes.'

'It's certainly,' says the woman, 'the sort of thing people say.' She has a northern accent – Midlands, north Midlands, somewhere like that. He doesn't really know the Midlands.

'I'm Tim,' he says, 'Tim Rathbone.'

'Susan Kimber,' says the woman. 'Maud's professor at the university. She called me this morning. She had a tutorial scheduled for this afternoon.'

'She called you?'

'She's conscientious. And they have a sort of phone on wheels, somewhere.'

'I brought her in last night,' says Tim. 'She was being sick.'

'It was lucky you were there.'

'Yes. I suppose it was.'

'You're a friend.'

'Yes.'

'Are you at the university?'

'I finished the year before last. I did English.'

'So you read novels for three years.'

'Actually, a lot of it was reading *about* novels,' says Tim. 'But it must seem a bit thin compared to what you do, you and Maud.'

'Not really,' says the professor. 'Or if it is that might be the point.'

'I would rather have done music. I should have.'

'You play something?'

'The guitar. Some piano. Mostly guitar.'

'Ah,' says the professor, her expression softening a little. 'You're the guitar player.'

'Yes. She's mentioned me?'

'I quiz all my students relentlessly, particularly about their private lives. Maud of course I had first to teach that she had a private life. I mean something between work and sleep. Something discussable.'

For a moment they both glance over at the bed, the sleeping girl.

'How well do you know her?' asks the professor.

'We've sailed a couple of times on the university boat. And once she came to a concert I put on. A lunchtime thing at the church at the bottom of Park Street.'

'You like her.'

'Yes.'

'You want to help her.'

'Help her?'

'Rescue her. You're not alone, I'm afraid. They flit around her like moths, though as far as I can tell she does nothing obvious to encourage it. Boys and girls. It's her pheromones perhaps.'

He nods. He is not sure what to say to this. She has started to remind him of his mother, though the professor is clearly sober.

'On the phone,' says the professor, 'she told me she had fallen from the deck of a boat. Presumably not into the sea.'

'The boat was in the yard. She fell onto brick. About twenty feet.'

'And then?'

'Then?'

'You were there, weren't you? What happened next?'

Tim frowns. For some reason – for several reasons – he has

failed to play it back to himself, the half-minute that followed. After a while, in which he seems to see pictures, like portraits hanging in a gallery – the welder under his shower of sparks, the man in the suit smoking, and some white bird, a gull or even an egret, wings spread in emblematic flight over the curled green heads of the trees – he says, 'She got up. She started walking.'

The professor smiles. 'Yes,' she says. 'Yes. That sounds like our Maud.'

For a second time he leads her from the doors of a hospital. He has a fresh set of guidance notes. She swings on her crutches at his side. The sky is tufted with small, perfectly white clouds.

He goes shopping again then cooks her a herb omelette with a side salad of imported leaves. She finishes her food, wipes her plate clean with a slice of bread.

He says he will play for her if she wants and when she agrees or does not tell him she does not want it, he drives the Lancia to his flat in one of the tall white houses overlooking the river, views of the suspension bridge on one side, the old bonded warehouses on the other. He rents the place with a Spaniard who works all hours at a restaurant, at two restaurants, at least two. Tim's share is paid from the family money stream, those trusts, the echo of old work, set up by his grandparents, and which provide him with an income never much more than modest but enough for this, the flat in the white building, the airy views.

The Spaniard's Spanish girlfriend is asleep on the window seat. She has a nose like a shark's fin and blue-black hair so thick you would have to cut it with gardening shears. He goes softly past her to his room, chooses a guitar, settles it into its case, clips the case shut and drives back to Maud.

She has showered, changed. Her hair is still damp. He asks if she is feeling better and she says she is. They drink tea (he has bought some milk). She reads for half an hour a volume entitled *Medical Physiology (2nd Edition)*, though her eyes are sometimes shut and the book teeters in her grip. As evening comes on he takes out the guitar and shows it to her. He tells her it's a reproduction of a René Lacôte and that Lacôte was a celebrated nineteenth-century guitar-maker. This is maple, and on the top, this is spruce. He draws her attention to the abalone rosette, the diamonds and moons on the headstock. He says, in fact, he has an original Lacôte, one that he bought at auction a couple of years ago. He keeps it at his parents' place. His parents have an elaborate security system. He laughs, then turns on the only lamp in the room and sits under its light.

He plays, she listens. He might imagine this a model of their future together. One piece, a short study by Fernando Sor, she asks to hear again. The guitar has a light sound compared to a modern guitar. It is clear and sweet and seems an instrument designed to play children to sleep.

At ten she rocks herself onto her good foot, readies herself for bed. When she comes out of the bathroom she has a nightshirt on and hangs between the crutches. He is thinking what to say to her – another quote from the hospital guidance notes perhaps – but it's Maud who speaks first. 'You can stay in my room,' she says.

'OK,' he says. 'With you?'

'Not to have sex,' she says.

'Of course,' he says. Then, more gravely, 'Of course not.'

In her bedroom the bed is not particularly large, not a full-size double. She gets under the covers, he quickly strips down to T-shirt and boxers. He gets in beside her. She smells – despite the shower – of the hospital, and when she reaches to put off the lamp he sees she still has the hospital ID bracelet on her wrist. She lies with her back to him. She has a small patch of shaved scalp around the wound on her head. They don't talk. He has an erection he knows will not subside for hours and he keeps his hips back a little so she will not feel it press against her. He listens to her breathing, thinks he hears the moment it settles into the rhythm of her sleep. He wants to stay awake all night and imagines that he will, that he will have no choice, but her warmth enters him like a drug and when he opens his eyes again there's a fine silt of dawn in the room. She is still there, the broken girl, the miraculous girl. All night they have lain like two stones in the road. He rests a hand on her shoulder. She stirs but sleeps on. In sleep, her nightshirt has ridden up a little and his right knee is touching the back of her left thigh, skin on skin. Under the window the occasional car drones past.

This was their courtship.

3

Maud alone for a moment, sitting on the bed nude as an egg, her foot sunk in the cast, no watch or bracelet or jewel of any kind on her, her skin lit by the light of an ancient and implicated city.

Her bedroom – as undecorated as the rest of the flat – is heated by a plug-in and possibly unsafe oil radiator that heats only a rose of air in the immediate vicinity of its grey fins. She has a good tolerance for the cold. All those hours of dinghy sailing in gravel ponds, on the Thames, the seaside. Wet shorts, wet feet. Then all the rest: the stubbed toes, rope-burn, your face slapped by a sail, a bruise on your thigh like a peony in full bloom from losing your footing among the weeds on the slipway.

As a schoolgirl she belonged to the school judo club. The club was in a kind of Nissen hut in the grounds of the boys' school across the road. It had no obvious ventilation and the small windows ran with condensation, summer and winter. The instructor was a middle-aged man called Rawlins, a one-time European

17

champion but by Maud's time a semi-cripple who chain-smoked throughout the classes and whose hands were huge and red and murderous. The smell of the place. The thump thump thump of bodies hitting the mat. How to grip up, how to point your feet. Your balance as a secret you carried and your opponent guessed at, reached for. Rawlins saw how she stood her ground, how she was not intimidated by bigger girls, never gave up even when giving up made sense. For a while he thought she might have the necessary oddness to do well in a fighting art. She reminded him of a dog he had once owned that had been killed by a car and that he still sometimes thought about. When she dislocated a finger throwing a girl with tai otoshi he asked if she wanted him to reset it, right there on the mat. This was one of his tests. With Rawlins everything was a test, a way of seeing who you were. She nodded. He took her white hand between his red ones, his gaze made crazy by the smoke drifting up from the cigarette between his teeth. You just keep looking at me, he said, you keep your eyes on old Rawlins, and she did, obediently, while his thumbs felt out the joint.

Tim calls to her through the door. 'You OK in there, Maud?'

'Yes,' she calls back.

'Decent?'

'Yes.'

He opens the door. 'Oh, Jesus,' he says. 'So sorry.' He blushes but she doesn't. Several seconds pass. 'I'll be in here,' he says.

4

In July they drive down to his parents' place. It turns out they grew up within a hundred miles of each other, in neighbouring counties, but while she was in a terraced house in a town, semi-industrial, a transport hub, he was among open fields, stables, copses, lawns. (The local hunt takes twenty minutes to cross his parents' land, a line of black and scarlet riders, mud like shrapnel from the horses' hooves.)

They bump up the driveway. It is the Rathbone summer gathering and there are already four other cars parked casually in the yard of the house, big cars dappled with mud. All the way from Bristol he has talked about his family. As they came closer to the house he became more convinced she would not get on with them, would not like them, would find them strange, difficult. Unpleasant.

'You won't want to speak to me afterwards,' he says. And then, 'Please be as rude as you like.' And then, definitively, 'They wouldn't even notice.'

In the hallway – if that's what it is, the room (with its own fireplace) that lies beyond the front door (if this is the front door) – a dog puts its snout in Maud's crotch while other, smaller dogs, chew at her heels. There are old newspapers, dog leads, twenty hats from straw boaters to waxed caps. Waxed jackets, rows of boots upturned on the boot racks, a riding crop propped against a windowpane. In a crystal bowl a dozen brass-ended cartridges are like loose change from somebody's pocket.

Between the hall and the kitchen are other rooms that seem to have the freedom to simply be rooms. There are dog baskets, armchairs, a table that looks even older than the house. From one of the armchairs a dog, very old, tracks them with milky eyes. Tim's mother is in the kitchen. She is doing something with flour and fat, her hands sunk in a glass bowl. She is tall with hennaed hair in a tight French plait. She has a floral dress on, laced patent leather boots, a butcher's apron. She offers Tim her cheek, smiles at Maud. 'I have cool hands,' she says, 'which is perfect for making pastry.'

Children come in – two boys and a girl, the eldest perhaps eight. They are chasing each other but, seeing Maud, become suddenly self-possessed. The girl holds out her hand.

'I'm Molly,' says the girl. 'This is Ish and this is Billy. Are you Tim's girlfriend?'

The children's parents arrive, Tim's brother, Magnus, and his wife, the former model. 'Is it gin o'clock?' asks the brother. He and Tim slap shoulders. Magnus looks at Maud, welcomes her to the asylum. Through the kitchen window, on the shining lawn, two teenage girls, their hair in heavy plaits, are playing croquet. There is nothing dainty in the way they handle the mallets. The balls fizz over the mown grass.

It turns out that it is gin o'clock. Magnus spends twenty

minutes preparing the drinks, slicing limes, breaking ice in a clean tea-towel, measuring, stirring.

The dog with the occluded eyes has got on to a bench and is eating a biscuit it has dragged from a plate. It has an expression on its face like a martyr in a religious painting.

At the sound of an aeroplane, a thin buzzing in the air, the children all run outside. Tim leads Maud out behind them. They walk towards the stable block. The plane has disappeared but suddenly reappears thirty feet above the road, skims the treetops, then the hedges. Magnus's wife calls to the children but her voice doesn't carry. They are running towards the field behind the stables, waving. The plane falls delicately to the grass, bounces, settles, slows, turns and taxis towards the stables. It is a very small plane, silvery and trembling in its movements. It stops a short distance from where the adults and children are now gathered. A door swings up, a large man struggles from his seat. 'Points for the landing?' he calls.

To Maud, Tim says, 'Meet Daddy.'

Lunch is long, noisy. The family has manners that are beyond manners. The food is delicious, clever. There is wine from a decanter; there are crystal glasses, none of which match. Maud has been sat next to Tim's father. She calls him Mr Rathbone and he says Peter will do or shall I call you Miss Stamp? He has red corduroys on, a thick wreath of grey hair, a weathered and immaculately shaved face, a voice that seems to have no back to it, that effortlessly subdues all others. He flew that morning over Salisbury Cathedral and felt proud to be of the race that built it. He says there was a queen called Maud, wasn't there? Married one of the Plantagenets. He wants to know about her work at the university, her research. She explains, carefully though not at length.

Pathological wound healing, tissue repair response, particularly in the elderly.

'People like me, you mean?'

'Older,' she says.

'Well, that's something.'

When she speaks about defects in oestrogen signalling, he seems able to follow her. He tells her he was in the army and since then a dabbler – reads a lot, does stuff in the workshops, a seat-of-the-pants pilot. He asks about her accident. The story of her fall has already been recited three or four times. The children particularly like it. The cast came off last week.

'Do you have any scars?' asks the ex-model.

'A couple,' says Maud.

'And tell me about this,' says Tim's father, taking hold of her left arm with hands utterly unlike Tim's. He has glasses on a cord round his neck. He puts them on, reads the ink along her forearm (ink that took four hours over two sessions to put in place, her arm bloody on a padded rest).

'*Sauve . . . Qui . . . Peut. Sauve Qui Peut?*'

'Every man for himself,' says Magnus, refilling his glass.

'I'm not sure it's quite that,' says Tim. 'Is it, Maud?'

'Of course it bloody is,' says his brother.

'Better,' says Mr Rathbone, 'than runes or some Maori non-sense. At least it means something.'

'By that token,' says Magnus, 'she could have had *Arbeit Macht Frei*. That means something.'

'Don't be an ass, Mags,' says his father.

One of the twins says, 'There's a girl at school who's going to have the Song of Songs tattooed in a spiral around her belly button.'

'No she's not,' says the other twin.

'But did you know what it meant, Maud,' asks Tim's mother, 'when you had it done?'

'Mum, please,' says Tim.

She smiles. 'It was just a question, dear.'

They are given the upstairs guest room at the western end of the house. This is sometimes called the blue room on account of the wallpaper, or the Chinese room on account of a framed scroll that hangs between the windows. They take their bags up there. The room is packed with afternoon sun. Tim frees a fly batting the glass of a window. 'The children already love you,' he says.

'They don't know me,' she says.

He puts his arms around her from behind. 'How long do you have to know someone before you love them?'

'More than a morning,' she says.

'Did you like any of them?'

'Of course.'

'Any in particular?'

'Your father?'

'When I was a boy,' says Tim, 'I was completely in awe of him. Everyone talking about him like he was God. But you need to be careful. I can remember all of us hiding behind a sofa, Mum too, while Dad went from room to room looking for us. It wasn't a game.' He holds Maud more tightly, draws her against himself. 'Anyway, they'll all be drunk in an hour,' he says.

The long twilight, blue and violet, blue and purple. They stroll in and out of the French windows. They drink gin poured from a blue bottle. The children chase the dogs around the croquet hoops. Tim's mother, speaking about the light, the loveliness of it, the way it seems to simply *fold* over everything, becomes incoherent and tearful and plucks at the material of her dress. To Maud, Tim's father explains that there are three twilights. 'This one,' he says, sniffing it, 'is civil. Later we will have nautical.'

Blue and violet, blue and purple. The twins, their big backsides in pale jodhpurs, kneel on the lawn and dreamily tear at the trimmed grass. Magnus wears an expression of tragic boredom. His wife, in a dress she has sewn herself, drifts after the children.

By the time they sit down to eat it's nearly eleven and no one has much interest in the food. Tim's mother has wept and recovered and is now elaborately precise in everything she says. When they have finished, the picked-at food is simply pushed aside. Someone is coming in in the morning. Everything will be taken care of.

The family disperses. Tim takes Maud's hand, leads her through a door into a passageway and along the passage to a short flight of steps. Here there is a door with a metal face, a keypad at the side of it. This, Tim tells her, is the treasure room. He laughs as he taps in the code and says it's like the burial chamber in a pyramid. Inside, the room is noticeably cooler than the rest of the house. The walls are whitewashed, lined with shelves and cabinets. There is no window.

He shows her things. 'I don't really know what any of this is worth,' he says.

There's some heavy Victorian jewellery. A portrait, palm-sized, attributed to Ozias Humphry, of a young woman with red hair. There's a first edition of J. M. Barrie's *The Little White Bird* (with a dedication to 'pretty little Lilly Rathbone'). There's a portfolio of watercolour sketches by Alfred Downing Fripp, mostly of children on the sea-shore. There's a wind-up gramophone, a Webley revolver someone in the family carried at the second battle of

Ypres. There's a ritual mask from somewhere in central Africa carved from a dark and oily wood, an artefact that seems to speak a dead or irrecoverable language but not itself to be dead, not at all. Tim poses with the mask over his face, the revolver in his hand. 'My place or yours,' he says, his voice muffled by the wood.

On a low shelf, in a creased brown case, is the guitar. He lifts it out, and after a second of hesitation, puts it into Maud's hands. Lacôte, Luthier, Paris 1842. Breveté Du Roi. It appears to be in almost immaculate condition. It is surprisingly light, buoyant. Around the sound hole is a pattern of tortoiseshell with gold and mother-of-pearl inlays. She hands it back. He sits on a stool and begins to tune by ear.

'Old guitars,' he says, 'don't necessarily improve with age. Most of them lose tone. But this one's exceptional.' He runs his fingers over the strings, sounds a chord, adjusts the tuning. He plays the beginning of something, fifteen, twenty bars of a dance. 'The acoustic here is shit,' he says. 'But you get the idea.'

In her own house – her parents' house – there was a laminating machine, the television, her mother's wedding ring. Some painted plates on the wall in the living room. Paperbacks.

'Why do you keep it in here?' she says. 'It's like having a boat you never sail.'

'It costs about the same as a boat,' he says. 'And it's a lot easier to steal.' He puts it back in its case, lifts the case back onto the shelf, turns to find Maud looking at the African mask as if the mask were looking back at her. He has not seen anything quite like that before. He decides not to think about it.

When the treasure room is locked again, sealed, the alarm reset to active, they move together, quietly, through the part-lit house. It's late. There's no one around. He opens doors for her, invites her to peer into the empty rooms. Each room has its particular smell. The drawing room is leather and flowers; the little drawing room is last winter's last fire. The study stinks of sleeping dogs. The music room smells of the beeswax worked into the black wood of the piano. Everywhere, on every surface, there are pictures of children and dogs. Upstairs, it seems they must be the last ones to bed, the last awake, but when Maud with her wash bag finds her way to the nearest bathroom the light is on and the shower running. She sits on the step opposite the door and waits. The shower stops and a minute later Magnus comes out with a towel round his waist. At supper, while topping up her glass with good wine he told her, in a voice he might, in other circumstances, have used to pass on sensitive financial information, 'This is an all-or-nothing family. We tend not to take prisoners.' Now, seeing Maud on the step, he grins at her, whips off his towel, slowly wraps himself again and plods away along the corridor. 'Goodnight,' he calls over his shoulder. 'Funny girl.'

In the blue room, the Chinese room, one o'clock in the morning, Tim hunches over Maud like a man who has stumbled, a man preparing to be flogged. Every few seconds he makes a quivering, doggish thrust, sinks into her, slides out a little. They have been lovers for five weeks. Each time they do it he wants to drive her mad but each time it's himself he drives mad. The gasps, the hushed exclamations, are all his. With Maud there's just a subtle thickening of the breath. Has she been louder with other men? He frets over whether he is doing it right; if he should, for example, be crashing into her frenziedly rather than this slow stop-start fucking that, at twenty-six, appears to be his sexual character, his sexual fate.

He has not told her what Professor Kimber said in the hospital about the flitting moths. He is not sure how much he wants to know. If she didn't encourage them, does that mean she didn't go with them? Or does it mean they didn't need encouragement, that Maud as Maud was encouragement enough? That quality in her he has not yet found the word for but that seems located in her gaze, something undesigned, vulnerable, subtly immodest, that might suggest to all manner of people who approached directly enough, boldly enough, she would simply lie down and let them do it.

What has he found? Who has he found? Is this a wise love?

The room is not entirely dark. Electric light seeps under the door from the corridor, and there's a scattered light in the air itself, the light of summer nights, like phosphorescence at sea. Her eyes are shut, her arms loosely by her head, *Sauve Qui Peut* a block of shadow on one palely gleaming forearm.

He changes the rhythm. The old bed jangles. It is, in some curious way, like a children's game. He kisses her throat and she lifts her hips to him. It's too much. He has a condom on but feels he is flooding her, has access to her blood and is flooding her. He buries his face in her shoulder, is briefly blind, erased. For a few joyful seconds the whole world rests on the peeping of a nightbird in the trees by the stream. Then the room reassembles itself. She reaches between them, touches the end of the condom. It means – for they have learnt this last month to read each other's sexual dumb-show – that he should come out of her and carefully. He kneels up. She shifts off her back and swings herself to the side of the bed. For a while she sits there looking towards the uncurtained window, then wipes the sweat from under her breasts with the blades of her hands.

27

5

A night sail to the Île-de-Bréhat in the university boat. Twenty-four hours if the wind is fair, the course as south as they can sail it, cut the shipping lanes at right angles, raise the La Peon lighthouse or Les Heux, pick their way in through the currents.

There are six of them – three young men, three young women. In experience there is little to choose between them though some, like Maud, know more about dinghies than yachts, are more at ease working purely with sail and wind than passage planning and tidal curves. As a matter of club policy they have (in the pub in Bristol) appointed a captain. The choice was made by ballot, the names written on Rizla papers, the papers folded and dropped into a clean ashtray. Tim won by a single vote and promised to flog them all for the merest indiscipline. Maud received two votes, one of them from Tim. As for whether Maud voted for him, he knew there were two who did not and prefers to assume she was not one of them.

They leave on the morning tide. The wind is from the west,

force three to four, the boat moving in stately rhythm and heeling just enough to make a pencil on the chart table roll slowly to the leeward side. As they come clear of the shelter of the bay there are cross-currents, fields of green water stubbled with short choppy waves that make the hull jitter and send wisps of spray to darken the wood of the deck. But this is sailing at its easiest, its most pleasant. Summer air, the boat's shadow like black silk hauled just beneath the water's surface, the crew fresh, fresh-faced, the forecast excellent. In the afternoon the wind backs towards the south. There's a rain squall they watch arriving from miles off that leaves the boat's hundred surfaces shining and dripping. England disappears in the murk astern then appears again in uncanny green detail as the weather blows through.

In the last good hour of daylight they prepare a supper of chilli con carne (chilli sin carne for the one vegetarian), have a single glass of wine each, mugs of coffee. They switch on the navigation lights and begin the watches. In another hour they will be up in the shipping lanes with vessels of fifty thousand tonnes, a hundred thousand tonnes, some moving so fast that a light on the far horizon could be on top of them inside of fifteen minutes. Ships that by rumour and repute travel blind or nearly so, some man or other dozing on a part-lit bridge sixty metres above the water.

At ten to three in the morning, Tim and Maud are woken for their watch and move from thin sleep into the life of the boat, the tilted world. The off-going watch has made hot drinks for them. A voice, amused, calls Tim 'skipper'. On the chart table under a red lamp the English Channel is pinned by weights of lead wrapped in leather. Soft lines show their progress. The last fix places them thirty miles west of Jersey. In the cockpit Maud takes the tiller. Tim goes forward to look for shipping. Off the starboard bow are the heaped lights of a RoRo ferry; something much smaller off the other bow – a trawler, perhaps, from the odd way she's lit up. He watches for a while, sees how her bearing changes, then makes his way back to the cockpit.

'OK?' he says.

'OK,' she says.

She has a blue Helly Hansen jacket on, jeans, sea boots.

'You should have a hat,' he says and points to his own.

The light of the binnacle on her face, the eeriness of that light. She's peering up at the mainsail, the dove-grey ghost of it under the masthead light. She lets the boat fall away from the wind then brings it up a point and settles it. Tim puts half a turn on the headsail winch. The ferry is already passing them. He thinks he hears its engines. Perhaps he does.

'Turn right,' he says, 'and we could sail for America.'

She nods. She's concentrating.

'Would you like that?'

'Yes,' she says.

'Good,' he says. 'I'll pop below and cut their throats.'

'OK,' she says.

'You may have to help me heave them over the side.'

'OK.'

'Or would *you* like to cut their throats?'

'Are you keeping watch?'

He reaches across, touches the cold cloth of her jeans. 'OK,' he says. 'I'll behave.'

At twenty-minute intervals they swap roles, one to the tiller, one to the slatted bench on the leeward side to keep watch under the foot of the sails. The urge to keep talking to her, to keep her attention, is disturbingly strong. Love is making him slightly foolish. Here they are, crossing the English Channel at night, and he, the nominal captain, is thinking of the chocolate in his pocket and whether she would let him feed it to her so that he could feel for a moment the slight damp heat of her mouth on his fingertips. He should shake this off. He should assume his responsibilities. Come on, Rathbone! But beyond all admonition is his belief that the world is secretly powered by people in exactly the condition he is now, melodic, lit up, the nerve-trees of their brains like cities seen from the air at night . . .

Over the eastern horizon, the morning star. At twenty to six the sun is rising. Briefly, sea and air appear as things new made and they are Adam and Eve drifting on a vine leaf, a morning in Eden. Then fog comes down as fog can, long fingers of it winding shyly around the things of the boat and thickening until visibility is down to thirty yards, then ten. Tim fetches the horn, shouts up the rest of the crew. They stand by to start the engine, to drop the sails. The sea rustles at the side of them. The fog is theatrical, impenetrable. Tim sounds the horn – one long blast and two short. There's someone below watching the radar, everyone else is on deck, leaning into the fog. They begin to hear the horns of shipping. They speak in whispers, see shapes, imaginary head-lands, vessels of smoke. On the VHF, the open channel, comes a sudden voice in a language none of them recognize. The cadence is unusual. It may be a warning of some sort but it sounds more like a recitation or a call to prayer.

6

In her pigeon-hole in the biology department she finds an advertisement for a job. It's been cut out of the *New Scientist*, and in the margin, in Professor Kimber's handwriting – *Interested?*

The job is for a project study-manager leading, in a year or two, to a position as clinical research associate. The company is called Fenniman Laboratories, American-owned but with a UK base in Reading. She applies and is called for an interview. She takes the train from Bristol. The journey takes her through Swindon, and as the train slows she looks up from the papers in her lap (the glossy folder of information about the company) and takes in the utter familiarity of the view – the car parks, the billboards, the old engine sheds and workshops, converted or derelict. The station is a bare half-mile from where she grew up and where her parents still live. Further off is the school she went to (not one her parents ever taught at) and beyond that, at the not-quite-visible edge of the town, the house on the estate where, at fifteen, she lost her virginity to the father of the children she babysat for. Twenty minutes on his marriage bed, the satiny counterpane, late-afternoon light on the wall and strict instructions about which towel she could use when it was over.

There is no one she knows on the platform, no girl from school with a pushchair, no one she remembers from the terraces of the football ground, the narrow turnstiles she used to push through to watch the team slide down through the divisions, the players steaming like cattle on the muddy pitch, the manager in his big coat tearing pieces of air to shreds. Then they are off again, past posters advertising days out by the sea, past warehouses, a trading estate ('Swindon Vehicle Solutions'), the rind of meanly windowed new-builds, the first fields . . .

She goes back to the folder. There are headings such as 'You and Fenniman Laboratories', 'Our Philosophy', 'Into the Future'. There are charts of company performance, market share. There is an open letter from Josh Fenniman, CEO (*I have a passion for excellence in all fields . . .*). At the back of the folder is a list, with short descriptions, of the company's current research areas – diabetic neuropathy, post-herpetic neuralgia, nerve blocks, kappa-opioids. One study in particular catches her eye, a project involving a chemical called epibatidine discovered on the skin of an Ecuadorian frog, a type of toxic sweat that has also turned out to be powerfully analgesic. Fenniman's has produced a derivative called Fennidine and is starting a phase two trial at a hospital in Croydon. If she gets the job, the study might, conceivably, become one of those she monitors.

The next time she looks up – alerted by some alteration in the quality of the light – they are passing beside water. It's the gravel ponds where she first went sailing in the Mirror Ten dinghy she and Grandfather Ray built from a kit in his garage. On the water they had nothing to guide them other than the how-to book that came with the kit. Grandfather Ray was a railwayman. He sat in the boat wearing his yellow fluorescent jacket with British Rail Western Region on the back. They had a tartan thermos, sand-wiches, no life jackets. They spent an hour crashing softly into the reeds that grew by the banks before they worked out how the boat was turned. She was two weeks short of her eleventh birthday.

At the interview she recounts something of this story. Professor Kimber, who has learnt, through patient questioning, much of Maud's past, has encouraged her to ('They'll like it,' she said. 'They'll like that side of you.') The interview is conducted by a woman from Human Resources and a man called Henderson, a South African, who is himself a keen sailor and grew up sailing out of Port Elizabeth with his father. He thinks it's delightful that Maud learnt to sail with a railwayman, that they sat on the bank of a pond with a how-to book.

The woman, however, has no interest in sailing. She is tall, impeccably turned out, has a small silver cross showing at the opening of her blouse. From the beginning, she seems suspicious of Maud, ill at ease with her, this candidate who shows no inter-view nerves, who makes eye-contact, who *maintains* eye-contact, in a way that is, frankly, not quite right.

For twenty minutes Maud and Henderson talk about the pathology of healing. Henderson uses the phrase 'the wound's journey'. They talk about methodology, health out-comes, trial protocols; about the pharmaceutical market place, the industrial angle. Maud is strong on the science, less so on commerce.

When the talk has lulled and Henderson has leant back in his chair, the woman from Human Resources says, 'If you were a drink, what would you be?'

After a moment Maud answers, 'Water.'

'With ice and lemon?' asks Henderson.

'No,' says Maud.

'Just plain old water? Straight up?'

'Yes.'

Henderson grins. The woman jots something onto her pad.

'Any questions for us, Maud?' asks Henderson.

She asks him about the trial in Croydon.

'Ah, yeah,' says Henderson. 'The little frog. Epipedobates. That's beautiful, isn't it? The chemical has a profile similar to nicotine. So maybe smoking will turn out to be good for us after all.' He smiles at her. 'I don't think I'm giving any secrets away if I tell you this is one of Josh Fenniman's pet projects. If there's a breakthrough, the consequences, human and financial, would obviously be pretty significant.'

From somewhere, someone's bag or pocket, there comes a faint electronic chime. Henderson looks over to the woman. The woman is looking at Maud.

'We don't,' she says, 'have an official policy, but do you mind if I ask what's written on your arm?'

She gestures to the half-word visible below the cuff of Maud's jacket. Maud undoes a button and pulls up her sleeve. She offers her arm, lays it on the table as if Henderson or the woman were going to take blood. The woman leans forward but keeps her hands in her lap. She has attended half-day seminars on appropriate and inappropriate contact. Henderson moves a finger in the air about an inch above the black ink, the white skin. He sounds out the words. 'Oh,' he says. 'Yeah. Yeah, I get it.'

After a second interview a fortnight later and a reference from Professor Kimber (*Maud is dependable, deeply resourceful and notable for the determined way in which she sees all projects through*

35

to conclusion), and despite the reservations expressed by the woman from Human Resources ('I thought she was arrogant. Is she going to get on with people?'), Maud is offered the job. She accepts.

7

Six weeks before Christmas, seven months into the relationship, Maud and Tim begin to live together. Tim finds a first-floor flat in a small, half-hidden crescent on the hill above his old place. It's hidden from the main road by three plane trees that have grown as tall as the buildings. The houses (that must once have belonged to wealthy and perhaps fashionable families) have been converted into flats by someone more interested in rent than architecture, but the big sash windows are unspoilt and admit a tree-filtered light that shimmers when the sun is low and throws shadows of branches onto the back walls of the rooms. Tim puts down the deposit, rents a van. The van is almost entirely taken up with his own stuff; Maud's few boxes are squeezed in by the rear doors. All of it – the relationship, the move – feels inevitable to Tim and several times, as they carry their things up the common stairs he says, 'Doesn't this feel inevitable?' After the first time, she's quick enough to agree with him.

They have a flat-warming party. Tim plays flamenco (not on

the Lacôte or the Lacôte copy but on a guitar of highly polished cypress from the workshop of Andrés Dominguez in Seville). Among the guests are Tim's former flatmate, Ernesto, and his girlfriend with the blue-black hair. While Tim plays, she dances some private version of flamenco then sits on a table and looks at Maud, studies her, before leaning over to Ernesto and whispering, '*Ella, la novia. Una bruja.*'

'*Una bruja? Qué va! Es como una chica que trabaja en una pastelería.*'

Professor Kimber is at the party, dress split to her thigh, a silk camellia in her hair. She has brought two bottles of prosecco and a bunch of small yellow hothouse roses. She has also brought three or four of the moths, who look innocent, sane and gentle, entirely unpredatory. At some point during the evening, the party in its last fling, the moths flown home, Tim finds himself alone with the professor. 'Congratulations,' she says, touching her glass to his, and when he thanks her she says, 'Now which do you think she is, Tom – very fragile or very strong?'

'Tim,' he says, 'rather than Tom.'

She smiles. 'I suppose you'll find out in the end,' she says. 'I suppose we all will.'

At Christmas they are invited to his parents' house. He puts them off with the promise of being there the following year, and he and Maud spend Christmas Day alone eating tinned sardines, peaches in brandy, chocolate money. He has bought for her several small lovely things. A little brooch of antique jade in the form of a salamander. A dozen bangles of thin, beaten silver. A trinket box of polished rosewood (though she possesses no trinkets). A book of Chinese poems full of lovesick minor officials setting off for remote provinces. Also, a pot of winter jasmine, flowering.

To Tim, Maud gives a sailor's knife with a cork handle and a marlinspike. 'This is perfect,' he says, not mentioning the two he already has in a drawer somewhere. 'A perfect present.'

On New Year's Eve, frigid air tangled in the branches of the plane trees, Tim prepares them a private feast. First, a dozen oysters that have been sitting in their woven basket on the narrow balcony; then steak tartare made by hand-mincing best fillet, a raw egg stirred in, a chopped shallot. She has never eaten steak tartare but is happy to try it. He cannot imagine what he might suggest that she would baulk at. Sago pudding? Calf's brain? In restaurants, when she chooses from the menu, he does not get the impression she particularly *favours* one dish over another. And he loves the way she steadily clears her plate, the way at the end she puts her knife and fork together, tightly, a dead knight and his lady.

With the meal over they sit on the sofa and drink gin. Glass after glass of it. The room is snug, a faint odour of seafood, the sea.

'Have you ever done anything you're ashamed of?' he asks.

'No.'

'Have you ever done something, you know, deliberately to hurt someone?'

'No.'

'Have you ever stolen anything?'

'No.'

'Did you ever lie to your parents?'

She shrugs. 'I didn't tell them everything.'

'Aha! What didn't you tell them?'

'Just not everything.'

'Like?'

'Where I'd been. Who I went with.'

'Who did you go with?'

'When?'

'I don't know. When you went.'

'We're drunk,' she says.

'Of course we're drunk,' he says. 'Have you ever kissed a girl?'

'What?'

'Have you ever kissed a girl?'

'Why do you want to know?'

'I bet you kissed Professor Kimber. I know she wants to.'

She laughs at this, that short laugh of hers that always seems to catch her unawares. 'Why don't you play the guitar?' she says.

'I want to know everything,' he says. 'Swindon 1975. Daylight. Your first breath.'

'That tune you played when I came out of hospital.'

'When did you start being you?' he asks.

'I don't know,' she says.

'Try.'

'I don't know.'

'You never ask about my girlfriends,' he says.

'Why would I ask about them?'

'Curiosity?'

'I'll ask if you want.'

'No,' he says. 'No. The past is the past. Isn't it?'

'Yes,' she says.

'It's just us now.'

'Yes.'

'Tim and Maud.'

He tops up their glasses. They've been drinking it neat. Their colour is high, their mouths burned with gin. They decide to go for a walk but get no further than the bedroom. They kiss, they topple on to the bed. The curtains are open but the room is unlit.

They seem to have been sewn into their clothes. Buttons do not operate in the usual way. He licks her wrists, she strokes his ears. Half an hour later he floats into the bathroom, kneels in front of the toilet and throws up. Oysters, raw meat, acid, gin. He's there a long time. When he comes back to the bedroom, cold, shaky, he stands in the doorway looking at her as she sleeps in a pool of thin light that falls past the netting over the window. His heart fails him for a moment, for there is nothing there, nothing in her shape on the bed, compact as a seed, to suggest she has any need of him, that she is not already complete. He has been fooling himself! He has not reached her, has not understood her at all. He should get out before it's too late. He should pack a bag and get out. He will change his name. He will work on a trawler. Maud, in time, will marry a passing god, a moth god. Or become a temple prostitute or an assassin or the first woman on Mars. She will think of him sometimes. She will look at the bangles, the jade salamander. She will not cry.

He whispers her name. She is snoring lightly; a girl, a woman, dreaming of snakes. Or whatever. You don't know. He unhooks his big towelling bath-robe from the back of the bedroom door, lays it over her with elaborate care, then settles himself on the bed beside her, shudders, shuts his eyes, plays music in his head, thinks wow, 2001. Wow.

In the morning, he remembers neither insight nor fantasy. He feels ill and cleans the kitchen. He decides – kneeling in the middle of the brightening floor – that the only thing that matters is being brave and he shouts this news to Maud in the bathroom and after a second or two thinks he hears her call back her yes.

She starts work at Fenniman's. She has bought two new outfits from the department store near the bus station. One is dark blue, one is black. Dresses with jackets that make Tim think of the sort of outfits a woman detective might wear to give evidence in court.

She gets up early, perhaps two hours before it is light. By lamplight he watches her dress. If she notices him she doesn't object. The clever way women put their bras on. Deodorant, camisole. He likes to watch her pull her tights on, how the act of pulling up the tights to her waist is somehow childlike, so that it's easy to imagine her at eight or twelve, dressing for school on a winter's morning. Depending on the outfit, she sits on the edge of the bed for him to zip up her dress. Each morning for the first two weeks he offers to make her breakfast but she doesn't want it. She cleans her teeth then leans in to say goodbye, her coat in her arms.

The first month is induction. She goes up on the train, eats a sandwich, drinks tea, looks out at the grey fields, houses in their morning privacy, the light coming up over England. Certain faces become familiar – the man who never takes off his cycling helmet, the man who appears to be meditating, the woman with eczema. When the carriage is very warm she sometimes falls asleep and twice in one week she dreams of the desert – or some place, scuffed, waterless, inchoate, that she thinks of as desert for lack of any term more exact.

At the laboratory they introduce her to everyone, including the cleaners. Fenniman's has bright, egalitarian policies. First names, no titles. The atmosphere is relaxed but focused. The walls are painted a fine silvery grey. The furniture is moulded plastic in primary colours. Here and there, on walls and doors, there are squares of board printed with inspirational quotes – Martin Luther King, Einstein, Gandhi. On the door of Meeting Room 2 there's a poem by Marianne Moore:

If you will tell me why the fen
appears impassable, I then
will tell you why I think that I
can get across it if I try.

The air of the place is odour neutral. The staff wear no per-
fumes or colognes, no one smokes. Even in the animal room,
where three hundred rats live in carefully indexed cages, there is
no strong smell. Heat in the room is strictly maintained at between
twenty-two and twenty-five degrees. The lights come on and off
at twelve-hour intervals. The animals themselves, or those not
subject to experimentation, are sleek with health, gentled from
regular, careful handling. At break-times, rather than sit up in the
staff room, Maud sometimes goes down to help the technician, a
man called Keith who plays at the weekends in a bluegrass band
and who sometimes winks at her as if he and she alone can see
through it all, the Fenniman vision, the Fenniman mission.

At the end of induction she is given two hundred business cards
and two lab coats (Fenniman Laboratories embroidered over the
breast pocket). She is given a phone, the Nokia 8260. She is given
a computer – one of the iBook 'clamshells' that come in a variety
of colours (Maud's is blueberry). There is also a company car, a
Vauxhall Corsa (purple), 78,000 miles on the clock, the driver's
seat moulded to the shape of someone larger than Maud, someone
who has left the company.

She will monitor three projects in three different cities. A study
of nociceptors and allodynia at the Radcliffe in Oxford, liver
enzymes at the Royal Infirmary in Bristol, and the epibatidine
trial in Croydon. Each project has its allotted day. One day a week
will be spent at the headquarters in Reading; the remaining day
she will be at the flat, working on the clamshell. She is not highly

paid but paid well enough and she will have more if she successfully completes her probation. Promotion to Clinical Research Associate could happen as soon as eighteen months. On the last day of induction, Henderson, despite the cold, the blustering wind, walks her the length of the car park to where the Corsa is waiting. 'For luck,' he says, and gives her a small origami crane he has made from red paper. It almost blows away as he passes it to her.

8

Spring comes, and with it the sly greening of the city. Doing yoga in the living room while Maud is at work, Tim is struck by a beam of sunlight and imagines himself a saint in a painting.

He decides to write a concerto, quite a short one perhaps, which he will call CYP2D6 after the liver enzyme that converts codeine into morphine and which, for the pleasures of her teacherly gaze, her fluency, he has made Maud explain to him at length and in detail. He will, of course, dedicate the concerto to her. For Maud, for M. For M with love. He will give it to her on her birthday or some other auspicious day. The little concerto! It will be proof of many things.

Elated by this – the prospect of the work, the already perfectly imagined moment of the presentation – he cycles to a music store at the bottom of Park Street and buys workbooks bound in blue card. Urtext. Merkheft für Noten und Notizen. He buys a dozen (they are so beautiful) then cycles to the delicatessen on Christmas Steps and has the plump girl lift ribbons of pasta from the wide floury drawer under the counter. He buys fennel sausages (that he will split from their skins), dried porcini, single cream, imported yellow courgettes. Also a bottle of red wine with a painterly label that seems to show Eve companionable with the serpent, the pair of them under an umbrella pine in some dangerous southern garden.

When she comes home – it's been a Croydon day, a three-hour meeting about the biosynthesis of alkaloids, then a talk, endless, entitled 'What can we learn from ABT 894?' – the wine is open, the mushrooms soaking in warm water, a large pan on the gas coming slowly to the boil. She takes a shower. When she comes back to the kitchen towelling her damp hair he says, 'Today was a true spring day, wasn't it?'

He watches her sit, watches her set up the little blueberry computer. He pours her a glass of wine. 'Check out the label,' he says. 'It may not be theologically sound.'

The sideboard by the cooker is spread with good things. His technique with garlic – crushing the clove with the flat of his knife, slipping it from its skin, dicing it – has an almost professional flair. He chatters to her over his shoulder. He hears the computer keys, now slow, now as though she is dropping fistfuls of dried peas. He has finished his first glass and pours himself a second. The wine, which had been interesting at first, with notes of rosemary and black tobacco, now seems bizarrely heavy, syrupy and heavy, with notes of tar, dead flowers, bath oil. How stupid it is to buy wine for the label! How stupid to go shopping because you have been touched by a beam of sunlight while practising yoga!

On the wall above her head the plaque of evening light is crisscrossed with the shadows of the plane trees. He takes a plate from the rack beside the sink, holds it at arm's length over the floor, waits some eight or ten seconds, then drops it. She looks at the shattered plate, glances up at him, turns back to the columns on the screen. 'Sorry,' he says, and fetches the dustpan and brush from the narrow cupboard at the far end of the kitchen where all the cleaning things are kept.

9

Something he would like to tell somebody. That when she sucks him it is no more lewd than if he were being sucked by, I don't know, a heifer, something of that kind. It is thorough and patient. And when he comes she drinks every last drop of him so that he wavers over the abyss and for several minutes afterwards is unable to meet her gaze or even say her name. In fact, there is no one he could possibly tell this to, not even his brother.

10

Though neither of them is now officially connected to the university, they are allowed to stay in the sailing club. They are the type of members the club cannot easily do without. They work on the boat, they pay their subscriptions, they know how to sail.

The boat is out of the water again but there is no caulking to be done, no bolts to replace. Some scrubbing of the hull and keel, on deck some sanding and varnishing. The most pressing job is replacing the stern gland around the propeller shaft. By the end of last season a steady drip had become a thin persistent trickle. It is not a job to attempt in the water, sea water flooding the engine compartment while someone flails with a spanner.

On the Saturday before Easter, they drive down to the coast in the Lancia. At the boatyard they meet two other members of the club, Angus and Camille. They pull on overalls. Camille, a fourth-year medical student, has brought two thermoses of coffee and a tupperware box of madeleines she has baked herself. Angus tucks copper dreadlocks under a woollen cap. Tim fetches the ladder and lashes the top rung to a cleat on the deck. He does not want Maud going up, feels his stomach turn at the sight of it, her blithe stepping from ladder to deck. He suggests she wears a safety line though he does not expect her to agree to it. She does not agree to it.

They work until two; coffee and madeleines sustain them. The men scrub the hull – neither is remotely mechanical – while Maud and Camille kneel either side of the access hatch on the cockpit sole, skinning their knuckles undoing clips and loosening bolts. To shift the locking nut they have to wrap four hands around the handle of the wrench. The capping nut is no easier. Camille hisses, '*Merde, merde,*' and when she catches her wrist, hard, on the edge of the hatch, is briefly tearful, then, laughing to find herself so ignored, comes back to the work. To free the old packing they need a tool they do not have – that may not, in fact, exist. Maud goes down the ladder and crosses to the boat shed. The shed is a hundred years old, an expanse of roofed air like a provincial railway station from the heroic days of steam, one of those places always grander than the town it served. There is no one in view – the yardsmen are still at lunch perhaps – and she is about to leave when a man leans from a shadowed tangle of ribs and struts, the beginnings or end of a boat, leans out and looks at her a moment and says, 'You're the girl whose flying lesson went wrong. I was here when that happened.'

His name is Robert Currey. He is forty, perhaps a little more, short and broad, his hair in dark curls. She tells him what she is trying to do, what she needs. He nods and crosses to a canvas tool bag, roots around (the bag is like an old canvas fish, a pantomime fish) and comes out with a tool, steel handle at one end, then a length of hawser, then, at the tip, something like a corkscrew. He smiles at her. 'Good luck,' he says.

The old packing is dragged out. Tim and Angus drive into town to buy crab sandwiches and a box of new packing. Maud and Camille wash in the marina toilet block. Camille brushes her fingers over the ink on Maud's arm. 'I love this,' she says. 'You want to see one of mine?'

She unbuttons the overall, peels herself, undoes her jeans and hooks down the waistband to show, just above the black cotton of her pants, a pair of elegantly drawn ideographs, Chinese, Japanese.

'What does it mean?' asks Maud.

'Fuck me until I cry,' says Camille. She rolls her eyes. 'Actually, it means harmony.'

'It's nice,' says Maud.

'Yes,' says Camille. 'It's nice but I like yours better. Yours is *speaking*.'

In watery sunlight they saunter in the yard. There are yachts on stilts, a few power boats, some upturned wooden boats like wherries or ships' pinnaces; a fishing boat hauled up on the slip, half-way through a fresh coat of blue paint. At the far end of the yard, the point where they will have to begin their loop back towards the water, Maud stops beside one of the chocked boats, looks up, walks slowly around it, first one way then the other. Everything suggests it has been there a long time. Even the wooden props are darker than those of the other boats, have more weather in them. The hull – fibreglass – is spotted with old red paint. The keel is long, deep, substantial. When she steps back she can see the end of the unstepped mast poking out like a bowsprit. All the rest is under a green tarpaulin streaked with bird shit and lashed so low over the transom they cannot see a name, a home port. From the mast tip, hanging like something someone has slung there and forgotten, is a small wooden board, the words 'For Sale' painted on it, and a telephone number, of which only the first few digits are legible.

They stand there looking up at it, two young women in overalls. Camille takes Maud's hand. 'It's like,' she says, 'one of those little houses you see in the country. You know, at the end of a long track. When you look through the window, there's a tree growing inside.'

When Maud returns the tool she asks Robert Currey about the boat. A nice boat, he says, an old Nicholson, but no one's been on it for at least two years. If she wants to know more she should talk to the broker, Chris Totten. Office by the car park. He gestures with his head. She thanks him, and is about to step out of the shed when he calls, 'Has it caught your eye, then?'

By four they have finished with the stern gland. The new packing – carefully cut loops of greased flax – is snug around the propeller shaft. Lock nut and capping nut are back in place, tight but not too tight. They won't know how successful they've been until the boat's back in the water but it looks right. They settle the hatch and go down to where Tim and Angus are sitting on drums of marine paint, eating chocolate. Camille tells Tim that Maud has found a beautiful boat for sale and that all he has to do now is pay for it.

'Maud?'

'Just a boat we saw,' she says. 'An old boat.'

He wants to see it and she takes him. 'It's probably too far gone,' she says. 'As for what it's like inside . . .'

'It might be fine inside,' he says.

They circle the boat, look mostly at the boat and sometimes at each other. She tells him what Robert Currey said.

'Two years?'

She nods.

He shrugs, makes a face. They both reach up to touch the boat, the red swell of it, then walk along the side of the boat shed and turn down towards the car park and the broker's office. The broker is at his desk, smiling as though he has been expecting them. He listens, nods, goes to the metal filing cabinet and pulls out a photocopied sheet with a picture of the boat that seems to have been taken during a blizzard.

'*Lodestar*,' he says. 'Not a vast amount I can tell you. The owner passed away. The family doesn't want it. It's got seventeen thousand on the ticket but if you made an offer that got their attention . . . Are you selling anything? That nice boat you've been working on, for example?'

'No,' says Tim. 'We were just curious about this . . . What was it again?'

'*Lodestar*,' says Maud.

'Well, she's a Nicholson 32. You probably don't need me to tell you about the pedigree. Serious blue-water cruisers. Wear their age very well. Potentially a lovely boat.'

'Is there a survey?' asks Maud.

'Not here,' says the broker. 'Perhaps not anywhere. As far as I know she's sound. Do you want to have a look at her?'

There is a hunt for keys. The keys are found. A ladder is found. The broker, who in his office looked like a character actor, someone employed to play the ex-husband, the ex-sportsman, his yellow hair slightly too long for his years, turns out to be both nimble and quietly efficient. He ascends (in leather-soled shoes), frees the tarpaulin, rolls it up to reveal the cockpit, the coach-house roof. There is no rigging of any sort; the deck is bare. He springs the padlock on the wash-boards, shoves back the hatch.

Maud and Tim stand behind him in the cockpit. The entrance to the cabin is set just right of centre. To the left are switches, a depth gauge. The tiller has been removed but the binnacle is there, the compass settled under clouded glass. Maud wipes the glass with her sleeve, sees the needle steady at 270. Due west.

The broker stands back and invites them to go ahead of him. Maud goes first, three steps down into the twilight of the cabin. A smell of damp fabric, a whiff of diesel, but mostly just contained marine air, a salty emptiness that comes cleanly to the nose. Galley, chart table. Brass-bound clock, stopped. Benches either side in some hopelessly faded green velour. Little green curtains. A folding table folded, a barometer; then the heads, the forecabin berths, sail locker, chain locker. Behind fiddle rails in the cabin a clutch of books that in the damp air have taken on the character of sea vegetables. Tim leans to read the titles. *The Shell Channel Pilot*, Joshua Slocum's *Sailing Alone Around the World*, a Penguin Classics edition of the *Dhammapada*. Near the books is a picture screwed to the bulkhead, a photograph of what appears to be the boat, moored somewhere, the hour of sunrise or sunset.

They go on deck though there is nothing much to see. There is not even a guard rail. Tim holds Maud's sleeve. 'She has a tendency to fall,' he says. 'I remember it,' says the broker, quietly. He smiles at Maud. 'They make them tough wherever you come from,' he says. 'Where do you come from?'

Outside his office they shake hands and the broker says those things that rise up in him effortlessly – have a think about it, a very nice example, hold their value, any questions don't hesitate. He knows he will not see them again, not to talk about that strange unloved old boat, but the next weekend they are back in his office and he walks them to the ladder, climbs up behind them.

The girlfriend, the girl who fell then *got up and walked*, has a torch with her, a little knife. In the cabin she removes the companionway steps and studies the engine. She lifts the cabin sole and peers into the bilges, tries the sea-cocks, wipes the beaded moisture from the steel surround of a window, comes up on deck and crouches over a cracked U bolt, rattles a grab rail, wears all the while a face that gives nothing away. The boyfriend sits in the cockpit. Now and then he calls to her but mostly he lets her get on with it. He's the friendly type, an amiable leaner against walls, an amiable loafer. The decision about the boat will, presumably, be hers. There is nothing that he, the broker, the salesman, can do to make it more likely, not really. The boat must sell itself or not at all. He lights a Café Crème cigarillo, talks to the boyfriend about the Camper & Nicholsons yard in Gosport, the history of the class, and when there is no more to say on it they talk about music. On his right hand the boyfriend has varnished nails, long nails for plucking strings. 'Be honest now,' asks the broker, 'who's the greater player, Jimmy Page or Jimi Hendrix?' The girlfriend is back below again, her shadow reaching into a sail bag. The boyfriend laughs. 'You've got to be kidding,' he says. 'Are you kidding?'

The following Thursday, at nine-thirty in the evening, they ring him at home. He is heating up his supper; he is halfway down a bottle of Argentinian red. They're sorry to call so late (it's the boyfriend, a bit breathless) but they've been talking for an hour and don't trust themselves to wait until morning. They call him Chris now. He calls them Tim and Maud. 'How does fourteen thousand sound?' says Tim.

'Fourteen? A good place to start,' says the broker. 'A smart offer.'

Next morning he calls the owners. He has never met them and never knew the man who sailed the boat. It's a London number. The woman who answers seems at first not to know what he's talking about, then: 'Oh gosh, Daddy's boat. Are they serious? Do they have the money? What are they *like*?' She accepts the offer immediately. She would, he realizes, have accepted a lot less. He puts the phone down and sits looking through the office window at the river, the wooded banks. Sometimes his life feels small, sometimes boundless. On the desk he lines up his tin of cigarillos, his ashtray, his lighter. He picks up the phone again and dials Bristol.

11

Among other things, Chris Totten passes on the name of a local surveyor. When Maud speaks to him the surveyor says, 'I'll be working for you. Not for the vendor, not for the broker. I'll say it as I see it.'

By the beginning of May they have the report. Items in green print are mostly cosmetic; those in blue describe work that should be undertaken in the next two years. Those in red are urgent and must be attended to immediately. On the list of urgent items – a list that runs to two pages – is a new cutlass bearing, replacement of engine mounts, of fuel hoses (compliance ISO 7840). There are two seized sea-cocks, no fire extinguisher. Stanchion feet one and two on the port side are unsafe. Likewise, the port-side coach-house roof grab rail.

'It's not going to sink,' says Tim. 'There's nothing here that says she's unsafe.'

Maud agrees. 'If we have to replace the engine mounts,' she

says, 'we might as well replace the engine. Put in something more powerful.'

'And we need new upholstery.'

'The spinnaker is torn.'

'How about red?'

'A red spinnaker?'

'Red upholstery. But a red spinnaker too, if you like. And new red curtains.'

'Red paint for the hull,' she says.

'Imagine her,' he says, 'freshly painted.'

'He hasn't even looked at the rigging,' she says.

'What does it say about osmosis?'

' "Consistent with the age of the boat".'

'Do you like her name?' he asks.

'What?'

'Her name. *Lodestar*.'

'The name doesn't matter,' she says.

'It sounds,' he says, 'like an intergalactic battle cruiser.'

They start to gather the money they need, to pool their resources. Much of what Maud earns she saves, not knowing what to spend it on, not desiring many things. Tim has savings too, of course, money that hangs slack in various accounts, fifteen or twenty thousand at the last look (he rarely opens the statements the bank sends) but that's money for an easy mind, a cash-mattress that ensures he can spend his days with his guitars, his yoga, his experimental cookery, his walks across the city, his not-yet-fully commenced life of serious composition, the music he will soon start to put down in the little blue Merkhefte, his concerto. For *Lodestar*, he decides to visit the money stream a little closer to its source. He goes home on his own during the week, says nothing the first day, then on the second, choosing the half-hour before evening drinks, he finds his mother in the kitchen, takes hold of one of her cool hands and explains, with an earnestness he knows she likes, what it is he wants. Money is called 'funds' or 'help'. She listens to him, a very slight smile on her face. They have horses, a plane, land. An old yacht is neither here nor there. She agrees the upholstery should be red. Not poppy red, not cerise. Brick, perhaps, or Morocco. She thinks young people should have a project. When she says 'strive' her cheeks tremble a little. He embraces her. The Aga sends out wave after wave of generous warmth. He fetches the gin, the blue bottle, the accoutrements.

'Maud's not who we would have chosen for you, Tim. Not, I suppose, what we expected. But love is love. If you're happy.'

'I am.'

'Are you?'

'Very.'

She nods and looks into her gin, touches the ice with the tip of a heavily ringed finger.

They never meet the boat's owners and learn almost nothing about the man who sailed her. Name of John Gosse. Retired from the law. Tim calls him ghostly Gosse and suggests they make an offering to him, placate his spirit to keep him from walking the decks above their heads at night.

'What sort of offering?' asks Maud.

'Our first born,' says Tim, then laughs at her, the strange, almost anxious expression on her face. 'I'm just kidding, OK? The Gosse has gone. He's not coming back.'

Maud puts in four thousand. The rest is gusted from Tim's mother's account to Tim's and then to the account (Coutts, the Strand) of Amelia Shovel (née Gosse). Ownership documents are sent together with a card from Chris Totten wishing them many years of successful sailing. It's suddenly theirs. A thirty-two-foot boat. A sloop, a blue-water cruiser. Deep-keeled. This thing they saw, she saw. The old boat. The new boat.

For a while the boat is everything. He pores over atlases; she researches engines – Bukh, Yanmar, Volvo, Ford. At the weekends, late Friday or early Saturday, they drive to the coast and spend hours clambering up and down the ladder. They have an account with the chandlers. In a single weekend they spend over six hundred pounds on paint, on nylon and polyester rope, on bolts and varnish. With the help of Robert Currey and the tools in his canvas bag, they replace the cutlass bearing. Other work is given over entirely to the yardsmen. Bills are pinned to the board in the kitchen, a fat sheaf of them fluttering in the breeze from the window. 'We'll die poor,' says Tim, 'but we'll die at sea.'

He writes a song about the boat in which *Lodestar* is rhymed with far and guitar; love with curve, rove, Noah's dove. He plays it for her while she sits on the sofa in a towel after showering. The song ends with ten bars of sea-shanty. He has tears in his eyes. He lays down the guitar and rests his hands on the roses of her knees.

'What about India?' he says. 'Or New Zealand? Cape Town?'

'I have a job,' she says.

'The Tuamotu Islands, the Red Sea, Tahiti, Cape Breton, Cuba.'

'I have three weeks leave a year.'

'It doesn't have to be tomorrow,' he says.

12

When she tells her parents about the boat – one of the every-third-Sunday phone calls – her mother says, 'Oh, Maudy. Whose idea was that?'

'Ours,' says Maud.

'No,' says her mother. 'It's always *somebody's* idea.'

13

She tells Henderson too. It's the Fenniman annual conference, a hotel in Surrey, a Victorian mock-Tudor mansion with notable gardens and a restaurant described in the information pack they have all received as 'imaginative'. There are sales people, research and development people, money people, legal people. The American leadership fly in from Orlando. Everyone has been asked to reflect on the question: 'Can I do my job better?'

Meetings with Josh Fenniman are scheduled throughout most of Saturday. Maud is booked in for eleven-ten sharp. The meetings are taking place in the Tennyson suite on the first-floor mezzanine. Maud takes a seat outside the door and a moment later a young male PA ushers someone out and with the briefest glance at his watch asks Maud to come through. Fenniman stands to greet her. He is wearing a white, open-necked shirt, a jacket of charcoal Italian cashmere, blue jeans, gleaming nut-brown brogues. They talk for exactly ten minutes. He asks her about the trials. He makes no notes – it's understood that he's remembering everything. As the morning is warm, a fine June morning out in the notable gardens, Maud is in short sleeves. '*Sauve Qui Peut*,' says Fenniman, reading her arm and pronouncing the words with a good accent. 'It's an interesting choice.' He regards her a while in the way his rank entitles him to. Then, 'We're all team players in this outfit, Maud. I guess you understood that?'

'Yes,' she says.

'You like your room?'

'Yes,' she says.

He holds out his hand to her. 'Hope we'll see you at the party tonight.'

The party is in the Gladstone room. An eight-piece mariachi band has been bused down from London. There's a bar, a free first glass of champagne. Maud wears a dress of dark chocolate silk, a short jacket of a lighter colour, the salamander brooch pinned on the left side, the Indian bangles around her right wrist. The dress has been her party dress for at least five years. On the back, under the jacket, is a small hole where somebody embraced her while holding a cigarette. She wears no tights. Her bra and pants are black and from the same department store where she bought her work outfits.

Henderson brings her a flute of champagne. 'Love this sort of thing or loathe it?' he asks.

'Neither,' she says.

'How did you get on with the great leader?'

'He wanted to know if I was a team player.'

Henderson laughs. 'I'm not sure you are a team player, Maud. I hope you don't mind my saying that. But you're twice the scientist he'll ever be. He's a Harvard MBA. I don't think he's opened a science textbook since high school. How's the sailing?'

'We've bought a boat,' she says.

'Bought a boat! Hey. I'm impressed. What kind of boat?'

She tells him, leans close to make herself heard over the noise of the band. Henderson, it turns out, has sailed Nicholsons – 32s, 44s – and thinks they're beautiful boats, beautifully put together. He says you could sail free of the known world in a boat like that, sail straight off the map. They have a second glass of champagne. He invites her on to the dance floor but she shakes her head. He leaves her alone for a while. Twenty minutes later he reappears carrying two shot glasses of tequila. 'For luck,' he says. She doesn't mind drinking, doesn't care that much what she drinks.

He tells her things about himself. The music is too loud to follow it closely. At some point he starts to speak of himself in the third person. Henderson was restless. Henderson got it into his head he should marry. What sort of man was this Henderson anyway? She nods, looks out at the dancers, sees Josh Fenniman making the rounds, is mildly surprised to find Henderson holding out another glass of champagne, which she drinks down for thirst's sake. Somewhere around eleven she goes up to her room. She has sat on the bed and taken off her shoes when there's a quick double tap at the door.

'A nightcap,' says Henderson, holding up a little bottle of brandy from a minibar. 'Two minutes?'

As soon as he is inside and the door is shut he puts down the bottle, speaks her name, touches her cheek, leans down – he's at least ten inches taller – and kisses her. She's tired but not very; drunk but not very. He's kissing her, kissing her, kissing her. One hand goes down to the hem of her chocolate dress, scrapes it up, strokes her thigh then moves round to press between her legs. He presses so hard it lifts her on to tiptoes. She slides off him and steps back. 'I know,' he says. 'You have someone, I have someone.

But this is not about relationships. It's two grown-ups alone in a room. It's what makes the world go round.'

He reaches for her again but she brushes his hand aside. He puts on an expression of offended puzzlement, exaggerated, theatrical. 'Come on,' he says. 'When you opened the door what did you think we were going to do?' He puts a hand on her shoulder. Again, with a movement of her own hand she breaks the contact. 'Jesus, Maud,' he says, 'you're behaving like a child. Relax, will you?' This time he reaches with both hands, takes hold of both her shoulders. There's a moment of dancing familiar to her from her years on the mat with Rawlins (lame Rawlins wreathed in smoke). She finds some space for herself, a half-yard between the desk and the trouser press. She has the television remote-control in her left hand. She swings it in a clean half-arc that catches him flush between temple and eye. He drops soundlessly, kneels on the carpet, both hands to his head. She steps clear of him and watches. Behind her the television has come on with its personalized message of welcome, its slideshow of the garden, the restaurant. Henderson gets to his feet and goes into the bathroom. There is the noise of running water. When he comes out he is holding a wad of damp toilet paper over the place where she hit him. He doesn't raise his voice, doesn't look at her. 'I'll tell you this,' he says. 'Someone like you comes to a bad end.'

He squints through the spy-hole in the door, opens the door, slips out and closes the door quietly behind him. Maud puts down the remote-control, then picks it up again to switch off the television. In the bathroom there are three small drops of blood on the lip of the sink. She washes them away, washes her face, cleans her teeth, sits on the toilet to urinate. In the bedroom she strips off, lays her dress carefully over a chair. The room is much warmer than the bedroom in Bristol. She climbs naked between the sheets and puts off the light. She is asleep very quickly but wakes an hour later, two hours, with dry mouth and dry lips, the shadow of Henderson's hand between her thighs. On the window, between the wooden slats of the blind, the glass is smeared with orange light. And there's a sound, a sound so soft, deep and continuous, it takes her several seconds to know it for what it is, the hushed tumult of the rain. She listens until it lies inside her like her own voice but when she sleeps again she does not dream of rain but of fog, and of herself, alone on deck, waiting for the noise of surf.

14

In July, *Lodestar* is lifted and laid in the water. The keel enters like a blade, the hull dipping then rising as if the touch of water has, in an instant, woken all the latent possibilities of its form. Tim whoops. Chris Totten opens a bottle of cava, pours it into plastic glasses. On board the boat, Robert Currey is freeing the sling. The crane operator polishes his sunglasses on the hem of his T-shirt. He looks at Maud and Tim then at Maud alone. Gulls circle. A day-trip boat on its way down river sounds its siren, idly.

All the work in red type on the report has been attended to. There is, as Maud wished, a new (a reconditioned) engine. The mast has been stepped, the hull is a glossy new red, a single line of cream at the boot top. Other work can be done while she is on the water. Anything that can't be done on the water will have to wait until she's lifted at the end of the season.

Maud has taken a week off work. For the first three days they are moored alongside one of the yard pontoons. They sleep in the forward berths, wake to seabirds and the singing of halyards.

They have bottled gas on board, a functioning galley. They make coffee, toast. They boil eggs and throw the empty shells into the water, watch them spin on the tide.

Tim takes up smoking. It is, he says, a considered decision. He rolls his cigarettes and smokes them up at the bow. He watches the life of the river, the ceaseless coming and going, the enchantment of it.

They have a list of jobs they will not come to the end of. Coming to the end of them is not the point. Tim sands and varnishes. Maud, below deck, is fitting the new diesel stove. People drop by. They want to see how the young couple are getting on, and because they are young the sense is that they are not simply fitting out their boat but fitting out their lives, their life together. Robert Currey helps Maud install the stove chimney (a five-inch hole drilled into the deck), fit the deck cap. He looks at Maud as other men do, puzzled and interested, looks sidelong at her face as she frowns at the work in her hands. He is not gallant or flirtatious, or he is both, though in ways she does not notice. ('That man,' says Tim, 'with the right tools, could build an entire city.')

On the fourth day – they have water on board and ninety litres of fuel – they move to a swinging mooring in the middle of the river. Tomorrow – at last! – they will sail. They will go out on the morning tide, raise their sails and see. They will learn what this boat of theirs can do. As night falls they sit opposite each other on the old green benches and eat bowls of mussels. They cannot light the stove because the pump is not yet fitted but it's not cold, not with a jumper on, a glass of wine in your hand. They stay up to hear the midnight shipping forecast then go to their bunks, their skin smelling of varnish, marine paint and mussels. Where the V of the bunks meet, their heads are close enough for kissing but their bodies slope away from each other. They sleep lightly.

The boat adjusts itself on the tide; water sounds the hull. In its locker the anchor chain shifts like money.

For the rest of that summer and on into the autumn, the coast of England is strung with helpful winds. The boat is at the centre of their lives; time away from the boat is time spent waiting to be back on board. Each weekend the Lancia heads south, then (sometimes by starlight, moonlight, ribbons of stray lights from the river bank) they row out in the tender with a holdall of clothes, bags of food. And there she is still, the river sliding beneath her, the deck gently dipping as they pull themselves on board.

The stove is functioning now and on cooler nights Maud twists a length of tissue, lights it and drops it into the burner pot. Then a bottle is hunted out of a shopping bag, there's food in tupperware boxes, things Tim has cooked while Maud was at work.

The boat becomes what perhaps it was before, in John Gosse's time. A true sailing yacht, sound, undecorated, dry where it matters, the cabin more workshop or garden shed than living room. They make few plans; they sail where wind and tide suggest, one weekend flying past Start Point on the tidal race, the next running across Lyme Bay on a westerly and spending the night anchored off Exmouth Dock. They are still sailing at the end of October. The pleasure boats, the few that keep going, are mostly empty. The banks of the river grow paler, barer. They tell each other that this is the season's long tail, that there's no real reason not to sail until Christmas, to have Christmas on board, sneak in to somewhere like Newtown and have the place to themselves. It's effortless. They're confident, increasingly careless. The second weekend in November they find themselves miles from home in a wind forecast to be four gusting five ('Isn't that what they said?')

but which feels nearer to six gusting seven, and rising. It comes suddenly, or seems to. No time to dog things down, to remember what's been left out below. Tim looks for the life jackets and safety lines, cannot find them. They furl the jib to a scrap then Maud crawls over the coach roof to reef the main. She knows how to reef but she's never reefed on *Lodestar*. While Tim keeps the boat on a close reach she eases the halyard, tugs at the sail, gets nowhere. Something is jammed or she's forgotten something. The boat's movement tips her against the mast, again and again. Tim is shouting advice or encouragement, she cannot hear which. She tears a nail dragging the cringle down to its hook, then moves along the boom to haul down the back of the sail, the rain and spray washing away the blood from her nail the moment it touches the deck. The sea heaps up. For a while it's exhilarating. They trust the boat, the boat can take it, but after an hour they are silent, their eyes fixed on the blurred and featureless coastline. They are motor sailing and doing the best part of seven knots but nothing seems to get any closer. The only other vessel in sight is some sort of coaster, steaming away from them. They are hungry, the light's going. They are children on an adventure that has gone wrong. From the cabin there have been two or three reports, gleeful smashings, and when Tim ducks below to snatch a handful of biscuits he sees the glimmering of broken glass, crockery. It's nine-something by the time they read the lights off the castle headland and know they are back. Forty minutes later they drop the main and motor into the wind's shadow. The wind falls from their faces. They see the lights of houses, the lit tower of a church, headlights of cars moving untroubled through the narrow streets of the town. Their hands are mottled from the cold; their fingers close stiffly. When the boat is moored they go below and stand among the broken things on the cabin floor, strip off wet clothes and pull on anything dry and warm. Tim makes tea while Maud sweeps up the mess. They slop whisky into their tea, tell each other it was quite a blow, that perhaps they were foolish but at least they know now how the boat performs in heavy weather. And where were the harnesses? Are they perhaps lying in the back of the car? They shake their heads, drink more whisky, climb into their sleeping bags, praising the boat in voices that grow quieter and quieter. The last voice is Tim's trying to explain something about the huts of Arctic explorers, and how everything was always hanging out to dry and the oil lamps were burning and someone in a white turtleneck was tamping tobacco into his pipe and it was so terribly, terribly snug . . .

In the early morning, tying on the mainsail cover, Maud steps briskly to the side of the boat, leans over the rail and vomits. Tim, in the middle of fixing breakfast, pokes his head out above the hatch. Maud wipes her mouth with the back of her hand, looks at him and shrugs.

15

It turns out she's pregnant. For the next six weeks she is sick every day, several times a day. She carries plastic bags in the pockets of her winter coat. When there is no bathroom to go to she can use one of the bags and drop it in the next bin she comes to. Tim asks: 'Is it supposed to be like this?' He tries to persuade her to take time off work but she says she's not ill, she's pregnant. In the car park of the hospital in Croydon she passes out, comes to a few moments later lying in grey snow. She cleans herself, picks up her briefcase and goes to the meeting where, after a few minutes, someone politely leans over to tell her she's bleeding, a little ooze of blood from above her left eye. Two days later she's in Reading, Fenniman HQ. The woman from Human Resources stops her in the corridor. She wants to know what happened in Croydon. 'Let's have a chat,' she says. In the course of the chat – red furniture in a silver room – the woman learns of Maud's condition and puts on, fleetingly, her disappointed face. Women who start work and then, a matter of months later, announce they are pregnant are no friends of the sorority of committed professional women. 'I see,' she says. 'Well, congratulations of course. Are you intending to leave us?'

'No,' says Maud.

'But you will need to take maternity leave.'

'Yes.'

'How long did you imagine you would need?'

'I don't know,' says Maud. 'Two months?'

'That would involve childcare for a very small baby.'

'Yes.'

'You might feel differently later.'

'About the baby?'

'You might want to stay with it. Him or her.'

'Perhaps.'

'Do you have a due date?'

'June the twenty-fourth.'

'Then let's schedule another chat for – what? – a fortnight from today? Obviously we need to agree on a timetable, get some firm dates in the diary. In the meantime you should have a look at your contract. Make sure you understand the relevant clauses. Our responsibilities, yours. Any questions for me at this point?'

To the woman, Maud looks like a child on a bench in a long corridor waiting for someone who is not going to come. A child with her knees politely pressed together, who does not even know she's lost. If she liked her more, she might pity her.

With Tim, she visits his parents, the Rathbone house. She is embraced by his mother who holds her for a full half-minute. She is thinner than Maud remembers her and has a number of small burns on her arms. Tim's father cups Maud's face then shakes his son by the hand. 'Bloody well done, the pair of you,' he says.

The twins, home on an exeat weekend, wrinkle their noses: 'Really preggers?'

Magnus, just back from a week of meetings in Stuttgart, all his movements weary and imperial, laughs at her but seems, like his father, genuinely touched by the news. His wife mouths, 'Caesarean.' Under the kitchen table the children sing, 'We hate babies! We hate babies!'

At supper – 'And all this is *very* baby friendly,' says Tim's mother, pointing to the dishes – Magnus asks where they will live when the baby is born.

'Where we live now,' says Maud.

'Well,' says Tim, 'we haven't given it much thought. Not yet.' Maud looks at him. 'What's wrong with where we live now?' she asks.

'A child needs a garden,' says Tim's father.

'Not to mention grandparents,' says his wife, peering at the buttered swede.

'Do you know,' says Magnus to Maud, 'why grandparents and grandchildren get on so well together?'

She shakes her head.

'They have a common enemy.'

Almost everybody laughs at this.

The next weekend they drive up the motorway to Swindon. The town has just twinned itself with somewhere in Poland and Maud's father points the place out in one of his atlases. 'Apparently it's quite pretty,' he says, 'as Poland goes.' While her mother is filling the kettle for tea Maud tells her the news. She looks round from the sink, the tap still running, something like fear in her eyes. Mr Stamp goes out to the garage to look for the bottle of wine he thinks might be out there. He comes back with home-made sloe gin he won in a school raffle. To his wife he says, 'I suppose Maudy can have some, can't she?'

'I wouldn't think so,' says his wife.

'I'll have tea,' says Maud.

'Do you want some, Tim?'

'I'm fine with tea too.'

'I'll pop it back then,' says Mr Stamp.

After tea they go to visit Grandfather Ray. He used to live two doors away but since his strokes (the year Maud went up to the university in Bristol) he lives at The Poplars.

'Maudy's got some news,' says Mrs Stamp. 'Haven't you, Maudy?' She wipes the old man's mouth. 'Look,' she says. 'They've put odd socks on him.' When Maud calls the old man Grandpa, Tim's heart staggers. This was the man who built the boat for her, who taught her to sail! British Rail Western Division. Very slowly, and with obvious effort, the old man turns his attention from Mrs Stamp to Maud. Impossible to say whether he understands what she's telling him. Mrs Stamp changes his socks. He has feet like a troll. On the wall is a picture of a steam train flying through a country station of the kind long since abolished. There is also a picture of a woman, his dead wife presumably, stout, friendly looking, sexless. They leave him. Find their way out through the large, frightening building.

At home the parents have work to do. They're sorry but there it is. Maud and Tim sit in the living room with the TV and a plate of sandwiches. When Mrs Stamp puts her head in Tim says, 'These are delicious.' They watch the last half of *A Room With a View*. When it's over and the news comes on he squeezes Maud's shoulder. 'Why don't you go to bed, love?' he says. She goes. He takes the plate through to the kitchen. Mrs Stamp has also gone to bed or gone somewhere (where is there to go in such a small house?) but Mr Stamp is still sitting in a circle of lamplight carefully tracing the delicate coastline of somewhere. If he wants to speak to Tim, to ask him perhaps for some account of his life with Maud, of his intentions, this would be a good moment, but he goes on with his work, utterly absorbed, a level of concentration, of lostness-in-the-task Tim has seen often enough in his daughter.

He has already been shown his bed in the spare bedroom – the only double bed in the house belongs to the parents – and he is about to step quietly out of the room when he sees a photograph on the cork board by the fridge. It's pinned between a milk bill and the dates for the Christmas bin collections, a girl in school uniform photographed standing against a wall, satchel over her shoulder, socks pulled up, skirt falling to somewhere about the knees. Her hair is shoulder length; her fringe needs cutting. You can see the curls, curls that would come again if she let her hair grow. He takes the picture from the board. On the back of it someone has written the date – 1987. That makes her twelve. Eleven or twelve. No grin, no frown. Nothing to say if this was a good girl, a bad girl, a humorous girl, an unhappy girl. A small badge on the lapel of her blazer. Could be anything. 1987. He puts the pin back in the board, puts the picture in the pocket of his shirt. 'Goodnight,' he says.

'Goodnight,' says Mr Stamp. He's looking at Tim now but if he saw the thing with the picture, the quiet theft of the little picture, he seems to have decided to accept it.

16

She stops being sick. She swells. The soft structures of her pelvis ache. She has certain cravings. One is for pomegranates and Tim buys them from a stall in St Nicholas Market. He cuts them open, scrapes out the seeds, feeds them to her, likes that dull look of pleasure that comes over her face at the taste of them. She also has what he calls 'an offal thing'. She keeps it in bags in the fridge. Kidneys, liver. Once a lamb's heart in a spattered bag on the shelf beside his yoghurts. He does not see her eat it. The heart is there and then one evening it's gone, the bag in the swing bin, empty, a fine haze of cooking smoke under the kitchen ceiling.

She has not become tearful or irrational. She is not subject to mood swings. The way she moves has changed, slowed, become a little clumsy. Now and then, watching her, he thinks of one of his mother's words – *slovenly*. He notes that she goes a week without washing her hair. He offers to do it for her; she says she'll do it herself but doesn't. And one morning, emptying the laundry basket on the floor by the machine, he sees a brazen shit-streak on the soft cotton of her knickers. He soaks them in hot water and too much detergent. He puts on yellow Marigolds and scrubs them. He would rather break a thumb than mention it to her.

There is not much sex, almost no penetrative sex. They touch each other, though on the last few occasions she has gently removed his hand from between her thighs then gone on with him until he was finished. It's a connection of sorts but it feels like something a paid woman does to a man in his car.

They watch television. They look at the house brochures his parents send them. *Lodestar* is out of the water, covered over until the spring. Spring or whenever, in this new world, they can get back to her.

'How do you feel?' he asks, taking her hand, a Sunday dusk in the living room, her four-month belly soft under a sea-blue jumper.

'I'm OK.'

'Really?'

'Yes.'

'Not just physically,' he says.

'Not just physically,' she says.

'And you're not sorry?'

'About what?'

'About this.'

'You know I'm not.'

'I'm checking.'

'I'm not sorry.'

'It would be OK to be a bit sorry.'

'I know.'

'You're going to be a lovely mum.'

'I hope so.'

'The Inkling will worship you.' Inkling is his name for the baby.

It's a name the Rathbones have used before for unborn children. The Inkling. 'Tell me if you're frightened,' he says.

'OK.'

'Are you frightened?'

'No.'

'A little?'

'No.'

'That's good.'

There's a white plate on the floor, white china with red gravy. She looks at him, he looks at her.

'Hello,' he says.

She nods and he thinks how close everyone is to a kind of madness. Maud, his parents, himself presumably. There is nowhere obvious to take this thought.

17

In April they settle on a house. As Maud has shown so little enthusiasm for the project the choice is mostly Tim's – well, Tim's and his mother's. It's a three-bedroom semi-detached cottage on the Dorset–Wiltshire border, a short drive from the Rathbone family house. There's a garden, beams, a big wood-burning stove, a Rayburn, a wooden gate with roses growing at the side, no onward chain. The money stream buys the place outright. Tim and Maud will pay the money back at so much a month.

At the beginning of May, Tim hires a van. Friends give up half a day to help them. Maud, heavy now, folds clothes into suitcases, wraps crockery and glasses in newspaper. She drops a glass and Tim's old flatmate, Ernesto, cries, '*No le toques, Maud!*' He sweeps up. He embraces her. He puts his hands on her belly, his expression like a priest officiating at the Mystery.

By mid-morning the following day the last oddments – a box of teabags, a pot plant, the cork board with *Lodestar*'s bills still pinned to it – are wedged into the back of the van and they set off, south then west. A-roads give way to lanes with lacy hedgerows and unmown verges. Tim's parents are waiting for them at the cottage. Also the twins and someone called Slad, a middle-aged man, four-square, who, if not entirely a servant, is something similar – a retainer, a housecarl.

All the windows of the cottage are open. There is honeysuckle growing around the door. The path is laid with a blue-grey stone that Tim's father, dropping stiffly to his knees, identifies as blue lias, ancient seabed of the Jurassic, rich in fossils, ammonites in particular.

Inside, in the cool of the low-ceilinged rooms, there is already some furniture, pieces the Rathbones had in storage. A dresser for the kitchen, dining chairs of dark varnished wood, a leather armchair, its leather mottled and dented as if the chair were made out of old heavy-bags from a boxing gym. There is even a bed – Slad has somehow wrestled it up the stairs – with a headboard of brilliantly polished walnut. Other things arrive in the afternoon: a fridge, a washing machine and dryer, things delivered by the vans of local firms the Rathbones have done business with for thirty years.

Slad lights the Rayburn. At first it stinks of oil but the fumes disperse. By dusk the house is a house to be lived in and they gather in the warmth of the kitchen to eat supper. Tim's mother has brought a casserole in a red Le Creuset pot. Tim's father brings in a half-box of Burgundy from the back of the car. Slad goes home. He makes a kind of shallow bow to them all. Everyone tells Maud she must be exhausted. She says she's not but falls asleep after supper on the leather armchair and only wakes when the others are leaving. She comes outside with Tim to wave them goodbye.

'They ran out of things to drink,' says Tim. 'But they'll be back in the morning.'

They stand, hand in hand in the doorway for several minutes after the car's engine note has dwindled to nothing. Over the silhouettes of the trees the sky is crowded with southern stars. An owl calls; an owl calls back. The moment rests against perfection.

'Let's leave the door unlocked,' says Tim, 'we're in the country for God's sake,' but later, when Maud is in bed, he finds the keys and locks it, puts the bolts over. If nothing else, he has the guitars in the house.

She begins her leave from Fenniman's. She is given a 'good luck' card signed by everyone, including Henderson who just puts his name, Karl Henderson. She will start back in October. After that Tim will stay at home with the child, an arrangement he seemed eager to accept but which his father mutters about, claims not to understand at all ('Is this modern? Is it modern to have a child and then simply leave it?')

A midwife is appointed. There are only two in the local town and Maud is given Julie – ruddy, stout, motherly, though only a year or two older than Maud. 'Are you planning on a big family?' she asks, and when Maud says no she laughs as if this is something she has heard before, women who seem not to really want babies but who end up with a houseful.

She examines Maud. 'You're very strong,' she says. 'It'll come out like a lemon pip.'

She plays the baby's heartbeat through a speaker while Maud looks up at the mobile of slowly drifting birds she thinks at first are swans but later, after watching them for half a minute, realizes are intended to be storks.

Julie shows Maud the unit. One mother who looks, at best, fourteen, sitting up in bed nursing her baby. One mother lying on her back as if shot. One walking slowly to and fro in the company of a man with a snake tattoo around his neck.

Back in the office Julie asks for the birth plan but Maud doesn't have one. Her plan is to do what is necessary when the time comes. That doesn't seem to need writing down. As for pain control, they agree she will simply ask for it if she needs it. She does not mention to Julie her work in this area, the project in Croydon, the trial packs of Fennidine she has in the glove compartment of the Corsa. So far, the trials have been extremely promising, though there have also been reports of side-effects, some of them worrying. One volunteer suffered extreme nausea and had, briefly, to be hospitalized. Another – who is suspected of having an undisclosed history of recreational drug use – claimed to have had hallucinations, both visual and auditory. This subject, known as Volunteer R, has been excluded from any future participation in the trial.

At the cottage, as advised, she packs a crash bag, something she can pick up in a hurry when the moment comes. Breast pads, nappies. Nightie, underwear, wash bag, torch.

'What's the torch for?' asks Tim.

'Just in case,' says Maud.

'Of a power cut?'

'Put it back,' says Maud.

He puts it back, suppresses a smart remark about adding a hand flare.

At about this time, in the morning post (the nice post lady who already seems to know them well), Maud receives an unsigned letter, or not a letter at all but a sheet of paper bearing a quote from someone called Marguerite Duras, and copied out in black ink, in careful handwriting. It reads:

Being a mother isn't the same as being a father. Motherhood means that a woman gives her body over to her child, her children; they're on her as they might be on a hill, in a garden. They devour her, hit her, sleep on her; and she lets herself be devoured, and sometimes she sleeps because they are on her body. Nothing like that happens with fathers.

She has no idea who has sent it to her, cannot tell if the writing belongs to a man or a woman. The postmark on the envelope is illegible. Nor can she tell if the words are intended to encourage her or warn her or simply inform her. She folds the paper and puts it between the leaves of a book (one that Tim's mother has given her, *What to Expect When You're Expecting*). A short while later she takes it out of the book and carefully slides it between two oak boards on the bedroom floor. Posts it into darkness.

She does small jobs in the garden, plants French beans and lettuces while Tim plays slow scales on the guitars (the Lacôte copy, the Andrés Dominguez, the Taylor with the ebony fretboard, the cocobolo backstrap). The people next door, a childless couple who seem to live a highly organized and orderly life, who dress each Sunday in black lycra and ride their expensive bikes for miles, have already said they have no objection to the sound of a guitar, though they hoped he did not have an electric guitar, did not belong to a rock band. Their names are Sarah and Michael. It is already perfectly clear there will be no intimacy between Sarah and Michael, Tim and Maud.

The due date comes, passes. Another week goes by. Maud

sweats in the July sun. Her ankles swell; whole days pass when she hardly speaks. She is awake when Tim goes to sleep, awake when he wakes up. Julie comes out to the cottage. There is no sign of distress from the child. Maud's blood pressure is a little elevated but not a cause for concern. They will wait a few more days then consider their options.

Tim's mother visits. She offers to massage Maud's belly, looks relieved when Maud turns the offer down. The twins, broad-hipped virgins, can barely look at her without squirming – the horrid, comical outcome of the secret act! – but it is the twins who are with her, sitting in the little front garden braiding each other's hair, when Maud's waters break. They gape at her as she lifts her dress to watch the fluid run down the inside of her legs, can do or say nothing as she trudges towards the cottage.

Inside, Tim's mother is sitting on the leather armchair, head back, eyes half shut. It's her second month on Seroxat and she has, after some adjustment of the dose, achieved a passage of glassy calm. 'I'll take you,' she says. 'Tim will only drive into a wall. He can come along later.'

She spreads newspaper on the passenger seat. Maud sits on it with the crash bag on her lap. A dog in the well of the seat licks her legs, timidly. They speed away, the car's dust falling on campion, moon daisies, creeping buttercup.

'Try and stay awake,' says Tim's mother.

'I haven't taken an overdose,' says Maud, who may as may not have intended this to be a sharp remark. The dog is still licking her, its tongue flickering around her knees.

'When I had Magnus,' says Tim's mother, her bone-thin fingers wrapped tightly around the wheel, 'when I was in labour, I had a sort of huge spontaneous orgasm. Very unexpected. Rather embarrassing if anyone noticed. But at that age I could lean against the tumble dryer and be in heaven in about a minute. I've never understood those things you read in the magazines about women who can't. Makes you wonder if something's missing. You know, anatomically. I'm not going to ask about you and Tim. It's obviously very healthy. I remember Magnus having an enormous collection of pornography that he used to rent out to other boys in his house at school. He always had a good business head. Very good. But babies are what matter, Maud. You'll know that soon. Babies and children. Especially babies but children too . . . Well, this is odd . . .' She brakes, hard. They are at the edge of a village of low, thatched houses. A man in white is riding on a beautifully decorated horse. Around the horse women in gold and green and red are tapping sticks together and singing.

'Looks like a Hindu wedding. There are only about two Indians in Dorset.' She slides the window down, edges the big car forwards, and to every surprised or frowning face says, 'This girl is about to be delivered of a child. Thank you! No time to wait, I'm afraid!'

When they've reached the front of the procession she puts up the window, accelerates. 'You can call it Shiva,' she says. 'Or what's the other one? Kali?'

In the unit two other women are giving birth, each with her attendant team. The noises are what you would expect – life tugged around its spindle. Maud is doing well, people tell her so repeatedly. It's lunchtime, it's three o'clock. She has an hour in the birthing pool (it's new and they seem keen to use it). She has, in her seventh hour, lungfuls of gas and air (this, too, they seem keen to use).

The midwife wears a plastic apron like a dinner lady. 'Good girl,' she says, 'almost there.' The feel of the midwife's hand, the sight of her own knees, her stirruped feet. And visions – caused no doubt by the gas – a woman, for example, walking naked through some barren place, a desert, a shiny grey desert like the moon, just the view of her back, her hunched shoulders, the relentless rhythm of her walking and no end in view. Her back, her hips like an anvil, her shadow rippling in the grey dust of the place . . .

Then the promised burn, Tim weeping at something she cannot see, and in two drenching pushes it's out and lifted, still roped to her, and settled on her pounding heart. She touches its seamed back, rests her fingers there. The clock over the door says ten past ten at night. A bus passes on its way to the station; a moth dances under the ceiling. She has given birth. She has given birth and she is a mother. A mother, come what may.

18

The baby is a girl and they call her Zoe. Neither Tim nor Maud knows any Zoes. It is a name with no shadowy parings of others, a name unhaunted.

She latches on. She feeds hungrily at Maud's breasts. Julie is pleased, the health visitor is pleased. When the health visitor, who is older than Julie, visits the cottage, she weighs the baby in a sling and writes the weight in a book that Maud keeps. The baby has a way of arching its back as though trying to shed its skin. Maud asks about it and the health visitor says it's fine, normal, completely fine. When in doubt, bosom out. 'It's the cure for most things,' she says. She laughs.

Maud loses weight. Her T-shirts have little yellowish crusts of dried milk on them. By early September she looks gaunt. Don't let baby eat you up, says the health visitor. She leaves some recipe cards that Tim drops in the wood-burner. He cooks a leg of pork with pistachio nuts and garlic. He cooks chicken with a sauce of cream and eggs (Madame Brazier's recipe). Maud picks at it. It's too rich, too something. She wants things like the electric-green lettuces still growing in the back garden. When Tim points out these are mostly water she says yes, she's very thirsty.

October is warm still. Hazy clouds collect in the distance. The last ragged stalks of evening primrose flourish in the dusk. Maud's parents visit. They say they are sorry they haven't been able to come before. First the walking holiday in Slovakia, which had been booked months ago, then the new term, an OFSTED inspection in Week Two, for heaven's sake. They bring a toy with them – coloured wooden blocks threaded onto curling wire, the whole thing screwed to a wooden base and designed to assist with hand-eye co-ordination, with motor control. Mrs Stamp has the baby on her lap. She looks quite comfortable. She does not look as if she will drop the baby. She handles the baby, thinks Tim, like a vase she has not yet decided to buy. Mr Stamp wrinkles his nose at her. He waves to her and says how nice she looks. He has a habit of glancing over at his wife for cues to the expected behaviour, the posture, the language. The only time he seems at ease is standing with Tim in the garden gesturing to the hills, evoking glaciers.

The Rathbones are at the cottage three times a week, sometimes more. They too bring gifts – a cashmere bonnet and blanket, a silver christening bracelet, a wooden goose, an onyx egg, a succession of soft toys, animals remarkably like the animals they imitate. They dandle the baby. Tim's father holds the child with real and obvious joy. In the warmth of the last warm afternoons he likes to lie in the unmown grass, the baby sprawled asleep on his chest, on the heavy cotton of his shirt. To anyone who visits him there he whispers, 'This is bliss.'

And there is a present for Maud and Tim. A belated

house-warming present, a new-baby present. Tim peels it from layers of bubble wrap and when he can see what it is he calls excitedly to Maud, holds it out to her. It's one of the Alfred Downing Fripp watercolours from the treasure room, a picture of a young girl with a basket of cherries. Big blue eyes, pink cheeks and pink lips, a straw sun hat askew on her thick blonde curls. The picture has been framed by some excellent people in Sherborne. It has been put behind non-reflective glass. It has been insured. Tim walks around the living room with it, trying it out in different places. His mother, from the centre of the room, gives her opinions. His father is holding Zoe, talking to her, softly, privately. Maud is looking out at a stranger's cat on the lawn. The rooted lightness of its walking. The purity of its attention.

At the end of the month she weans the baby. The baby is frantic, pushes away the teat of the bottle, writhes in Maud's grip. Tim tries. He sits with her on the leather armchair, wets her lips with the milk, forces nothing. It takes the best part of an hour. The noise is remarkable, inhuman. Then, with a sudden uncoiling of her body, the child gives in. She lies back in Tim's arms and feeds, the new appetite as blind and powerful as the old. Tim looks at Maud, grinning. Maud goes upstairs and sleeps.

A week later she starts back at Fenniman's. Within days the drive to work through morning darkness, the drive back through evening darkness, feels entirely familiar. The Bristol project is with someone else now, the Oxford project is finished, but she still has Croydon, and is given a new project in Southampton investigating the use of kappa-opioids in short-term pain relief, including pain during labour. Because she herself has recently experienced the pain of labour this is, perhaps, thought to be a suitable project for her, though no one says this.

When she comes home in the evenings she often finds Tim and Zoe asleep in the warmth from the wood-burner. She does not wake them. She eats then sits with them a while. Sometimes the baby wakes first, sometimes Tim, sometimes they wake together as if, through the course of the day, the week, the several weeks, they have become perfectly synchronized.

There's nothing wrong with the baby, nothing at all. She loses her raw look. Overnight, it seems, a face appears. 'Christ,' says Tim, 'it's little Maud. Look!' Though to Maud it's obvious – the brow, the chin, the eyes above all – that the child is a Rathbone.

On winter Sundays they wrap up and go on walks. Zoe hangs on Tim's chest in a baby carrier, a kind of back-to-front rucksack called the Snuggler. He has a stick and on his thinning hair a Barbour waxed cap. They climb the stiles, cross shallow streams, walk up the blown green faces of Dorset fields. There's a pub they stop at for lunch, with swept stone floors, an open fire, a stuffed fox in a glass case. People there like to see the child. They learn her name, ask after her, admire her hands, her wispy hair, her mild, intelligent gaze. Soon, she is crawling over the stone flags. She pats the dozing dogs. The dogs, warming their bellies, ignore her. In the spring she experiments with standing and takes her first steps not at the cottage but in the pub, sliding from the bench to the floor then swaying into the lounge bar where she stops under the fox in the glass case, looks up at it warily, the sharp snout, the dead bird in its mouth, the brilliant eyes. She is laughed at; she is gently applauded. Tim follows her at a respectful distance. He is, he thinks, like a monk put in charge of a reincarnated lama. How did he fill his days before this? What were his days for?

'Whoops,' he says, returning her to her feet for the ninth, the tenth time. 'Whoops.'

*   *   *

Her first birthday: all manner of tender celebrations. In the morning, Tim mixes red paint – non-toxic, entirely safe – spreads it in a pyrex baking dish, and while Zoe and Maud watch him, lays his hand in the paint then presses it on the white wall by the back door. 'There,' he says, looking at the mark, the red ghost of his hand. 'Now you guys.'

Zoe goes next, excess paint dabbed from her wrist with a paper towel. Tim steadies her, helps her flatten her hand against the wall. The child looks with amazement at the mark she has made. She makes three more, each a little fainter. 'Now Mummy,' says Tim. 'Come on, Mummy.'

And Maud wets her hand with the paint, leans over Zoe to make her mark. 'Keep going,' says Tim, who is dipping his own hand again.

The fainter prints are more detailed, more truly a copy of the hand that made them, the pattern and texture of the skin. With a felt-tip pen, Tim writes the date on the wall, then they wash their hands together in the kitchen sink, red paint, red water, swirling round the plughole.

At noon the Rathbones arrive – Mr and Mrs Rathbone, the twins, Magnus's wife and children (Magnus himself is in Zurich).

A little later, Maud's parents arrive in a yellow car, the make and name of which nobody recognizes but which will do over sixty miles to the gallon. They park it carefully, though not too close to the Rathbones' Range Rover, and come in under the rose bush and along the path, the old seabed, in single file. In the crowded living room, Tim's mother kisses them both and this they endure with the flushed miming of a type of conviviality that is utterly foreign to them. For several minutes the women pair off and Mrs Rathbone speaks to Mrs Stamp like the prime minister's wife to the consort of an African president, a prime minister's wife who has started the day with some Qi Gong exercises and then a few drinks, or one particularly strong one. Mrs Stamp, who is clever, who has a face like a small flower or like an insect looking out of a small flower, says, 'Oh yes, yes,' a great many times and tries not to stare at Mrs Rathbone's hands when Mrs Rathbone touches her.

The men have their own kind of failure. Mr Rathbone does not know how many miles to the gallon his Range Rover will do, which is, anyway, his wife's car. He is not interested in roads or the different routes one might take to get somewhere, unless of course one were in a plane at, say, ten thousand feet, when he likes to follow the courses of rivers. He asks where Mr Stamp went to school, nods and says nothing when he answers. Mr Stamp does not ask where Mr Rathbone went to school, though not because he has anticipated the answer but because he is largely unaware of the basic rules of conversation. They stand at a distance that precludes any accidental touching, where they will not even have to smell each other.

'Let's go outside!' says Tim, watching it all from beside the front door. 'Come on, everyone!'

There are bees in the foxgloves, rose petals scattered by the gate from yesterday's rain. They sit on the warm, slightly damp grass. The adults, even Mr and Mrs Stamp, drink champagne, Perrier-Jouët, quite a lot of it. A dab of champagne is put on Zoe's lips and everyone agrees she seems to like it. Tim's father is a favourite of the child. She has a name for him, an apparent name. 'Ubu!' she calls whenever she catches sight of his scarlet corduroys. 'Ubu!' This, it seems, is the name Tim's father (Major Peter Ensleigh Rathbone JP, son of a general, great-nephew of a viscount) has secretly been waiting for. 'I'm Ubu!' he booms at Sarah and Michael as they wheel their thin bikes from the shed, the expressions on their faces suggesting they have been driven from their house by the noise of the party. 'I'm Ubu!' he calls to the new young vicar walking with his wife in the lane.

There are party games – pass the parcel (with a present in every layer), hide and seek, pin the tail. There is a cake of mashed banana, cinnamon and yoghurt, a single candle on top. The older children pick Zoe up and put her down. They squeeze her and push their faces into hers. Now and then she looks for Tim, his assent to these strange happenings. By three o'clock she's dazed, pale, the rosebud mouth (the juicy perfection of that mouth), smeared with what looks like earth. 'Why don't you take her up, Maud?' says Tim's father.

'Yes,' says Maud. 'Do you think she's tired?'

'Of *course* she's tired,' says Tim's father. He chuckles but there's no humour in it. 'She's out on her feet. Don't you think?'

So Maud lifts the child and Tim's father looks at Tim, who looks away and starts collecting plates, carrying them through to the kitchen where the dry handprints on the wall have taken on an unintended character. He should not, he thinks, have chosen red.

In August they make the trip down to the coast. Maud drives her new company car, a cherry-coloured Honda, a great improvement on the Corsa. Tim sits in the back with Zoe, keeping her mild with dried apple rings, milk formula, songs. They stop at a service station to change her nappy. In the boot of the car they have a great bundle of things devoted to the baby. The pushchair alone (a rugged cross-country affair) fills half the space.

When they pick up the key from Chris Totten's office, the broker makes friendly noises to the child, lets her leave small fingerprints on the stainless steel body of his lighter, asks Tim and Maud about their sailing plans.

'Nothing too ambitious,' says Tim. 'We'll have to see what sort of sailor this one is first.'

Lodestar is on her mooring in the middle of the river. Maud frees the tender from where it has wintered on the pontoon boat rack. Curious small things have found their way into the boat. A mussel shell, a bottle top, a feather. Most curiously of all, the shed skin of a snake, papery, almost weightless.

Zoe has fallen asleep in the Snuggler but at the first pull of the oars she wakes and begins to twist her head in what is obviously a mounting panic. By the time they reach *Lodestar* and she is passed over the guard rail she's howling. They take her below, console her, but each time she's brought up (each time with soothing words), her terror is reignited and she is hurried below again. They had planned to stay down for the bank holiday but after a day and a half they drive back, service station by service station. The second attempt is equally hopeless; the third, if anything, slightly worse, the child staring at the water as if at some old enemy, suddenly, monstrously, present. They cannot speak to her, cannot reassure her. Robert Currey, witnessing some of this, the child writhing in her father's arms, a sound like heartbreak, says maybe it's just too soon. All that water, and a world that tips when you step on it. Why wouldn't that unsettle a body? He smiles at them. He has tiny corkscrews of metal shavings in his hair. 'None of my business, of course,' he says. But Tim agrees with him, vigorously. 'Too much too soon,' he says, and laughs with the relief of it.

Two weeks later, Maud goes down on her own. There are jobs that need doing, things that cannot wait, or can be seen that way. Tim will go next time, though when the next time arrives he says, 'It's OK. You go.'

'Don't you want to go?'

'I'm OK,' he says.

'You're sure?'

'Yeah.'

'I don't mind staying,' she says.

'I know.'

'I can look after her.'

'Of course you can. What are you talking about?'

They look at each other a while. She shrugs. 'If you're sure.'

'I am. Completely.'

'OK.'

'Mummy's going down to the boat,' says Tim to the child in his arms. 'But Zoe's going to stay here with Daddy.' The child gazes at him then turns to Maud, regards her with big, solemn eyes. From her fingers she unlaces a scrap of green ribbon and holds it out.

'The young queen's favour,' says Tim. 'All new discovered lands must be named in her honour.'

Maud takes the ribbon. 'Thank you,' she says, and after a moment, softly, 'Yes.'

Though she must have more than five hundred hours alone in small boats she has never sailed a yacht on her own. On Sunday morning, dressed in jeans, trainers, a thick blue shirt like a working man's shirt, she motors out of the harbour on the ebbing tide. It's the last of the high season and boats criss-cross the river ahead of her, a good many of them little bobbling motor-boats rented by the hour from the kiosks and commanded by people who have, perhaps, never been on the water before. Here, then, is a first difficulty – being in the cockpit at the tiller, being five foot six, and having no one up front to call a warning, to watch for the ferries, spot a length of drifting rope ready to wrap itself around the propeller. She's on edge for a while, dances from one side of the cockpit to the other, keeps glancing back as though the river were full of silent liners that would overhaul her in minutes, reduce *Lodestar* to splinters. Then she stops. She can see enough, and the movement of her boat is a proper part of the river's morning business. The engine thumps reassuringly beneath her feet. She likes the smell of diesel. She likes the unexcited way the boat is moving, like a confident swimmer pulling out, stroke by steady stroke, for deeper water.

Between the two castles, their headlands, she passes the invisible line that takes her from the keeping of the harbour to the keeping of the sea. The wind is a westerly, force two or three; the light is excellent, the coast visible for miles. She steers in a slow arc until she is more or less head to wind, then lashes the tiller and goes forward to hoist the main before running back to the cockpit, freeing the tiller and bringing the boat around until the green ribbon, tied now to the starboard shroud, blows at right angles to the deck. The boat heels. She turns off the engine, unfurls the jib, spends fifteen minutes shifting between the tiller and the winches, balancing the boat. Suddenly, there is nothing more to do, nothing but rest a hand on the curve of the tiller, narrow her eyes against the brilliance of the sea. She is sailing. She is alone. Ahead of her is the world's curve and beyond that, everything else. The known, the imagined, the imagined known.

Her most difficult moment is coming back to the mooring. She has not thought it through, not properly. Engine dead slow she passes the buoy, turns and comes up again hoping the tide will bring the boat to a gentle halt. It does, but by the time she has run to the bows the boat has drifted and the buoy is out of reach. She takes the boat around for a second try, then a third. This time she drops a weighted rope over the buoy, a lasso that draws tight as the boat is carried past on the stream. She's not sure if she's remembering this or if she is improvising. It doesn't matter. It is, evidently, the solution. She turns off the engine. The river's silence rises to meet her. Below, she scoops soup out of a tin into a saucepan, sits on the companionway steps to watch it heat. Everything is as it should be; nothing has gone wrong, or nothing serious. She took the boat out and she brought it back. There are skills to sailing alone that she will need to learn if sailing alone is to become a regular occurrence, and she makes a mental checklist of what she would need if she were to set sail not for a morning or a day but – say – for a week. She wonders how John Gosse managed, ghostly Gosse, who she and Tim have always imagined sailing on his own. Above all, she would need some sort of self-steering, a wind vane, an auto-helm. She will do some research. She will talk to people in the yard. To Robert Currey, perhaps.

Her phone is in a mesh pocket above the chart table. The little blue message light is blinking. She watches it. The call, she assumes, is from Tim, wanting to know when she'll be back, or if she can pick something up on the way home or to tell her something about Zoe. What does he want to tell her about Zoe? She turns off the gas under the soup, pours the soup into a cup and goes on deck. In future, she thinks, she might leave the phone in the car.

19

When Zoe is three and a half she gets chicken pox. Several other boys and girls in the playgroup have it. The illness does not distress her much and when she is better she seems to have moved into some new phase of life, to look out at the world with an alertness that wasn't there before, as if her infancy was being stripped from her, layer by layer.

She is strong, full of play, precociously musical. Tim buys her a pink ukelele. Because his own instruments are so valuable he will not let her do more than touch them, stroke the grain of the wood, the bright strings, with fingertips that have been carefully inspected for honey, chocolate, snot. All the guitars are at the cottage now, even the Lacôte from the treasure room at his parents' house. When not in use they are kept upstairs in the spare room in a locked cupboard.

She has lots of dolls, some beautiful ones from Ubu. She disciplines them harshly, smothers them with kisses. She pretends to be a kitten, a phase that lasts many weeks. She wants Maud to be a kitten with her. Tim, half hidden in the doorway to the kitchen, watches them, Maud on her hands and knees, a kitten that seems to have learnt its kitten nature out of a book. Nor can Maud make up stories, or only in the most laboured way. And asked to shake the hand of some invisible man or woman, someone newly sprung from her daughter's head, she is flummoxed. Was this how she was as a child? Tim thinks of the picture he stole from the cork board in her parents' house. Girl with brick wall, girl with white socks, girl unfathomed. When he asks her (gently, not wishing to appear to be probing her like some manner of therapist) she says she was like any other child. 'They're not all the same,' he says. 'I know,' she says. It's one of those discussions with Maud that goes nowhere.

He can see Maud in the set of the child's mouth, in the curls of her hair, the shape of her toes (Rathbone toes are very straight), but it's a long time before he sees any mannerism, any behaviours, that come distinctively, unarguably, from her mother. Then, one afternoon, just the two of them at home, he catches Zoe standing on the lawn watching nothing obvious with that same rooted calm, that uncanny stillness, he has witnessed so often in Maud. A switching off or a switching *in*. Something weirdly primitive about it; a posture, an expression, you might find painted on a piece of pottery buried with a Babylonian princess. He is not sure how much he likes to see it there, in his daughter's face.

A fortnight after this, stripping Zoe in the steam of her nightly bath, he sees black marks, black smudges, on the underside of her left forearm. He asks her to show him but she doesn't want to, holds her arm against her naked flank. When he asks again she does a little dance on the bathmat and as the last gesture of the dance presents him with her arm. He gets it then. The marks, a dozen loops and squiggles made with a felt-tip pen, are her version of her mother's tattoo, of *Sauve Qui Peut*. He tries to soap it off in the bath but she won't have it. It fades slowly. Thankfully, she does not attempt to renew it.

With Maud, there are discussions, at night mostly, sometimes in bed, about having another child.

'You were an only child,' he says. 'Wouldn't you like Zoe to have a brother or sister?'

'If you asked her she would say no.'

'If we asked her,' he says, 'she would have us sell the house to buy chocolate. She would certainly have us sell the boat.'

These discussions reach no conclusion. He does not attempt to insist; she does not say no, never. In the years since Zoe's birth they have used a variety of contraception (condoms; the pill; briefly, a diaphragm). Sometimes they go for weeks without touching each other. They are often tired. Her work, the long hours of travelling; his work caring for the child. By ten at night their appetite is more often for sleep than for each other, the physical labour of making love. And then the spell is broken. He notices her pulling her jumper over her head, the stretch of her girlish body. Or he says something that makes them both laugh and the tension between them, the almost unnoticeable tension, is instantly dissolved. They do it in the bedroom, once or twice in the bathroom under the shower, but it's better downstairs where they don't have to worry about the child waking. Maud is light enough to hold against a wall, her knees up by his shoulders. Or he has her sit astride him in the kitchen, her tights on the floor, her skirt up by her hips, her strong legs flexed, supper plates on the table still, the ticking of the kitchen clock, night pressed against the uncurtained window, a darkness thick as felt.

* * *

Their friends – their country friends – are Jack and Maggie, Chris and Bella, Lally and Tish. Friends, supper guests, fellow parents with children in the same toddler group as Zoe or with older children already at St Winifred's, the well-regarded local primary where, in September, Zoe will start. There is also childless Arnie, a friend of Tim's from prep school, working in estate management now, newly divorced and having 'the time of his life' but looking jowly and distracted and ten years older than he should.

All of them live within a dozen miles of the cottage, and with the exception of Tish, who has a Burmese mother, they are white, university educated and with money in the bank. Maud is the only one not to have been to public school (King's Bruton, Eton, Cheltenham Ladies' College, Roedean, Charterhouse); she is also the only one to have studied pure sciences. Sitting around each other's tables they talk about children, marriage, country living. They talk about politics (only Arnie unapologetically on the right); about the arts (the Royal Academy, the Edinburgh Fringe, HBO). Tish and Lally, who describe themselves as Dorset lesbian royalty, know all the local gossip. They know, for example, that the young vicar's wife has run away, that the young vicar is in disgrace, and that the old vicar – who is, reputedly, more interested in paleontology, in bone fragments and flint arrowheads than the forty-two articles of the Church of England – has been summoned out of retirement to keep the parish from drifting into Hinduism or devil worship.

'God, it's like Trollope!' says Jack and the others nod, all except Maud who has not picked up a novel since GCSEs and *Jude the Obscure* and to whom the name Trollope means nothing. She does not shine at these gatherings. She is friendly, speaks when spoken to, remembers to ask questions about the other children and has a small store of remarks about her own child, but she does not suddenly say, as Maggie does one day, that she is in love with the new plumber; does not, as Tish does, mimic the pompous blathering of a minister of state, does not (Lally) give a tearful defence of euthanasia, or tell (Bella) a risqué story about her year as an au pair girl in Rome.

'She's obviously incredibly bright,' says Chris, as he and Tim drive back from playing tennis on Jack and Maggie's grass court. 'Yes,' says Tim, 'she *is*,' but he's afraid something else has been meant, something more nuanced. Only Arnie seems to get her, or says he does. He appoints himself her champion, so that when Maggie – a night when Maud is late home from work and the party has begun without her – says how much she admires Maud, her quality of the *naif*, he looks up from his plate (his place at the table with its gravy splashes, its spilt wine) and growls, 'Piss off, Maggie,' a moment that takes some smoothing over.

Tim hopes that one or other of the women will become Maud's particular friend. He thinks it will be good for her if she has such a friend. Who *are* her friends? Professor Kimber? The people at work? The moths? He thinks Tish might be a possibility, Bella at a push. He encourages her to accept the invitations that come. A girls' night out in Bath, a spa day at a local hotel, the inaugural meeting of a new book club. Finally, she goes. It's an evening at Chris and Bella's house, ladies only. She wears her dress of chocolate silk, the lighter jacket with its little burn. She's back by eleven-fifteen. When she comes in, Tim is sprawled on the sofa watching the end of *The Sopranos*. She watches it with him and when it's over he switches off the television and asks if she had a nice time. She says she did.

'What sort of nice time?'

'We saw a film. Then we had supper.'

'Sounds fun. What did you talk about at supper?'

'The film.'

'Just the film?'

'Other things too.'

'Come on, Maud. What sort of things?'

'They were talking about their dreams.'

'Did you tell them about yours?'

'What?'

'Your dreams. I know you have them because I hear you talking in your sleep. Quite often, in fact.'

She shakes her head. 'They asked me to explain what an enzyme is.'

'An enzyme?'

'Yes.'

'Let me get this right. They're talking about their dreams and they ask you to explain what an enzyme is?'

'Yes.'

'And did you?'

'Yes.'

'Do you think they understood?'

'I'm not sure,' she says, her jacket folded over her knees, 'but I don't think so.'

20

A fortnight before Zoe's first day at St Winifred's her parents have a row in the kitchen. 'Of *course* we must be there,' says Tim, waving a serving spoon. 'Her first day! We must *both* be there.'

Maud, sitting at the table, arms folded over her breasts, explains for the third time that she has a meeting at Southampton University at nine in the morning. A scheduled meeting. An important meeting.

'How can it be more important than *this*?' cries Tim.

'If you had a job,' she says, 'you'd know.'

'If I had a job,' he says, 'who would look after Zoe? You?'

She does not withdraw from the meeting (she is tabled to present the five-year follow-up results from the Kappa-opioids trial) but she tells them she will be late. When she tells them the reason they say that's fine, Maud, come when you can. This surprises her slightly. Perhaps the meeting was not as important as she thought.

* * *

The first day, the hush of early morning, the lamplit bedroom; Zoe, solemn queen, stands in her nightie and looks at her uniform laid out on the bottom of the bed. White vest, white pants, white shirt, grey tights, grey dress, scarlet cardigan, all of them clearly marked with her name, Zoe Rathbone. She can, of course, dress herself but this morning allows her parents to draw on her clothes. Her hair is brushed. She wears it much longer than her mother, too long perhaps, a mass of chestnut curls that Tim crushes in his fist then twists into a coloured band.

When breakfast is over they set off in Maud's Honda. The car, chilly when they first get into it, slowly warms up. The radio is on – warnings about congestion on roads many miles away. Maud turns it off. Behind them, the school bus swings out of a narrow turning, brushing rain from the hedgerows. It's a coach chartered from a local company. It looks too big for the lanes. 'One day, Zoe,' says Tim, sitting with her in the back of the car, 'you can go on the bus. All the coolest kids go on the bus. Did you go on the bus, Maud?'

'Sometimes,' she says.

Zoe sits upright in her booster chair, her cardigan buttoned, her new coat folded on the seat beside her. She has barely spoken since breakfast. Somehow she has surrounded herself with an atmosphere of sacrifice, as if the two people she most loves, most depends upon, have decided to sell her, and she – at barely five – must accept the inevitability of it.

It is not a long journey. At the school she walks between them, holds her mother's hand, her father's. The headmistress is waiting in the playground. The girls in their red cardigans, the boys in their red sweaters, are gathered around her. She smiles at each child and they look at her with awe. On the tarmac surface of the playground are the faintly chalked lines of old games.

The parents talk in quiet voices. Rain clouds pass overhead but no rain falls.

'Time to say our goodbyes,' says the headmistress, who has now been joined by her assistant, Miss Beazley. Zoe holds up her arms to her father. She embraces him then looks at her mother. Maud leans down and kisses her. 'Bye bye, Maud,' says the girl who has, this last summer, started addressing her mother by her name.

The parents are drifting away. Some children cling on, frantic. Miss Beazley is dispatched; she has the skills of separation. In they go, red and grey through the open doors behind the headmistress (who, at this distance, does not seem much bigger than a child herself). The parents wander back to their cars. Some are weeping. They cry, laugh at themselves, touch their chests as if to calm their troubled hearts.

Beside the Honda, Tim has his face against Maud's shoulder. Because he is so much taller than her there is something comical in the posture. He speaks into her shoulder, his hot breath, the trembling in his back. Bella appears. She has just dropped off the twins, who are in the year above Zoe. She tells Maud she'll take Tim home. She'll look after him. 'It's vile at first,' she says, 'an awful wrench. But by next week it will just be the new normal. Trust me.'

The driver of the school bus is standing by the open door of the coach, smoking, sucking his teeth. He winks at Maud. He's a young man who looks old or an old man who looks young. Maud gets into the car, checks her phone. As she drives out of the car park, Tim and Bella turn and wave to her.

It is, of course, as Bella said. Wise Bella! The first week, the second. The cottage has a new rhythm. Is it games today? Is it

Miss Beazley or Mrs Luckett this morning? Where are your shoes? Hey! It's ten past eight already! The smell of toast, the voices on the radio, the day still shadowed.

Sometimes Maud is with them but often she has left the house before the others are out of bed. Three, four hours of travelling, whole sections of motorway she can scroll across the shut lids of her eyes in the moments before sleep. She's a senior clinical research associate now. She earns just over thirty thousand a year, has her own cubicle on the top floor of the building in Reading. At the annual conference (Brighton last year, the hotel the IRA bombed) Josh Fenniman sees her sooner and for longer. She has proved her worth, her reliability, and though she is not one of those he has marked down, secretly, for high office, she is the type of employee he wishes to retain, and the management in Reading have been tasked with seeing she has enough to keep her interested. That tattoo still sounds alarm bells. What possessed her? But Josh Fenniman can recall moments from his own youth (he's still a youthful-seeming man), instances of exuberance before he saw the world for what it is. Someone should mention laser removal or that it might be wise to keep it covered up more, might certainly be a smart move to cover it up when she goes for a one-to-one with the CEO. It's not just the team player thing. Is she respectful? Is there some issue around respect? Henderson thinks she's on the spectrum but Henderson does not always see clearly, which is why his name, like Maud's, is not to be found on the list (the very short list) of those who will one day have the best things.

Sauve Qui Peut! Big indelible letters!

What *possessed* her?

21

They have Christmas at the Rathbones again. Gin, sloe gin, charades, midnight mass, a turkey so big Magnus tells the children it's an Alsatian. Zoe is swept up with her cousins, young teenagers now. Trails of gold foil from chocolate coins. Dogs held up on their hind legs and made to dance. On Boxing Day they walk over Rathbone land. Tussocky grass, the hills bled of their colour, the streams, shallow and broad, where the dogs lap their reflections. They have come out to see the hunt, and at last it comes, tiny figures working their way down the edge of a hill, then the ground reverberating, the pack spilling and reforming, the brute horses bullied on, Zoe on her father's back lost in a thrill of looking.

January, and welcome back children. Tim on the school run. Have you got *everything*? Then stopping to talk to Bella or one of the other mothers. Their names, the children's names – Sue who has Daniel and Zadie, Jenny who has Tamsin, Lu who has Maya and Rupert, Claire who has the little one whose name Tim can never remember, the one with the glasses and the red hair, the unfortunate limp.

Miss Beazley shutting the gates.

At home in the cottage he brews coffee and rolls a cigarette. There's a sheltered place by the back door and though sometimes it smells of fuel oil from the tank and is therefore probably not the safest place to smoke a cigarette, it has become a place of contemplation. Smoke, drink the coffee, try to think how it's all going (his life, his *relationship*), and when you cannot think any more or make it lie down, stop thinking and imagine music.

He is, at last, making progress with CYP2D6, the concerto he planned (and thought he would write in a month) when they were still in Bristol. He has a nice opening, a theme in common time, a minor key, the guitar a solo voice quietly establishing itself. Later movements will recycle the theme in new and unexpected guises – ragtime, for example, and then a slow movement like a stately, droll flamenco. He has his own computer, a slightly better one than Maud's, with software that rigs the screen with staves and offers orchestration at the press of a button. The dedication will read, 'For Zoe' or 'Zoe, with love'. Or just 'For Z'.

The mornings grow lighter. In the garden there are already spikes of new green and by the end of the month the rooks are busy in the bare trees opposite the cottage. On the drive to school a low sun slants across drenched fields. Sometimes there is ice, sometimes a steady green-seeming rain, the water from the road flung up onto the Lancia's windscreen, Tim leaning forward at the wheel.

In the cottage, blotchy paintings of houses or cats or smiling, schematic people, are Blu Tacked to doors or the kitchen cupboards. There are wands, there are pictures made from leaves, there are loo rolls rolled in glitter, there are jars with earth in them and twigs.

When Maud gets back to the cottage at night Zoe is often in bed. Tim says, 'Go up and look at her,' and so she goes, up the stairs in her work clothes to stand in the part-open doorway looking into the room's subtle blue and seeing the shadow of the bed then, after a moment, her eyes adjusting, the pale of her daughter's face on the pillow.

Sometimes Zoe is still awake, and in a whisper she calls to Maud and Maud sits on the bed while the child talks. They speak like prisoners, like escapees, or as if the night were sternly conducting its own strange music and must not be disturbed. She tells Maud urgent stories. There is something luxurious in her capacity to invent. All of it seems to mean something. She asks Maud where she has been and Maud tells her, her plain words accepted in silence. When they kiss goodnight they can hardly see each other's faces. Kiss an eye, kiss a nose, an eyebrow. Then the slow walking back to the door, the last goodnights, the very last a bare whisper like a sigh, the door pulled to but never shut.

Downstairs, Tim, angling a log into the stove or putting out a plate of reheated supper or listening to some programme on the radio about the burial practices of early humans (a grave in Vedbaek, Denmark, of a woman buried with a hundred and ninety teeth of red deer and wild boar around her head, and beside her, a child – hers, presumably – laid on a swan's wing, a flint dagger at her waist), asks Maud how Zoe was and Maud, sitting down to the reheated food or opening her laptop or just standing there, Maud style, looking at God knows, says, 'Zoe? Oh, she's fine.'

22

'Should we talk?'
    'If you want.'
  'It's not really about that, is it?'

Nights are like the bottom of somewhere, a kind of seabed. As for the days, they have a cunning of their own.

23

It's a morning in March, a month before the Easter holidays. Tim plays some of the new piece, twenty bars or so, for Bella. It's raw outside, damp and raw, and they are sitting in the warmth from the stove, their clothes unruly on the floor around them, the bell of the church tinkling the quarter-hour. It's an odd thing to play the guitar naked, the wood cool on your lap. And odd, too, to play for a naked woman who is sitting smiling in a half-lotus on the rug, her neck and cheeks still a little flushed from before. An odd thing but pleasant.

They've talked about it; they've gone into this with their eyes open. Bella will not be leaving her husband. Tim will not leave Maud. Nothing in the outward form of their lives needs to change. If Bella left Chris he would fall apart. He is, she explains, much more fragile than he looks. When his mother died he wouldn't get out of bed for a month. He became briefly incontinent. Regressed to an age somewhere around seven months.

As for Maud, what would become of her? Tim has – many

times – imagined himself telling her it's over, that he's leaving, taking Zoe with him. He is not sure when these thoughts began. He suspects the first time was probably about a month after the baby was born. The hard part is imagining Maud's reaction. Tears? Silence? Or would she wait until his back was turned then sink a boning knife between his shoulders?

There are moments when he believes that in the last six years he has learnt nothing important about her at all, nothing that *shows* her to him. More frequently now, much more frequently, are those occasions when he simply shakes his head and walks away, cannot be bothered to try to figure it out. Was his mother right about her? And smart-arse Magnus ('I can see why you wanted to fuck her, old boy. I just don't see the rest of it')?

But this is Maud, for Christ's sake! Maud who flew past him, lay dead on the ground then stood and walked. Who else has entered his life like that? Has entered his life with the force of myth?

'We take people on,' says Bella (Bella who *genuinely* likes Maud). 'It doesn't always make much sense. And then the children come along.'

Two or three times a week they are together. No great subterfuge is required, they just follow each other back from the school. The neighbours are both at work, there's no one else. If he said he felt guilty he'd be lying. He's put up with a lot; he deserves Bella. He is dazzled by her tallness (as tall as he is). He likes to arrange her limbs on the sofa as though he were going to sketch her. Once, when he was in her from behind, rooted in her, their four knees on the generous width of the sofa, her back hollowed, her backside tilted up a little, shining, he found himself looking out of the window and straight into the gaze of the old priest who was peering owlishly past the garden gate. He didn't tell Bella, didn't think the old man could see anything, though the thought that he *might* see, see life at work in the fucking of this long-armed woman, her streaming hair, did not displease him. Nor is his conscience much troubled by those occasions when a small deceit is needed for Maud – or possibly isn't needed, for who knows what she notices. Half the time she seems in a dream, the other half she looks at you and your skin is glass.

He tells himself he's a lizard but the thought only raises a moment of grim laughter. Less comfortable is the realization that driving his daughter to school is a sort of foreplay, so that he is aware of himself talking to her too much and too excitedly, sometimes wanting to tell her everything, to make her his little confidante. It also makes him drive faster than he should, the Lancia, the much-repaired Lancia, dancing through the lanes.

Then the holidays arrive and for three weeks he barely sees Bella. When he does it's with the children or with Chris or Maud. Between the lovers there's all the usual play of fleeting glances, the backs of their hands touching as they pass each other, the social kiss pressed a little harder than before. They have exchanged tokens. He gave her a silver moon on a silver chain; she gave him a ring bought years ago in Cairo that takes the form of twining snakes. He wears the ring on the first day of the new term, slips it on in the car, then drives past Bella in the school car park, his window down, his hand, the glinting ring, displayed.

They resume. The sofa, the stove. Sometimes music. The light is generous now, falls past the deep-set windows to find them in their innocence, their nakedness. One morning they have to hide from the postman. One morning the fuel-oil man comes and Tim has to drag on clothes and smooth his hair and banter with the man while the tank slowly fills. And one morning, the last week in May, her knees up by her chin, his body braced across her, braced like a gymnast, the phone rings, the answer phone comes on and the voice of Maud's mother fills the room saying Grandfather Ray is dead.

'We should stop,' says Bella. 'Timmy?'

But they don't stop. They keep going until they are done.

Zoe isn't with them at the crematorium. She only met Grandfather Ray twice, both times at The Poplars when he gave no sign of understanding who she was, and where she played contentedly with his Zimmer frame until it was time to kiss his bloodshot cheek and leave. Ubu has promised to take her up in his plane ('Don't fuss, Tim. It's a damn sight safer than a car').

The crematorium is new. From the road it looks like an inexpensive hotel or the clubhouse for a municipal golf course. Most of Swindon's dead come here now. In the car park, lines of hearses wait their turn in the shade of young trees.

Maud and Tim are in the front row of the chapel with Mr and Mrs Stamp. The row behind them has four people and the one behind that is empty. Across the aisle is a nurse from The Poplars and half a dozen old railwaymen in dark jackets.

When the coffin comes in, a young man with a top hat walks in front of it. None of the bearers seems to have a suit that fits them and this gives them, slightly, the look of clowns or exiles. The coffin is laid in the alcove. The young man takes off his hat and makes a solemn bow to the coffin. It is part of his work but the gesture carries with it something startling and profound. Who ever bowed to Grandfather Ray in life? Tim glances down the row, but if the moment has struck home there is no outward sign. Mrs Stamp has a ball of tissue in one hand but so far has had no use for it. Mr Stamp occasionally nods as if being secretly addressed, perhaps by the spirit of his dead father. They are invited to sit. On the order of service there is a roughly copied photograph of Grandfather Ray looking sixty, vigorous, a man cut out for work. A dependable man, a nice man.

The vicar is a woman. Is the cemetery a good posting? She makes a joke; the old men cough. There are no poems, nothing of that sort. A single hymn, a five-minute eulogy that the vicar has somehow constructed from two visits to The Poplars and a brief conversation with Mr and Mrs Stamp. There is a sentence about sailing with his beloved granddaughter (a smile here from the lectern to Maud). At the end, the curtains close with a curious jerking movement, like the end of a puppet show. The young man with the hat makes another deep bow and the doors of the hall are opened (not the way they came in, of course, where others will be waiting). The mourners shuffle out to the early summer air, a pathway next to raw beds of self-tending plants. Floral tributes have been laid out – one from the care home, one from the union. Over the low walls are views of the country, of sunlight on sheep-cropped hills.

The Stamps have invited people back to the house. There are sandwiches, biscuits, cups of tea, bottles of beer. The old men gather in the living room, stand together in a line as if on a platform in some hard wind, looking for a train that is already hopelessly delayed. Each in turn shakes Maud's hand and to each she speaks a few words before moving on to the next. Tim, sipping tea and keeping out of the way, feels his scalp prickle. What is she? The young Queen of the Night? Are they paying tribute to her? Renewing their allegiance?

When it's done and the crumbs have been hoovered and the glasses washed and put to dry on the rack and a mark like a hoof print, a mark made by one of the old men's boots, has been sponged from the carpet, Tim and Maud and Mr and Mrs Stamp sit in the kitchen. The wine in the garage has still not been found but there is beer left over from the wake and this is poured carefully into four tumblers. Tim asks questions about Grandfather Ray. He is hoping someone will tell a story about him but no one does. Quite casually, Mrs Stamp lets drop that Maud is to inherit everything, but then (in the next breath) that everything amounts to very little. Some savings, some of Grandmother Dot's old jewellery. Anything of real value was sold years ago, the money spent on care.

They eat supper – shepherd's pie in a pyrex dish – and afterwards sit in the living room for an hour drinking tea. No one says so but clearly it would not be appropriate to have the television on. At ten, Maud goes up to take a bath. Tim excuses himself and goes out to smoke in the street. He texts his mother: *How was the flight? Zoe OK?* He texts Bella: *I wish I was drunk. I wish I was with you. I'm a stranger here.*

From the houses opposite come small reports of life. Light spills from kitchen windows, from frosted bathroom windows. The parked cars give the impression of great patience. He tidies his cigarette into the gutter, goes into the house, pads up the narrow stairs. Maud is in her room sitting on the bed. She has a towel wrapped around her and is using another towel to dry her hair. White walls, a white MFI wardrobe, a small, frameless mirror. The room has only one picture, something cut long ago from a magazine, laminated on the laminating machine in the kitchen, and tacked to the wall at pillow height. A boat in heavy weather, a woman in yellow oilskins in the cockpit. He's seen it before and knows it's Clare Francis on her solo transatlantic run, mid-1970s.

'Quite a day,' he says. 'Eh?' He sits on the bed beside her, drops a kiss on her shoulder, then, when she looks at him, her bare face washed back to the brightness of bone, he leans, a little wildly, and kisses her mouth.

TWO

It is human nature to stand in the middle of a thing,
but you cannot stand in the middle of this . . .

Marianne Moore

1

Having eaten a sandwich upstairs in her cubicle, she has come down to spend half an hour in the animal room gentling rats and listening to the technician talk about the history of bluegrass – Bill Monroe, Earl Scruggs, 'the high lonesome style'. He talks softly. He doesn't ask questions. Now and then there are playful asides. Josh Fenniman he refers to as Uncle Jo. Trouble, he says, always starts on the ground floor – or better still, the basement.

She lifts the rats from their cages, picks them out by their tails and settles them on an arm folded across her chest. They're albino Sprague Dawley rats, bred for their easy natures, their docility. They push their heads into the crook of her arm. She strokes behind their ears, strokes their restless warmth, then lifts them back into the cage by the loose skin behind their necks.

It has been raining for days, perhaps for weeks. Slate-coloured November rain, the rivers suddenly muscular, old bridges overwhelmed. There are wild geese in the flooded fields. In cities the offices have their lights on at midday. Even in the windowless animal room you are aware of it, a background rattling, unlistened to but registered somewhere.

The history lesson has moved on. He's laying down the ancestry of a sound. Red Smiley, Don Reno, the Greenbriar Boys, the Country Gentlemen. Uncle Josh Graves from Tellico Plains, Tennessee. The names are like old shoes or old hats or old notebooks, notebooks with creased and marbled covers, the pages inside scrawled with dense handwriting you are never going to read.

Her phone rings. It's in the hip pocket of her lab coat. When she answers, there's a sound, a confusion of sounds. No one responds to her hello. She goes on listening. Someone who has her number in their phone has accidentally called her, someone out in the street or perhaps even standing by a television or a radio.

'Hello?' she says. 'Hello?'

Recitation. Song. As in a dream where some animal, a jaguar, rests its black head beside you on the pillow and speaks in a voice you know as well as your own.

She ends the call, looks at the phone, and after a moment puts the phone back in her pocket.

'Have they summoned you?' asks the technician. He's concentrating but quite at ease, an anaesthetized rat on the bench in front of him, a glass microcapillary tube angled to the back of one of its eyes.

Fifteen minutes after the call, a few minutes before the end of the lunch break, the woman from Human Resources comes in. She looks like herself yet also somehow strange, altered. Her beautiful shoes, her hair with the tawny highlights. She says, 'Can you come with me, Maud?' She holds out a hand to Maud. She has never done that before.

Between the animal room and the staff room are two flights of stairs. The woman is explaining to Maud that some people have come to see her. On the second flight it turns out that the people are from the police, that they are the police. A policeman and a policewoman. 'I'll stay with you,' she says, 'unless you want me to go.'

In the staff room the officers are standing with their hats in their hands.

'Hello,' says the policewoman. 'Are you Maud Rathbone?'

'She's Maud Stamp,' says the woman from Human Resources.

'But Henley Rathbone is your partner?'

'Tim,' says Maud. 'Yes.'

The policewoman nods. She manages a sort of smile at Maud, though her colleague looks mostly at the floor.

'Could you sit down for me please, Maud?' says the woman officer. She gestures to where four of the brightly coloured chairs have been arranged, two facing two, in a part of the room beside one of the tinted windows. The others wait until Maud is sitting before taking their own seats.

When they are finished – it doesn't take long – the woman from Human Resources goes to collect Maud's coat and work bag. Maud has already told them that she will drive herself to the hospital. This is not the usual way and some effort is made to change her mind, but she appears to be in control of herself, is quietly insistent, and it cannot be absolutely forbidden. She takes off her lab coat, takes the phone from the pocket, puts on her outdoor coat. The policewoman is watching her very closely. She and her colleague walk behind Maud as they leave the staff room. Anyone coming onto the corridor – a cleaner, Henderson even – might imagine at first that she was being arrested.

In the car park the woman from Human Resources holds an

umbrella over Maud's head. 'Have you got everything?' she asks. 'Are you sure?' Maud settles herself in the driving seat. The woman, leaning in under the umbrella, touches a brown half-curl of Maud's hair. Has the odd, immediately suppressed desire to kiss her.

Though it's not yet three o'clock the motorway is clogged. There are speed restrictions. Most cars have their lights on and as they pass they send up a wash of spray that lands brown and finely granulated on the windscreen. At the first service station after Swindon she stops, parks, and goes to the toilets. When she's finished she buys a pack of sandwiches and a bottle of water. In the car she drinks from the bottle, opens the sandwiches and puts them on the passenger seat. It takes another hour and a half to reach the turn-off for Bath. Twice during that time her phone rings but she makes no attempt to answer it. She follows the signs to the hospital, tries to leave the car in several small car parks in the hospital grounds before finding one with a space. She walks through the rain to A&E. When she speaks to the receptionist she is told that no one of that name has been admitted and then, with a little startled 'Ah!', the receptionist tells her that Mr Rathbone is in ICU and that he's there more as a precautionary measure really and someone will come out in a minute and take her to him. Have a seat.

She sits. Some of the people around her look calm and brave and some look frightened and brave and some just frightened. A young nurse comes and leans over her. 'Hello,' she says. 'Do you want to come with me?' She's younger than Maud, a young black woman, twenty-five or -six to Maud's thirty-four, but at some point on the walk to ICU she calls Maud 'sweetie'.

At the unit Maud is given into the care of a male nurse. The unit is hushed, heavily furnished with technology. There is no banter here, no attempt at homeliness. The temperature feels very similar to the animal room at Reading.

The male nurse leads Maud to Tim's bed. He is lying with his eyes shut, the side of one eye raw-looking, swollen, a small dressing in place. There's a canula in his left arm, a clear hose leading to a bag of fluid. His parents are sitting on chairs either side of the bed. His mother is holding his hand. His father is staring down at his own knees but glances up for a second to see who it is, then drops his gaze again. Tim's mother stands and comes over to Maud. There's a quick embrace, stiff-limbed, then – in the voice of someone who has decided that there must be at least one person who remains clear-headed – she explains the nature of her son's injuries. A concussion, two broken ribs, a fractured femur, a broken thumb, contusions. He has been examined, X-rayed, sedated. Tomorrow he will be moved to an observation ward and his leg will be put in a cast. He is not in any danger. They were worried about his eye but his eye will recover. They do not expect him to remain in the hospital longer than a week.

'Do you understand what I'm saying?'

'Yes,' says Maud. They look at each other. The older woman's face spasms. Her fingers tremble at her throat. Maud helps her back to her chair and stands beside her, looking down at Tim. At some point another nurse comes, a senior nurse in a dark blue dress. She has epaulettes. To Maud she says, 'Are you . . . ?'

And Tim's mother says, 'Yes, yes she is.'

The nurse smiles at Maud. 'Tim's doing very well,' she says. 'Shall we go down to the family room for a while? It's nice and quiet in there. We won't be disturbed.' She waits. Tim's father makes a noise in his throat. In other circumstances you might take it for laughter.

*   *   *

When she leaves the hospital the rain has stopped. It's a little surprising, and several people, emerging through the doors after long visits, peer up into the darkness suspiciously.

Her car smells of eggs. The open packet of uneaten sandwiches is still on the passenger seat. She looks for a bin, spends fifteen minutes wandering the grounds with the sandwiches in her hand before leaving them on top of some sort of metal junction box.

By the time she gets back to the cottage it feels late, the middle of the night, but it's not yet ten o'clock. The air is colder than in the city, apparently thinner. To the south, through breaking cloud, a dozen stars are visible. Sirius between two trees, and above it, the constellation of Orion.

She unlocks the cottage door, glides her fingers over the wall, feeling for the light switch. She has had some idea the cottage will be in chaos but of course it is not. Why would it be in chaos? She goes through to the kitchen. On the table are two unwashed cereal bowls and two spoons. She collects them, washes them, puts each thing away in its place then goes back into the living room. The room is cold and she thinks about lighting the stove. The phone rings. She watches it until it stops then takes off her coat and shoes and lies on the sofa, her coat pulled over her as a blanket. She is almost asleep when she sits up and rummages in her coat pocket for her phone. She opens it and scrolls through the log of recent calls until she finds the one she answered in the animal room. She does not expect to find a number and she doesn't. It's listed as unknown. An unknown caller.

2

In ICU the next morning they tell her Tim has already been moved, that she has just missed him. She sets off along broad corridors, the sick being wheeled in their beds, visitors frowning at signs. The usual smells, the predictable smells. When she finds him, a semi-private bay at the far end of the ward, his parents are with him again. They have stayed the night in a Bath hotel. Tim's mother says, 'You went home, I suppose.'

Tim is awake. He watches her approach the bed. When she leans down to kiss him he turns his face away. She waits. He will not look at her or speak to her. She leaves and walks around the hospital grounds. Sunlight glitters on every drenched surface. She decides to make a list of things she has to do – the dozen, the twenty urgent things she must attend to – but when she finds a pen in the glovebox of her car and smooths out the back of a Trial Volunteer Disclaimer form (TVD-1), she can think of nothing except calling her own parents, which she does, immediately, sitting in the car with the door open. They are both at work of course. It's a school day. She leaves a message asking them to call her, then goes back to the ward. Now there are three people by the bed. One of them is Bella. When she sees Maud she flinches, then recovers herself, smiles, begins to spill fresh tears, embraces Maud and whispers, 'Anything, anything at all. You only need to ask.'

It's another two days before Tim will speak to her and even then he will not meet her eyes. He tells her he will be discharged the day after tomorrow, that he'll have crutches and the use of a wheelchair. He says he'll stay with his parents. They will collect him and he'll stay with them.

'Where will you be?' he asks.

'At the cottage,' she says.

'Don't move anything,' he says.

'OK.'

'Nothing.'

'I won't.'

'Upstairs.'

'I haven't been there.'

'Nothing,' he says.

'No,' she says.

'Nothing.'

'I won't.'

'If you do . . .'

'I won't.'

Later the same day she's in the living room kneeling in front of the stove breaking kindling. She hears the garden gate and stands up in time to see a policewoman, plump and blonde, brushing droplets from her shoulders, raindrops that were strung on the thorns of the rose bush and which the shutting gate has shaken down on her.

Maud lets her in. She wipes her feet, looks at the wood in Maud's hand, the open mouth of the stove. 'I could help you with that,' she says. 'I've got one like that at home.'

Maud tells her the Rayburn has gone out and that the Rayburn runs the heating for the house. She thinks the oil tank is probably empty. She hasn't looked.

'Do you know how to get more oil?' asks the policewoman, and Maud says yes, she just has to call and the tanker will come.

'Good,' says the policewoman. 'It's important to stay warm.'

They sit. The policewoman has a plastic document wallet on her lap. She unzips it and takes out a thin sheaf of paper. She's from victim liaison and she starts by saying a few simple, kind things, then moves on to the papers and goes through them item by item, stopping after each to ask Maud if she has understood. The driver of the school coach has been arrested. His blood tests were negative but he has been charged under Section 1 of the Road Traffic Offenders Act. There will be an arraignment at the magistrates' court. There's no need for either Maud or Mr Rathbone to attend. At any future trial Mr Rathbone is likely to be called as a witness, though obviously not Maud. The coach itself is still being examined. Preliminary findings suggest it was mechanically sound, that there was, for example, nothing wrong with the brakes. Likewise, Mr Rathbone's car. Mechanically sound.

'You mean Tim,' says Maud. 'Tim's car.'

'Yes,' says the policewoman. 'I mean Tim.'

'Have you seen him?'

'A colleague has been to see him. To take a statement.'

Maud nods. The policewoman turns the page. There will be a

coroner's inquiry, she says. It's triggered automatically by a situation like this though if there's a trial the inquest may be adjourned until the verdict. 'Someone from the coroner's office will get in touch and talk you through it all. You will be invited to attend but you don't have to. It's up to you. Do you understand?'

She tells Maud that the children on the coach, the ones who were hurt, are back home now. One little boy has a broken arm and another a fractured cheekbone. The others just suffered bruising and shock. Counsellors will be going into the school next week. Experts.

She gives Maud her card and a sheet of paper with the numbers of various agencies and helplines. 'I'll let myself out,' she says, zipping up the wallet and standing. 'Don't forget to ring about the oil.'

Maud watches her through the window, sees her shake the raindrops onto her shoulders again. As if she had forgotten, or didn't care.

Magnus calls. Somehow he has been given the task of organizing things. He leaves businesslike messages. If there's something you want, he says, something particular, music for example, you need to let me know as soon as possible. If (the third message) I don't hear from you I'll assume you're content to let the family make the choices.

Then the vicar comes. It's the old vicar who replaced the young vicar whose wife ran away – who has presumably not come back, who is still running. He knocks softly, asks softly if he might come in for a moment. He's very tall. He has to bow his head to avoid the beams. Maud leads him through to the kitchen. There is still no oil for the Rayburn. For the last week she has been heating the room with a fan heater. For cooking she uses the microwave. Mostly she lives on cereal, toast, fruit.

She flicks on the kettle, squats to switch the heater on. The vicar watches her. The cuffs of his jacket are frayed. He is a scholar. He has a heart complaint that will not get better now. When she sits opposite him and passes him his mug he brings to bear fifty years of sitting in kitchens with men and women. It is, he thinks, a truth to be noted, how often the fire is out, the range unlit.

'I had a call from Father Wylie at the hospital. He's a Catholic of course, but in these situations we set such things aside. The differences, I mean. Is your husband here?'

'We're not married,' she says. 'He's at his parents' house.'

'Major Rathbone.'

'Yes.'

'Well, I'm sure he'll have all he needs there.'

He has seen rage, he has seen shock, he has seen derangement. Mostly he has seen bewilderment. This girl, this young woman looking into the steam of her tea, it's hard to say.

'You have been on your own then?'

'Yes.'

'Are your parents still with us?'

'What?'

'Might you also spend a little time with your family? As your, as Tim, is doing.'

'No,' she says.

'No?'

'No.'

He tries to draw her out, to make a space for her to pour herself into. He does not try to make any physical contact. Touch can be quite explosive in such circumstances but he has a half-dozen

131

clean tissues folded in the right-hand pocket of his jacket and these, at the appropriate moment, he will offer. He sips his tea, noticing on the wall by the kitchen door a pattern of red hand-prints. Adult hands, a child's hands. He asks if she is sleeping, if she is eating. If he can help her with some practical matter? She is polite. She appears to be listening to him. Is she listening to him? Sometimes there is a noise in their heads they cannot hear past.

'Maud,' he says. 'Would you like me to say a prayer? We can stay just as we are. And it doesn't matter about being a churchgoer or even a believer – I mean whether or not you would describe yourself as a believer. We are all of us free to pray at any time. Any time we feel it might be helpful.'

'OK,' she says.

'Yes?'

'All right.'

He nods, smiles, shifts his gaze to the surface of the table, gathers his thoughts. His prayers have a noted conversational tone. His intention is to speak to her, the suffering woman, and speak to whatever may be with them in that place. He shuts his eyes; he assumes she has shut hers. He listens for a squeak, some catch in her breathing, but there's only the fan heater, the sound of a distant, apparently circling, helicopter, his own voice. 'Amen,' he says at last, 'amen,' and looks up to find her looking back at him with a gaze that predates his religion. He falters. He has not seen that for a long time. The hieroglyphic stare. The impression of a mind like a shaped and painted scapula, a mind like a horse's, moral as grass. The first time he saw it, it came from a girl of ten or so, looking down at him (a gangling schoolboy hurrying home) from the heaped rubble of a Bristol bomb site. The last time, ten years ago now, it was a man he was ministering to in the old jail at Shepton Mallet, one of those in whose presence you were not allowed to carry even a pencil for fear of what might be made out of it. It was not a theological matter. Why should we imagine we are all fruit of the same branch? We know so little of our own story. A few bones, artefacts. Something on the wall of a cave, misunderstood.

He smiles at her, a lopsided, apologetic smile. 'I've taken up enough of your time,' he says. 'More than enough.' He gets to his feet. She walks with him to the front door and he is thanking her for the tea and starting to think of the little reward he will give himself when he reaches home, when she says, 'On the day it happened I was at work. My phone rang and I heard her voice.'

'Oh?'

'The call was made afterwards. The time of the call.'

'Afterwards?'

'Yes.'

'You are sure?'

'Yes.'

'And since?'

She shakes her head. She has lost that unsettling dawn-of-the-world gaze now and her face, tilted up to him, is just a face, pale, plain as a dial, pretty in its way. He was, perhaps, mistaken in what he saw, what he thought he saw. Just an ordinary girl after all, a girl in trouble. He smooths the hair on the sides of his head. He would like to offer her the protection of a formal blessing but instead finds himself looking away into the garden, the black tangles of old growth like a kind of scribbling. 'It might be best to leave here for a while,' he says. 'Go somewhere you are less reminded. Where you feel safer. Can you think of such a place, my dear?'

3

The day itself then, a dozen moments beyond speaking of. The sense, among many, of something like indecency.

She sits with her parents. She sees Tim arrive in his wheelchair, his father pushing him, Tim's face like marble, his father's red, raw, scalded from the inside. As they move towards the front of the church hands settle on their shoulders and their backs, men's hands, women's, light as wings. These are noticed or not noticed, certainly they are not responded to. Behind them comes Mrs Rathbone, the twins, Magnus and his wife with their children, the girls in black velvet coats, the boys in the uniforms of their distant, expensive schools. Only Magnus notices Maud. He nods to her then busies himself with his family.

The church is in the town. Memorial plaques, thin pillars, thin November light through the windows. A lectern in the form of a bird, a tight screw of stone steps up to the pulpit. The vicar is not the old vicar who visited the cottage but a much younger man, someone known to the Rathbones. The church has a sound system, a loop of some sort, so that his voice comes untethered out of the middle air.

There are candles – everyone has been invited to hold a small candle. There is coughing, whispering. Now and then a noise, a groan, like something out of the lion house.

The little headmistress is there with her assistant, Miss Beazley, and some of the children from the class, a half-dozen selected from among the steadiest, the most reliable. When necessary, Miss Beazley touches a child to settle him, to bring him back.

Tish and Lally are four pews back on the Rathbone side. They have dressed in dark suits like men's suits but each wears a brightly coloured scarf, something out of Asia, something that pressed to the face would smell of sandalwood or attar of roses. In front of them are the twins who, in the last year, have become almost beautiful, their piled hair a lustrous, shadowed gold. Tim's mother holds Tim's hand. She keeps her back very straight. Tears run off her chin. The candle in her hand, the flame, is trembling.

The choir sings. A woman – a woman Maud has never seen before – reads a poem by Eleanor Farjeon.

Then the vicar invites Magnus Rathbone to come forward and speak on behalf of the family. He does it well. Three or four minutes, a graceful thanking of those who have shown their love and support, who have travelled long distances. The school, the choir. No trace of cynical, frivolous Magnus, Magnus who whipped off his bath towel to show himself to his brother's new girlfriend. He sits down and his wife leans to whisper something to him. There is not much more to be done. Maud's father has rolled up the order of service, holds it in his fist like a baton, taps the side of his knee. Mrs Stamp is taking care not to spill the wax from her candle onto her quilted coat. The simplest thing now, the simplest gesture, could burn the place to the ground. No one can move, no one can stay completely still. There is not enough air in the church. Soon, surely, someone will faint.

In the dying notes of the final piece of music, Tim's father lurches upwards and swings blindly out of the pew, smacking one of his heavy thighs against the woodwork. The vicar asks everybody to blow out their candles. One candle will be left burning on the altar and this, he explains, perhaps for the benefit of the children, is a symbol.

'Come on, Maudy,' says Maud's mother. 'Everybody's leaving.'

The children go first. They are ushered out by Miss Beazley and then collected and counted by the lychgate. A coach is waiting on the road, a coach from a different company. The driver, in jacket and tie, stands ready to guide the children on board.

By the church door (where yellow leaves have fallen in complicated patterns onto the dark of the wet path) the vicar is listening to something Tim's mother is saying. There is no sign of Tim's father. Slad – Slad who carried the great polished headboard up the stairs at the cottage – has been given the job of pushing Tim's chair. Each time Tim turns his head Slad pauses and Bella bobs down to hear what Tim has to say. When she straightens up it's the signal for Slad to go on with the pushing.

Maud is standing under a tree at the bottom of the yard, a chestnut crazed and magnificent with age. She is wearing one of her work outfits. Her head is bare. She has lost some weight, seven or eight pounds. Despite the cold she stands with her coat folded over her arm. She is waiting for her parents. She is not quite sure where they are, if she needs to go and look for them. People steal glances at her. Some of them murmur to her, words that are lost in the dampness of the air, absorbed by it. Someone, approaching from behind, touches her elbow. It's the policewoman, the blonde one who shook the rain onto her shoulders. She is not in uniform now.

'Mr Rathbone said it was all right to come,' she says. 'We sometimes do. Not always. I hope you don't mind?'

She waits for Maud to say something, then nods to her as if silence is as good an answer as any and perhaps the expected one.

'Why don't I wait with you?' she says. 'Until you're ready?'

4

Her parents drive back to Swindon the same day. They leave in the dark. Her mother has tidied the kitchen and her father has lit the stove for her, and this she understands as her parents working at the far range of what is possible for them. When they have gone she puts more wood in the stove and watches it for a while. She wonders if someone will come but no one does. In the kitchen she looks in the cupboards. She is not sure when she last ate anything. She thinks it was probably yesterday. She finds a tin of Morello cherries and she opens these and picks the cherries out of the syrup with her fingers. Tinker tailor soldier sailor. At midnight she listens to the shipping forecast.

A card from Josh Fenniman. It arrives with her bank statement, a charity mailshot, the parish magazine. The front of the card shows a boulder-strewn American landscape photographed at first light. Inside, in his own hand, there are expressions of sympathy, assurances of the company's support. The feeling behind the words is that he, Josh Fenniman, is someone who has known extremes of experience, that he has faced these and found the inner resources to master them. He signs himself *Joshua*. He includes his PA's direct line. Maud reads the card through once, quickly, then places it flat on the mantlepiece above the stove. In the afternoon she calls Reading and says she would like to come back to work the following week, or if that's not possible, the week after. It's not the woman from Human Resources she speaks to but someone in the same department, a woman with a Northern Irish accent she can't quite put a face to. It's clear from her voice, however, the tone of it, that she knows who Maud is and knows her story. Perhaps she even saw Maud that day leaving the building in the company of the police.

She shops in the supermarket in town. It's a place the Rathbones sometimes use but she doesn't see any of them. Before she unpacks her bags in the kitchen she takes from the big store cupboards above the worktop the animal pasta, the fruit bars, the lunchbox orange juice cartons, the peanut butter, the rice cakes, the little boxes, smaller than matchboxes, of California raisins. She moves it all to a cupboard at the other end of the kitchen where things rarely used or needed are kept on paper-lined shelves. She also finds various medicines – Calpol, junior disprin, syrup of figs. These she puts in a plastic bag and lowers the bag into the swing bin.

Three or four times a day the phone rings. A message from her mother saying the important thing is to eat nutritious food. A call from the police wanting to speak with Tim. A call from Arnie who, when the call was made, was clearly on his way to being drunk. He will come to her, he says, at a moment's notice.

Whatever she needs, anything at all, anything. And later, a second call, when he is fully drunk, saying there is obviously no God, that there are things she should know about, that she can call him in the middle of the night, it's not as if he's sleeping anyway and for God's sake she mustn't do anything stupid, mustn't, I don't know . . . Are we in control of our lives? Obviously not. And what then?

These messages from Arnie are the first she pays close attention to. A shout that carries above the noise of a shouting crowd. The unexpected value of incoherence.

The oil man comes. He whistles. He fills up the tank. He says it's usually her husband he sees. He says, 'We could all use a little sunshine, eh?'

One evening, walking in the lane, she sees an owl flying along the road in front of her. She assumes it's an owl. A large pale bird, silent and suddenly swerving into the dark of a field.

She thinks, as she walks home, she's about to come on. She's very regular, a day or two either way. In the downstairs toilet of the cottage she looks in her pants, touches herself. There's nothing. Nothing the next day or the next or the one after.

A visit from Slad. He has, he says, been asked to collect the picture, the little watercolour of the girl in the straw hat with the basket of cherries. He doesn't say why they want it back; it may have something to do with the insurance. He lifts it off its hook and puts it into a cloth bag he takes from one of his pockets. The bag is like those used to keep a pair of expensive shoes in, or that is pulled over the head of a man about to be hanged. He asks Maud if she wants him to take the hook out of the wall but she says he can leave it. There is nothing brusque or unfriendly in his behaviour. He spends a lot of his time around horses and his movements are measured, predictable.

At last the kitchen is properly warm. She sits at the table in lamplight drinking a glass of water. The night is wild and the wind is knocking a window somewhere upstairs, a window she should probably go up and secure.

There are flowers in the sink, white chrysanthemums she found on the doorstep with a card (*Deepest Sympathy*) signed by the neighbours, Sarah and Michael. White chrysanthemums, some greenery, cellophane, thin green ribbon. People know. All over the place people know. It may even be in the parish magazine. It doesn't matter. It's all right.

On the worktop between the bread bin and the toaster the child monitor is sitting in its base beside the plug socket. A red light shows that it's on, a green light that it's connected to the unit upstairs, that it's receiving. Sound is played through a speaker; it is also registered in a rippling fan of lights on the face of the monitor. She sips her water and watches the lights, the way they leap forward until almost the entire face is lit up then drop back for a moment before pulsing into life again. She watches. She drinks her water. She slowly drains the glass.

When she goes back to work the first person she sees is Kurt Henderson. Perhaps no one told him she was coming back. In his stare there is deep discomfort, a profound unreadiness. He says, hoarsely, 'I'm so sorry.' After a pause, he adds, 'Yeah.' He holds out the papers in his arms to indicate work, and shoulders his way into Meeting Room 2. *If you will tell me why the Fen appears impassable . . .*

She spends twenty minutes with the woman from Human Resources. It's agreed she will, for the time being, work a four-day week, that she will drop the Kappa-opioids project which is, anyway, pretty much running itself these days. She asks Maud how she is coping, how she and Tim are coping. She knows Maud well enough now not to expect much in return, much beyond some vague assurance, and when it comes she nods and smiles and says, 'Good, good.' She makes no mention of how Maud has been remembered in her prayers or how, at the church in Reading city centre where four or five services are held each Sunday, where there are bands and young faces wet with tears and the minister in jeans and a T-shirt struts the stage like a successful comedian, she has had Maud's name read out, thrown like a rose to the fluttering hands of the faithful.

Sweet Jesus Lord lay your healing hands on this woman!

Day two at work and she drives down to Croydon. There's a seminar, the latest in a series about the reporting of side-effects, a topic they can never quite get free of and that is starting to worry the team in Orlando. The assumption is that Fennidine/epibatidine is acting on the receptors for the chemical acetylcholine, but it's unclear what else it may be interacting with, what else is stimulated, released. On a screen they look at colour slides of positron emission brain scans. On one of these – image twelve, middle-aged female – there is a shadow shaped like a bird in flight.

During the coffee break a man strides over to Maud, leans over her and says, 'I hope Fenniman's aren't playing games with us. I hope they're serious about seeing this through. It would be a bloody disgrace if they don't see it through . . .'

He is interrupted, tapped on the elbow by a woman, a

colleague, and later, when he's been told, he is quiet, will not look at Maud, turns a pen through his fingers.

Mid-December: cold air descending from high latitudes. In the morning she scrapes ice off the windscreen then leaves the engine running while she goes in to make coffee. The kitchen is not untidy. She does not let the dishes pile up, does not forget now and then to sweep the floor. It is not untidy but it is different, like a ring no one wears any more or a path no one walks on, no one but her. She checks in her bag to see she has what she will need for the day. She looks, for perhaps a full minute, at the monitor on the worktop. One morning (ice on the tips of the grass, on the rosehips, on the stumps of cut maize, the steel bars of field gates) she passes a car that has come off the road, ridden up a bank and wedged itself in the hedgerow. She slows and sees a man standing beside the car with a scarf tied round his head. He's like a man from the year 1200. He grimaces, calls something she does not catch, waves her on.

It is at the end of this season, this three weeks of tumbling air that is written about in the newspapers, that she comes home to the cottage and finds the front door open. It's been dark for hours, no moon, no lights in the house. She calls then goes in and works her way through the house, visits almost every room. In the spare room she sees the guitar cupboard is open and empty. She goes downstairs. Someone is knocking on the door, a gentle but persistent knocking. It's the neighbours, Michael and Sarah. Michael has a torch. They are both wearing dark blue or black fleeces.

'Is everything all right?' asks Michael.

'We were very worried,' says Sarah.

'We didn't know what to do,' says Michael. 'We wanted to call someone but we didn't know who. We thought of calling the fire brigade.'

They wait, and when they see she has no idea what they are talking about, they begin to tell her, passing the story back and forth between them.

They had been off work for two days, the vomiting virus everybody has. At about half past three – they know the time because they were watching a programme on the television and it finishes at half past – they heard a car and a car door and looked out in time to see Tim going into the cottage. He was using a single crutch, he was on his own. They didn't think anything of it, not really, but then, from their kitchen window, they saw him go into the garden. He had a guitar with him and that *did* seem odd because it was cold and already starting to get dark and why would he want to go and play in the cold? But instead of playing he put the guitar on the grass and went back to the house and a few minutes later came out with another guitar, put that on the grass beside the first and went back to the house again. They had no idea what he was doing but they began to be anxious. Three or four guitars – and they knew he had good guitars, very good and very expensive – all just lying on the grass. The rest of it happened very quickly. He poured something on them, lit a match. It was like an explosion. It *was* an explosion. At first the flames were as tall as he was and he staggered back and nearly fell. Then he just stood there, watching until the fire was almost burnt out. Afterwards he went back into the house and a minute or two after that they heard the car again.

'We're not unsympathetic,' says Michael. 'We're just worried.'

'We're worried about fire,' says Sarah.

'The fire brigade,' says Michael, 'cannot be here in less than twenty minutes. More like half an hour.'

Maud has never heard them speak so much. They had seemed to be people of few words, people who moved about their lives almost silently. Now she sees this impression was wrong. They are full of words, words that were waiting for something to happen that would release them. She thanks them and closes the door. There's a torch on the kitchen windowsill. She turns it on and goes out to the passage between the kitchen and the oil tank. The back garden is small. A parcel of land with vegetable beds at the bottom, a low red-brick wall separating it from the neighbours' garden, a beech hedge on the lane side. The fire, what's left of it, is on the lawn close to the swing. There are embers still, a residual heat, the smell of an accelerant. She squats with the torch and lifts out the head of one of the guitars, wipes it with her thumb, sees the smutted inlay of diamonds and moons, feels how the wood is warm as a hand, then lays it back with the rest, the ashes, the heat-tangled wires, the blackened nuts and little cogs, the debris.

In the house the answer phone is flashing. A message from Tim's mother. 'Is Tim there, Maud? Have you seen him? He's taken one of the cars. It's the automatic so he can drive it. Will you please get in touch *immediately* if you see him?'

Then another message, weary. 'He's back. Will you kindly call when you get this? I think we should at least have a talk. We need to start making some sense of things. We need to find some way to go on with our lives.'

5

She does not warn them she is coming. Or she does not warn herself that she is going. It's a Saturday afternoon. She drives through patient country rain, parks in the courtyard. Dogs run out to greet her. They follow her through the rain to the door. There is an old stirrup bell here but no one ever rings it. She goes into the room with the waxed jackets, the cut-glass bowl with its shotgun cartridges. In the kitchen she finds Slad's wife, a heavy woman dicing meat, a bone-handled knife in one hand, its blade as long as Maud's forearm. She has never shown much friendliness to Maud, though Maud has never seen her show much friendliness to anyone other than Magnus, who treats her as a serf, a serf's chattel. Mrs Rathbone, she says, is lying down. Mr Rathbone is in his workshop and won't thank anyone for disturbing him.

'And Tim?'

'In his room,' she says.

'Upstairs?'

'How could he manage stairs?' says Mrs Slad. 'He's in the little room. Off the music room.'

Maud thanks her. She does not say that he managed the stairs at the cottage, managed them all right and carried things down. She goes out of the kitchen, through the morning room and along a short windowless passage to the music room. Rain-light on a faded carpet, on the scuffed black of violin cases, the glass face of a tall-clock. On the piano, the photographs are arranged in tilted rows like a solar farm. Children kneeling by a Christmas tree. Children in their school uniforms, hair neatly parted. Children with dogs, children on the knees of their parents. There are, she knows, at least three generations of them there, children smiling for the camera, or caught between one stride and the next, one gesture and the next, arms flung out, hands and fingers blurring into air.

To the left of the piano is another door. Through it, softly, a woman's voice.

She taps on the door and goes in. Tim is in bed, a single bed with wooden legs on casters, perhaps a child's bed. Bella is on a chair beside the bed, a book in her hand. She is wearing a turtle-neck dress of light grey cashmere, her hair scraped back and held with a clasp of muted silver.

'Hello, Maud,' she says. 'Would you like to speak to Tim? He's a bit drowsy, I'm afraid. A bad night last night.'

She too looks tired, a slight shadowing under her eyes as if, self-lessly, she shares the burden of bad nights. She stands, puts the book on the chair, and with a quick smile at Tim she leaves the room.

In the bed, Tim has the covers pulled up to his throat. He is not looking at Maud. Perhaps he is not looking at anything. On the small round table under the window are various medicines. She can see that one of these, from its trade name, is a benzodiazepine. She could, if she chose, tell him the drug's metabolizing enzymes. Could recite them to him like lines of poetry.

'The neighbours were scared,' she says. 'They're afraid you'll set fire to the house.'

'I thought about it,' he says.

'Did you burn them all?' she asks.

He nods.

'Even the Lacôte?'

'Yes.'

'Don't burn anything else,' she says.

'What do you want?' he says.

'Are you staying here?'

'Yes.'

'You're not coming back to the cottage?'

He moves his head on the pillow, rolls it in a narrow arc.

'Are you with Bella now?'

'For fuck's sake, Maud.'

'What?'

'Is that relevant? Who I'm with? Who you're with? Is it relevant?'

He shuts his eyes. He looks very like his mother. The book on the chair is *Vanity Fair*, a paperback with a creased spine, a man and woman on the cover, dancing formally.

There are things she was going to tell him. Things whose relevance she thinks he would not question. Now she sees that if she tells him these things he will start to scream.

In the music room Bella is sitting on the piano stool looking as if it is only a kind of politeness that keeps her from playing.

'Goodbye,' she says.

'Goodbye,' says Maud.

*   *   *

When she returns to the kitchen Mrs Slad has gone but Tim's father is there, leaning against the sink, arms folded, apparently studying the toes of his shoes. He looks up. 'Come through,' he says, and leads her to what the family call the small drawing room. There is no one else there. At one end of the room is a sideboard too large for the room, its shelves filled with porcelain dogs and more pictures of children. In the grate is the remnant of a morning fire. Tim's father leans down to it, prods it, then picks out from the wood basket a quarter log and lays it in the embers. All the wood comes from his own land.

'A drink?'

'No thanks.'

He goes to the table under the window, one of several about the house known as a 'drinks table'. Into two heavy glasses he pours two measures of Scotch.

'Never trust a man who doesn't drink,' he says. 'Applies to women too, I think.'

He grins at her. She takes the glass, touches it to her lips, feels the small burn where her lips have cracked.

'So you've been to see Tim.'

'Yes.'

'And how did you think he looked?'

She considers for a moment – the sallow face on the plumped-up pillow, the eyes that seemed, the moment before he shut them, to be pleading with her. 'Tired,' she says. 'Sad.'

'Sad?'

'Yes.'

'Sad. Mmm. Well, yes, we're all of us, over here Maud, a bit sad. You appear to be bearing up, however. I'm told you're back at work. Got the old lab coat on again.'

'Yes.'

'Good. Good for you.' He looks away from her. His face is flushed. When he speaks again it is with a voice that comes from somewhere much deeper inside of him, a voice he has been keeping hidden.

'Tim is not sad, Maud. Tim is devastated. My wife is devastated. I am devastated. Even bloody Magnus is devastated. Only you, you and perhaps your extraordinary parents, seem to be managing.'

He empties his glass, carries it over to the drinks table. With his back to her he says, 'I always rather admired you. The way you didn't try too hard to make people like you. Most people do, don't they?'

He pours another two fingers of Scotch into his glass, turns to her again. 'We used, in the family, to talk about you quite a lot. Does that surprise you? Two schools of thought, really. One, that you were a bright girl, a bit shy, a bit gauche, a bit unworldly but basically all right. The other school, quite a big one, had you down as cold-blooded, entirely self-absorbed and not really all right at all. One thing that both schools were agreed upon was that you hadn't the slightest interest in being a mother.'

'That's not true.'

'Oh, I think it is. I never saw the least evidence of any maternal instinct. I don't mean you were cruel. That would have taken a measure of engagement, some effort of imagination. No, no. In your own rather pathetic way you tried. But something was missing. Something fundamental. You reached for it and it simply wasn't there.'

He acts it out. The reaching, the clasping at air, the expression of open-mouthed surprise.

'Why are you saying this?' she asks.

'We saw you, Maud. I saw you. Everyone did. It wasn't difficult.'

He moves closer, close enough for her to smell his leathery aftershave, the whisky. He takes hold of her left hand, lifts her arm, slides up the sleeve of her sweater.

'Look at it,' he says. 'Who would want this on themselves? I'm sorry, but there's something very wrong with you and I wish to Christ Tim had never laid eyes on you. I wish none of us had.'

There are tears on his cheeks thick as varnish. He has given way to something, or something has given way inside him. She frees herself from his grasp, turns away from him towards the door.

'Don't you *dare*!' he shouts. 'Don't you . . .' He lunges at her. He is, in his fury, very strong. For half a second she is in pure flight, then her feet tangle with the end of the sofa and she slams into the base of the sideboard, lies there, dazed, while porcelain dogs and picture frames tumble onto the floor around her. Slowly, she gets to her knees. He reaches down for her and helps her to stand. He says he is sorry and sounds as if he means it. He draws her to him, holds her tightly, one hand smoothing the hair on the back of her head. His shoulders are heaving; his breath is very hot. 'Please,' he says, 'don't ever come back. Do you understand? Don't ever come here again.'

6

She spends Christmas with her parents in Swindon. As a present she is given a jumper, oatmeal-coloured; also the receipt in case she wishes to change it. No one comes round.

In January she is sick. A virus – perhaps the same one Michael and Sarah had. Acid in her throat, her nose. The impossibility of being warm. She keeps the stove going until she runs out of wood then lies thirty-six hours on the sofa wrapped in a heavy blanket. For part of this time there is a pain in her head and neck so intense she hardly dares to swallow. She doesn't bother with aspirin or ibuprofen. She takes one of the Fennidine from the box stamped FOR TRIAL USE ONLY. It's not the first she's taken. Several of the team involved with the trial have used them.

She sleeps or passes out, comes to in the cold room, in utter darkness. She has for a moment no idea where she is, then feels the rough weave of the cushion against her cheek and remembers. After a while she becomes aware of the sound of her own breathing and a few seconds later of something else, like the subtle echo of her breathing but an echo that does not stop when she holds her breath.

She turns her head. Whatever it is it seems to be coming from the stairs, the top of the stairs, and she frees her arms from the blanket and pushes herself, as quietly as she can, into a sitting position. She imagines a cat up there, crouched on the top step. She imagines a fox, aware of her, utterly still. Or a bird like the pale bird she saw flying low along the lane that night. At the same time she knows perfectly well there is no bird or fox or cat, nothing of that sort. She waits, listens, then climbs from the sofa and gropes her way towards the stairs, to the wall at the bottom of the stairs, the light switch. Half a minute of running her fingers over the wall to find the switch. The light changes everything, rocks her like a soft yet powerful blow to her chest. She screws shut her eyes and clutches the bannister. When she can open her eyes her view is the rise of carpeted steps, an angle of wall on the landing, the light itself in its red shade, which sways slightly in one of those currents of cool air that flow unstoppably about the cottage and are, perhaps, an integral part of how the building has survived. For two or three minutes she remains there, looking up the stairs. The temptation to speak a name, to loft a name into the lit air of the landing. Then she pads to the kitchen, drinks from the tap and sits on the floor, her back hard against the iron of the old Rayburn. When has she been this cold? She cannot think when she has ever been this cold.

It's another week before she's strong enough to go back to work. Even then she doesn't seem quite right, does not feel it or look it. On the day after St Valentine's, the woman from Human Resources comes to her cubicle, leans down by her ear and says, 'Can I borrow you for ten minutes?'

They go to her office. They sit opposite each other. The woman smiles. 'You're very pale,' she says.

'Am I?'

'Yes.'

'It's winter,' says Maud. 'And I was ill.'

'I know,' says the woman. 'But it's more than that, isn't it? You've been incredibly brave. Unbelievably brave. But it's all too soon. People are worried about you, Maud. People here, people at Croydon. They're worried. Concerned. They don't think you should be back, not yet. And I have to think of them too. Of their needs. The truth is a lot of them are uncomfortable. They want to support you as a colleague but they don't know how. Do you see what I'm saying? Does it make sense? I've been in touch with Orlando. The view there is that you should take more time. What they'd like is for you to finish the week and then begin a period of leave until the end of the summer. September, say. That will enable us to offer at least six months to your replacement. You'll be on full pay for the first three months and a sliding percentage thereafter. I'll get in touch with you in July and see how you're doing. See what you're feeling ready for. Now how does that sound, as a package? Does it sound fair to you? Maud?'

So she sits at home; her work clothes in the wardrobe; her laptop on the kitchen table, shut; her work bag, mostly empty, against the wall by the front door. In a shoebox in the kitchen, beneath scraps of paper with tradesmen's phone numbers and various oddments such as a postcard from Tish and Lally (Buenos Aires) and a small photograph of herself as a schoolgirl standing against the wall at the back of the house in Swindon (a photograph Tim must have asked her parents for), she finds some of Tim's tobacco and cigarette papers. She hasn't smoked since she was fifteen, when the man whose children she used to babysit for gave her cigarettes from his pack after what he called *sessions*. The tobacco is dry and hard to roll but by concentrating and trying several times she ends up with something like a cigarette. She smokes half of it, drops the rest into the dregs of her tea.

She receives a letter from Arnie. It describes, over several pages, the descent of his life, his struggle with weakness and mystery, his ailments, his insomnia, his stab at poetry. It is written on office notepaper. It is, apparently, a love letter.

On the same day that the letter comes she drags the heavy furniture to the edges of the living room to vacuum the floor. Under the sofa she finds a red marble and a green one. She also finds the torn and empty envelope of a condom, the type *ribbed for mutual pleasure*. She examines it, turns the little silvery envelope through her fingers; would perhaps have put it on the stove if the stove were lit. At what point would she have minded this? She's not sure. It feels mostly like old news. Old news about Tim and Bella. Old news about herself. Old news about the race, the species. Very briefly, and in an almost academic way, she imagines breaking one of Bella's very white and beautiful wrists. Then she reaches up and places the envelope beside Josh Fenniman's card on the mantlepiece. She goes on with the vacuuming.

For a long time she does not go upstairs other than to fetch clothes or use the bathroom. She sleeps on the sofa and then, one evening, as if for a moment she has forgotten everything, she goes upstairs and sleeps in the bedroom, in the bed with the walnut headboard. Some of Tim's clothes are folded over a chair by the window. A book he was reading is on the floor by his side of the bed. She hears mice run across the roof spaces above the bedroom ceiling.

She thinks of them chewing the insulation from the wiring, thinks she should buy traps for them, poison, but knows she won't, not now.

Whole days are passed either sitting in the kitchen or sitting on the sofa or sitting on the stairs or standing somewhere between these places. She could not account for these days, could not begin to.

When she needs to, she drives into town to buy things. She has a glimpse of Slad's wife in the supermarket looking through packs of meat. She thinks she sees the blonde policewoman go past in a car but may have imagined it. She sees Arnie talking on a street corner to an older man in a tweed suit and the man saying something and Arnie laughing as if he hadn't a care in the world.

Some nights, rather than go to bed, she watches the television, often with the sound turned down. The oddest programmes on at three in the morning. Sales channels selling a kind of mock jewellery. Detective shows, ten or twenty years old. Educational shows about daily life in Lima, the formation of valleys, beginners' Gaelic. On one of these shows – the Gaelic primer? – there's a woman about her own age, with rosy cheeks and short blonde hair. She's wearing a black swimsuit of the kind that comes down to mid-thigh like a pair of cycling shorts. She's standing on the deck of a boat, a big old wooden boat, anchored in some northern sea. It's quite obvious how cold everything is – the air, the woman, the green water. She seems to be speaking to someone behind the camera. Now and then she breaks off to look, a little apprehensively, at the sea, and all the while she is edging towards the side of the boat until at last she's standing on the wooden gunnels, supporting herself by holding the ratlines. For a good fifteen seconds she stands there in her black swimsuit, the camera settled on her back, her strong legs, her shoulders reddening in the wind.

Then she lets go of the ratlines, balances, sways forward a little, bends her knees and launches herself into a brief arc in which her heavy body is suddenly graceful. She breaks the water. The camera watches. The water settles. There is no sign of the woman.

That same night, when at last Maud climbs into the old bed, falls into it with that strange exhaustion that comes from doing nothing, she has a dream that feels as if it is a continuation of the dive, though there is no sea, or wooden deck or shyly smiling woman. Instead, she is in the presence of a very old man. He is turned away from her, his head, what she can see of it, like a bag of damaged plush in which a metal ball is kept, an iron ball. She is explaining to him what has happened to her. She doesn't miss anything out. Among other things she tells him about the phone call in the animal room, about the lights on the monitor in the kitchen, about the night she felt herself observed from the top of the stairs. When she has finished telling him these things he turns to her and she sees that it's Rawlins the judo instructor, Rawlins old, ancient, perhaps dead.

She sleeps until nearly midday, wakes with the sense of his having said something to her, something she should have taken note of and cannot now remember, but standing in the bathroom, stripping for a shower, she catches sight of her arm, of *Sauve Qui Peut*, and wonders if that is what he said. That.

She showers, pulls on clothes, goes downstairs. She makes coffee, rolls a cigarette and goes into the garden. On the lawn, a black circle on the grass from the fire. Unexpected sunlight, unexpected warmth. She smokes and sips her coffee, looks up at the windows at the back of the house. When she has finished her coffee she goes back into the house, leaves her mug on the kitchen table, goes up the stairs and opens the door of the nursery or what, half jokingly and right at the start when they were painting it, they called the nursery. She strips the bed, bundles the sheets, the duvet cover. The pink ukelele is lying in the middle of the floor. She had forgotten about the ukelele, that it existed. She leans it against a wall then changes her mind and lays it on the stripped bed before changing her mind again and leaning it against the wall. She shuts the not quite perfectly shut window. She folds the scattered clothes. She takes the bedding down to the kitchen, puts it in the washing machine, sets the programme, starts it.

The way the drum swings one way and then, after a pause, swings the other.

How one moment you are not ready and the next, somehow, you are.

In the bedroom she puts the big holdall at the end of the bed, starts with a layer of pants, bras, tights, vests. Then jeans, shirts, shorts, a pair of black cotton culottes that Tim called her coolie trousers. A jumper of oiled wool she has had for years that smells like rope treated with Scandinavian tar. The soft blue jumper, a little moth-eaten, she bought the winter she was pregnant. Thermals. Salopettes, rolled tight. Helly Hansen jacket rolled tight. Every pair of thick socks she can find. Deck shoes. Musto half-length sea boots. A red travel towel. A striped beanie, fingerless gloves. From the bathroom her toothbrush, toothpaste and a half-box of tampons, though she still hasn't come on, not for months, a fact she has shared with no one, not even the dreamed head of old Rawlins.

A tube of SPF 25 face protector. Nail clippers, deodorant. She zips the bag, heaves it, lets it slide down the stairs ahead of her. Back in the bathroom she takes off her top and uses a pair of heavy dressmaking scissors (she who has never made a dress) to cut her hair. Cuts it so close you could hold the back of her head in your hand like the shell of something. Here and there the skin shows through. In one place, by the crown, she has nicked herself.

She carries the holdall out to the car then goes back to the kitchen, moves the washing to the dryer, sets it to run for an hour. She unplugs the monitor, locks the back door, puts her phone and charger in her pocket, shuts and locks the front door. It's the middle of the day. Other than birds provoked to song by the warmer weather, she cannot hear a sound. She walks on the path, the old seabed. The gate swings shut behind her. She does not look back.

THREE

And so, into our darkness life seeps,
keeping its part of the bargain.

John Ashbery

1

Through his window (where pictures of boats are displayed on boards, pictures with curling edges yellowed by the light) the broker is looking at an imagined building. The owners of the yard – men who always arrive in convoys of 4x4s, like a shooting party – have plans to build a marina hotel, something with two hundred bedrooms, a spa, a gym, a couple of restaurants (one to be called The Olde Yard and to have a theme of boat-building and be decorated with parts of boats and boat-builders' tools). He has seen the architect's model in the marina office, the clever trees, the people sized like grains of rice. His own office will go, of course. Everything improvised, everything merely makeshift, will go. On the model he has gone already.

He opens the tin of cigarillos, takes one out and taps the end of it on the desk. The air today is heavy with rain waiting to fall. The river, the boats on their moorings, the hazed green of the far bank, all of it held in that stillness that comes just before or just after the event.

At two o'clock – the schedule! – he has an old boat to see, a big ketch, ex-charter, beautiful and impossible, a boat that will devour time and money and must be sold to someone who knows exactly what he's doing, or to some romantic, some moneyed fool, who will pin a picture of it to a wall in his house and sigh over it.

Next high tide is 16.15. Low tide at 21.15. Where are we now? Springs? Just past springs? He tries to recall if he saw the moon last night, tries to reconstruct some fugitive moment of the night, himself in T-shirt and boxers standing over the toilet bowl (light off because he cannot bear the light on at such a moment, the mind softened from sleep) and thinks he *did* see it, a moon with a bite out of it sliding towards the hills between the town and the cliffs (those fields where careless farmers occasionally drive their tractors into thin air), and he's nodding at this, pleased to have recovered something that would otherwise have been entirely lost, nodding and holding up the unlit cigarillo like a conductor's baton, when the door of his office is pushed open and without a single measurable instant of hesitation, he meets her eyes, smiles at her and says, 'Your season starting already?'

The boat is in the yard, on its legs of chocked wood. It has been there since the previous September when it was hauled out after a summer of four or five weekend sails. This, as the broker knows, is the common fate of boats. Bought, loved, sailed. Then loved less, sailed less. Because there is always money to be spent – mooring fees, yard fees, endless repairs, refits – the boat becomes a burden. Finally, someone makes a decision they refer to as 'sensible'. They come to the broker's office. They smile sadly. They look a little ashamed.

Between them – Maud at the front – they carry a ladder. *Lodestar* looks tired, a boat not entirely convincing any more. If it were a car you might consider stripping it for its parts.

'A dab of paint,' says the broker. 'A scrape down. Always look a bit sorry for themselves at the end of the winter.'

She knows all this, of course. He's talking for the sake of talking.

She goes up the ladder. Legs, backside, steps over the rail.

'Everything OK up there?'

She is already undoing the tarpaulin. From the nearside shroud a scrap of ribbon lifts to the breeze.

'Rob's around somewhere. Or at least his car's here. Nice to have you back, Maud. Please be careful up there.'

She has, he thinks, walking back to his office, cut her hair with blunt shears, a bread knife. Something like that. Or it fell out? She's had chemo and has spent the winter sitting in a ward with a drip in her arm, a view of the incinerator chimney. Yet she doesn't look frail, sickly. She looks like a woman it would be a serious mistake to force into a corner. Does he like her? Trust her? He has, he imagines, seen her type before (or perhaps just read about them). Women who step out of a burning town and who, later, turn out to be the reason the town was burning. One of those wide-eyed girls who carry a kind of wreckage in their wake.

The boat's cabin is a shell, a skin, a form blown in glass, slightly unreal. She sits on one of the benches, the Moroccan red upholstery that has not lasted well, that already looks to have absorbed too much weather. There is so much to do – so much! – but after sitting a while doing nothing there seems less. She goes through to the forward cabin, begins to look through lockers, reach into sail bags. She touches the coiled anchor chain, the anchor, the spare. In the saloon she finds things left behind from the previous summer and the one before that. An almost empty tube of sun cream, a sun hat, a crumpled T-shirt. It's all her stuff, or hers and John Gosse's. His books are still behind the fiddle rails, *Sailing Alone Around the World*, *The Dhammapada*. Also the picture, the boat at sunset or sunrise, the frame screwed to the bulkhead.

On deck she picks her way up to the pulpit rail, checks the rail, the forestay, the plate, the bow roller, cleats, fairleads, walks slowly backwards, touching everything as she comes to it, testing it. It is at first just an impersonation of purpose but by degrees becomes what it mimicked. At the mast she looks up, following the ascent of ropes to where they disappear into the sheaves like streams into the earth. Spreaders, reflector, the masthead light. She moves to the cockpit and uses her fingers to dig out leaf rot, dig out God knows what from the cockpit drains. She opens the left-hand seat locker and connects up the gas bottle for the galley stove. She stands by the tiller. The boat, lifted, is on course for the upper boughs of oak trees. She has hardly noticed that it's raining, gusts of it crossing the river, beading her hair, the whole valley swallowed in a cloud.

Below her, the yard looks deserted. She wipes the water from her face, steps through the companionway, shuts the hatch and lies down on one of the benches, cold hands between her thighs.

When she wakes it's late afternoon. Through the delicate crazing of the saloon window she watches the reinvention of colour, the low sun flooding the valley, the oddness of a day that grows brighter rather than darker at its close. A figure in red is crossing the yard towards her. She watches him then pushes back the hatch and steps into the coolness of the rain-cleaned air. He waves to her, and when he's closer, standing at the foot of the ladder squinting up at her, he says, 'Chris told me you were here. Want me to run a cable up?'

'Yes,' she says. 'Please.'

'Tomorrow morning OK?'

'Yes.'

'So you're down for a while?'

'Yes.'

'When do you want to get her in the water?'

'I'm not sure. A week?'

'Well, you're ahead of the crowd. That shouldn't be a problem.'

Silence.

'I'll see you in the morning then.'

'Yes. OK.'

He waves again and turns back towards the boat shed. On the far side of the river the sun is dropping behind the hills. There are patches of gold on the bank behind her but the yard and the river are already being sifted into the first blue of twilight. She will need to find things before it's dark – the lantern, the torch, the sleeping bag that has overwintered in the quarter berth. People are not supposed to sleep on the cradled boats but she has made no other arrangement. She can use the sink and toilets at the marina. There's tinned food on board, a bottle of water in her bag. She will not be noticed. Other than the broker and Robert Currey, there's not a living soul who knows she is here.

Twice during the night she comes to in the dark with all her senses alert. The first time she does not know where she is, can feel only the constriction of the bag, the nearness of unlit walls. It is the boat's smell and the dank odour of the unaired sleeping bag that bring her back. Then again, hours later, opening her eyes to a glassy light and the sketched clutter of the cabin, the barometer's brass edge like a setting moon. In between – between one waking and the next – hours of dreamless sleep and a rest truer than she has known in months.

At seven-thirty she's in the cockpit dismantling a winch that does not, perhaps, really need dismantling. Robert Currey arrives waving a thermos and a white paper bag that turns out to have a bacon sandwich in it.

She comes down the ladder to him. The sandwich smells delicious. As soon as he passes it to her she takes it out of the bag and starts to eat.

'I guessed you were going to sleep up there,' he says. 'No skin off my nose but it's against the rules. And you don't have a great record for knowing where the edge of a boat is.'

'That was once,' she says, her mouth full of bread and bacon.

By quarter past nine she has power cable and a plan of work. By ten she's wearing overalls and goggles and using the jet spray to sluice the bottom of the boat. What she can't clean off with the spray she scrapes off with the edge of a palette knife then rubs down with wet-and-dry. The sun comes out and she steps from under the shadow of the boat, holds her face up to the warmth of it.

After lunch she begins to patch-prime the gel-coat, then crosses to the town on the chain ferry to buy anti-foul. The ferry has only four cars on it and a recycling truck, a few foot passengers. The money is collected by a man with a leather saddlebag. The crossing takes seven minutes and everything he does, the little conversations, the handing out of change, the stroll to the ferry gates, is timed to perfection. He cannot help it.

In the town the cafes and seafront kiosks are mostly shut, their flyers still announcing the previous summer's fishing trips, the motor-boat rentals whose prices will go up by a pound or two this year. A man on a stepladder paints the woodwork of his souvenir shop. A traffic warden sits on a bollard looking at the water.

The chandlery is smaller than the chip shop next door to it, but inside, over two floors (and on the edges of the stairs) is almost everything a boat, a boat-owner, even a boat-builder, might have need of. Snap shackles, ratchet blocks, battery boxes, hand flares, sea boots, fenders, tidal atlases, bilge pumps. Drums of coloured polyester braid, shock cord, PVC hose by the metre. Skin fittings, cable glands, grapnel anchors. The woman who works there – sometimes there is a girl too but the woman is always there – knows what you need better than you know it yourself, yet she looks as if she has no particular interest in boats, does not sail, does not perhaps much care for the sea. She points Maud towards the shelves of paint along the back wall then watches her from the end of the aisle, this young woman she has, she thinks, seen before. Quite what is wrong with her – and something is – she cannot say. Tempting to imagine she's on the drink – boat people often are. But her skin looked clear, her eyes. Nor, when she comes back to the counter, does she smell of drink. She pays with a card, carries the paint, a pot in each hand, towards the door, but stops beside the charts, puts the paint down and stays for nearly forty minutes, her fingers walking to and fro across the tops of the plastic envelopes. With another customer, a different sort of customer, the woman might have offered some assistance, but this one either knows exactly what she's doing or she hasn't a clue. When she comes to the counter again she has Admiralty charts 4011 and 4012. 'And these,' she says, a little burr to her voice, not Devon though. The woman puts them in a bag. The North Atlantic Northern Part and North Atlantic Southern Part, respectively. It all seems clear enough now, and when she leaves the shop, steps into the street where two gulls are scrapping over a chip in the gutter, the woman leans by the window to watch her go and thinks *we won't be seeing you again*, and this thought strikes her like a prophesy, so that for several minutes she does not know whether to make more tea or rearrange the footwear display on the first floor. And this is not like her. It is not like her at all.

2

The next morning Maud pulls on her overalls over jeans and jumper, brews coffee, eats a banana, eats a square of chocolate and goes on deck. She sits on the coach-house roof, looking up river to where the water and the light meet. She rolls a cigarette from a pouch bought in the town. She is becoming better at rolling, better at smoking.

When she has finished her cigarette she goes down the ladder with one of the tins of anti-foul. Yesterday, in the late afternoon, she taped the boat's waterline. Now she walks slowly around the hull, checking her work. When she is satisfied, she opens the tin and pours some paint into a tray, coats the mohair roller and begins to paint. She's been at it for an hour, her eyes starting to smart, when Robert Currey comes over with a box of disposable gloves and a pair of plastic goggles.

'There's a reason it keeps stuff off the bottom of boats,' he says.

In one of his pockets he finds a rag, finds a corner cleaner than the others and wipes a splash of anti-foul from the back of her right hand. It takes only a few seconds and during those seconds neither of them speak.

By lunchtime she has the first coat finished and steps away from the boat to get the smell of it out of her mouth. The yard is busier today though most boats still look unattended. On the slipway, Robert Currey and another yardsman are working on a pleasure boat, a converted survey boat once called *Skagen*, now called *Tinkerbelle* and strung with bunting. Robert Currey, disappearing down a hatchway, stops to wave and Maud waves back.

The second coat of paint goes on the following day. According to the instructions the paint should have the thickness of a business card, like those cards, mostly unused, she has in a box in the car – Maud Stamp, Senior Clinical Associate.

By mid-afternoon the paint is dry enough to peel off the tape. It's not a perfect job but it's good enough. She touches up, wipes away any unevenness with a rag dipped in solvent. She is booked in with the launching crane for next Monday. That gives her two more days to do whatever must be done in the dry. What is not done, what is missed, will have to stay that way. This she has already decided. On Monday the boat will go into the water and she will go into the boat. There are no alternatives, certainly none she can think of. Go back to the cottage? Go back to those things she spoke of to the dreamed head of Rawlins? Behind her the way has closed. She has closed it herself or something beyond her closed it. It hardly matters. She cannot wait any longer. The one thing that feels genuinely dangerous is stillness.

The night before the launch she goes down to the marina toilet block with her towel and wash bag. It's late and there's no one else in the block, no one she can hear. She undresses, puts her clothes in a locker, steps into the cubicle, puts a pound coin in the slot, turns on the shower. The water's cold. It shocks her. Then it starts to heat up and the cubicle fills with steam and her skin glows pink. She looks at herself through the steam. A blackened thumbnail; three little bruises on each shin, a long graze high on her left thigh from some forgotten collision, perhaps with the edge of the saloon table while she manoeuvred in the dark. The timer ticks. The water slides in sheets of light over her breasts and belly and thighs. She remembers Camille showing her her tattoo, saying it meant fuck me until I cry and making a face like a girl crying. She has not had a single sexual thought in four months. Neither, in four months, has she bled. Are these things connected? She touches herself, very lightly, a ringless ring finger in the dark hair between her thighs, presses at the lips of her sex then lets the tip of her finger slide into the heat inside her. She leans against the wall of the cubicle, hooks her finger a little deeper, a little deeper. She's not a fool; she's not naive; she knows that desire, memory and grief are wound together like strands in a wire. What she does not know is what she should do about it. She slides her finger out. The ticking of the timer grows louder, then stops. She does not have another coin. She dries herself quickly, pulls on clothes over skin still clammy. When she comes out into the washroom she sees that she is not alone, though she heard no one come in. A woman is at one of the sinks, a woman of sixty or more, stripped to the waist and soaping herself under her arms. On the woman's back, either side of her spine and running down from her shoulder blades, are two lines of scar tissue. The mirror shows a weathered face and eyes of narrowed gold. For a few seconds she studies Maud in the glass as if trying to decide whether or not she knows her. Then she nods and smiles. It might be taken for approval. It might be taken for 'Keep going!'

3

The crane driver is a young man basking in the last of his youth. He has red-blond hair that will be blond entirely by midsummer, a face that is starting to talk about him, to give him away, though looked at casually he can still be whatever you want him to be. He lounges by the ladder to his cab watching Robert Currey and Maud make last-minute preparations for the lift. The morning's rain has blown through. In a painted box outside the marina office a half-dozen awkward daffodils are dotted with the rain. On the road down to the yard one shade of green is slowly moving through another.

Chris Totten comes out to watch. Over the next few weeks many of the boats in the yard, those that are not forgotten, will find their way back into the water, but *Lodestar* is one of the first and he never tires, not quite, of that moment when a boat is settled onto its reflection. He makes remarks to Maud, compliments her on how the boat is looking (would, perhaps, like to compliment her on how *she* is looking, which is slightly better than she did when she arrived), then goes over to smoke with the crane driver. 'Your busy time now,' he says, and the crane driver nods.

On the boat's topside Robert Currey is bolting shut the sling. He hangs off the shackle, swings off it, then calls, 'All right. She's yours!' The crane driver climbs into his cab. He puts on sunglasses. All his movements are confident. He takes up the slack in the wire and for an instant the weight of the boat and the force of the crane are perfectly balanced. Then the boat lifts free and the sling creaks and everybody is perfectly still.

When it's in the water and free of the gear, Maud goes on board to take it round to a visitor's berth on the pontoon. This is where she will do the next phase of the work, but when she turns the ignition key there's a belch of smoke, a brief thudding of pistons, then silence. She slides below, lifts off the companionway steps and looks at the colour of the fuel in the separator. Not clear red, not even amber. She drains the bowl, finds a spare filter in the locker of spare and useful things under the starboard berth in the forecabin, fits the filter, slacks off the bleed screw, works the fuel pump, tightens the screw, clambers up into the cockpit and turns the key again. The engine starts. She casts off and brings the boat round to the pontoon. Robert Currey takes her lines.

'You're good with that engine,' he says.

'I should have checked it before,' she says.

'Even so, you sorted it. And no one checks everything.'

She steps onto the pontoon, fusses with a bow spring. When she has it as she wants it she stands and says, 'I need some things.'

'Oh yes?'

'A self-steering vane.'

'OK.' He walks to the stern of the boat, examines it for a

moment. 'No problem getting a vane on there,' he says. 'Want me to source one for you?'

She nods. 'And lazy jacks for reefing. And a new mainsail halyard.'

'You'll want a rigger then. Unless you fancy trying it yourself? I'll give Mal a call. When he's sober he's about the best you'll find on this piece of coast. What else?'

'I'm going to take the guard rail off. Fit more U bolts.'

'Clip on,' he says, 'rather than wait for the rail to catch you nicely behind the knees. OK. And what about a jackstay?'

'Yes,' she says. 'Down the centre line.'

'Wire or rope?'

'I don't know.'

'Wire will be noisy. You can get plastic-sheathed stuff but then you can't see if there's a problem with the wire.'

'Rope.'

'Rope it is.'

'I can do a lot of it,' she says.

'I know that.'

'I don't have all the tools.'

He nods. 'You're going out on your own.'

'I've done it before.'

'But you're going further this time.'

She shrugs. 'I don't know.' Then, 'yes.'

'Can I ask you something? What's the furthest you've been on your own?'

'Cowes.'

'The Isle of Wight?'

'Yes.'

'Have you sailed at night on your own?'

'No.'

He nods again, looks up river to where the tide is sliding from the mud flats. There are a few dinghies out, the usual comings and goings around the foreshore.

'I'm no sailor,' he says. 'I can build most of a boat but that's about it. The boats here, Maud, all these boats here, they're basically sound. They're not going to suddenly open up. They won't go to the bottom the first time a wave breaks over the deck. The question is always who's sailing them. And sailing alone, well, it's a frame-of-mind thing, isn't it?'

He waits, gives her a chance to reply, to reassure him. A chance even to tell him to keep his nose out, to back off. When she says nothing, just stands there on the slats of the pontoon looking at him in a way that makes it impossible to know if she has understood him, he says, 'Can you be ready to start at seven tomorrow morning? I can do a couple of hours with you before I have to go back to *Tinkerbelle*. Maybe we can do some more in the evenings. There's plenty of light now.'

'I'll pay you the proper rate,' she says.

'Let's worry about that later,' he says.

'I haven't lost my job,' she says. 'I'm on leave.'

'On leave?'

'Yes.'

'That's all right then,' he says.

4

With Robert Currey beside her, nothing in the work feels too difficult, nothing overwhelms. The canvas tool bag – the pantomime fish – always seems to have what they need. Several times during these mornings and evenings with Currey she remembers working with Grandfather Ray, the pair of them in his garage with the pre-cut parts of the dinghy, the smell of glue and resin, the Calor gas from the heater. Her hair in a plait then, her small hands passing out the tools. The radio on. The old man quietly whistling. Some slung lamp on a flex they worked beneath.

She does not mention any of this to Robert Currey. When they talk it's about the boat, the work in hand. They fit a new bow roller, a new samson post. They fit the U bolts – one either side of the cockpit, low down, so that she could, in theory, clip on before leaving the cabin; two each side going forward, all of them with steel backing plates and lock nuts.

The rigger comes. He's sweating cider. He has eyes like a frightened horse. Robert Currey speaks to him, calms him as though he were indeed a frightened horse. The rigger gets to work, hauls himself to the top of the mast, rope coiled over his shoulder. He takes half a day, and when the job is done he seems returned to some less disastrous version of himself. He accepts a mug of tea from Maud. He grins and shows the remnants of his teeth.

Day by day the weather sweetens. Maud works in T-shirt and jeans, her feet bare when she's on the boat. A van delivers the wind vane – a three-year-old Hydrovane from a yard in Chichester. With its parts laid out along the pontoon it looks at first like the wreckage of a small plane that has flown into the side of a building. At half five, Robert Currey crosses the yard from *Tinkerbelle*. He puts the tender in the water at *Lodestar*'s stern, measures up, then drills the fibreglass while Maud, leaning through the pushpit tails, holds the mounting brackets in place. Ten minutes in the boat shed produces six three-quarter-inch backing plates. By twenty to eight, after wrestling with a seized bolt at the base of the drive unit, and a moment of vexation when it appeared the nylon vane cover was too small, the system is in place.

'This will be your new best friend,' says Robert Currey, tilting the vane on its axis and watching it swing back to its centre line. 'Most people give them names. You got a name in mind?'

'For the vane?'

He laughs at her, her expression. 'You don't have to give it a name,' he says, 'but we should drink a toast to it. That would be a nautical thing to do. Got any drink on board?'

She goes below and comes up a moment later with a bottle of dark liquor and two plastic glasses.

'Navy rum,' says Currey, squinting at the bottle. 'I wouldn't have put you down for that.'

'Tim bought it,' she says.

'Right,' says Robert Currey. 'For emergency uses.'

'He thought it was something the boat should have.'

'He was probably right.'

'Yes,' she says.

He holds the glasses and she pours a measure of rum into each. 'Thank you,' she says.

'You're welcome,' he says. Across the water a light comes on in a house on the side of the hill, a farmhouse perhaps, a light that leaps like a spark from the darkness.

Two days later she takes the boat out into the bay. Ten knots of wind, an April sky fretted with high cloud, the headlands gleaming. When she has the boat balanced she secures the tiller, removes the vane lock-pin and angles the leading edge of the vane into the wind. She wedges herself into a corner of the cockpit and stares at it, the delicate tilting and twitching of the vane in its orange nylon cover. She checks the compass, looks at the boat's wake. It's working but it's over-correcting, the boat crossing and recrossing its heading. She goes back and adjusts the angle of the vane, leans it away from the vertical. This is better, steadier, but it takes another three adjustments before she has it as she wants it. She's on a close reach doing five knots, the sea ribbed and sparkling, a gull flying at deck height off her port side. Improbable as it seems, *Lodestar* is holding a course and the gear bolted to the transom is steering it. She is free! Free to do whatever she needs. Trim a sail, keep watch. Go below to make coffee. Go below to sleep.

With the control lines she moves the vane's leading edge and the boat arcs gently away from the wind. She lets out the jib a little, feels the boat settle again. She is lost in it, this new game in which she mediates between the wind and the gear. Her role on the boat has changed. It already seems strange that she managed on her own before, scurrying between one task and the next like a figure in a silent film. Now she is a type of technician. No more lunging for a winch as the boat comes around. No more running forward to free a line only to find the boat immediately starting to luff. She reaches into the cabin for her tobacco pouch and squats on the cockpit sole to roll a cigarette out of the wind, then sits up wondering where the vane's weak points are, what a big wave might buckle, how she might repair it in the middle of the night. Everything can break; she knows that. Everything will break in the end; she knows that too, for what it's worth. But the vane – all that calibrated simplicity – has the look of something that will go on for a long time. She even likes the bright orange cover. It is a flag, a banner. She finds it comforting, and for that, if nothing else, she is grateful.

She has four more days before her pontoon booking expires. After that she must either renew or move to the swinging moorings in mid-river. Working with Robert Currey – sometimes so late they must wear head torches to see what they're doing – the boat is fitted with tubular steel 'goalposts' over the head of the vane, and onto the crossbar they mount a pair of fifty-watt rigid solar panels. This should answer most of her electrical needs – it will at least mean significantly less time running the engine. Currey promises to fit an AC inverter for her. 'You'll be able to plug stuff in,' he says. 'CD player, hairdryer, power tools. You can charge your phone.' Apparently, there's someone he knows who might have a spare Victron out in a shed. Someone who might part with it for beer money.

She fills up with water and lays in some food. On the morning of the fifth day she casts herself off from the pontoon and motors out to the old mooring. When the boat's secure, the bows parting the incoming tide, she goes below and pushes all the sail bags out through the forward hatch, then sits under the mast passing canvas through her hands looking for tears, loose stitching, signs of chaffing. Her mainsail and the furling jib she is not worried about. The others came with the boat, or all except the red spinnaker she has hardly used, that she does not quite trust herself to manage on her own. There's a genoa she could hank onto the spare forestay (this extra stay an innovation from the days of John Gosse). Another foresail, already much repaired around the tack; and a little storm jib, suitably stiff and battered, though with no obvious signs of weakness.

She bags them and drops them back through the hatch into the forecabin. It's mid-afternoon. She cooks eggs, eats them sitting on the companionway steps looking into the cabin. To her right is the VHF, the new battery monitor, the charge controller for the solar panels. Below these, the Navtex, the GPS, the radar, the chart table itself, chartless at the moment, just a coffee mug, an ashtray, the Breton plotter and a pair of brass dividers. In the deep shelf at the back of the table is a *Reeds Almanac*, a book of ocean landfalls, John Gosse's old Channel pilot. Above, in the mesh pocket, is a Garmin handheld GPS, a pair of lighters, her phone (off), a pair of sunglasses, her pass for the hospital in Croydon. The Zeiss binoculars are in the wooden cubby beside her cheek, a torch in the same cubby, another torch somewhere among her bedding in the quarter berth. Behind her, in the cockpit lockers, she has parachute flares and handheld flares (she saw Robert Currey checking the dates on them). Also fenders and spare warps in there. Harnesses, foghorn, a canvas bucket of decent size, big enough perhaps to be used as a sea anchor.

Some items – the sail thread, the fishing line – are already lost or have somehow become absent from the plan of the boat she carries in her head. Others – a soldering iron, a measuring jug, a spare wristwatch, writing paper, a swimsuit (though she has shorts and T-shirts and these, surely, will serve) – she simply does not have. But if her lines were cut in the night and she woke at sea, she has enough, more than enough, to survive, to keep going. The boat is ready. It is ready, and there is nothing now except to decide what it has all been for.

She is a woman alone on a boat. What is strange about that? Yet it feels as if she has taken her place in the heart of the impossible, and for the space of four or five breaths an immense physical weakness overwhelms her. The thought of hauling on ropes, of doing the thousand things the most ordinary day at sea will demand of her, is intolerable. Also, weirdly remote, as if she were thinking of things she will never do.

She pushes herself away from the steps and puts her plate in the steel sink. She kneels on the cabin sole, opens a locker under the port-side bench, rummages there a while and pulls out a green backpack. She unzips it, looks inside, sniffs it, then starts to collect things from various parts of the boat, laying them first on the red bench before packing them carefully into the bag. This will be the crash bag, kept at hand to be snatched up when all else is lost – the bag of last resorts. She will not need breast pads or a spare nightie for this one. She will need a hand compass, a pair of smoke flares, a signalling mirror, a good knife. She will need, if she can only find it, the fishing line. The line, the hooks and lures . . .

5

In Chris Totten's office it's the hour he laughingly refers to as closing time. No one has been in all day. In the late morning he spoke on the phone to a broker in Brixham. He has sent three emails. He has eaten a ham sandwich he prepared in his kitchen at home while listening to the early morning news on the radio (swine flu, fifty dead Taliban, an earthquake in Cumbria). And now it's closing time and he is standing from his desk and starting to stretch when Robert Currey taps on the window and a moment later, comes through the door.

They were not at school together, and neither would remember the first time they met because to neither would the occasion have felt important. They live in different areas of the town but the town is small and each is dimly aware of the other's life, sees the other in a bar or a convenience store or in the street. And each of them lives alone and so can guess at something of the other's private routine because it must, in some way, be like his own; a thought that might, perhaps, be comforting, but isn't.

'Chris.'

'Rob.'

'What's new in here, then?'

'Well, this is not a good time to sell boats.'

'The rich are still rich, aren't they? Recession or no.'

'I tend not to sell to the rich. I sell to the moderately well-off.'

'And they're holding on to their pennies, are they?'

'I was thinking I should get myself a little day boat. Go out in the mornings and catch a few mackerel.'

'Become a fisherman?'

'Or take tourists out to the castle.'

'You'll find there's a bit of competition for that.'

'Maybe I'll get something at the new hotel. Park people's cars.'

'You'll be all right.'

'We're going to have to reinvent ourselves a bit. Even you, Rob.'

The yardsman nods though it's hard to say if he's listening. He's looking through the office window towards the river. Without turning he says, 'What's she up to, do you think? On *Lodestar*?'

'Maud? You'd know better than me.'

'Would I?'

'You spend time with her.'

'I spend time with the boat.'

'She's on the boat.'

'Something's not right. Where's the husband? Where's the child?'

'As you say,' says the broker, 'something's amiss.'

'So you don't know what she's got planned, then?'

'I don't know she's got anything planned.'

'She's got something planned. Just spent the best part of three and a half grand on the boat. Self-steering. Solar panels.'

'You didn't ask her?'

'You know what she's like.'

'Cards close to her chest.'

'It's like it doesn't occur to her anyone might want to know.'

'And you want to know.'

'Nothing wrong with that, is there?'

'Nothing at all.'

'You know what she told me? The furthest she's sailed on her own is the Isle of Wight.'

'She looks the part, though. Don't you think? Looks handy.'

'I don't know.'

'You're worried about her.'

'I wouldn't say that.'

'Come on.'

'I'd say she's a good sailor. I'd also say she'd be a fool to head off into blue water in the state she's in now.'

'Isn't that what sailors have always done?'

'What?'

'Cut and run.'

'Bollocks.'

'You're worried about her.'

'You saw what she looked like when she came down here.'

'Not good.'

'No.'

'Cut her hair with a penknife.'

'God knows.'

'Like Joan of Arc.'

'What are you on about?'

'Joan of Arc. You know.'

'And what's his name isn't coming down, is he?'

'She ever mention him?'

'Not really.'

'Tim.'

'Yes. Tim.'

'I don't think he's coming down.'

'She's on her own.'

'She looked on her own even when he was with her.'

'She's on her own now.'

'And you're worried about her.'

'I don't want to read in the paper about a boat on the rocks or a boat found drifting.'

'You want to help her.'

'Help her?'

'Rescue her.'

For a few seconds the yardsman says nothing. He seems to be considering it. Then he steps to the office door, pauses and looks back. 'You've got a dirty mind, Christopher Totten,' he says. He opens the door and goes out, crossing at a measured stride to where his car is parked. The broker stays where he is. His office is full of shadow, and to the shadowed floor, almost inaudibly, he says, 'Not.'

6

On the boat the masthead light looks frail, as if a small white flame were burning there, unpredictably. Another light, broader, shows at the cabin's uncurtained windows and forms a restless slick on the water below. Maud, leaning over the chart table, a thin cigarette in one hand (the last of her tobacco), is walking the brass dividers over the outspread chart of the Atlantic Ocean, west, then south, then west again. At the edges of the table she has her books of pilotage open at the relevant pages. Photographs of headlands, lighthouses, diagrams of channels, leading marks, transits and light sectors. Back and forwards go the points of the dividers. She makes notes on a pad, pulls on the cigarette, brushes ash away, carefully, from the Azores. The brass-bound clock says five past eleven. She looks about herself, reaches to drop the end of the cigarette into the dregs of a mug of tea in the sink, rubs her eyes, stretches, looks back for long minutes at the chart, then breaks off suddenly, goes to the heads, cleans her teeth, spits out into the toilet bowl, urinates, pumps out the bowl.

In the saloon she takes off her jeans, climbs up into the quarter berth, wriggles into the bag and reaches up to put off the light. Within minutes she is asleep (her face, her posture, like those drawings of people sleeping in the Underground during the London Blitz) but minutes later she is awake again, all drowsiness fled, every sense straining. Someone is on the boat. Someone's feet are walking over the deck above her. In one movement she swings herself out of the berth. Her hand, from memory or luck, falls onto the dividers. She listens, waits. The sound of movement has stopped but out of the silence comes the noise of breathing, the gentle rasp of breathing on the other side of the washboards.

A tap on the wood of the boards. As if someone had tapped on her chest, her ribs.

'Who is it?' she asks. Her voice is steady.

He gives a name but she doesn't recognize it. 'The crane driver,' he says. 'From the yard?'

After a pause she says, 'What do you want?' and after another pause he replies, 'I was passing. Thought I might stop and say hello. I've got a bottle.'

'A bottle?'

'It's Saturday night,' he says. 'I'll go if you want.'

Is this how it always is? A man tapping on wood; a woman trying to catch her thoughts in flight? She turns on the chart table light, pulls on her jeans. 'It's not locked,' she says.

The hatch slides back. The crane driver's head is there. All the angles are odd. He grins and holds up his bottle. He lifts out the top washboard and slides down into the cabin.

'Where's your boat?' she asks.

He nods towards the bow. 'No guard rail makes it nice and easy to get up. It's snug in here, though. Lovely.'

She does not know if he is drunk and if he is, how drunk. There is the smell of drink on his breath but rowing in the dark will have sobered him a little. He puts the bottle on the folding table. He has a windproof jacket on, the round neck of a T-shirt underneath.

'Shall I get us some glasses?' he says.

'I'll get them,' she says.

'I saw your light,' he says. 'Then it went out. But it seemed a shame to turn back.' He opens the bottle, a screw-top bottle of red wine, and when she puts the plastic tumblers on the table he fills each to within half an inch of the brim.

'Love and life,' he says. He drinks his wine with two big swallows. 'There's quite a tide running,' he says. 'It's thirsty work.'

The light on his cheeks, on the red threads of his hair, his eyelashes. He doesn't remind her of anybody. She leans her back against the edge of the chart table. 'Have you got any tobacco?' she asks.

He looks pleased at this, immediately delves into pockets. 'Want me to roll it for you?'

She shakes her head. He watches her, is ready with his lighter. 'I half expected to find Rob on board.'

'Who?'

'Rob Currey. I thought you were friends.'

'He works on the boat.'

'It's nothing to do with me,' he says. He laughs. 'You mind if I have a poke about?'

'OK,' she says.

He moves down the saloon, looking along the shelves. He leans into the heads, the unlit forecabin with its ghostly sail bags. He looks at the framed photograph of the boat at sunset or sunrise, then comes back up the other side of the table, looks at the charts on the chart table, at the quarter berth, the electronics. He is standing very close to her. His jacket makes a rustling sound with each small movement.

'You going far?' he asks, tapping the chart, but he doesn't wait for an answer. His eye has been caught by a white card box among the pencils and spare fuses in a small open drawer at the back of the chart table. 'Trial use only,' he says, reading the label on the box. When he looks inside, one of the blister sheets is empty and the other has two of the small green capsules missing. He looks at her.

'It's called Fennidine,' she says.

'Nice,' he says. 'Fennidine. Should I take one?'

'They're for pain,' she says.

'Then I should definitely take one.' He laughs, pushes the blister sheets back in the box and puts it back where he found it. He pours them each another glass of wine. 'You get a lot of headaches? Or is it the curse?'

'I'm a scientist,' she says. 'I work for a company that develops medicines.'

'And you take them.'

'They like us to,' she says.

'Terms and conditions,' he says.

'No one tells us to,' she says.

'What's it like, then? Aspirin?'

'It has a structure like nicotine.'

He nods. 'I don't see you going to the office much.'

'I'm on leave,' she says.

'On leave.'

'Yes.'

'Should I believe all this?' he says.

'Why not?' she says.

'For a start you've got a tat,' he says. 'I've never met a scientist with a tat before.'

'Do you know any scientists?' she asks.

'At school,' he says. 'But they weren't like you.'

'What were they like?'

'Not like you.'

She nods.

'Have you got anything else to drink?' he asks. 'I don't really like wine.'

'I've got rum.'

'Perfecto.'

She turns from him to reach into the cupboard where the rum is kept and where she replaced it after drinking the toast to the new vane. The crane driver steps across the distance between them and settles his hands on her shoulders. She does not move. The weight of his hands on her shoulders, his breath on the back of her head. When she turns he takes the bottle from her and puts it on the folding table. 'We're just two lonely people,' he says, 'in a lonely old world.' He kisses her brow. He strokes her thigh. 'This is nice,' he says. He shifts his hand from her thigh to the unbuttoned steel button of her jeans, tugs at the opening until the zip unfastens. He flattens the palm of his hand against her belly, slides his hand beneath the waistband of her jeans and her pants, his middle finger settling into the groove over her sex and moving there, quite gently, until he can slide a finger inside her. He does this for perhaps a minute, working his finger inside her then drawing it out a little and pressing it back in. They don't speak. When he takes his hand out of her pants they shuffle across to the companionway steps. She sits on the middle step and takes off her jeans and pants though not her T-shirt or bra. He takes off his jacket and drops it on the sole. He doesn't take off his trousers but pushes them down to mid-thigh. His arms hook under her knees, his hands on her upper arms. For a moment it feels like she has closed against him, sealed herself over. He's pressing and getting nowhere. Then, as if her skin has opened at the bidding of a thought – hers rather than his – he's inside her, his weight forcing her against the step. She pushes back at him and he feels the strength of her legs, her belly, the strange restlessness of that strength. He knows he won't last long. It's not going to be like that – controlled, patient. He grunts, rhythmically, like a man doing bench presses. Now and then she looks at him and when she does the plainness of that look makes him turn his head away. He's fucking her, this woman he first saw with her husband when the boat was new to them, he's fucking her, but he begins to worry that he's losing his hardness. He wants a sex picture but this is not quite a sex picture. Should he have rowed home when he saw her light go off? Should he have rowed back to the landing steps, the parade with its friendly flags? He shuts his eyes and concentrates. He thinks of other girls, girls as enthusiastic, as indifferent as he was himself. He imagines her as a prostitute; he imagines rape; he imagines love. At last he feels himself starting to come and is pulling out of her when she says, quietly, but quite clearly, 'You can come inside me.'

Women – he knows full well – cannot be trusted, but the moment is upon him, and it's like those creatures, God knows, whose organs lock for the duration. He cries out, 'Christ fuck!' He grabs at her clumpy hair, takes what he can of it in his fists. Three big spasms, his stuff flying into her. Then ten more thrusts to end it all and at last the longed-for stillness, the pair of them panting like runners, the first brief kiss, the last.

They separate. They pull on their clothes. She asks for a cigarette and he says, 'I'll roll you a couple so you've got one for the morning.' They smoke together. There seems some agreement between them to pretend that what has just happened has not just happened. It's not shame exactly. Perhaps just the knowledge that it was one of those events whose awkwardness will not be lessened by time, that time cannot make beautiful. They do not touch again. He puts on his jacket and zips it to the neck.

She goes on deck with him, stands there while he slithers down into his inflatable, settles himself, finds the oars. She undoes his line and throws it to him. 'Cheers,' he says, and nothing more. She can hardly see him. The little boat is carried by the current. She hears the quick rhythm of the oars as he shapes a course, then a steadier rhythm as he pulls away.

Below again, she feels cold. She washes out one of the glasses they used, fills it with water and drinks it. She puts the washboards in, draws shut the hatch, bolts it, takes off her jeans again and climbs up into the quarter berth. There's clean underwear, five or six pairs in one of the lockers, but she can't be bothered, it doesn't matter. She puts out the chart table light and lies on her back in the dark, the sleeping bag pulled up to her chin. She's shivering a little, she hurts a little, mostly in her lower back, the back of her hips. As she warms, so the shivering eases and becomes almost pleasant. Perhaps half an hour has passed since he left her and she is nearly asleep, drifting in a tangle of after-images, aftershocks, when she hears for the second time the sound of movement above her, but softer this time, softer and lighter. Light feet along the deck. Light feet stepping onto the cabin roof. Light feet moving along the roof and stopping at a place she guesses to be exactly above her face. It could be a bird, of course. But a bird landing on the deck in the dark? She reaches up and touches the bulkhead, rests her fingers there.

7

Though it is a Sunday and he has no official business there, Robert Currey parks in the yard in his usual place and walks down to where the yard abruptly ends in a short drop to the water. Over the river the fog is so thick you could spin a coin and lose sight of it before it came into your palm again. On the road along the headland he was able to look over the top of it, the table-smooth upper surface of the fog, and on either side, like things finished while the rest was still dreamed, the green of woodland and high fields.

He does not think it will last much longer now. Everyone who lives along this coastline knows these fogs well. Sometimes they linger half a day but once you can see them thinning, once the sun gets into them, they burn off in an hour.

He steps away from the water's edge (too much staring into the fog starts to do odd things to you) and goes back to lean against the side of his car. On the back seat, in an orange Sainsbury's bag, he has a Victron inverter that he will, when it's clear, take out to

Lodestar. His friend brought it round last night and the yardsman paid him from the petty cash he keeps in a plastic wallet in the fridge. It will not take him long to fit it. He has already pictured in his mind where it should go. And while he is fitting it he will talk to her and find out her plans (if she has any, which he is starting to doubt). He will speak plainly to her in the way he has earned. He will press her and hear the truth from her.

Away from the fog it's already warm. He rubs his neck and throat. He has shaved this morning and cannot think of the last time he shaved on a Sunday morning. He even came close to putting on a few drops of aftershave from the bottle with dusty glass shoulders on the shelf above the sink, but the thought of being in the confines of the cabin and everywhere smelling himself, unable to escape the smell of himself, made him leave the bottle where it was. It has a foolish name. He finds it slightly odd that he ever bought it.

The masts of the yachts along the nearest pontoon are clear now to the upper spreaders. This is how it goes, from the upper air down to the water where the last of it will drift for a few minutes like wisps of smoke. He opens the car door, takes out the Sainsbury's bag, looks in at the inverter, fetches a cordless drill from the boot of the car and strolls to the gate leading to the pontoons. He taps in the four-digit code and walks down the sloping duckboards to where they keep the yard tender, a small black rib with a two-stroke outboard. The rowing boat that's usually tethered to the rib isn't there this morning, which is a little surprising, though such boats have a way of coming and going, of being viewed as a kind of public property. It's not his problem, certainly not this morning. He stands on the pontoon watching the fog dissolve. All the yachts on the pontoons are in the sunlight now, and the river to twenty yards out is bright as spring water.

In the middle of the river the fog is at its most stubborn. He shades his eyes, bides his time. A bird lifts out of the fog, and taking the sun on its wings seems for a second to blaze with silver flames.

He can make out the mast of the boat at the town end of the swinging moorings now – a nice little sloop called *Aphelion*. Along from her there's *Black Witch* and then, still ghostly, a motor sailer called *Jacqui*. *Lodestar* is astern of *Jacqui* but the fog hasn't given her up yet. He waits, turns away to get his bearings, looks back, counts off the boats again. He can see *Lodestar*'s mooring buoy, a grey ball becoming a pink ball. There is no sign of *Lodestar*. He stays there, unmoving, until he can see down as far as the fuel barge and up to where the river curves and the tower of a church stands out faintly from the land behind it. There is no confusion. Nor, he finds, is he much surprised. With one hand and with the bobbing of his head he makes a small courteous gesture to the water, then he picks up his bag, the cordless drill, and starts back to the car.

FOUR

This is the Hour of Lead –
Remembered, if outlived . . .

Emily Dickinson

1

She spends the night in Fowey, a visitors' mooring opposite the town quay. The next morning, with the VHF turned up to catch warnings from the gunnery ranges off Dodman Point, she follows the coast, counts off headlands, finds herself at three in the afternoon riding the swell in Falmouth Bay, the lighthouse looking freshly painted, cliffs of siltstone, slate, tumbled sandstone, rising to grazed fields and slow-moving cloud. She drops the sails and starts the engine, follows another yacht past the eastern breakwater to the inner harbour and on to the marina. Two men, idling on the pontoons, take her lines. They compliment her on the boat, try to engage her in conversation, then, seeing there will be none, wander off, unoffended.

She puts the boat in order, checks her fenders, tightens the mooring lines, runs a cable to the mains socket on the pontoon. When she has finished she cooks pasta and stirs in a tin of tuna with its oil, sits in the cockpit to eat it. A woman from the marina office comes by. She's sorry to disturb her. 'How long do you think you'll be staying?'

'A night,' says Maud, her lips and chin slicked with oil.

When the woman has gone, Maud washes the pot and plate in water warmed by the engine on the run in. She is tired but tiredness does not signify; she will, she knows, be more tired later, much more. She goes into the town just as she is, in her shorts and summer sweater, the trainers she has had for years, size 4. Now and then she sees herself in the windows of the shops she's passing but feels no strong ownership of that shadow. Once, as though walking on unmarked ways through a forest, she stops and glances behind her, suddenly anxious she will not know her route to the boat again. It's only a moment, then a bare slim shoulder, some teenage girl on her phone, jostles her on the narrow pavement and she goes on.

At the supermarket she takes two trolleys, pulls one and pushes the other. She has not written out a list but there is a list in her head. Dry food, tinned food, twenty packets of boil-in-the-bag rice, all varieties. Vacuum-packed bread, vacuum-packed bacon. Rye crackers, rice cakes. Coffee, tea, chocolate. Powdered milk. Three dozen eggs. Twenty oranges and twenty lemons. Potatoes, carrots, spring greens, onions, cabbages.

People passing her, women passing her, must imagine she has a family of six at home, six at least, and has been left (poor love, poor fool) to do this on her own, a husband dawdling by the magazines, the kids larking in the aisles.

Four packs of tobacco. A dozen packets of Rizlas, the ones with the cut corners in the green packs. It's what Tim had. It's what she's become used to.

Torch batteries, batteries for the radio. Various items from the pharmacy.

At the checkout she pays with her card and wonders if there will be some problem, if Fenniman's have remembered to pay her, their absent employee. She asks for her bags to be delivered to the marina, gives her name and the name of the boat. The super-market is used to making deliveries to the marina, and because she has spent a good sum of money the delivery will be free. They give her a discount voucher for her next visit. She looks at it a moment, then folds it and slides it into the back pocket of her shorts.

On board again she listens to the six o'clock shipping forecast. Winds from the south-east, three or four, rain for a time in the morning, then showers. On the boat beside her – a wooden boat, a cutter with a name like one of the heroines in those old novels she has not read – a party is starting. Two men with glossy beards, two women with braided hair, a boy squatting like a buddha on a varnished hatch, the pop of a cork, a voice pretending to scold, then laughing. The women's movements are languorous. The men touch things with the confidence of ownership. The boy is mysterious, beautiful, his glances quick as light on water. One of the women, carrying a plate of food, notices Maud, seems on the verge of saying something, then looks away.

She's asleep on one of the saloon cabin benches when her shop-ping arrives. The deliveryman is cooing to her from the pontoon. He has a dunnage trolley loaded with orange carrier bags. He offers to carry the bags below but Maud says it's OK. He hands her the bags two at a time and she arranges them along the sides of the cockpit and the top of the coach-house roof, then signs the electronic pad, her name a spider's web on the machine's glass.

'I used to sail a bit myself,' he says, putting away his machine, nodding to the boat. 'Then life came along.'

It's dark before she has packed away the last of it. She has endeavoured to be methodical but many items are simply squeezed in wherever they will fit. When stowing anything on a boat you should consider the boat turned upside down. What will come away? What will fly and shatter? She looks about herself, the little space – four steps to the saloon bulkhead, four steps back to the companionway – and knows that a great deal would fly, that the air would be full of it.

She rolls a cigarette, leans at the chart table – that cluttered shelf – leans over 4011, North Atlantic Ocean, Northern Part, and beneath it, 4012, North Atlantic Ocean, Southern Part. It is not possible to memorize an entire chart but she could make a passable sketch of certain coastlines, could mark in a dozen soundings, the locations of certain features – Craggan Rocks, Vrogue Rock, the Longships Lighthouse.

Her plan is to quit Falmouth three hours before high water (Dover) and reach the Lizard an hour later. From the Lizard she will turn south-west and ride the ebbing tide across the shipping lanes. She has a waypoint in mind, a buoy, ODAS Brittany, a hundred and fifty miles off the French coast at Brest. Two days' sailing – less if the conditions are favourable – though time on such a passage hardly matters. She is not expected anywhere.

In the morning she will top up with water and diesel then leave the marina at half twelve to be clear of the harbour a little after one. All this is plain enough. It is plain and sensible and readily understood. At the same time it feels whimsical and fatally private, a plan that will disappear like a shout and leave no trace of itself.

She goes on deck with a torch to check her lines. The party on the cutter is over or they have moved it ashore. She steps onto the pontoon, reties one of the springs, steps back on board, switches off the torch and gazes at the clustered lights of the town – then turns seawards, investigates the shadows, the silvered channel, the lit buoys that mark the way out. This is all she needs for now. It's a readiness of sorts, and she stands there a long while meeting it all in silence, her breath like a feather laid along her tongue.

In the morning, she rises to the sound of the promised rain, boils two eggs (from her great supply), makes coffee, makes more coffee, pulls out the washboards and leans against the companionway steps under the shelter of the hatch, blowing tobacco smoke towards the town.

By ten, the rain has softened and lies in the wind, drifts with it. She busies herself with twice-done jobs and notices – four seconds of peering at herself in the little mirror screwed to the back of the door in the heads – that her hair has grown long enough to begin to curl.

At eleven she no longer knows how to distract herself. She pulls on her coastal jacket, steps down onto the pontoon, unplugs herself from the electrics, goes to the marina office to settle up, then comes back and begins to loosen her lines. In the textbooks of sailing, particularly the textbooks of short-handed sailing, the leaving of moorings – marinas, pontoons, harbour walls – is listed among those evolutions most likely to cause trouble. State of the wind, state of the tide, and all around her, packed tight, other people's boats, some of them – most, perhaps – worth a great deal more than *Lodestar*. She frees all lines except the bow warp and the stern spring, puts both of these on a slip. She starts the engine, then goes forward and begins to pay out the bow warp. One of the men from the cutter calls, 'Want a hand?' but it's too late for that. She slips the bow warp, hurries to the cockpit to put the engine in gear, slips the back spring, hauls it in and drops it in crazy loops round her feet.

'Where're you headed?' calls the man, leaning over the stern rail of his beautiful boat.

'West,' calls Maud in return, and the man, if he has heard her at all, simply nods, raises an arm in farewell and turns away.

By the time the light is failing she's mid-Channel and beating into wind and tide. She switches on the navigation lights; the Hydrovane is steering, the needle in the lit bowl of the binnacle floating over 235, 239, 237, 235.

During the first hours, moving south from the Lizard, the shipping was heavy; now it is quieter and her course should take her well clear of the lane around Ushant. Off her port bow a freighter is heading up channel; to starboard, a pair of fishing boats are rolling in the swell fifty yards from each other. She is not sure if they are fishing, can see no black cones hoisted and they have not put on their lights yet. She watches them; she has been watching everything – seabirds, flotsam, the shifting light. Watching the boat, too; watching and listening.

Before it is properly dark she decides to go below and eat, use the heads, put on more clothes, prepare for the night. She has not, since her eggs at breakfast, eaten more than a few oatcakes. Her stomach is tender, her appetite less than it should be. It would be wise now to make a proper meal but she settles for a cereal bar, a mug of black tea, a couple of Kwells (less sleep-inducing than Stugeron).

Sitting on the leeward bench she strips down to her T-shirt then layers up, pulling clothes from the lockers beneath her. She puts on her salopettes, her coastal jacket, her sea boots. It is May and the wind is temperate but at some point in the night she will be cold. Fatigue will see to that.

A last mouthful of tea, then she goes to the companionway

steps, pauses, reaches over and takes her phone from the mesh pocket above the chart table. It is not clear what has prompted this other than a fleeting thought about whether or not to wear her beanie and hearing in that thought something of Tim's voice. She does not question it. Her hand reaching out is argument enough.

On deck she looks for shipping, checks the compass, the Hydrovane, then fits herself into the angle between the cabin and the edge of the cockpit and switches on the phone. The battery is down to about thirty per cent, and as Robert Currey did not install the inverter she will not be able to charge the phone at sea. There are two missed calls, both more than a week old. One number she recognizes immediately as the office in Reading; the other she has seen before but is less certain of. She thinks it is probably the police, perhaps the woman officer who came to the cottage, who waited with her in the churchyard.

There is only a single bar of reception – it flickers at the top of the screen like a faltering pulse – but she types in the number, listens to several seconds of hissing, then a ring tone that sounds unfamiliar, as if the call is being routed through a foreign exchange.

'Tim's phone,' says a woman's voice, brightly, and then, after a short pause, 'Hello?' and after a second pause, during which each perhaps can hear the other's breathing, 'Maud?'

Maud ends the call, powers down the phone, slides it into one of the deep pockets of her jacket. She had thought some automated voice might tell her she was out of range, that the number she was calling was unreachable. As for what she would have said if Tim had answered rather than Bella, she had nothing prepared. Told him where she was? How the boat was handling? That the green ribbon was still tied to the starboard shroud though the weather had washed and bleached it almost white? Or she could have simply held the phone out to the sea – even tossed it over the side to let him listen for a few seconds to whatever that sounded like, a phone sinking.

She imagines him asking Bella who it was, who called, and Bella saying, 'I think it was Maud,' and when asked what she had said, answering, '*Nothing*,' and Tim saying, 'Yes, that sounds like her.'

One of the steadiest patterns of their time together – in place from their earliest days – was a kind of call and response whereby Tim would ask her questions and she would answer them. As time went by her answers became less and less satisfactory to him. He had an expression that told her this – the unsmiling mouth, the eyes briefly widened. And certain phrases: 'That's it?' 'Yes . . . ?' Even (something a teacher might have said to him at his school) 'I'm waiting . . .'

He said to her once, 'Men complain all the time about women talking all the time. But I have the original silent woman.'

He described – more than once and each time with different emphasis – a cartoon he had seen in a magazine, or that someone had seen, Magnus perhaps: a caveman on the phone to his friend, the caveman's wife standing in the background. 'I'm thinking of teaching her to speak,' says the caveman. 'That can't do any harm, can it?'

She thinks of the last time she saw him, his head on the pillow, his eyes turned away from her, his medicines on the table, the open book, the sound of the rain, the willows by the stream. And she remembers – it's the stream itself that joins the two thoughts – the Boxing Day morning they all went out in boots and scarves to watch the hunt ride through, how they spotted them, still half a mile off, and watched them work their way down past the black hedges then zig-zag through empty fields until they were suddenly there, a hundred yards away, fifty yards, the horses big as cavalry horses, the master at the front in his faded coat, his face like bronze, raising the bone handle of his whip in salute . . .

The memory of it laid down in the moment like a rune in the soft matter of her brain.

On the VHF, after a burst of static, the Falmouth coastguard invites all mariners to switch to channel 79. She ducks her head below the hatch, dials in the new channel and hangs there, waiting.

Sunrise has no fanfare, just a cautious brightening, a hairline crack of gold bright enough to leave a line across the eye as you turn from it. The sea, that all night has simply been a sound, becomes again a particular set of distances, a thing she can study, that scatters under her gaze, that is both patterned and shapeless. She wonders if she has, for much of the last hour, been sleeping. The night, her memory of it, is not coherent. Lights that did not approach. The noise of a plane heading for France or some destination beyond. A shower of rain that lasted no more than a few minutes, that made the skin of her hands shine. A little later, the night unbroken still, the cautious calling of birds. Twice she went below to brew tea, roll a cigarette, use the heads, squint at the GPS. And there was a moment – before her last visit below? Afterwards? – when she felt she was falling and reached out urgently for something to hold on to only to find she was sitting, perfectly safe, in her wedge of cockpit, the boat riding forwards in easy sequences.

And now the dawn drifting towards her, small waves rising blue and silver out of the grey. She scans the horizon, climbs stiffly down the companionway steps, unzips her jacket and drops it on the leeward bench. The latest forecast from the Navtex is for force four, five by nightfall. No gale warnings, sea state moderate. She takes off her boots, her salopettes. She sets her alarm clock for thirty minutes, gets up into the berth. She's on a port tack and the heel of the boat rolls her against the skin of the hull, the water's infinite rhythms. She has never slept at sea before – not as a solo sailor – and for a while she fights it, the recklessness of it. Then sleep swallows her in the skip between instants, leaves her dreaming she is a woman alone on a boat too anxious to sleep. As if her sleeping head could think of nothing more fantastic.

When she opens her eyes again she knows from the light that the morning is well advanced and sits up so suddenly she hits her head and cries out, the first time she has heard her voice since speaking to the man on the cutter.

She goes on deck in her socks as though the seconds it would take to put on her boots might be the time she needed to avert a collision with the bow of a super-tanker, but when she stands in the cockpit the only vessel she can see, a good mile off her starboard beam, looks like a tall ship, a sail trainer perhaps, all sails set and heading west into the deep Atlantic.

For over two hours *Lodestar* has sailed unattended. Nothing has gone wrong. The course is good still, the sails sweetly curved, the boat balanced and making the best part of six knots through a low swell. There is even a hint of warmth in the wind, some promise of the light and air of the south.

Below again, she reads off her co-ordinates from the GPS, finds herself on the chart, then puts the kettle on the gimbaled burner and discovers her appetite is back. She scrambles three eggs, eats them on ham and bread, rolls a cigarette, smokes it in the cockpit, coils rope and sluices out the cockpit sole with a bucket of sea water. Then she goes forward to inspect the rigging, to look up the mast, to test the lashings on the little Bombard inflatable, check shackles, touch the sails. She kneels at the pulpit rail and looks down at the boat's stem smashing the green tiles of the sea. She has been underway for not quite twenty-four hours but already a sense of pattern is emerging. The unspectacular doing of the necessary, the looking out, the tending, the slow ceasing of expectation. A hermit in her floating cell, a pilgrim, an exile, a woman out of a Book of Hours who works her life like a garden, who suffers in it if necessary, who rarely looks up.

In the late afternoon, clouds descend. For hours the world is grey and she has the company of silent grey birds. The sea is muffled. It's not raining but somehow she still gets wet.

At ten, she fries up cabbage and caraway seeds, eats it out of the pan standing in the space between the galley stove and the companionway steps, the boat humming under her boots. She catnaps in the cockpit, her head lolling onto her chest, each short sleep with its brief luminous dream, each dream immediately forgotten as she wakes to the sound of wind and water.

At three in the morning she reaches the continental shelf, its contour lit by the lights of fishing boats, a great curve of them she cannot see the end of, a line running south and east towards Bilbao, north towards the coast of Ireland. She hears the fishermen's voices on the VHF, alters course to sail between two of their boats, bracing herself to feel *Lodestar* caught suddenly in the hatchwork of a net. As she passes them, as she leaves them behind, the depth gauge in the cockpit shifts from a hundred metres to three hundred to five hundred then, going beyond what it can measure or display, the screen is suddenly blank.

When she can pick out the first signs of day she goes down to sleep, not in her berth – she is afraid she will not wake up – but on the leeward bench, her head on one of the little velvety cushions embroidered with the boat's name that Tim's mother gave them as a Christmas present the year after they bought the boat together. She sleeps for an hour, gets up to check the course, goes on deck to tack, comes down and sleeps a second hour on the other bench, the matching cushion.

The middle of the day is given over to repacking some of her store cupboards. The fresh food has already taken on a smell of boats, the inside of a boat. The radio is on, a test match at the Oval, the commentators passing sly remarks about each other's clothes. Then a few minutes after six she sights her way marker, ODAS Brittany, spots it first with the naked eye – a black stick in the distance off the boat's starboard shoulder – then finds it with the Zeiss, a black and yellow buoy with a ring of lights on top, the sea beyond it swept with shadow.

She marks her position on the chart – a dot within a circle. She makes a sandwich, makes coffee, puts a splash of rum in the coffee. The rum is to mark the relief she feels, the slight astonishment that she has found it, a buoy no bigger than a family car, upturned and tethered out here at the top of a cliff of green water. She carries her coffee up to the cockpit. The taste of the rum brings back the touch of the crane driver, the scent of him, certain things he said (Perfecto, Cheers, Christ fuck). Brings back, too, how that night on the swinging mooring had become uncontainable, how (almost invisible to herself on the deck) she crept out of the harbour through the forming fog, and halfway to Fowey, below for a moment using the heads, found his sperm in the crease of her pants, the crease of herself, and thought *what if?* while deciding immediately and with whatever certainty she could muster in the face of such recklessness, that nothing of his would grow in her, could grow in her.

She is due to come on next week but won't – the absence of those secret tides she hardly noticed until they were gone. She will be dry again, dry as stone, and this is another kind of silence, something in her like those shocked clocks found at the scene of a disaster, the hands stopped at the instant.

(The first time she bled her mother left at the end of her bed a roll of those bags you find in budget hotels and the toilets of aeroplanes for the disposal of what cannot be flushed. Also a newspaper article, laminated, about teenage girls getting pregnant, a picture of them sitting with their babies in some kind of day centre, smiling like those Flemish Madonnas in the old paintings where the frames are decorated with wildflowers.)

She sets a new course, a little to the west of the old one. Her next waypoint is a patch of water twenty nautical miles off the coast of Terceira in the Azores. She will only stop there – Terceira or Faial – if she needs to, if there's some problem with the boat. Otherwise she will keep sailing, drop down to somewhere on a line with Senegal, then across to wherever it is she is heading, her destination . . .

To the man on the cutter she said simply 'west' but everything, approached, becomes specific, like it or not, and sooner or later west must take on a name, a set of co-ordinates. All those evenings at the yard and on the mooring, when she stayed up late with the charts walking the dividers across the sea like dowsing rods until, each time, they hesitated somewhere in the mid-Atlantic. She has ruled out the United States – she has no entry visa and does not want to try to explain herself to the Department of Homeland Security. Several times she has travelled to Fenniman HQ in Orlando and knows the US customs force is made up of young men fierce for category and that nothing she could say about her situation would fit between the narrow lines of any form they possessed (how many others like her? How many at any given time had purposes and business only really explicable through a medium like song?).

Cuba is possible, Cuba via Bermuda. Then work her way south to the Windward Islands. Or Mexico? She has not rejected Mexico. In the drawer at the back of the chart table she has the *Book of Landfalls* (a book as thick and heavy as her old textbooks of biology). She will find somewhere. She will not sail off the edge of the world. Cayo Largo, Île-à-Vache, Montego Bay. She is most tempted by those places she fails most completely to imagine. For example, a place called Progreso on the Yucatán coastline where nothing else seems to exist, nothing the Admiralty thought worth depicting. A dot on the mustard yellow the chart uses to distinguish the land from the sea. A dot, and beside it a blot of purple to indicate a light. Some manner of settlement off the waters of the Campeche Bank. A place whose ambition for itself she could not begin to guess at.

Day after day, the tasks she allots to herself, the little cleaning jobs, the meals taken standing up by the galley. Nights under the waxing moon, silver wake, green phosphorescence. Sleeping for an hour, for half an hour, waking to the same scene her eyes closed to.

She wears shorts and a shirt now, bare feet growing brown and bruised. Hair lightening, face darkening. Little cracks, salt-sores, on the skin of her hands.

In the early hours of her tenth night at sea the boat wakes her with a new angle, a new noise. There's a front passing overhead and she goes on deck, one hand fumbling with the zip of her jacket, one hand clutching at the shadows around her. In the cockpit she pulls up her hood only to have it immediately blown down again.

There is no sense of the boat struggling, but after watching it a while, the bows thudding into the swell, her face becoming streaked with drifts of sea water, she furls the jib to roughly half its full surface then struggles into her harness, clips on, and goes to the mast to free the main halyard and drops two reefs' worth of mainsail into the lazy jacks. The boat slows, quietens. In daylight she might have left it to sail hard but it's half four in the morning and she wants to get below again.

There are no lights visible other than her own. She has not seen a ship for forty-eight hours. As she passes the depth gauge she flashes her torch beam at it, wipes away the moisture with her thumb. It's blank, of course, but she knows from the chart there's more than five thousand metres of water beneath her.

She is sailing an average of ninety nautical miles a day, noon to noon. When she closes her eyes she sees only the sea, its ceaseless motion, neither rough nor quiet, neither away from nor towards, a view unburdened with anything resembling meaning.

Forty degrees north, twenty-four west. She is, she judges, a day and a half from the island of Terceira. In the late morning she is sitting, smoking in the lee of the mast, when a plume of feathering water rises, thirty, forty metres from the boat. A slick back appears, a fin, then just a patch of seething water, settling. She stands, one hand gripping the mast, her gaze sweeping the surface of the sea. And there it is again! Ten metres closer, a noise like the steam whistle of a drowned factory, the high plume dispersing, the great back rolling. Two of them, she thinks, two at least. If one rises under the boat then the boat is finished. She glances at the life raft in its orange canister, pictures the crash bag beside her berth. Do they know she's here? Can they hear the boat, see it?

She waits. She is ready for them, but still gasps the next time one surfaces. A clear view of the flexing blow-hole, a mottled fin, detailed and living. An eye? Does she see an eye? And if she sees it, is it blank, remote? A plaque of shone metal, a green stone washed and washed? Or a thing that glances at her, that is full of kinship?

Another plume – but further off, further ahead. They are passing her, finished with their investigation of her, if that's what it was. It is understood of course that such creatures are on a journey, their tonnage in constant purposeful flight, but when they have gone she misses them with an intensity she could not have anticipated. She stands on the coach-house roof, damp from the mist of their breath. Her cigarette is out and unsmokeable. Their breath had no strong smell to it, was not, as she might have imagined it, like the puddles on a fish dock. In its temperature, it seemed to carry the warmth of their blood, their four-chambered hearts.

All day the wind is southerly. She's sailing close-hauled on a short sea, jib and main winched tight. The knocking makes her ribs ache or her ribs were aching anyway. Her longest sleep since leaving England is three and a half hours. She is tired; she supposes she is tired. Sometimes she looks at the chart or the GPS or the battery monitor and there's a moment, no more than a second or two, when she doesn't know what she's looking at.

The fourteenth night, drowsing in the cockpit (her life rising and dipping with the rising and dipping of the boat), she wakes with the sense of having been touched, caressed, and looks out to see a light on her port bow like the light you might see from an aeroplane, the first spark of the sun on some huge, sluggish river thirty-five thousand feet below. She watches it double and dance in the lenses of the binoculars, watches it slowly fade with the hushed blue rising of the day, then sees in its place the unmistakeable smudge of an island.

All day she sails towards it. With each hour some new detail appears. The shocking green of trees, of vegetation. Every time she goes below then comes on deck again, she stares at it with an impatience she has been free from for many days. A ship comes out from the port, a coaster, a supply ship. It passes her in a long curve, a red ship, or a white ship red with rust, a dozen figures leaning over the rail. One of them – brown arm, white singlet – waves to her, and after a moment she remembers to wave back.

By mid-afternoon she can pick out the white tower of a church, white houses straggling up from the port into the green volcanic hills. She tacks to put herself on course to round the island's eastern end. The port is there, tucked away from the long weather of open sea. She is almost in thrall to the place, an island green as Dorset – greener – and crowding the eye after so many days of emptiness, grey sea.

It's evening before she's passing the breakwater. She sees the first lights come on (the lighthouse flashing red in sequences of four) then the lights along the front, the headlights of a car climbing into the hills. For several minutes, the thought of being tied up in port, of going below and sleeping eight hours, sleeping without setting the radar alarm, without some part of her seeming to be on deck still, watching for ships, for weather, for some rope or wire to wear through and stream along the wind, it tempts her. It's not too late. Just start the engine, drop the sails, put the boat about. But there was a cost involved in getting this journey started (she doesn't know what it was, perhaps it was almost everything) and to break the rhythm of her movement even for a night puts it all at risk. She's thirty-nine degrees above the equator. Below thirty-five – thirty for sure – she should find the trades, and once she's in the trades she can pole out the sails and have the wind behind her all the way to Havana, to Progreso, to wherever.

She looks at the island – whale-backed, spangled – looks and turns away. Ahead of her each rising lip of water carries the light of the setting sun. Stars rise. A planet on the old moon's shoulder.

(To sailors, the night sky turns about the earth, a shell of glass around a globe.)

2

Two days south of the island, two days of good sailing, the wind dies and the boat drifts over a sea clear as tap water. (She should of course have gone via the Canaries or the Cape Verde Islands, but this is the route Nicolette Milnes Walker took on her way to becoming the first woman to cross single-handed, and Maud, who was given the book of the voyage on her twelfth birthday – a picture on the cover of Milnes Walker taking a sunsight in a bikini – has never forgotten it.)

Shoals of little fish gather around the boat, eating the weed from the boat's hull. The sails hang. She leaves them up because they offer her some shade. She moves about the boat in shorts and a T-shirt, then in shorts, then in nothing but a hat. She has a choice of hats – her own blue cotton baseball cap and a straw hat she found long ago in one of the lockers in the forecabin, a battered type of Panama, the straw watermarked and fraying but still serviceable. Was it Gosse's hat? It fits her well and is cooler to wear than the cap.

She stretches (she remembers some of Tim's yoga). She smokes with her back against the metal of the mast and when the mast is too hot, against the canister of the life raft. An event is the vapour trail of a plane, graze pink in the light of the evening sun. Or a bird almost indistinguishable from its element.

She could start the engine – a whole tank of diesel – but the silence hangs sheer and the engine would shatter it.

She thinks of swimming, and once the thought has occurred to her – such benign and cool-looking water – it grows into an appetite, a kind of thirst. The boat is travelling on a current at about the speed of an old man walking with a child, but in the water she will travel on the same current. She can see no risk.

From the stern of the boat she trails a length of buoyant rope then goes forward until she is standing by the pulpit rail. She lays her hat on the deck – feels nude beyond the mere stripping off of clothes – and for half a minute observes the faded green ribbon on the shroud for some sign of a breeze but the ribbon, though it trembles, hangs slack. She shuffles forwards, curls her toes over the edge of the deck. She is thinking of the woman she watched on the television, small hours of the morning, standing as she now stands, at an edge, a divide, her back flushed with the cold as Maud's is reddened by the sun. Fellow feeling – not exactly sisterly, but something, a recognition, the awareness of lines like surgeon's thread sewn through the hearts of strangers and now and then drawn taut. She looks to the horizon, teeters, slightly giddy in the midst of so much light, then leans into her dive, her head breaking the water into pieces of gold.

When she surfaces and looks up at the weird brightness of her own boat the first thing she sees is the green ribbon lifted from the shroud and floating in a curve like the sine wave on the screen of an oscillator. The sails draw breath, the boat tilts away from her. She cannot, from the water, see the rope she trailed. She kicks out. The water is cold and the boat is two hundred yards from her before the ribbon lies down again and the sails empty themselves and hang slack. She finds the rope, pulls herself along its length, then grapples herself aboard beside the Hydrovane. She sits in the cockpit streaming water. She is shaking a little (adrenaline that prepares the body for a wound, that anticipates the wound), and when she tries to roll a cigarette in the church gloom of the cabin her hands are unsteady and the tobacco spills onto the cabin floor.

That night she sleeps on deck and watches satellites. The boat drifts. The sound of the sails is like the sound of someone turning restlessly in their sleep. She's in the bag, her head on a folded jumper, the sea blue one she wore in the flat in Bristol that winter she was first pregnant, the flat smelling of toast, of dust scorched by the elements of the heaters.

She sleeps for twenty minutes, ten minutes, forty minutes. Each time she wakes she feels a hand on her thigh, a hand against her cheek, sees through slitted eyes the stars heaped up on the horizon.

Things pass her by, creatures of some sort. She hears one of them circle the boat twice, quite slowly, before moving off. Other sounds play from below through the muffle of her jumper. They are an effect of the water perhaps, of the cabin's bundled acoustics, the way the whole boat has always been a type of instrument. Tempting, though, to free herself from the sleeping bag and run on light feet to the cockpit, thrust her head under the hatch and *see*.

(See what?)

In the morning, sweating in the bag from the heat of the sun, she wakes out of a dream of slow trains passing to find the boat in the middle of an island of light bulbs. There are thousands of them, and at every touch of the boat each glass shell rocks against its neighbours and sounds them. Gently, she stirs them with the boat hook. Some are broken, their filaments open to the air, but most are whole and seem – their glass skins signalling the light of the sun – to be switched on.

How long have they been in the sea? How far have they drifted together? With her bucket she scoops some out and examines them. General Electric. Sixty watts. Clear glass. Bayonet fittings starting to crust with salt, to react. She keeps one and lowers the others back into the water.

It's like glass spawn.

By midday the wind is back, a breeze from the south-east, a bare breeze, but enough to make headway. The bulbs rattle past the hull, then she is free of them and the sea is darker and she puts on clothes again. She is businesslike, she works the boat. She has come, by the log, one thousand four hundred and eighty nautical miles since Falmouth. Below her, marked on the chart, a submerged mountain called Atlantis.

3

It might have gone on like this forever, her parish a thirty-two-foot boat, her days both empty and purposeful, her nights as the lonely caretaker of a vast, unlit theatre. So much of the journey has gone as she might have wished it to – no gross difficulty, nothing beyond her reach – that when she is woken (three-fifteen in the morning, her twentieth night at sea) by the crazed insect-call of the radar alarm and swings out of her berth to find herself ankle deep in water, the moment feels due; feels, in truth, long awaited.

She climbs – runs – through the open hatchway, jumps down into the cockpit, misjudges something – the heel of the boat, her own velocity – and only avoids going over the side by snatching at one of the steel goalposts at the stern. A sudden heat in her left hand, felt and dismissed. She steadies herself, wraps an arm around the post, stares out into the darkness around the boat. Sees nothing, hears nothing.

Whatever triggered the alarm has come and gone. Sometimes a wave can do it. Dolphins. A whale.

She goes below again, puts on the red nightlight and tastes the water to be sure it's salt and not coming from some breach in the fresh-water tank. It's salt – salt mired with diesel and whatever debris accumulates in the hidden places of the boat, now carried up.

She tries to judge if the boat is sinking. She does not think it is. The boat is still sailing. It has not appreciably slowed, it is not wallowing. If the water is rising inside it's rising slowly.

She reaches for the torch, flashes its beam at the crash bag then follows its light into the forecabin. Her black bin-bag of empty tins and cartons is moving in the water as if it contained something living. She goes to the anchor locker. If one of the anchors has worked loose it might have done some damage, but other than the usual slick of moisture the locker is dry. She works her way back, throws everything from the cabin sole onto the berths. She needs to pull up the floor but when the fingers of her left hand touch the brass pull ring she shouts with pain, turns the light onto her own hand and sees how the tip of her third finger is bent backwards, an angle of fifteen, twenty degrees. She wedges the torch into the V of the bunks and uses her right hand. She has not lifted these panels in a long time. They feel jammed, sucked in – then the first comes away so abruptly she topples backwards into the water on the saloon floor. She writhes there a moment, finds her feet, slings the panel through the folded door of the heads and kneels by what she has opened up. Plenty of water here. One of the through-hulls gone? Which one? The log? She reaches deeper, up to her elbow, up to her shoulder. By stretching out her fingers she can touch a jagged crown of plastic, the water pouring through it like the bubbling of a secret spring.

And there is something else down there, a small, shaped piece of metal or plastic she assumes is part of the broken fitting but which, when she pulls it out and holds it to the light of the torch, turns out to be a little heart-shaped hair clip of painted tin, and for several seconds, squatting barelegged in the half-dark, in the pooling water, the hurt boat, she simply stares at it.

A hair clip painted with red enamel and little white flowers.

She does not know where to put it – she almost puts it in her mouth – then she reaches up, slides it into her hair and snaps it shut.

With the torch she walks backwards into the saloon. She hauls up the next panel and slings it beside the first. She knows what she needs but she is not sure where to find it. She starts to dig things out of cupboards, pulls them out and drops them any-where. She protects her left hand. She pauses to think, to think hard, then crosses quickly to the other side of the boat, opens a compartment by the galley, rummages, and comes out with a shaped, softwood plug. She kneels by the bilges, gropes for the broken fitting, pushes in the plug, strikes it with the flat of her palm, then hammers it home with the waterlogged mallet of Captain Slocum's journal.

She's working well now or that's her impression. Who's to judge it? Old Rawlins? From the cockpit locker she fetches the two-foot-long anodized steel bilge-pump handle (a good-sized pump for a boat like this), slots it into its socket between the companionway steps and the quarter berth and pumps, hard, for twenty minutes, rests for half a minute, then pumps for another fifteen, rests and manages another ten minutes before the burning in her back, the nausea of it, forces her to stop. The bilges are still full but the water has dropped to below the level of the sole. She checks on the wooden plug, drinks from the galley tap and goes back to pumping. Day is breaking before she is shifting more air than water. She drags herself up into the cockpit. The morning is faultless – crystal blue with a dozen small clouds like the smoke from silent guns. She holds her damaged hand in her lap, feels out the joint, seizes it, pulls, twists, pulls again, then leans over the side of the boat to dry-vomit. When she has recovered, when the two or three big shudders are over, she goes below to the deranged cabin, finds a roll of electrician's tape and binds the reset finger to the finger beside it. In the daylight she can inspect the plug more thoroughly. The wood, saturated, has darkened and swelled (as it is intended to swell) and pressed itself into the pattern of the broken fitting. If water is coming in it's coming at the rate of a dripping tap. For now, at least, the boat is secure. No reason to turn back for the Azores. Certainly no reason to send out any kind of distress call.

She takes off her wet clothes, finds dry clothes, sits heavily on the starboard saloon bench, feels for the hair clip, slides it out of her hair and stares at it as if to make sure – she's drunk with tiredness – that it's not some figment, some invention out of the night's emergency.

For a few wild seconds she imagines fetching her phone from the pocket of her coastal jacket and calling the old priest, imagines it being possible, and her telling him what she has found and hearing him sigh (sitting up alone, not in the nice old vicarage in the village but a brick box on an estate in the town) and say, 'My dear, my dear, is there somewhere safer you could go?'

She sits there. She does not look pretty; she does not look easy to like. She's afraid, of course, but fear does not consume her. She spends a while trying to think of some plausible explanation as to how the clip came to be there, tucked away in the boat's flooded lungs. All she can come up with by way of an answer is her own foolishness in imagining she could sail free of anything. Isn't that one of the rules of running away? Never to assume that what you're running from isn't somehow ahead of you?

Someone like you comes to a bad end, said Henderson that night at the hotel, the wadded toilet paper against his cut head. What do people know in such moments? What do they see? Anything? And she remembers something else he said – not then, but during her interview for Fenniman's – a little phrase that must have been related to her work with Professor Kimber in Bristol. The wound's journey.

The wound's journey.

She sighs – sighs like an old woman who, in the dead of night, has started searching for something she cannot remember the name of, will never remember the name of. Then she sweeps everything from the bench onto the cabin sole and lies down, just as she is, the hair clip clutched to her chest, a fist that even in sleep does not soften.

4

The plug, the bung, is holding. Strange that something so simple – so cheap! – should work so well, but it does.

The boat sails on a broad reach, six knots according to the GPS screen, sometimes seven. In darkness, she cuts the line forty degrees west – a line that followed northwards would take her to the coast of Greenland. Followed south it would land her a few hundred miles from the mouth of the Amazon.

Her twenty-ninth night – a field of dry lightning in the sky ahead. It is miles away but she finds the handheld GPS and puts it in the oven in case the boat is hit. A boat hit by lightning can lose all its electrics but an oven is supposed to function as a Faraday cage. A boat hit by lightning can also lose its keel bolts. About that there is nothing to be done.

The tap and press of water, the rustling of the sails, the boat's ceaseless small adjustments, her own movements, her own breath, her own thoughts, the voice of those thoughts.

The wind creeps up; she takes in sail. The boat is flying – a hundred and twenty, a hundred and thirty miles in a day.

Through the binoculars, a ship ploughing eastwards. Hard to see at first what kind of ship it is. Two smaller ships are following. They are slim and shadowy and fast. The bigger ship, she realizes, is an aircraft carrier. They are soon gone, and the sea is empty again. Perfectly empty.

Her reset finger is acutely sensitive. She seems to catch it with everything she does – cooking, washing, using a winch, coiling a rope, adjusting the Hydrovane. She makes a splint by splitting off the edge of a wooden ruler and taping it into place, a job that takes her half the morning. Rolling cigarettes requires a new technique (she rolls them on the chart table and leans down to lick the gum).

When the pain is troublesome or if it keeps her from sleeping, she cuts a tab of Fennidine in half, swallows it with tea or water. Sometimes a sip of rum.

The weather is becoming hard to guess. The Navtex is out of range; the long-wave radio does not offer reports for the mid-Atlantic. If she sees a ship she could call on the VHF for a forecast but other than the aircraft carrier and its escort she has not seen anything in nearly a week. She should have an SSB on board or a satellite phone, but she has her barometer, her book of clouds, her eyes. She tells herself that others have managed before her and that she too will manage. She recalls to herself sometimes the fact that people have rowed across the Atlantic in open boats.

*　　*　　*

On deck, making her rounds, dead centre of the night, she grips the starboard shroud and looks up at high cloud scudding across a hazy moon. The next morning, a fine slanting rain begins, light but relentless. She is glad of it at first and stands bareheaded to have it wash the salt out of her hair. Then it starts to bother her, to make her restless. It goes on all day, patient and unceasing. In the night, two hours into sleep, she's roused by the sound of something flogging on the deck and goes up with the torch. As soon as she is outside she's aware of how the wind has strengthened. It's getting under the inflatable on the foredeck, lifting it and dropping it down. She spends forty minutes redoing the lashings. She could have done it in half the time but she's using one hand and her teeth. Only when she has finished does she realize she's not wearing her harness, is not clipped on.

Below deck she wipes her face dry with a tea cloth. The barometer is down a point and she decides to tidy things away, put things in their proper places, secure the lockers, clear the galley. Instead she sits down and reads two pages of the *Dhammapada*, sees a note in the margin, presumably written by Gosse, and spends several minutes trying to decide if it says *Doctrinal* or *Doctor's at 1*. Then she puts the book down and goes out to do what she should have done the last time. She furls the jib to something like a fifth of its full size, takes in two reefs' worth of the mainsail, does it all clearly, cleanly, robotically, then slithers back into the cabin, glistening with the wet and making, with each action, a little grunt of effort. She lifts a panel from the cabin sole to inspect the bung, replaces the panel, and is glancing round for her tobacco when the boat lurches and she ends on her back in a comical tangle between the saloon table and the port-side bench. She's not hurt; bruised perhaps but not hurt. She gets her boots off, hangs her jacket to drip in the heads, gets up into the quarter berth and is asleep within seconds.

For an hour the sea rolls her but cannot wake her. When she does wake there's a grey light in the cabin. White water and darker water are swirling past the port-side windows. She can read the anemometer from where she is lying. Thirty knots, gusting thirty-five. She gets up and goes in a series of short, staggered vectors to look at the barometer. It's down to a thousand millibars. She taps it, hard, but the reading is steady. She puts on her salopettes, her jacket, her boots, her harness, and gets out through the hatch. The rising sun is unobscured but to the north there is a wall of cloud that appears to grow directly out of the sea – brown, purple, at its base a luminous soaked black.

Statistically, this should not be happening. In September perhaps, the height of the storm season, but not in June.

The swell is shorter, steeper. Much steeper. At each crest she has a view that stretches for miles; in the troughs she is hemmed in by water. She needs to make a decision but puts it off for an hour, sitting below smoking and nibbling biscuits, then comes up to see the port-side toe rail under the water, water streaming along the deck like molten glass, and decides to run south, have the sea behind her, the sea, the wind and whatever the wind is bringing.

She disengages the Hydrovane and takes the tiller. She brings the bows down to 110. She is worried the boat will gybe but she has the mainsheet in tight – the boom would not have much of an arc to swing through. The jib, in the shadow of the main, starts to flap. She ignores it.

Now that she is running, the movement is easier. She is pitching rather than yawing, the seas plunging under her stern, accelerating her, then leaving her to slide into the trough. She helms for an hour then reconnects the Hydrovane, spends twenty minutes playing with the angle of the vane before she decides she can trust it. She goes below. Out of the wind, out of the worst of the noise, she stands on braced legs at the chart table, stares at the chart, the GPS, shuts her eyes and sleeps for several seconds before waking to the sound of water shooting through the ventilation slats in the washboard.

She's trying to remember everything she knows about riding out a gale. She has, at least, no shortage of sea room – better to face this out here than in the whipping tides of the English Channel, some lee shore becoming invisible in the haze. She tries the radio, picks up, very faintly, an orchestra playing music she would guess was either Korean or Chinese, Indian perhaps. Then a voice in a language she thinks belongs to some ex-Soviet state, a woman's voice speaking with great sobriety as if announcing the demise of the president, the fall of a city. She switches it off and kneels on the cabin floor, groping in a food locker. The kettle launches itself from the galley and bounces off the table by her head before disappearing through the opening to the forecabin. She finds a can of baked beans, peels off the lid, gets a spoon and eats them cold, the whole can, tomato sauce on her fingers, her chin, her jacket. She's briefly nauseous, then better. She would like something hot to drink but it is not safe now to have boiling water down here and she would need first to find the kettle. She spends quarter of an hour rolling a cigarette then sits at the bottom of the steps to smoke it, one booted foot against the chart table to keep herself in place. There is no restful space. As the boat is struck by the seas, so she is struck by the boat.

A new unpredictability has entered the boat's movements. It is, she realizes, starting to surf, and a boat that surfs is not under control. She turns up the collar of her jacket (it is not the most expensive model, not the one she needs now), tapes shut the Velcro bindings and climbs the companionway steps. The moment her head is above the hatch the wind opens her mouth, pushes at the lids of her eyes. She clips on, squirms her way into the cockpit, draws the hatch tight shut and stands with her back against the washboards squinting through the tunnel of her hands at the cloud wall behind her, the storm wall that has blotted out half the sky and is now closing on her at a rate she cannot possibly outrun.

She turns to the sails; the boat is over-canvassed, that much is obvious. Somehow she must find a balance between maintaining steerage and keeping the boat from overreaching itself. She wants the storm jib up. The storm jib is a good strong sail but it's stowed in the forecabin and she cannot risk opening the forehatch and having the sea plunge through it. She will have to bring it out through the cockpit, take it forwards. She stands there a moment, gathering the wherewithal, then unclips herself, drops back through the hatchway – waits – feels the movement of the boat, runs down through the saloon and arrives in the forecabin in time to brace against the impact at the base of the wave. The storm jib bag is small but heavy. Getting it out through the cockpit hatchway, dragging it, thrusting it ahead of herself, the cabin rearing around her, is a dumb-show of gross effort.

In the cockpit she clips to the central jackstay and works her way forward a yard at a time until she is sitting on the foredeck, her boots by the pulpit rail. She starts to pull the sail from its bag. A kindly hand has written in black indelible marker which corner of the sail is which. She shackles the tack to the base of the spare stay then hanks on until she reaches the head. Every thirty seconds the sea sweeps over her legs. Water forces itself up the inside of her salopettes, forces itself under her jacket, down the back of her salopettes. She crawls to the mast, drops the remains of the mainsail, binds it with bungees, then bangs her shoulders against the mast while she finds a halyard for the storm jib. She uncleats the halyard, slithers back to the jib, undoes the halyard shackle with the marlinspike she once gave to Tim as a present but which later, somehow, became her marlinspike. She attaches the head of the jib, frees the sheets from the furling jib, reties the bowlins through the clew of the storm jib, hoists the jib from the mast, regains the cockpit, sheets in the jib, cleats it, and sits on the grid of the cockpit sole, her chest heaving, her clothes soaked through.

She's cold; she needs dry clothes, but the thought of trying to undress and dress in the confusion below makes her hang on in a blood warm, blood cold huddle. Thoughts arrive; none of them are about boats and the sea. When at last she moves, her limbs are stiff, slow to react to the boat's bucking. A dozen times on her way down she is thrown against some unforgiving edge but she makes no sound or nothing you might hear above the wind. When she tries to get out of her clothes they cling to her. She scrapes them from herself, leaves them where they fall, tugs dry clothes from the holdall in the locker under the chart table, climbs into them while clinging to whatever will take her weight, puts on her salopettes again, her heavy jacket. She looks for her hat, her beanie, wants it very much and spends a crazed quarter-hour searching for it and fending off the cabin before remembering the hat is in the pocket of her jacket.

The light outside is a dusk light, though it is the storm's dark rather than the day's. She clips on and looks down the length of the boat. She watches the bows. With each descent they dig a little deeper, and each time they rise the whole boat shudders with the weight of the water. How far, how deep would the bows have to go before they could not struggle back and the whole boat sailed itself under the sea? This is not a fantasy; there are records of such things.

She disengages the Hydrovane and takes the tiller. At the crest of the next wave she puts the tiller over to come down the face of it at an angle. At the bottom she straightens up, takes the sea under the stern. She's never had to do this before – it's pure theory – but the bows are drier and the boat feels a little safer. As for how long she can keep it up she doesn't know. It means timing things carefully; it means staying alert, watching for the wave that comes from a different angle. The wind shoves at her continually. She needs both hands around the tiller, and she cannot sit – she must see what is happening, must look down the long field of the wave, use all the strength of her belly to hold the rudder against its force.

She manages for the best part of two hours then gives it up – she has no choice. Her eyes are raw from salt and wind. Nor can she trust what she is seeing, not now when the difference between the last of the light and the first of the dark is so small. She will lash the tiller amidships, let the boat find its own angle to the wind, its own luck. And she has ducked down, searching in the shadows around her legs for a rope to lash with, when she hears her name, quite clearly shouted, and because it seems to come from behind her she unbends and looks back to see a wave bigger than any she has ever seen, a grey wall with a grey crest crumbling down its face like masonry, the whole thing apparently at right angles to the wind. She turns from it, flings her arms around the boom, locks her hands to her wrists. Three seconds later it comes aboard (this thing that carries its own unanswerable truth), smashes the air from her lungs, breaks her grip, lifts her, accelerates her, whips her against the wire of the starboard shroud and flings her into the sea.

The sea. The sea is ready for her. It spins her, rakes at her clothes, pushes at her mouth. She has no idea which way is up.

Her brain is lit with an entirely new light, pinkish, as if she were looking out through the meninges of her own skull. Then her line comes taut, she's hauled briefly into air, and as the boat heels towards her, the sea – those five square yards she's thrashing in – lifts her with strange exactness and she arches herself, extends herself like a dancer, hooks three fingers of her good hand through a grab rail and is raised up as the boat rights itself.

For a time – a bare minute perhaps – she clings to the ledge of deck, her face, the smacked flower of her mouth, pressed against one of the coach-house windows. Misjudge her next move and she will be in the sea again; she cannot hope to be so lucky a second time. She tries to guess from its movement how the boat is lying to the sea, decides it's beam on or thereabouts, waits for her side of the deck to swing up, then breaks cover and scrambles head first into the cockpit.

There's a foot of water in the cockpit, though as it must have been brimful after the wave it's evident the drain holes are clear and working.

She is sitting on rope. She gathers it, makes one end fast to a cleat on the side of the cockpit, puts the tiller amidships, takes three turns around it with the rope, and makes it off to the cleat on the far side. She gets to her knees, to her feet, looks forward. The mast is still there; what else is there or not there she cannot tell.

She pushes back the hatch and drops through it with black water following, closes the hatch and bolts it.

The temptation to creep into her berth, to go there just as she is in her layers of soaked gear, is almost overwhelming. Instead, she switches on the nightlight and starts to pump, bends herself blindly to it, the pain in her ribs – the wound she sustained going over the side – making her cry as she cried that time she caught her hand between the trailer and the dinghy, and Grandfather Ray hovered around her not knowing what to say or how to comfort such a creature, a hunched girl in her anorak getting her crying out of the way before standing, smudge-eyed, and wanting to get onto the water.

If nothing else, the pump is something to hold on to, and if she can keep the boat dry, if she can keep whatever water is inside it to manageable levels, then there is hope of coming through. She remembers what Robert Currey said, how all the boats were basically sound, that they would not suddenly go down, would not open up like the old wooden ships in the stories (some of which must be true) seam by rotten seam. But how many had been tested like this? On the anemometer the wind speed is moving between fifty-four and fifty-eight knots. She knows her Beaufort. Storm force ten, violent storm eleven.

How long can a storm last? It can last for days.

She stops pumping; and there is only a little water over the sole. She sits on the nearest bench, undresses with one hand. When she gets below her T-shirt she sees the rhubarb-coloured welts across her ribs, touches them, then pulls on what might be her last dry top, puts on the sea-blue jumper above it, puts on a pair of tracksuit trousers, then the salopettes. One of her sea boots was left in the sea. She takes off the other and wedges her damp feet into her trainers.

As for food, there's food on the floor, an apple among other things that has been cannoning towards her, cannoning away, for the last ten minutes. She picks it up and bites it. It's salty, tastes of bruises, has grit on its skin. She eats it to a slender core, tosses the core towards the galley sink, misses. Also on the floor, the white box, TRIAL USE ONLY, its cardboard sodden but still somehow intact. She swallows two of the capsules with her own spit. (She has never taken two before but it was a dose they sometimes discussed, and one Josh Fenniman himself was said to look favourably upon, a subject referred to in Reading as the 'high-end' question.)

The quarter berth is too wet to lie in. Water must have come down when the cockpit was flooded; the lockers must have flooded too, and leaked. She works her way back to the nearest bench. Under the seat is a triangular canvas lee-cloth. She pulls it out, hooks its eyes over the fittings on the cabin ceiling. The canvas smells ancient, smells like a scrap of sail from a ship-of-the-line in Admiral Shovell's time. With one hand gripping the handhold at the edge of the chart table, she climbs behind the cloth and onto the bench. The instant she is in she is thrown against the canvas so that her whole weight is on it. It does not split, the eyes do not unravel. A moment later she is being forced against the padded back of the seat.

It should not be possible to sleep with such violence but she shuts her eyes and for minutes together there is something very like sleep. The storm does not abate. The storm has resources beyond imagining. An hour after lying down she feels the wind veering and knows that out there in the dark a hammer is swinging.

Get up?

Do what?

She could trail warps.

She could put down oil (but she is not carrying enough oil).

She could start the engine, increase manoeuvrability, take the helm.

She is sick with tiredness. More tired than when the baby was born, infinitely more, but she cannot leave the boat to struggle on its own, cannot hide away down here in its belly. She starts to scrabble free of the bench, the lee-cloth – it's like Lazarus climbing from his grave – and she is crouching by the side of the bench, waiting for her moment to cross to the companionway when she hears a noise she might have taken for the roaring of surf if she didn't know there was three thousand metres of water below her, the nearest land a thousand miles away. She waits but does not need to wait for long. The boat is struck on its starboard side, overwhelmed and flattened to the water. Maud somersaults across the table to the port-side bench, on top of her a rain of clothes, charts, books. The brass dividers like a throwing knife. They miss her, just.

At ninety degrees, the mast in the water, the boat pauses as if to play out some subtle reckoning of the forces, then goes on with its roll. The speed of its turning is like the sweep of a second hand on a clock: not fast, not slow. She is tipped onto the cabin ceiling, falls with everything that is free to fall with her. At one-eighty the boat stops again, keel to the sky (and what does *that* look like? To see it, even in a dream . . .). She fights her way upwards but up has become a confusing place and among those objects lying on her is the top of the saloon table that has freed itself from its gear and landed – three hinged leaves of oak – across her chest. She knows what's happening but knowing does not help. Nothing she does or does not do now will make the slightest difference. The boat begins to move again. It gives out some frantic sound of its own effort, slides from one-eighty to two hundred, snags again (Maud and all else spilling down the starboard bulkhead) then swings up and rears out of the sea as if revolted by its former state. This last quarter of the wheel is the most violent, the most difficult to defend against. Before, she was falling; now she is dropped, flung down. Her forehead misses the edge of the lower companionway step by perhaps two inches. The tabletop lands across her ankles. Her face is in a swill of water. When she can stand she is in the

kind of darkness the eye immediately sketches shapes onto, outlines, faces, things that cannot be there. She finds the pump
handle, clutches it with one hand and reaches around herself with
the other. How much of the boat is still there? Cabin window.
Cabin roof. The washboards, miraculously; the hatch apparently
(though she can't quite reach it). If she could find the torch she
could see what else is there, but the torch has taken flight with the
rest and she is not sure she wants to see what it would show her.
There is no glow from the VHF, no comforting light from any
screen or dial.

She touches herself, frisks herself; she does not seem to have
broken a limb, to be bleeding from anywhere obvious. Though
she can see nothing, she can hear everything, but the sound she
attends to above all others is the thudding on the hull, a noise like
a giant fist beating drunkenly at the side of the boat not far from
where she is standing. She knows what it is, or she can guess. She
needs the bolt-cutters and the bolt-cutters are in the forepeak.
She starts to grope her way through the saloon, something prima-
tive and crazed in her movements, something insect-like in the
way each time she is thrown off her path she immediately returns.
And she has some luck. The heavy tools are where they should be
and it is not difficult to feel out the cutters. Four, five times on
her way back to the companionway she falls. She does not know
what she's falling over, cannot see it. It doesn't matter. All that
matters now is getting on deck.

She drags back the hatch but leaves in the washboards, slithers
over them like an otter. In the cockpit she clips on, shuts the
hatch, and on hands and knees makes her way along the deck. The
mast has gone, or part of it has – she cannot see how much – but
whatever was torn away is now hanging from the rigging and
beating, with each roll of the boat, against a layer of fibreglass half

the width of her thumbnail. Wire, rope, anything holding it to the boat must be cut through. It takes twenty minutes; it takes forever. Most of the work must be done lying down, her feet lodged against whatever she can find that still feels solid, the water breaking over her head again and again, her eyes burning from the salt. She cuts; she creeps forward. A last piece of wire – the starboard shroud? – and then she knows it's gone, feels it go, feels the sea suck it away.

She rises up: two quick strides put her back in the cockpit. She cowers there until the boat, lifting on the back of a wave, has a motion that is briefly predictable, then she opens the hatch, climbs down into the greater darkness, and shuts the hatch behind her. At the bottom of the steps she kicks away whatever is beneath her. She widens her stance, takes hold of the pump handle with both hands, and with a steady, an irrepressible rhythm, she starts to work it.

(Strength is weakness rearranged, a rope plaited from grass.)

5

For another fourteen hours the storm is undiminished. It drives the boat south, scatters it south like a leaf down an alley. All day she hides in the cabin waiting for something to give. She crouches, she clings on, she even sleeps a little. At dusk she goes on deck. To get the hatch open is an immense and exhausting struggle but she gets it open. The first thing she sees is that half of the mast and all of the standing rigging has gone. The boom has sheared off at the neck, the inflatable is gone, the life-raft canister. When she looks sternwards there is no sign of the steel goalposts with the solar panels, the aerials. The Hydrovane too, all of it, gone without a trace.

The wind is no more than a five now, a stiff breeze, but the seas are still big, each wave, if it came aboard, if it broke over the boat, capable of doing more damage, of finishing it perhaps. Somehow the boat is riding them – the stubbornness of form, the clever lines, the clever men who built her.

She goes below, closes the hatch. She drinks from the galley tap, staggers about scavenging for food, finds shattered jars, burst containers, floating vegetables. There's a Dundee cake wedged behind the stove chimney. She breaks off a fistful and eats it. She thinks of the life raft and whether, torn from the deck, it inflated, as it should have. Whether it is out there now, already many miles away, a life raft traceable to the boat. Empty.

She sleeps behind the lee-cloth. When she comes to, the light through the salt-greasy windows illuminates a disorder that can only be thought of as total. Even the little fridge is face down at the far end of the cabin.

On deck the sun is high, blinding. She is dressed in her heavy-weather gear still. She sits on the cockpit seat like an actor who has wandered off the set to smoke a cigarette. The movement of the sea has changed, the swell, in foaming green fractals, slower and more regular. She is hot from the sun, hot from fever too perhaps. She gets her jacket off. The clothes below have dried onto her, or almost dried. She strips down until her top half is bare to the wind and sun, her lower half still swathed in Neoprene. The skin of her arms, breasts and belly is dead white. There are fewer bruises than she expected. The worst is around her ribs – her whole flank starting to flower. She puts her T-shirt on, pulls up the braces on her salopettes. She already knows the main GPS is dead, has tried it twenty times and got nothing, but the hand-held is down there somewhere and she goes below to search for it. During the search she finds other things that are useful – the tin opener, her Green River knife, a pouch of tobacco still in its cellophane – but the handheld has disappeared and she is wondering, in her fevered state, if it could somehow have fallen out of the cabin and over the side, when she opens the door of the oven and finds it where she left it the night she saw the lightning.

Hard to believe it could still function after the battering it must have taken but when she turns it on it vibrates in her hand, lights up. She takes it to the cockpit, shades the screen, peers at it and reads off the co-ordinates, reads them aloud.

'North zero five one. West zero zero two.'

She switches it off, switches it on again, reads off the same figures. North zero five one. West zero zero two. She knows those co-ordinates, she doesn't need to look on any chart. If she plotted them the dot would sit over the cottage in Dorset. Some sort of reset? Did she test it once at the cottage? Did Tim? She reboots it, several times; nothing changes. She turns it off, puts it in the thigh pocket of her salopettes, looks up with narrowed eyes at the perfect wilderness around her. At least the binnacle compass seems trustworthy (not much in there to break – inch-thick glass, a card, some manner of alcohol). It shows a heading just west of south. Since the storm's beginning she may have travelled several hundred miles in that direction. She tries the engine. The starter battery is flat. She tries wiring in one of the other batteries but in the capsize they were flung from their mountings and have, apparently, discharged in the water on the cabin floor. One of them produces a flicker of light in the ignition indicator but the engine remains silent. And even if she could get the charge she needs, the engine itself must be full of water, the fuel lines clogged with sediment from the tank.

For a long time she tries to puzzle out how to jury-rig a sail. Has someone explained it to her? Has she read about it? One of those ingenious Frenchmen for example, part engineer, part poet, who, in the dead centre of the Pacific, rebuilds his boat out of its own ruins . . .

She has twelve feet of mast, possibly more. The first thing is to secure it with some rigging and she starts to collect, out of the sail locker, the cockpit lockers, whatever she has left in the way of sheets and halyards and spare blocks. The deck is far from steady but she judges it steady enough to work on. She does not bother with a harness and line though it is not many days since these saved her life.

With a pencil, on the back flyleaf of the *Dhammapada*, she makes a sketch of what she needs to do, then she goes to the mast, rope slung like a bandolier across her shoulder. She secures the mooring steps (they're metal, lightweight, telescopic) to the base of the mast and goes up until she can reach the top of the stump. First she makes the backstays with a pair of red Dyneema sheets, running them back to the cockpit and taking up the slack on the winches. Next, she ties on a brand new thirty-metre rope and leads it forward and under the through-pin of the samson post, sweats it until it's as taut as her weight and strength can make it, makes it off on the post, goes back to the cockpit to take another turn on the winches.

The sun is reddening the back of her neck. She loses herself for a moment, sways, recovers, and goes up the mooring steps with a block, attaches it to the top of the stump with wire lashed in place with shock cord and an entire roll of two-inch-wide plastic tape. She threads a polyester halyard through the block, secures one end to the cleat at the base of the mast. The other end has a Wichard snap shackle spliced into it. This will take the head of the sail.

From its locker she drags out Gosse's old number four jib, thrusts it out through the forehatch, cannot, in her condition, haul herself out after it, and goes out through the main hatch. She attaches the shackle, ties on a sheet at the clew, raises the sail and makes it off at the big wooden cleat behind the tiller. The wind is light – the storm's echo, ghost winds. The sail is her attempt at a trysail. It looks, she thinks, like the laundry of the poor, but it fills, briefly, and the boat slides forward. If the wind stays light then the rig is feasible; if it strengthens then the number four jib will join the other debris she has left across an arc of ocean. All this is the work of many hours. It is the best she can do. It is all she can do.

Four or five times a day, she pumps the bilges. Everything, even survival – especially survival – has its routines.

The wooden bung in the broken fitting is still secure, but water is seeping in from somewhere else, probably from several places. She should, ideally, work the pump once an hour, and would do if she had the strength. She makes herself eat but cannot always keep the food down. To do more than lie for hours in the shade of the sail requires a doggedness that each time is a little harder to summon.

In the sea during the day, clumps of sargasso weed, the blue shadows of dorados, triggerfish. In the sea at night, globes of drifting light like the wax in a lava lamp. Dinoflagellates, copepods. Struck by the boat they break, swirl past, reform.

She uses stars, dead reckoning and the colour of the sea to estimate her position. She is close to the equator, perhaps south of it already. She has seen the Southern Cross but can still see northern stars.

The chart, stained, frayed, beginning to split apart, is folded to show an area of ocean and land that includes Suriname, French Guiana, the shoulder of Brazil. At the centre of her square is the Vema Fracture Zone. She is, she believes, somewhere on that square.

*　　*　　*

The things the sea carries to her. An object off her port bow she thought at first must be a creature of some sort, something sleeping in the water, a dolphin, a pilot whale. She even thinks of the seals she has seen sleeping in the mouths of certain bays, at the edges of loughs. It turns out to be a suitcase, and though she might have guessed herself to be beyond curiosity, the effort of it, she catches the case's handle with the boat hook (the boat hook that has survived everything), hauls it into the cockpit and sits, hugging her ribs, panting, and looking at it, a suitcase, bronze-coloured, quite new and not, it seems, much damaged by the sea. It has an Air France label on it and a name, illegible other than for the initial R.

She assumes the case will be locked but it isn't. She assumes the contents will be heavy with water but that too turns out to be wrong. She leans over it, the open case with its quilted, silvery lining, reaches down to touch a white shirt still neatly folded. There's a hesitancy to her touching, as if the shirt were not merely a stranger's possession but the stranger himself (she who has no history of making the first move). A white shirt, only slightly damp, and beneath it two more, then a black jacket with black satin lapels, black trousers, a man's underwear, several pairs of thin black socks.

There's a wash bag of fake leather with half a dozen disposable razors inside, a brand of toothpaste called *Sorriso*, a condom, a tube of cream that, from its listed contents, is for the treatment of a chronic skin condition.

A phrase book, French to Portuguese.

Two novels, one in English, the other in Spanish, though after a moment she realizes it's the same novel – *The Last Adventure of Sanchez Coello, Conquistador/La última aventura del conquistador Sanchez Coello.*

Tucked beside the books is a box of *Garoto* chocolates; also a copy of the *International Herald Tribune*, the date of the paper the day after she sailed from England ('76 Feared Dead in South African Goldmine').

One of the hip pockets of the jacket has a small religious medal in it and three used tickets for the Paris Metro. The other pocket is full of red petals from some large, possibly tropical flower. She holds the petals in her hand, dazzled by their colour, and when she pours them back into the pocket (its opening dark and moist as a mouth) they leave a faint red stain on her palm.

During the night the boat passes more cases – big ones, small ones, some with stout buckles, some wrapped entirely in layers of plastic film. She does not see them. She is asleep, splayed to the cooler air, her split lips parted, dreaming of someone called Sanchez Coello, conquistador in a tuxedo, dragging the petals from the heads of flowers as he passes them . . .

She has been at sea for forty days. She does not go below more than she needs to; below is hotter than above, and below the shadows loll, heap up in a nook or hang suggestively in the narrow places. She goes down to drink water from the galley, to forage in the lockers for unspoiled food, to pump the bilges. In the mornings there's always an inch or two of sea water over the cabin sole. She is almost used to it, the water pearly dark and cool around her bare feet.

She notes the sharpness of her joints, the rising bone, her breasts like a twelve-year-old's, the thin brown hardness of her thighs. It does not alarm her. She has been alive long enough to know that women's bodies are endlessly plastic, can remember herself in her third trimester, a ripeness that had a kind of violence at the back of it. And now she is turning into wood like one of those nymphs Tim told her about, daughters of river gods running for their lives through the forest. She does not remember their names. The stories were as dense and strange as anything she ever told him about eukaryotic genes, monoclonal antibodies, catalysis. When she asked him if such stories had a purpose, he said yes, yes of course, but he could not tell her what it was. Just grinned. Wanted to kiss her.

Forty-third day. The water tank is empty. Yesterday a flow, a lace of water, today nothing. She counts the bottles of water. Several burst their skins in the capsize. There are six left, each containing a litre and a half. She wraps each one in a piece of clothing, stores them in a locker where no sharp edge can find them.

In the night a flying fish lands on the deck. She hears it floundering about in the cockpit. She gets up and kills it. In the morning she cuts off its wings, guts it and cuts two pink-white fillets from it. Though she has gas she does not trust the connections and does not want to blow up the boat. She makes sashimi, throws the remains over the side where some larger fish, a small shark perhaps, immediately seizes it. To finish her meal she eats some of the sweets from the yellow box in the suitcase. There are various kinds. Her favourite is called *Serenida de Amor*. Of the others, she likes one that tastes of hazelnuts and is called *Surreal*.

Half an hour after eating all this she throws up over the stern.

How everything is terribly fragile. A girl at school, for example, who came off her push bike and knocked her head, a bruise no bigger than a primrose, no blood. She lay a month in a coma then died.

How everything is insanely strong. Those men and women she has come across in her work, children too, who lie on their beds or sit on their tall chairs with eyes wide and wild as if receiving unbearable news from distant galaxies. And that film she was shown in the Radcliffe – something made in the 1960s when science had not entirely given up on the freak show – a man whose skin was so sensitive to any impression, any touch, the technician could make him writhe with the gliding tip of a feather. But such people survive. They cut up their food and live for years.

Forty-sixth day. She wakes in the late afternoon from a long drowsing on the foredeck to find herself looking at distant clouds. The clouds are new. A line of them, white, blue white, stretching down the western horizon. She looks at them with that all-her-life animal talent for looking, that composed and hunkered gazing that seems to be the nub of her, the thing she is burning back to. Then she makes herself look down. When she looks up the clouds are still there. Three hours of this – a sort of game. Looking, turning away. Then the clouds flush red, ignite, fade to blue. Night falls with that suddenness she is not yet accustomed to. No moon rises. The boat creeps forward, the water hisses. She lays her head on a pillow of rope and is woken hours later by a breeze crackling the sail. She turns to the sky. Rain, like the sudden spilling of small coins. She strips off. She opens her mouth. In two minutes the rain is over but her grey shadow glistens and her mouth tastes of something miraculous. She sits up. She is almost cold and relishes it. By instinct she turns to the west again. There is a light there now, a spark at the edge of the night, a light trembling with distance.

A setting star? But she knows at once it is not a star.

A ship? Then why does the bearing not change?

If the light is on land then there are certain calculations to be made. Height of observer above the water; height of the light observed. She does not know the height of the light. On the shore? The top of a cliff? In the end it is nothing but a guess. The light, she decides, is twenty miles away. Twenty nautical miles or less. At the speed she is making (the speed she thinks she is making) that's ten hours of sailing, of drifting.

Long before sunrise she loses the light, but by the middle of the morning the clouds are back and two hours later she sees through the Zeiss an uneven black line beneath the clouds, the kind of line a young child might draw across a sheet of paper spread out on the floor, the beginning of something but not something yet, just a line heading out, its tip a point containing everything.

She lowers the binoculars, closes her eyes. 'Where have you brought me?' she asks, her voice a rasp. She feels no heavier than a blade of grass; a puff of wind could send her spinning over the water. She creeps below, opens the last can of fruit, sits in the dark of the cabin with it, water swilling over her feet. When she's finished with the can she simply drops it.

She could take the tiller now but the current and a south-east breeze is slowly bringing her in. Sooner or later a coaster will appear, a fishing boat, a Customs launch. Perhaps they have seen her already, the good people of Progreso, of Île-à-Vache, but when she scans the shore she can make out no houses or boats, no smoke, no glitter of glass.

By late afternoon she is heading towards a scatter of small steep islands half a mile from the mainland. She does not want to be among those islands in darkness. She fetches the crash bag, brings it up on deck, checks on the flares, the Lumica light sticks, the torch. She has, at most, another three hours of daylight.

Through the binoculars she watches birds wheeling about the peaks of the islands, how they slide from the sheer edges of the rock in silent avalanches, fall towards the surface of the sea then, with two or three powerful beats of their wings, rise again.

The smell of land! Like putting down your window on the motorway at night after rain. Breathing in, deeply.

She passes the islands, slides past close enough to hear the birds, their endless calling. Under the hull a network of local currents is edging her ever nearer to the shore. The water is green and perfectly clear. She lies on the foredeck and stares down, sees the shadows of fish, the shadows of small rocks. The boat has a draft of just under six feet. She waits for the first touch. When it comes – this boat, this keel that has sailed above canyons – it is very gentle. A slight checking of its motion, then afloat again, then a second contact, more certain. The bows swing; the boat dips towards the shore. She drops the plough anchor over the leeward side, lets go all the chain she has. From below she fetches her phone, a few clothes, a half-full packet of raisins, her passport, her wallet. The little hair clip, the heart of tin, which she has kept safely in a zipped pouch in the wallet, she threads onto a length of shock cord and ties the cord with a double knot around her neck.

In the cockpit she steps over the stranger's suitcase (it's bone dry now and dull like a pebble brought home from the beach). She lowers the makeshift sail, bundles it. The day is settling into its short twilight; the boat's keel growls on the sand. She puts on her trainers, ties one of the straps of the crash bag to her wrist, looks about herself as if, surely, she has forgotten something, then sits in her shorts and T-shirt, feet dangling a little way above the water. She remains there for several minutes staring at the shore, the low bluff of red rock, the curtain of trees above it. No one appears. There is nothing, to the naked eye, to suggest anyone has ever set foot there before. She eases herself down into the water. It is awkward to swim with the bag, with the pain in her ribs, but soon she can feel the ridged sand below her and she wades ashore, spilling the sea from her shoulders, then her belly, then her knees, until she is standing on the beach in the land's shadow, the water behind her lit like coals, the boat crouched like a thing at prayer.

FIVE

I hope you will forgive me if I use the word 'truth'. The moment I say 'truth' I expect people to ask 'what is truth?' 'Does truth exist?'. Let us imagine that it exists. The word exists, therefore the feeling exists.

Hélène Cixous

1

She climbs the scarp – red rock and shadow. She is not steady on her feet. The land has no give in it, cannot be trodden upon as the sea could.

At the top she sits to catch her breath. In fifteen minutes she has walked further than she has in weeks. The air is warm, the moon rising out of the sea with a face of finely meshed gold, a soft and intricate moon, but bright enough for her to make out a landscape of bare grey trees, darker bushes, the suggestion of low hills in the distance. With the binoculars she scans for a light, perhaps the one she saw from the boat, but there is nothing, and nothing to tell her the direction she should take – no path, no signs, only the scarp and the grey trees, the moon creeping out of the sea.

She decides to keep to the coast if she can, and as the way looks slightly clearer in one direction than the other she turns left – south – and walks the fringe of open ground at the top of the scarp until the trees press her to the edge and she is forced to turn inland. The moon is higher now and in its light the tops of the grey trees have become silver, the ground below them bare, dark, uneven. Often she has to shift her route where the scrub rises up in a black fence directly ahead of her, and once, brushing against the edge of one of these thickets, she feels something slice the skin of her arm with the ease of a razor. After this she is more careful.

She hears the singing of insects, though the place where she is moving is always quieter, the singing always at a distance. She's land sick, heavy on her feet, but keeps up a steady pace, her shadow crossing bones of moonlight, then lost for a moment in something darker than herself, then out into moonlight again.

She startles a bird. It passes close in front of her face with an angry beating of wings and she stumbles backwards, loses her balance and falls. When she gets up she is unsure of her bearings. Which way is the coast? Which way was she headed? She digs out the compass from her pack. The luminous tip of the needle wavers delicately. She finds herself, heads off again, swimming between the silver trees, following paths more imagined than real, the trees and the light laying themselves down in patterns on her brain, a game of minimal differences, a kaleidoscope of moonlit branches that ends with such abruptness she teeters and rocks on her heels as if at the edge of a precipice. In fact, she's standing at the edge of a road, or if not a road then a track of packed earth but certainly wide enough to take a car. She finds her torch, shines it both ways, then shines it by her feet, looking for tyre prints, and thinks she can see some though it's hard to be sure. Again, she must decide on a direction. Again she chooses left.

On the track she goes more quickly, feels safer, more certain of finding help, and soon. Either side of her is the same scrub and bare trees she walked through from the scarp but ahead of her, surely, even if she has to walk all night, there will be a farm, a settlement, the edge of a city perhaps, and she pictures herself (she's half asleep in the monotony, the rhythm of her walking) passing suburban gardens, silent roundabouts, traffic lights signalling to no one.

The moon is overhead now, its light pixellating the air, the uncertain distance. She pauses to drink some of her water, to eat some of the raisins, then puts the pack on and sets off, last woman on earth, first woman on earth, her shadow rippling over the dust of the track, her feet in her trainers making a dull sound, a soft sound, surprisingly soft. Another hour of this, then another, burrowing into the silence of the night, the night's outrageous amplitude, her nose full of the scent of whatever is growing at the side of the track. Slowly – or she is slow to notice it – the land to her right is altering. The silver trees are thinning out; then they have gone entirely and in their place there are palm trees, very tall, gently curved, their heads sparked with moonlight, the ground below them splashed with each tree's starburst of shadow.

She wanders into the midst of them; it's difficult not to. Are they coconut palms or some other kind? Does someone harvest them? They do not look to have grown randomly but to stand in rows. She takes out the torch again, shines it around her, the beam breaking on the trunks of the trees. When she puts it off she's blind. She considers letting off a flare – she has two in her bag and someone might see. Instead, she squats at the base of the nearest tree. The air is still warm. The blood thuds in her head and seems to mimic the beat of her walking. She drinks some water then lies down, pillowing her head on the pack. The ground smells like a spice but when she shuts her eyes it is the sea that appears to her, grey, green-grey and endless. She sleeps, dreamlessly, the fronds high above her sometimes making a noise like rain though no rain falls.

*   *   *

In the early morning, uncoiling from the base of the tree, she looks about herself, the grove, the visible world, its colours bleeding through the muted air – the red of the earth, the tattered green of the palm fronds, some bird threading the grove, a blur of living yellow.

The ground is cracked, almost grassless, and not, as she might have hoped, strewn with fallen coconuts, though the trees have some sort of fruit, high up and well out of reach. She eats a handful of raisins, drinks more of her water, then walks about the grove hoping to find a building of some sort, or failing that, a wall, a fence, a fresh track, something – anything – with writing on it. She finds nothing except the blackened remains of a fire with an empty fire-blackened tin at the edge of it in which a large insect is living. She returns to the track. For the first hour she is listening for the engine note of a truck, a car. After that she just walks, her trainers red with dust, her shadow shortening, the light starting to dazzle so that for long periods she keeps her eyes lowered to the surface of the track. There is no shade. She thinks of the hats on the boat, Gosse's hat, her own. She takes sips of water, falls prey to the idea she is walking in circles, then lies down in the shade through the worst of the heat and sets off again in the mid-afternoon. Her watch says nine o'clock; her watch is useless to her. As the day cools, the whiteness of the sky settles to blue. A half-dozen clouds appear though none obscure the sun, even for a moment.

On the right-hand side of the track there are cacti, some as tall as two men. On the other side, and for some time now, she has been walking next to bushes of small yellow flowers, and beyond these the vegetation is denser and greener, the bare trees replaced by trees with broad leaves that reflect the light like green mirrors.

She longs for the sheltering dark, the cool of the night. She keeps going because the track keeps going and because stopping feels like the harder choice, certainly the more dangerous one. The gathered heat of the day radiates from the track and comes up to her in warm gulps.

With the dusk, bats appear – frantic dartings at the edge of sight. A beetle whirrs across the air in front of her. A moth, large as a saucer, settles for a second on her shoulder, from each wing a false eye staring. And there – at last! – the moon, moving through the upper branches of the trees then rolling clear into a sky that's briefly green, then ten different blues with black at the back of them.

Again, she has that stubborn fantasy of arriving at the edge of a town, a city, with its subways waiting patiently for the first train of the morning, but it's a fantasy thin as celluloid. The rest of her is head down and head deep in the actual, in red dust and moon-light, in the tide of her own breathing.

And then – like an entirely unexpected move in a game you thought you were starting to understand – the track divides. It's the first thing that has frightened her. One way curves into the bare country on her right, the other enters the woodland, the green place to her left. Each path is of a similar width. There is of course no post or sign. Or perhaps there is a sign, for *something* is there, at the tip of the island where the ways divide, but sunk in such deep shadow she has to go close – close enough to smell it – before she understands what it is. A cow's dry hide, propped up on a maquette of sticks, the long skull (she's turned her torch on it now) growing through the skin, a thing transitioning, a thing leaving itself behind.

She chooses left again – isn't that how you find your way out of a maze, always turning in the same direction? After twenty yards she's under the canopy of the trees. This way, she decides, will lead her back to the coast. She should not have allowed herself to lose sight of it, to become lost in palm groves, to walk on a track that leads nowhere. She thinks of the boat, of how much she wants to see it again, the thing that almost killed her, the thing that saved her. Was it still there? Or had it dragged its chain and drifted into deeper water, an unlit boat wallowing off the coast, a menace to navigation?

She tries to work out how many hours she's been walking since the palm grove. Ten? Twelve? She trips over roots, walks several paces at a time with her eyes shut. Twice, she wanders off the track entirely and has to find her way back (there are cells in the hippocampus that help her to do this).

In the treetops and at ground level she hears the movement of small creatures, or creatures she prefers to picture as small. She hears – a bare yard away! – something climb on quick claws the trunk of the tree she is passing. Then the track enters a clearing and she looks up to see stars, the freewheeling night, a patch of it at least, its edges like cut paper where it meets the leaves and branches of the trees. She sinks down into the rough grass, gets the pack off her back, lies down and draws up her knees. Certain tedious songs are playing in her head, the kind children are supposed to like and perhaps do. Part of her is still working on a plan; most of her suspects the time for plans is over. She cannot move a finger. She is pressed to the ground, crushed to it. The life of the forest, its ten thousand separate sounds, pass through her unencumbered . . .

At the edge of the clearing a sleek head slides past the wall of tangled black. Eyes that do not flinch, that do not waver, take in the shape of the sleeping woman. Nostrils quiver. The forest holds its breath. Then the head withdraws and the surface of the forest closes over it like water.

*   *   *

262

When she wakes there are butterflies overhead, and on her leg a centipede long and thick as a pencil. She flicks it off, examines the rash it has left behind, then forgets her leg and looks at the car. The forest has tried to tidy it away so it looks like a car that might have appeared on a 1970s album cover, the unmistakeable shape of a car but bound with vines and tendrils and studded with large red flowers. She crosses the clearing towards it. She is not so confused, so far gone, that she does not know some things are unreal. Close to, however, it's real enough. She feels the sun-reflecting heat of its metal, sees the light ripple on the windscreen – there's even an aerial, neatly wound with some delicate climbing plant. She walks around it. It's a long car, an estate of some sort, a shooting-brake, long and low. Beneath the greenery the sides of the car are a sort of mock wood or, examined more carefully, real wood. There's no hope of getting any of the doors open, not without a half-hour of sawing at stems, some of them as thick as her thumb.

She parts the curtain of leaves by the driver's door. The glass has its own ecology, a fur of green – a type of lichen? – and she rubs some of it away with the heel of her hand, puts her face close and peers inside. Whatever has happened to the outside of the car, the interior seems untouched, or just to be changing more slowly. There's a steering wheel bound in what looks like padded maroon leather, red trim on the doors, broad seats of a paler colour. A radio, an open ashtray. A key in the ignition, a second key dangling from it. Bench seats, and on the passenger side a pack of cigarettes and Zippo lighter, a flag on the side of the lighter which, pressing herself to the glass, she identifies as the flag of the Confederacy. A fine dust over everything, everything sleeping in the red shade of the trim, the green shade of the creepers. When she circles the car again (studying it like a prospective buyer) she finds the part-devoured remnants of a bumper sticker that reads *DO YOU FOLLOW JESUS THIS CLOSE?*

She wants the car to tell her something. Someone must have driven it to this place. Did they come down the track she walked yesterday? Or up the track, the way she will have to go today if she is not to retrace her steps? But the car is facing neither one way nor the other. The car is parked. It has no clear message, offers her no clue. As for who drove it there, where did they go? Where *is* there to go?

She returns for the bag. There are only two or three mouthfuls of water left, perhaps a fifth of a pint. She drinks, screws on the top, eats the last of the raisins, put the bag on her back, the straps immediately finding yesterday's rawness. The rash on her leg is swelling. She can also feel she has been bitten on the face – mosquito bites, or one of the other insects that thickened the air above her as she slept.

She stops in front of the car again. It is, she now realizes, a tomb of some sort, albeit an apparently empty one. The scent of the red flowers is not sweet, nor are the flowers themselves pretty. They sit with their large petals open in a mime of exhaustion and make her think of those carnivorous plants that close at a touch, though above them a score of yellow butterflies (not the yellow of English brimstones but as if cut from yellow card or scraped from an old yellow-painted wall) drift on the car's thermals and do not look threatened. She takes her leave of it, walks backwards for several steps, then turns and enters the shade of the track, its curving descent between the trees. It must be possible to find food in such a place – berries, roots, leaves, types of fungus – and throughout the morning, the first hours of walking, she breaks things off, scrapes things between her teeth, begins, in a small way, to eat the forest.

At noon – call it noon – the light plunging through gaps in the canopy, she hears the whooping of monkeys and going closer looks up to see a crowd of them on a tree whose bark is mottled like a eucalyptus, but on this tree there are clusters of black fruit the size of ping-pong balls growing directly on the trunk in a way she has never seen before. There's a term for it, this sort of growth, but she cannot remember now what it is. The monkeys are eating the fruit, feasting on it, and though they scream at her and bare their gums, she shrugs off her pack and climbs into the lower boughs, picks the fruit and breaks the skin with her teeth. Inside is a veined, milky pulp, sweet as a grape. She spits out the seeds, then takes off her T-shirt and makes a bag of it, fills it with the fruit and clambers down to sit at the base of the tree, ignoring the monkeys' rage and pressing the fruit, one after the other, against her teeth and tongue. She puts the remaining fruit into her pack, puts on her T-shirt and starts to walk again. A large green bird flies down the track. It carries the light on its back. It's like learning green for the first time.

She has gone no more than five hundred yards when she is seized with stomach cramps and squats at the side of the track gasping and emptying herself, then goes on for a while in a waking nightmare in which the car, riding its heavy suspension, is coming down the track behind her, coming very slowly yet closing on her all the time. But the mood, the fear, ebbs away, and something else begins, some fresh effect of exhaustion, of the black fruit perhaps, and she walks as if gliding, without effort, without pain. 'I can't stop!' she cries, her voice, her English words, more exotic in this place than any green bird. At times she is almost running, her feet pressing lightly on the deep litter of the track, a woman right at the edge of flight. Everything that she is travels with her. There is no long scarf of memory, no extraneous thought. She walks, she runs, her hair in damp whorls plastered to the skin of her face and neck. Her heart is a wingbeat, her mouth dry as a stone. And like this she dances out of the forest to find the world has stumbled into night, that there are stars at the level of her feet, a horizon of some pale violet colour, and the sea, slack, tipped with starlight, the smell of it like something poured out of her own veins, like sucked brass.

Ten steps to the left would take her into the air. She stands there a minute, her breath frayed almost to nothing, to rags and threads, bare threads. Then she lies down exactly where she is, curls up on the path listening to the deep reflection of the sea while above her the Milky Way glitters in a blue smoke and lines of light streak for a second and burn to nothing.

2

Though she is a girl as curious as the next she has learnt in her short life to have a proper caution. She is, after all, in charge of the goats, and the animals, twelve of them, spill around her as she squats on a convenient rock and looks at the figure sprawled across the path at the point where the path enters the forest. At this distance she cannot be sure if it's a man or a woman but she's certain it's not a child and not anyone she knows.

She's a blonde, gap-toothed girl with a band of freckles across her cheeks, a straw hat on her head, an oversized black T-shirt with a picture of Luke Skywalker on it. And though barely past her tenth birthday, she has already seen a good many dead things – dead goats, dead cattle, dead chickens, a dead turtle once. Not yet, not properly (because it doesn't count when they're under a sheet and you can't see the face) a dead person.

The old billy, who has been cropping the dry brown heads of plants at the edge of the path, stops, wary for a moment, then picks his way past the open, outstretched hand, and the others follow him, one by one, into the shadow of the forest. The girl slides off her rock. She doesn't want the animals to get too far ahead of her. There are things in the forest that will eat a goat and only a month ago she did lose one and did not dare (she who dares a great deal) go far from the track to search for it.

So who is this, who does not wake at the sound of goat bells? She can see it's a woman now. Shorts and T-shirt, a green bag beside her. Her face burnt and bitten, sores on her lips. Her shoes red with dust.

'*Você fica cansada?*' she says. She prods one of the woman's legs with her stick and the woman makes a noise in her throat. It's a little funny to watch someone coming so sleepily up the long stairs of themselves, to see them squirm in the dust of the track as if they had, two minutes ago, been made out of that same dust.

The eyes open, brown like the brown hair.

'*Você tem sede?*' The girl has a camouflage-green, military-style drinking bottle across her shoulders and she unslings it, unscrews the cap, squats and holds it to the woman's lips. Most of the water slides down her cheek but then she's suckling like a baby. When the girl decides she's had enough she takes the bottle back, screws on the top. For a moment she's distracted by the woman's arm, the black writing there, then she remembers her manners and asks, '*Qual é o seu nome?*' She waits. For long seconds the woman says nothing, just looks at her with eyes that could swallow you whole. Eventually she pushes herself into a sitting position, looks about herself, looks at the sea, looks back at the forest. When she speaks the girl does not understand her then, suddenly, she does, and in her head the honeycomb of words is changed.

'My name is Leah,' she says, listening to herself, the charm of her own voice. 'Please wait here. I must find my goats.'

*   *   *

With frequent stops, the girl and the woman make their way along the coast. The path leads them down to the edge of the sea and after that the only path is the girl's own footprints and those of the goats. They cross a spur of headland, descend to a second beach, then up a shallow rise to where the sand gives way to ochre earth and a white church stands looking out to sea like an old white boat drawn up out of the surf. At the side of it is a second building, also white, with a row of small shuttered windows above three dark archways.

As they come closer, other children appear. Some are about the girl's age, some much younger. They do not speak to Maud. They look at her with grave expressions, expressions of wonder. In whispers they ask Leah questions and several times Maud hears the girl speak her name, or a version of it – 'Moor . . . Moor'.

The walk from the edge of the forest has taken two hours, perhaps two and a half, and has cost Maud the last of her strength. She leans on Leah's stick and waits for one of the children to bring an adult and for that adult to tell her where she can lie down. One of the children – a boy running furiously – has been sent as a messenger to the church but instead of an adult, two older children step from the door, an adolescent girl and boy, and for a while they simply look on as if they were expecting someone else. Then the girl strides forward, parts the circle of children and stands in front of Maud. She is, perhaps, thirteen, though at least as tall as Maud. Copper-coloured skin, her hair a slightly darker version of the same colour. The dress she is wearing, with its orange polka dots, has at one time belonged to somebody larger, heavier, and has, at the waist, been gathered into pleats and tightly belted.

'*Ola*,' says the girl.

269

'I need to sit,' says Maud, and does so, almost tumbling to the ground in the middle of the children, the goats.

The older girl speaks to Leah then kneels at Maud's side. 'You are American?'

Maud nods. American will do.

'You are lost?'

She nods again. She has shut her eyes. When she opens them and looks up at the girl, the girl smiles. She is missing one of her front teeth but it doesn't make her less beautiful. 'I am Jessica,' she says. 'I will help you.'

Before Maud can answer, the girl has stood and begun issuing orders, scattering the younger children, one of whom returns a moment later with a plastic beaker of water and a slice of mango. Maud drinks some of the water but she cannot manage the fruit. They watch her, then one of them takes the cup from her and they raise her up – the older girl, Leah, and two other girls, twin's surely, black girls with bright astonished faces. They prop her onto her feet. Maud reaches an arm around the older girl's shoulders, and they set off, step by halting step, towards the nearest archway.

Inside the building they climb a flight of wooden stairs to a corridor or gallery where three unglazed windows, their shutters partly open, look from the back of the building, a view consumed by light. Opposite the windows are four or five doors and the older girl opens the first of them, the one nearest the top of the stairs. 'This is my room,' she says. 'You can stay in here.'

It's small and simple, a narrow bed along one wall, a table and chair under the window. The window, like those in the corridor, has green shutters but no glass.

Maud sits on the bed. Life is happening to her; she has no part to play, or her part is like that of the blind men, madmen and cripples in the Bible stories, people lowered from a roof or touched miraculously in passing.

A small boy comes in carrying, with great care, a bowl half full with water.

'Thank you, Caleb,' says the older girl, in English, perhaps for Maud's benefit. The boy sets down the bowl, spilling some of the water onto the boards. He has a yellow, short-sleeved shirt on, red shorts down to his knees, bare feet. He looks as if he has some Indian blood in him.

'It's not polite to stare,' says the girl, and though it's hard to tell if the boy understands the words, he understands enough – the tone of voice, the young schoolmistress – and he looks down, leaves the room.

'You can go ahead and wash now,' says the girl. 'The children won't come bothering. I'll have Leah sit outside. When you need me you just send her to get me.'

Maud nods.

'You got all you need?' asks the girl.

When she has gone Maud sits there looking at the trembling in her legs, the thinness of her legs. She does not wash, she does not undress, does not take off her shoes. Eventually she lies down. She can smell the girl in the rough linen, can smell herself too, the bitterness of her skin, or a bitterness that rises from somewhere deeper. Outside, the children are calling to each other and the sounds are like the cries and whoops and chattering of the forest. She listens. Surely now some man or woman, some clear, rational voice, will speak over them and she will hear the heavy footfall on the stairs and she will ready herself to tell her story.

She listens. She waits.

*   *   *

Once she has fallen asleep she is like a child into whose room the parents can come and go without fear of waking her. Leah, the doorkeeper, in exchange for small gifts, admits, one at a time, her particular friends. All the friends are girls; certainly no boys will be allowed. So Jenna, a black girl, seven years old, stands at the end of the narrow bed imagining herself as a baby again. So Bethany, pale as Leah, daring to lean over Maud to examine her dirty face, her broken fingernails, the writing on her arm that seems almost readable but not quite. So Summer, eight, snub-nosed and frizzy-haired, not knowing if the woman is twenty-five or fifty-five, and wondering why she wears around her neck a piece of string with a child's hair clip on it.

Jessica is also a visitor, and like the younger children she stands over the sleeping woman, but on her face the expression shifts between something like anxiety and something like relief, pro-found relief. In the evening she covers Maud with a blanket then holds out her hands, palms down above Maud's sleeping head and speaks a dozen words, hushed and fervent.

Below, when the girl comes down, the children are waiting for her. They pester her with questions, hang from her hands, tug at the polka-dot dress. She shakes them off, gently, and crosses to the church, walks down the unlit length of it to the door beyond the altar.

She opens the door; the boy is in there. By the light of one of the wind-up lanterns he's doing something with the boxes on the bench and she stands very still until he has finished. He has on a baggy checked shirt and a pair of jeans as tightly, as awkwardly belted as her dress. The room is whitewashed, a small window just above head height. There's a desk with metal legs, a metal filing cabinet, a pair of tubular steel office chairs, a calendar for the year 2007 open at the month of December, a photograph of snow on the mountains.

'She's still sleeping,' says Jessica. 'Maybe she has a bad fever. Should we give her something?'

'Give what?'

The girl shrugs. 'An Advil?'

The boy laughs at her. 'Did you look in her bag?' he says.

3

Through the middle watches of the night, delirium flourishes. Old Rawlins is a regular visitor, slumped at the end of the bed like the night itself, a man lit only by stars but unmistakeable. He seems pleased to see her, though also distracted by what he calls tactics. His chest bubbles. He addresses her as Minnehaha, as he used to in the Nissen hut in the car park of the boys' school where they trained. He laughs to himself. Did I ever tell you about my dog? he asks. My dog, Lady? One, he says – sitting up in his tracksuit and coughing his way towards song – one is the loneliest number.

At another time she can hear her parents outside the door, a sharp to and fro of anxious whispers, and even, seeping from somewhere, the warm plasticky whiff of the laminating machine.

Other voices, speaking to her or about her. Bella saying, Anything at all. You need only ask. The woman from Human Resources saying, That would involve childcare for a very young baby.

The last voice is the man from the cutter in Falmouth, or that man transfigured to a grey-bearded Captain Slocum leaning over the stern rail of *Spray* and demanding, with terrible urgency, where she is headed. She does not have the breath to call back an answer . . .

She sleeps for a while but it's still dark when she wakes again. There's a blanket over her and she pushes it down to her waist. Her T-shirt is stuck to the skin between her breasts, her hair is damp on her forehead. She feels nauseous but does not think she will actually be sick. For long minutes the only thing that ties her to any sort of reality is the whine of a mosquito somewhere by the window. Then something joins it (as if out of the hollow wire of the insect's throat), a noise that makes her remember lying in bed as a girl in Swindon, those nights they were firing on the ranges, the rumble of artillery, bombs too, a drumroll that stood outside all other sounds – the night bus, a neighbour's television – not because it was loud when it reached her but because of what it was where it started out, a force that opened up the sides of hills. And here? Here perhaps it was thunder or some trick of the sea. She holds her breath, tilts her head, listening until it's impossible to know if she is still hearing it or if the sound now plays only inside her own head.

The next time she wakes, a bar of sunlight is simmering on the wall opposite the window. She sits up, spends half a minute wondering why she is not on the boat, and with a grunt of effort swings her legs out of the bed.

The wash bowl the boy brought in – yesterday? Two days ago? – is still beside the bed. She cups her hands to drink from it, then strips and crouches by the side of it to wash herself. As she can see no towel she dries herself with her T-shirt. The rash on her leg from the centipede has blistered – four, five little sacks of fluid.

The backs of both ankles are blistered raw. There are numerous fine cuts on her arms and legs and hands, though none look to be infected. She is, she considers, in better shape than she might have feared, though her ribs – as they remind her when she stands – can still stop her dead, make her gasp.

Draped at the end of the bed is a pile of clothes. She does not think they were there when she lay down. She picks through them. A nylon dress that she is neither tall enough nor wide enough to wear. A nylon slip, a white nylon blouse, a pair of tan slacks with a waistband that would circle two of her. The only wearable item is a shirt of heavy, faded blue cotton – a man's shirt, surely, and perhaps brought in by mistake, part of an armful carried from a wardrobe, some deep drawer. When she puts it on it hangs to just above her knees, but with the sleeves rolled up it's comfortable and cool.

She leaves the room (her feet are bare) and in the passageway pushes back the shutters of the window opposite the bedroom door. The view is over the building's landward side, and to the right, some hundred yards away, is a piece of walled-in ground, half an acre perhaps. Over the top of the wall she can make out tilled beds, low trees, trellises strung with climbing plants. Also the heads of three or four children, one of them with a pitchfork taller than he is, much taller, another with the blade of a machete resting on her shoulder like a broadsword. Beyond the garden is the shallow dome of a water cistern, and at the side of that, a line of palms, their trunks shaped by the onshore wind.

Leaning a little and looking the other way, she can see a single-storey building of mud and sticks, a clutch of hens investigating the dust around an open door, a young girl squatting in the building's shade, apparently in conversation with the cockerel. There's a flagpole where no flag is flying, some pieces of a dismantled tractor, and a track of red earth like the one she walked on that first night, heading in an almost perfectly straight line towards low, round-topped hills. There are no houses in the distance, no telegraph poles. Nothing like that.

She comes down the stairs and arrives in a large open room cross-lit by the light coming in through the arches, brighter on one side than the other. At the far end there's a long table and against the wall, rows of shelves where plates and cups give off the dull gleam of themselves. An animal she mistakes at first for a cat is scavenging on the floor – the packed earth – between the chairs. Noticing Maud, it trots to her on quick small feet, tail erect, and she can see it's some other kind of animal, the size of a cat, but looking more like a monkey or even a small, fur-covered pig.

She walks out through one of the archways and shades her eyes to look at the sea. There's a little boat coming in – blunt prow, dirty-white lateen sail. She's seen pictures of this kind of boat before, knows it as a craft peculiar to these coasts – a jangada. As it reaches the surf the lone sailor slips into the water and leads the boat like a horse, pulling it up onto the sand. She can see who it is now – the older boy who watched her from outside the church when she arrived. From a box on the deck (it's as much a raft as a boat) he lifts two large fish the colour of red coral. He whistles and she wonders for a moment if he's whistling to her but then a child comes sprinting past her, a boy who can be no more than five, his feet kicking up the sand in little spurts as he runs. He takes the fish, holds them with his hands through the gills. They look too heavy for him but he manages them, just, a grimace of concentration on his face. As he passes Maud he squints up at her then disappears with the fish along a path of sunlight between the church and the building with the arches.

Maud waits for the older boy to come closer. He must have

seen her, but he sets off along the edge of the beach and only once he has walked beyond the tree that grows where the sand gives way to the red earth does he turn away from the sea and towards the church. Maud takes the shorter line across the front of the church and meets him as he arrives at the steps of a trailer home. She was not expecting this – an oversized caravan parked on salt-whitened breeze-blocks along the far wall of the church. She stares at it, the plastic and metal flank of it much punished by the sun, then looks back at the boy and says, 'Do you speak English?'

'Of course,' he says.

He has on a T-shirt at least two sizes too small for him, his belly taut and brown between the shirt's hem and the waistband of his shorts. His forearms glitter with fish scales.

'I came on a boat,' she says. 'I lost the mast in a storm. I left the boat along the coast here.' She points in what she hopes is the right direction. 'Have you seen it?'

'No,' he says. His eyes keep flickering over the shirt she is wearing. Something about it obviously disturbs him.

'It's red,' she says. 'A red boat.'

He nods and turns to go up the steps to the door.

'Will you look for it?'

He nods again.

'What is this place?' she asks.

'The Ark,' he says.

'The Ark?'

'Yes.'

'Who looks after the children?'

'They are not here now,' he says.

'When will they be back?'

He shrugs. 'Soon.'

'Today?'

'Soon,' he says, and turns away, opens the trailer door and goes inside.

She stands there a moment examining the trailer, the yellowed sticker above the door that reads, *The Ten Commandments are not multiple choice*. She cannot tell if the boy is shy or for some reason angry with her. She turns and looks down the beach to where his boat is drawn up. If she took it now and sailed it along the coast would she find *Lodestar*? And if she did, what then? Despite the damage (not all of which might be obvious and visible) she still believes the yacht could be salvaged, that a well-equipped yard and several weeks of work could make it sound again. There is, of course, the question of cost, of how this hypothetical yard would be paid. She does not think she has more than a thousand or two in her account, even if she could find a way of accessing her account (this place where she has not yet found a farm, let alone a bank).

She walks to the door of the church and slips inside. It's cool as evening in there and as dark. What little light there is – the light from the door and from the shuttered windows above – lies in shallow pools on the tiles of the floor and in frail, trembling grids on the grey walls. There are no pews, just a dozen chairs that look to have come from an old schoolroom, gathered in a semi-circle below the pulpit. The pulpit itself is some tight-grained wood riddled with wormholes and something about its appearance suggests to Maud the timbers of a ship, and that it was, conceivably, once part of a ship and cut away by people who dismantled their vessel on arriving, who did not intend to return anywhere.

She moves around the walls squinting at memorial tablets. The earliest she can find is from 1658, the latest 1780. Ribbons of faded Latin; some imagery, including what seems to be a whale.

The Portuguese names are like tables laid with too much silver. Other names look as if they might have belonged to servants or slaves. Nearly all of them – slaves and masters – appear to have died young.

Outside again, she walks to the tree. It's a mango tree, a pair of macaws in the head of it helping themselves to the fruit. She watches them, and they tilt their yellow faces to watch her as they eat. Then she curls up in the shade of the tree and sleeps. When she wakes, the older girl is sitting beside her.

'You just sleep and sleep and sleep,' says the girl. 'You're the most tired person I ever met.'

First, they clear up the question of her name, so that the girl learns to say Maud rather than Moor. Then the girl tells Maud where they are, though it seems to Maud the girl's geography is a kind of hearsay, and that she carries no clear map of things in her head. She wants to know about Maud and Maud tells her about the boat, the voyage, the storm, her landfall on the coast. All of it, it turns out, can live in a score of simple sentences.

'I talked to the boy,' says Maud. She points towards the trailer.

'Theo,' says Jessica.

'He said the people who look after you are away. That they are not here.'

'Pa,' she says. 'He means Pa.'

'Pa? Your father?'

'He was Pa for all of us.'

'Where has he gone?'

The girl shrugs. 'Maybe Huntsville?'

'Where?'

'Huntsville, Alabama.'

'Pa's American?'

'There was Ma too,' says the girl. 'But she passed.'

'She died?'

'Yes.'

'And Pa went away?'

'You're wearing his shirt,' says the girl.

'Is that Ma's dress?'

'Yes,' says the girl, looking down at herself and lightly touching the material.

'The boy,' says Maud, 'Theo. He said Pa would be back soon.'

'Oh yes,' says the girl. She smiles. 'He will.'

'Do you have a phone here?'

'Pa has the phone.'

'He took it with him?'

The girl nods, grins. 'Pa can make anything,' she says. 'Pa will fix up your boat.'

'Was it Pa who taught you to speak English?'

'Pa and Ma.'

'How long have you been here?'

'Oh, a long time,' says the girl.

'And Theo?'

'Yes,' says the girl. 'And Theo. Since babies. Since little babies.'

At the Ark, the day's main meal is in the late afternoon, the last full hour of light, and for the first time Maud sees all the children together. They gather at the ringing of a goat bell and take their places at the table between the arches. There are fourteen of them, the youngest a boy of four. Each child seems to know his or her place.

Maud is sitting next to the older girl at one end of the table. The boy, Theo, sits at the other end. When he arrives, walking quietly through the end archway, appearing to them as if sinking – calmly, a philosopher – from the world of light (the beach) to their world of shade and shadow, the children become hushed and respectful. The food has been cooking for the last hour on a brick-built griddle at the back of the building. The fish, their pink skins charred, are brought to the table and divided up, quickly and neatly, by Jessica. There's sweetcorn and sweet potato, bowls of rice, a chewy, unsalted flatbread, a salad of leaves (a type of spinach?).

Before anyone starts their food they bow their heads while Theo says grace. 'Heavenly Father we thank you for this food we are about to receive for the nourishment of our bodies. Please cleanse it from impurity in Jesus' name.'

The little animal is present, the one Maud mistook for a cat and which Jessica now tells her is called a coati. Theo shoos it from the table then throws it a piece of sweet potato, which the animal eats, turning the food in the dirt with its sensitive-looking snout. Throughout the meal the children stare at Maud for as long as they dare. Beyond the arches the building's shadow stretches towards the beach. No one comes, no one goes.

After the cooked food there is fruit – mangoes, and something that looks like red bananas and may be, in fact, bananas. Then Jessica leaves the table, and after a theatrical pause, a shy grin at Maud, she pulls up by a rope ring a trap door in the floor, descends with a wind-up LED lantern and returns two minutes later with a biscuit barrel. Each child is given a biscuit – a charcoal-black Oreo – then the barrel is closed and returned to whatever place it has below the floor. A second grace ends the meal. The children carry their plates to a metal tub into which Jessica pours water from a pan that has been heating on the embers of the griddle. Each child washes his own plate, cup, fork and spoon. Three children – Leah is one – have cloths and are in charge of drying. Two others carry the clean things to the shelves where Jessica oversees the stacking. No instructions are given; all of them clearly know what is expected of them. By the time they have finished, all that is left of the light is a narrow band of paler blue at the horizon.

With the work done, Jessica places a chair over the trap door, winds up the lantern, sits and places the lantern on the floor in front of her. This is a signal. The children, like a flock of sparrows, settle at her feet, the faces of those at the front etched with light, while those further back are almost hidden.

She begins a story – Jonah and the whale. She tells the story in English, though now and then some word of Portuguese or some brief aside in that language is added. Maud, whose knowledge of the Bible is like her knowledge of certain cities – accurate and even detailed for small areas, entirely vague for the rest – is unsure if the girl is telling the story as it is written or some more private version of it. She leans against the end of the table, and at the point where the whale vomits Jonah onto the shore she looks through one of the arches to the beach and sees the glow of a cigarette. For several seconds she assumes it must be Pa, that he has made his expected return. Then the ember arcs into the sea and she sees the boy's silhouette slouching towards the church or the trailer.

The story ends. The children are readied for bed or ready themselves, trooping off in small groups to the lean-to latrines beside the garden wall or wiping their faces with makeshift squares of cloth, cleaning their teeth with small brushes. To Maud, Jessica says, 'Every night I tell them a story but they've heard all of them many times. Do you know stories, Maud? Maybe one night you could tell the story?'

She invites Maud to see the children in bed, and together – Jessica holding the lantern – they go in and out of the rooms off the corridor where the children are lying in metal-frame beds, four or five to a room, the younger children mixed in with the older. They look up at the light, at the girl, at Maud. Some of them have tattered soft toys in their arms. Some call out their goodnight in English. One boy, as Maud passes his bed, shouts, 'Goodbye Mama!' and immediately pulls the sheet over his face.

When they come downstairs again, Maud asks Jessica where she will sleep and the girl says she's in the trailer now and that Maud can use her room as long as she wants. It can be her room now.

'Does Theo sleep in the trailer?' asks Maud.

'The trailer's big. We got plenty of room.'

'That was Ma and Pa's trailer?'

'Pa drove it down one year. All the way from Huntsville.'

The lamp is drawing in a haze of insects. Some with their white wings look like the ghosts of themselves, others seem whimsical, balletic. The girl shows Maud where the lamps are kept, hanging from nails between two of the arches. She turns off the lamp, and for a moment they are invisible to each other, then the white walls of the building begin to glow and with a quick goodnight and the merest touch of her fingers on Maud's forearm, the girl takes her leave.

Maud goes out the other way, towards the latrines. All around her on the path, the slow zig-zagging, the green light of fireflies. The latrine has four cubicles with doors like the swing doors to an old Western bar. There are drifting green lights inside the cubicles too. The toilets themselves – it has already been proudly explained to her – are compostable, the dried humus used in the garden.

When she comes out she can hear a dull ringing from the jostling of the goats, though she does not know where they are penned and cannot see them. She looks along the path, wonders what would happen and where she would reach if she followed it towards those hills that are nothing now but a starless dark beneath a dark pitted with stars. She has seen no maps at the Ark. Perhaps there are none, or the maps travel with the man, with Pa.

She walks back through the fireflies, past the hen house, through an archway. She feels her way to the water container, drinks the water that tastes of iron, rubs at her teeth with a finger, then goes up the worn wooden edges of the stairs to her room. She does not take off the man's shirt but slides under the blanket still wearing it and drifts into a dreamless sleep, only to be woken, minutes later, by a child crying in the room next to hers. A voice speaks over the crying, a fierce whispering until the crying stops. After that, nothing but the small sounds of the ocean.

In the morning she is again the last to rise. It seems strange that so many children have passed her door without waking her. Are they under instructions to pass voiceless on bare feet so that the stranger, the sleeping woman (this woman who has, they might imagine, walked out of the sea in fulfilment of a prophesy none of them even knew about) can wake in her own time?

Downstairs, she finds the trap door open and looks down to see a flight of metal steps such as you might find leading to the engine room on a ship. The older girl appears in a pool of light at the bottom, and though the steps are steep she comes up them nimbly, the wind-up lantern in one hand, a large saucepan of rice grains in the other.

'You want to see?' she asks. She puts the saucepan on the end of the table and climbs back down with Maud following her. The space below is larger than Maud had pictured it, some fifteen feet by ten, and high enough for someone taller than either of them to stand upright. She thinks immediately of the treasure room at the Rathbones' – an odd, dislocating thought that seems to spread her hair-thin across the whole Atlantic – though on the shelves here, in place of watercolours and African masks there are rows of tins, of packets, labelled boxes. She follows the lantern – Hershey's cocoa, California olives, red bean gumbo, instant grits, pancake mix, Oreo biscuits, SpaghettiOs. There are even cigarettes, four cartons of Lucky Strike, three of them still in their paper wrapping, the fourth half empty. At the end of the room are bins of rice, dried beans, flour, demijohns of maize oil, red palm oil. None of these are full – none of the shelves are full – but even without the walled garden and the fish the boy catches, there is enough food here to last the children many months.

Between the bins, a door opens to a second room. Drums of whitewash, loops of cable, hand saws, drill-bits. Also, exercise books, boxes of coloured chalk, of pencils. Against the far wall there's a generator with wires hanging like pale roots from the ceiling above it. Maud lifts one of the steel jerrycans.

'No gas,' says Jessica. 'No gas for a long time.'

On a shelf beside the generator there's a small machine of some type half hidden under a drape of black velvet. When Maud raises the cloth she sees that it's a film projector, a Bell & Howell super 8 that looks to have been well cared for, its glass and steel parts gleaming with a medical brightness.

'Oh, we have movies,' says the girl, and she points with the light to a pile of slim boxes on the shelf above the projector. 'We miss them.'

They climb back into the upper air. The coati is waiting for them. It sniffs them, observes them with sad, gum-coloured eyes. Jessica closes the trap door, locks it with a combination padlock, the shank threaded through a stout U bolt.

'You want me to tell you the number?' she asks.

'I don't need to know it,' says Maud.

For a moment the girl looks crestfallen, unexpectedly checked. Then she brightens. 'The children will eat something now. Us too. Then we have school time. You want to teach the children a lesson?'

'A lesson?'

'Yes. School time.'

'What should I teach them?'

The girl laughs. 'You're an adult. You know lots of things.'

'Do they all understand English?'

'Some more, some less.'

'Ma and Pa taught them.'

'Then me and Theo.'

'What happened to Ma?'

The girl shrugs. 'Snake bit her.'

'A snake?'

'Pa's bit three, four times and never even gone to the doctor.'

'Did Ma go to the doctor?'

'There are no doctors here, Maud.'

'Is she buried here? Her grave?'

The girl points through the middle arch and out along the path. 'Pa chose the place. Worked all night making a box for her. He said her dying like that didn't mean he was wrong about things.'

'What things?' asks Maud.

'Oh,' says Jessica, picking up the goat bell with hands, ringless like Maud's, that seem to belong to a fully grown woman, 'about everything, I guess.'

After they have eaten they gather in the shade of the mango tree. Maud has her back to the trunk, the children sit in a fan around

287

her, all except for two boys whose absence is not explained, and Theo who is out in the boat. She teaches them how a body breathes, how the lungs are like bags filled with little structures like the roots of a plant, how oxygen travels in the blood pumped by the heart, how the air we breathe out is different from the air we breathe in. She teaches them that a tree like the mango also does a kind of breathing and that the energy of the sun makes this possible. At one moment – sliding into some state parallel to sleep – she hears herself talking about plasma membranes, and looks at the children only to find them listening to her as if she were telling them about Goldilocks and the bears. She talks for twenty minutes. At the end, Jessica claps and the children join in.

'You're a good teacher,' says Jessica when the younger children have scattered.

'I've never taught children before,' says Maud.

'A real good teacher,' says the girl.

'Thank you,' says Maud.

'You want to do it again tomorrow?' asks the girl.

In the afternoon Maud finds the children who missed her class on breathing. She has been walking – first along the beach in the direction she had not taken before, then inland, through sharp-edged grasses and the remnant of some long-disappeared settlement, the keels of ruined houses, the outline of what might have been a street. After walking the best part of an hour she comes to the church again, the back of the church, where she sees, propped against the wall, a hutch or pen with a sloping metal roof and two wood-frame doors covered in chicken wire. She goes up to see what kind of animal is kept here, and finds the children, boys of about eight who she remembers from the previous evening's meal. She does not know their names. One is a black boy with a bounce of ginger hair. One is paler, naked apart from a pair of pants or swimming trunks. When she crouches in front of the chicken wire she can see how the whites of his eyes are pink, the eyelids raw.

'Why are you here?' she asks but gets no answer. On their cheeks, through the dirt on their cheeks, there are tear stains, though long since dry. They look at her with expressions beyond resentment or fear. They are like machines turned to their lowest setting.

The doors are held in place by small steel bolts. Maud draws the bolts and opens the doors. 'You can go,' she says, but neither boy moves. 'It's OK,' she tells them, and thinking it's her being there that stops them coming out she straightens up and walks around the far side of the church, passes the trailer home and goes down to the mango tree in time to see the jangada riding up to the beach on the smallest of breezes, and the boy, who may or may not have noticed her under the tree, stepping down into the surf.

At the evening meal, he does not join them. Jessica says grace. The children are unsettled, uneasy. Throughout the meal they look at Jessica, look at Maud, look later at the embers on the beach.

'He's mad,' says Jessica to Maud when the children are in bed. 'Someone opened the forno.'

'The forno?'

'Behind the church. When the children are bad.'

'I opened it,' says Maud.

Jessica nods. 'I know.'

'One of the boys has an eye infection,' says Maud. 'Do you have eye-drops?'

The girl shrugs. 'Pa says the best medicine is prayer from a pure heart.'

'He needs to keep it clean,' says Maud.

'Jesus heals,' says the girl, though she seems to be listening.

They walk outside together. A warm muggy night, starless and very dark.

'I'd like to smoke,' says Maud. 'Can I have some of the cigarettes from the store room?'

'The store room?'

'Where you keep the food.'

'Oh, sure,' says Jessica. She sounds pleased. 'I'll go get them.'

Maud walks towards the sea, the sound of the sea. When she sees the grey edge of it sliding towards her she takes off the shirt, takes off her pants, makes a bundle of them and puts them down where the sand is dry. Her body is a poor light she follows into the water. She has to walk a long way before the sea covers the tops of her hips and she can lean in and start to swim. Though her ribs ache as she pulls – the muscles on that side feel shortened, tight – she keeps it up for fifteen minutes, then stops, floats onto her back looking up into the black mirror of the sky, her hands pooling the water.

She has slept many hours since she came here, to this house of children, but she is tired still with a tiredness she has begun to suspect she will never quite be free of now; a weakness, like a withered arm or palsied foot she will have to find some way of going on with. And she supposes that she will find a way – for isn't that what she does? The thing that marks her out as her? Strange then, this sudden longing for stillness, for surrender, for letting this swell that gently lifts her up and drops her down, keep her.

Who or what has ever held her as the sea does?

Her parents must have held her when she was small. Held her, sang to her even. And she has a memory of Grandfather Ray, something retained not as a picture but a loose knot of sensations – the rise and fall of his big smoker's chest, the heat flooding up from the gas fire, drugging them both . . .

Tim, of course, and she had liked that and not questioned it, though it was only really restful a dozen times or so somewhere near the beginning, those occasions when they had not wanted anything from each other beyond bare presence.

The last person to hold her was the crane driver (whose name she cannot remember). The thump of his heart, the thump of hers. Those minutes that could not be kept entirely free of tenderness.

Is that a lot? Is that what others can remember, more or less? She doesn't know, has no idea. It is, she thinks, the sort of question she would have to ask Professor Kimber, who would laugh at her and sit her down and say, 'Maud, dear Maud, let's go through this step by step . . .'

And she is thinking of Professor Kimber, the pretty shoes on the big feet, the silk camellia she sometimes wore in her hair even to work, when she hears, not far away from her – though it's difficult to judge – the water moving, some sound not made by the sea itself, and her head empties out and her whole being becomes a kind of arrow. She lets her feet drop and tries to see what's there. She knows that sharks hunt at night, that there must be sharks off this piece of coast, but on *Lodestar* she developed a feeling for them, their presence, and would often look up a second or two before they showed themselves. She does not think it's a shark nearby. A turtle? Wrong season. A dolphin then, or some big fish, a marlin or tuna, come to investigate what manner of creature is out here in the dark with it.

She can feel herself standing in a current of cooler water she imagines running parallel to the shore but the shore itself is invisible – utter darkness both ways – and she is no longer confident of the direction she is facing. If she struck out now she might be swimming further and further away from the land, a mistake not understood until it was too late.

And there, again, the movement – a swirling she both hears and feels – a tremor like the flick of a big tail, and she prepares herself for some manner of contact, turning and turning, not wanting to have her back to whatever is with her. Her heart rate is up but there's no panic, not yet. If it wanted to attack her she thinks it would have done so without announcing itself, and she has a series of compressed, possibly confused thoughts, one of which is that this life circling her own is lonely.

Then, from far off, she hears her name called, the sound of it coming to her like one of those birds that fly so low over the water the tips of their wings seem to touch the waves with each beat. A fragile spark of light appears, growing stronger as the lantern is wound. She starts to swim, wondering if she has left it too late, if she has the strength to get back. Then she finds the strength and burrows through the water, its dense black grain, until at last she sees the lines of surf, untethered in the dark, and her feet brush against the ridged sand. The first time she tries to stand she falls and the surf breaks over her head. She tries again, steadies herself, looks over her shoulder at the sea and walks up onto dry sand.

'Maud?'

'Yes.'

'Oh, Maud, I was scared.'

'I wanted to swim.'

They look for her clothes with the lantern, find them. Jessica casts shy glances at Maud's nakedness, then runs to one of the archways and comes back with a towel. Maud dries herself and dresses. They walk up the beach together, sit down where the sand is soft and still warm. They sit side by side. The lantern is off now, now that Maud has been found. Jessica gives her the pack of cigarettes and Maud strips off the cellophane, takes one out. Jessica lights it for her with a match – a quick blue flaring, their blue faces anonymous as masks.

'Are these Pa's cigarettes?'

'Yes.'

'The cigarettes Theo smokes?'

'Yes.'

'Will he be angry?'

'Pa?'

'Theo.'

'Theo's always angry. He's angry since Pa went away.'

The chill from the swim is slowly wearing off. Blue smoke from the cigarette floats just above their heads. There's no breeze to blow it away.

'Maud?'

'What?'

'Can I ask something?'

'If you want.'

'Why do you wear the thing around your neck? It belongs to a child.'

'Yes.'

'To your child?'

'Yes.'

'A girl.'

'Yes.'

'Maud?'

'What?'

'Has she passed?' Something in the girl's voice here. Kindness, yes – but something else, something alert and sinuous.

'Yes. She's passed.'

'I can tell things like that.'

'Yes.'

'Are you angry with me?'

'No.'

'What was her name?'

'Zoe.'

'Zoe?'

'Yes, Zoe.'

'And is that why you were on the boat on your own?'

'That was part of it.'

'Because you were sad?'

'Yes.'

'Maud?'

'What?'

'What happened to her? To Zoe?'

'She was in an accident.'

'You were with her?'

'No.'

'She was alone?'

'Her father was with her.'

'Has he passed too?'

'No.'

'Didn't he want to come on the boat with you?'

'No.'

'How old was she, Maud? When she passed?'

'Six.'

'You must think about her all the time.'

'Not all the time.'

'You dream about her?'

'Sometimes.'

'Maud?'

'What?'

'You ever feel she's reaching out for you?'

'Reaching out? How can she reach out?'

'Well, you ever see her, Maud?'

'No.'

'You ever think you *hear* her?' The girl waits. She's not a fool, did not spend nine years of her life with Ma (Ma's ways, Ma's games) and end up a fool. She listens for a catch in Maud's breathing, for the cigarette to tumble to the sand, for something. When none of this happens she says, 'If Pa was here he would help you.'

'Help me?'

'He would know how to help you.'

'How would he help me?'

'Maud?'

'What?'

'Maybe I can help you?'

'I don't need you to help me.'

'I'd really like to help you, Maud.'

'It's too late for help.'

'No,' says the girl, emphatically. 'No, you just have to want it. Don't you want it?'

For a minute, as if they have forgotten whose turn it is to speak, they are silent. Then, out of the dark, comes a sudden breeze. 'Rain wind,' says Maud, lifting her face to it, and almost before the words are out, it begins, fat drops, just a scattering, striking the sand around them. One breaks on Maud's cheek, one on her knee. As they get to their feet the rain begins in earnest – black sheets chasing them up the beach as they run, drumming on their skulls, blinding them.

The girl and the boy are not lovers, though Ma and Pa used to joke about it. They have not kissed, would never think of letting the other see them naked. So the boy is troubled and does not know what to think when Jessica sits on his bed in the dark and leans over him, rain dripping from her hair onto his face, her hair smelling of rain, and her face so close he feels her breath on his skin.

'What?' he says. '*O que você quer?*'

'The woman,' she says.

'She's gone?'

'Where could she go?'

'Then what?'

'I think she's here for a reason. A purpose.'

'What purpose?'

'I don't know,' says the girl, 'but maybe it's a test for us.'

4

The only sign of the rain on the following day is a speckling of flowers, some of them appearing out of cracks in the ground or from the mouth of a stone-coloured pod – something, the previous day, you took for dead. The sea has shifted its blue a little, and from the window of her room (water pooled on the floor beside the table) Maud guesses that offshore, beyond the bay, a big swell is running. The air is fresh, cool, but by the early afternoon the heat is back, the flowers wilt, and those woody fists that broke open to show intemperate colour have sealed themselves again.

Today, under the mango tree, Maud teaches Evolution. 'Think of two birds,' she says. 'They both want to eat the same food but one bird has a beak' – she makes the shape with her hand – 'that is good for eating the food, while the other has a beak with a different shape that's not so good. The bird with the good beak grows stronger. The children of that bird are bigger. It has more children, and most of those children have the good beak too.

'Everything changes,' she says. 'Everything is moving very slowly from one state to another, one condition to another. Birds, mountains, rivers. People like us. Like you. Like me. Very slowly . . .'

She mentions Darwin's name and when she has finished the lesson Jessica smiles at her and says, 'Devil Darwin. Pa told us about *him*.'

Neither of them speaks of their night on the beach. In the afternoon Maud helps Jessica prepare the evening meal. They walk up to the walled garden together. The rain has washed the dust from the leaves of the plants. They pick sweetcorn, tomatoes, cassava, gourds. They light the griddle, boil water, start to cook. Later, they lay up the table with forks and spoons and cups and plates. They put out the precious bowl of salt. They make loaves of flatbread with flour from the store cellar. They talk a little as they work, mostly about the characters of the younger children, about Pa's prodigious skill of fixing up, the way a screwdriver looked small as a pin in his hand. It's sisterly, easy enough, entirely sane. Now and then Maud leans against one of the arches to smoke, whole minutes in which nothing urgent needs to be achieved. When they are ready, Jessica offers Maud the goat bell. She rings it and the children appear as if out of the day's slowly cooling crevices. They gather, they circle around Jessica. The bolder ones come up to Maud. They say, 'Hello, how are you?' then scatter before she can answer.

They sit at the table. The food smells wonderful – smells like the kind of food she sometimes dreamt of on the boat. The coati is under the table; some of the hens wander in and two of the girls get down to harry the birds back to the coop where someone has forgotten to close the door. They are waiting for Theo. They look out through the arches, the empty beach, and Jessica is about to send one of the children running to the trailer to fetch him when he comes into view, Theo, or some version of him, sauntering along the beach parallel to the building, the arches, the table, then turning and walking towards them. It's a game, a piece of theatre. He is wearing a suit, a dark suit – a black one, in fact. A black suit with a white shirt underneath (bare brown feet below). Unlike everything else Maud has seen him wear the suit seems to fit him perfectly. A black suit. A tuxedo with satin lapels. He stops at the end of the table. He does not sit down. He looks at them all. The children are silent, Jessica is silent. He looks very briefly at Maud as if (what is he? Fourteen?) she has not yet earned it, the weight of his regard. Then he reaches into the right pocket of the jacket, brings out a spilling fist and flings red petals into the air above the table, red petals that shimmer down, one of them landing, like some fat splash of blood from an upstairs murder, on the back of Maud's wrist.

Next morning she waits on the beach while he drags the jangada down into the surf, then she wades into the water and climbs onto the boards with him. It takes her a few minutes to become used to the boat's skittishness, then they sit together, hunkered down side by side (the boy back in his usual clothes), as the church, the house with the arches, the figures on the beach, lose all particularity and are folded into a landscape. The boy does not talk, or no more than a few words. He has his fishing gear with him and perhaps later he'll fish. They have also brought the two steel jerrycans from the store cellar, and these give off a tired though undispersible whiff of fuel.

It takes less than two hours to reach *Lodestar*. Her route away from it – that march along the red track and through the forest – must, viewed from above, look like a tangled thread and not at all the line, the almost straight line, she thought she was walking. The yacht has shifted a little, dragged its anchor some eighty yards across the face of the bay but looks, at a distance at least, much the same as when she abandoned it – a vessel carrying its history, a vessel that seems to have been shot at, but still recognizable as the boat that made her stop that day in the yard with Camille.

A pair of large white birds are sitting on the coach-house roof and only take to the air once the jangada comes alongside. Maud pulls herself onto the deck, takes the jangada's line and ties it to a cleat. The boy, in a single neat movement, climbs onto the deck behind her.

When she goes below there is water up to the level of the benches. Has the boat, technically, sunk?

She goes down, splashes about. She flicks on the VHF – more life in a stone. She picks Captain Slocum's journal out of the water, puts it on the chart table. She can hear the boy in the cockpit rummaging in the lockers there.

Her sleeping bag is still in the quarter berth. She hauls it out and hangs it over the companionway steps; it might be useful. She finds some of her clothes and puts these up with the sleeping bag; finds – floating like the last remark of some urbane and drowned man – the straw sun hat. In a drawstring PVC bag in the heads are two bottles of wide-spectrum antibiotics and an antibiotic cream, together with a hundred US dollars rolled tightly in cling film that she had completely forgotten about. She searches for her mobile phone adaptor but cannot find it. There is no trace of the suitcase that was in the cockpit, nor of any of its contents. She does not ask about it. It's the boy's prize for finding the boat.

They bring the jerrycans up from the jangada. Maud finds the fuel-cap key hanging in its not very secure or secret place in the starboard cockpit locker. In the same locker are oddments of hose. One length of hose will carry the fuel; a second, slipped into the tank alongside it, is to blow down to start the fuel running without swallowing a mouthful of diesel. They fill both cans and lower them onto the jangada along with the other things Maud has pushed inside the sleeping bag, then cast off and sail back. With the fuel on board it takes both of them to draw the boat up onto the beach. They unload; the children touch the sleeping bag, the soaked book, the clothes, even the old sun hat that has dried on Maud's head on the sail back.

They have been out for half the day. Maud – as usual now after any exertion – finds herself reaching for reserves of energy she has not yet recovered, and after eating she goes upstairs to sleep for an hour. When she comes down again the trap door is open and she descends the metal steps and goes through to the second room where the boy, lit by two of the wind-up lanterns and stripped to the waist, is looking furiously at the generator, both fists balled in frustration.

'It won't work,' he says. 'It has the gas and it won't work.'

There's a blue metal tool box beside the generator (one of those that you open like a mechanical mouth, and in the act of opening, on either side of the box, a series of hinged drawers appear). Maud gets on her knees in front of the generator. Some manner of albino lizard scurries away between the film projector and the wall. If the generator was run until it was empty there is almost certainly air in the fuel pipes. She works her way along the black rubber tubing, loosens off clips and bleeds out air until the diesel seeps over her fingers. The boy is watching her, her or what she's doing. She has noticed already how much heat the boy gives off, how when you're close to him you feel it. She loosens the nut by the fuel injector, pushes the run/stop lever to run, turns the key and cranks the engine. Nothing wrong with the pump. She tightens the nut, finds in the tool box a folded rag, wipes up the fuel she has spilt. She takes one of the lanterns and runs its light over the engine then puts the light down, unscrews the electric fuel valve on top of the pump, sniffs it, decides it has probably burnt out and removes the plunger. She tells the boy what she is doing, explains the function of the valve, explains that from now on he will have to use the throttle lever to stop the generator. She turns the key again. The engine starts. The boy knows the rest of it. He hooks up the dangling wires. One of these powers the extractor fan (where does *that* come out?). When they speak they have to raise their voices though they do not need to shout. Jessica comes down. She's laughing with pleasure. They let it run for several minutes then Maud shuts it off and cleans her hands on the rag.

The children have heard the generator and most of them are there to witness Maud rising out of the ground, her dirty knees, her gas perfume, a speckling of fuel oil on her right arm, black as the lettering on her left.

Now that the Ark is electric again they long for darkness. Thirty litres in the fuel tank will give them forty hours of power, probably more. Maud takes her pack of Lucky Strikes onto the beach, sits cross-legged, lights up and looks at the horizon. The sound of the generator has started something in her. She thinks of the batteries on *Lodestar*. If they can be charged – or just one – then, in theory, the engine can be started, the boat pumped out, and she can limp along the coast until she reaches a port. And she's picturing this, picturing it while knowing full well the boat is going nowhere, that it needs a crane rather than a battery, when Jessica sits in the sand beside her and says, 'Tonight we're going to do something special. OK? We're going to do something for you.'

'If you want,' says Maud.

The girl puts her hand on Maud's shoulder and though Maud may be mistaken it feels like the girl is trembling. They look at each other; it's a little like the moment before a kiss, then the girl jumps up and runs back to where Theo is standing in one of the archways, half in, half out of the light.

They eat at the usual time. There are pancakes, biscuits, even some little rubbery sweets in the shape of simple objects like clocks and guns. Then Maud goes down to the store room with Theo and starts the generator. The projector has already been carried up, the screen also, unopened on its stand but in position by the bottom of the stairs. The projector bulb with its snapped filament has been replaced. The film has been chosen, wound on. The older children have seen it many times; the younger ones once or twice. They gather on the floor under the screen. Some find it impossible to sit still, and one boy, seized with the spirit, hops from foot to foot, his little shadow on the screen, a thing in itself, so that soon the others jump up to join him, dancing and watching their shadows dance, the wildness of it. Only when the screen bursts into colour do they sit down, holding hands, their mouths gaping. Below them the generator thrums; they can feel its vibrations through their sitting bones. On the screen now a night sky, a drawn sky – *Through the snow and sleet and hail, through the blizzard, through the gale, through the wind and through the rain, over mountain, over plain, through the blinding lightning flash and the mighty thunder crash, ever faithful, ever true, nothing stops him, he'll get through* . . .

Storks. Then a whole arkful of baby animals dropping by parachute. Dumbo's mother unwraps her package. Dumbo looks at his mother's feet then up, up, up, to her face . . . It is not just the young children who are watching this as if it were life itself unfolding in front of them. Theo and Jessica too are taut with attention, and even Maud, half sitting, half leaning against the end of the dining table, stares at the screen, the richness of the old film's colours unlocked by the light. Everything around the frame of the screen is flat, silent, nothing but a canvas backdrop. The children laugh. They shriek at the scenes of chaos, at the precariousness of everything, the speed, the hooting, the flames, the flights that always threaten to end in disaster. It is not a long film. When it ends the children want to watch it again, immediately. They are all crying out for it and Jessica is trying to explain that they must not use up the fuel in the generator watching *Dumbo* all night, and then, with no warning, there is something else on the screen, and the children fall silent. A man in a checked shirt is smiling at them. He has a cigarette in one hand and is talking, bantering, with the person filming who, talking back to him, turns out to be a woman. The man is in his forties perhaps, a heavy handsomeness, his hair thick, black as an old telephone, and swept back in a wave from his forehead. A rockabilly. A man you can imagine dancing and dancing well. He's in high good humour. The sound quality is poor and his accent heavy with the south but some of it carries clearly enough. 'Hey, Ginny, what shall we do in the dry?' And the woman answers, 'Blow away, I guess.' And the man says, 'Asses to asses, bust to bust,' and the woman, laughing, says, 'A-men to that,' and the man looks away at something out of view and his smile fades and you see how big his face is and how shadowed. Then it's over. The film flicks out of the gate. Theo turns off the motor, puts out the light. Maud takes one of the lanterns and goes down to the generator.

When the children are in bed, Maud swims again. There's a crescent moon, thin as the paring of a nail. She has a towel with her. She doesn't know where Theo and Jessica are, but she doesn't mind much who sees her. She makes a pile of her clothes and goes into the water. She doesn't swim far tonight. She's killing time, something like that. She swims towards the moon then swims away from it. There's no one on the beach when she comes out. She finds her clothes, her towel, dries herself, dresses in her shorts and a sweatshirt she brought from the boat and dried in the afternoon sun. She smokes a cigarette then starts up the beach towards the building with the arches. There are no lights in there, none she can see, and she has stepped into the building's greater dark when a hand grips her arm. She breaks free immediately. She knows it's the boy, can smell him, feel the heat of him.

'Jessica's in the church,' he says. 'She's waiting on you.'

For some seconds there's a silence between them, then she says, 'OK,' and walks out of the building, walks across to the church door, pulls it open and goes in. At the far end of the church a single candle is burning.

'Maud?'

'Yes.'

'Can you see?'

'Yes.'

She walks towards the candle. When she reaches Jessica, the girl takes her hand and leads her into the small room with the desk and chair, the little window, the calendar on the wall from December 2007.

'Sit here,' says the girl, pulling the chair away from the desk into the middle of the room. Maud sits. The girl puts the candle on the floor. She is wearing make-up. Maud has never seen her with make-up before. She looks excited. A girl on a date, a first date.

'Don't be afraid, Maud,' she says.

'I'm not,' says Maud.

'Didn't I say we would help you?'

'What are you going to do?' asks Maud.

'You only have to open your heart,' says the girl. 'Can you do that, Maud? Can you open your heart?'

Maud looks away from the girl to the boxes on the bench at the side of the room opposite the window. There are three of them, the size of foolscap box-files, each with a pattern of small holes in the top and each with a hasp and lock.

'Where's Theo?' asks Maud.

'He's coming,' says the girl.

'What's in those boxes?'

'Oh, Maud,' says the girl, 'I'm going to put this little light out now.' She squats and pinches the wick between her fingers. 'Think of your little girl, Maud. Think of her and open up your heart.'

'I'm going now,' says Maud. 'I'm going to go to bed.'

The girl fumbles for Maud's hands, clasps them. 'Wait,' she says. '*Please . . .*'

Very faintly at first, but so unexpectedly Maud makes a small, involuntary noise in her throat, the clear bulb hanging directly above their heads begins to glow. The boy has started the generator. The light grows brighter. A minute later the boy himself comes in, swiftly and softly, shuts the door behind him. He's wearing a clean checked shirt. It's not the one Pa was wearing in the piece of film they saw but one very like it. It hangs off him, his narrow, hard frame. 'You ready?' he says, perhaps to Jessica, perhaps to both of them.

He goes to one of the boxes (the young technician, the young master of ceremonies), quickly frees the lock then, more slowly, opens the lid, peeps inside, closes it again without locking it. He comes and stands at the side of Maud's chair, takes one of Jessica's hands, takes one of Maud's. He starts to pray. He's speaking in a rapid, low voice. The words spill over each other. The girl is staring at Maud, her face bright as morning. It's hard to look away from her.

The boy is working up to something. He's getting louder. Maud stands. It feels awkward to be sitting, foolish. She looks at them both, looks from one to the other, these children who have opened some secret cupboard and found things they ought not to have found. She should tell the girl to wash the make-up off her face. She should send them both to their beds. She does not understand why she has not already done it.

The bulb with its faultless skin fades and brightens; the room's shadows soften then grow hard again, hard-edged. The boy lets go of her hand. He goes to the box, he nods to himself, opens the box and reaches in. When his hand comes out it's wearing a living branch of snakes. Now, truly, they have her attention. The snakes, with their slender, triangular heads, look like vipers of some type. The boy pours them gently from hand to hand. He gazes at them, enraptured. All this is real enough. And she's heard of something like it, those little churches in the hand-written, misspelt far south of the United States, the stubborn descendants of slow readers, people Christ himself might have been uneasy about but understood and even admired. These are Pa's snakes or Pa's example or both. But who would have guessed the power of it, or these children's ability to channel it? The snakes move slowly, drowsily. The boy holds them up like a slow green fire. The girl is cooing. Whoever she was before, she's someone else now. Her face with its make-up (Ma's make-up?), its sheen of sweat, seems caught in a panic of happiness, some-thing urgent, bodily, ancestral. Maud has dreamt none of this, has had no convenient previsions. It turns out, however, that none of it is out of her range.

The boy holds out the snakes to her. She does not flinch but her breath does something odd – goes from shuttling in her throat to sinking like a glass rod to somewhere, some point in the knot of nerves between her legs. She takes the snakes from him, threads the fingers of both hands through their looping bodies. Cat's cradle, carding wool. The boy is moving like a figure in an old film. He is moving like a man with Parkinson's disease, a boy with Parkinson's disease. She holds the snakes. They are not heavy. How many are there? Five, six. Not easy to see where one ends and another begins. The girl touches her own breasts as if they're beginning to hurt her then puts her hands above Maud's head. Maud passes the snakes to the boy who brushes them against his forehead then carries them back to the box. The rest of it feels very private, though in some way the gibbering of the children makes it possible. She sits on the floor under the bulb and begins to cry. It breaks out of her, comes out of her in waves. Her eyes, her nose, her mouth. She speaks her child's name, mutters it thickly. Zoe, Zoe . . . The boy and girl are kneeling either side of her now. They are chattering and crowing, touching her shoulders, her head. All three of them are rocking, swaying. All three in a small boat adrift. And then it stops. For a moment Maud imagines the bulb has gone – blown – but it hasn't. The boy is standing. He's staring at her, clownish in his big shirt. The girl is also staring, though she is still on her knees and her expression is different. Maud looks down at herself. On the inside of one of her thighs there's a heavy web of blood; blood too through the cotton of her shorts, blood on the floor beneath her. She's shaky but she manages to stand up. She's never bled like this before. She goes to the door. She crosses the unlit body of the church, trips over a chair, bangs her knee, gets up, reaches the door to the outside and walks down to the sea, walks straight in until the sea is around her waist in a black skirt on which the moonlight shines like threads of silk.

5

In the night she hears again the sound like distant artillery. Hears it at the edge of the audible but is sure this time it is not thunder. When she wakes in the early morning she lies a long time looking at the light on the wall. She cries again, though without any violence, the tears following the creases at the corners of her eyes and finding their way down to her throat.

Before getting into bed she made a rag for herself by tearing the back out of one of her T-shirts. She looks at it now, looks to see if she has bled onto the sheet below her, then gets up, dresses in jeans (the denim stiff with salt but wearable) and goes down the stairs. She's very hungry and goes straight to the cupboard where, in tupperware boxes and old biscuit tins, any uneaten food from the main meal is kept. She eats cold roast vegetables, a piece of flatbread, three of the little plantains, two tomatoes. She goes out to the girl looking after the chickens to ask if she has any eggs and the girl gives her two, which Maud breaks and swallows raw. She sees Jessica coming down from the walled garden. The girl greets her with just a moment of unease. She looks somehow younger today and perhaps feels it.

'Where's Theo?' asks Maud.

'He's in the trailer.'

Maud goes to the trailer and knocks at the door until he opens it. He's just wearing shorts.

'Can you take me to the boat?'

He will not look at her, not directly.

'I'm tired,' he says.

'OK,' she says. She smiles at him but he is already turning away from her, closing the door.

She goes back to find Jessica and has her take the lock from the trap door. In the room below she tops up the fuel in the generator and takes an empty jerrycan down to the beach. She does not believe she will find the jangada hard to sail. She drags it into the surf, climbs in over the stern. The boat is steered with a rudder oar and there's no more to the rigging than a mainsheet but for the first twenty minutes she thinks she's made a mistake and has to reach back to skills learnt in her teens, the club days when she raced shallow-hulled Lasers and Fireballs on the Thames. Even so, the church is out of view before she starts to feel comfortable, to know where to put her weight, how to aim the sledge prow at the swell, how close to the wind she can go.

By the time she reaches *Lodestar* there's almost no wind at all. She brushes alongside the yacht, ties on and climbs aboard. She fills the jerrycan with diesel – there's still plenty in there – then goes below into the water. In the sliding-door cupboard in the heads she finds the tampons she took from the bathroom of the cottage, and pushing down her jeans (she's up to her knees in water) she unwraps one and makes use of it then and there, a side-glimpse of herself in the mirror, her face darker than her hair, the white line of the shock cord around her neck.

Back in the saloon she looks for what else she can take. As before, she makes a pile on the top step of the companionway, then packs the smaller items into a pair of canvas buckets and puts the rest into a sail bag. She collects the boat's title document, registration and insurance (all in a plastic file still above the waterline). The last thing she does is tear out an endpaper from the *Book of Landfalls* and with a pencil she finds floating between the benches and rubs dry until it functions, she writes a note that will serve as the final entry of the log she did not keep. *My name is Maud Stamp, joint owner of the yacht* Lodestar. *I set sail from Falmouth on the English coast at the end of May 2009, was dismasted in the mid-Atlantic and driven south by a storm . . .* It's a short account, at the end of which she writes Tim's phone number and the address of the Rathbone house. As an afterthought she also puts down Chris Totten's name and the address of the yard. She hangs the page from one of the brass hooks holding the curtain wire at the window above the chart table and is about to step through the companionway when she sees, below the framed photograph of the boat, a piece of buoyant light in the water and she wades over to it and lifts it. It's the bulb she picked out of the sea south of the Azores. General Electric, sixty watts, the glass skin undamaged, the filament unbroken. She turns it in her hands. She is almost afraid of it. She is also smiling at it, and for a moment she considers taking it with her – this object carrying its own improbable news – but she settles it onto the water again and climbs the companionway steps for the last time, drops in the washboards, and after tugging, hard, three, four times, drags shut the hatch on its runners.

The boy is waiting for her on the beach when she gets back. He runs into the surf to take hold of the boat, take possession of it. 'You must never take it!' he shouts. '*Isso não te pertence!*' Something strangled in his voice. He's close to tears.

'You were tired,' says Maud.

'It's not yours!' he shouts. He grabs one of the canvas buckets and flings it onto the beach, scattering the contents. Maud walks around the front of the boat to where he is standing. 'I'm sorry,' she says.

He stares at her, then looks down at his feet. 'It's not yours,' he mumbles.

She lifts the other bucket from the boards, lifts the sail bag, puts them on the sand and crouches to collect the contents of the spilt bucket. Some of the children have been drawn to the sound of shouting, and outside the door of the church Jessica is looking on. No one comes any closer – then one of the children breaks ranks and runs down the beach towards Maud. It's the boy with the bounce of ginger hair she found in the punishment box, the *forno*, at the back of the church. He flicks a nervous glance at Theo, then picks up one of the buckets and carries it behind Maud to the arches. Three other children carry the sail bag. It's like the head of a giant they have just watched slain.

There is no film that night. At the evening meal Jessica tells them they must save the gas. Next week perhaps they will watch another; it will depend on how good they are, how obedient. Theo says nothing other than the grace at the start of the meal. As soon as the meal has finished he leaves the table. The atmosphere is exactly that of a household where the parents have reached some impasse.

Maud, carrying one of the wind-up lanterns, goes to her room half an hour after the children are in bed. She did not accompany

Jessica on her rounds. She's tired, drained, restless. Has she become unused to bleeding? So much blood last night she half imagined a miscarriage. She undresses, puts on Pa's shirt that she now uses as a nightshirt and lies on top of the bed with Captain Slocum's journal. Most of the pages are stuck together and when she unsticks them they feel, between finger and thumb, like old fake money. She props the lantern at the head of the bed and reads paragraphs at random, moths touching the edges of her face with the edges of their wings. *After righting the dory for the fourth time, I finally succeeded by the utmost care in keeping her upright while I hauled myself into her and with one of the oars, which I had recovered, paddled to the shore, somewhat the worse for wear and pretty full of salt water . . .*

She settles the book on her chest, looks up at the ceiling where a house lizard is looking down at her. All there is, she thinks, is this, just this. This and nothing more.

The lantern, unwound, is growing dim, and she puts it on the floor, switches it off and has rolled beneath the thin blanket when she hears her door being quietly opened. She waits – it's too dark to see who's there – but when they do not speak she sits up and asks – with no great kindness in her voice – who it is.

'It's me,' says a small voice. A child's voice, a girl's.

'You want to see me?'

'Yes.'

Maud feels for the lantern, winds it, holds it up (as Captain Slocum might on a wilder night to see what rattled the dog-house door). It's Leah.

'Come in,' says Maud.

The girl comes in and behind her come two black girls, the twins, who helped Maud to stand that first day. They gather at the end of the bed while Maud looks at them and they look at her.

'Are you OK?' asks Maud. Leah nods.

'Did you have a bad dream?'

The girl shakes her head.

'Are you hungry?'

'No,' says Leah. 'No,' chime the girls behind her. (Everybody knows the word 'hungry'.)

Then Leah – perhaps prodded – comes around the end of the bed and stands directly in front of Maud, in front of her knees. Only now does Maud understand what they have come for. She opens her arms, the girl steps in and Maud holds her for some ten or fifteen seconds. After her comes one of the twins and in her turn, her sister. When it's over, and without another word, the three of them file out and the last carefully shuts the door.

This, then, becomes the pattern of Maud's nights. The tap on the door, the face of the boldest child leaning in. Three or four of them at a time, each one patiently waiting his or her turn to be held, then quietly leaving. She doesn't tell Jessica about it but somehow she finds out. 'So you're a mother now,' says Jessica, coming to sit next to Maud under the mango tree.

'I was a mother before,' says Maud.

'But now you're their mother.'

'No,' says Maud. 'They have their own mothers somewhere.'

There's a long silence between them. The girl rubs a piece of red earth between her fingers.

'You,' says Maud, 'you're like a mother to them.'

'When Pa comes back,' says the girl, kneeling up and grinning, 'maybe you can marry him.'

'Do you think he's coming back?' asks Maud, in whose head

has appeared, in all its weird detail, a picture of the car in the forest clearing.

'Sure,' says the girl. 'Why wouldn't he come back?'

That night she hears it again, those guns firing at the edge of sound. It wakes her and she lies listening to it for a while, then gets up and goes to where her watch is on the table. When she opens the shutters there's enough moonlight to see the dial, and though the time it shows is local to itself – she has seen no clocks at the Ark – she makes a mental note of it and goes back to bed.

In the morning she walks out with Leah and the goats. She asks her about the noise, thinks it unlikely the girl will know what she's talking about, but she nods immediately, looks at Maud and says, '*O trem.*'

'*Trem* . . . train?'

'Yes. Train.'

'Have you seen it?'

'One time. With Pa. He likes to walk at night when it is cool.'

'Is it a train that carries people?'

The girl points to the sky. 'On top,' she says.

'People on top of the train?'

She nods.

'And inside?'

She shakes her head.

'It passed last night,' says Maud. 'When will it come again?'

'Not tomorrow,' says the girl, nudging one of the goats with her stick. 'Not tomorrow tomorrow. Not the next tomorrow. The tomorrow after that.'

Maud holds up her hand, her fingers. 'Four days?'

'Four days,' agrees the girl.

* * *

For two of those days she's undecided. She's keeping an open mind, or that's what she tells herself. There are practical questions, of course, but she's Maud Stamp, and the practical holds no terrors for her. So what else? The children? The children were on their own for months before she arrived. And she cannot be certain Pa will *not* return, though she no longer wants to see him, the magician, the old dancer, the man whose shirt she has been sleeping in. There's food, water, shelter. Looked at from a certain point of view, their situation is enviable.

On the third day she puts on her trainers and walks up the path towards the hills. As she passes children – children working, children playing, children making work into a game and getting the work done – they stop to watch her and some run over to her and she spends a few moments talking to them before moving off. After fifteen minutes of walking the ground starts to rise. On either side of the path the land looks barren, though here and there some leathery succulent grows, or patches of silvery grass, or a cactus (one with a small white bird on its highest limb she mistook for a flower until the sound of her walking put it into flight).

Halfway up the hill she enters a belt of trees, their trunks no higher than her head but with large, intricate crowns of branches and tangling twigs where cicadas sing their tireless, mechanical song. Beyond the trees, she comes to the bare summit of the hill and climbs onto a cinnamon-coloured rock to look out over the country. No buildings, no herded animals, certainly no sun glinting off rails, just the low hills repeating themselves and rolling on towards the watery outline of bigger hills, mountains perhaps. She should have brought the Zeiss with her though she does not think she would see more than emptiness magnified.

She turns back, gets among the trees again by a different route, and there, at the base of a larger tree, one that rises above the others like a yellow fountain, she finds a wooden cross and a grave covered in patterns of fallen leaves. Carved into the wood of the cross, the lettering still sharp: *Ginny Plautz August 2 1967 – December 13 2007. A True follower of Signs.* She had known it was up here somewhere, the grave, but she was not looking for it, and to come across it like this, by chance, feels important in a way she could not easily explain. She sits beside it. She's tired and hot and the shade of the tree is welcome. And there is the sense of a meeting, overdue, with this woman whose presence has not quite ebbed away from the old buildings on the beach. Ginny Plautz, dead of a snake bite. Ginny Plautz not healed by Jesus or Pa or anyone. No way of knowing what kind of woman she was, what kind of guardian to the children. Maud has not even seen a picture of her, has nothing to go on other than her clothes, her voice on a clip of film, and cannot quite remember what she said. *'What shall we do in the dry?'* Or was it Pa who asked the question and Ginny who said something about blowing away? It would be good now to have her company, to sit here in the shade of the tree with her, talking in low voices, the sort of conversation Maud has had so rarely but now feels a sudden appetite for. Ginny Plautz might offer confidences about Pa (there would be many, surely). And Maud, when her turn came, would tell her things you cannot tell to children; tell her, for example, about that winter morning she drove through the rain to the Rathbones' house, Mrs Slad in the kitchen, Bella reading to Tim that book with the man and woman on the cover, dancing. And she would tell her about Tim's father waiting for her in the kitchen and leading her through to the little drawing room. The fire, the drinks table, the way the whisky burned her lips. And she would tell her what he said and before Ginny Plautz (the dead woman is her friend now) could cry,

'Why, the devil!' she would say that she did not think he was wrong, not entirely. Had she ever been interested in being a mother? In motherhood? Interested in the way the other mothers were or seemed to be? Was she not, in truth, perfectly content to let Tim be the one who fed Zoe, who bathed her, comforted her, knew which of her soft toys was her current favourite, knew which drawer her winter vests were in, knew when she was tired, when she had had enough? A bad mother, then. Or not a good one. And this perhaps should trouble her more than it does. A bad mother who worked long hours, who sailed, who liked to sail on her own, who liked to be on her own. The simple reason Tim was with Zoe that morning on the way to school was that he was with her most of the time, whereas she, her mother, was not. But about the rest of it, her being cold-blooded, unmoved, about that he knew nothing at all, and she would not let him knock her down a second time.

She lays a hand on the grave's wooden crosspiece, lets it rest there a moment, as you might on another's shoulder. Then she gets to her feet, looks down through the twisting avenues of trees. If you have a talent for surviving – as poor Ginny Plautz did not, as Pa, too, may not have done – it does not seem wrong to use it. Is it wrong?

Anyway, she'll use it.

In the room that night, after the children have visited, she goes through the things she brought from the boat, puts some of them – clothes, her phone, her passport, the boat's documents – into the green backpack, then lies awake a long time wondering if Leah's counting can be relied upon. In the morning she cuts up the sail bag and uses the cloth to make two parcels. Into one she puts the antibiotics, fifty American dollars (the other fifty is for herself), the last of the Fennidine with clear, careful instructions written on the side – how much and in what circumstances. Also, half a dozen tampons – nothing in the store rooms below to suggest Pa or Ma had thought that far ahead. In the other parcel she puts Captain Slocum's book, the tattered charts, the binoculars, her Green River sheath knife and two of the hand flares – then changes her mind and puts one of the flares into Jessica's parcel.

They watch another film that evening – *The Empire Strikes Back* – and though several yards of the film seem to be missing (at one point the soundtrack gives way to that of another film entirely – *Mutiny on the Bounty*?), the children cheer as if watching a football match and afterwards run on the beach, flinging themselves at each other, tumbling over each other in the sand.

It takes almost half an hour to round them all up but when the last of them has washed and the last boy, weary on his feet, has wandered back from the latrines, Maud goes up with Jessica to say goodnight, then says goodnight to the girl herself at the top of the stairs, a quick touching of hands in the dark, a dozen soft words. Ten minutes later, four children come in to be held – Jenna, Conner, Caleb and Faith. She holds them and they go. She checks the time, straps on her watch, lies on the bed, sleeps for an hour dreaming of a night sky thick with the migration of fabulous birds, the moon rippling on their wings as they pass. Then she gets up, changes into jeans, T-shirt and sweatshirt, though does not yet put on her trainers (what's left of them). She has been tempted to cut her hair again, cut it short, but instead she uses a strip from the sail bag, pulls her hair into her fist and binds it.

The parcels are under the bed. There's a T on one, a J on the other. She takes them downstairs, listens, then goes to the door of the church. The door does not open silently but she does not need to open it far. Once inside she turns on her torch and follows the beam the length of the nave to the room behind the altar. She imagines suddenly confronting the boy there but the room is empty.

On the bench the boxes are where she last saw them. She lifts them in turn. Two she can immediately feel are empty; the other is heavier, a weight that wakes in her hands. This one she sets on the floor and in its place puts the sail bag parcels, then grips her torch between her teeth, picks up the box and goes back to the church door where she stops, turns off the torch and slides it into one of the back pockets of her jeans. She has thought carefully about what she is going to do next. Her first instinct was to release the snakes but the thought of leaving behind a half-dozen pit vipers combined itself in her head with pictures of the children's bare feet. Nor could she carry them with her. Nor could she leave them in the little room – it's barely even a matter of conscience. Without Jessica the children might not survive. Without Jessica, Theo might simply follow the shade of Pa to wherever it is he thinks Pa has gone.

She carries the box down to the surf, walks out and sinks it in the water, holding it there until the weight of water running through the air holes is enough to anchor it to the sand. It only takes a minute, perhaps two.

In her room again, she sits a while, getting her breath. What's done is done. She looks at her watch, puts on her trainers. She is starting to tie the laces of the second shoe when the door opens and a figure slips inside. It's Leah. She's dressed. They had no arrangement, or perhaps the girl thought they did. Either way, Maud is pleased to see her. She puts on the backpack. Everything now is touch and whisper. They go down the stairs and out through the back of the building, past the chicken house, past the walled garden and the latrine. Leah has her stick in one hand; her other hand has hold of Maud. She guides her away from the track towards the shallow grey dome of the water cistern and the palm trees. The half-moon throws thin shadows from solitary trees, or from cacti or black rocks. They do not use the torch, nor do they speak much. Maud has water with her, some mangoes and biscuits, a piece of flatbread. Leah has brought her camouflage canteen, the one she held to Maud's lips the first time they met. The walking is not difficult. The ground is solid and true, though walking at night is never like walking in the day. The eyes change; the brain too, presumably. Some afternoon in her third year at Bristol, sitting in the library, Maud skimmed through a paper on it in a journal – *Cell*, perhaps, or *BioEssays* – and can remember things about cones and rods and photoreceptor proteins; can remember herself, too, sitting by the window with a view of afternoon clouds over office blocks and ancient churches, a young woman who sometimes disconcerted people though never tried to . . .

Leah stops. They don't seem to be anywhere.

'Here?' asks Maud.

The girl points. It looks at first – the metal smudged with moonlight – like rivulets of water, little streams, but it's the rails, a hundred yards away, running on a shallow bank between the open country and the rising ground beyond.

They sit in the dust and take a mouthful of water each, eat a biscuit. They wait; the moon glides; the train, of course, is not coming. It is impossible to even imagine a train. The girl rests her head against Maud's shoulder, then slides down to her lap and sleeps. Maud looks at her watch again. She did not really have a plan for the train failing to come and she cannot stay out here all night with the child. Another hour, an hour at most, and they will have to go back. She will have to face the boy's rage.

Then a new sound enters the world. The child opens her eyes and sits up. She leads Maud by the hand to the cover of a low, scrubby tree, a thing within a thin, twisted trunk as if its growing had been an agony. It's not clear to Maud which direction the train is coming from but Leah knows and is staring down the track – south? – for several seconds before the light appears. Everything now depends on the speed of the train, on whether Leah's memory of it (out here in the cool of the night with Pa) is a true memory, but from the way the light – a neat cone of yellow light – is creeping towards them it's clear that it is, as the child promised her, a train you can outrun.

But the noise of it! Rumbling, jangling, screeching. It's like an old world army on the march, a column of conquistadors with their siege towers and loot and tarnished armour. The light sweeps the dark before it, shows the land unreal, martian. They stay hidden by the trunk of the tree, watching, fascinated. Then Maud leans down to the girl and into her ear says, 'You want to come with me?' The girl shakes her head, says something in which Maud can only catch the word goats (in fact it sounds like 'ghosts'). Maud nods. It's too late for speaking now. She lifts the cord from around her neck, the hair clip, and puts it around the girl's neck.

The engine is almost level with them, a soft wash of light behind the double windscreen, a ten-second view of the driver sitting as if stunned in a dream. After the lead engine a second, pouring fumes through high vents. Then the first of the wagons, some painted white, some a darker colour, some with words on the side – ALBRAS, HANJIN, FMC Chemicals – some swirled with graffiti. And on top of the wagons, huddled as if at the top of a high wall, the shadows of people, scores of them, dark blue against the paling blue of the sky . . .

How many wagons have passed? Forty? Fifty? The base of the

wagons is at least four feet above the rails but all of them appear to have mounting steps and little ladders, a whole superstructure of handholds and footholds. A red glow, soft and somehow lovely, indicates the end of the train. Maud reaches round to touch Leah's hair, the warmth of her. Then she squats with the pack on her back, and when the red light draws its colour across her face she rises up and starts to run.

In truth, the girl does not see her climb aboard, not the actual moment when she must have leapt and seized hold of something, but the train, which took so long to arrive, takes only a few minutes to disappear, and when the lights have gone so has the woman. She calls her name, two or three times, but nothing comes back. The track is empty and the world has settled into silence again.

6

In the car park at the boatyard, Chris Totten and Robert Currey are standing either side of a cherry-red Honda. They lean, peer into the car, can see the other's blurred face through the opposite window. Robert Currey tries the door but it's locked of course. They walk around the car, change sides, peer in again as though, from a new perspective, they might see something helpful. Thirty yards away, a man in a yellow hard hat and hi-vis jacket is waving directions to the rear-view mirrors of a reversing concrete-mixing lorry. When the beeping stops you can hear the gulls again.

Recession has meant a scaling-back of the plans for the marina. The hotel will only have one restaurant and there is a new emphasis on conference facilities, but the money doesn't come from British banks or banks in Zurich or in America. It's money moving to a different music altogether, and stage one – the clearing of the ground – is underway and on schedule. A film of dust from the work has settled over the Honda. Notices have been left on the windscreen ordering the owner to move the car. The date mentioned on these notices has already passed. It's the only vehicle remaining in this part of the car park.

There's not much inside the car. A water bottle on the front seat, a road atlas on the back seat, and what looks like a little box of business cards on the rubber mat below. Next to the tax disc (only a month to run) is a pink and green parking permit for Croydon University Hospital.

'It can't stay here,' says Robert Currey, as both men slowly circle the car again.

'Nothing can stay here,' says Chris Totten. He's in a suit and has good shoes on, though the toes of the shoes are scuffed.

'I've got room at mine,' says Robert Currey. 'We'll just have to get it lifted.'

'To yours?'

'Yeah.'

'You've got room, then?'

'Yeah.'

'OK,' says Chris Totten, bending down for one more look – that bare, that unremarkable interior. 'Sounds like a plan.' They step back from the car. The lorry is reversing again. This is the future.

'See you at close of day,' says Chris Totten, his voice smothered by the beeping. Then both men turn their backs on the car and walk towards the water. On the side of the car, the driver's door, one of them has drawn a small heart in the dust.

ACKNOWLEDGEMENTS

With thanks to James McKenzie, to Liz Baker and Jon Pritchard. Thanks also (once again) to Beatrice Monti della Corte and the Santa Maddalena Foundation in Tuscany where this book was started. And thanks, as ever, to my agent Simon Trewin at WME, and my editor Carole Welch at Sceptre.

Writing is a solitary task; it is also a communal one.

Extracts from 'Self-Portrait in a Convex Mirror', copyright © 1974 by John Ashbery, and 'Voyage in the Blue', copyright © 1972 by John Ashbery, from *Self-Portrait in a Convex Mirror*, used by permission of Carcanet Press and Viking Books, an imprint of Penguin Publishing Group, a division of Penguin Random House LLC.

Extract from 'I May, I Might, I Must', copyright © 1959 by Marianne Moore, renewed 1987 by Lawrence E. Brinn and Louise Crane, Executors of the Estate of Marianne Moore, from *The Complete Poems of Marianne Moore*. Used by permission of Faber and Faber Ltd and Viking Books, an imprint of Penguin Publishing Group, a division of Penguin Random House LLC.

Extract from 'A Grave', taken from *The Complete Poems* by Marianne Moore, copyright © Estate of Marianne Moore, reprinted by permission of Faber and Faber Ltd. Also reprinted with the permission of Scribner, a Division of Simon and Schuster, Inc., from *The Collected Poems of Marianne Moore*, copyright © 1935 by Marianne Moore, renewed 1963 by Marianne Moore. Permission for the electronic use of the extract from 'A Grave' is granted by the Literary Estate of Marianne C. Moore, David M. Moore, Successor Executor of the Literary Estate of Marianne Moore. All rights reserved.

Extract from *Three Steps on the Ladder of Writing* by Hélène Cixous and Susan Sellers, copyright © 1994 Columbia University Press. Reprinted with permission of the publisher.

THE WRONG SIDE OF THE GALAXY

I, the Great Gaggenow, dedicate this book to those who have recognised my true genius. That is to say...umm...well, anyway. I dedicate it to all my fans out there!
Hey, hold on a minute, this is my *book!*
Quiet, Thomson, you're nothing but a jumped-up typist – without me, you're nothing!

ORCHARD BOOKS

First published in Great Britain in 2014 by Orchard Books

3 5 7 9 10 8 6 4

Text copyright © Fabled Lands, 2014
Courtesy of Advocate Art: Cover artwork Mathew Britton
Internal artwork by Jamie Lenman

The moral right of the author has been asserted.

A CIP catalogue record for this book
is available from the British Library.

ISBN 978 1 40833 026 5

Printed and bound in Great Britain by
Clays Ltd, Elcograf S.p.A.

The paper and board used in this book are made from
well-managed forests and other responsible sources.

Orchard Books
An imprint of
Hachette Children's Group
Part of The Watts Publishing Group Limited
Carmelite House
50 Victoria Embankment
London EC4Y 0DZ

An Hachette UK Company
www.hachette.co.uk

www.hachettechildrens.co.uk